NEW DIRECTIONS IN SCANDINAVIAN STUDIES

TERJE LEIREN AND CHRISTINE INGEBRITSEN,
SERIES EDITORS

NEW DIRECTIONS IN SCANDINAVIAN STUDIES

This series offers interdisciplinary approaches to the study of the Nordic region of Scandinavia and the Baltic States and their cultural connections in North America. By redefining the boundaries of Scandinavian studies to include the Baltic States and Scandinavian America, the series presents books that focus on the study of the culture, history, literature, and politics of the North.

The Power of Song

NONVIOLENT NATIONAL CULTURE
IN THE BALTIC SINGING REVOLUTION

Guntis Šmidchens

UNIVERSITY OF WASHINGTON PRESS   *Seattle and London*

MUSEUM TUSCULANUM PRESS   *Copenhagen*

THIS BOOK IS MADE POSSIBLE BY A COLLABORATIVE GRANT
FROM THE ANDREW W. MELLON FOUNDATION.

This publication is supported by a grant from the
Scandinavian Studies Publication Fund and the Baltic
Studies Program at the University of Washington.

University of Washington Press
www.washington.edu/uwpress

Published in Europe by Museum Tusculanum Press
126 Njalsgade, DK-2300 Copenhagen S, Denmark
www.mtp.dk   ISBN 978-87-635-4148-0

Library of Congress Cataloging-in-Publication Data
Smidchens, Guntis, 1963–
The power of song : nonviolent national culture in the
Baltic singing revolution / Guntis Smidchens.
pages cm. — (New directions in Scandinavian studies)
Includes bibliographical references and index.
ISBN 978-0-295-99310-2 (hardcover : alk. paper)
1. Song festivals—Political aspects—Baltic States.
2. Choral singing—Political aspects—Baltic States.
3. Music—Political aspects—Baltic States. I. Title.
ML3917.B37S65 2013
782.4209479—dc23   2013029860

Life's greatest moments are so simple. A people singing.

—Ivar Ivask

CONTENTS

ACKNOWLEDGMENTS

In writing this book I have had the aid of a number of institutions and individuals whose role I gratefully acknowledge. The Ralph Rinzler Folklife Archives and Collections provided copies of sound recordings that are at the center of this study. The University of Washington Libraries ensured access to most published sources quoted here. The EEVA Digital Text Repository for Older Estonian Literature, the Digital Collections at the National Library of Latvia, the Lithuanian Folk Culture Centre website, and Google Books gave easy online access to rare publications. The National Library of Estonia helped locate numerous songbooks in its collection. In Estonia, Latvia, and Lithuania, musicians and singers opened their homes and rehearsals to me and invited me to sing with them. People whom I interviewed in person or by email gave insights beyond any information found in published sources. Their names appear in notes, but I wish to emphasize here that their generosity and friendly assistance enriched this work immeasurably.

The University of Washington Department of Scandinavian Studies provided a Junior Faculty Release Quarter and a Summer Research Grant, and made possible several expeditions to the Baltic. In 1991–1992 and 1997, my fieldwork was supported in part by grants from the International Research and Exchanges Board (IREX), with funds provided by the National Endowment for the Humanities, the United States Information Agency, and the US Department of State. In 1999 and 2000, travel grants from the Open Society Support Foundation Group Research Support Scheme allowed me to meet colleagues in Latvia for valuable discussions about national identity formation. The UW Chamber Singers and UW Chorale invited me to travel with them on their Baltic concert tours in 2000, 2005, and 2010, allowing me to witness firsthand the power that songs have in creating bridges across language barriers.

Portions of the manuscript were read and commented on by Geoffrey Boers, Mimi Daitz, Thomas DuBois, Ulrich Gaier, Heather MacLaughlin Garbes, Terje Leiren, Lalita Muižniece, Živilė Ramoškaitė, and Rimas Žilinskas. Kanni Labi offered a particularly incisive reading of several chapters. The entire manuscript was read by Dace Bula, Kevin Karnes, Violeta Kelertas, Aldis Purs, and Zinta Šmidchens, whose critique and encouragement were invaluable. Students in classes I taught at the University of Washington have provided a sounding board for ideas and translation attempts. Scandinavian Department research assistants Sean Hughes and Axel Thorson helped index my archive and edit the manuscript. The editors of the New Directions in Scandinavian Studies Series gave support and suggestions for improvements. Tim Zimmermann, Kerrie Maynes, and the editors and anonymous readers at the University of Washington Press helped shape the manuscript's final version.

Illustrations for this book were possible thanks to the assistance of the directors and staff at the institutions mentioned in the credits. Silvestras Gaižiūnas, Ojārs Grīķis, Ain Haas, Inta Kaņepāja, Andres Kasekamp, Veiko Lukmann, Angonita Rupšytė, Valters Ščerbinskis, and Aušra Valančiauskienė also offered critical help in acquiring images and other resources. Zinta Šmidchens crafted a map of place names mentioned in this book.

All of these institutions and people have improved my work considerably, but I alone remain responsible for this book's content. I thank the four teachers who opened up Baltic worlds for me: Violeta Kelertas, Lalita Muižniece, Harri Mürk, and Toivo Raun, and my father, who sang with his children to pass the time on long car trips.

The Power of Song

Introduction

Three Nonviolent National Cultures

"A nation who makes its revolution by singing and smiling should be a sublime example to all," wrote the Estonian artist Heinz Valk, in the June 1988 editorial whose title, "Singing Revolution," gave the nonviolent Baltic independence movement its name. "It is impossible to even imagine in Estonia's city streets the riots, barricades, burning automobiles and similar features of mass revolt by large nations. This is not our way!"[1] The Baltic way had begun a year earlier when courageous Estonians, Latvians, and Lithuanians publicly broke through Soviet restrictions on free speech and assembly. It gained force as attendance at political meetings grew from handfuls to hundreds of thousands. It culminated in the election of the three governments that in spring of 1990 declared independence from the Soviet Union and established civilian-based defense as the means of liberation. The movement's non-violent foundations were tested from January to August 1991, when Soviet soldiers killed people in public displays of violent force. Estonia, Latvia, and Lithuania nevertheless sustained policies based on non-violence, and achieved their goal of political independence when they established diplomatic relations with the Russian Federation from July 29 to August 24, 1991. At this great moment, the power of nonviolent political action was reconfirmed. What Estonians, Latvians, and Lithuanians did, exclaims a leading scholar of nonviolence, "stands as a major milestone in the history of the modern world."[2]

Why did the struggle for Baltic independence come to be called the Singing Revolution? What did they sing? And what role did singing play in the Estonian, Latvian, and Lithuanian campaigns of political mobilization and nonviolent action? Many scholars have documented and analyzed the events that led to Baltic independence; most have focused on the parliamentary processes by which nonformal Baltic citizens groups created the three governments that severed ties with Moscow.[3] Some have studied the movement's nonviolent tactics and expanded the Singing Revolution's history to include events that took place many decades or even a century earlier.[4] Few, however, have gone to the heart of Baltic nonviolent political action in the late twentieth century: the songs and singing that gave the movement its name.[5]

At public gatherings, Balts sang. This book offers a small selection of their choral, rock, and folk songs in English translation. Following traditions of "thick description" in folklore studies, song texts are presented in their historical, cultural, and poetic context.[6] The goal is to interpret meanings as Balts themselves may have imagined them when they sang, or, following the lead of Anthony David Smith, to enter the participants' "inner world."[7] Ideally, Estonians, Latvians, and Lithuanians should be allowed to speak for themselves, selecting, performing, and commenting on their own songs. This is why the sixteen songs in the book's first chapter carry particular weight. They were documented at the 1998 Smithsonian Folklife Festival, in a concert in which native participants remembered their Singing Revolution.[8] Songs presented in later chapters, too, were usually first selected by persons other than the author. At some point in national history, each of the one hundred and twelve songs in this book was identified by an Estonian, Latvian, or Lithuanian, or in some cases by an outside observer, as a key text, worthy of inclusion in the discourse on national identity. Some songs, for example, were foregrounded by persons who placed them first or last in a songbook or a concert program, or by audiences who enthusiastically requested encores. Some songs were selected because they entered national tradition, to be quoted and adapted by poets and songwriters in new, popular songs. Many of the songs in this book were sung during the Singing Revolution. Documentary filmmakers and memoir authors have quoted them as a means of capturing the movement's spirit.

In 1998 at the Smithsonian festival, my job as interpreter for Baltic singers and speakers as they performed on stage was to convey to the English-speaking American audience, within a split-second, a sense of what the singers were singing. On paper, there is more time to ponder and translate each word, but the sounds of the singing and the faces of the singers are gone. The written words on this book's pages are voices from the past, "textual shards of a once-living work of verbal art," removed by decades from their original performances, transcribed and translated into a language and cultural context very different from their own.[9] Space restrictions do not allow inclusion of musical notation or texts in the original languages; these sources may nowadays be easily retrieved online, or found in the publications listed in notes. This book needs to stand alone, too. It should contain poetry that might, albeit distantly, recreate the feelings of the people who once sang it. My English translations attempt to use sounds and rhythms that might help a reader "hear" them, perhaps, as a native might experience them in Estonian, Latvian, Lithuanian, German, or Russian. Some of the translations follow the original meter precisely, others retain some poetic form but are not "singable," while still others sacrifice poetic form to reproduce content or intertextual connections. Together, these texts make up a web of songs and performances in cultural and historical context, recreating meanings beyond the sum total of individual texts.

The chapters of this book offer some pieces in the puzzle of the Singing Revolution. Why were songs particularly resonant symbols of national identity and political action? The story begins in chapter 2 with the eighteenth-century philosopher Johann Gottfried Herder, who identified songs as symbols of heritage and as models for effective poetry, and used them as rhetorical tools that would bring about social change. How did these ideas diffuse to the masses of the three nations? Chapter 3 sketches out the transition from Herder's philosophical interest in folk poetry to the nineteenth-century construction of Baltic national cultures, and to the birth of singing nations in song festival traditions. Singing traditions established a fundamental means of nonviolent political change, but parallel strands of violent national military songs also emerged; these are engaged in chapter 4. Chapter 5 introduces the ideologically charged traditions of Soviet mass culture that were imposed upon the Baltic under Stalinism, and presents a mechanism by which individuals could maintain non-Soviet identities, most notably by singing songs that did not follow the officially prescribed rules of Soviet socialist realism. Chapters 6, 7, and 8 outline non-Soviet singing that emerged in three styles: choral, rock/pop, and folk. All of these traditions converged in the Singing Revolution.

This book aims to expand our knowledge of Baltic national cultures and nationalism. It also contributes to our understanding of nonviolent political movements. In the international study of nonviolence, many books have been devoted to political tactics, and to the

biographies and moral and philosophical writings of movement leaders.[10] The past two decades have produced many ethnographic descriptions of conflict resolution in "peaceful societies."[11] We know less,
however, about the shared texts and traditions through which large
masses of individuals assumed ownership of tactical and philosophical principles and joined these movements to give them their "people
power."[12] Singing is often overlooked. The standard history of nonviolence by Peter Ackerman and Jack DuVall, *A Force More Powerful*, a companion volume to the six-part PBS broadcast, lists in its
index many key words related to nonviolent struggle: ahimsa, armed
struggle, boycotts, Catholic Church, civil disobedience, doctors, elections, financial sanctions, general strikes, hunger strikes, Internet, leaf-
lets, marches, media, negotiating, noncooperation, petitions, refusal
to work, resignations, self-rule, sit-ins, strikes, (withholding) taxes,
underground press, violence, work stay-aways—but no singing, and
no songs. A case study of the Baltic Singing Revolution may help add
these key words to the study of nonviolence.

Because the Baltic independence movement combined nationalist
and nonviolent ideologies, this book engages a well-known problem,
the question of whether it is possible to reconcile nonviolent principles with a pursuit of nationalist power.[13] In the Baltic, Mark Beissinger finds that "non-violence and passionate ethnic identity need not
be incompatible," and argues that the emotional bonds created by
nationalism were a resource for peaceful mass politics.[14] The three
national cultures provided Baltic activists with much more than ethnic
solidarity. They contained a powerful arsenal of symbols that could
inspire and sustain faith in nonviolent struggle. Connections between
the ideology of nonviolence and Estonian, Latvian, and Lithuanian
national identities reach back two centuries, drawing deep strands
from the nineteenth-century works of native Baltic nation builders.
In 1873, the Latvian national poet Auseklis exclaimed, "The power
of songs drove away war!" Auseklis's poem passed into the national
choral canon, and resurfaced a century later at the national song festival of 1990. In the Baltic, nonviolence and the struggle for national
political independence were not merely compatible—they merged in a
powerful, unified current of songs. To be Estonian, Latvian, or Lithuanian in 1988–91 meant to be politically nonviolent. True to Heinz
Valk's assertion quoted above, Auseklis's song and many other songs
of the Baltic Singing Revolution offer inspiration to the nonviolent
people and nations of our world.

CHAPTER ONE

Balts Speak to America, July 4, 1998

They walk onto the main stage at the Smithsonian Folklife Festival in Washington, DC: one hundred fifty Estonians, Latvians, and Lithuanians, carrying the three national flags: blue-black-white, red-white-red, and yellow-green-red. Lithuanian shepherds' horns and Latvian bagpipes play fanfares, answered by enthusiastic applause from the audience that fills every available seat. This concert celebrates the ten-year anniversary of the Baltic Singing Revolution.[1]

[First to speak is Estonian ethnomusicologist Ingrid Rüütel:]

A large empire can assert itself with the power of a Goliath.
A small nation like the Estonians needs the wisdom and cleverness of a
   David.
Living under foreign powers for hundreds of years, we have developed a
   strategy of self-preservation.
It is external adaptation, but internal remaining ourselves.
We could not liberate ourselves by brandishing weapons.
For the renewal of our independence, we needed to find our own path.
At the critical moments we managed to unite diverse political forces,
   and diverse sectors of the people, in the name of a common goal.
And we fought ourselves free singing, raising our blue-black-white flags.
The victorious, bloodless singing revolution of a small nation is unique
   in the history of the world.

The Singing Revolution was a process, not an event, and because of that
   it is difficult to determine its beginning.
It was the heritage protection movement.
It was the demonstration in Hirve Park, where the so-called dissidents,
   who had maintained the idea of freedom throughout the Soviet period,

now were first to unfurl the slogan of renewed independence.

It was the Song of Estonia event on the Tallinn song festival grounds, organized by the largest people's movement, the Rahvarinne [Popular Front], and other mass events.

It was the crowd of people who assembled on Dom Hill, who with their cold-blooded calm, and with their self-control, dispersed the crowds of the Russian so-called Interfront which had attacked the government building of Estonia, and sang and danced through the night, defending this building.

It was the 1990 National song festival, which ended with spontaneous songs and dances, and much much more.

Besides the Estonian national character, which is quite stubborn and obstinate, but at the same time level-headed and determined,

Besides the entire Estonian people's unshakeable desire for independence,

Our cultural traditions also played an essential role.

For centuries, the rituals of Estonians have been accompanied by group singing.

In the second half of the past century an essential activity of the antifeudal and national liberation movement was the battle for an Estonian-language school.

Another of its essential activities was the large folklore collection project led by Jakob Hurt.

And the massive song festivals.

Song festivals maintained their role as confirmation and expression of national and cultural self-awareness throughout the Soviet period.

During the days of the Singing Revolution, old patriotic songs and old traditional songs came back into circulation,

Also popular songs that appeared at the beginning of this century during the period of Estonia's political independence.

But during the days of the Singing Revolution, entirely new songs were born, too. Among them songs by the young composer Alo Mattiisen, in which the characteristics of the oldest Estonian folk songs were combined in an original way with elements of modern rock music.

Those songs were performed at mass political meetings by the youth ensemble In Spe, with the popular lead singer Ivo Linna.

His hypnotic, incantation-like verses were repeated by thousands of people.

With one such song I would like to end my brief talk, and after that we will sing a few other songs of the Estonian singing revolution.

[The audience applauds enthusiastically. Heavy-metal electric guitar chords explode over the loudspeakers, and the Estonians on stage sing along to the recorded, amplified refrain of a Singing Revolution anthem:]

Guarding the beautiful fatherland, fighting against the enemy:

Remember, remember, remember, remember!

[The exhilarating feeling of national revival has ominous undertones. Ivo Linna's voice chants incantations in the eight-syllable meter of *regilaul*, the archaic Estonian folk songs, and the singers on stage repeat after him:]

If you truly trust yourself (If you truly trust yourself),
And the wisdom of wise people (and the wisdom of wise people),
And the shoulders of strong people (and the shoulders of strong people),
And the power of the ancients (and the power of the ancients),
And the quickness of the young men (and the quickness of the young
    men),
And the sisters and the brothers (and the sisters and the brothers),
And above all, trust yourself (and above all, trust yourself):
Then you'll get a better life (then you'll get a better life).

Guarding the beautiful fatherland, fighting against the enemy:
Remember! Remember! Remember! Remember!

If you trust the wolf's slick stories (If you trust the wolf's slick stories),
If you fear the hounds' mad howling (If you fear the hounds' mad
    howling),
If you listen to the landlord's cursing (If you listen to the landlord's
    cursing),
If you trust the servants' snitching (If you trust the servants' snitching),
And the glutton's greed for more (and the glutton's greed for more),
And the views of the vile person (and the views of the vile person),
And the scolding of the senseless (and the scolding of the senseless):
        Then you won't get anything.

Guarding the beautiful fatherland, fighting against the enemy:
Remember! Remember! Remember! Remember!

If you sink into false stories (If you sink into false stories),
If you drown yourself in dreams (If you drown yourself in dreams),
Grovel when you're given orders (grovel when you're given orders),
Bow down low before the ruble (bow down low before the ruble),
You'll get lice between the legs (you'll get lice between the legs),
You'll get hives inside your heart (you'll get hives inside your heart),
Sores on your skull, bones in your belly (sores on your skull, bones in
    your belly):
        Then you'll go to hell.

Guarding the beautiful fatherland, fighting against the enemy:
Remember! Remember! Remember! Remember!

If you truly trust yourself (If you truly trust yourself),
Then you'll truly trust the people (then you'll truly trust the people),
Family farmstead, worldly wisdom (family farmstead, worldly wisdom),

Truthful teachings, objective justice (truthful teachings, objective
    justice),
And the birch grove of your birthplace (and the birch grove of your
    birthplace),
And the swallow-bird in the blue sky (and the swallow-bird in the blue
    sky):
Courage will be powerful,
And you'll get a better life.

[Loud applause. Another recording played over the loudspeakers shifts the
mood from heavy-metal to soft-rock anthem. On stage in Washington,
DC, the Estonians raise clasped hands in the air, singing along, conjuring
feelings they had a decade earlier when Ivo Linna sang on stage:]

A thousand times over and again,
A thousand years of rising, not a final flight;
To renounce your own nation
Is like selling yourself into slavery.

> I am and I'll stay Estonian; I was created Estonian.
> Proud and good to be Estonian, free like our forefathers.
> Yes: free like our forefathers.

A thousand people's questions thundering,
Sacred soil, free sea, native farmsteads.
A thousand times one thousand people there
Hold the sacred flame alive defiantly.

> I am and I'll stay Estonian; I was created Estonian.
> Proud and good to be Estonian, free like our forefathers.
> Yes: Just like our free forefathers, just like those courageous men.

> I am and I'll stay Estonian; I was created Estonian.
> Proud and good to be Estonian, free like our forefathers.
> Yes: Just like our free forefathers, just like those courageous men.

[Whoops of support and applause from the audience recede when the
sound of a lone trumpet introduces the next melody. The Estonians on
stage, and some in the audience, too, sing along, clapping hands to the
rhythmic marching-band music that streams from the loudspeakers.]

The waters in our sea
Are free, they surge and roar.
And forests of our homeland
Shall greet us from afar.

> Stay free, Estonia's sea!
> Stay free, Estonia's shore!
> Then every proud Estonian
> Shall fear not snow nor storm.

Stay free, Estonia's sea!
Stay free, Estonia's shore!
Then every proud Estonian
Shall fear not snow nor storm.

Our fisherman may sail now
And freely cast his nets;
And field and forest echo
With ringing songs of joy.

Stay free, Estonia's sea!
Stay free, Estonia's shore!
Then every proud Estonian
Shall fear not snow nor storm.

Stay free, Estonia's sea!
Stay free, Estonia's shore!
Then every proud Estonian
Shall fear not snow nor storm.

The sun will glimmer brightly,
On waters by our shore,
And fields will hold rich harvests
In their bosom of black earth.

Stay free, Estonia's sea!
Stay free, Estonia's shore!
Then every proud Estonian
Shall fear not snow nor storm.

[The audience continues to clap in rhythm as the Estonians walk off
stage. Three Latvian bagpipers enter, playing the stately traditional
dance tune "Garais dancis," while a group of about forty singers
walks on. Silence. Helmī Stalte chants the first line of an incantation
that they sang in Rīga in July of 1988, at the opening of the Baltica
Folklore Festival, where the Latvian Singing Revolution began:]

Shine, sun, shimmering, shimmering, shimmering,
Shine, sun, shimmering, shimmering, shimmering,
Shine, sun, shimmering, shimmering, shimmering,
Shine, sun, shimmering, shimmering, shimmering,
Shine, sun, shimmering, shimmering, shimmering,
Shine, sun, shimmering, shimmering, shimmering,
Shine, sun, shimmering, shimmering, shimmering,
Shine, sun, shimmering, shimmering, shimmering!
    Drive darkness to the sea, clothe yourself in white,
    Let the daughters of the sea strike it with their oaken clubs!

Shine, sun, shimmering, shimmering, shimmering,
Shine, sun, shimmering, shimmering, shimmering,

Shine, sun, shimmering, shimmering, shimmering,
Shine, sun, shimmering, shimmering, shimmering,
Shine, sun, shimmering, shimmering, shimmering,
Shine, sun, shimmering, shimmering, shimmering,
Shine, sun, shimmering, shimmering, shimmering,
Shine, sun, shimmering, shimmering, shimmering,
Shine, sun, shimmering, shimmering, shimmering!
   Drive darkness to the sea, clothe yourself in white,
   Let the daughters of the sea strike it with their oaken clubs!

Shine, sun, shimmering, shimmering, shimmering,
Shine, sun, shimmering, shimmering, shimmering,
Shine, sun, shimmering, shimmering, shimmering,
Shine, sun, shimmering, shimmering, shimmering,
Shine, sun, shimmering, shimmering, shimmering,
Shine, sun, shimmering, shimmering, shimmering,
Shine, sun, shimmering, shimmering, shimmering,
Shine, sun, shimmering, shimmering, shimmering,
Shine, sun, shimmering, shimmering, shimmering!
   Drive darkness to the sea, clothe yourself in white,
   Let the daughters of the sea strike it with their oaken clubs!

[Scattered applause. Latvian musicologist Valdis Muktupāvels, seated
with the stringed Latvian musical instrument, the *kokle*s, in his lap,
recalls (in English) his own participation in that historic festival. His
group, Rasa, reconstructed folk poetry as it might have been sung in
Old Prussian, a language that went extinct in the seventeenth century:]

And in 1988 the Prussian songs that were performed by Rasa Ensemble, they reminded very many people what can happen with a folk that
becomes oppressed by a bigger folk, and reminded once more again
about the terror of extinction.

   And this Prussian songs program was a success during the festival,
and woke many people, made them conscious of their Baltic ancestry
and helped them regain confidence in their traditional singing.

   And so I will sing a song from those Prussian songs in an old,
reconstructed Prussian language, exactly as it was sung ten years ago:

Ei, skīja skīja
Be jāu etskīja
Iz Gillijas mistīkan
Jāu geltāinan laiwīkan.
Iz Gillijas mistīkan
Jāu geltāinan laiwīkan.

Ei, bratrīk bratrīk,
Tū bratrīke majs,
Grēnzimai kwei laiwīkan,

Wērpimai kwei ziglīkans?
Grēnzimai kwei laiwīkan,
Wērpimai kwei ziglīkans?

Anga ān-jurin,
Anga ān marin,
Anga ān stan kaimīkan,
Kwei aūg majā mergīka?
Anga ān stan kaimīkan,
Kwei aūg majā mergīka?

Neggi ān-jurin,
Neggi ān-marin,
Ter an debban kaimīkan,
Kwei aūg majā mergīka.
Ter an debban kaimīkan,
Kwei aūg majā mergīka.

[The song's language is not spoken anywhere in the world. Only a handful of specialists in Indo-European languages may decipher its words.[2] Muktupāvels expands the melody's final notes with the eerie harmonies of throat singing. Again, scattered applause. The Latvian folklorist Dainis Stalts comes to the microphone:]

We had our own weapons to keep us from the fate of the Prussians,
    which was planned for us during the grim years of the Soviet
    occupation.
We had weapons:
The wisdom, the conscience, and the song of the nation.

[The Latvians on stage sing a series of three soldiers' songs, with no commentary other than brief summary translations by the Smithsonian presenter. The first two songs are unaccompanied. The third is joined by an accordion and hand drum. With these upbeat melodies, the audience's applause also gains energy.]

Brother dear, oh brother dear, take the sword in your hand,
    Take the sword in your hand, and defend your fatherland,
    Take the sword in your hand, and defend your fatherland.

Better that they take my head than they take my fatherland,
    Better I be killed in war than I die beside the road,
    Better I be killed in war than I die beside the road.

Lead me, God, on my pathway, and protect my body,
    So that I may honorably defeat the enemy,
    So that I may honorably defeat the enemy.
Why do you weep, my dear sister? I'll return home from the war;
    Wait for me, I shall return, see the sun gleam in my sword,
    Wait for me, I shall return, see the sun gleam in my sword.

[audience applause]

Our troops are not so great in number,
But feel our spirit, great and free.
   We know the scales of fate are tipping,
   The balance shifting to our side.
   We know the scales of fate are tipping,
   The balance shifting to our side.

We do not have many soldiers,
But sunlight shimmers on each face.
   The foe will know the words they've spoken,
   By the nation's heart and blood.
   The foe will know the words they've spoken,
   By the nation's heart and blood.

Our troops are not so great in number,
But feel our spirit, great and free.
   We know the scales of fate are tipping,
   The balance shifting to our side.
   We know the scales of fate are tipping,
   The balance shifting to our side.

[audience applause]

High up in the air, two doves,
Both coo softly as they fly;
   Aijā, aijajā, both coo softly as they fly.

Riding off to war, two brothers,
Both now ponder as they ride,
   Aijā, aijajā, both now ponder as they ride.

Should they ride, or should they wait,
Should they turn and stay at home,
   Aijā, aijajā, should they turn and stay at home.

Life is good at home, they know,
Young girls made the bed at home,
   Aijā, aijajā, young girls made the bed at home.

Who will make the soldier's bed,
Smoothe the blankets where he sleeps?
   Aijā, aijajā, smoothe the blankets where he sleeps?

Just a sword, just a stone
Are pillows in the soldier's bed,
   Aijā, aijajā, pillows in the soldier's bed.

[The stage empties for the next song, and Julgī Stalte sings, accompanied by Zigmārs Kristsons on guitar:]

Lord, you hear each tiny blade of grass, you protect and calm its pain,

Hear the words that burn and smoulder, inside every Latvian heart.
There are words which echo in our veins on our first day of life,
For you decreed that in this land my brothers and I were born,
My brothers and I were born.

It can't be your wish, that foreign shackles come and bind our hands,
Once we've seen the sun, that we should now fall down back into
night!
It can't be your wish, that Latvians be forced down on their knees,
Free today, but then tomorrow we'll again be locked in chains,
We'll again be locked in chains.

It can't be your wish, to hear our prayers in a foreign tongue,
You, who are our father, you, who gave this land to us!
Do you hear us singing sweetly? No, a slave can't sing like that!
Therefore on the Latvian children your sun should always shine,
Your sun should always shine.

So we pray to you, oh Lord, do not let the Latvian people die,
Let us feel your warm sun high above our heads forever free,
Through the ages that today are known to nobody but you,
Let the Latvian eagle spread its wings and fly, forever free!
Through the ages let us walk toward the future days unknown,
Father, give us strength, and bravery, and unity, we pray!
Through the ages let us walk toward the future days unknown,
Father, give us strength, and bravery, and unity, we pray!

[An accordionist strikes up a waltz tune, "Ķemermiestiņā," and Dainis
Stalts interprets:]

Those who have not been in Rīga during the time of the barricades,
Maybe they do not know that
Between the shots and explosions
It was exactly this song melody to which
Our people danced this waltz
That was once danced by our fathers and grandfathers.

[The dancers cheerfully spin and sway, filing off of the stage. Loud
applause continues as fifty Lithuanians enter. The Lithuanian ethnomusicologist Zita Kelmickaitė speaks:]

Since ancient times, the song was always very important to the
Lithuanians. For Lithuanians, the song was patience; for Lithuanians
the song was strength; for Lithuanians the song was a foundation of
survival.
Lithuanians sang a lot when they were happy; Lithuanians sang a lot
when they were sad.
In 1988, when the entire nation needed to go and be together, they all
were again united by song.
People stood, sleep deprived, freezing, but they all sang.
Foreigners who had arrived in Lithuania asked, "How did you preserve

that singing tradition?" And it was our countryside that preserved
that singing tradition, the village people that you see before you
today.
But those songs which we sang in Independence Square during the
Soviet times were not tolerated, and they were not sung frequently.
Really, people sang them only at home, and in very small groups.
But truly the foundation of the song is the folk song, a song like the one
we are about to sing. This song resounded in the city squares; this
song resounded at all of our difficult occasions, and also at times
when people gathered and had a good time.

[A lead singer, Veronika Povilionienė, starts the first words, and the
others join her in sonorous two-part harmony:]

On a hill there stood a maple tree,
    On the maple's·branches, shining leaves,
    On the maple's branches, shining leaves.

On the maple's branches, shining leaves,
    Brother proudly sat upon his steed,
    Brother proudly sat upon his steed.

Brother proudly sat upon his steed,
    Talking to a maiden, young and sweet,
    Talking to a maiden, young and sweet.

Talking to a maiden, young and sweet,
    Promised that their wedding soon would be,
    Promised that their wedding soon would be.

[Kelmickaitė's narrative continues:]

The great Lithuanian scholar of mythology, Norbertas Vėlius, took
    many students along on folklore collection expeditions,
    but later, in 1972, the KGB warned him not to take students along,
    and not to lead those expeditions.
He said, "When I returned from the folklore expeditions, the KGB
    representatives always said, 'You go ahead and study the folk song,
    but don't try to get the youth to sing. There is no need for the youth
    to sing, and be so kind, do not take them along on expeditions!'"
But the youth of Lithuania sensed that they could say much with song,
    that song is a weapon,
    and an expression of ideas,
    the kind of ideas that could not be expressed out loud at that time.
And when the young people of Lithuania sang,
    then the old people of Lithuania said,
    "Truly, songs will resound in Lithuania for a long time to come."
This song here that you will hear now,
    it was the very most popular song of 1989,

it was sung by all Lithuanians,
and truly,
tears flowed from every person's eyes:
"Oh, don't weep, dear mother, when your young son / Leaves home to
defend his dear country, / When he falls, like an oak, to the forest
ground / To await the Last Day of Judgement."

[Povilionienė leads the song, and her voice resonates above the fifty
other voices that join hers, the men's voices reverberating in harmony
a third note lower:]

Oh, don't weep, dear mother, when your young son
Leaves home to defend his dear country!
    When he falls, like an oak, to the forest ground,
    To await the Last Day of Judgement.
    When he falls, like an oak, to the forest ground,
    To await the Last Day of Judgement.

So don't wring your hands, like the boughs of a birch
When wind crashes through the forest,
    You still have other sons; if you lose your land,
    Even prayer won't give you another.
    You still have other sons; if you lose your land,
    Even prayer won't give you another.

There, beyond the wide rivers, our shimmering troops
Defend our dear Lithuania;
    And the angels of heaven lift each fallen man
    And weave him a crown of diamonds.
    And the angels of heaven lift each fallen man
    And weave him a crown of diamonds.

[Kelmickaitė continues:]

People avoided singing such songs during the expeditions.
    But if one asked for them, then they would cover the windows
    so that the neighbors wouldn't see,
    because nobody knew how it might end if such songs were sung.
Lithuanians are a very peaceful nation.
    And truly even in the old historical war songs the singing is always
    only calm.
And Veronika, our—
    truly, we could say, the mama of our folk songs,
    from the Dzūkija region,
    will sing a few stanzas of
    "Oh, dear son, dear soldier, / Why did you turn into an oak?"

[Povilionienė sings the mother's lament, solo:]

Oh, dear son, dear soldier,

Why did you turn into an oak?
Why did you turn into an oak,
And your steed into the north wind?
And your rider's staff into a willow stick,
And the saddle into stone?

[Kelmickaitė continues:]

On January 12, people stood by the television tower
    and around the television broadcast building,
    with no weapons,
    and their only shield was the song.
Nobody believed that they would truly see a tank driving up,
    and a cannon being aimed.
    And that you could be only singing.
When we stood together with the students,
    a woman,
    when the tanks were really rolling into the courtyard,
    grabbed me by the arm and asked,
    "I wonder which would be better to do, to sing, or to pray?"
    That is, the Lithuanian had only two things to depend on:
    He had faith, and he had song.
And our noble resistance using only the song, of course,
    today seems rather unbelievable to everybody.
    But truly we are already a free nation,
    and we came to your free country.
    And the roadside cross that was blessed today in our exhibit territory
    also testifies that we are truly in the company of free people.
Now there will be one stanza, because time is passing very quickly, one
    stanza of a hymn. When it was very, very difficult for Lithuanians,
    they would always turn to Maria.
    And today, when we stood by the sacred cross,
    then there was a hymn to Maria.
    And now we will sing that one stanza,
    because all of the time,
    whenever it is very difficult for our fatherland,
    that hymn is always sung, and we hope for guidance.

[Povilionienė begins the Roman Catholic hymn, joined by all on stage,
and many voices from the audience, in two-part harmony:]

Maria, Maria, most beautiful lily,
You shine high in heaven above.
Oh come, ease slavery, save humankind, come, rescue from the terrible
    foe,
Oh come, ease slavery, save humankind, come, rescue from the terrible
    foe.

[Kelmickaitė concludes the Lithuanian presentation:]

Thank you to you all, who were with us
    at a very difficult time
    for us, for Lithuania,
    our Lithuanians,
    and our friends from all the countries of the world.

[The lengthy applause—twenty seconds—testifies that the Lithuanians
on stage have touched people in the audience. The bagpipes strike up
a concluding melody, droning an accompaniment to Dainis Stalts's
remarks:]

I have the honor-filled responsibility
    to speak on behalf of all three delegations of the Baltic countries,
    and to say what we all have in our hearts.
With our flags in the wind, today we are here,
    in this place,
    in this place which is most important of all for America,
    in order to say what we think.
And we think that a half century under Soviet occupation
    would probably have been too difficult to bear,
    if for all of those fifty years
    we could not have listened to the voice of liberty
    coming from America.
And our hearts grow warm, seing you, hearing you, and looking at you.
    Because among you there are so many of our people,
    to whom you have given refuge, education, and strength,
    and a belief in the fatherland and liberty.
All of this we say with our songs and our music,
    having arrived here once in a hundred years.
    Thank you, America!
    Believe in liberty,
    and believe that we also believe in it,
    and we will never give it away.

[Applause. The audience claps in rhythm to the bagpipes, as the Estonians, Latvians, and Lithuanians file off of the stage. But people linger.
The performers and audience join hands in a large ring. One of the
performers speaks off-microphone, and the Smithsonian festival presenter translates, "A quick translation: There was a demonstration in
1989 in the Baltic lands, when all the Baltic people joined hands in a
chain from Tallinn through Rīga to Vilnius, the human chain of hands
across the Baltic. And we invite you to also join hands as we did in
1989." They sing in Lithuanian:]

Dear Lithuania, land of my fathers,
Land where the heroes rest in their graves;
Beautiful in the blue of your sky!
Loved, because you endured through the ages.
Beautiful in the blue of your sky!

Figure 1. Singing Revolution concert at the Smithsonian Folklife Festival,
Washington, DC, July 4, 1998. Lithuanian, Latvian, and Estonian performers join hands with their American audience to represent the Baltic Way
demonstration of August 23, 1989. Photo by Donald Hurlbert. Courtesy of
the Ralph Rinzler Folklife Archives, Smithsonian Institution, 98-8268, #25.

Loved, because you endured through the ages.

[An Estonian speaker comes to the microphone, addressing the audience in English:]

You can see one Estonian flag there in the crowd.
    But you can see another one on the stage.
    And that particular one on the stage was secretly made by
        Estonian people for the folklore festival in Moscow in 1988,
        when it was still forbidden.
    It was hidden, and the Estonian delegation carried it to the Red
        Square, and when they entered Red Square, they let it fly.
Now, it was— [applause].
That was in 1988 in Moscow, in the capital of a big country.
    Now, in 1998, ten years later,
    we have brought it here to show [it] Washington, a capital of
        another big nation,
    before the flag retires and a new one takes over.
    Thank you.

[Applause. A conductor steps forward to conduct the choir on stage:]

Decorate Estonian homesteads in three colors of our land,
Under them Estonian sons can congregate in unity;
Let them strive as one, together, brothers unified by love,
Let our call be powerful: Estonia, Estonia, long may you live!

Blue the color of your sky, homeland dear, Estonia,
If you are in pain, in danger, lift your eyes up to the sky;
Black the color of your earth, tended through the centuries,
Black the overcoat of the Estonian since ancient times.

Let the blue and black and white decorate Estonia,
Let the fields grow and flourish, bountifully giving fruit.
Let Estonian households echo with brave minds and brotherhood,
Let the heart call to the heavens: Estonia, Estonia, long may you live!

[Applause. The event concludes with a song about the Daugava River
and national culture, which join Latvia's three historical regions:]

Daugava's two shorelines, joined as one forever:
Kurzeme and Vidzeme and Latgale are ours.
    Rai, rai, rai radi rai rā, Kurzeme and Vidzeme and Latgale are
        ours.

Laima, grant your favor, come protect our land,
The one land, the single soul, the language that is ours.
    Rai, rai, rai radi rai rā, the one land, the single soul, the language
        that is ours.

Daugava's two shorelines, joined as one forever:
Kurzeme and Vidzeme and Latgale are ours.
    Rai, rai, rai radi rai rā, Kurzeme and Vidzeme and Latgale are
        ours.

[In the background, a hand drum accompanies the song, and continues, softly, as the audience and performers gradually disperse.]

REMEMBERING THE SINGING REVOLUTION

On July 4, 1998, American Independence Day on the National
Mall, the Estonian, Latvian, and Lithuanian pavilions fell silent
at 4:00 pm, and 150 delegates from the three Baltic countries converged around the main music stage in the central festival tent.
The event was framed by Smithsonian representatives, and understood by Balts, to be a moment when they would speak to the
American people, in this place which is America's most important
speaking ground, a "once in a hundred years" moment when they

would be heard. The transcript translated above makes available, for the first time in English, the words that Estonians, Latvians, and Lithuanians spoke and the songs that they sang on this historic occasion.[3]

Time was short. The festival organizers asked the Balts to limit this event to ninety minutes. Their leaders met on July 2 and quickly reached consensus on a sequence of groups and themes, separated into four twenty-minute time slots: Estonians would come first, because the Baltica Association was established in Tallinn in 1989—this was the moment that set the three countries on a unified path. Latvians would center their memory on the watershed event of the 1988 Baltica festival in Rīga. Lithuanians would remember the January events of 1991 in Vilnius. Finally, the three nations would converge in Baltic unity, as they had done in 1989 during the "hands across the Baltic" mass demonstration.

But it was then no easy task for each of the three groups to select, out of many hundreds of songs, the sixteen songs that would on July 4 represent their entire movement. In their twenty minutes, the Estonians presented a narrative history, and sang along with three recordings made by the Estonian performers who originally sang and played them during the Singing Revolution. The Latvians squeezed six songs into their allotted time, sacrificing interpretive commentary. The Lithuanians, on the other hand, abbreviated all four of their songs to leave time to narrate a contextual frame. Each of the groups sang one more song at the conclusion. Much remained unsung.

For the Balts on stage, songs bridged a decade back to 1988. While singing, they recalled not only words and melodies but also feelings. Ninety minutes could barely suffice, it seemed, to bridge the cultural gap between the Baltic and the United States. Kalev Järvela, whose Estonian folk dance ensemble "Leigarid" performed at the festival, later recalled the core problem: "The Singing Revolution was based on emotions. One can describe emotions, but one can't easily revive them. The event was important for the Estonians, but did it say anything to Americans? This was our inner affair. We can show what was there, but—," his voice trailed off.[4]

Songs, a combination of language and music, are time capsules of emotion. Their meanings and effects were created, and are created, out of many associations with experiences, individual and collective, recent and centuries-old. In order to revive not only the words and melodies but also the feelings that accompanied each song and story, the translation must be expanded, with a semantic field of native references in historical and cultural context. That is the goal of the remaining chapters in this book.

CHAPTER TWO

Herder's Discovery of Baltic Songs

These oaks, three feet in diameter, could be two centuries old. The linden is larger than her neighbors, but probably younger. Beneath the three towering giants stands the white-bearded Oskars Stalts, together with his daughter Helmī, his son-in-law Dainis, and granddaughter Julgī. Around them are their singing group, Skandinieki, locked inside a circle of folklore performers from many countries. We are in the Latvian Ethnographic Open-Air Museum on the outskirts of Rīga on July 11, 1991. Julgī will soon light a fire to open the international folklore festival, Baltica. Dainis Stalts speaks, ascribing meaning to the trees and landscape that surround us:[1]

> They give us strength, and, we hope, they will do the same for you.
> For this is no ordinary place.
> It is an ancient place, a place visited not only by our ancestors, the
> Livs and the Latvians,
> But also by persons who came from distant lands.
> And this is a significant place in another way, too:
> Here, many years ago, Johann Gottfried Herder witnessed our folk
> celebration, listened to our songs, and carried news of them to the far
> corners of the world.
> Folk song: This concept emerged in Herder's mind, having been heard
> here, on the shores of Lake Jugla.

The opening of the 1991 Baltica Folklore Festival identifies a point of interest on the map of Estonian, Latvian, and Lithuanian singing history. Many roads lead to the German philosopher Johann Gottfried Herder, and he is well remembered. In 1778–79, he published

Figure 2. Baltica Folklore Festival opening celebration at the Open Air Ethnographic Museum, Rīga, July 11, 1991. Dainis Stalts, Oskars Stalts, and Julgī Stalte light a ceremonial fire near the place where Herder witnessed a midsummer celebration in 1765. Photo by Guntis Šmidchens.

two volumes of folk songs, *Volkslieder*, that inspired nation builders throughout Europe, among them also Balts, to go forth into the countryside and seek and publish oral poetry in their native languages. Herder's collection included a small sample of Lithuanian, Estonian, and Latvian folk songs that would remain close to the the heart of the national repertoires even two centuries later, during the Singing Revolution. Some of these songs are translated here from Herder's German into English for the first time.[2] Herder also pioneered ethnographic methods that remain useful today. He aimed to document humanity as experienced by people "from inside," in their own words. Songs have an effect on people who sing them; Herder aimed to translate, annotate, and publish songs in a way that would extend their effects to his readers. Such is also the goal of this book. The reader is invited to follow Herder's discovery of songs; if we can revive the feelings of empathy that he felt, then perhaps we can also reexperience the emotions that permeated songs during the Singing Revolution.

In the summer of 1765, Herder was twenty years old and not yet world famous when he visited acquaintances on the shores of Lake

Jugla, near where Skandinieki sang their songs on July 11, 1991. The oaks towering above them might have been thin saplings 226 years ago.

HERDER'S FOLK SONG PROJECT

Herder arrived in Rīga in November of 1764. Rīga was then a thriving port city and the center of economic and intellectual activity in Lifland Province of the Russian Empire. To the southwest across the Daugava River lay Kurland, a duchy of the Kingdom of Poland. These places warrant special mention in the history of eighteenth-century European philosophy: Rīga was home to the publisher Johann Friedrich Hart-knoch, who printed, along with many of Herder's books, Rousseau in German translation and Immanuel Kant's first major treatise, *Critique of Pure Reason*. "The Magus of the North," Herder's mentor, Johann Georg Hamann, lived twenty five miles to the south, in Kurland. Herder lived in Rīga for four and a half years, teaching in the Dom Cathedral school, serving as second city librarian and as the pastor of two German Lutheran congregations. Herder's time in Rīga, argued Kurt Stavenhagen, was the time when he became "Herderian" in his ideas about literature, history, nations, religion, and humanity.[3] There he wrote the first of many volumes of literary, philosophical, and theological essays. A glimmer of his later folk song project appeared in a 1765 prospectus for an essay about the literary ode, the "firstborn child of poetic empathy," and the related genres of elegy, pastoral poetry, and "songs" (Lieder). Herder planned to describe the odes of differing nations, epochs, and languages.[4]

His attention soon shifted from written odes to oral poetry. Seeds of folk song studies were sprouting in Europe. Five years earlier, in 1760, James MacPherson had announced his discovery of the Scots Gaelic equivalent of ancient Greek epic poetry, which had been preserved in old manuscripts and through oral tradition. In 1765, Thomas Percy rescued a manuscript of traditional ballads from oblivion in his *Reliques of Ancient English Poetry*. The German philosopher Gotthold Ephraim Lessing discovered two Lithuanian songs that proved to him that poetry could be found where it had not been seen earlier, and that all human poetic expression, written or not, had value. Herder would quote Lessing's groundbreaking essay in the introduction to *Volkslieder*:

> You should learn . . . that under every part of the Heavens, poets are
> born, and that lively sensations are not the sole privilege of civilized

nations. Not long ago . . . I came upon a rarity which amused me to
no end. A few Lithuanian *dainos*, or little songs, namely in the manner
as they are sung by the common girls. What naive wit! What lovely
simplicity![5]

Herder was well read in English, German, and French scholarship.
But later, in 1771, he declared that the genesis of his enthusiasm for
the songs of wild nations, and specifically for MacPherson's Ossianic
poems, did not lie in library books, for then his ideas would be "delu-
sion, a mere apparition." Herder's inspiration came at the moment
when he left the armchair and entered the field: "You must know that
I myself have had the opportunity to observe the living remnants of
ancient songs, rhythms, and dances in living nations." [6]

Historians have attempted to parse out a detailed sequence of
Herder's biography to determine the date and place when he could
have seen those "living" song traditions that stirred his enthusiasm.
The strands of evidence lead to the Baltic. It was in Rīga that Herder
first began writing about folk songs.[7] But did he actually encounter living Latvian folk poetry during that stay? Where? Herder himself did
not explicitly say.[8] Latvian folk song traditions were certainly widespread in Herder's day, in the countryside as well as in the city of Rīga;
it is likely that he saw singers during a trip to Mitau (Jelgava), where
Hamann lived, and also during his visit to the Gravenheide estate on
the outskirts of Rīga, on the shore of Jagelsee (Lake Jugla) in June of
1765, when the Latvian serfs would have been celebrating midsummer. Herder knew that the local German landowners heard midsummer songs performed by their serfs, because he quoted a 1764 article
by Johan Jacob Harder describing such an occasion.[9] This, then, is
the evidence presented by Stavenhagen and Leonid Arbusow, however
circumstantial, that Herder's life-changing encounter with folk poetry
happened at a Latvian midsummer celebration in 1765, near the city
of Rīga.

Later, in August of 1770, Herder fell in love with Caroline
Flachsland. His thoughts and feelings, and the poetry that inspired his
emerging folk song project, may be traced in his love letters to Caroline.[10] In one of the four long letters he wrote to her in the days after
they first met, Herder describes how he was affected by reading a love
poem, and mentions a plan to compile a book of songs:

I've had a foolish fancy to make a small collection of the few German
pieces that seem to me to be the true expression of sensibility and the
entire soul; wouldn't that be a pretty songbook?[11]

Caroline compiled about two hundred such poems and songs that he sent her, in a notebook named the "Silver Book" after the color of its cover.[12] They were married in 1773, and continued work on the book of folk songs. These early years of idyllic bliss, as Caroline would later remember, were the "golden years of our marriage," "our paradise" in which they shared poetry.[13]

Soon afterward, Herder submitted to a publisher the first manuscript of a book titled "Old Folk Songs." But the notion that a printed work could embrace words coming from the mouths of uneducated people was new. The publisher Christoph Friedrich Nicolai openly mocked the folk song project, and Hamann disparaged his use of oral colloquialisms. Herder's self-assurance on the issue was at its lowest point in 1774, when he recalled the manuscript.[14]

Up to this point, whenever Herder mentioned Lithuanian songs, he only echoed Lessing's surprise and joy upon discovering that uncivilized nations have poets with "naive wit" and "lovely simplicity."[15] But in 1775, Herder received two packets of seven Lithuanian *dainos* in German translation sent by a professor at Königsberg University, J. Gottlieb Kreutzfeld.[16] Herder's view of folk poetry changed after he received these songs, possibly because their content resonated intertextually with the Old Testament Song of Solomon, with German folk songs, and with love letters that the Herders wrote to each other during their courtship. After 1775, Herder saw Lithuanian *dainos* in a new frame of universal humanity, as a fundamental expression of human love. In 1777, Herder wrote, "The Greeks, too, were once wild. . . . If the wife, Sappho, and a Lithuanian girl sing love in the same way, truly the rules of their song must be true, they are the nature of love and reach to the ends of the world." Herder would later place three of Kreutzfeld's songs at the very beginning of *Volkslieder*.[17]

While translating and editing songs, Herder wrote two essays to lay theoretical foundations for the songbooks that he would publish in 1778 and 1779.[18] His 1777 essay about "poetry's effect on the customs of people in ancient and new times" argues that throughout history poetry's power lay in its closeness to nature. When poetry is transferred from oral to written form, it loses its effect:

> *Book printing* has brought about much that is good; [but] it has *robbed* the poetic art of much of its living effect. Formerly poems resonated in living contexts, accompanied by harp, animated by the voice, the valor and heart of the singer or poet; now they stand here black on white, beautifully printed on pages made of *rags*.[19]

This was a challenge, however, that Herder planned to engage. In a second essay published that year, he offers his vision of an anthropological overview where song texts would allow many nations to represent themselves:

> Anthropology has greatly expanded the map of humanity: We now know so many more nations than just the Greeks and Romans! But how well do we know them? From outside, through hideous copper engravings, from foreigners' accounts that resemble such engravings, or from inside? Through their own soul? From sensation, talk, and action? This is how it should be, and it rarely occurs. The pragmatic writer of history or travel accounts describes, paints, portrays; he always portrays what he sees, it comes from his mind, one-sided, civilized; he thus lies, even if he wishes to lie as little as possible.
>
> The sole measure that can be taken against this is easy and obvious. All unregimented peoples *sing* and *work*; they sing what they are working and sing an exposition.[20] Their songs are the archive of the people, the treasure trove of their *science* and *religion*, their *theogony* and *cosmogony* of the deeds of their ancestors and the events of their history, the impression of their heart, the picture of their domestic life in joy and sorrow, by the bridal bed and the grave. . . . A small collection of such songs, taken from the lips of each nation, describing their work and the conditions of their life, in their own language, at the same time thoroughly understood and explained, accompanied by music: . . . From this we would gain a much better perception than from the idle chatter of travellers' accounts.[21]

Herder, like the self-reflexive "culture broker" Richard Kurin, who two centuries later would direct the Smithsonian Folklife Festival, grappled with the questions, how are cultures translated? and how are differences understood and bridged?[22] Herder formulated principles that would guide his work as a song compiler and translator: a scholar of poetry, he wrote, should be an expert historian; he should also be a specialist in the study of language and literature (a "poetic philologist"); and he should be a philosopher who knows the world well. All three perspectives were required "so that he would know the spirit of the nations surrounding him, and find among the scattered shells of examples the kernel that they nurture."[23] Out of many scattered examples of folk songs that Herder collected and edited, there soon emerged the kernel of a universal human emotion, love.

In 1778, two books of translated songs complemented Herder's essays. One was *Songs of Love* (Lieder der Liebe), a commentary and new German translation from Hebrew of Solomon's erotic Song of Songs. These passages had been censored from a recent German

edition of the Old Testament, and Herder presented theological arguments for keeping them in the canonic Bible. But in the context of his
earlier essay about "poetry's effect," this book presents German translations of effective Hebrew oral poetry that existed prior to the shift of
religious traditions to written texts. The Song of Songs is, according to
Herder, a collection of folk songs from Solomon's times that powerfully expresses humanity, effective because its poet and audience were
close to nature.[24]

Herder's other 1778 book, *Volkslieder,* and its second volume,
published in 1779, presents songs and poems from eighteen nations,
grouped according to content, giving concrete form to his vision of
poetry in a unified archive of humanity.[25] The ordering of the 162
songs in *Volkslieder* has long puzzled Herder's biographers. He himself explicitly directed his audience to read each song "in its place and
order." But subsequent readers, most notably Bernhard Suphan and
Heinrich Meyer, editors of Herder's collected works, could not identify a principle of ordering—ethnographic, aesthetic, or otherwise.[26]
Clearly there is a structure to *Volkslieder*: two volumes, each containing three "books," with twenty-four songs per book in volume 1, and
thirty songs per book in volume 2. The German scholar Ulrich Gaier,
in his annotations to the new edition of *Volkslieder,* uncovers a semantic framework related to Herder's earlier writings on poetry, finding
that the two volumes and six "books" were organized according to
fundamental eighteenth-century anthropological problems: Herder's
ordering of songs was to guide a reader through a sequence of emotions in the depths of his soul. Step by step, the reader would become
more human without himself being aware of this transformation.[27]
This was a frame in which Herder foregrounded the Lithuanian songs.

EMPATHIZING WITH LITHUANIAN SONGS
OF LOVE VERSUS WAR

The first songs in *Volkslieder's* first chapter, "Book One," echo love
poems and letters that Johann Gottfried wrote to Caroline two years
before they were married; among them are three Lithuanian songs
that may have inspired him to revive his folk song project in 1775.[28]
The next chapter, "Book Two," expands a new, broader theme:
love's opposite is war. It begins with five songs telling the tragic
story of a bride whose beloved was killed in war. First comes a six-
teenth-century German poem recounting a dialogue between a bride

and the hazelnut bush in her garden; she took the bush's advice and didn't foolishly go to a dance where she might lose her bridal wreath. Three Lithuanian songs continue the story: First, the maiden's garden was ruined. Then an enthusiastic son left his weeping father to go fight in foreign lands, soon to discover that his journey was a "black morass" with no end. Herder added three dashes here, indicating that he considered the song incomplete; the story continued in the next song, where the rider sank in a river, holding a willow branch in his hand.[29] Although this Lithuanian song does not explicitly say that the bridegroom perished, the German song that follows it is unambiguous: a maiden found a young man in the forest, red with blood, dead. Her mourning would never end. These three Lithuanian songs connect the experiences of two German songs about an unmarried woman and a widow:

SONG OF THE MAIDEN ABOUT HER GARDEN (LITHUANIAN)

Rise, maiden, sing now,
I won't! Oh, why not?
Why do you lean so weakly?
Your frail arms cannot hold you.

How can I sing
And be cheerful?
My garden devastated,
Oh, cruelly devastated!

The rue is trampled,
The roses plundered,
Crushed are the white lilies,
The dew all dried up!

Alas, I could not
I could not stand,
I sank in the rue garden,
Holding my wreath so brown.

SONG OF THE YOUNG WARRIOR (LITHUANIAN)

In early morning
My horse has just been fed.
As soon as day breaks,
Along with sunrise
I must ride far from here.

There stands my father,
He stands by my side
My dear old father

Pressed close to my side.
He stands and speaks to me;
He speaks, and he advises,
Weeping as he advises.

Hush, don't weep, my father!
Hush, don't weep, my elder!
Just as lively as I ride off,
I'll ride back so lively,
And I'll worry you no more.

Hey, my stallion,
Hey, my brown one,
Where will you fly?
Where will you neigh?
Where will you take me?

Hey, off to war!
To foreign lands!
To there you'll fly,
To there you'll neigh,
To there you will take me.

Will your wide road
Become too bitter?
And too heavy
This sack of oats
Or this young horseman
In his riding livery,
With the shining sword?

Yes, too bitter
My long road will be,
And this pitch dark night,
And these green moorlands,
And this black morass—

THE UNLUCKY WILLOW (LITHUANIAN)

Hey, my horse, my good horse
You, my dear brown one.
You, why don't you eat
Pure and pretty oats?

Is it now too bitter,
This, your distant journey
This, your distant journey,
Twice-one-hundred long miles?

Nine times we did swim,

Swimming through the waters;
Now let's plunge again
Into this tenth one!

Horse swam to the shore,
Brother sank below,
And while sinking brother
Tightly holds a willow branch.

Oh you, willow, willow,
Will you stand again?
You'll be green no longer
When the summer ends.

Yes, I want to fell you,
Cut your branches off,
And out of your trunk
I want wooden boards,
Small white wooden boards.

Out of them I'd make
A white little cradle
For my dear young maiden,
And out of your branches
I'd make wooden floorboards
For my horse's stable.

Herder brought together the two German and three Lithuanian songs to present an image of love destroyed by war, a theme of deep emotional meaning in Herder's own life. He had once moved to Rīga to evade conscription into the Prussian army. "One can only empathize with, and not describe, how his delicate mind was influenced by the daily feeling of danger that he could forever be removed from his studies, and that his inclination up to that point would be suppressed," Caroline would later write, adding, "These early influences of military power and slavery left him with a lifelong distaste for the military order in several German provinces of the time, which he would sometimes bitterly describe as crude and inhuman, a fundamental perversion of customs and implantation of ignorance and laziness."[30] An Estonian "Song about the War" that Herder placed in a later section of *Volkslieder* resonates with this personal aversion. There is only traumatic estrangement, and no love or heroism in a soldier's return from battle.[31] A sister advises her brother to stay away from the battle and come back alive; when he does return, he tells her that in war, there is no human love:

News of war has now been issued,

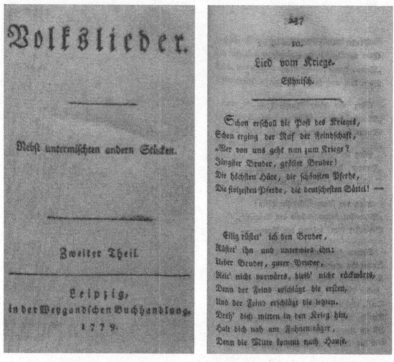

Figure 3. Estonian "Song about the War": "Full of haste, I help my brother, I prepare him and instruct him. . . . " Johann Gottfried Herder, *Volkslieder*, vol. 2 (1779), 237. Courtesy of the Department of Special Collections, Memorial Library, University of Wisconsin-Madison.

> Hostile dispatches rang out.
> Who of us will go to war now,
> Youngest brother, biggest brother!
> Highest hats, the fairest horses,
> Strongest horses, German-est saddles.
>
> Full of haste, I help my brother,
> I prepare him and instruct him:
> Dearest brother, my good brother,
> Don't ride forward, don't stay back,
> Enemies will kill the front lines,
> Enemies will kill the back lines,
> Keep yourself near the flagbearer,
> Move into the army's middle,
> Because the middle comes back home.
>
> Brother came back to his home,

Went before his father's door:
Father, come, and know your son!
Father came and knew him not.

Went before his mother's door:
Mother, come, and know your son!
Mother came and knew him not.

Went before his brother's door:
Brother, come, and know your brother!
Brother came and knew him not.

Went before his sister's door:
Sister, come, and know your brother!
Sister came and knew her brother.

How then did I know my brother?
I knew him by his short overcoat,
I knew him by his low cloak.
Dearest brother, my good brother,
Tell me, tell about the war!
Speak, how does one live in war?
Is the wife still dear in war?
Sweetest wife, the faithful spouse?

Dearest sister, little sister!
Take from me the dusty mantle,
Wash for me the bloody sword,
Then I'll speak about the war.

No, in war the wife is not dear,
Not the wife, the faithful spouse!
The shiny sword is dear in war,
The valiant horse is dear in war,
It will save the man from war.
Dear, because it sways the foe's sword,
Moves the gun from the foe's hand.

In folk poetry, Herder uncovered a gentle counterworld. Each nation had its "natural way of thinking": "The *warlike* nation sings the feats of its ancestors, inciting itself to perform similar feats," he wrote in the unpublished manuscript of 1774. "The *gentle* nation sings *love songs* full of nature and naiveté."[32] Herder repeated this contrast in the folk song project's mission statement that he wrote in 1777: "The warlike nation sings feats, the gentle sings love."[33] Among Herder's "gentle nations," then, the Lithuanians undoubtedly held a central place. Even their war songs revolved around a core of love and marriage; the soldier's "feats" were erased, and all that remained was the pain that his death caused his bride. But the first volume's Book Two ends on the theme of "love transforms everything."[34] Its next-to-last song is again Lithuanian: "The First Acquaintance" resolves the tragedy begun when the young man departed for war. Here, at the book's conclusion, begins a new love story, when a traveller drank to the health of a young maiden distant from his life's painful experiences:

> Deep in night, in darkness,
> Deep in the thick forest,
> My dear maiden was far off,
> Ere I knew her yet.
>
> Not knowing who she was,
> I arrived unmindful,
> Sat down in the corner
> By the clean white table.
>
> I sat with a full heart,
> Weeping to myself,
> Then I saw the dear girl
> By my side, above me.
>
> Now a little glass comes,
> Bubbling white with foam,
> Ho! That was my life!
> To whom is this glass raised?
>
> The glass is raised to her!
> Raised to her, fresh maiden!
> Right before me, yet how distant!
> Now my love!

Book Two then ends with love restored in a German poem, a "little song of yearning," where the singer, having fallen in love, can no longer enjoy food nor drink: "And I hope that you will not abandon me for long, or I would submit to the force of bitter death." The story that began when a young man left his bride for war is resolved: if love is alive, then death has no power. And the reader's trauma, caused by songs of war, is healed by the poetry of love.

AUTHENTIC ESTONIAN AND LATVIAN
ORAL POETRY VERSUS SLAVERY

The second volume of *Volkslieder*, writes Gaier, would show how man himself construed and took responsibility for the relationships portrayed in volume 1. Finding an effective means of expression was key. To Herder's earlier thoughts about oral poetry this volume's introduction added a context of meanings shared in performance. Folk songs, wrote Herder, should be sung, not written. "Singing loves the large group, the harmony of many: It connects the ear of the hearer and the chorus of voices and feelings." Herder's greatest fear was that folk songs, "wildflowers," might lose their charm in print and be, like weeds, plucked out of the "garden of white paper" by a refined public.[35]

This second volume was again divided into three "books," of which the first, as interpreted by Gaier, was devoted to the theme of "internal and external human," the second to "authenticity and artificiality," and the third to "fate and self-determination." The second book of this volume thus focused on the most authentic poetry—living oral traditions. It began with a cluster of Estonian, Lithuanian, Sámi ("Lapp"), Latvian, and Inuit ("Greenlander") songs, and two songs from ancient Greece. Herder quoted ethnographic reports to prove the Nordic and Baltic songs' authenticity and oral sources. He quoted August Hupel's descriptions, for example, to report that Estonians "all sing only in unison, but usually in two choirs, so that every line sung by one group is repeated by the other," and that Latvians "choose one or two maidens who sing the text, and the remaining people maintain only a single tone, somewhat like the bass note of a bagpipe."[36] Herder added yet another comment to an Estonian song to reiterate its ethnographic authenticity, but also to argue that no ethnographic evidence was needed to prove each stanza's beauty: "Here one can talk about the true, genuine, characteristic songs of a nation, and not about an abstract ideal of a song. The following songs which I present here are merely examples selected out of a large number of songs."[37]

Estonian and Latvian songs were not easy to get. In the unpublished manuscript of 1774, Herder had placed in print the meager fragments that he could find, one of which, he noted, was not qualitative or representative. It was with the help of Hamann's acquaintances that Herder finally acquired more suitable texts late in 1778, after the first volume of *Volkslieder* had already been published.[38] Herder wanted songs that would exemplify oral poetry's power. The new Estonian and Latvian songs did that, and more, when Herder added rhetorical comments about social justice. Back in Rīga, Herder's contemporaries discussed Rousseau and other Enlightenment thinkers in their relation to slavery as it had developed in Lifland Province, an issue directly related to Baltic German identity. Over the centuries since German-speaking crusaders had conquered the region in the thirteenth and fourteenth centuries, Latvians and Estonians had gradually been enserfed. For Herder, this was a land of contradictions. It was, he wrote, a "province of barbarism and luxury," a place of intellectual freedom for Germans and slavery for Latvians and Estonians.[39] Just as Herder had once empathized with and understood a Lithuanian maiden who sang love songs, he now could feel in folk poetry the crushing pain of the Estonian and Latvian serfs subjugated by German masters.

The second "book" of volume 2 begins with "A Few Wedding Songs," a single title for four Estonian songs.[40] These differ from many songs of love and longing that Herder placed elsewhere in *Volkslieder*. There is no happiness on the bride's wedding day, because she will inherit a life of grief.

> Dress yourself, adorn yourself, girl,
> Dress yourself in the same jewelry
> Which your mother carried once,
> Decorate yourself with ribbons
> Which adorned your mother once.
> On your head, a band of grief,
> On your forehead, a sash of sorrow,
> Seat yourself in mother's seat:
> Step into your mother's footsteps:
> Don't weep, don't weep, little maiden,
> If you weep in your bride's dress,
> You shall weep your entire life.

The song is followed by four others that continue the story of a maiden's marriage. She is praised by her own relatives for remaining innocent until her wedding. She meets her in-laws. And finally her husband tells her that she belongs to him, although he does not belong to her. There is a dissonance between these Estonian wedding songs and the love poetry of other nations. Herder brings the divine nature of poetry down to earth, orchestrating a clash between the songs' gentle poetic sensitivity and the barbaric reality of their Baltic singers: slavery. These songs offered to Herder stark, painful images of real humans whom he had seen in Lifland and Kurland. To the next song, also Estonian, Herder added a rhetorical title, "Lament about the Tyrants of the Serfs," and a stylistic note merged with social criticism: "A shorter text would surely be more beautiful; but it should not be abridged. The true groan that comes, not from poetic situation, but rather from the powerfully felt situation of a suffering nation, should resound as it is here."[41] In a footnote, Herder indicates that Jaan, the man mentioned in line 3, is the name of "her husband," interpreting the song as a continuation of the wife's experience that began in the previous wedding songs:

LAMENT ABOUT THE TYRANTS OF THE SERFS (ESTONIAN)

Daughter, I do not flee work,
I do not flee berry bushes,
I don't flee from Jaani's land;
I flee from the evil German,
From the horrid evil master.

Penniless farmers by the posts
Get a bloody whipping.
Lowly farmers locked in irons,
Men are rattling their shackles,
Women knocking on the door,
Bringing eggs held in their hands,
Egg patterns adorn their gloves,
Chicken shrieking in their arms,
Gray geese screaming by their sleeves,
The sheep bleating on the wagon.
When our chickens lay the eggs
All are for the German bowl.
Our sheep gives a spotted lamb,
It, too, for the German's oven.
Our cow gives its first young ox,
It, too, for the German's fields.
Our horse gives a sprightly foal,
It, too, for the German's sleigh.
Mother has an only son,
For the German's whipping post.

Our life here is purgatory,
Either hell or purgatory.
Eating burnt bread at the manor,
Moaning, drinking from their mugs,
Blackened bread and burning crust,
Sparks inside the crumbs of bread,
Whips below the crusts of bread.
If I can flee from the manor,
I will run away from Hell,
I'll escape from the jaws of the wolf,
I'll escape from the throat of the lion,
From the sharp back teeth of the pike,
From the bite of the spotted dog,
From the bite of the black dog.

You won't bite me anymore,

Spotted dog, and you, the black one!
I have bread for you, you dogs,
In the hand here for the black one,
Under the arm here for the gray one,
In the bosom for the small dog.

The word "tyrants" did not appear in the text sent to Herder by Hupel, who first translated the song into German and titled it, "A Song in Which Slavery Is Greatly Lamented."[42] In the songs and language of the Estonian peasants at the time, the word *saks* was a synonym for "master" on the estate, and did not denote Germans as a nation.[43] In his translation, Hupel seemed unsure which word to use; like other Baltic Germans, he misunderstood the word's meaning, and defined it for Herder as a word with primary connotations of ethnicity: "German, here as usual it means the masters of the estate." Herder then understood the word to denote Germans as a nation, and created the title that presented Germans as shameful tyrants. Herder's use of the "Lament about the Tyrants of the Serfs" may be interpreted broadly. Unlike contemporary critics of serfdom and slavery, Herder saw Baltic serfdom in national terms, as the oppression of one nation by another. He thus exposed what is today called colonialism.[44] The "Lament" is followed by a Greek wedding song that invokes the god of weddings, Hymen, so that, Herder wrote, the "delicate Greek soul" would "console" the Estonian song's "barbarism."[45]

The Greek song was also to "console" the Lithuanian text that followed it. Of all the Baltic songs in *Volkslieder*, "Bridesong" probably received the widest attention in German culture. It had been one of the songs that Lessing quoted, and Goethe would later quote it in his play *The Fisherman's Wife*. It was this song to which Herder referred earlier when he compared Greek and Lithuanian songs. But in *Volkslieder*, Herder seems to have lost interest in this particular text. Whereas in the unpublished *Alte Volkslieder* he had placed it first among the "Nordic" songs, now it is buried among others, and, although he formerly equated the singing "Lithuanian maiden" with Sappho, he did not place these poets next to each other.[46] Perhaps, in contrast to the Lithuanian songs of Books One and Two, this song did not resonate with Herder's personal experience. In the context of the Estonian songs before it, it is yet another lament about unhappy separation from loving parents, and about submission to fate and the tasks of a married woman.

Herder did, however, sense textual resonance between ancient Greek poems and contemporary Latvian oral poetry, as apparent in two titles:

"Fragments of Greek Songs of Sappho" and "Fragments of Latvian Songs." Both Greeks and Latvians seemed to be close to nature. Sappho felt solitude under the dark night sky: "The moon has set already, / The seven stars have waned, / It's midnight! And the hour / Has passed, and I, poor thing, / Am still alone."[47] Latvian singers, too, spoke to the sun in moments of loneliness; the sun was a comforter of orphans or a companion bringing light to a very small wedding party:

FRAGMENTS OF LATVIAN SONGS

Dearest sun, oh why so tardy?
Why did you rise up so late?
Tarrying beyond those hills, I
Warmed the orphaned children there.

Won't you shine still, dearest sun,
Through the cracks into our dwelling?
Are there no more lovely guests here
At this wedding, than we five?

Similarities, however, were not to be overemphasized. Herder added a footnote that he had inserted the "Fragments of Greek Songs," again, as an "apology" for the Latvian songs. Latvian serfs faced harsh reality in relationships: They did not sing poetry about being happily lovesick, like Sappho. A woman sees that a manservant has become haughty when he mimicks his landlord, but he is still only a serf. Serf girls should beware of their master's promises, which are as untrustworthy as tying a boat to a reed, or hitching a horse to stalk of grain:

What does master's servant lack?
Isn't he so proud and haughty:
Sitting in the master's saddle,
With the master's spurs and horse.

I would promise my son's daughter
To a young master;
I tied my ship to a reed,
Tied my pony to an oat stalk.

The remaining two "fragments" of Latvian songs again resemble Greek songs of love. Women come to sing songs and give flowers to a man, urging him to find happiness in marriage.

Up the hill I climbed and looked
All around at golden girls.
In a crowd came all the girls,
They all danced around the hill,

> They all sang such pretty songs,
> In their hands were apple blossoms, etc.
>
> Jingling, my horse was bridled,
> Jingling with a harp's strings.
> I rode him to foreign lands,[48]
> Echoing,
> Cantering,
> In foreign lands I saw maidens,
> Fair as flowers, fresh as roses,
> Young man, when you live alone,
> You have only woe and torment;
> Young man, find a woman friend,
> You'll have happiness for life.

Herder's "etc." at the end of the first stanza is puzzling. From a much longer manuscript sent to him, he selected only these few stanzas. It is possible that in this excerpt Herder saw similarities to a passage from Solomon's Song of Songs, where the bride saw her beloved when he "Springs over the hills, / Leaps over the hills. . . . / One soon sees blossoms on the ground, / The time of singing is here. . . . / Stand up, my beloved, / Stand up, my beautiful one, / Come!"[49] and he might have believed that such Biblical references would be obvious to his readers.

The Latvian stanzas also resemble Sappho's songs in which she calls on the goddess of love to offer golden nectar to her lovely boyfriends: "Come, o Cypris, come with your / Goblet full of golden nectar, / Give it to these lovely boys, / Friends of mine and also yours.[50] Sappho's trochaic meter also appears in another series of Latvian songs, titled "Spring Song":

> Come, oh come, oh nightingale!
> Come with your warm summer;
> Otherwise my dear young brothers
> Wouldn't know the time for sowing.

The image of farmers who harmonize the start of planting season with birdsong and the seasons offered poetic evidence for a Romantic description of Latvians that Herder quoted from a 1778 Baltic German novel: "In the little songs that are unique to this people, gentle, rural nature predominates."[51] The Latvians' closeness to their natural landscape would sustain spiritual and physical existence:

> Honeybee, dear little mother,
> Honey she has plenty;
> But she can't provide for all.

Summer, though, gives bread to all.

In the third and fourth stanzas of the five that Herder compiled under this one title, marriage is decreed by tradition:

> Fathers, fathers, build the paths,
> Children, children follow them;
> Grant us God that our children
> Follow after on our paths.
>
> Pony with your feet so white,
> Will you balk, or trot right through?
> Son, you must ride through it all,
> Bring a bride home for yourself.

Herder had read that Latvian folk songs preserved remnants of ancient solar mythology. This observation resonated well with the mythology of Greek poetry, and with the idea that the human institution of marriage reached back to the beginning of time. But the songs Herder had at hand did not have such content. It is likely that the final Latvian stanza was invented by Herder or his correspondent, because, unlike all of the other songs, its ties to oral tradition are questionable.[52]

> Long ago, not yesterday,
> Then the sun was still a bride;
> Long ago, not yesterday,
> That's when summer first arrived.

In *Volkslieder,* Baltic songs presented German readers with effective oral poetry, composed by singers with whom they could empathize. Readers would recognize that the singers were humans, too. With regard to Estonians and Latvians, Herder's German readers were not to feel comfortable in their empathy, because the singers' poetry emerged out of suffering. Elsewhere, and particularly in his historical writings, Herder attacked Baltic serfdom explicitly.[53] But in *Volkslieder*, Herder subverted slavery by subjectivly appealing to his German audience's conscience. An empathetic reader of these songs would discover the suffering humanity of these enslaved singers.

AFTER *VOLKSLIEDER*

In the closing pages, Herder writes, "I could be very eloquent in chattering about the use of this work, how the few withered branches of our poetry could draw refreshment from these humble dewdrops from foreign clouds. I leave this to the reader and pupil, who may desire to employ and make use of my efforts." Now, he wrote, he had said all he wished to say, and he swore not to write about folk songs anymore.[54] Herder's translations of international poetry into German were recognized in his day as a groundbreaking expansion of German poetic traditions. Herder did not simply reproduce literal content but rather aimed to "be true to the tone and the manner of each song and poem."[55] The leading literary critic, poet, and translator August Schlegel wrote to Herder, "You have brought to a never-before attained level the art of portraying the most varied kinds of natural poetry and folk poetry, each in its own tone and its own manner."[56] In 1803, Schlegel began lecturing on the significance of Herder's song collections and translations, ensuring that they found a prominent place in German and European cultural history.

The very last song in *Volkslieder* is "Eveningsong," a Christian hymn written by Herder's gentle friend Matthias Claudius.[57] Herder had argued in his 1777 essay that the original character of poetry was preserved in hymns; in the conclusion of *Volkslieder* he explains that he wished to give readers "a glimpse at the kind of content that the best folk songs have and will continue to have. The hymnal is the Bible of the folk, their consolation and their best respite."[58] After finishing *Volkslieder*, Herder shifted his energies to church chorales, compiling a Lutheran hymnal published in 1795.[59] For him, this was a logical continuation of the *Volkslieder*.

Herder resurrected his folk song project at the turn of the century. In November of 1799, Caroline wrote to a publisher that there would be a new collection of folk songs, "with a different configuration and title,"[60] and in 1803, shortly before his death, Herder described his goal: "A resurrected collection of such [folk] songs, expanded, ordered according to lands, epochs, languages, and nations, and clarified according to these contexts, *as a living voice of the nations and of humankind itself.*" [61] Herder mentioned "the voice of the folk, of scattered humankind" in an 1803 poem that he probably intended to publish in the new book's introduction. How he intended to present that "voice" through song texts is not known.[62] Had Herder himself published a revised collection, it is likely that he would have written new essays to introduce the book and its chapters, and added notes explaining song details, as he had done in *Volkslieder*. In view of Herder's other essays and poems written in 1803, it is likely that the themes of love and war would have provided at least one frame. He might have included, for example, James MacPherson's songs of Ossian, which to him proved that "epic songs can exist also without bloodthirstiness and murder, without an eagerness for conquest, fanaticism, superstition and idolatry, without apparitions and the devil: these were the gifts one had wished for."[63] Perhaps Herder would quote songs of the past to construct a future where "humans would be friends of humans, and no nation on earth sharpens its sword anymore."[64] Such a frame would follow from Herder's philosophy of history, where he synthesized the opposing ideologies that Isaiah Berlin has called "cultural pluralism" and "monism": Herder saw humanity as a diverse array of nations moving toward the fixed end of God's plan.[65]

The folk song project, writes Ulrich Gaier, was one that Herder pursued throughout his life, and he was always developing new perspectives on the topic.[66] Herder passed away leaving only a few hints about how the project's next steps might proceed. It is not known which songs from his large collection he would have included. Caroline Herder and Johannes von Müller took it upon themselves to continue, well aware of the fact that their new book would be "only a shadow of what he intended." Guided by a brief outline that Herder had titled "Voices of the Nations," they edited a new and expanded book to which they gave the title *Voices of the Nations in Songs* (*Stimmen der Völker in Liedern*). They could not include all of the nations mentioned in Herder's outline, because there were no such songs in his collection. They did not attempt to create the outline's concluding chapter, which Herder had titled "Universal Voice of Humankind. Moral Songs. Songs (Gesänge) for the Folk."[67] Caroline Herder and Müller did, however, revive most of the folk songs from Herder's earlier books; they published all of the Baltic songs of both *Volkslieder* and the earlier, unpublished 1774 *Alte Volkslieder* manuscript, including the fragmentary Estonian and Latvian songs that Herder thought were of inferior quality. They added one Estonian and two Latvian songs that Herder, it seems, translated after publishing the 1779 volume. Among them was a series of Latvian midsummer stanzas, perhaps a clue that Herder was, as Stavenhagen argued, originally inspired by a midsummer celebration near Rīga.[68]

The editors of *Stimmen* shared Herder's love for humankind. They remarked that the book contained "fragments of a glorious Odeum" (an ancient Greek stage for poetry competitions), where singers would sing in the most diverse national intonations to express the spirit of each people, while universal human nature would allow "a harmony of all lineages" to emerge.[69] Today, however, there is consensus that

Caroline Herder's and Johannes von Müller's book did not succeed in resurrecting the project interrupted by Herder's death.[70] A dissonance is most evident in their new title: whereas Herder had envisioned a *single,* universal voice (*eine Stimme*) of humankind expressed in the songs of many nations, the editors produced a book of *many* voices (*Stimmen*).[71] Ironically, it is this title and book, and not *Volkslieder*, which is usually attributed to Herder and has been reprinted most often over the subsequent two centuries. This new anthology, in which all songs are segregated by nation, inclines a reader to skim through the international table of contents in order to focus on the songs of one's own people, reading only those particular texts out of the many that Herder once integrated and celebrated. This seems to be what Balts and other Europeans usually did in the centuries after Herder's death, when the study and revival of folk songs grew and flourished. Many quoted Herder, but few paid attention to songs that weren't of their own nation.

It is not surprising that Herder is remembered today in Estonia, Latvia, and Lithuania as one of the Balts' first true foreign friends, a welcome advocate in an epoch in which these countries were still shackled in chains of serfdom. But the Baltic debt to Herder extends beyond his discovery and elevation of their folk songs, and beyond his arguments for the emancipation of Baltic serfs. Herder's *Volkslieder* and other essays shaped the work of nation builders for years to come. When Estonians, Latvians, and Lithuanians of the nineteenth and twentieth centuries recalled Herder, they also saw in his work an assignment for themselves. Baltic patriots pored over Herder's works, quoting him as an authority, compiling his references to their particular nations, studying the songs that he had published. Texts from *Volkslieder* took on a new life in traditions of national culture. Some were revived as heritage of the nation's golden age, others were included in national epics, and still others passed into the traditions of choral songs.

Regardless of whether Estonians, Latvians, and Lithuanians were or weren't nonviolent nations before Herder, what he wrote about them left an imprint on later interpretations of current national spirit and future national missions. Wedding and love songs, for example, were prominent in Herder's portrayal of the world's humans and their love, and they retained a celebrated place in Baltic national cultures. The idea that their songs were as valuable as those of the ancient Greeks stimulated Lithuanian, Latvian, and Estonian national pride.

Balts likewise would continue to believe that, unlike the more industrialized nations of Europe, they had not lost an ancient, close connection to nature. In the nineteenth- and twentieth-century era of military heroism, it was more problematic to accept Herder's notion of Balts as gentle farmers, not warriors, but this image, too, took root in Estonian, Latvian, and Lithuanian national identities.

The seeds that Herder planted grew into massive national movements. Like Herder, cultural activists everywhere recognized in folk songs effective poetry, to be revived as poetic and historical heritage; they studied songs to discover the "spirit" of their nation, and to find its place among other nations. For them, empathetic revival made songs into weapons that could be used in a struggle for cultural equality and social justice. Herder built a bridge to the world of songs, and subsequent generations followed in his footsteps across that bridge into the future.

Herder also demonstrated an ethnographic method that this book about the Singing Revolution hopes to reproduce. Deeply moved by living, singing voices, Herder collected, translated, and printed songs that, he hoped, would transmit a similar effect to his book's empathetic readers. Song texts on a printed page could be a bridge to emotions that moved people in the past.

A BRIDGE OF FOLK SONGS FROM HERDER
TO THE SINGING REVOLUTION

And many branching strands of Herderian traditions reconverge here, on July 11, 1991, on the shores of Lake Jugla, at the opening of the International Folklore Festival, Baltica. On the first page of the festival's printed songbook is a song whose first stanza once appeared, in German translation, in Herder's *Volkslieder*. The song comes to life when Skandinieki sing the text and tune documented by Herder's correspondent, Hupel. Its melody is strange, only three notes, and its performance style is archaic: Dainis Stalts calls out lines, and the group repeats them. Some singers repeat his melody, while others drone the repeated words on a single note, like a bagpipe:

Fathers' fathers building bridges, / Children's children crossing bridges;
    (repeat)
God grant that our little child / Finds the path across the bridges;
    (repeat)

Figure 4. Latvian folk song published by Herder's correspondent, August Hupel: "Fathers' Fathers Building Bridges," *Topographische Nachrichten*, vol. 3 (1782), printed insert. Courtesy of the Department of Special Collections, University of Minnesota Libraries.

> Fathers' fathers building bridges, / Children's children crossing bridges;
>   (repeat)
> Children, when you cross the bridges, / Keep enough to last a lifetime.
>   (repeat)

This is the same song that Herder once published in *Volkslieder*—and yet it also isn't the same song. For Herder, it was a song about marriage. He added a stanza in which a father advises his son to bring home a wife, and he added two more stanzas to place such parents and children in a mythical frame of natural bounty and the ancient wedding of the sun. The singers at the folklore festival, on the other hand, sing a second stanza with a variant line collected from oral tradition.[72] These words add rhetoric that is directed, first of all, at the lead singer's own children, and perhaps at his wife and her father, who are all there, singing with him. In a broader context, the song speaks to all of the folklore festival participants, audience and singers alike, urging them—the children's children—to keep and carry through their lives a legacy that their ancestors created. This folklore festival holds on to heritage of the past: "The human spirit endures, enshrined in traditions which, over the centuries, have lovingly preserved the traces of all those who have passed this way before," writes the folklorist (and future president of Latvia) Vaira Vīķe-Freiberga.[73] The song and festival also gaze into the future, to the children's children: "Even if some day the door to the family of free European nations is opened for us, the traditional folk culture is still going to be of important and lasting value for us in order to retain and safeguard our national as well as cultural identity," writes a founder of the Baltica festival, the ethnomusicologist (and future first lady of Estonia) Ingrid Rüütel.[74] Rüütel's words will gain new force a month and a half after this folklore festival, when in August of 1991 the Soviet Union will dissolve and the Baltic countries will again be independent.

This song and this festival of many songs combine a memory of the past with rhetoric that shapes the political future. Singers follow past tradition and adapt the song to new contexts. The song is most powerful in the immediate present, during performance. The sung words resemble Herder's, but their texture is different. Herder's was a silent, written text permanently printed on the pages of a book, but this song comes alive on the lips of singers and in the ears and hearts of listeners. It is oral poetry, a true folk song as imagined by Herder when he exclaimed, "Song must be *heard*, not *seen*!"[75] Voices converge and resonate, sending a chill down a participant observer's spine. This singing moves and transforms people rationally and emotionally, intellectually and viscerally. And when people are moved this way, history's course can change.

Three Singing Nations and Their Songs

They pass at a rate of one hundred people per minute, or more. Thirty thousand singers, walking with their choirs in a long procession from Old Town Tallinn down Narva Street, past the building near Kreutzwaldi Street where we perch in a small fourth-floor apartment balcony, and continuing on to the great Estonian song festival stage on the outskirts of town. They sing as they walk. Fragments of songs in my sound recording are overpowered by the cheers of thousands who line the sides of the street; melodies played by marching bands sometimes converge, sometimes drown out the singers' voices.

... *Läks aga metsa mängima, läks aga laande lauluga* ...
... Stepped in the forest with a tune, went into the woods with songs...

... *Mu isamaa armas, kus sündinud ma* ...
... My dear fatherland, land where I was born ...

... *Saa vabaks, Eesti meri, saa vabaks* ...
... Be free, Estonia's sea, be free ... [1]

These songs, and many others, are part of an informal national repertoire. Created by individual poets and composers in the nineteenth and twentieth centuries, and diffused by the mass media, the songs entered oral tradition. They are sung at family celebrations and community gatherings, and, of course, while walking in the song festival procession. But they are rarely performed on stage to a passive, listening audience.

Figure 5. Latvian song festival procession at the crossing of Brīvības and Miera Streets, Rīga, July 7, 1990. Photo by Guntis Šmidchens.

The cheering expands to a roar when the crowd greets the Vilnius Conservatory Choir, whose leader proudly carries the gold, green, and red flag of Lithuania:

> . . . *žirgelių girdyt, žirgelių girdyt* . . .
> . . . to give their horses water, give their horses water . . .

A Soviet military helicopter thunders over our heads. An ominous warning from above, we think? No, our Estonian friends calm us; it was rented by the city to film the historic song festival procession today, June 30, 1990.

A week later, about two hundred miles to the south, in the capital city of Latvia, the street is lined with masses of people; we lean across the windowsills of an apartment building at the crossing of Brīvības and Miera Streets. It is not only the choirs in the procession who are singing. The Latvian spectators sing, too. Songs flow in a constant, never-ending stream.

> . . . *Šeit ir Latvija, šeit ir Gaujmala* . . .
> . . . This is Latvia, these are Gauja's shores . . .

> . . . *Latviet's esmu, latviet's būšu, latviet's mūžam palikšu* . . .
> . . . I am a Latvian, I'll be a Latvian, forever I'll remain Latvian . . .

As in Estonia, the spectators often call out to the choirs walking past: "Long live teachers!" (to the Sidrabene schoolteachers' choir); the choir answers with a cheer. "Long live Bauska!" (to a choir from that city); the choir answers with a cheer. Or sometimes a singer calls back: "Long live the ladies up there on the roof!" or "Long live the inhabitants of this great building on Freedom (Brīvības) Street!" Or the choir replies as a group, in four-part harmony:

Sveiks lai dzīvo, sveiks lai dzīvo, lai dzīvo sveiks!
Long may he live, long may he live, may he live long!

As the procession passed on that day, Latvians sang more than thirty different songs, most of them more than once.[2] These songs were common knowledge, sung alike by choirs in the street and spectators on the sidewalks. Latvians, too, shared a national repertoire from which they retrieved texts appropriate to any occasion. In the summer of 1990, two months after Latvia's declaration of renewed independence, the patriotic texts quoted above were most frequent, as may be expected. But most songs had no explicit nationalist ideology. The happy "Long May He Live" is one example, to which may be added many, many other songs of love, work, and life in the preindustrial countryside. The typical length of these *dainas*, archaic folk songs from oral tradition, is four to seven two-line stanzas, each line repeated twice.

. . . *Ciemā teku, ciemā teku meitas celt* . . .
. . . Going to the village to wake up the girls . . .

. . . *Pati māku sienu pļauti, pat' izkapti asināt* . . .
. . . I know how to cut my own hay, I can sharpen my own scythe . . .

. . . *Pa vienāmi saule lēca, pa otrāmi norietēj'* . . .
. . . Through one door the sun was rising, through the other door it set . . .

. . . *Uz akmeņa malku cirtu, strautā kūru uguntiņu* . . .
. . . On a stone I chopped the firewood, in a brook I lit a fire . . .

While thousands of singers walked by, spectators strained to see the people they knew, running out into the street to hand a flower to a relative or friend in that particular choir. Each flower came from someone among the nation's masses. The singers' hands were full. In the Baltic, at national song festivals, the relation between the individual and the nation was mediated by songs and singing traditions. The idea that every nation has songs came, of course, from Herder. For Herder, too, songs expressed the spirit of their singers, but it is no simple step from Herder's writings to modern-day individuals who sang together by the hundreds or even thousands, in agreement that their songs were both a means and a goal of the nation's existence.

HYMNS BEFORE ANTHEMS

As elsewhere in Europe, print media created conditions necessary for the formation of modern nations in the Baltic.[3] The authors of religious literature, and Protestant Christian literature in particular, standardized print language across a territory of diverse dialects, and produced native-language hymnals to launch congregational singing traditions. These, then, were the first printed texts that could be shared on a mass level. Baltic people were not yet "nations" as defined by Anthony David Smith, groups bound by explicit public rituals and a centrally organized official national culture. At the outset of their national movements in the nineteenth century, however, Estonians, Latvians, and Lithuanians could be loosely described by Smith's term, "ethnie," a "named, self-defined human population with myths of common origins, shared historical memories, elements of common culture, and a measure of ethnic solidarity."[4] The formation of Baltic ethnies coincides with the history of choral singing among Estonians, Latvians, and Lithuanians; in fact, singing, more than any other cultural activity, was instrumental in national group formation.

The Protestant Reformation provided ideological foundations for a choir singer's identity. Martin Luther argued that congregational singing was a means for individuals to establish a direct relationship with God; he wrote and popularized hymns sung in German, enabling all singers to actively participate in the Eucharist. Lutheran pastors continued the tradition of translating or composing hymns in the native languages of their congregations (Herder, too, was a Lutheran pastor). For Baltic Protestants, and, later, Catholics, church singing traditions established a new form of public singing, apart from the folk traditions practiced by kin and household groups. The introductions and title pages to these native-language hymnals testify that they were printed for the "Estonians," the "Latvians," or the "Lithuanians." National self-identification came later, coinciding with the awareness of a song repertoire held in common with others who spoke, read, and sang the languages.

The Lithuanian ethnic minority of East Prussia, a population of about 33,000 in the sixteenth century, was first to be officially converted to Protestantism.[5] Native-language church services were fundamental to Protestant ideology, and thus from the very start Lithuanian was supported institutionally. A Lithuanian language seminar was established at Königsberg University to provide training for theology students who would serve as pastors in Lithuanian-speaking congregations, and Lithuanian-language parish schools were established in 1568. With the very first Lithuanian-language book—a catechism that included ten hymns—a long, rich tradition of published Lutheran hymnals began mainly with translations of German texts, and later expanded to include folk melodies and hymns from oral tradition.[6] The number of Lithuanians in East Prussia expanded sevenfold by the end of the seventeenth century, but the plague of 1709–11 killed about half of them, leaving a population of about 100,000. The region was colonized by Germans (among them also Herder's parents[7]), and over the short period of a few decades Lithuanians became a minority in most districts. From then on, they gradually assimilated into German culture, and the Lithuanian language faded from public life, surviving only in church services and primary school religion lessons. Despite the fact that hymn texts were printed in books, national choral music traditions did not emerge. Lithuanian Lutheran congregations sang in unison, not choral harmonies; they also did not follow the standardized melodies of Lutheran German hymns but instead sang hymns in the style of oral folk song traditions to yield new melodies not shaped by printed musical notes.[8]

Congregational singing traditions were different for Lithuanians to the east, across the border in the Commonwealth of Lithuania and Poland, where the Roman Catholic Church was dominant. There, from the fifteenth century on, music was performed by trained singers during services, but the language was Latin. Little changed after Lithuania was annexed by the Russian Empire in the late eighteenth century. Around that time, Catholics also began to sing hymns in Polish, the language of the rural gentry and urban elite. The first records of Lithuanian-language church singing date from the 1860s. Unofficial Lithuanian-language "folk" hymnals (*kantička*) were printed in 1820 and 1859 and saw many reprintings, but melodies varied from place to place because the hymnals did not include notes. Official, standardized, and professionalized church musical traditions took root only at the turn of the twentieth century. The Catholic Church provided less stimulus to popular schooling and literacy than its Protestant counterpart across the border, and when parochial schools were established, lessons were usually conducted in Polish, not Lithuanian. After the Polish and Lithuanian rebellion of 1863, the government print ban on Lithuanian books, along with restrictions on public choirs, slowed the spread and standardization of singing traditions among Lithuanian Catholics in the Russian Empire until the beginning of the twentieth century.[9]

In the German-speaking congregations of Rīga and Tallinn, Lutheran musical traditions were established in the 1520s, when professional cantors were hired to perform music and teach it at church schools.[10] The first Latvian- and Estonian-language hymnals were published soon afterward,[11] and traditions of both literacy and congregational singing slowly took root among the Estonian and Latvian serfs, despite the reluctance of the local nobility to educate them. Unlike the Prussian government, which encouraged and often enforced German language use among Lithuanians, the Baltic German nobility's consistent policy was to exclude non-German serfs from German-speaking society. Protestant singing traditions took hold at the grassroots level in Lifland and Estland Provinces during the early 1700s, in Moravian Brethren congregations established by the followers of Nikolaus Ludwig von Zinzendorf, who wrote that songs were "the best method to bring God's truth to the heart and preserve it there."[12] Zinzendorf's followers, like Lutheran pastors, produced both handwritten and printed hymnals in the native languages. Although the Brethren were officially banned in the Baltic Provinces in 1743, their traditions of both written and musical literacy spread through informal home instruction. The Duchy of Kurland banned all Moravians throughout the eighteenth century, but Pietist ideas inspired Lutheran pastor Gotthard Stender to advocate literacy for Latvians and publish books with secular content, including also songbooks. Among the folk songs and early Latvian poetry that Stender documented was a poem printed in 1685 that began with the words, "Shine, sun, shimmering!"[13]

Throughout the 1700s, formal schooling was rare in the region, and minimal for non-Germans. Nevertheless, various sources document that by the end of the eighteenth century, some Estonians and Latvians attended German-speaking parish schools and served as cantors in rural churches. Congregations or schoolchildren's choirs sometimes even sang in four-part harmony. In the first half of the nineteenth century, reports appeared with increasing frequency about Estonian and Latvian singing in rural choirs.[14] The repertoire of Lutheran choral music moved toward standardization in 1839, when Johann Punschel published his *Evangelical Chorale Book, Coordinated with the German, Latvian, and Estonian Hymnals of Russia's Baltic Provinces*; over the next seventy-five years, the book was reprinted in fifteen editions.[15] Choral singing traditions were now on firm, mass-mediated foundations in Latvian and Estonian Lutheran congregations, fertile ground for the seeds of nationalism that were planted in subsequent decades by native activists.

Along with a mass-mediated, shared language, a shared national choral culture was one of the cultural preconditions for the emergence of Baltic national movements. The history of church music illuminates a similarity between Estonian and Latvian singing traditions on the one hand, and their differences from Lithuanian singing on the other hand. The Lutheran regions where most Estonians and Latvians lived were first to see native-language congregational singing that followed standardized, published hymn texts and melodies. While such standardization existed to some extent in the Lithuanian Lutheran congregations of East Prussia, it did not occur until the beginning of the twentieth century for Roman Catholics in the Lithuanian and east Latvian (Latgale) regions of the Russian Empire.

The Estonian and Latvian "ethnies" thus had relatively uniform cultures of choral singing. Singing by itself, however, does not make a nation. Songs accumulated new meanings tied to national identity when, beginning in the early nineteenth century, local intellectuals studied the indigenous Baltic cultures and cultivated symbols that later were used to construct modern national cultures.[16] Prominent among these new national symbols was the oral poetry that had once energized Herder's folk song project.

SONGS BECOME NATIONAL HERITAGE

In the nineteenth century, the study and revival of Baltic oral poetry continued at the desks of educated individuals who had sufficient leisure time for reading and writing. The ethnic backgrounds of these individuals varied, but by education they were usually acculturated into a German-speaking world. They were interested in the antiquities—including indigenous languages and songs—of their locality; sometimes they went out into the field to collect Estonian, Latvian, or Lithuanian folk songs, and then converted oral poetry into written monuments of culture. When they mentioned Herder, it was usually to point him out as a prominent outsider who validated the study of that nation's folk songs.[17]

Among others, Herder's *Volkslieder* correspondents continued to collect, translate, and publish folk song texts. It was probably J. Gottlieb Kreutzfeld, for example, who contributed two Lithuanian songs to a Prussian journal in 1780.[18] August Hupel continued to write detailed ethnographies of Estonian and Latvian serfs in Lifland Province, and Gustav Bergmann printed his private collections of Latvian songs, commenting, however, that their artistic value was negligible: "They cannot be freely compared to the masterpieces of the Greeks and Romans, but they do have a unique scholarly attraction, because they are the only thing we have in this language, from this nation which itself cannot write."[19]

Others published songs as part of a broader project of human liberation. Christian Schlegel and Garlieb Merkel published Estonian and Latvian songs, respectively, adding rhetorical comments that songs were proof of those nations' creative potential if emancipated from serfdom: "Had they been appropriately evaluated earlier, perhaps they would already now be free of their shackles," wrote Merkel in 1797.[20] Merkel and his contemporaries catalyzed a new, speculative branch of Baltic folk song scholarship, using *dainas* as a source for the study of Baltic prehistory and mythology, creating images of the past that spoke to the present. They constructed what they believed to be ancient pantheons, and in doing so they also constructed an argument that these nations had cultural roots comparable to those of the ancient Greeks and Romans.[21]

Research on prehistory and mythology supported contemporary rhetoric. Merkel argued that the Latvians had always been nonviolent. He imagined that the ancestors of the Latvians and the Lithuanians did not know war before the medieval Christian conquest, finding proof in a chronicle that supposedly quoted Baltic travelers in 559 AD: "In our land there is neither iron nor war; we live in constant peace, and know no better pursuit than music." Merkel celebrated the supposed Latvian god of love and friendship, Līgo, whose name he thought to have survived in the popular refrain of Latvian midsummer songs. Regarding Estonians, whose prehistory Merkel considered to be the same as that of the Finns, he asserted that they had never pursued conquest of foreign territories. They appeared to have loved music and poetry; a medieval chronicle account gave evidence of their receptivity to harmony: "When the Estonians were once attacking a Latvian fortress, a Latvian Christian priest stood on the fortress wall and began to play on an instrument: Suddenly the Estonians halted the attack and finally

Figure 6. Illustration in Merkel's history of Lifland Province, *Vorzeit Lieflands*, vol. 1 (1798), 229. Traditional Estonian clothes are demonstrated by "Vaina-Möinen, Orpheus of the Finns," whose music, Merkel notes, was said to be so beautiful that even wild bears came to listen. Courtesy of the Department of Special Collections, Stanford University Libraries.

departed."[22] Merkel shared his research with Herder, at whose home he was a frequent guest, and Herder praised Merkel's 1796 book *The Latvians*, "which," wrote Herder, "has accomplished much good."[23]

Merkel's writings about prehistory blended seamlessly with his literary creations, most notably *Vanem Ymanta*, a dreamlike narrative interspersed with descriptions of singing at ancient pagan rites, telling the story of a Livonian chieftain whose lands were invaded in the thirteenth century by the armies of Christian crusaders.

Artistic creativity also lay close to the roots of Lithuanian folk song scholarship. In the late eighteenth century, a student at Königsberg University, Liudvikas Rėza, began writing German-language poetry. He participated in the university's Lithuanian seminar, and identified with the ethnic Lithuanian heritage of his birthplace on the Couronian Spit, assuming the middle name Jedimin in honor of the medieval Lithuanian Duke Gediminas. In 1809, he published his first book, *Prutena* (Latin for "Prussia"), a collection of sixty-one German-language poems arranged around ten poems with the subtitle "Lithuanian Folk Song."[24]

Rėza later recalled that some of these "Lithuanian songs" in *Prutena* were true translations of songs from oral tradition, while others were free adaptations or individual creations.[25] His sources have been identified by Albinas Jovaišas, who found that Rėza had not yet read *Volkslieder* but was familiar with several of Herder's Lithuanian songs reprinted elsewhere. Among them was "Song of the Maiden about Her Garden" (quoted in chapter 2), which Rėza revised and expanded in *Prutena* under the title "Lament of a Maiden for Her Garden of Rue":

> Your blue eyes so sad?
> No wreath 'round your locks?
> Why do you weep, lovely maiden?
> Rise! sing us a daina for a dance!
>
> How can I now sing a daina,
> My garden devastated, desolate!
> How can I weave myself a wreath,
> The rue plants have all been destroyed!
>
> The little tree has no leaves,
> No longer offers its shade,
> Roses trampled in dust,
> Lilies scattered all 'round!
>
> Did the storm wind strike it,

Unleash a foaming flood,
Did Perkono from the angry chariot
Sling arrows of fire?

The storm wind has not struck it,
Nor torn open a foaming flood,
Perkono from the angry chariot,
Did not sling arrows of fire.

With sword in hand,
Came men of war
From the sea onto shore,
Brought destruction here.

What have the men from the sea done
To you, my innocent garden?
Here I sit and grieve in tears,
Whatever shall I do now?

The little tree has no leaves,
No longer offers its shade,
Roses trampled in dust,
Lilies scattered all 'round!

Like other "storm and stress" poets of his day, Rėza studied folklore as a source of artistic inspiration. In *Prutena*, he conjured up ancient Lithuanian mythology and history, combining oral poetry with new stanzas based on his studies of Old Prussian mythology. The scholarly basis of his poetic lines is expounded in annotations such as the one for "Lament of a Maiden": "'Percono from the angry chariot.' Percono, the god of thunder, together with Picollo, god of the dead and Potrimpo, god of fertility, were the three primary gods of the Old Prussians. Still to this day, Lithuanians say of stormy weather: 'Percon is riding his chariot, or he is is angry.'" Rėza's fourteen pages of such notes are in fact the first substantial published overview of Lithuanian folk song and mythology scholarship.[26]

In 1807, Rėza began teaching at Königsberg University, and eleven years later he was appointed professor of Oriental languages and theology. It was during this time that he compiled a scholarly collection of *dainos*. Failing to find a publisher, Rėza himself financed the book's printing in 1825.[27] "There is nothing in this collection of mine which I could call my own property. It all belongs to the Lithuanian people. Only the translations and annotations are mine," he wrote in the introduction. Rėza's reference to Herder in his 1809 survey of Lithuanian folk song scholarship proves that at that time he had not yet read

Volkslieder, but the 1825 introduction notes that he had translated several songs found in that book from German to Lithuanian, because the original Lithuanian texts were not available.[28] These texts, however, also contain Rėza's innovations. In translating Herder's "Song of a Maiden," for example, Rėza gave it a new title, "Ruin in the Garden." He changed the color of the maiden's wreath from brown to black, but, most important, he added to the new Lithuanian text the stanzas that he himself composed in 1807, about the storm wind, the god of thunder, and the men from the sea. He added still more new motifs to that text when he imagined the foreign invaders to be "Bearded men, men from the seas, arriving onshore."

Rėza's unpublished manuscripts reveal that he in fact fabricated all of the mythological poetry found in the 1825 book.[29] Although Rėza's collection led the scholars of ancient mythology into a quagmire of pseudomythology, it also left lasting legacies in two modern Lithuanian cultural traditions. The first was artistic. The mythological images that Rėza presented offered to generations of Lithuanian (and also Latvian) patriots literary references akin to those of classical mythology, affirming the idea that Lithuanian and Baltic culture had inherent value. The second legacy was a model for subsequent folklore research. Rėza's annotations and comparative notes set high standards for knowledge of the published literature. He initiated genre studies in Lithuanian oral poetics when he distinguished *dainos* from *giesmės* (religious hymns) and the less common genre of *raudos* (laments). And, most notably, after Rėza published seven folk song melodies together with his eighty-five verbal texts, later scholars followed suit and printed Lithuanian melodies collected from oral tradition—decades before comparable publications appeared in Latvian or Estonian scholarship. The book was reviewed by Goethe and by Jacob Grimm, whose favorable remarks about Lithuanian songs, like Lessing's and Herder's before them, would later be quoted by Lithuanian patriots as international validation of Lithuanian folklore studies.[30]

To the north, in Estonian lands, it was an 1815 edition of Herder's collected works, among them the revised collection of folk songs edited by Herder's wife Caroline and Johannes Müller, that elicited the first "Herderian" traditions of folk song interpretation.[31] To be sure, scholars collected Estonian folk songs before that year, but they usually didn't reference Herder by name, and Herderian ideas regarding the beauty or inherent value of folk songs were not characteristic, particularly in the ethnographic writings of August Hupel.[32]

The most prominent case of a conversion to Herderian interpretations appears in the long-lived ethnographic journal *Beiträge zur genauern Kenntniss der ehstnischen Sprache*, established in 1813 by Johann Heinrich Rosenplänter. The second volume published that year included four Estonian folk songs, to which the editor added a note that questioned their value. "Permit the editor to append a comment to these so-called songs, because they are hardly songs in any other way than by name. . . . How much is there still to do, particularly for the Estonian pastors, to awaken a better spirit in the Estonian, and to plant in him a noble intellect."[33] But three years later, Rosenplänter changed his opinion, and to a new corpus of folk song texts he added a note about their great poetic significance, referring to Herder's *Stimmen der Völker in Liedern* as his source: "What he says there about the German language and literature, it seems to me, may easily be applied to Estonian."[34]

Jaan Undusk has recently pointed out that here Rosenplänter actually copied passages not from *Stimmen* but rather from Herder's essays about Ossian and about the relation of German and English poetry. In the 1815 Stockholm edition, these essays were published in a single volume as *Stimmen der Völker*. Rosenplänter replaced the word "German" with "Estonian," and did not explicitly quote his source. Later Estonian folk song scholars, most notably Jakob Hurt, also repeated Herder's words in the Estonian adaptation, establishing a tradition of scholarship that was not overtly aware of its source in Herder's writing.[35] Another prominent propagator of this Herderian "synechdoche" in Estonian folk song scholarship was Arnold Knüpffer, who contributed many Estonian songs to Rosenplänter's journal, and in 1817 argued that modern Estonian poetry should adopt the native meter and style of Estonian folk poetry, or it would forever remain "foreign and unpalatable" to the Estonian spirit.[36]

The journal's Estonian folk songs were avidly studied by Christian Jaak Peterson, who found rich comparative materials in Kristfrid Ganander's 1789 Swedish-language overview of Finnish mythology. Peterson translated that book into German, adding extensive comparative notes on Estonian variants, and sometimes modifying Ganander's ideas to fit his own view of the ancient pantheon.[37] To Peterson, the Estonian folk songs proved that the ancestors of the Estonians had also once sung epic songs about the god of song whom Finns called Väinämöinen: "The deity described in them, however, has completely disappeared, or one finds a singing farmer instead."

I had a dear brother,
He went on the hill to play,
He went on the hill to play,
To make a stringed instrument for himself
From the wood of the apple tree,
From the wood of the hazel bush,
From the wood of the white maple.[38]

Over the subsequent centuries, the folk songs studied by Peterson and other Estonians would resurface numerous times as expressions of Estonian national tradition, while Johann Gottfried Herder's view of folk songs as a universal human expression receded to the background.

The early Baltic folklorists, like their peers elsewhere in Europe, usually saw oral folk poetry as a dying tradition. Some were content to collect and publish the songs as "monuments" of an earlier era.[39] Others saw a potential for adapting oral poetry into their nation's written literary culture.[40] Baltic nation builders gradually constructed an image of Lithuanians, Latvians, and Estonians as "nations of singers." Herder had once focused on songs of love as the core of Lithuanian folk poetry, but when Simonas Stanevičius published his first collection of Lithuanian folk songs in 1829, its first song was about singing; the thematic grouping of "songs about singing" was also adopted by leading Latvian and Estonian folklorists.[41]

EUROPEAN NATIONALISM COMES TO THE BALTIC

The national anthems of England and France sparked a transnational movement that produced at least one national anthem for every nation and country in the world. Both of these eighteenth-century songs were established in state policies that aimed to mobilize popular loyalty. England's "God Save the King" publicly premiered in 1745. It built on England's tradition of Protestant chorales that united singers in collective prayer, asking God to protect the monarch and "scatter his enemies, and make them fall." The simplicity of the words and melody of England's anthem was envied and copied by political leaders, composers, and poets on the continent throughout the nineteenth century.[42] In the Russian Empire, an 1815 translation of the English anthem by Vasilii Zhukovskii, "Prayer of the Russians," served at official occasions for nearly two decades, but borrowed anthem content and melodies soon lost their luster, and Zhukovskii's was discarded in 1833 when Tsar Nicholas I wearied of listening to its "English" melody and commissioned a new anthem. Zhukovskii's new text, "God Protect the Tsar," followed a poetic structure similar to the English anthem but had a new melody composed by Aleksei L'vov. Although it was also a prayer, Russia's new anthem differed from England's. After a one-line prayer to God for the tsar's protection, the collective nation addressed its absolutist political ruler directly, in second-person singular: "Powerful Ruler, / rule for our glory, / rule to the terror of enemies, oh Orthodox Tsar!" Tsar Nicholas I decreed in 1833 that the song be performed at all ceremonial occasions, and, as in England and France, the national anthem was required at theater performances.[43] A choir of one thousand singers sang it at the coronation of Alexander II in 1856, accompanied by an orchestra of two thousand. Submission to the tsar as God's representative on earth was affirmed in mass rituals; in 1883, Alexander crowned himself, then stood during the prayer while the public kneeled before him; at the tercentennary celebration of 1913, the public kneeled before Tsar Nicholas II as the anthem was played. Another new song in the Russian nationalist canon was "Glory, Glory to Our Russian Tsar!," the finale chorale of Mikhail Glinka's 1836 national opera, *A Life for the Tsar*. It, too, confirmed the nation's submission to the monarch's divine rights: "Given to us by the Lord, oh sovereign tsar, / let your royal lineage be eternal, / through it let there be happiness for the Russian people!" Glinka's arrangement of "Glory" was later revised by Tchaikovsky to transition into the national anthem, and was performed by eight hundred singers at Alexander III's coronation in 1883.[44] In the late nineteenth century, both songs were required in the curriculum of all schools in the Russian Empire and were officially performed at most public events.

   A second European tradition of anthems had a military function. In France, "La Marseillaise" was disseminated widely by the mass media immediately after an army officer created it in 1792, to sustain popular enthusiasm for war. Instead of a prayer for or to the monarch, the French anthem's core was a call to arms and resistance to a foreign invasion, a declaration of war in the name of "liberty," and a prophecy of victory: "Our dying enemies witness your triumph and our glory."[45] Napoleon's armies proved the power of these patriotic, morale-boosting songs that were copied across the continent in attempts to repel foreign invaders.[46] Along with poetic texts and melodies, myths were created about anthems' origins. It was said that soldiers won battles with the song on their lips, that crowds broke spontaneously into the song upon hearing of the current government's rise to power, that audiences requested multiple encores, that beloved leaders were overtaken by emotion and tears when they heard the songs, and so on. Songbooks were published for soldiers on both sides of the frontlines. An Estonian-language military songbook (to be discussed in chapter 4) appeared in 1807, on the eve of Napoleon's invasion. In Prussia, in 1813, Rėza, serving as a military chaplain, authored a book of German-language songs.[47]

Throughout Europe, governments began using songs to mobilize populations. The task was not simple. The French directorate intensively subsidized the production of new songs for political propaganda, but it quickly learned that popular anthems could not simply be created on demand. The test of time was weathered best of all by texts that allowed multiple interpretations. "La Marseillaise" was created by a monarchist, but later propagated by revolutionaries, liberal democrats, and supporters of Napoleon's imperial expansion alike. A tight system of censorship was needed, however, to prevent parodies of official songs.[48]

In the Russian Empire as elsewhere in Europe, various movements of nationalism, liberalism, and constitutionalism "from below" loosely merged in a political movement that strove to achieve rule by "the people," a group whose ethnicities in the Baltic were not identical to that of their absolutist Russian monarch. The transnational movement of subversive liberal nationalism emerged in the Baltic through the activities of three non-Russian national cultures: Polish, Finnish, and German. Poland and Finland were annexed by Russia in 1795 and 1809, respectively, and the German-speaking elite classes of the Baltic Provinces also predated the 1710 arrival of tsarist rule. Throughout the 1800s, nationalists of all three ethnic groups maintained historical memories of an era before incorporation, and pursued national identities apart from the imperial autocracy. Their movements and songs, in turn, later provided models for the nationalist singing traditions of Lithuanians, Estonians, and Latvians.

Polish nationalism radicalized after the 1772–95 partitions of Poland, during which Poland's eastern territories, including that of present-day Lithuania and three quarters of Latvia, were annexed by the Russian Empire.[49] Nationalism and military objectives merged in the Polish insurrection of 1794, and a few years later the ideology of

"La Marseillaise," whose words opposed domination by foreigners, found even more force among Poles during Napoleon's eastern campaign. After Napoleon's defeat and the return of Poland to Russia's rule, Alojz Feliński was inspired by England's anthem to write "Boże, Cóś Polskę" ("God Who Holds Poland," 1816). The word "king" in Feliński's refrain "Protect our king, oh Lord!" was later replaced in written and oral tradition with "fatherland," signifying a loyalty shift from monarch to nation. Sung to Jan N. Kaszewski's melody, the song was later incorporated into the conclusion of the Polish Catholic mass. Many new songs—not only political songs of liberty but also parodies—were written to its melody.[50]

Among such texts written to Kaszewski's Polish tune was the Lithuanian-language ballad "Biruta," by Silvestras Valiūnas, which is the earliest example of a Baltic nationalist song to achieve lasting importance as a national symbol. The poem, written around 1823, celebrated a fourteenth-century event that was at the time entering the Lithuanian national cultural canon: the marriage of Grand Duke Kęstutis to Birutė, whose son Vytautas would in the fifteenth century expand Lithuania's borders across the continent of Europe. The content was adapted from historical chronicles, while the lexicon and style embraced both native Lithuanian folk songs and international ballads. Three variants were published during the author's lifetime—in 1824, 1828, and 1829—and other variants seem to have existed in oral tradition, because contemporaries noted that the song was sung differently by the folk. The version printed in 1828 may be closest to the poem as originally written by Valiūnas[51]:

> On the shore of the lagoon, in the town of Palanga,
> Which was stolen by our enemies,
> Is a great hill called Biruta,
> With green pines on its peak.
>
> There, where our land was happy once,
> When we ruled Prussians and Belarusians,
> Gentle and pure as the rose and the rue
> Lived the duchess Biruta.
>
> She was not a queen of any kind,
> But a poor girl from Palanga.
> She did not don golden earrings or pearls
> When she went out to walk by the shore.
>
> She wore her work shirt,

And a short, striped apron,
On her golden braids—a little wreath of rue,
On her white neck—a string of amber.

Once when her brothers decided
To ride out to fish in the lagoon,
Their sister, carrying dinner in a basket
On the road met the bright duke.

It was Keistuts, uncle of Jogėla,
Who ruled the Samogitians and Lithuania.
He was riding out to destroy the crusaders,
Who aimed to lock us up in shackles,

On a gray steed, with a bearskin cap,
With a bright weapon, and a quiver of horn,
Spurs kicking in golden stirrups,
And the horse's hooves beat the forest ground.

When he saw on the shore this true beauty,
He said these words to the young Biruta:
"Whoever you are, a goddess or maiden,
Here on this road, take my hand."

I have always been the master of your land,
But from now on I shall be your husband,
And where I first saw you at this place,
I shall have built a beautiful palace.

And the hill where you first saw Keistutas,
Shall from now on have your name, Biruta.
There you shall live, loved by your husband,
You, who found a place in my heart.

Though for me it is not a sin to have many,
Before you, all others shall be nothing."
Hearing this, the bashful maiden,
The pure and wise young Biruta—

She lowered her pretty blue eyes,
She sighed, and bowed to the ground,
"Though," she said, "long ago to god Perkūnas
I vowed to remain chaste in body,

But if, oh master, such is your wish,
Then let there be loving mercy."
All was done as Keistutas had said,
And on the hill a castle was built.

Biruta herself, joined in marriage,
Brought a son, Vitoldas, into the world.

Some of the poem's meaning was on the text's surface level. For example, there was an explicit protest against the transfer of Palanga ("stolen by enemies") from the administration of Kovno Province to that of Kurland Province in 1819; the town was returned to Kovno in 1827, and consequently this line disappeared in most later variants. But the poem's meanings among Lithuanians of its day, and the reasons it became popular, were multiple. Valiūnas was a student at Vilnius University in the 1820s, at the time when tsarist repression of political activities among university faculty and students had begun. The well-known tune would call to mind Polish constitutionalism and nationalism, and resistance to Russian rule. But the text was also subversive among Polish nationalists, who argued that Lithuanians should assimilate into Polish culture. For Lithuanian singers, it recalled a national history that was Lithuanian, not Polish, where it was not Poland's king Jagiełło but Vytautas, grand duke of Lithuania, who won the great Battle of Žalgiris in 1410.

The song's popularity could also have also been related to fictional, not factual, content. Its focus on a submissive Birutė, mother of the grand duke, may have resonated in secular harmony with Catholic images of Mary, mother of Jesus.[52] In biographical details the text diverged from well-known historical sources. Contrary to chronicle accounts describing Birutė as the daughter of a local leader, Valiūnas wrote that she was of common birth—reflecting the French and Polish revolutionary ideals of equality. Contrary to the primary sources, which stated that Kęstutis abducted Birutė by force, Valiūnas's ballad asserts that she forsook a religious vow and agreed to marry him, reflecting Enlightenment ideas of rational choice over religious belief. The song also portrayed Kęstutis as smitten with love at first sight, swearing to stay true to Birutė. The ballad was thus not only a song of national pride but also a story about two Lithuanians who crossed boundaries of class and religious differences for the sake of monogamous love.

The poem's author Valiūnas went on to fight in the rebellion of 1829–30, hoping to restore a constitutional government to Lithuania and Poland. The revolutionary army was vanquished by the tsar, and Valiūnas died of a bullet from his own rifle, possibly by suicide. Perhaps for this reason, his name was sometimes omitted in nineteenth-century publications, but the ballad lived a life of its own. It was repeatedly published in nineteenth-century collections of Lithuanian folk songs, and today has been documented in about two hundred oral variants. Two melodies were written for the poem in the mid-nineteenth century: the older one by L. Koreivienė resembled Kaszewski's, mentioned above, and the second, which became most popular, was created around 1860 by Antanas Beresnevičius. The words have also been sung to other folk melodies.[53] Valiūnas's song would reemerge as a national symbol a half century after its author's death, revived by singers among the small Lithuanian minority of East Prussia. In Lithuania proper, however, Lithuanian national activism was repressed after the revolution of 1830; serfdom and the near-absence of schools restricted the spread of Lithuanian literacy until emancipation in 1861, and after the 1863 Polish-Lithuanian revolution, the tsar imposed a ban on the printed Lithuanian alphabet that was lifted only in 1904. Thus Lithuanian literacy and mass media, and along with them the possibility of a mass national movement, were restricted until the very end of the nineteenth century.

In Finland in 1848, the Swedish poet Johan Ludvig Runeberg published *The Tales of Ensign Stål*, an immensely popular book of poems about the 1808–9 war in which Russia acquired Finland from Sweden. That same year, the University of Helsinki's music instructor, Fredrik Pacius, set Runeberg's first poem to music, and his choir, the Academic Singing Society, performed the song at a university student festival. Witnesses reported that it was repeated several times with great emotion, and national historians thus identify this as the moment when "Our Land" ("Vårt land"), later translated into Finnish by Paavo Cajander, became Finland's national anthem.[54] In 1869, its melody would be borrowed by the author of the Estonian national anthem, as discussed below.

Polish and Finnish nationalism were providing some models for Baltic culture builders, but the most powerful influence on Baltic singing traditions came from German culture. Herder's writings played a role in the early nineteenth century, revived by Schlegel, and spurred on by several editions of Herder's collected works. Beginning with Achim von Arnim's *Des Knaben Wunderhorn* in 1806, secular songbooks and singing came into vogue. In the many German-speaking countries of Europe, men's singing societies received their founding inspiration from the Swiss music teacher Hans Georg Nägeli. In 1809, he published the first of two booklets about secular choral singing, in which he saw a means for developing the German national movement. Europe's first Liedertafel singing society was established in Berlin that same year by Carl Zelter. The ideas of liberal nationalism, which supported rule by "the people" rather than by hereditary monarchs, and of state unification based on national belonging, all found followers in university student fraternities. In Jena, the heart of the *Burschenschaft* movement, these student associations were banned in 1819. While the students continued their traditions underground, nationalism found public expression in purportedly nonpolitical organizations of singers, gymnasts, and marksmen, who all maintained organizational singing traditions. In 1848, there were about 100,000 singers in more than one thousand singing societies throughout the German-speaking lands of Europe; the first pan-German singers' festival of 1847 featured a combined choir of 1,100 men.[55] In Königsberg, the first Liedertafel choir was established in 1810, and the singing movement quickly spread to the German-speaking towns of East Prussia, and to schools, fraternities, and choirs founded by ethnic Germans in the Russian Empire.[56]

The cultural factors that standardized Baltic singing traditions were discussed above; a mass singing movement, however, would not have been possible before the abolition of serfdom. In the Baltic Provinces of Estland (northern Estonia), Lifland (southern Estonia and northern Latvia), and Kurland (western and southern Latvia), the serfs were emancipated in the years 1816–19, and the transition to new agrarian laws was completed around 1830. Serfs in eastern Latvia and Lithuania were emancipated two generations later, in 1861.

Some of the first free Estonians and Latvians, even under the continued burden of corvée labor and restrictions on land ownership, were able to pay for their children's schooling. Others were sponsored by Baltic German benefactors. The future Latvian cultural leaders Jānis Cimze and Krišjānis Valdemārs were educated at existing parish schools. Estonians Adam Jakobson and Johann Voldemar Jannsen studied privately with Lutheran pastors, gaining not only reading literacy but a basic education in music as well. There followed dramatic developments in Estonian and Latvian culture. In 1844, Jakobson established a choir in Torma that was the first to perform Mozart's Requiem in Estonian translation. Beginning in 1845, Jannsen translated and published a new series of widely used Lutheran hymnals. Three years later he began publishing a popular annual journal, *Sannumetoja* (Messenger), and then in 1850, when he was barred from full membership in a German choir because of his ethnicity, he left that choir and founded his first Estonian choir.[57] Valdemārs established an association in 1848 that sponsored the first Latvian public library as well as the first Latvian men's choir. Among the founders of Estonian or Latvian choirs were also Baltic Germans such as Martin Wilberg, whose choir in 1843 performed in eight-part harmony to the astonishment of the local pastor, eliciting, it is said, the exclamation, "Is it possible that Estonians are able to sing so beautifully?"[58]

Estonian and Latvian students first sought the job skills needed to become a rural church sexton (köster, ķesteris), who would usually serve as church scribe, organ player, and teacher in the parish school. The need for sextons and teachers was growing, and in 1839, the government of Lifland Province established a pedagogical seminar in the town of Valmiera for ethnic Estonians and Latvians. The seminar's director, Jānis Cimze, was sent abroad to Prussia to study pedagogy at the Weissenfels Seminar and the University of Berlin.[59] Cimze brought back to Lifland new Pestalozzian methods based on respect for the individual child; he also carried home an enthusiasm for singing. Over the next four decades, and particularly after the seminar moved to Valka in 1849, Cimze left a lasting imprint on Latvian and Estonian choral history. In 1857 alone, for example, his graduates started Latvian choirs in four towns (Vietalva, Aizkraukle, Burtnieki and Beņislava).[60] In total, about one hundred Estonians and three hundred Latvians studied under Cimze, resulting in a new generation of schoolteachers, poets, composers, and choral leaders.[61]

The choice of German language for instruction, as opposed to Estonian or Latvian, was the rule at the Cimze seminar and at its siblings, the Irlava seminar in Kurland Province (1841–1900), and at the Baltic teachers seminar in Rīga, later moved to Kuldīga (1870–1919). Before cultural Russification policies were decreed in the 1880s, curricula followed contemporary Prussian models, and students acquired the culture of German national traditions; among the most popular songbooks was Das Rüttli, a collection of German nationalist song arrangements for men's choirs. One effect was acculturation. At a meeting of Latvian teachers in 1863, students sang "What Is the German's Fatherland?" and in 1869, schoolchildren under the direction of a Cimze seminar graduate performed the song "I Am a Prussian, Do You Know My Colors?."[62] A dramatic contrast between German cultural wealth and the poverty of non-Germans was apparent to all. In 1857, the first Baltic German festival in Tallinn gathered together two hundred singers. In attendance was Jannsen, who wrote in 1858, "I feel sad and sick when I think of it: What a miserable situation in our land regarding songs."[63]

Strong German influences permeated the early Latvian and Estonian-language choral repertoire. Jannsen's 1860 Estonian song book,
for example, contained 125 songs, all of them adaptations of popular
German texts and melodies. The reason for the book's existence was
language. Most, if not all Estonian singers could have just as well sung
the songs in their original German. But the book's goal was to provide choirs with modern arrangements of songs that they could sing in
Estonian. As the author points out in his preface, "An Estonian also
has his own fatherland, social standing, law, and rights; his own fields,
meadows, forests, and rivers (for some, these are already their own
property). Why shouldn't he sing?"[64] Although inspired by German
songs and melodies, the book was not a mere Google-translated text;
Jannsen's songs diverged significantly from the traditions of German
nationalism. The book's first song is a vivid example.

"Where Is My Dear Fatherland?" was, on the one hand, a translation of the most popular German nationalist song "What Is the
German's Fatherland?"[65] Both songs were similar in their claim that
national identity crossed existing political boundaries. The two songs'
geographical references differed, of course, because Jannsen listed ethnic Estonian rather than German territories. But the differences went
far deeper. In the German song, the singer simply asserts in the third
person that all Germans belong together, and concludes with a prayer
for unity and fatherland-love to be granted from above: "O God in
heaven, see to it! / And give us true German courage, / that we would
love it, true and good!" Jannsen, on the other hand, wrote in the first
person, expressing a personalized, individual feeling of belonging, joy,
and love which sprang from within him: "Wherever sings the Estonian
tongue" is "my fatherland and my happiness!" A tradition began of
Estonian nationalist songs that resembled Protestant hymns in their
theme of personal, first-person-singular communion not with God but
with the Estonian landscape, language, and nation. Estonian nationalist songs also digressed from the transnational tradition established by
England and France, and continued by Russia, of mentioning national
enemies. Whereas the seventh stanza of the German "What Is the German's Fatherland?" identified foes (in one variant, blasphemers, and
in another variant, Frenchmen), Jannsen's version did not mention
any:

I.

Where is my dear fatherland?
Is it Estonia[66]? Is it Latvia?

Is it the narrow western shoreline?
Is it Narva River, Peipus Lake?
   (refrain:)
   Oh no! no! no!
   My fatherland is larger still. (repeat twice)

2.

Where is my dear fatherland?
Is it Harjumaa? Is it Virumaa?
Is it where the people with wide overcoats
And sharp tongues are?
   (refrain)

3.

Where is my dear fatherland?
Is it Kurland? Is it Finland?
Is it the bread-rich Järvamaa?
Is it Tallinn, with its sprats and herring?
   (refrain)

4.

Where is my dear fatherland?
Is it Hiiumaa? Is it Muhumaa?
Is it along the narrow shore of Sõrve?
Or the fertile Kuressaare?
   (refrain)

5.

Where then is my fatherland?
Now I want to name it:
Wherever sings the Estonian tongue,
Remaining true to God above!
Yes, that is it! (repeat four times)
My fatherland, and my happiness!
Yes, my happiness, yes, my happiness!

6.

Here I live, an Estonian man,
In my Lutheran faith,
I do work and God I thank,
He does good to me each day,
And I feel joy (repeat four times)
That God's truth and merciful love
Will not forsake me, though I am dust.

7.

The entire Russian state and land
Is also my dear fatherland!

Oh God in heaven, come and bless
Our land and the tsar, too!
This is the land! (repeat four times)
My dear, beloved fatherland!
My fatherland! My fatherland!

The two last stanzas reflect Jannsen's uniquely Estonian context, balancing as he was between two centers of power and culture. His pledge of allegiance to the Lutheran faith meshed with the political agenda of the Baltic German nobility who maintained religious autonomy in the Lutheran Church of the Baltic Provinces. Jannsen's prayer for the tsar of Russia reflected another political axis. Explicit declarations of loyalty to monarchs were required in the Baltic public culture after the constitutionalist or liberal nationalist movement was defeated in the Polish revolutions of 1794 and 1830, and in the Russian Decembrist revolt of 1825. The song's loyalties were thus divided among three groups: one stanza each was devoted to the Russian tsar and the Lutheran Church, and five stanzas were devoted to the Estonian language. Jannsen's declarations of allegiance to the Lutherans and tsar both also carried subversive meanings. For him, Lutheran identity was on the same level as Estonian identity, and he rejected the chauvinist opinion that the non-Germans (*Undeutsche*) or farmers (*Bauer*) were lesser people. Jannsen also prayed *for* the tsar—not *to* the tsar, as was the rule in Russia's national anthem and symbolic political culture. Jannsen's song's primary meaning, however, as confirmed in his foreword to the songbook, was its medium: it was above all a song to be sung by Estonians, in Estonian.

German national activism in Europe developed through a variety of conduits. Student fraternities were among the first organizations that incubated nationalism, and choirs assumed a greater public role after fraternities were driven underground in 1819. For Baltic Germans, the history of associations followed the western European pattern, with student fraternities appearing at the University of Tartu soon after it was reopened in 1802. Curonia (established 1808), Estonia (1821), Livonia (1822), and Rigensis (1823) congregated students, mainly ethnic Germans, from their native provinces of Kurland, Estland, and Lifland, and from the city of Rīga. Baltic German singing societies appeared later in the cities of Rīga (1834), Tallinn (1849), Tartu (1851), Pärnu (1854), and elsewhere.

The sequence was reversed for Estonians and Latvians. Their first generation of emancipated serfs already sang in church congregations and choirs, but it was only in the 1850s, two generations after emancipation, that Estonians and Latvians began enrolling at universities and joined what were then Baltic German fraternities. The future Estonian folklorists and national leaders Friedrich Reinhold Kreutzwald and Jakob Hurt were members of Livonia. Latvian activists Krišjānis Valdemārs, Krišjānis Barons, and Juris Alunāns first joined Curonia, but left it in 1857 to establish Fraternitas Academia Dorpatensis, a mixed-ethnicity organization including Estonian, Jewish, Russian, and German students. That fraternity's rights were rescinded in 1861. During the 1870s the Estonian Students' Society unofficially adopted customs and attributes like those of fraternities, among them the traditions of dueling and a tricolor flag, blue-black-white, but Estonian students were not permitted to organize a fraternity until 1907.[67] In 1882, ethnic Latvians acquired government permission to incorporate the first ethnic-Latvian fraternity, Lettonia.[68]

A full examination of the role played by fraternities and other university student groups in Estonian and Latvian cultural life is beyond the scope of this chapter. Here, it is important to note that fraternities practiced highly formalized traditions of singing. All fraternities, regardless of ethnicity, sang the Latin-language academic anthem "Gaudeamus Igitur." German *Burschenschaft* ritual songs such as the "Landesvater" were sung at both single-group and interfraternity celebrations; these were translated into Estonian and Latvian, but kept their original melodies.[69] Nonritual singing customs also diffused off campus. Fraternity rules of conduct allowed any member to conduct songs at group meals, and required that all others either sing along or remain silent. Some early customs of the Estonian and Latvian national song festivals, among them the tradition of patriotic oratory at festival banquets, may also have roots in fraternity customs. Jānis Lapiņš, biographer of the Latvian national poet Auseklis, argued that the spirit of German fraternities inspired the optimism and public bravura, as well as the sense of individual honor and pride, that are characteristic of early Latvian cultural activists.[70]

In fraternities, one would learn that the *Burschenschaften* were banned in Jena in 1819 and went underground, with history preserved in the song *"Wir hatten gebauet"*: "We had built a grand house," but "The bond/ribbon has been cut, / It was black, red and gold, / And God has allowed this, / Who knows what he intended. // The house has crumbled. / What then can cause despair? / The spirit lives in us all, / And our fortress is God!" The melody had an alternate text in the

contemporary Prussian military anthem *"Ich hab' mich ergeben"*: "I
have given myself / With heart and hand, / To you, oh land full of love
and life, / My German fatherland! . . . / Let me acquire the strength /
In heart and in hand, / To live and to die, / For the holy fatherland!"[71]

Both of these texts, and along with them the melody's meanings,
were probably known to Martin Körber, son of the pastor who educated Jannsen. He studied at the University of Tartu in the 1830s. At
that time, the fraternity, Livonia, was banned, but Körber's brothers
were members, and he probably participated in underground meetings. It was no accident, for example, that when Körber later founded
a choir in Anseküla, its flag contained Livonia's red-green-and-white
colors. Nevertheless, Körber's 1866 song, like Jannsen's quoted above,
differed greatly from its German siblings. There was, for example, no
lament over a lost heritage, and no hint of a hidden conspiracy, as in
the German fraternity anthem. In the German military song, the individual's fate is sealed ("I have given myself") and he asks only for
the strength needed to die for his fatherland; the Estonian singer, in
contrast, pledges allegiance while singing, and swears to protect and
remain true until death.[72]

> My dear fatherland,
> Land where I was born!
>   I shall love you forever,
>   And honor you in song,
>   (repeat two lines)
>
> No cedars or palm trees
> Grow in our land,
>   But pretty pine trees grow there,
>   And spruce, and birches, too.
>
> In our land one finds neither
> Silver nor gold,
>   But everywhere around us
>   We have rich, fertile soil.
>
> I'll always defend you,
> And stay true to you,
>   Until the day I die
>   And go into my grave!

"My Dear Fatherland" was first published in a popular Estonian songbook of 1866; it was subsequently folklorized in several oral variants.[73]

The tradition of translating and adapting foreign songs also embraced
Estonia's "big brother" to the north—Finland. Jannsen was aware of

the argument that Germans were "culture carriers" who supposedly civilized the Estonian savages, and, like Kreutzwald before him, looked across the "Finnish bridge" for symbols that would distinguish Estonians from Germans.[74] He wrote a new Estonian text to the melody composed by Fredrik Pacius for Finland's national anthem. Jannsen's song was first published under the title "Finnish Melody" with no reference to the Estonian text's author.[75] It clearly was not a translation, however, but rather a variant in the ongoing tradition of Estonian patriotic poems that included, among others, Jannsen's own "Where Is My Dear Fatherland?" and Körber's "My Dear Fatherland." Whereas Finland's text was in the plural first person ("*Our* land"), Jannsen's was based on individual, not collective emotions:

> My fatherland, my happiness and joy,
> How beautiful you are!
> I shall not ever find anything
> In this great, expansive world
> Which would be as dear to me
> As you, my fatherland!
>
> You have given birth to me,
> And you have nurtured me!
> I shall always give thanks to you
> And until death I'll stay true to you!
> You are dearest of all to me,
> My dear fatherland!
>
> May God above watch over you,
> My dear fatherland!
> May He be your protector,
> And may He give his blessing
> To all that you should undertake,
> My dear fatherland!

Despite Jannsen's enthusiasm for Estonian songs and singing, and for German culture, his views were not "Herderian." Whereas other European nationalists such as Richard Dybek, author of Sweden's national anthem, followed a Herderian spirit in borrowing folk melodies and motifs to create patriotic songs,[76] Jannsen explicitly rejected a revival of supposedly primitive Estonian oral melodies and poetry:

> "Aido raido, ellad vennad," "Külla neiud, norokesed," and "Tere ella ämma eita" and others like them are also called "songs," but they have no substantial words, no real melody, no sense or end; a word taken from here, another from there, all put together like a patched up bagpipe, and this should be called a *song*? . . . All of the German song

intellect and song festivals will not help us at all, if we don't ourselves
learn to sing better than this empty, bare "aido raido," which we
should leave for the drunks to sing.[77]

Jannsen established a view of Estonian national singing traditions
that prevailed for more than a century. *Regilaul* singing was relatively
rare. Some nineteenth-century authors of patriotic poems may have
employed alliteration as a reference to folk poetry, but they did not
favor the trochaic meter of archaic songs. The three Estonian patriotic
songs quoted above, for example, are in iambic or pyrrhic, not trochaic, meter, and the three most frequent public songs sung during the
1990 song festival procession, as quoted at the beginning of this chapter, were also not *regilaul*. Instead, many popular Estonian national
songs followed Jannsen's model of non-*regilaul* meters; a recurrent
theme was the individual singer's first-person-singular marriage to the
nation, akin and not opposed to a Lutheran's relationship to God.

As time passed, Jannsen's secular songs, with the exception of the
national anthem, faded in popularity; this may have been due to their
content, often overly pious, or their language, sometimes unwieldly,
or their melodies, whose foreign, usually German origin was unmistakable. Even as Jannsen was writing the national anthem, a new generation of songs emerged through the combined activities of native
poets, native composers, and, of course, native choirs.

NATIONAL POETS, NATIONAL SONGS,
NATIONS OF SINGERS

Baltic singing "ethnies" transformed into singing nations at national
song festivals, which established a distinct public culture to carry the
message of nationalism. Members of the nation arrived from many
distant places to converge on one stage, singing together in what
Benedict Anderson calls "unisonance," a "physical realization of the
imagined community." The years when the three nationally singing
nations were born are well documented: 1869 for Estonians, 1873
for Latvians, and 1924 for Lithuanians. These events were the result
of organizational work by individual cultural leaders, who built on
foundations of new national literary and musical traditions.[78]

Historians often identify the beginning of the Estonian and Latvian
mass national movements as being a bit earlier, in the late 1850s or
early 1860s.[79] National self-identification was one milestone. In 1856
at the University of Tartu, Krišjānis Valdemārs posted a card on his

door to announce his nationality as "Latvian." In that same year, also in Tartu, Johann Voldemar Jannsen published an editorial in which he gave a name to the Estonians, Eesti Rahvas (Estonian People), replacing the commonly used terms *Maarahvas* (country people) in Estonian, and *Bauer* (farmer) in German. This new national identity was shared among individuals in groups. Also around 1856, ethnic Latvian and Estonian students at Tartu University began meeting to discuss the issues of their languages and cultures, focusing on new works of literature, such as the first book of Latvian secular poetry, *Dziesmiņas* (Little Songs) published by Juris Alunāns in 1856, and Kreutzwald's epic poem *Kalevipoeg* (1857–61).

The futures of the Estonian and Latvian languages were debated. A prevalent idea at the time was that Latvian and Estonian were "farmer languages," while German was a language of culture. Kreutzwald published his epic in a bilingual Estonian-German edition, believing it necessary to preserve the epic's story after the demise of the Estonian language. German intellectuals discussed whether the Estonians and Latvians should be Germanized, and whether they were even capable of Germanization. But, regardless of academic debates, when restrictions on the press were relaxed in 1856 after Alexander II's accession to the throne, a market of readers emerged for two new native-language newspapers: *Postimees* in Estonian and *Mājas Viesis* in Latvian. These were the first mass-mediated vehicles for the ideas of cultural nationalism, albeit very reserved in their politics.[80]

"Imagined communities" could exist in the virtual world of print media, but live, face-to-face communication was also necessary for nation building to achieve tangible results, in the Baltic as elsewhere. In 1863, the first Estonian secular singing society, Revalia, was established in Tallinn; two years later, two such societies were born in Tartu: Estonia and Vanemuine. The latter, established by Jannsen, was named after the god of song who was born in the romantic folkloristics of Garlieb Merkel, Christian Jaak Peterson, Friedrich Robert Faehlmann, and, most important, Kreutzwald, who, in his epic *Kalevipoeg*, invoked the god as the Estonian bard's muse.

The late 1860s saw a transition in Estonian singing culture. Earlier poets, among them writers of Lutheran hymns, worked in the context of non-Estonian literary and musical traditions as they translated and adapted foreign poetry, squeezing and sometimes forcing Estonian words and grammar into borrowed molds of rhythm, rhyme, and melody. Their poems for the most part did not withstand the test of

time; a new generation of poets, however, began writing and composing works that followed poetic patterns more attuned to the native
language, songs that still function as effective poetry today. Foremost
among these authors whose works established lasting national singing
traditions was Lydia Jannsen, daughter of Voldemar Jannsen, known
by her pen name, Koidula.

Koidula helped her father edit the popular weekly newspaper *Pärnu
Postimees*, and, after the family moved to Tartu in 1863, the *Eesti
Postimees*. Because social mores forbade the mention of unmarried
women's names in print, Koidula did not receive public credit for her
work. Her experience in editing and authoring content was the training ground where she learned the crafts of writer, political analyst (she
often wrote summaries of international news), and publisher who had
to reckon with the paper's political censors. She also engaged political
and social injustice in her work, and was the first Estonian author to
write prose fiction about human oppression. Koidula's sources of political inspiration are well documented. In her copy of Merkel's *Vorzeit
Lieflands*, for example, the passages about Estonians are underlined in
red. Koidula was particularly moved by the fate of a young Estonian
man, Peeter Peterson, arrested and deported in 1864 for circulating a
petition requesting that the Russian government assume more control
over local affairs dominated by Baltic Germans.[81]

Koidula's first collection of poetry, *Meadow Flowers* (1866), contained popular love poems translated and adapted from German. Her
second book, *Nightingale of the Emajögi River* (1867), was the work
of a mature poet, intense in feeling, balancing a very personal anguish
over her nation's present condition with optimism about the future.[82]
Like her father before her, Koidula spoke in the first person singular,
declaring eternal love, and vowing fidelity in a marriage between individual and nation:[83]

MY FATHERLAND IS MY BELOVED!

My fatherland is my beloved
To whom I gave my heart,
I sing to you, my greatest joy,
My blooming Estonia!
Your sorrow boils within my heart,
I feel your happiness and joy,
My fatherland!

My fatherland is my beloved,
I will not forsake it,

And even if for this I must
Then die one hundred deaths!
When foreign envy slanders you,
You still live on within the heart,
My fatherland!

My fatherland is my beloved,
Here I would rest in peace,
Upon your lap I'll fall asleep,
My holy Estonia!
Your birds will sing me into sleep,
You will grow flowers on my grave,
My fatherland!

This second book struck a strong chord in Estonian literary circles. The journalist and teacher Carl Robert Jakobson praised the author's "Estonian heart—a heart beating with powerful lyric passion!" and prophesied that "the verses mentioned above will ring and live in the ears of Estonians as long as the Estonian language exists."[84] Jakobson is credited as the creator of Lydia Jannsen's pen name, Koidula, "poet of the dawn," symbolizing her role in awakening the Estonian nation to cultural activism. In 1867, Jakobson compiled a popular school reader that included twelve of her poems. Among them were "My Fatherland Is My Beloved" and "You, until Death"; these were set to music by a Cimze seminar graduate, Aleksander Kunileid, and performed in 1869 at the first Estonian national song festival's grand finale.

Song festival history may be traced to 1855, when several Estonian choirs sang together in Põlva at the first documented joint concert.[85] It is, however, another concert that is usually recognized as the tradition's beginning. In 1863 in Anseküla on Saaremaa Island, an audience of 500 came to listen to a secular music concert organized by the local pastor, Martin Körber (author of "My Dear Fatherland," discussed above). Two years later in Jõhvi, northern Estonia, a teacher named Saar organized a joint concert of 119 singers from three towns. In 1867, the joint concert of seven choirs in the city of Pärnu attracted an audience of 1,500; that event included a procession with flags, speeches, a banquet, and a boat ride in the sea. These concerts were reported by Johann Voldemar Jannsen's newspaper to a growing pool of readers. The notion of an all-Estonian festival was born after Jannsen founded the Vanemuine choir, whose singers discussed such an event at their choir's one-year anniversary on Midsummer Day 1866. Jannsen then formulated the plan to celebrate the fifty-year anniversary of the emancipation of serfs in Lifland Province, an event that, he argued, could happen only with the help of choirs. These were the only Estonian social organizations that existed in sufficient numbers. Most choirs were associated with churches, and existing administrative structures simplified communication. There began the long process of acquiring government permission for this public assembly. A permit was granted in early spring of 1869, and work could begin in earnest. The program was selected quickly, and musical notes were printed and distributed in May.[86]

Then, one month later, on the morning of Friday, June 18, 1869, the festival opened in Tartu with a procession of choirs led by the pastors of many congregations. They walked to the park on Dom Hill for a Lutheran service beginning at 10:00 am. The honorary president of the festival committee, Adalbert-Hugo Willigerode, a Lutheran pastor from Tartu, gave a speech about the festival's significance. He recalled the ancient past, "when Estonians freely and independently served their god, Taara, and listened to the songs of Vanemuine." The arrival of the Germans brought culture, Christianity, and new songs to the land; Estonians were now "true Christians" who felt that "praise of Christ was much dearer than the singing of Vanemuine."[87] Several other pastors spoke; a brass band accompanied congregational hymns, and individual choirs performed. After the service, the procession of singers, accompanied by the band, went to lunch at 2:00 pm, and assembled again an hour later for a procession to an outdoor stage near St. Peter's Church on the opposite shore of the Ema River. On this sunny, windy day, Jannsen and Aleksander Kunileid conducted the concert of ecclesiastical music performed by 845 men from fifty-one choirs before an audience of over 10,000.

Dark clouds gathered on Saturday, and a heavy rain was falling when the singers' procession again arrived at the outdoor stage for their concert of secular music. Should the concert be cancelled? "If the listeners remain seated, then the singers may not flee the stage" was the consensus. The conductors maintained high spirits, and introducing songs with words such as, "Friends, let's sing to dry up the weather!" Johann Voldemar Jannsen reminded the choir and the audience that the rain that was soaking their clothing was at the same time also giving great benefit by watering their fields, and it should not be allowed to extinguish their flame of joy now, when they had finally been given the opportunity to assemble.[88] The concert program of fifteen songs was a rousing success. The audience of about 12,000 responded most enthusiastically to four songs in particular. Two melodies by Finnish composers—one of them the future national anthem, with Estonian text by Jannsen—and the grand finale of the two Koidula poems mentioned above, conducted by their composer, Kunileid.

Two speeches held between the songs were memorable. A pastor from Viljandi parish, himself a singer in the choir, gave a humorous, uplifting speech in praise of the song festival's "father," Johann Voldemar Jannsen: "Barely had he spoken the last words, when loud hoorays erupted from the lips of the singers." The second speech was by Jakob Hurt, who presented his famous "three wishes" for a program to build the national culture: that Estonians buy and read newspapers and books, that they maintain a feeling of national self-esteem, and that they establish schools for Estonian higher education. "While song and music elevate the spirit," wrote an observer, "speeches satisfy the intellect and carry thoughts on the festive path. This two-part satisfaction has become a necessity for the Estonians." Thus began the long-lived tradition of oratory at Estonian song festivals. The festival concluded with the national anthem of Russia, with an encore requested, as was the tradition, by an enthusiastic audience. There was reluctance to leave the concert area, but finally, accompanied by the marching band, the procession waded back to town, with their flags, footwear, and clothes soaking wet, but hearts joyful.[89]

The festival banquet took place in the evening, outdoors, its cheer not damped by the continued, heavy rain. Among the many speakers that night was Jānis Cimze, at whose pedagogical seminar many of the festival's participants had studied. The festival's third day was sunny, and after a series of performances by individual choirs in the morning, the afternoon saw a competition of twenty-two choirs. An observer noted that only one of the choirs sang in the "old-fashioned" manner, with all singers tapping their feet and conducting with their hands. Nine choirs were awarded prizes: first prize went to an urban choir, the Estonia Society, second prize to a rural choir from the village of Kursi, and third prize was shared by seven other choirs.

The departing singers carried their experiences back home. They disseminated not only news of the festival's events but also a redoubled singing energy. Of the 789 Estonian singers surveyed by a member of the Vanemuine Society, more than half (398) were teachers in district, village, parish, or church schools.[90] When they returned to their classrooms and singing lessons, the singing Estonian nation multiplied and began to prepare enthusiastically for another national song festival.

The year 1869 may be marked as the birth of Estonia as a nation of singers not only because 845 men gathered to sing on stage but also because that year saw the first explicit attempt to build a national repertoire of songs that contain uniquely Estonian melodies as well as words. Carl Robert Jakobson published a songbook of such native songs shortly before the song festival. In the introduction, he retold the story of Vanemuine, god of song, whose songs were lost over centuries of slavery: "But we hope that this winter of Estonian songs has ended and a new age of songs begun, where our singers will be unified by the old Estonian spiritual power, and where it will no longer be necessary to wear foreign jewelry and hide our own creations. Most of our songs at our first song festival still follow foreign melodies, but we hope that the story will be entirely different at the next festival."[91] The title of Jakobson's songbook and its sequels, *Vanemuine's Kannel Tune*, created a mythical principle upon which Estonian singing identity could be based. The myth assumed poetic form in October of that year. A poem by Friedrich Kuhlbars, "The People of Kungla," celebrated "Kungla," a place that Kreutzwald had invented as the home of the ancient Estonian pantheon. It told a story in which a song was created by Vanemuine, a deity similar to the one imagined by Peterson a half century earlier. Although the poem's dominant meter was not trochaic, *regilaul* form was referenced with alliteration. "Etc." marked the poem's refrain, a feature unknown in *regilaul* tradition, nevertheless revealing that the author intended his text to be experienced as a song, not simply read:[92]

> Once, in the golden age of Kungla,
> People held a banquet,
> And Vanemuine on the grass
> Played music on his kannel.
> He stepped in the forest with a tune,
> Went into the woods with songs.
>
> From this the bird and the tree leaf
> And beast received their songs;
> The forest sang, and the sea,
> And all the Finnic family.
> He stepped in the forest, etc.
>
> The melody was beautiful,
> And wreaths were on their heads then.
> And forest fairies, too, appeared
> To the Estonian people.

He stepped in the forest, etc.

I sing in fields and on the hill
And late at night in farmyards,
And Vanemuine's kannel tune
Is beating in my bosom.
He stepped in the forest, etc.

The poem, set to music by Karl August Hermann, was soon popular nationwide, although its line about "all the Finnic family"—referring to speakers of Balto-Finnic languages—was revised to "Estonian people's family." In 1890, a prominent Estonian asserted that this was the most beautiful Estonian song of its day. Other Estonians unmasked the song's mythology as an inauthentic, recent invention, but, regardless of historical accuracy, singers loved to sing it, and the "pseudo-myth" of a singing god became reality.[93] The story about the origin of the Estonian people's songs concluded with a testimonial, sung in the present-tense first-person singular to express identity: Vanemuine's kannel and song are within the singer, and within all of the people of Kungla. The singer sings because he or she is Estonian; to be Estonian is to sing.

Among ethnic Latvians in the Baltic Provinces, the administrative foundations for a mass choral movement also took shape. In 1857, in southern Lifland, Juris Neikens, a graduate of the Cimze seminar and the University of Tartu, was ordained pastor of the Lutheran congregation in Dikļi. He established four parish schools with singing as the core curriculum. Together with Ernests Šveichs, in 1864 Neikens organized the first Latvian song festival, a joint concert by seventy to eighty singers representing six Latvian men's choirs, and another 120 children from the four schools.[94] Neikens started an annual tradition of concerts by combined choirs, changing locations each year, and, after 1867 his festival, assembled in two places each year. In 1870, across the Daugava River in Kurland Province, Jānis Kaktiņš, a graduate of the Irlava teachers seminar, and the Lutheran pastor Augusts Bīlenšteins were key organizers of the first province-wide festival in the town of Dobele.[95] At this concert, Latvian choral music and cultural activities were transformed from relatively isolated, small community events to mass meetings. Four hundred singers representing fifteen choirs came to Dobele from places as distant as Durbe (seventy miles); an instrumental orchestra traveled fifteen miles from the Irlava pedagogical seminar. Four thousand persons paid admission, yielding a substantial profit that was donated to the Kurland school for the deaf.

In Rīga, the first concert by a Latvian choir was organized in 1868 by Jūlijs Purāts, another graduate of the Cimze seminar. This was also the founding year of the Rīga Latvian Society (RLS). The society's overt purpose was not nationalism. It was founded as a charity to raise funds for victims of the 1867 famine, and thus it was incorporated under the name "Latvian Assistance Society for Estonians Suffering Poverty." Its effect, however, was also local, because fundraising events—among them concerts, theater performances, and lectures—were occasions for the advancement of Latvian culture. The first Latvian Singing Festival of 1873 was the result of these two interests, financial and cultural: a need to raise funds to build the society's meeting hall, and the wish to advance Latvian national singing traditions. Government permission to organize a festival was granted in February of 1873, allowing four months' time to organize the event. The musical repertoire was selected quickly; this would be a "Latvian Singing Festival" and not a "Latvian Song Festival," because many of its melodies would be by foreign composers. A total of 1,019 singers (126 sopranos, 86 altos, 365 tenors, and 426 basses, accompanied by 16 musicians) performed; memoirs recall that some rural choirs continued to rehearse even as they rode to the festival. Twelve university students (among them some founders of the ethnic Latvian fraternity Lettonia) volunteered as honor guards for festival ceremonies.[96]

The 1873 Latvian Singing Festival opened in the newly constructed Rīga Latvian Society meeting hall with a ceremonial assembly of choirs, each carrying its own flag. In brief opening remarks, the society's chairman, Jānis Baumanis, pointed out that regional festivals had taken place in Lifland and in Kurland, but that this was the first occasion for Latvians of the two provinces to sing together. There followed a historic premiere of the song that would later become the national anthem, "God Bless Latvia," performed by students of the Baltic Pedagogical Seminar conducted by a student, Jānis Dreiberģis-Dreibergs. Its words and music were by Kārlis Baumanis. Each stanza is repeated twice:

> God bless Latvia,
> Our precious fatherland,
> God bless Baltija,
> Give it your blessing!
>
> Where Latvian daughters bloom,
> Where Latvian sons sing,

Let us rejoice in happiness,
In our Baltija![97]

The song gave a unified name, Latvia, to the territory inhabited by ethnic Latvians—the southern half of the so-called Baltic Provinces ("Baltija"), administratively divided between Kurland Province and southern Lifland Province. On the other hand, it placed Latvia in Baltija, a region of the Russian Empire, and thus made no claim to political independence (in the twentieth century, "Baltija" would be replaced by "Latvia"). The song's effect lay partly in its resonance with the poetic content and musical structure of other well-known national anthems, most notably Russia's and England's.[98] Its text, however, clearly distinguished it from the hymns of monarchies. In accord with the ideology of liberal nationalism, it requested a blessing for a country, not for its monarch or leader, and it was a prayer to God, not to the tsar. National enemies were absent. And the Latvian national objective, for which God's blessing was requested, according to the text, was happiness for the land where Latvians blossomed and sang.

The national anthem also defined the nation. Unlike the Estonian national anthem, the Latvian text did not recognize the individual singer as a member of the nation, however, its use of first-person plural ("us" and "our") explicitly identified both men and women as subjects, mirroring the singing festival's mixed choir of men and women. It also bridged class differences. In his memoirs, Matīss Kaudzīte recalled that the chairman of the song festival committee, Richards Tomsons remarked after the song was sung that not only were Latvians from two provinces singing together, but that their singing expressed the festival's egalitarian nature:

> The time has come when Kurlanders [kurzemnieki] and Liflanders [vidzemnieki] have united at their nation's festival, testifying that borders, rivers, and distance cannot divide them. People from various classes and various levels of education have gathered today to revive their ancestors' Līgo midsummer festival. All nations at a higher level of culture have such festivals, and they are useful as a weapon for developing and inspiring the nation. So it is also with us! This festival testifies not only to our feelings, but also our goals and our culture, revealing what cannot be hidden, that is, that the Latvian nation is striving for light and the beauty of culture.[99]

It was a sacred and uplifting moment, states the printed report of the organizing committee, when Richards Tomsons presented to the

Latvian nation the newly created festival flag, carried by the society's chairman and two officers, accompanied by the nine women who embroidered it and twelve honorary guards. On the flag stood the Latvian shaman of antiquity, as interpreted by Tomsons: "The old *krīvs*, the *vaidelotis*, teaches that, wherever peace reigns, there is happiness and joy."[100]

As in Estonia, the Latvian festival's lasting legacy was not in its opening concert of religious songs but rather in the second concert's folk songs arranged in four-part harmony. These were first published in 1872 by Jānis Cimze in the second volume of *Dziesmu Rota* (Garland of Songs; the songbook's first volume contained translated texts and melodies from the international repertoire, mainly German, including the celebratory song, "Long May He Live!").[101] One particular Latvian folk song carried extraordinary cultural weight:

> Rīga rings! Rīga rings!
> Who is making Rīga ring?
>   Trallallā, trallallā,
>   Who is making Rīga ring?
>
> Three good brothers for their sister
> Forge a wondrous dowry chest.
>   (repeat as above)
>
> Father's brother forged the chest,
> Mother's brother made the key.
>
> My very own true brother
> Cast the lid of purest gold.

The text's meaning was publicly contested on the evening before the concert, at the festival banquet. As later recalled by Matīss Kaudzīte, first to speak was the festival's guest of honor, Jānis Cimze. He likened the Latvian nation to the "sister" in this song, and asserted that the three "brothers" who forged her dowry chest were German schools, the Baltic nobility, and (Kaudzīte wasn't certain if he recalled Cimze's third metaphor correctly) the city of Rīga. Cimze's speech was followed by a stinging rejoinder, orated by Atis Kronvalds, "eyes blazing, words crackling like sparks." German schools, Kronvalds countered, had existed for many years without producing a festival; the credit and honor belonged instead to Latvian mothers, who had taught their children the language; to the Rīga Latvian Society; and to the Latvian national spirit, which had survived six centuries of slavery. Shouts of joy followed Kronvalds's speech, recalled Kaudzīte, like a powerful

Figure 7. Flag of the first Latvian Singing Festival, 1873. The *vaidelotis*, a Latvian shaman of mythical antiquity, raises an offering to the heavens, teaching Latvians that "wherever peace reigns, there is happiness and joy." Courtesy of the Museum of the History of Rīga and Navigation.

flood breaking open the gates of a great movement. "They did not even want to stop, and rose again and again. It is unlikely that any other speech has ever aroused more enthusiasm."[102] Offended, Cimze left the banquet.

The war of words did not calm down. Another speaker at the banquet was Bīlenšteins, an organizer of the 1870 Kurland song festival and a leading scholar of Latvian folk songs. His speech, as summarized by Kaudzīte, noted that the concert of ecclesiastical music had shown the high skill of Latvian singers in performing songs of foreign nations, but that the next day's concert would feature the singers' own folk melodies, songs arising from the distant past of the nation's childhood. Once again, Kronvalds strode to the speaker's stand, spurred by applause and cheers. He had misunderstood Bīlensteins's speech, and gave a second, powerful barrage of oratory to defend the beauty of Latvian folk songs and attack the notion that they were songs for children. "Again," recalled Kaudzīte, "unending applause, not questioning whether the preceding speaker actually deserved such an enthusiastic rejection." Bīlenšteins, too, rose to depart, but was persuaded to stay.[103] Needless to say, the public thronged to the next day's concert of Latvian folk songs, which opened with Imperial Russia's national anthem (sung in Latvian translation), followed by "Rīga Rings."

A third speech at the festival banquet by the Lettophile Aleksandrs Vēbers, himself of Baltic German ethnicity, told a story about Latvia's mythical golden age, inspiring a poem that would enter the national canon of songs. As reported by Jānis Lapiņš,

> He recalled an old legend told in Kurland, about a sunken Latvian fortress. This fortress looked far across the free land of the Latvians. But along with the loss of Latvian liberty, this fortress of the nation sank deep into the earth. But the fortress's name was entrusted to an old oak tree. If the name were guessed, then the ancient Latvian fortress would again rise from the bosom of the earth. According to the speaker, this fortress is rising again and has already risen high, across all of Latvia. The riddle of the fortress's name has been solved, and it is—Light. Let God, who is neither old nor young, the same God whom Latvians once worshipped in the shape of Pērkons, let that ancient God protect this risen Latvian Fortress of Light.[104]

Among the banquet attendees was Miķelis Krogzemis, a singer in the bass section of the national choir who was well known as Auseklis (Morning Star), the pseudonym under which he published a book of patriotic poetry a few weeks before the festival.[105] Lapiņš points out that Vēbers's speech piqued the poet's interest in this particular folk legend, of which an oral variant appeared in Auseklis's notebook.[106] In 1875, Auseklis expanded the story into a poem that copied the trochaic meter of Latvian folk poetry:

Kurzemīte, God's own country,
Mother of a free nation,
Where have the grey gods departed,
And the free sons of the nation?

They sang līgo in the old days
High atop the hill of light.
Great spruce forests grew around
The nation's very brightest castle.

Golden columns, roof of amber,
The foundations made of silver.
Neither stormy winds could crush it,
Nor the crashing waves of war.

Bloody days dawned in the valley
Of the ancient fatherland,
Nation locked in chains of slavery,
Heroes killed on battlefields.

The proud fortress disappeared,
Sank into the hill of light.
There lie the gods of our fathers,
And the nation's splendorous soul.

To the ancient graying oak
A final sacrifice is made:
Deep inside its scarred heart
Hides the castle's holy name.

If the name would once be guessed,
The old fortress would arise
And proclaim the nation's glory,
Glimmering with rays of light!

Flags of red and white would flutter
High up in the deep blue skies,
Deep, deep voices would resound:
The singing of the ancient spirits.

The sons of the nation guessed
The long-forgotten, sacred riddle:
They called light! Light dawned,
Light's Fortress is rising upward!

Auseklis died in Saint Petersburg in the winter of 1879. His body was transported by train to Rīga, where many thousands attended his funeral, the first such mass public commemoration in Latvian history. Several of his poems posthumously entered the national song repertoire. First among them was a song honoring the Latvian god of beer, Trimpus, set to music by Kārlis Baumanis and performed at the second national song festival of 1880.[107] But Auseklis's most remembered poem was "Fortress of Light," which premiered at the 1910 song festival with a melody composed by Jāzeps Vītols.[108]

Vītols belonged to a generation of Baltic composers and musicians with higher musical education. Many of them were graduates of the recently established music academy in Saint Petersburg. Vītols completed his studies at the academy in 1886 and remained there as a lecturer, and later, as a professor of composition. Among his students were leading Baltic composers of the late nineteenth and early twentieth centuries: the Estonian composers Juhan Aavik and Artur Kapp, Latvian composer Andrejs Jurjāns, and Lithuanian composers Juozas Tallat-Kelpša and Juozas Žilevičius. Besides Vītols's direct influence on students as a faculty member, memoirists recall the frequent interaction among the Baltic composers and conductors who lived in Saint Petersburg. The Estonian composer Miina Härma, who was Vītols's classmate at the academy, recalled that he often came to events led by conductor Johannes Kappel and composer Mihkel Lüdig in Saint Petersburg's Estonian Welfare Society. Vītols was also a friend of the Estonian national leader Jakob Hurt, and a guest of honor at one of the nineteenth-century Estonian song festivals.[109]

The nineteenth-century Estonian and Latvian choral music movements, energized by national song festivals,[110] laid the foundations for the twentieth-century festivals that brought many thousands of singers together on stage. Composers and musicians with more education now had performers and audiences for their works in the native languages. Professionalization of Estonian and Latvian music assured a growing repertoire and a steady rise in the artistic quality of mass choral traditions.

The "discovery" of Lithuanian folk songs, together with ethnographic research on Lithuanian oral traditions, predated similar studies of Latvian and Estonian songs. The classic works of Lithuanian literature were also printed well before comparable Estonian and Latvian books, but they were written and read by only a small number of educated individuals. A "singing ethnie" of Lithuanians had not emerged even as late as the turn of the twentieth century. As mentioned above, most Lithuanians lived in the Russian Empire. Lithuanian serfs were emancipated in 1861, four decades later than Estonians and Latvians, and from 1864 to 1904 Russia's government banned Lithuanian publications in the Latin alphabet. Secular public organizations and assemblies were also forbidden until 1904, making it impossible to organize Lithuanian choirs like the ones singing in Latvia and Estonia. Only behind the closed doors of the Kaunas Catholic seminary could students secretly rehearse secular works composed by their teachers.

The first public concerts of secular Lithuanian choral music took place across the border in East Prussia, in the ethnic Lithuanian communities of "Lithuania Minor." During the second half of the nineteenth century, and particularly after the new school language policies of the 1870s, assimilation into German culture was accelerating. The 1861 census registered 171,000 Lithuanians in East Prussia, but by 1890 the number had decreased to 131,000, falling further to 114,000 in 1910. In 1890, the ethnic Lithuanian population was concentrated in three districts: Šilutė (Heydekrug), Ragainė (Ragnit) and Tilžė (Tilsit), with a total of 62,197 ethnic Lithuanians; an additional thirty thousand Lithuanians comprised half of the population of the city of Klaipėda (Memel).[111] As an ethnic minority Lithuanians were thus a small group, but their national community was much larger, extending into the Russian Empire. Lithuanian-language newspapers found a large market when they were smuggled across Prussia's eastern border. Authors in Lithuania Major smuggled manuscripts westward and published them under pseudonyms in East Prussia. In 1904, when the print ban in Lithuania Major was lifted and underground cultural activities came out into the open, East Prussia provided models for the emerging movement. In those early years of national awakening, a song repertoire was shared on both sides of the border.

A key Lithuanian choral activist was himself not of Lithuanian ancestry. The German polyglot Georg Sauerwein supported multiculturalism in Germany, and was an advocate of the Lithuanian and Sorbian languages. In 1884–85, he published a series of polemic articles arguing, from the perspective of a German patriot, in favor of maintaining Lithuanian culture. Sauerwein petitioned the German government to repeal its assimilationist policies, and worked with Jonas Basanavičius to activate Lithuanian culture from within. He stood at the cradle of the Lithuanian Literature Society, established in Tilžė in 1879, and of the first Lithuanian newspaper, *Auszra*

(Dawn), established in 1883 in Ragainė; in 1885, he was elected honorary member of the newly established youth society, Birutė. Sauerwein was also a multilingual poet, and probably intended for his works to be sung as songs. He wrote about three hundred poems in Lithuanian, of which the best known was (and is) "We Were Born Lithuanians," first published in 1879.[112] On February 17, 1895, the poem was sung at the ten-year anniversary of the Birutė Society, to a melody composed by Vincas Nacevičius, an organist in Lithuania Major; the poem's text was published in a 1905 collection of East Prussian Lithuanian folk songs.[113]

We were born Lithuanians,
And we must be Lithuanians!
At birth we received that honor,
And we cannot let it die!

Despite the many who are determined
To turn us all into triviality,
The fruitful land of the Lithuanians
Will still give birth to Lithuanians.

Even if dark clouds should gather
And storms threaten to disperse us,
Despite the many who would loudly scream
And want to erase our language:

Strong as the oak by the Nemunas,
The Lithuanian will not tire!
Green as the spruce tree by the Šešupė,
Flourishing green in storm and cold.

Hold strong, and stand strong,
Lithuanian family,
And speak Lithuanian courageously,
Let ignorance be angry!

Let anger come to whoever doesn't know
How dear the ancient language is,
In which dear father and mother
Taught us to pray "Our Father"!

We shall still truly love the emperor,
We shall still love the great empire,
We'll only say what is in the heart,
With Lithuanian lips.

(repeat first stanza)

Sauerwein later wrote a Lithuanian-language parody of this poem, perhaps lamenting the futility of his efforts at awakening Lithuanian national pride.[114] In 1899, he moved to exile in Norway, where he soon joined the campaign for the Nynorsk language and translated "We Were Born Lithuanians" into Nynorsk, replacing "Lithuanians" with "Norwegians."[115]

In the Russian Empire under the print ban of 1864–1904, Lithuanian cultural activities took place underground. The language was taught by home schooling; books and newspapers were smuggled in from the West; and concerts took place in secret.[116] Authors sent their works across the western border to East Prussia, where they were printed and smuggled back. The best-known poet of this period was a Roman Catholic priest with the pen name Maironis who lived in Kaunas and Saint Petersbug while publishing his works in East Prussia. Many of his written poems were conceived as songs, as evidenced by the word *daina* (song) in their titles, and by textual features such as refrains.[117] The poems were, in fact, often sung, although their original tunes, some by Maironis himself, were soon forgotten when professionally educated composers such as his friend Juozas Naujalis wrote new melodies. Among such songs was the one which was first titled "Tautiška daina" (National Song) but was better known by its later title, "Where Šešupė Flows." Its was probably first set to music by Naujalis in 1898, but a later melody by Česlovas Sasnauskas became the standard.[118]

Where Šešupė flows, where Nemunas runs,
Our fatherland, beautiful Lithuania;
Our brothers, the plowsmen here speak Lithuanian,
Birutė's song sounds here, high above villages.
Let our rivers flow swiftly to the deepest seas!
Let our songs ring out over the farthest lands!

Where pearl flowers bloom red, where rue grows green,
And our pretty sisters decorate their braided hair,
In the orchard sings the speckled cuckoo-bird—
There, a traveller will find our farmsteads.
By pearl flowers and green rue, by the speckled cuckoo,
Is the fatherland, and the farmlands, and our dear old mother.

Whenever the bright days of springtime are dawning,
Whenever the hay scythe is cutting bluebells,
Whenever the harvested rye field stands in frost,
Forever our fatherland stays beautiful.
Whether spring dawns, or rye harvest sweltering approaches,
Lithuania, dear mother, you are always fairest.

If sun shines upon us, or skies are darkening,
You are our dearest land of ancestors!
The land here was watered by sweat from our labor!
The heart finds so many memories here!
Whether happy or suffering, you are always our mother!
Resounding with memories, and dear as the soul.

Here Grand Duke Vytautas ruled in glory,
Defeating fierce enemies by Žalgiris.
Here ancestors fought for freedom through the centuries.
Here was our fatherland, here it shall be.
Here, where Vytautas ruled and protected us.
Through the centuries, Lithuania, fatherland forever!

Protect, oh Highest One, this dear land,
Where our farmsteads are, and ancestors' graves!
Your fatherly grace is all powerful!
We are Your children, wearied by centuries.
Full of grace and all powerful through all times,
Oh Highest One, don't foresake our dear fatherland.

Nation builders in Lithuania Major and Lithuania Minor were participants in the same national project, as is clear in the images in Sauerwein's and Maironis's poems. The rivers Nemunas and Šešupė flowed along the border between Germany and Russia, through the region inhabited by Lithuanians of both empires. The song of Birutė that Maironis mentions was written by Valiūnas in Lithuania Major, then revived by activists in East Prussia, and thus it could easily become a symbol of ancient poetic heritage that was shared by all Lithuanians. Lithuania's heroic golden age was in the Grand Duchy of Lithuania, whose 1410 victory over Prussia's Teutonic Order on the Žalgiris battlefield was that epoch's defining event. For Maironis, the "plowsmen who speak Lithuanian" of the first stanza were "wearied by centuries" of both German and Russian domination and assimilationist policies. To these national symbols Maironis added the religious motif of a prayer for God to protect the land.

Maironis consolidated firm links between Lithuanian nationalism and Roman Catholicism. He defined Lithuanian identity, and along with it Lithuanian religious identity, in opposition to the Polish language and culture that was dominant among nineteenth-century clergy and the rural gentry in Lithuania.[119] It is in this context that he wrote a poem of prayer to the Virgin Mary that was soon incorporated into the Lithuanian-language mass:

Maria, Maria, most beautiful lily,
You shine high in heaven above.
Oh come, ease slavery, save humankind, come rescue from the terrible foe,
Oh come, ease slavery, save humankind, come rescue from the terrible foe.

We are straying people,
We pray for grace;
Maria, deny not our prayers!
Between weeping seas
Come lead and strengthen
These fallen mortal soldiers!

The weakness of flesh,
And earthly goods,
The black spirit of hell,
Pulls most humankind
Down to its destruction,
And kills with the darkest power.

Like a river's currents
So also our habits
Pull us downward each time;
Will everyday troubles
Like iron shackles
Ever stop binding us?

So weak and hopeless,
We see only in you
Our very last hope;
You, through your grace,
Are able to give strength
For this earthly struggle.

Maria, Maria,
Most beautiful lily,
Bright queen of heaven above!
Speak for the smallest of people
Before the Highest
You are able to call to God!

Across the Prussian border in Lithuania Minor, Jonas Basanavičius and Georg Sauerwein produced the newspaper *Auszra* (Dawn), which was often smuggled to Lithuania Major during the print ban. In the late 1880s, a teacher in Marijampolė passed this contraband on to his students, one of whom, Vincas Kudirka, recalled in his memoirs the semi-religious experience of his own awakening as a Lithuanian patriot upon reading the newspaper's first issue.[120] When *Auszra* ceased publication in 1888, Kudirka assumed the task of editing a new newspaper, *Varpas*

(Bell); his manuscripts were smuggled to East Prussia, and the printed copies were smuggled back into Lithuania Major. Although others also contributed articles, much of the newspaper's content was written by Kudirka himself, working more for love than money. The Lithuanians of Kudirka's home city, Vilnius, were splintered politically into mutually opposed factions of socialists, Catholics, and nationalists, and the political parties in turn consisted mainly of small clusters of urban intellectuals who had few ties to the broader Lithuanian population in the countryside. Kudirka hoped to unify Lithuanians of all factions, and in 1898, on the occasion of his newspaper's ten-year anniversary, he published the words and melody of his "national hymn":

> Lithuania, fatherland, our land of heroes!
> Let your sons gather strength from history.
>
> Let your children only walk upon the paths of virtue,
> Let them labor for your good and for all humankind.
>
> Let the sun in Lithuania overcome the darkness,
> Let the light and the truth guide us in our steps,
>
> Let love of Lithuania burn in our hearts,
> In the name of Lithuania, let unity blossom.

Upon Kudirka's death in 1899, the author of his obituary wrote that this was Lithuania's hymn. It premiered that year in Saint Petersburg, performed by a student choir. At the time of its first performance in Vilnius in 1905, disagreements ran deep over the song that would represent all Lithuanians. Atheist socialists and religious nationalists could find no compromise on religious themes, but they could agree on pride in history and the importance of education (light) and justice (truth). Kudirka focused on images that could build unity, and omitted God. Merkelis writes that the text was "a creation of reason, not feelings. . . . It is not surprising that it moved Lithuanians, and continues to move them not only with its melody but also with its deepness of thought and noble ideas, which, one can say, are eternal."[121] Not all contemporaries agreed on the value of the song's melody. It was criticized for its musical similarity to the anthem of the tsar's elite Preobrazhensky Regiment, to a Polish hymn honoring Vilnius's "Gates of Dawn" (Witaj Panno), or to a German student song by Albert Methfessel. The composers Mikas Petrauskas, P. Stankevičius, and Juozas Dryja-Visockis all tried to set Kudirka's words to alternate melodies, but none of these variants caught on in public life.[122]

Several songs competed for the title of national anthem. Stasys Šimkus (a student of Jāzeps Vītols) abbreviated Sauerwein's "We Were

Born Lithuanians" to three stanzas and composed a new melody that was performed often, usually alongside Kudirka's anthem.[123] Maironis's song "Where Šešupė Flows," with a new melody composed by Česlovas Sasnauskas, also filled the role of second anthem, most notably at the Council of Vilnius in 1905.[124] But in the end, the simple melody and concentrated patriotism of "Lithuania, Our Fatherland" found consensus, and in 1919 Kudirka's song would be institutionalized as Lithuania's national anthem.[125]

In 1904, the print ban was lifted and laws forbidding public assembly were relaxed. There followed a flood of public Lithuanian cultural activities. "Lithuanian Evenings" featuring performances by choirs, actors, and dancers were publicized by Lithuanian newspapers, which also reported on Estonian, Latvian, and Finnish song festivals, arguing that Lithuanians should follow these examples. In 1906, for example, an author proposed a modest festival of about three hundred to five hundred singers from Lithuania and the ethnic communities of Rīga, Liepāja, Saint Petersburg, and Odessa; all that was needed, he wrote, was a committee of five to twelve people in Vilnius to organize it. A few weeks later, the newspaper reported that nothing would happen because nobody had volunteered: "Besides that, money is also necessary, and . . . donations will be difficult to collect."[126] The Lithuanian choral movement continued to grow, however, and choirs held joint concerts and even a small song festival in the city of Kaunas in 1910. A larger regional festival and choir competition was planned for 1914, but plans were cancelled when World War I broke out.[127] The first national choir concert took place in 1924, in the independent republic of Lithuania. In Estonia and Latvia after 1918, too, song festivals took on a new life as part of official culture in independent nation-states.

SINGING, LIBERATED NATIONS

At the Latvian Singing Festival of 1873, the poet Auseklis enthusiastically participated in the competition of choirs, called the "Song Wars." It was here that he came across the idea that songs were weapons. An essay he wrote soon afterward included guidelines for a nonviolent political movement:

> How lucky the nation whom the dear, kind *Mother Nature* has led
> to the precious, beautiful *book* [of oral poetry], to learn how to trill
> such glorious, magnificent songs. The nation in whose breast there
> flow and thunder waves of immortal song spirit, akin to the crashing

waves of the sea, lives in golden happiness. That nation does not stain
steel swords and spears with the precious blood of people. *Peace* is its
stately, proud flag; a shield of songs which repels the spear.[128]

Then Auseklis wrote the poem that became the founding myth of Latvian song politics. Its content came from an episode in the thirteenth-
century *Chronicle of Henry of Livonia*. Garlieb Merkel, too, had once
quoted this passage about a Christian priest's song that miraculously
caused the invading Estonian army to lift its siege. For Merkel, the episode demonstrated the predisposition of Estonians to music. But Auseklis changed the singer's identity in the story to that of a pagan shaman (*vaidelotis*), and thus ascribed magical powers to the traditional
songs of the Latvians:

THE BARD OF BEVERIŅA

In proud Beveriņa Fortress
Tāluvaldis ruled the land,
Far and wide throughout his kingdom
He was praised and loved by all.

The Estonians, brother nation,
Raised a feud in Latvia,
Laid a siege to her great fortress,
Sent sharp arrows flying high.

Storms of war! Storms of war! Beveriņ' shall be destroyed!
    Ai, ai, aijaijā, Beveriņ' shall be destroyed!
Oaken maces, clubs of spruce—skulls of heroes shall be crushed!
    Ai, ai, aijaijā, skulls of heroes shall be crushed!

High above, upon the ramparts
There appears a vaidelots:
Silver hair, silver beard,
In his hands the priestly *kokles*.

Strumming the *kokles*, the elder one sang,
Estonians' weapons fell from their hands;

Now the drumbeats of war fell still,
Now the bagpipes of war fell silent.

Arrows were stopped by a shield of songs,
Noise was drowned out by the sound of songs,
War was ended by the power of songs,
The nation was saved by the spirit of songs!

The poem was set to music by Jāzeps Vītols in 1891 and premiered
at the fourth national song festival of 1895. Another performance at

that festival demonstrated not only the political power of songs but also the power of singing to transform the meaning of a song's text. The festival's opening concert was to include a speech by the metropolitan of the Russian Orthodox Church in Rīga, a staunch supporter of cultural Russification. An eyewitness would later describe how, at this event, the anthem of Imperial Russia paradoxically became an expression of resistance to Russian cultural domination. At the moment when the dignitaries entered the hall, conductor Ernests Vīgners led the choir in greeting them with Russia's anthem. As was the official custom, they and the audience applauded to request an encore, and then another. After the third repetition, however, a group of conspirators in the audience continued to applaud, calling for yet another encore, and another, and another. In one of the intervals of applause between encores, the metropolitan climbed up on the conductor's stage and tried to talk to the conductor, but Vīgners replied in a stage whisper, "Batyushka, publika trebuyet" (Father, the public demands it!) and continued to wave his baton. The anthem was repeated again and again, until the metropolitan departed from the hall, making a sign of the cross in the choir's direction before he left.[129]

That confrontation of 1895 displayed a meaning of Latvian song festivals that could no longer be derived from song texts alone. The context of the song festival, and the act of singing in itself, had become means of expressing an independent Latvian identity. Singing would become part of national institutions after the Republic of Latvia declared independence in 1918. National poets, composers, and song festivals would be incorporated into the nation's canonic history, and in 1935 a row of choir singers would be engraved in the national Freedom Monument. It is no surprise that in 1926, "The Bard of Beveriņa" was performed in the opening concert of the independent republic's first national song festival.

Under Russia's rule, Estonians often framed national activism as an expression of loyalty to the tsar, declaring, for example, that a song festival be held to honor Tsar Alexander's liberating the Estonian serfs. Such contrived meanings were dropped beginning with Estonia's declaration of political independence in 1918. The prime minister of Estonia pointed out, "The goal of national and political expression at the Estonian song festival has changed in the free Estonia. We no longer need to write and read between the lines, or to speak in half words."[130] In 1923, the first national song festival held in this new era of liberty concluded with the premiere of "Dawn," and presented songs as the medium for expressing the nation's hopes and belief in the future:

> Songs are now flowing in beautiful music,
> Crossing our country in powerful streams. (repeat line)
>
> Beauty is flourishing in verdant gardens:
> Fatherland's earth now awakens to bloom.
>
> Dawn is now glimmering on the high mountains.
> Let the flame of our hope rise to the sky! (repeat line)

In the early 1920s, Lithuanian choir leaders visited Latvian and Estonian song festivals to learn from them; they compiled national statistics about singers and choirs, and congregated regional rehearsals for choirs to learn to sing together. The first national song festival, cautiously named the "Day of Songs," took place in Kaunas in August 1924. Three thousand singers of seventy-six choirs performed at the festival, which, although hampered by rain, showed great potential for the future. Maironis dedicated a poem, "To the Song Festival," and its singers would place their voices into a context of national history:

> Dear songs of songs, in sounds of sounds,
> Resounding broadly, firmly, powerfully,
> Fly over hills, forests and fields
> Harmoniously, solemnly, gently,
> And wind into a single thread,
> Around Lithuania-fatherland
> Resounding broadly, powerfully.
>
> Dear song of the nation, you alone
> Survived, when heroes perished;
> Oppressed in times of suffering,
> You endured so much, oh so much.
> But you survived, strong and unbroken,
> In the unbendable villager,
> Though many heroes perished.
>
> Dear song of the nation, you revived
> Our soul through endless centuries;
> Alone you stood guard, when in their graves
> The giants dreamt of the beloved land;
> You stood on guard, and rocked a cradle,
> And calmed the youth and the elder,
> You nurtured the nation's soul.

Songs did continue to nurture the Lithuanian soul, but national unity faltered after the authoritarian coup of 1926. The festivals of 1928 and 1930 were marred by boycotts and disagreements between political factions, and between religious and secular organizations. Nevertheless, the second Lithuanian song festival featured about six thousand singers from 170 choirs, with a growing contingent of secular choirs, among them twenty from schools and ten from chapters of the nationalist "Šiauliai" associaton. The third song festival of 1930 was the last national song festival before World War II. It brought together a choir of 6,500 singers from 180 choirs to perform twenty-four works by Lithuania's leading composers.[131]

Cultural activists struggled to explain why national choral music traditions were faltering. Some argued that amateur choirs did not have sufficient technical training; some pointed to class differences, noting that the educated intelligentsia and government officials did not wish to sing together with farmers and servants; still others saw stagnation in a song repertoire that bored audiences. There was consensus, however, that choral singing was the "people's culture," in which all could participate, and that it should therefore continue.[132]

The musical skill of Lithuanian choirs improved steadily over the two decades of independence. In the early 1920s, churches were first to establish Lithuanian choirs; by 1930, rural church choirs had mastered four-part singing. New secular choirs, too, were led by professionally trained conductors, touring both nationally and abroad, and gaining a solid foothold in urban culture during the 1930s. Successful regional festivals in four cities assembled choirs averaging 1,500 singers, and organizers tested new ways of popularizing and advancing artistic quality, but the national festival that was to have been revived in 1943 was forgotten when World War II broke out.[133]

MASS-MEDIATED NATIONAL SONG REPERTOIRES

Back in the late eighteenth century, Baltic serfs recited oral poetry to ethnographic fieldworkers, aware of each text's connection to their own lives but unaware of the fact that their folk songs and singing would, after Herder, become national symbols. In contrast, twentieth-century Estonians, Latvians, and Lithuanians consciously participated in modern national cultures and were aware of themselves as "nations of singers." Some songs continued in the informal oral repertoires of individuals, families, or communities. But other songs found new life in mass-mediated national culture. These modern transformations were well known to Estonian singers; they embraced a folk song arranged by Miina Härma, "Singer's Childhood," which was performed by ten thousand singers at the 1910 national song festival and disseminated throughout the land during the 1920s and 1930s in many thousands of printed songbooks and schoolbooks:[134]

> When I was a little child, al-le-a, al-le-a,
> I grew like a little violet, al-le-a, al-le-a.
>
> Mother took me down to the meadow,
> Carried the cradle to the hayfield,
>
> Placed the cuckoo by the cradle,
> Bid the bird to rock the baby,
>
> Then the cuckoo bird it cuckoo-ed,
> Summer bird sang many songs,
>
> I remembered and I listened,
> I remembered and I learned,
>
> All of it I put on paper,
> Out of it I built a book. (repeat stanza twice)

The song's words embraced the idyllic agrarian landscape of a hayfield as well as modern forms of communication, writing and books. The composer likewise led oral folk songs to adapt and embrace a world in which educated audiences expected complex harmonies. Härma's melody, like many other early twentieth-century choral arrangements of folk songs, was no longer a simple tune from oral tradition; it combined melodies from several oral variants, elaborated melodic details, and added four-part harmony. Each of the first four stanzas had a dramatically different tune, imitating the varied warbling of birds in the countryside. Thanks to cultural traditions nurtured over several generations yielding ten thousand skilled singers from all parts of the country, Miina Härma could express her artistic creativity at the 1910 song festival.

From 1918 to 1940, national independence placed Baltic singing traditions on firm institutional foundations. Public schools provided jobs for an expanding corps of teachers trained in music pedagogy, and also ensured that children throughout the country would share a repertoire of songs. Singing professionalization was advanced by the three national conservatories; by artists who earned their living in nationally based operas, orchestras, and religious organizations; and by a growing infrastructure of mass-mediated music publications, recordings, and broadcasting.

Some Baltic singing traditions were supported by nationalism. Some songs, like the ones quoted in this chapter, explicitly defined national identity and political ideology. Authoritarian governments of the late 1930s sponsored songs of national unity.[135] But nationalism was not the only fuel for singing traditions. As singing traditions expanded, the national song repertoires also expanded and diversified. A significant portion of song-festival concert programs, for example, was devoted to religious hymns, which were sung year-round in church. Between song festivals, social democrats sang songs of socialism, scouts sang about scouting, and fraternities and sororities maintained their own private singing customs. Folk songs, mentioned above only in a few examples, covered a broad spectrum of singing communities from diverse political backgrounds; these songs about nature, love, and country life also comprised a large part of the national song festival repertoire. The four fragments of Latvian folk songs quoted at the beginning of this chapter give a representative sample: the first is about a rooster running over to the neighboring farmstead to wake sleeping women, among them the singer's bride; the second is a song of a woman who is capable of doing difficult farm work on her own and makes a shirt for the man who works alongside her; in the third song, a bride asks her brothers to build a house with one door facing the sunrise, another facing the sunset, and a third for her to walk through on her wedding day; the fourth song speaks to a brother who rides a horse across a swift river and makes a fire for people who wish him harm, to warm themselves. Each of these songs, on the one hand, was known to be part of the unique national heritage and thus meshed with nationalism, but, on the other, it was also about human relations and love.

Estonians, Latvians, and Lithuanians were now nations of singers, and, thanks to schools, songbooks, and song festivals, many individuals in each nation shared a large repertoire of songs. These were not homogenized singing nations. Hundreds of songs circulating in print and oral tradition had diverse semantic fields, allowing for a large range of variation in song meanings within personal repertoires. Individual singers could easily call up the song that expressed a feeling at a given moment, and they would usually find others who knew the text and could share the moment by singing. Identities were thus individual and communal as well as national, connecting a person to a small group and to the nation of singers; they, too, knew the songs and could sing along, for example, when a singing choir passed by during the song festival processions of 1990.

CHAPTER FOUR

Songs of Warrior Nations

The 1990 Lithuanian National Song and Dance Festival published a songbook for public singing events. On the first page is a song with a motif common to Lithuanian folk songs about war: a group of brothers riding horses. The singer tells the riders to stop, listen, and look at the mystical black poplar. There is music coming from the mythical tree, whose branches, Lithuanians know, stretch up into the heavens while its roots reach down into the netherworld.[1] (The refrain words *Slaunasai žolyne rugeli* [proud dear rye plant] sung after each line do not carry literal meaning but add a meditative atmosphere):

> Black poplar standing by the roadside,
>
> *Kankles* ringing at the roots,
> Honeybees humming in the center,
> Hawk's little children nest at the top,
> There rides up a squadron of brothers,
> Stop now, stop, oh young brothers,
> Listen to the ringing *kankles*,
> Listen to the humming bees,
> Look at the hawk's little children.

The Singing Revolution's historian must likewise stop and listen to its songs. At the core of a nonviolent, singing political movement, one might expect songs of peace and unity, and songs that reject or at least avoid martial themes. But nine out of thirty songs in this 1990 Lithuanian songbook are explicitly about war. Among them are two of the five songs that Lithuanians would sing in 1998 at the Smithsonian festival: "On the Hill There Stood a Maple Tree" and "Oh Don't Weep, Dear Mother."

More than a century of war songs were deeply embedded in the national cultures—as deeply as the peaceful songs presented in the preceding chapters. War has long played an important role in the formation of ethnic identity, and it is a common theme in the discourse of nation building.[2] It is, however, a theme that is contested in conflicting attitudes toward the soldier's experience and killing enemies. Herder's assertion that "the warlike nation sings of feats, the gentle nation sings of love" offers a starting point for interpretation. Some war songs valorize the defeat of enemies, and others empathize with the trauma of soldiers and civilians. At the outset of the Singing Revolution, both kinds of songs were available in the Baltic national song repertoires.

SONGS OF WAR, REAL AND IMAGINED

Herder's folk song project belonged to his study of differing national identities, based in his belief that a nation's spirit was revealed in its songs. He brokered this worldview particularly well when he published the Estonian folk song in which a sister pragmatically advised her brother to avoid getting killed in battle. The song preserved images of war as truly experienced by Estonian serfs in the late eighteenth century. When it depicted a returning soldier who was not recognized by his parents, for example, it described the true experience of men conscripted into military service for twenty five years, returning home in old age. The song's singers, like the soldier in the song, could intensely experience the absence of love and separation from kin that was part of every soldier's life. For a lowly serf, war was involuntary, a brutal carnage with no higher purpose, and its violence was to be avoided. Estonian serfs expressed this experience in oral poetry, and Herder's published translations brought their world to life for readers.

In Herder's writings, this particular song connected well to a rhetorical image of peaceful, gentle nations of farmers who, in contrast to Europe's warlike nations, were not preoccupied with pride and bravery. Another Estonian song in *Volkslieder* evoked empathy for serfs, and Herder's comments nudged Baltic German serf owners toward emancipation. But this song embraced a wider readership, Baltic and other, by giving voice to a soldier who was also a victim of war. The true nature of war lay not in proud victory and loyalty to leaders but rather in killing and alienation from humanity. This Herderian view of war was marginalized by nineteenth-century European govern-ments who followed Napoleon's model of national mobilization, and by poets and singers who embraced policies of military nation build-ing. These added new songs to the mass-mediated national repertoire, displacing problematic oral texts such as Herder's Estonian war song. Poets imagined more useful pictures of war, and their imagination extended to the soldiers who sang their songs before battle. An indi-vidual soldier's fear of being killed, or his meek love and longing for his bride, his family, or home, were all easily drowned out by images of masculine brotherhood and proud service to a mighty monarch blessed by God. The new militaristic songs excluded feelings of real-life empathy, projecting instead a sense of duty and honor that would extend into an imagined afterlife, if a soldier were to willingly die.

In 1807, with Napoleon's armies at the borders of the Russian empire, a Lutheran pastor in Tallinn printed a booklet of five songs adapted from German into Estonian, aiming to enlist ethnic Estonians in the local militia.[3] The songs followed blueprints used by many mili-tary culture builders. Images of war revolved around polar opposites: bravery and cowardice, pride and shame. Irony and ridicule would convert passive nonviolence into active violence:

Whoever is not prepared for war

When the enemy approaches,
And whoever wants to stand aside
When help is necessary,
This is a despicable man,
Let's give him a spinning wheel
Or let him knit us stockings
Together with the women.

And when he sees the enemy,
He should run and hide in the forest,
And he should watch the enemy
Bring his clan to an end;
Then he himself will shrivel when
He comes out of the forest
And, God forbid, discovers that
He has no bread or children.

Or if he stays there on the spot
When enemies approach:
Well then, let him open wide
His barns and chests to thieves
And today let him give up his harvest,

And then tomorrow his money,
And then his last shreds of clothing,
And finally his own skin.

And then let him drive out his wife
And children to be beggars,
And after them his gray-haired father,
And also his ailing mother
And finally then he himself,
Feeling his deep shame,
Should roam along the forest's edge,
Like a rabbit, full of fear.

Oh, disaster strikes a people
Who has men like these!
They will fall and never rise,
And their children's children will weep.
Like a tree without bark,
Such is this poor people,
They are scorned by all,
And suffering always.

But praise and honor shall go to him
Who stands for fatherland,
And whose firm and manly mind
Reveals itself in wartime!
He is a gift from heaven,
All shall look toward him,
And all are calmed by him,
And all depend on him.

He goes to the fore in battle,
Like an angel sent from heaven;
All others follow behind,
Not one shies from the troubles,
And children, wives, and parents,
All give to him their blessing,
And in their eyes the tears
Speak their praise to him.

And like a lion he battles,
Because he fights for the tsar,
Fearless in the valley of death,
Because he defends his own land.
His mind is firm as a rock,
His valor like a river,
Terror and death walk before him,
Power is in his footsteps.

This enemy is struck down,

And falls into his pit;
And the rescued people
Sings a song of thanks.
The girls of the land rejoice,
That the young men are brave,
And their gray-haired parents
Call for a wedding feast.

And oh! what joy for the man
Who defended the Fatherland,
And so ensured new happiness
For his kindred people!
All children shall sing of him,
All shall honor him,
And young and old shall try
To bring him happiness again.

And when he departs from the world
In old age,
Then every man shall mourn,
And every man shall weep.
And the people's prayers shall send
His soul before the Creator,
And the angels of heaven shall give
To him the crown of life.

The song declares that a man who avoids military service is not masculine. Furthermore, it warns that if he refuses to enlist, he will lose
his personal property and allow his kin to be harmed. On the other
hand, the man who proves his worth in battle will gain honor before
society and be rewarded: on earth he will get a bride, and in heaven he
will get immortality. The song omits both killing and death in battle.
The enemy simply falls "into his pit," and the hero will someday die
of old age. In 1807, prior to emancipation, the words "fatherland"
and "tsar" did not yet have the meaning that they acquired later in the
Estonian language, because an Estonian serf did not have national (or
imperial) identity; he did not own "his own land," and hardly had any
contact with rulers other than the noble gentry of his native district.[4]
The song focused on individual self-interest, not collective identity; a
soldier would fight to defend his property and kin, or to earn a wife.
After emancipation, as individual identities expanded through literacy
and mass-mediated communication, the rhetoric of military mobilization would shift further from individual experience to that of a larger,
imagined community. Indeed, another song in this 1807 songbook
belonged to this cultural transition. "Now, Men, Let Us Be Strong!"

tells how a soldier's heart is strengthened when he leaves behind his weeping family and realizes that he is fighting for the tsar with the conviction "God is with us!" That song's soldier is killed in battle, and his dying words are addressed not to his bride but to his military brethren and the fatherland. "Now, Men" lasted for several decades in Estonian military marching tradition:[5]

> Whoever falls from our midst,
> He calls out as he dies:
> "Oh brothers, men, fight!
> Think now of the Fatherland!"
> And he dies joyfully,
> And he dies joyfully.

The martial tactics and technologies of nineteenth-century Europe required massive armies of soldiers who were trained to suppress their own fear as they charged and killed enemies. War songs played a critical role. Their melodies stimulated confidence and enforced rhythmic discipline in large marching, shooting, reloading, and shooting regiments. Song words presented simplified ideology that enabled a soldier to attack. In the nineteenth century, the ideology of armies was built on imperial or national loyalty.

Herder's idea of national spirit was revived during nineteenth-century nationalistic movements. But instead of deducing differences between nations based on whatever songs could be collected from oral traditions, as Herder would have done, patriotic scholars now aimed to find or create poetry that would enhance the valor and thereby also the perceived value of their nation. In 1822, a young Estonian student at the University of Tartu, Christian Jaak Peterson, rediscovered two oral variants of the song that Herder had once quoted. In the spirit of his times, Peterson began with a postulate that the Estonians were ruthless fighters in ancient times, and that their national spirit extended into the contemporary world:

> The Estonian however went confidently into the war. How he experienced it, is shown in the following excerpt from a song. The sister asks the brother returning from battle:
>
>> Is the wife dear in War?
>> Dear the wife, true the spouse?
>
> The brother answers:
>
>> In war, it is the bright sword that is dear,
>> The sturdy steed is pretty;
>> There the heads of men fall

> Like tree stumps in the forest;
> There the men's blood flows
> Like water in the watermill.

> Even nowadays one finds traces of the old ruthlessness and the hard
> disposition of the Estonians, but—Hail Alexander! He led them
> toward the morning dawn of a high education—In the name of my
> entire people I cry out, "Hail Alexander! For him every brave Estonian
> will be willing to spill blood!"[6]

Peterson manipulated data to serve his rhetorical conclusions. He had
two oral variants of the "Brother's War Tale" at his disposal, and he
chose the one that did not include the sister's pragmatic advice for her
brother to avoid battle.[7] Then he abridged the song that he quoted,
omitting the tragic story of the brother who returned from war and
was not recognized by his relatives. According to the folk song that
Peterson selectively quoted and interpreted, the heroic Estonian soldier felt no regret for participating in war.

Peterson's assertions, however, found little resonance in nineteenth-century Estonian national culture, in no small part because
Friedrich Kreutzwald, the author of the national epic *Kalevipoeg*,
espoused nonviolence. Twice in that work, Kreutzwald faithfully
quoted complete, tragic variants of the "Brother's War Tale," injecting a dissonant note into episodes in which the hero calls his people
to battle.[8] Later in the epic, the national hero himself is disarmed
and then abandons war. Kreutzwald inserted an antiwar poem into
the epic to clearly state his ideological stance. In a pivotal episode,
a singer is commanded by the king to announce that war is coming,
but on his way he meets messengers of blood, carnage, hunger, and
plague, and

> I took to mulling the matter over, coaxed my senses into thinking:
> will any gain grow from my errand . . . ? . . . Why should I strew the
> wretchedness of bloodshed, the raging of murderous swords onto a
> time of peace? . . . And I tore the commands from my wallet . . . and
> cast them into the bottomless sea . . . that is how strife's crackling was
> stilled, the rumbling of war made to vanish.[9]

After Kreutzwald, images of glorious war and demonized foes would
falter in Estonian national culture.[10] In more than a century and a half
of Estonian national song festivals, the national choir would sing only
two songs that called for violence against enemies: the tsarist anthem
of Russia (quoted in chapter 3) and the Stalinist anthem of the Soviet
Union (to be quoted in chapter 5).

The image of war in Kreutzwald's epic is that of tragic defeat and destruction: wars of the past were worthy of sacred memory but they were not a model for future military campaigns. A passage of the epic was set to music by Karl August Hermann, to be sung in 1923 at the first national song festival of independent Estonia and taught to children in schools.[11] "Fatherland Commemoration" centered on the land's destruction and the nation's soldiers' suffering, and not on glorious victories over evil enemies. It thus remained true to the nonviolent ideology of the national epic from which it came.

> Guarding the beautiful fatherland,
> Fighting against the enemy,
> Brave counties crumbled,
> Districts perished
> Under the ancient earth.
>
> May their sad suffering,
> Their tormenting wounds,
> Precious ancient memories
> Sound among us without ceasing,
> Sound among us without ceasing,
> Sound among us without ceasing.

The Latvian national song discourse also saw tension between aggressive and empathetic images of war. The lack of epic songs in oral tradition was hailed by some as evidence that the Latvian nation was peace loving, but others imagined this to be shameful evidence of national cowardice. Folklorist Fricis Brīvzemnieks argued that Latvians had once sung heroic epic songs but had forgotten them under the yoke of serfdom.[12] In 1888, the poet Andrejs Pumpurs, himself a veteran of the Russo-Turkish War, would publish his literary epic *Bearslayer,* about a fictional military leader of the Latvian golden age who would someday return to lead his nation to liberty and happiness. Latvians, too, desired songs that would not only generate national pride but could also mobilize tangible armies for real wars. One such song was Cimze's "Farewell Now, Dear Vidzemīte," first published in his 1872 *Garland of Songs,* a collection of *dainas* that he and his students had collected from oral tradition. The song saw ovations and encores at the conclusion of national song festivals in 1873 and 1880. In the broader context of the Russian Empire's nineteenth-century military expansion into Central Asia and the Caucusus, which seems to have enjoyed public support among Latvians in the 1870s, the concluding stanza evoked confidence in an easy military victory over a conventional enemy:

Farewell now, dear Vidzemīte,
I'll not stay here anymore,
I'll no longer wander freely,
Calling at the village doors.

Let the wheat grow, let the rye grow
Where they proudly ride along,
Soon I'll have to proudly ride, too,
In the handsome cavalry.

If, dear mother, you could see
How they decorate your son,
Then you would no longer weep
For the sake of your dear son.

They'll put on a fine war coat,
They'll put on a fine war hat,
They'll strap on a fine steel sword,
Lift him on a sturdy horse.

Singing songs and playing music,
We shall ride off to the war,
Singing songs and playing music,
We shall come home from the war.

The song would be sung by the Latvian folklore ensemble Skandinieki in June and August of 1991; in that new historical context, the last stanza's meaning would change dramatically, to both depict and enact the means by which Latvians fought for and gained liberty: singing.[13] But in the late nineteenth century, and then during World War I, when it was sung by the Latvian Riflemen, the song maintained, first and foremost, optimistic confidence that Latvian soldiers would win military victories. The folk song's archaic references to swords and steeds became a stable Latvian poetic metaphor, a euphemism for modern wars in which real soldiers carried rifles and boarded trains that carried them to battlefield trenches.

Other folk song texts in Cimze's book would also reappear in military service. One of them, a song arranged by his brother, Dāvis Cimze, could hardly bolster fighting morale because it ended with the soldier killed on the borders of a foreign land: "Where is my dear brother, / The flag bearer?, / Aijā, aijajā, the flag bearer? / The rider stayed there, / On the Lithuanian border."[14] But later, during World War I, these last stanzas were dropped, preserving more heroic stanzas in popular tradition, among them "High Up in the Air Two Doves," as remembered at the 1998 Smithsonian festival (chapter 1). Another song, "The Soldiers Are Uneasy," juxtaposed two images of the sunrise: one pensive and bloody, the other hopeful and silvery. In 1915, although this song's melody was not a marching tune, its hopeful concluding line became the motto of a Latvian Riflemen's battalion. The image of the rising sun appeared in early wartime versions of the national flag, and in 1921, it was included in the Republic of Latvia's official coat of arms.[15]

SINGING WITH REVOLUTIONARY VENGEANCE IN LATVIA

The late nineteenth and early twentieth centuries saw an explosion of militant songs fueled by socialism. "The Internationale," whose French words and melody were composed in 1871 and 1887, respectively, was translated into Latvian by an anonymous author during the 1905 Revolution.[16] Its text was adapted to fit local preparations for a violent battle against the tsar:

Awake to battle, working people,
You crowd of slaves from every land!
You've snoozed under the curse of labor,
Our spirit thirsts for struggle now.
We'll crush the throne of violent oppression,
Poverty and injustice shall fall,
We'll build a new world for ourselves
Where work and justice shall prevail.

This is the final battle,
Which will bring victory,
With the Internationale
Each person is reborn!

Not tsar, nor heroes, nor the gods
Will bring to us the new age.
Only our own hands, our own strength
Bring happiness, shatter the chains!
And so that we may now capture
Our own happiness with a strong hand,
Off with the chains! Let us forge spears,
While the iron is still hot.
    (refrain)

We are the ones who sweat in work's yoke,
We are the workers of all lands.
To us belongs the world, we shall rule,
Off with exploiters and parasites!
And while anger's furious thunder roars

Over crowds of servants of the tsar,
Above us, with its crimson rays
The sun will pour down fire of life.
   (refrain)

"The Internationale," "La Marseillaise," and other translations
merged in performance with many new socialist fight songs in native
Baltic languages. The poem "Broken Pines," for example, was written
by the Latvian poet Rainis in 1901 and set to music by Emīls Dārziņš
in 1904.[17] It had originally referred to the tsarist repression of 1898,
when, among many others, Rainis himself was arrested for socialist
activism; its meaning expanded dramatically during the 1905 Revolution, reasserting that the battle against the "hostile enemy" would
never end:

The wind snapped the tallest of pines
Which stood on the dunes by the shore,
Their gaze reached for the horizon,
They could not hide, nor bow their back.

"You broke us, oh hostile enemy,
The battle against you shall not end!"
Their last groan breathes toward the horizon,
With undying hatred in every branch!

And the tallest pines after breaking
Rose up from the water as ships,
Their chests raised proudly against the storm,
The fight roars anew against power:

"Crash your waves, you hostile enemy!
We'll reach the horizon of happiness!
You may splinter us, you may break us,
We'll reach the horizon, and the rising sun!"

The poem was a beacon of Latvian resistance to tsarist rule. Next to
it stood another poem by Rainis that supported cold-blooded violence
as a means of advancing social justice, arguing, "You must know: The
greatest idea knows no human compassion."[18] The song of the 1905
Revolution that penetrated most deeply into Latvian national memory
was "With Cries of Battle on Your Lips," a poem that Jānis Akurāters
dedicated to the civilians killed by the tsar's soldiers on January 13,
1905. Its words were printed a few days after the event and set to
music by an anonymous composer. The song reaffirmed an ideology
of vengeful violence. It would be reprinted in nearly every Latvian
socialist songbook of the subsequent decades:[19]

With cries of battle on your lips,
You fell with burning hearts.
But your death, holy, free,
Is a precious talisman for us.

And the innocent blood
Burning on the white snow
Will not fade for years—
In our flag it will smolder.

Peace to you! Your lips are now silent.
But their silence calls loudly,
And a thousand new brigades for battle
Will grow out of the people.

But for you, oh tyrant on the throne,
Our sword was sharpened long ago!
At dawn your murderers and killers
Shall all be punished and repaid!

Those who live, shall go to bloody battle,
And thrones and castles will be crushed!
To you, the dead, eternal glory!
We, the living go to avenge you!

The song's last two lines caught fire in the summer of 1905, when Latvian revolutionaries went on a violent rampage in the countryside, burning manors and killing clergymen. The lines would be quoted often by Latvian Bolsheviks for the next decades and throughout the Russian Revolution, continually reasserting the fundamental importance of vengeance in their ideology and tactics.

But the 1905 Revolution also contained powerful currents of non-violent politics.[20] Rainis renounced violence in his 1905 play *Fire and Night*, in which the national heroine, Spīdola, urged the national hero, Bearslayer, to "change upward" and reject revenge.[21] In 1909, Emīls Dārziņš set to music a poem, "Restlessness," that the poet Kārlis Skalbe had dedicated to the martyrs of the 1905 Revolution. A controversy immediately arose over the changes that Dārziņš made to the original text. Skalbe's poem, for example, addressed the readers directly and exhorted them to rise: the enemy has shattered "our" sacrificial vessels, and the homeland is "covered with stars of blood." Dārziņš defused this rhetoric of revenge, replacing "our" with "ancestors'," and "blood" with "fog." He also deleted Skalbe's words "martyrs" and "curse" and replaced them with "heroes" and "ancient story." It is not possible to reconstruct the reasons why Dārziņš revised Skalbe's text, but it is clear that his text no longer carried a threat of immediate violence[22]:

> Latvia's hillsides are blue forever;
> In shadows of birches restless forever
> The *kokle* will weep above Latvia's hillsides.
>
> Sacred ancestors' vessels lie shattered,
> Fields of the homeland hidden in fog,
> Below the spruce grove's gray branches
> The ancestors' spirits cannot rest.
>
> The crashing rapids of Daugava carry
> The ancient story through stone crags forever,
> Daugava rapids restless forever,
> Spirits of heroes restless forever.
>
> (repeat first stanza)

"Blue Forever" would premiere on the Latvian national song festival stage in 1926, after Latvia had won its war for independence. It was now a song of national military commemoration, no longer tied to the specific historical event from which it arose. The dead heroes, it declared, would always be restless, reminding the living to weep for those shattered lives. But the song did not call for revenge.

REVIVING LITHUANIA'S GOLDEN AGE OF MILITARY VICTORIES

In Lithuanian national song culture during the late nineteenth and early twentieth centuries, the combined forces of nationalism and religion produced lasting traditions of violent rhetoric. For this strand of literary creativity, folk poetry was not a useful source of inspiration. Early Lithuanian folklorists, like Herder, had observed that their songs, and by extension also contemporary Lithuanian identity, were related to love, not war. In 1809, Liudvikas Rėza even defined the entire category of *daina* as an "erotic genre," that is, secular love songs. He repeated the idea in the introduction to his 1825 book:

> Most Lithuanian folk songs, as shown by this collection, belong to the erotic type: They sing about the feelings of love and joy, portray the happiness of domestic life, and in the simplest fashion they place before our eyes the relations of love among the members of a family and their relatives. From this perspective, this entire collection as a whole comprises a cycle of love, from its very beginnings through various levels to its embodiment in marriage.[23]

At the same time, however, Rėza, like Peterson in Estonia, wished
to establish military heroism in the canonic history of Lithuania. He
argued that Lithuanian heroic epic poetry must have existed in the
fourteenth and fifteenth centuries, when Lithuania was a European
military power. Rėza had not found such songs in East Prussia, but he
believed that they might still exist in Lithuania Major. Across the border, however, Simonas Stanevičius responded to Rėza's writing with a
resigned account of ethnographic reality in Žemaitija, the northwest-
ern region of Lithuania: "It is an empty hope that there might still
exist songs of the ancient Lithuanians and Žemaitians, as formerly
sung by the Waydelotay, the elders and bards of our land." What is
more, he wrote, the dominant theme in Lithuanian folk songs was
love, not war: "The topics of Žemaitian songs of our age are words
of love between a youth and a maiden, between parents and sons or
daughters. If war is mentioned somewhere, then it is always in a story
of love."[24]

The second half of the nineteenth century saw a new generation of
songs that turned to military history—and not war as depicted in oral
tradition—to construct symbols of national greatness. In East Prussia, the nation builder Sauerwein hoped to stimulate German respect
for Lithuanian culture when he wrote poems about medieval Lithuania's military defeat of the Teutonic Order. But Sauerwein was also
a member of the International Peace Society. The Lithuanian language
"moved his heart," because he saw in it a connection to the Indo-European people, the ancestors of the Europeans, who, he believed, had
once lived in harmony: "It was the youth of humankind, / A dawning
of the ages; / And friendship of mankind was still / Like that of house-
mates, not like now."[25] Sauerwein's opposition to German assimilation policies and his advocacy of the Lithuanian language were tied
to hopes for peaceful coexistence among the nations of Europe, and
certainly not an attempt to mobilize Lithuanians for a war of vengance
or national liberation.[26] Sauerwein's poems, however, could, and did,
stimulate feelings of national military pride.

Across the border in Lithuania Major, memories of real war were
recent and visceral, and were directly related to contemporary violence. The 1863 revolution in particular, but before it the revolutions
of 1830 and 1794 as well, were remembered by Lithuanian national
leaders (many of whom were Catholic clergy) as an ongoing conflict between Eastern Orthodoxy and Roman Catholicism. Memories
were refreshed by current violence, for example, when Russian troops

destroyed the Roman Catholic church at Kražiai in 1893. This was the context in which Maironis's poem titled "Song of Ancient Times" once again revived the memory of medieval Lithuania's military leader, Grand Duke Vytautas, and of his war against enemies in both the East and the West. The motivation for battle was vengeance. War was framed in religious, Christian images, according to which Lithuanian soldiers killed in battle went to heaven and received crowns of diamonds from the angels. Lithuanians sang the first three stanzas at the 1998 Smithsonian festival (translated in chapter 1), and four more stanzas complete the song:

OH, DON'T WEEP, DEAR MOTHER (CONTINUED)

Many sons fell there, like the autumn leaves:
Pale sweethearts will weep for their love!
But the Nemunas River shall hold less water
Than the enemy blood that flowed there.

Here the troops of heroes that Vytautas led
Once shattered the enemy's glory!
And the mighty crusaders were all driven out
Beyond distant seas and forests.

In the graveyard of Vilnius the red setting sun
Shone over the gathering soldiers,
And they buried their brothers among the great ones,
And the Lord God embraced their souls.

So, don't weep, dear mother, when your young son
Leaves home to defend his dear country!
When he falls, like an oak, to the forest ground,
To await the Last Day of Judgement.

Maironis's original poem of 1895 had named the enemy in the line, "the Belarus blood that flowed there," specifying that enemies came from an Orthodox land to the east. But in 1913 he changed the word to "enemy," allowing the song to be used in wars against other nations, too. It is this later text that eventually passed into national singing tradition.[27] In other poems, too, Maironis revived the memory of Vytautas as Lithuania's defender against demonic German crusaders from the west. His 1895 poem "Graves of Giants," later transformed into a song by Juozas Tallat-Kelpša, depicted Lithuanians mobilized in revenge for the deaths of sons and husbands. In the twentieth century, this song, retitled "Where the Plains Are Level," would maintain its position as a core text in the Lithuanian national military repertoire[28]:

Where the plains are level, where the dark forests sleep,
Bearded Lithuanians tend fires;
They whet their axes and sharpen their swords
And saddle the black-bay steeds,

From the Prussian land, like the wings of a cloud, (repeat line)
    Dark smoke coils up to the heavens;
The blazes of war turn the night into day: (repeat line)
    In flames are the forests and castles.

In the wilderness it is not the howling of beasts:
Oh no! Those are Lithuanian widows;
They weep for a son, or for a dear young man,
Who has fallen, and no longer defends them.

The crusading men, who once came as guests (repeat line)
    Now advance through Lithuania, feasting;
For glory they thirst, but when morning will dawn, (repeat line)
    The most fiery hopes will be answered.

The scouts report that Lithuanian troops
Ford the Nemunas River by Kaunas;
Through the village a rider, his horse white with sweat,
Summons the Lithuanians to battle.

The forests are thick! Only blazing flames (repeat line)
    Light up the path through Lithuania.
The darkened sky throws a storm of lightning bolts; (repeat line)
    The guests now tire of wandering.

The forests rumble, like thunder on high
In a flash, by surprise, the Lithuanians
Like fire flaring up on a straw roof
Surrounded and charged at the crusaders.

Oh, it was a fight! The dusk of night (repeat line)
    Was ashamed to reveal it when day broke;
The corpses laid high, by the hundreds in piles (repeat line)
    Would lie there still for a long time.[29]

World War I broke out in 1914. After a brief Russian attack into
East Prussia, Germany counterattacked and quickly occupied Lithuania and southwestern Latvia. The front lines stalled at the Daugava
River from 1915 to 1917, when Germany advanced to occupy the
entire territory of the present-day Baltic countries. Songs played a role
in the Russian Empire's war propaganda, particularly among the Latvian Riflemen's regiments that were established in 1915. This was the
context in which "Brother Dear," "Our Troops Are Not So Great

in Number," and "High Up in the Air, Two Doves" (all translated in chapter 1) spread in Latvian song tradition. (The future Latvian national anthem was also part of every evening's official ceremony, sung after "God Protect the Tsar."[30])

Songwriters also aimed to mobilize Estonians for the Russian Empire's battle against Germany. A songbook published at the war's outset adapted earlier patriotic images to the current hostilities. A modification of Karl August Hermann's song urged, "Go across the mountaintops, / Hurry, Estonian brothers, / Unified with Russia's forces, / Hasten to Austria!" A variant of the national anthem specified that the singer would stay true until death in war: "My fatherland, you truly are / My happiness and joy! / To you I shall always sing, / That you are dear until death, / If even in the din of war, / I must die for you!" And a sequel to "People of Kungla" stirred up a historical hatred against Germans:[31]

> Once, in the ancient times of yore
> Estonians lived free,
> Our happiness was everywhere,
> And pain and need were distant,
>> Stepped in the forest with a tune,
>> Went to the woods now with a song,
>> Stepped in the forest with a tune,
>> Went to the woods now with a song
>> Went with a song, went with a song, went with a song!
>
> Then Germans came across the sea
> And freedom disappeared,
> We fell in chains of slavery,
> There came grief, pain, and suffering!
>> Did not go to the woods with a song,
>> Went to the manor to toil instead!
>> (repeat as above)
>
> Gone now the whips of slavery,
> The master cannot beat us,
> Slave labor gone, and German yokes
> No longer press our shoulders:
>> Now we go gladly out to fight
>> To meet the Krauts and vanquish them!
>> (repeat as above), Yes, vanquish them!

In the Russian Imperial army during World War I, Estonians and Lithuanians were not organized into ethnic units like those of the Latvian Riflemen. Estonian songs such as the ones quoted above thus would not have been sung by marching regiments, and perhaps this is a reason why they did not last long in the national repertoire.

Baltic military nationalism switched to a new course after Lithuania, Estonia, and Latvia declared independence in February and November of 1918. The three governments organized armies to fight the war for national self-determination, and here, native songs and poetry were sung to raise and maintain the soldiers' morale. The Lithuanian children's song "Father Went Out to the Forest" was one that all recruits knew well, and this is probably why it became a popular military marching song during Lithuania's war for independence.[32] Earlier songs, among them the texts by Maironis and Sauerwein quoted above, energized images of a national mission. In Estonia and Latvia, new poems and songs defined national symbols. The Estonian military song "Be Free, Estonia's Sea" was born in 1916.[33] In that same year, Rainis wrote a patriotic poem, "Daugava's Two Shorelines," that would enter the national canon when it was set to music by Jānis Norvilis (these two songs were translated in chapter 1).[34]

After the successful war for independence, the soldiers themselves became national symbols. In Lithuania, as in Latvia and Estonia, the memory of fallen soldiers played a central role in national symbolism of the 1920s and 1930s.[35] National military culture flourished in hundreds of new songs. Patriotism spurred both amateur and professional poets to adapt older songs or recombine images from folklore. Soldiers compiled such songs in handwritten notebooks and popularized them after returning home from service. It was during this period that Lithuanian songs such as "In the Forest Grew an Oak Tree" became popular, documenting a transformation from agrarian identity to national identity that placed military service above farming. The variant translated here also preserves the memory of interwar hostility between Lithuania and Poland.[36]

> In the forest grew an oak tree, (repeat three times)
>   And a son grew by his father. (repeat twice)
>
> Worrying, the father said
>   That his son was very small.
>
> Don't you worry, oh dear father,
>   Your son soon will grow much bigger
>
> Your son soon will grow much bigger,
>   He'll be Lithuania's soldier.
>
> I don't need a little soldier,

> I need only a good plowsman.
>
> I'll not plow those hills so high,
>   For Lithuania I will fight.
>
> Farewell, my dear, we'll meet no more,
>   From Vilnius we'll drive the Poles.
>
> Make a wreath of mint so brown
>   So that Poland would burn down.
>
> Make a wreath of rue so green
>   So Lithuania would be free.

Lithuania's unresolved dispute with Poland over the city of Vilnius overshadowed international politics in the Baltic region during the 1920s and 1930s. Lithuania's preparations to regain the cherished city nourished a national military symbolism that was much more intense than in Estonia and Latvia. Images of the Grand Duchy of Lithuania as a military power were already thriving in the memory of previous nation builders, and now they zeroed in on Lithuania's central fortress in Vilnius. Songs solidified the foundation of rhetoric that surrounded Lithuania's stolen capital, for example, when Lithuanian folklorist Jonas Basanavičius gave a lecture, "Vilnius in Lithuanian Folk Songs."[37]

The 1930 commemoration of the five-hundred-year anniversary of Grand Duke Vytautas's death was a symbolically rich expression of Lithuania's statehood, and is remembered as one of the most significant events in all of twentieth-century Lithuanian national culture, enshrining symbols that retained their power even into the twenty-first century. The year's central event was an eight-week, semireligious public ritual that reenacted Vytautas's triumphal procession through the country in 1424. A portrait of the ruler was carried through all of the cities and towns, beginning on July 15, the date of the 1410 Battle of Žalgiris (Grunwald) where Vytautas defeated the Teutonic Order, and concluding on September 8, the date when the grand duke was once to have been crowned king. Accompanied by military displays and armed guards, the assemblies surrounding the portrait unmistakably stressed not only historical pride but political issues of the present day, bound to an anticipation of future military conflict. A celebratory biographer wrote, "Vytautas's politics may be summarized thus: In the East—offense; in the West—defense; and within the country . . . Lithuania for the Lithuanians!" "Offense" unmistakably referred to Vytautas's capital city, Vilnius. The national song festival

that year featured the song "Without Vilnius, We Shall Not Rest!"
Another song that premiered that summer was incorporated into the
official repertoire of the Lithuanian armed forces:[38]

> Oh, Vytautas the Great, the fatherland's leader!
> You decorate centuries with wreaths of glory.
> Awaken, oh eagle, an age of heroes—
> The land will yet rumble with the steps of the giant! (repeat line)
>
> Reborn is the power that ancient times foretold.
> Our men on steeds thunder through the forest.
> Like the ancestors riding, clothed in armor,
> Young defenders of the fatherland have risen.
>
> To Vilnius! To Vilnius! The glorious castle!
> For it, our sword will strike the enemy.
> Here the souls of the ancestors lie in dead silence,
> Here your vigilant eye once stood guard.
>
> From here you threatened the mighty crusader,
> From here you trod the paths into battle.
> Echoes of our warrior ancestors ring out here,
> For ages the Lithuanian was here, and shall be!

Not all rhetoric surrounding Vytautas was military. Some speakers directed attention to tasks that the grand duke left undone. At
a new primary school's ceremonial opening, a speaker pointed out
that Vytautas had not bequeathed to Lithuania any educational institutions, and that this was a duty to be assumed by Lithuanians in
the present. Lithuania's minister of education also wrote that, back
in Vytautas's day, it was the sword that weighed heaviest in international relations, but that nowadays that weight had passed to schools
and education.[39] It is clear, however, that in the heroic symbolism of
Lithuania's armed forces, Vytautas's policies of military defense and
territorial expansion stood at the fore. In a 1935 military songbook
produced in ten thousand copies, for example, "Where the Plains Are
Level" and "Oh, Vytautas the Great" provided a historical frame
for songs that stimulated excitement over powerful modern warfare,
including the new, invincible twentieth-century weapon: "Ra-ta-ta-ta,
when that noise / flies over the snow-covered fields, / when machine-
guns sing out loudly, / who will dare to march against us?"; it was a
weapon that filled a soldier with glee: "But Maksimas only guffaws,
/ howling, whistling like crazy, / beating his sides, / he's now sown a
field full of corpses."[40]

SONGS OF RESISTANCE

Lithuania's preparations for a war to regain its historic capital turned out to be unnecessary when in September 1939 the Soviet Union invaded Poland and transferred occupied Vilnius to Lithuania while establishing massive military bases on Lithuanian territory. In the following summer, the Soviets removed the governments of the three independent Baltic countries and absorbed their military forces into the Red Army. Germany attacked the USSR a year later, in June of 1941, occupying most of the Baltic region within a few weeks. Like the Soviet Union before it, Germany soon began conscripting Balts into its military forces. Although official songs of loyalty to the Soviet and Nazi governments were required in schools and public events, folklorists would later find few if any traces of such songs in oral tradition.[41] Underground, however, the illegal prewar patriotic songs thrived, along with parodies of the official songs, and new songs created in response to the Soviet or Nazi occupation.

After 1941, Grand Duke Vytautas was temporarily embraced by Soviet war propaganda, when "Where the Plains Are Level" was played over the radio to celebrate battles against the Germans. Later the Soviets would suppress this song because it retained popularity as a celebration of Lithuanian, not Soviet, bravery, but for the time being, it was useful in the Soviet battle for the Lithuanian public's loyalty. In Latvia, the Soviets recycled Latvian nationalist rhetoric of World War I against Germany. As in earlier Bolshevik songs, violent revenge was a core image in the refrain of a 1941 poem by Fricis Rokpelnis, "Riflemen's Song":

Whoever hopes to capture us gets
A bullet in the forehead!

The song "Be Free Estonia's Sea" (quoted in chapter 1), among others, was popular among Estonian conscripts in the German army, sustaining a false belief that war against the Soviets would bring independence back to Estonia. Latvian soldiers, too, sang upbeat, optimistic marching songs about victory:

Rīga girls now have sorrowful faces;
Latvian boys are going off to war;
Some will cry, but others only laugh,
In farewell, they call out to the girls:

(refrain:)

> Oh, farewell, my little friend!
> Our love was very nice!
>> Wait for me, I'll come back home, dear,
>> When the cherries start to bloom! (repeat last two lines twice)

> And we drive forward, only forward,
> Our enemy will soon meet defeat;
> Our girls will not smile for another,
> They will wait until we come back home:
>> (refrain)

Parodies of this song's refrain, however, revised the last line with a pessimistic metaphor that said that returning home was impossible: "Wait for me, I'll come back home, dear, / When the owl sprouts a tail!" Others squeezed in a cynical interjection "When the cherries start to bloom, if I'm not shot" after the refrain. Another popular marching song identified both the Soviets and Germans as enemies: "We'll go and give the Reds a beating, again, again, / And then give the Gray-Blues a beating, again, again!"

In the Estonian, Latvian, and Lithuanian songs that were popular in oral tradition during World War II, dominant themes were the departure to an unknown future or death, and longing for family and one's bride. Political ideals, national honor, victory in battle, and even hatred of an enemy were not core motifs in the worldview of the soldiers conscripted into the Soviet or German army, or of their civilian kin behind the lines.[42]

Songs bolstering military morale and resistance reemerged in non-official culture in 1944 and during the subsequent years of Soviet occupation. Sometimes the singers would perform in public. For example, a group of Lithuanian university students in the obligatory two-month military training program marched through the streets of Kaunas singing, "Sister, sow the rue so green, / So Lithuania shall be free!" (translated in chapter 8).[43] More often, however, such songs were sung underground, literally, in the bunkers of Baltic partisan fighters during the brutal war waged by Soviet military forces from 1944 to 1953. Lithuanian partisans were particularly successful in sustaining armed resistance. The partisan war would falter after the Soviet mass deportations of May 1948 and March 1949.[44]

Songs about political prisoners and deportees, some of them created by the prisoners themselves, expressed a critical foundation of partisan ideology: living under Soviet rule left life empty of meaning. The partisan war was the only alternative. Such is the core idea of the song "In Springtime the Birds Fly" (to be translated in chapter 8), which is remembered to have been written by a political prisoner in 1946,[45] and "But for the Golden Summer Days," a deportee song that was diffused in more than one hundred oral variants with at least three different melodies, a song that would later be sung as an anthem of Lithuanian deportee commemoration:

> But for the golden summer days,
> And the rye flower blue,
> We would not be in this place
> Where dreary days drag by.
>
> We shall depart on the great roads,
> Depart and not return,
> The rye flowers will bloom again,
> But we will never see them.
>
> We left out on the crossroads
> Everything that we once owned:
> Our youth, our laughter, and our tears,
> And people whom we loved.
>
> Walk with me, dear mother,
> If only to the village gates,
> And kiss me, dear mother,
> For the very last time.
>
> Walk with me, dear mother,
> Up to the boxcar doors,
> And kiss me, dear mother,
> As a son of the fatherland.
>
> But that long train, covered with dust,
> Has travelled oh so far.
> I still remember, mother dear,
> The meadows that were once green.
>
> But that long train, covered with dust
> Has travelled oh so far.
> It carried our brothers, Lithuanians
> Barely breathing, up the hill.
>
> And if that train were once to stop
> In that faraway land,
> I would then write a letter
> To my dearest girl.
>
> I do not long for father or mother,
> Nor everything we owned,

I long for Lithuania,
Which we so dearly loved.

Farewell, my dear Lithuania,
Did we not once love you?
But never did we once believe
That we could not remain here.

And the gray summers drag along,
The flowers bloom and wilt.
Quietly we wipe our tears.
And bury our days of youth.

Many songbooks circulated during the partisan war, some of them printed by the underground partisan press, and others copied by hand. Paper and ink were in short supply, and thus the songbooks usually did not include the best-known songs. They disseminated instead the new texts created during the war. The fact that Maironis's song "Oh, Don't Weep, Dear Mother" was widespread in oral tradition is evidenced not by its appearance in songbooks but rather by the new adaptations in which the effect was intensified if a singer knew the original text and melody. One such adaptation documented the harsh cruelty of this war. Partisans captured alive were tortured by the Soviet police (*chekists*) to force them into betraying companions in the forest; their corpses, and those of partisans killed in battle, were mutilated and placed on public display ("thrown down on the pavement") to demoralize and frighten the civilian population into submission. The song also confirmed the Lithuanian partisans' determination to fight to the death rather than make any compromises with the Soviet occupation regime:

Oh, don't weep, dear mother, when your young son
Is killed by a chekist wolf,
When he's thrown down upon the pavement stones,
Buried there by scornful Stalin.

So don't wring your hands, if hundreds today
are bitterly weeping from sorrow,
When the five-pointed star from Moscow will shine,
We'll burn in a bloody fire.

Out in the green forests our shimmering troops,
Every one of us marches with them,
Our roads soaked in blood, our paths strewn with the dead,
But we do not lie to the fatherland!

Don't weep, dear mother, when your son lies
Torn to pieces, by the churchyard,

> This oppression of the fatherland will not last,
> The Russians won't lock us up forever.

In the first year of the partisan war, morale was sustained by the belief—supported by false dispatches from the West—that the Western powers would intervene and help restore Baltic independence either by diplomatic or military means. But illusions faded quickly when the partisans heard radio reports of meetings between Western and Soviet government representatives. Around 1949, partisan tactics shifted from aggressive violence to a sustained underground resistance whose existence, they believed, would undermine Soviet legitimacy and outlast Soviet power. It was a battle for moral justice. The politics of the Western democracies, as seen by partisan leader Lionginas Baliukevičius, were defined by greedy self interest. For them, "What matters most is to keep that imperial British lion from getting too thin and the American dollar strong."[46] For Lithuanian partisans, however, abandoning the war would, first of all, achieve nothing. Previous false amnesties had shown that the only result would be arrest, torture, and execution or deportation to Siberia. It would also be an immoral betrayal of the partisan's deported relatives and the comrades who continued to fight. It would thus be treason against Lithuania. There was no moral alternative to death in the forests. Partisans gave an oath that, if battle were to become impossible, they would commit suicide rather than compromise and be captured alive.

A new image of war emerged in Lithuanian partisan songs. In it, death was inevitable, because victory was hardly possible. But death was preferable to a betrayal of truth and justice. Human empathy and love grew as core emotions in the ideology, while killing or hatred of enemies faded. "The Linden Tree Bowed Low" was a new song that emerged during this partisan war, written and set to music by anonymous authors, disseminated in oral tradition. More than 125 variants of the song have been collected in recent years. One such variant, written down in 1947 or earlier, appears in a handwritten songbook held by the archives of the Museum of Lithuania's Genocide and Resistance in Vilnius.

> The linden trees bowed low by the road,
> A mother broke out into tears:
> Dear son, the fatherland calls you,
> Lithuania will be free again.
>
> But if some day I must depart
> From this dear land that I love,

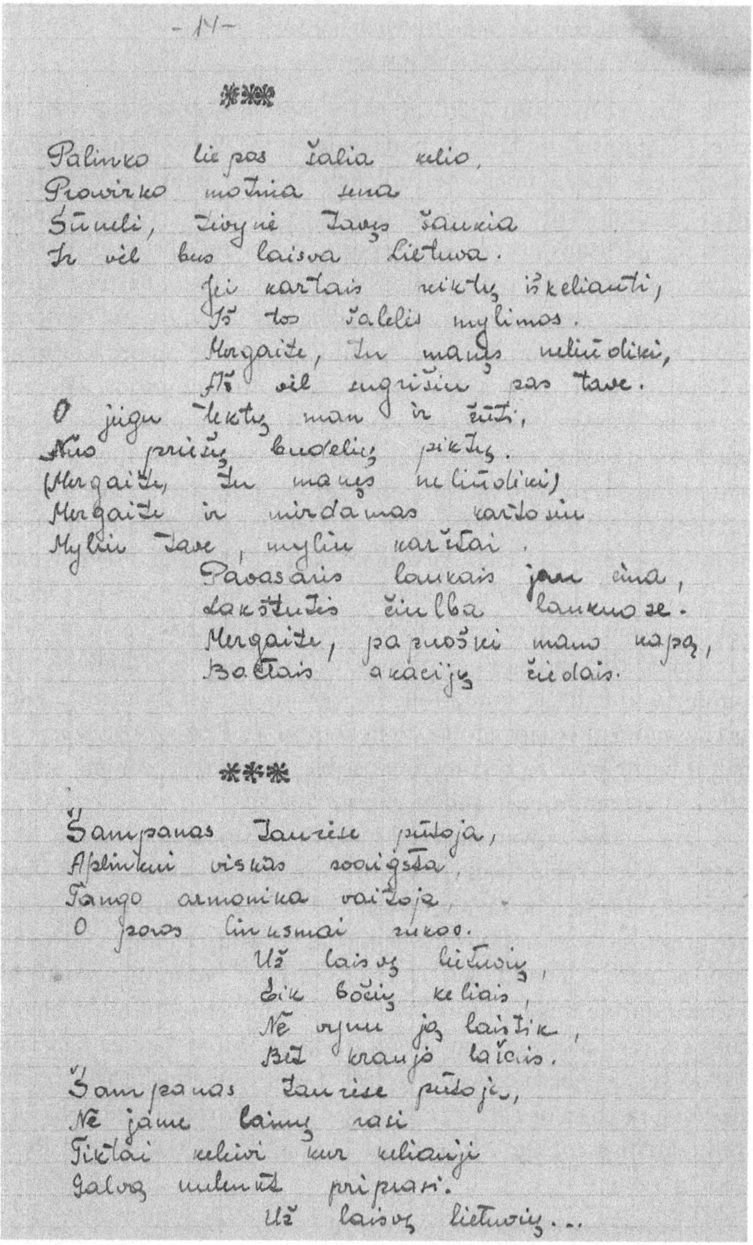

✳✳✳

Palinko liepos žalia relio,
Prauirko motina sena
Sūneli, Tėvynė Tavęs šaukia
Ir vėl bus laisva Lietuva.

Jei kartais nieko iškeliauti,
Iš tos šalelės mylimos.
Mergaite, tu manęs neliūdėki,
Aš vėl sugrišiu pas tave.

O jiegu tektų man ir žūti,
Nuo priešų budelių piktų.
(Mergaite, tu manęs neliūdėki)
Mergaite ir mirdamas kartosiu
Myliu Tave, myliu karštai.

Pavasaris laukais jau eina,
Lakštutis čiulba laukuose.
Mergaite, paruoški man kapą,
Baltais akacijų žiedais.

✳✳✳

Šampanas taurėse putoja,
Aplinkui viskas rausgsta,
Tango armonika vaitoja,
O žavos linksmai rūkos.

Už laisvę lietuvių,
Eik bočių keliais,
Nė vynu ją laistyk,
Bet kraujo lašais.

Šampanas taurėse putoja,
Nė jame laimę rasi
Tiktai nežinai kur nežengi
Galvą nuleidęs pripirsi.
Už laisvę lietuvių...

Figure 8. "Linden trees," in a Lithuanian partisan songbook written c. 1946. "Girl, even as I die I'll say again: I love you with a burning love. . . ." *Paliokienės sąsiuvinis*, 14. Courtesy of the Genocide and Resistance Research Centre of Lithuania, P-Loo6/14.

Girl, don't you mourn for me, because
I will return to you again.

But if it happens that I die
By an angry enemy executioner,
(Girl, don't you mourn for me, because)
Girl, even as I die I'll say again:
I love you with a burning love.

In the fields, springtime is beginning,
The nightingale sings evening songs,
Girl, come and decorate my tombstone
With blooming white acacias.

The song had first appeared toward the end of the German occupation in 1944.[47] It was, perhaps, not so new after all, even if its content emerged in the mid-twentieth century history of a captive Lithuania. The experience of war in this song is real. The mother's tears are not tears of gratitude for the son's heroic feats. She weeps because his death cannot be avoided. The girl's experience is like that of the maiden whose garden was once ruined in Herder's *Volkslieder*. A reader of the translated text is struck with empathy for the killed soldier, his mother, and his bride. The song is yet another variant in the Lithuanian traditions of folk poetry about love destroyed by war.

GENTLE NATIONS, NEVERTHELESS

Herder once presented three Lithuanian folk songs that told the story of a man who broke his engagement to a woman, went to war, and was killed. The song focused on the bride's love and loss, not the man's brave feats, building an image of a gentle rather than warlike Lithuanian nation. Many of the war songs sung during the Singing Revolution follow a similar theme. At the 1998 commemorative concert in Washington, DC, the Lithuanians opened their performance with a song like the one mentioned above. Its content may not have been clear to that particular audience, or even to people who understood Lithuanian, because the singers omitted its last two stanzas to save time. But back in the Singing Revolution, the song always ended, like the text quoted by Herder, with the young man's death:

ON A HILL THERE STOOD A MAPLE TREE (CONTINUED)

Promised that their wedding soon would be,
    But he rode to war upon his steed.
    But he rode to war upon his steed.

But he rode to war upon his steed,
  And laid down his head for fatherland,
  And laid down his head for fatherland.

The Singing Revolution was a confrontation between civilians and the armed soldiers of a military superpower. It is clear that war songs invigorate a struggle against violent power, infusing its individual participants with bravery and calming their fear of death. The question is not whether war was a critical theme in Baltic songs. The question to ask, rather, is which war songs out of the hundreds in each nation's centuries-old repertoire would be selected and sung during the Singing Revolution. Nearly all of the songs that were sung, like the songs that Herder presented to his readers two centuries earlier, embraced neither personal glory nor heroic defeat of enemies, but rather the human, personal emotions of love and death, set in the context of national struggle. The songs and their singers reaffirmed a gentle identity based on love, even in war.

CHAPTER FIVE

Soviet Power versus Power of the Powerless

Soviet power was established in the Baltic by military force. On August 23, 1939, Stalin and Hitler divided eastern Europe into spheres of influence. In September, World War II began when first Germany then the Soviet Union invaded Poland, and a second Soviet-Nazi treaty on September 28 expanded the Soviet sphere of influence westward. On that same day, Stalin issued an ultimatum to Estonia: the Soviet Union must be given permission to establish military bases in Estonia, or the Soviets would invade within twenty-four hours. Similar ultimatums went to Latvia and Finland on October 5, and to Lithuania on October 10. Estonia, Latvia, and Lithuania submitted to the threat, and Soviet troops crossed their borders. On October 11, the Soviet secret police began plans to deport 10 percent of the Baltic population to Russia and Siberia. After Germany's invasion of France in June of 1940, with Soviet military bases in place, Stalin presented another ultimatum: that the Baltic governments must resign. In August of 1940 Stalin incorporated the three countries into the USSR. The three Baltic armies were absorbed into the Red Army, and most of their officers were executed or deported to Siberia.[1] A year later, Nazi Germany attacked the Soviet Union and occupied the Baltic from 1941 until the end of the war. Germany's war crimes in the occupied Baltic left deep scars: the Jewish population was killed in the Holocaust; tens of thousands of Estonians, Latvians, and Lithuanians were executed; and the remaining men were conscripted into the army or forced into labor units.[2] After the Red Army's return in 1944–45, the Soviets quickly reestablished power in urban centers, but in the Baltic forests and in the countryside, Soviet military forces fought for eight years to defeat Lithuanian, Latvian, and Estonian partisans numbering in tens of thousands.[3]

The Soviet government took control by violence, executing or deporting potential resistance leaders—not only the soldiers mentioned above but also civilian government officials and prominent members of society. Political terror served Stalin's policies of social and biological engineering, an attempt to create humans who would have only collective identity and no sense of individual ownership.[4] The Soviets confiscated property and killed or deported its owners. Large and small businessmen and homeowners in the cities and owners of farms over thirty hectares (sixty acres) in the countryside were arrested and deported, along with their spouses and children. Hundreds of thousands of immigrants from Soviet Russia, Ukraine, and Belarus arrived in the Baltic to take their place. The threat of violence kept public culture under control. None of the Balts who remained after the deportations could feel safe from arrest when even seemingly loyal political and cultural figures were publicly ostracized.[5]

Culture, as seen by Stalin and the Soviets, contained a mechanism that would transform the people who remained after the military violence ended. Poetry, songs, and mass events such as the Baltic song-and-dance festivals played an essential role in Stalinist and post-Stalinist policies. Government offices were established to administer all arts, including songs. The writers union and the composers union organized the creation of poetry and its setting to music; the philharmonic oversaw professional performances; and people's arts centers organized public singing events. Membership in and cooperation with these institutions was mandatory for persons to legally earn money by publishing or performing their art. The work of union members was planned and guided by incentives and punishments. Members were paid with money and in other material rewards for art that adhered to government policy, but if they did not conform, artists were ostracized or expelled from the unions, which in turn would elicit persecution by the Soviet political police.[6] Each song or poem, each detailed concert program, had to be approved by the Soviet Artistic Affairs Board before it could be performed in public; organizers or performers who did not obey these orders would be held criminally accountable.[7] Censorship of the mass media was ensured by an administrative network whose existence was a Soviet state secret. Forbidden publications were removed from libraries and destroyed; the head of the library at the

University of Latvia, for example, reported in 1949 that he had over-seen the destruction of 341,622 "ideologically harmful" books from that collection.[8]

Jazz music was banned, because it was of Western origin and there-fore a tool of enemy agents. The Vilnius Jazz Ensemble was disbanded in 1946, the internationally famous jazzman Eddie Rosner was arrested and deported to Siberia, and the adjective "jazzy" denoted undesirable sounds in musical composition.[9] But what, exactly, this "enemy style" sounded like was unclear; it is said that in Estonia, Raimond Valgre's work survived because he transposed his earlier jazz tunes from minor to major, to obey government demand for optimism in music.[10] But minor keys were not officially forbidden, of course, and the reason for the survival of Valgre's music probably lies elsewhere.

The purpose of culture, as imagined by Stalin, was to physiologi-cally condition humans to adopt new behavior. Guided by the bio-logical principles of Trofim Lysenko, who asserted that environment, not genes, determined physiological traits across generations, and Ivan Pavlov, who postulated that all behavior is a conditioned response to physical stimuli, Stalin and his ideological followers sought to control the entire Soviet environment and all of the stimuli that would con-dition people's behavior—linguistic signals in particular.[11] Their goal was the creation and cultivation of a new breed of people, the "Soviet Human."

SOVIET SOCIALIST REALISM, BEHAVIORISM, AND SONGS

Beginning in 1932, the principles of "socialist realism" officially defined and regulated culture in the Soviet Union. Art was defined as a political act the purpose of which was to construct a communist soci-ety. Its guiding principles were encapsulated in four Russian principles. The first was *partiinost'* (party-ness), which stipulated that art's pur-pose was to unambiguously submit to the leading role of Joseph Stalin and the Communist Party. The second, *ideinost'* (idea-ness), required that art enact these leaders' ideas. The third, *klassovost'* (class-ness), later replaced by *kollektivnost'* (collectiveness), aimed to unite indi-viduals in group action. The fourth, *narodnost'* (people-ness), postu-lated that art should be accessible and appealing to the masses. Art's appealing nature would derive from its adaptation of earlier art tradi-tions, either folk or national. Accessibility required that texts have no hidden meanings that might send confused stimuli to their recipients.

An artist should explicitly take sides in politics and declare loyalty to the ideas of the Communist leaders.[12]

The historical roots of Soviet culture were identified in folklore. Defined as communal folk culture, folklore would display "collective-ness" and "people-ness." The rural farmers who once performed folk-lore were identified as an exploited working class, displaying "class-ness," too. But oral texts of the preindustrial epoch could not express loyalty to the current ideas of the Communist Party. "Party-ness" and "idea-ness" had to be added. And so folklore was redefined as emer-gent communal art, raw materials that would be developed and trans-formed for use in modern Soviet society through processes of "folk creativity" or "folklorism."[13] Beginning in the late 1940s, state-spon-sored expeditions systematically combed the national territory to find gifted performers of songs and stories, and archived thousands of texts that would ostensibly demonstrate the nation's support for Sovietiza-tion.[14] Fieldworkers found such "Soviet folklore" in local newspapers and on workplace bulletin boards, or they coached folk performers to create it, and sometimes the folklorists themselves wrote the required texts:

> Lenin is our shining sun,
> Lenin is our happiness,
> Stalin is our noble leader,
> Stalin is our dearest friend![15]

"Active intervention in the folklore process" to inject "party-ness" and "idea-ness" into folklore had been Soviet praxis since the 1930s; Balts merely had to use templates established by earlier Russian folk-lorists and administrators.

Authors of written literature would likewise follow Soviet models. A typical Soviet socialist realist work portrayed a leader who trans-formed reality into an ideal world, imprinting the hero's behavior on the recipient reader's or listener's mind. The hero would be an opti-mist who confronted an enemy (conceptual or human) by explain-ing a political idea to the people, thereby enacting that idea to defeat the enemy.[16] The hero's ethnicity should be Russian, or some positive stimulus from ethnic Russians should be demonstrated, affirming the leading role of that nation in social evolution.[17] In music, the nonver-bal elements should conform to "people-ness," with a work's beauty determined by its closeness to folk music and nineteenth-century Rus-sian or native classical music. Works with a verbal component (songs) would be given precedence, because they could follow the rules of socialist realism with the least ambiguity.[18] Singers and dancers, in addition to propagating Soviet values in the texts they recited, would create an "emotional and psychological state" of optimism and joy in audiences.[19]

A new chapter in Stalin's song politics opened in 1944, when he adopted the Soviet Union's new anthem. "The Internationale" was no longer appropriate, in Stalin's view, because the Soviet Union had eliminated social classes and was now constructing a Communist society. The anthem's key line about Stalin illuminated his method of creating the "Soviet Human." The past tense of the verb *vyrastil*, translated below as "trained," has three meanings in Russian that converged in Stalin's adherence to the postulates of Lysenko and Pavlov: "raised/reared" (as in raising and educating children), "bred" (as in physiological manipulation of livestock), and "cultivated" (as in agriculture). Stalin's role was defined even more precisely by a perfective grammatical form that does not translate into English. Whereas the battles of war and revolution mentioned in the third stanza also "trained" (*rastili*) the Soviet people, the prefix *vy-* asserted that Stalin's work completed the action.

> Great Rus has united forever
> The unbreakable union of free republics!
> Long live the unified, powerful Soviet Union,
> Created by the will of nations!
>
> (refrain:)
> Glory to our free Fatherland,
> Reliable defender of the friendship of nations!
> Let the Soviet banner, the people's banner,
> Lead from victory to victory!
>
> The sun of freedom shone to us through the storms,
> And Lenin the great illuminated the path for us:
> Stalin trained us to accept the truth of the people,
> Inspired us to labor, and to victories!
>
> (refrain, second line changed:)
> . . . the happiness of nations!
>
> We trained our army in combat.
> We will sweep the vile invaders off of the road!
> In battles we are deciding the fate of generations,
> We will lead our Fatherland to glory!
>
> (refrain, second line changed):
> . . . the glory of nations!

This song was one of the linguistic stimuli that Stalin believed would mold the psychology and behavior of the Soviet people. The change that should take place in a person's psychology was expressed in grammar. Over the three stanzas, singers were incorporated into the text to an increasing degree. The subjects of the first stanza ("Rus" and "nations") were in the grammatical third person; the first-person plural appeared in the second stanza as a passive recipient ("us") of stimuli from Stalin, and then became an active subject ("we") in the concluding stanza. Singers acted as a collective ("we"), and not as individuals in the singular first person ("I"). Nations had "will," individuals did not.

The new Soviet anthem's melody by Aleksandr Aleksandrov exhibited allegiance to party, idea, and class in its resemblance to the anthem of the class struggle led by Communists, "The Internationale." For example, both songs' first two chords followed an upward fourth interval, and both had rousing refrains. Aleksandrov's melody also conformed to the principle of people-ness in its echoes of nineteenth-century Russian nationalist music, most notably in the refrain's resemblance to the first notes of Mikhail Glinka's "Glory to Our Russian Tsar."

True to the rules of socialist realism, the song's words by Sergei Mikhalkov explicitly declared an ideal vision of transformed reality, presenting heroes who showed the way by which the country's population would build its future. Its three stanzas moved from the past, where it claimed the historical legacy of Kievan Rus, into the present, where the socialist hero Stalin had transformed the people, and then on to a future of military victory over vile invaders. The reference to medieval Rus signaled a shift from internationalism to Russian nationalism as a core of Soviet ideology; its refrain, "*slavs'ia*" (glory) integrated earlier songs and traditions of Russian Orthodox religion and nationalism, most notably Glinka's chorale mentioned above. The second stanza recognized the role of the authoritarian Soviet leader, Stalin. The third stanza focused on the Soviet nation's mission: the military defeat of its enemies. In 1944, the enemies would have been understood to be Nazi Germany, which had not yet capitulated, although its defeat was not in doubt. The term "vile invaders" was flexible, however, and could later apply just as well to the "capitalist" nations thought to encircle and threaten the Soviet Union after World War II.

The new anthem of the Soviet Union was adopted on January 15, 1944. Over the next few years, similar songs were created as anthems of every Soviet republic. Latvia's and Estonia's prewar anthems, which mentioned God, were replaced immediately.[20] In Lithuania, Kudirka's pre-Soviet anthem "Lithuania, Our Fatherland" remained in the role of national anthem until July 15, 1950, when a government decree established the new anthem of the Lithuanian SSR.[21]

As was done in Moscow for the all-Soviet anthem, in the Baltic, local governments announced competitions to create these new songs. Poets wrote words, and composers set those words to music. The competitions were won, predictably, by persons who had already earned Soviet credentials and held high places in the Soviet cultural administration. These anthems will be analyzed here as representative texts of Baltic Soviet Socialist realist song traditions.

At first glance, the three Baltic SSR anthems seem nearly identical to the all-Soviet anthem. It is difficult, however, to document the extent to which this was planned and enforced by Moscow. The Soviet Latvian government, for example, referred to an all-Soviet decree when it stated that the new anthem's text should include three things: the Latvian nation's struggle against invaders, the Russian nation's friendship, and the need for Latvia to be a component of the USSR. It did not give guidelines for composing the song's poetic structure or melody.[22] Tomas Venclova, son of the Lithuanian SSR anthem's author, suspects that competition organizers and prospective authors were informed orally, not in writing, that the winning works should resemble Aleksandrov's and Mikhalkov's.[23] The Latvian and Lithuanian texts are rather similar to the USSR text in their basic melodic structure (three stanzas with a refrain). But, although the Estonian anthem closely resembles the USSR anthem's melody, it does not have a refrain, indicating that its authors were not following the same template as their Baltic peers. Had there been an official written directive to copy the USSR anthem's form, then all three new anthems would have had refrains.

None of the authors of the Soviet Baltic anthems seems to have been aware of the relation between Stalinist culture and Pavlovian behavioral psychology. Whereas in the all-Soviet anthem, Stalin "trained" the people, as discussed above, in the Lithuanian anthem he "led," reflecting submission to an authoritarian leader but not transformation of human nature; in the Latvian anthem he was only in the heart, suggesting love but not submission or transformation; and in the Estonian anthem he was not an active subject, although the singers walked on a Stalinist path.[24] The Lithuanian text followed the three-stanza structure that drew a singer into the text: (1) third person, (2) passive first-person plural ("us," "our"), and (3) active first-person plural ("we"), but the Latvian and Estonian texts did not. All three Latvian stanzas placed the first-person plural in the role of the subject, while in Estonian there was no active first-person subject at all. Thus these three songs, as compared to the all-Soviet anthem, would be less effective tools in Stalin's plan to create the New Soviet Human by conditioning behavior.

The three Soviet Baltic anthems did, however, follow the general rules of socialist realism: they were explicit in their party-ness (deference to Lenin and Stalin), idea-ness (enthusiasm for agricultural and industrial production, defense of the fatherland, and the shining lights of Communism), and collectiveness (plural first-person "people"). Their optimism was profuse: the singers were happy and strong as steel, the land of socialism was blossoming, the fields bloomed, factories pulsed at full speed, and the sky above was clear. And their "people-ness" appeared in intertextual references to an earlier heritage of national tradition, as described below.

The Latvian SSR anthem incorporated images of earlier songs, most notably "Rīga Rings," in the first stanza, and an inversion of a line from "Broken Pines," where the new anthem asserted that the "enemy" was broken. Its second stanza confirmed the leading role of the Russian nation. "Breaking the chains" echoed a line in "The Internationale." The nationalist word "fatherland," which in earlier times denoted Latvia alone, was modified to explicitly denote the broader Soviet land in whose wreath Soviet Latvia now glimmered.

> We gained freedom in this most precious land,
> Generation upon generation will be born happy here,
> Our sea crashes here, our fields bloom here,
> Our cities resound here, Rīga rings here.
>
> > (refrain:)
> > Soviet Latvia, forever may it live,
> > May it glimmer brightly in the Soviet wreath!
>
> We arose to break the chains of slavery,
> Every place tells of century-long battles.
> Only in comradeship with the people of the proud Russian land
> We became a power that breaks the enemy.
> > (refrain)
>
> Along Lenin's path to happiness and glory
> We will go forever with Stalin in our hearts.

We shall defend our Soviet Fatherland
To the last drop of blood, every one of us.
  (refrain, repeated twice)

The Lithuanian SSR anthem's first stanza incorporated the word "justice" from Kudirka's national anthem, and its line "Where ancient Vilnius and the Baltic Sea are" resembled the syntax of the banned prewar song "Where Šešupė Flows." Geographical references confirmed the new borders of Lithuania, which included places of significance in national history. A reference to Vilnius resonated with memories of the historic capital city annexed by Poland in 1920 but returned to Lithuania after the Soviet defeat of Poland in 1939; a reference to the Baltic Sea likewise hinted at the return of Klaipėda, taken from Lithuania by Germany in 1938 but returned after the Soviet defeat of Germany in 1945. The second stanza confirmed the leading role of the Russian nation. As in Latvia, the word "Lithuania" was consistently coupled with the modifier "Soviet." The word "fatherland" was reframed to denote a powerful country that was building Communism:

The people created Soviet Lithuania,
Having long fought for freedom and justice.
Where ancient Vilnius and the Baltic Sea are,
There our cities and fruitful fields flourish.

  (refrain:)
  In the glorious Soviet Union,
  Equal among equals and free,
  Live through the centuries, be happy,
  Dear Soviet Lithuania!

Lenin illuminated the road to freedom for us,
The great Russian nation helped in battle.
Stalin leads us to happiness and power,
Our friendship of nations is strong as steel.

  (refrain)
  Our country is powerful, we do not fear dangers,
  We shall defend the Fatherland from all enemies.
  We step forward to a proud tomorrow,
  The lights of Communism will glimmer in the clear sky.

  (refrain)

Like all of the anthems discussed above, the Estonian SSR's anthem harnessed an earlier national symbol, the national epic (people of the Kalevs), to merge it with a Soviet future. It followed the Estonian poetic tradition of addressing the country in the grammatical second-person singular. Curiously, the first-person plural appeared only in passive roles ("work of ours" and "our Union"), never as "we," forsaking the image of Estonia's singers as active subjects in Soviet history. More strangely yet, while it declared allegiance to Lenin and Stalin, the text omitted the leading role of the Russian nation; instead, the anthem asserted that Estonia walked at the front of all Soviet peoples. Whereas "fatherland" in the Latvian, Lithuanian, and all-Soviet anthems clearly denoted the Soviet Union, in the Estonian song, the word "homeland" had local connotations. In the first stanza, it was the homeland of Estonians (the people of Kalev), and in the third stanza it was a homeland that must still be exhorted to become powerful:

> Continue to endure, oh strong people of the Kalevs,
> And stand like a rock, our homeland!
> Your valour didn't weaken in distress,
> You burst through the centuries,
> And grew into a blossoming land of socialism,
> So that the sun could shine into your days.
>
> Rumble now, oh factory, cut, oh sickle, in waves
> The crops in the meadow, strike the anvil, oh hammer!
> Pulse at full speed, oh Soviet life,
> Bring happiness to the people, oh fine work of ours!
> In our Union of peoples and countries
> You, oh Estonia, step firmly at the front!
>
> You carry the Leninist flag high,
> And firmly walk the Stalinist path,
> The Party gives direction to our steps,
> And it leads us from victory to victories.
> Under its firm leadership, you must grow,
> And become strong and beautiful, our homeland!

None of the three Baltic anthems celebrated war of the future, diverging significantly from the all-Soviet national mission of sweeping vile invaders off of the road. In Latvian and Lithuanian, the concept was rephrased as defense of the Fatherland, and in Estonian, the meaning of "victories" in the final stanza was unclear, because no military images were presented on the Stalinist path. This and other differences, even divergences, from the content of the all-Soviet anthem might be significant if the songs' function were, as Stalin intended, the physiological conditioning of human behavior. But Lysenko-Pavlovian psychology, particularly the idea that culture and language condition behavioral responses across generations, is not supported by true science. Alexei Yurchak documents that unchanging loyalty rituals became particularly important after Stalin's death, but, ironically, their unchanging form enabled diverse and unplanned meanings.[25]

A more productive frame of analysis views Soviet socialist realist art in its historical context from the mid 1930s on, as an effective instrument of political coercion.[26] Because specifics were open to interpretation by political leaders, any artist could be found guilty of breaking the rules. The practice of naming persons who purportedly transgressed the rules of socialist realism was very effective in controlling art.[27] Accusations of "formalism" (a focus on form instead of content) and "Western influence" or "cosmopolitanism" (most notably references to non-Soviet works, or perceived influences from jazz), when made by persons in political power, meant, in the best case, public humiliation, and in the worst case, arrest, deportation, or death in a prison camp. Being apolitical or passive was also a crime. Attacks on the Russian literary journals *Zvezda* and *Leningrad* demonstrated that "any advocacy of unprincipledness, apoliticalness, or 'art for art's sake' is alien to Soviet literature and harmful to the interests for the Soviet people and state," and the implications were clear to composers as well.[28] Fear of punishment was the most powerful reason why poets wrote, composers composed, and singers sang loyal songs in the Stalinist era.

The psychological trauma of writing praise poetry for the dictator who ruled by terror appears to have been intense. The Latvian poet Jānis Sudrabkalns experienced several nervous breakdowns; the Lithuanian composer Juozas Tallat-Kelpša collapsed and died in 1949 while conducting his cantata to Stalin.[29]

Several years after Stalin's death in 1953, his name was purged from the four Soviet anthems translated above, and revised texts were officially reinstated as anthems in the 1970s.[30] Many other songs were created in the traditions of Baltic Soviet socialist realism. Few if any of them lasted long in the national song festival repertoire. Most such songs were commissioned, awarded government prizes, and performed at a national song festival or two, then shelved forever. Stalin's principles of behavioral conditioning faded, but loyal songs still functioned as public displays of submission to Soviet power. The hazy definition of Soviet socialist realism and its enemies remained an instrument of official exclusion and an obstacle to free artistic expression until the late 1980s, when censorship collapsed.

CULTIVATING SOVIET PEOPLE IN MASS SONG
AND DANCE EVENTS

The new Soviet government embraced pre-Soviet Baltic choral traditions. The song festival's image of an entire nation singing in unity was as appealing to Stalin as it had been to the organizers of the prewar festivals. The content of the festival repertoire, however, was revised.

Soviet mass events followed the Soviet socialist realism principles outlined above. These events were, first and foremost, never apolitical. Parades demonstrated unambiguous "party-ness" in visual form, with the leaders carrying red flags and portraits of Communist Party leaders. Others carried banners with current government slogans, demonstrating "idea-ness." "Collectiveness" was given visual and kinetic form by thousands of people walking together, wearing symbolic clothes. When their clothes resembled nineteenth-century peasant apparel (long, colorful skirts for women, vests and felt hats for men), it signified a connection to folklore as stipulated by the principle of "people-ness." Orchestras projected loud optimism with happy marching tunes. The official visual messages of processions carried over to the concert stage, where red Soviet flags and banners with political slogans provided a backdrop for the mass of performers.

Musical performances were "national in form, socialist in content." Dancers emulated Igor Moiseev's Folk Dance Ensemble of the USSR, which displayed "people-ness" by adapting folkdance motifs into awe-inspiring ballets and acrobatics—signifying progress from archaic traditions to modern Soviet life. "Idea-ness" was manifest in new choreographies ("The Partisans" and "A Kolkhoz Street").[31] Songs from folk or national traditions would likewise be adapted into an explicit frame of Soviet patriotism and progress.

The first mass song festivals of 1946–48 were administered and choreographed by a large government apparatus of "people's art centers." Lithuania came first, on July 21, 1946. The official plan was to gather the largest ever Lithuanian choir. Voluntary participation was encouraged materially: "Performers were given paid vacations from work; they were placed in the military barracks with cafeterias, clinics, and free meals. During free time between rehearsals and competitions, they were treated to concerts and films, and visited by the republic's leaders."[32] In the Lithuanian countryside, the partisan war raged with full force. Perhaps this was a factor that led the Soviet Lithuanian government to retain some national symbols of independent Lithuania, co-opting their use by the partisans. The 1946 concert began with the new all-Soviet anthem, but Kudirka's national anthem came next. Soviet loyalty songs were not as pervasive as in later years; of the twenty-two songs in the program, fourteen were arrangements of folk songs, most of them by composers who were well known in the pre-war national repertoire.[33] It is likely that the Lithuanian singers at the festival experienced the concert not only as a government propaganda event but also as a "celebration," an inversion of the deprivations and fear that pervaded everyday life. Such juxtaposition of public festival and political terror were typical of Stalinist culture in the 1930s.[34]

"It would be too little to say that it is Lithuania's song festival. It is an event of much greater significance," declared Justas Paleckis, chairman of Lithuania's Presidium of the Supreme Soviet; "It is the festival of the Lithuanian nation's resurrection!"[35] Song festival history began under Soviet rule. The 1946 festival's name, "First Soviet Lithuanian Song Festival," may be read in two ways. It was "Soviet" Lithuania's first song festival, but the name also gives an impression that this was Lithuania's "first" song festival; official history books reported that Soviet Lithuania had been established in 1918.[36] Although the 1946 festival lasted for only one day, it was called a "song festival," unlike the 1924 festival, which had two days of concerts but was called a "day of song." For a decade and a half, prewar song festivals would be mentioned only as failed attempts: "Little was done to advance people's art during the period of bourgeois rule," the story went, and if festivals did take place, then choirs were "poorly prepared, and the performance level was low." The steady growth of 1930s regional festivals was forgotten. Not all national culture was resurrected, either. The first Soviet song festival omitted works by eight established pre-Soviet composers, some of whom now lived in the West.[37]

Later in the summer of 1946, Andrei Zhdanov attacked the insufficient political activity of two Moscow literary journals, and the Lithuanian composers union assembled to discuss the implications. A representative of the architects union, Jonas Kumpis, arrived at the meeting to point out, "Such an important event as the republic-wide song festival was not discussed sufficiently deeply by the [composers] union." The composers union's leader, Abelis Klenickis, criticized inactivity: "As a result of political backwardness, we, the composers of Lithuania, have done little in our creative work to participate in the reconstruction of the country. The important genre of mass song with Soviet text has hardly been touched, and the feelings and texts of many songs (even when written by a Soviet author) hardly reflect our battle for Communism." He pointed out in particular the "intolerable inactivity" of union members M. Šteimanas, Jonas Bendorius and Jonas Nabažas, and his attack was echoed by the head of Soviet Lithuania's arts board, Juozas Banaitis: "This apoliticalness is condemned by the Party."[38]

In 1948, two years after Zhdanov publicly attacked the Soviet composer Vano Muradeli, criticism in the "Bolshevik spirit" began in earnest. Klenickis attacked the composer Juozas Karosas, who was not striving to correct formalist mistakes in his work; Balys Dvarionas, whose folk song arrangements played with sounds instead of developing folk music; and Stasys Vainiūnas, whose "high mastery" in folk song arrangements was spoiled by formalistic distancing from Lithuanian traditions. Musicologist Zita Kumpienė stressed the need for principles of "party-ness" in music criticism, and attacked the head of the Kaunas conservatory, Juozas Gruodis: "Where is the professor's authority, what battle is he leading against these tendencies, what has been done? Nothing." And the composer Tallat-Kelpša summarized the causes and consequences of formalism: "But if the reclusive individualist does not himself reject the remnants of bourgeois worldview, then he, like unnecessary ballast in a rising airplane, will be thrown out of life."[39]

More active political oversight, combined with more political initiative in creative work, led to a more loyal Soviet Lithuanian song festival in 1950. The event was dedicated to the ten-year anniversary of Soviet power in Lithuania, and subsequent titles of "jubilee" festivals would likewise refer back not to the first festivals of the pre-Soviet era but rather to 1940 as the beginning of history. The pre-Soviet repertoire faded. Songs by three pre-Soviet composers—Juozas Naujalis, Vincas Kudirka, and Domas Adrulis—were still sung in 1946 but gone in 1950. Lithuanian music suffered one blow after another. Public ostracism of Juozas Gruodis was probably probably a factor in his sudden death. The young Juozas Pakalnis died in hazy circumstances.[40] Balys Dvarionas, however, survived the accusations of formalism and appeared in the 1950 song festival program, as co-author of the new Soviet Lithuanian national anthem. Others also moved quickly to demonstrate loyalty: "Our Song Resounds for Stalin" and "Cantata to the Decade of Soviet Lithuania" provided a grand opening, and the concert's conclusion confirmed the Russian nation's leading role with Anatolii Novikov's "Hymn of the Democratic Youth of the World." The brotherly friendship of Soviet nations was expressed with Russian, Belarusian, and Ukrainian folk songs, as well as, interestingly, the song that was unofficially becoming a non-Soviet Latvian anthem, "Oh Wind."

In 1946, the Soviet Lithuanian government could easily employ extensive mechanisms of Soviet cultural administration to surpass the pre-Soviet song festivals in number of participants, mathematically demonstrating the superiority of Soviet cultural production. The task was more challenging at Estonia's first Soviet festival in 1947. It was decreed that the festival had to have more singers than ever before. Organizers quickly increased the total by six thousand by adding children's choirs to the program. But to ensure massive adult participation, the concert needed to balance between explicit national submission as demanded by the Soviets on the one hand, and truly popular Estonian songs on the other. In the two-day song festival of June 28 and 29, 1947, the latter songs dominated. The opening concert began with seven Soviet songs: the anthems of the USSR and the Estonian SSR, a song about Stalin by Soviet composer Muradeli, and four other expressions of Soviet patriotism by Estonian composers. But this first set was followed by an old text: Koidula's poem "My Fatherland Is My Beloved," set to a new, majestic melody by Gustav Ernesaks. Political content diminished over the remaining series of twenty-six songs, concluding with Miina Härma's happy "Tuljak," traditionally sung to accompany the national folk dance. The second day's concert omitted Soviet anthems, beginning instead with "Song to Joy," a poem by the nineteenth-century German romantic Friedrich Schiller, set to music in 1890 by Aleksander Läte. "My Fatherland Is My Beloved" was repeated, and the concert again concluded with "Tuljak."[41]

Repression began in the following year. Zhdanovism was particularly harsh in Estonia, where it overlapped with a large-scale purge of the Communist Party.[42] The organizers of the 1947 song festival were severely criticized by a Moscow commission: "A feeling of pride for the dear Soviet homeland emerged spontaneously from the working people at the song festival. . . . There was a marked discrepancy, however, between these people's patriotic feelings, and the content of the festival's songs."[43] A Moscow newspaper added directions for future Estonian song festivals: unlike this one, they should include songs from Russia, Ukraine, Belarus, and Georgia.[44] Public criticism was followed by punitive action. Three organizers of the festival were expelled from the 1950 festival organizing committee, arrested, and sent to labor camps in Russia and Siberia; Alfred Karindi, Riho Päts, and Tuudur Vettik were imprisoned for from four to six years each, to be freed only after Stalin's death.[45] A few months before the 1950 festival, more Stalinist songs and songs in Russian were added, and guest performances by two Russian choirs were inserted into the final concert. Finally, the practice of numbering festivals according to pre-Soviet history was pronounced "bourgeois" and abolished, with festivals now numbered, as in Lithuania, according to jubilees of Soviet Power established in 1940.[46]

The two-day festival's opening concert began with the combined choir singing anthems of the USSR and the Estonian SSR, followed by "Song about Stalin," "Song for Stalin," and "People's Power." Then children's choirs sang four songs of Soviet patriotism and a Russian folk song. Men's choirs sang six Soviet songs, followed by women's choirs singing "In the Name of Stalin" and five other Soviet songs, one of them in Russian. Finally, the mixed choirs sang four songs about work, "A Wedding in our Kolkhoz," and "Glory to Soviet Power!" The second day's concert repeated many pieces from the first day, but added three songs performed by the miner's choir and five songs by the Soviet army chorus. Included in the two-day program were international folk songs—Chuvash, Hungarian, Latvian, Lithuanian, and Russian—but no Estonian folk songs, only two compositions based on Estonian folk tunes. Two songs by pre-Soviet Estonian composers were included in the program: "I Devote Everything to My Beloved," by Miina Härma, and "The Most Beautiful Songs," by Friedrich Saebelmann. These two songs, along with others composed or conducted by persons who were popular before Stalinism, regardless of their propaganda content, may have placated the singers' wish for meaningful songs.[47] But in all other respects, the program of the unlucky thirteenth Estonian song festival remains as a cold monument to Stalinism in Estonia.[48] To the organizers as well as audiences, the Stalinist festival program demonstrated the Soviet power structures.[49] Party loyalty framed the event, and Estonian songs were placed in a multinational program where the Russian-singing military choir occupied a special place.

In Soviet Latvia, Stalinist repression began in mid-1946, within weeks of Zhdanov's public attacks in Moscow on Russian authors Mikhail Zoshchenko and Anna Akhmatova. In August, the head of the Soviet Latvian government accused the editors of the leading arts periodicals of poisoning Latvian minds with bourgeois nationalism, and the literary journal *Karogs* was castigated for not including a single political poem in its summer issue. Latvian authors soon began to publicly confess their own ideological shortcomings. In March of 1948, when Zhdanov attacked "cosmopolitan," "decadent" theater critics in Moscow, Soviet Latvian leaders quickly followed suit.[50] Soviet control over composers was established in person when Latvian-born composer Nilss Grīnfelds, who had lived and studied in Soviet Russia during the 1930s, returned to Latvia to head the Soviet Latvian composers union from 1944 to 1946 and to serve as artistic director of the Latvian SSR State Philharmonic in 1945–46 and 1948–54. Vladimir Muzalevskii was sent from Moscow in 1946 to organize the music history faculty at the Latvian conservatory, and Moscow-born Anatols Liepiņš, composer of the Soviet Latvian anthem's melody, also lived in Latvia from 1945 to 1950.[51]

After Zhdanov's 1948 attack on Muradeli's opera "The Great Friendship," and that composer's public atonement in Soviet praise songs, political demands intensified in Latvian music. But the search for Soviet socialist realism's enemies, the "formalists," was not as dramatic in Latvia as elsewhere. In 1948, an attempt to pin the "formalist" label on Nilss Grīnfelds failed; even a Latvian Communist Party leader's loud accusations that Grīnfelds's music was "incomprehensible" were shelved, and Grīnfelds was instead appointed director of the philharmonic, where he oversaw all professional music performances in Latvia through the period of most intense Stalinist repression.[52] By 1950, formalism was no longer even a pretext; the Soviets demanded explicit, active declarations of loyalty. The elderly composer Jēkabs Graubiņš was accused of being apolitical. He was found guilty and dismissed from his professorship at the conservatory in the spring of 1950, and his song was immediately removed from that summer's song festival program; in autumn he was arrested, interrogated for several months, sentenced to eight years in a labor camp, and deported to Siberia. Among other conservatory faculty and students punished to various degrees for insufficient loyalty were professors Mirdza Paleviča, Jēkabs Kārkliņš, and Emilis Melngailis; concertmasters Irēna Bergmane and Tija Goba; and students Jānis Līcītis, Krišs Deķis, Jāzeps Lindbergs, and Vija Muške.[53]

The Soviet Latvian song festival of 1948, like its Lithuanian and Estonian peers, proclaimed loyalty in its historical numbering. It was named the "First Song Festival of Soviet Latvia," and subsequent Soviet festivals were numbered accordingly; besides asserting these

Figure 9. Stalinist Latvian national song festival, Rīga, June 23, 1950.
Above the singers are portraits of Lenin and Stalin, and the slogan in Lat-
vian and Russian "Glory to the Great Stalin." Courtesy of the National
History Museum of Latvia.

numbers in their titles, the festivals also celebrated jubilees of Soviet
power in multiples of five.

The next festival took place after a wave of mass terror in all three
Baltic republics. In March of 1949 alone, the Soviet government
deported to Siberia at least 60,000 Estonians and 43,000 Latvians,
and confiscated their land. From the end of the war to the summer of
1949, about 350,000 Lithuanians were deported. Fear of deportation,
combined with real estate taxes raised to levels that were impossible
to pay, forced the remaining landowners to give up their property and
become workers on collective farms.[54] But the stage of the 1950 Second Song Festival of Soviet Latvia was decorated with a large portrait
of Joseph Stalin and a banner that declared in Latvian and Russian,
"Glory to the Great Stalin."[55] Against this backdrop the choir sang the
Soviet anthem "Stalin Trained Us to Accept the Truth of the People"
and "We Will Go Forever with Stalin in Our Hearts." The song texts,
the visual documents, the speeches and reports in the mass media—all
were choreographed to testify that the Latvians (like the Estonians and
the Lithuanians) were loyal followers of Stalin, and, by extension, that

they supported his policies of deportation and execution as a means of sweeping vile enemies off of the road to Communism.

CAPTIVE MINDS, LIVING WITHIN A LIE

"Party-ness"—explicit recognition of the Communist Party's leading role—was manifest at all mass events. Alexei Yurchak argues that some people truly felt such loyalty; during the later years of Soviet socialism, repetition of government slogans was a ritual that enabled people to bond in groups "outside" (vnye) Soviet reality, but this was "not necessarily . . . opposition to communist ideals and goals and often precisely in the name of these ideals and goals."[56] Others document that under Stalinism there existed a multiplicity of beliefs pertaining to official ideology and policies, even if disloyal beliefs usually remained out of sight.[57] The Soviet-era choirs and dance ensembles who performed loyal music were not necessarily followers of the Communist Party and its ideology.[58] Their repertoires were integrated into the official culture of the Soviet Union and regulated through established processes of punishment or payment to leaders; but dancers also felt national pride and, perhaps, imagined that they danced and sang for reasons other than state propaganda.

Such secret meanings belonged to a mechanism of imprisonment that Czesław Miłosz once called "spiritual Ketman," where people would nurture an addictive feeling of aesthetic satisfaction that depended only on internal, not external opposition to political power. Perhaps it was more pleasant to secretly imagine dissent, Miłosz speculated, than to hope for real liberation and a world where one would actually be free and responsible for one's own actions. "A poet muses over what he would write if he were not bound by his political responsibilities, but could he realize his visions if he were at liberty to do so? Ketman brings comfort, fostering dreams of what might be, and even the enclosing fence affords the solace of reverie," wrote Miłosz in 1951.[59] In a similar vein, Aili Aarelaid-Tart points out that the very existence of song festivals and "singing nationalism" depended on their "carnivalesque" dialogue with the dominant Soviet ideology.[60] Thus Baltic singers might have held an ironic stake in maintaining the repressive government.

Regardless of the beliefs within people's minds, symbolic public displays of submission maintained Soviet power structures, confirming the Communist Party's leading role in the Soviet Union. Vaclav Havel writes that, for the Soviet system to persist, individuals would not need to believe government spokesmen and slogans:

> They must behave as though they did, or they must at least tolerate them in silence, or get along well with those who work with them. For this reason, however, they must *live within a lie*. They need not accept the lie. It is enough for them to have accepted their life with it and in it. For by this very fact, individuals confirm the system, fulfil the system, make the system, *are* the system.[61]

"Living within a lie" continued after Stalin's death in 1953, as the Soviet system mutated into what Vaclav Havel calls a "post-totalitarian" system where power over the population was no longer derived primarily from military might and violence.[62] It continued even as formerly forbidden musical forms were brought into the fold of official Soviet culture. In 1955, for example, a series of articles in the Soviet press signaled that jazz would now be allowed in "*estrada*" (a category of light entertainment or dancing music named after the "stage" or "bandshell" on which it was played). The saxophone, banned under Stalin, was rehabilitated, national *estrada* competitions and music education programs were established, and there began a jazz-fuelled campaign to convert *estrada* into "serious" listening music.[63] Several Baltic stars rose to success in the Soviet recorded-music market, among them Latvian composer and pianist Raimonds Pauls. The roots of his success clearly lay in his original, interesting melodies and arrangements, and in his skill at improvising melodic variations to liven up performances. In Latvia, Pauls's song lyrics released emotions formerly repressed under Stalinism: local patriotism (for example, a song about the city of Liepāja, and another about the Baltic Sea) and romantic love ("I look at your lips—amber glimmers there!" and "Wild Rose Blooming with Fiery Red Blossoms"). Even here, however, official sanction was required and Soviet rules were obeyed. Pauls would sometimes set to music poems that might otherwise be censored and perform them at live concerts; but, regardless of the songs' popularity, Party censors forbade recordings and broadcasts, maintaining the lie that such songs did not exist.[64]

Because song festivals were officially, explicitly framed as celebrations of Soviet loyalty, their primary meaning, as exposed by Vaclav Havel, would still be the singers' submission to Soviet power. No anti-Soviet songs were allowed. A singer would follow the approved concert program, in Havel's interpretation, to display that "I know what I must do. I behave in the manner expected of me. I can be depended upon and am beyond reproach. I am obedient and therefore I have the right to be left in peace" or "I am afraid and therefore unquestioningly obedient."[65] As long as singers continued to sing only songs allowed by Communist Party censors, albeit with secret, unspoken meanings of dissent, the political mechanism of Miłosz's "spiritual Ketman" might be an effective tool for describing what happened at Baltic song festivals. But Havel's notion of "living within a lie" opens a different interpretation, because it is paired and contrasted with "living within the truth."

POWER OF THE POWERLESS, LIVING WITHIN THE TRUTH

In the Baltic, singing traditions are difficult to categorize under the labels of loyalty or opposition to Soviet power. For example, the Lithuanian composer Jonas Švedas authored numerous songs of Soviet loyalty, among them the national anthem of Soviet Lithuania. But in 1946, he led the Lithuanian SSR Folk Music Ensemble, which often performed "We Were Born Lithuanians," to the consternation of a Soviet overseer who wrote, "The choir's artistic directors Ilčiukas and Švedas performed these songs, as they say, 'to raise the spirit' of the audiences at concerts. But it must be pointed out that such songs only 'raise the spirit' of a certain number of listeners, those who have non-Soviet ideology."[66] Švedas's main cultural work lay somewhere between the two ends of the collaboration-confrontation continuum. The ensemble performed mostly instrumental music and traditional dances, neither of which engaged Soviet politics. Other musicians also found that they could choose to not participate.

In Latvia, the program of the 1948 Soviet song festival announced that Alfreds Kalniņš would be one of the head conductors. However, Kalniņš was not at the concert, supposedly for reasons of poor health. In 1950, he was again appointed honorary head conductor, but again was absent (another honorary conductor, Emilis Melngailis, also did not attend). Folk memory recorded that this was a protest against too many Soviet propaganda songs in the program.[67] In 1949, Kalniņš openly composed music based on explicitly non-Soviet religious themes; the Latvian musicologist Joachim Braun calls this the first Soviet Latvian "artwork of dissent.[68]

The words "dissent" and "dissident" are not appropriate for describing Alfreds Kalniņš. Vaclav Havel writes that the people called "dissidents" "are not primarily denying or rejecting anything. On the contrary, they have tried to affirm their own human identity, and if they reject anything at all, then it is merely what was false and alienating in their lives, that aspect of 'living within a lie.'"[69] A black-and-white distinction between "dissidents" and "collaborators" is likewise problematic. To focus on Kalniņš, who decided to be visibly absent at the song festival, is to wrongly assume that the tens of thousands of people who did sing and listen at that festival were collaborators; it would also marginalize Kalniņš as an exception to the rule. In fact, nonparticipation involved more than several dozen "dissidents." Four decades after Soviet power was established, many Lithuanians were not participating in the Soviet anthem, as indicated by a 1983 government decree which reiterated that learning it was obligatory in schools, and that "persons preparing to join the Komsomol or Pioneers be required to know, from memory, the texts of the USSR and LTSR anthem."[70]

It is true that most singers and audiences hardly ever, if at all, sang songs that explicitly attacked Soviet power structures. There were no "anti-Soviet" texts sung at the Baltic song festivals of the Soviet period. The songs that met particular public resonance had an unclear connection to socialist realism's requirement of "partyness." Their truth lay in omission: they did not repeat the official, explicit lie, and thereby remained outside of the lie, in a non-Soviet identity. Some songs which otherwise would not be considered political became political, precisely because they were not political at a time when political expression was required. Audiences heard explicit texts of loyalty alongside apolitical texts, and requested encores of the latter, non-Soviet songs. Their singers could, for a moment, feel that they were not participating in the official politics of mass festivals.

Among all Baltic song festivals of the Stalin era, both of the Latvian festivals, in 1948 and 1950, stand out for the sheer weight of non-Soviet folk songs and pre-Soviet nationalist songs, among them "Oh Wind," "Broken Pines," and "Fortress of Light." Inclusion of the latter song and other works by Jāzeps Vītols must have been particularly complicated, because the composer had fled to the West to escape the Soviet occupation. Nevertheless, he was included.[71] These nonverbal meanings were not lost on the singers or their audiences, who could, for a moment, live in a world more real to them than Soviet culture.[72]

A revolution could be imagined in the posttotalitarian Soviet world, wrote Vaclav Havel, if a person stepped out of "living within a lie":

He rejects the ritual and breaks the rules of the game. He discovers once more his suppressed identity and dignity. He gives his freedom a concrete significance. His revolt is an attempt to *live within the truth*. . . . Most of these expressions remain elementary revolts against manipulation; you simply straighten your backbone and live in greater dignity as an individual.[73]

After Stalin's death, such attempts were no longer life-threatening, but an individual would still risk career and livelihood by every decision to not participate in the public lie. As more persons stepped out of the Soviet ideological façade, the entire system would melt away. This was the mechanism for political change in the Soviet bloc that was outlined by Havel in "Power of the Powerless." The essay was not read in Estonia, Latvia, or Lithuania until after the Baltic Singing Revolution was well underway. It is useful, however, as an analytical framework for understanding the mechanisms that operated in the Baltic mass movement. Havel's action plan for Czechs under Soviet control in the 1970s resembled what happened in the Baltic in the 1980s, despite the fact that Balts did not articulate these tactics beforehand, as Havel had, in the form of a political tract. Baltic mass activism during the Singing Revolution came from a pre-existing blueprint that emerged in a different expressive genre: singing.

Havel's classic example was that of a greengrocer who regularly receives from headquarters a delivery of onions, carrots, and posters with political slogans for display in the shop window. Everybody does it, and although nobody reads it, refusal to display the poster would cause trouble. Such transgression was treated as an attack on the Soviet system, and, wrote Havel, it was indeed a genuine denial of the entire system. And if the greengrocer did in fact refuse to post the slogan, it would be the beginning of the system's end, because "every free expression of life indirectly threatens the post-totalitarian system politically." As individual after individual would choose to live within the truth, parallel structures would emerge through society's self-organization. These transformations would be openly visible, unlike Milosz's Ketman, because parallel structures were not an escape from reality into secret meanings.[74]

Change, Havel predicted, would first take place in society, not government, and its effect on power structures would not be immediate. Its agents would address the hidden sphere, demonstrating that living within the truth was a social alternative. Steps taken to live within the truth would change the world by changing perceptions and attitudes: "They help—even though it is, of course, indirect help—to raise the confidence of citizens; they shatter the world of 'appearances' and unmask the real nature of power. . . . They leave it up to each individual to decide what he or she will or will not take from their experience and work." Havel offers a framework useful to writing a history of the Baltic Singing Revolution. He points out that political movements such as the Czech Charter 77 movement of the 1970s were not the cause of awakening but rather the final outcome of awakening, because

> in the post-totalitarian system, the real background to the movements that gradually assume political significance does not usually consist of overtly political events of confrontations between different forces or concepts that are openly political. These movements for the most part originate elsewhere, in the far broader area of the "pre-political," where "living within a lie" confronts "living within the truth," that is where the demands of the post-totalitarian system conflict with the real aims of life.[75]

The Baltic Singing Revolution's beginnings may likewise be traced to the first Stalinist song festivals of the late 1940s. Here, Stalinist anthems were juxtaposed in concert programs with non-Soviet songs, bringing into public view the contrast of "living within a lie" and "living within the truth." Over four decades of Soviet rule, the contrast was displayed at hundreds of singing events, most notably, but not exclusively, the national song festivals that were organized in each country every five years.

What is to be done? asked Vaclav Havel in 1979, repeating the question made famous by Vladimir Lenin, but coming to a radically different conclusion. Whereas Lenin in 1901 had argued for collective discipline and purging of dissent in Communist Party ranks (the principle of "party-ness"), Havel turned to individual moral values. The goal was to find new relationships among humans, and to rehabilitate trust, openness, responsibility, solidarity, and love.[76]

Before 1988, mass singing events in the Baltic were framed, in both visual form and in content, as expressions of Soviet loyalty. This was not the true meaning of singing. In all three Baltic countries, a shift to unambiguous politics and the mass movement for political independence happened in early summer 1988, and, in all three countries, the shift was publicly displayed at singing events, among them a rock concert in Estonia, a choral song festival in Lithuania, and a folklore festival in Latvia. At these moments, the movements defined the political meaning of their public assemblies with an unambiguous visual cue: the flags of pre-Soviet, independent Estonia, Latvia, and Lithuania.[77] The disappearance of red flags of Soviet loyalty also clearly showed that these masses of people were no longer participating in the Soviet Union. All three events featured songs and singing, and therefore converge under the title of the "Singing Revolution." But each event featured a different form of singing traditions: choral, rock, and folk. Each style had its own historical background, as will be outlined in the next three chapters. But in the big framework of the Baltic movement for political independence, singing—whether choral, rock, or folk—was a means of rehabilitating the values that Havel had seen as the key to political reform driven by the power of the powerless: trust, openness, responsibility, solidarity, and love.

CHAPTER SIX

Living within the Truth in Choral Songs

Lithuania's song festival traditions became explicitly non-Soviet in Vilnius on July 1, 1988. During the opening concert of Gaudeamus, a Baltic university students' song festival, singers in the combined choir unfurled, for the first time together on stage, the three national tricolors: Lithuania's yellow-green-red, Latvia's red-white-red, and Estonia's blue-black-white. Soviet officials rushed to confiscate the flags, which at that moment were still illegal in Lithuania, but they were not able to push through the choir of seven thousand singers, clustered together tightly, singing, and so those who had revealed the festival's true colors remained unpunished. Baltic flags then emerged at every festival event, unmindful of the scores of policemen who looked on. Choirs in the festival procession carried at least four Lithuanian, seven Latvian, and many more Estonian flags, with all singers carrying lapel ribbons of their national colors. From this moment on, public singing events in Lithuania would always include the flags that marked them as being non-Soviet.

As usual under Soviet rule, the official government newspaper at first did not report these ubiquitous non-Soviet activities, instead reminding its readers several times that the festival was dedicated to the seventy-year anniversary of the Soviet Komsomol. But directly below its description of the opening concert, probably not by coincidence, there appeared an unrelated article about international trade with the timely title "All Flags Are Our Guests."[1]

Two years later, in the summer of 1990, the national flags fluttered freely, and the Soviet Union's red flag was absent at the three Baltic

Figure 10. Estonian, Latvian, and Lithuanian flags at the Gaudeamus Baltic students' song festival, Vingis Park, Vilnius, July 3, 1988. The photographer, a singer in the Šviesa choir, recalls that many Estonian and Lithuanian banners fluttered in a "forest of flags" on the festival's third day, but he could find only one Latvian for a picture of the three brother nations. Photo by Antanas Bajoriūnas.

national song festivals. There were no songs of Soviet patriotism, and no deferential references to the Communist Party, to Joseph Stalin or Vladimir Lenin, or even to the Soviet leader of the day, Mikhail Gorbachev. But the memory of previous Soviet song festivals was still fresh on the singers' minds. During an intermission, friendly Estonians explained to me why they, along with thousands of others, once sang songs of loyalty to the Soviet state:

Astrid: Do you like our song festival?

Guntis: Yes, very much.

Leidi: But ten years ago [when you were in Estonia] you didn't see the festival?

Guntis: No. That was in August.

Leidi: No, so you can't compare.

Juta: You didn't see it in Rīga either?

Guntis: No.

Leidi: Yes. Earlier there were was a speech by the first
secretary of the Party, of course. They spoke Estonian
with an accent, a much heavier accent than yours.

Guntis: Aha.

Juta: He doesn't have an accent at all!

Leidi: Then they would always greet the guests from Moscow.
Sometimes it would be a cosmonaut, sometimes a
Party officer whom they greeted very warmly.

Juta: Mikoyan was here once. And didn't Andropov come once?

Leidi: Yes, I think.

Astrid: The song festival always began—

Juta: There were ten anthems: the anthem of the Soviet Union—

Leidi: And all kinds of Lenin songs.

Astrid: A song about Lenin, a song about Stalin, about
the Party, then one or two of our own—

Leidi: And songs of the peoples of the Soviet Union. They had to
be included. They allowed only a couple of Estonian songs—

Astrid: —after all of that.

Leidi: In the entire festival program, only
a couple of Estonian songs.

Juta: But people all waited for those couple of songs. They
were willing to sing all of the Stalins and Lenins.
The most important thing was to sing those couple of
songs, especially "My Fatherland Is My Beloved."

Astrid: And when they sang this song—and they didn't allow it
to be sung often—then all the people stood up and sang
along, and this song has always been sung [unofficially].

Leidi: And then, what was done so that people wouldn't
sing those fatherland songs: then at the end, a brass
band was ordered to blast away so that people—

Astrid: —couldn't sing.

Leidi: And they were ordered to leave the stage. The brass band
played so loudly that it wasn't possible to sing anymore.
That's what our festivals were like.[2]

They exaggerate a few details. None of the Soviet festival programs began with ten anthems, for example. More than a couple of Estonian songs always appeared in the program. But the intent of their hyperbole was to better explain to me, an American, what it might have felt like to finally stand with the choir and audience, singing the unofficial anthem.

Latvians and Lithuanians also remember mandatory songs of explicit loyalty to the Soviet government. Those Soviet songs, they also explain, were given unto Caesar, sung to the Soviet government, as payment for the chance to sing the non-Soviet songs that the people themselves wanted to sing. "If you have to pay to sing, then pay!" wrote the Latvian poet Imants Ziedonis in 1971.[3] Not all songs could be purchased in this way. Some were banned from the Soviet stage— the Estonian and Latvian national anthem, and after 1950, the Lithuanian national anthem; "Estonia's Flag"; "Be Free, Estonia's Sea"; "We Were Born Lithuanians"; "May You Live Forever, Latvia"; and songs which mentioned God, for example, "God, Protect Estonia" and the last stanza of "Where Šešupė Flows." Religious hymns existed, but only in church services that were repressed by means other than song control; outside of church, a song like "Maria, Maria" was not allowed on public stages, and was not even included in scholarly Soviet editions of Maironis's *Collected Works*.

The list of songs that might land their singers in prison was not very long, and the list of mandatory songs was also relatively short. In between there were hundreds of other songs, and some of those acquired particular public resonance somewhere in a labyrinth among various government institutions, composers, conductors, sponsors of choirs, singers, and their audiences. That these songs were important is obvious. But the qualities that could turn a song into an "unofficial national anthem" are difficult to define, as fuzzy as formulating the rules of Soviet socialist realism. In fact, in some respects the unofficial anthems even followed the government guidelines quite well. Among their characteristics there was most definitely "people-ness," because the public easily understood the songs and they evoked well-known national or folk traditions. They could display "collectiveness" and sometimes even "idea-ness" and "party-ness," as will become clear below.[4] But, unlike Soviet socialist realist songs, they also contained the truth that allowed singers to step past the boundaries of Soviet everyday life.

SINGING TRUTH

The unofficial national anthem of Estonia was born in 1944. Its original role was to be that of a Soviet anthem. Since the 1930s, the official image of the "Friendship of Peoples" in the Soviet Union included the selection and propagation of a classic "people's poet" for each nation: Pushkin was established as the voice of the primordial Russian nation, Shevchenko represented the Ukrainians, Yanka Kupala stood for Soviet Belarus, and so on.[5] For Estonia, the role of people's poet was to be filled by Lydia Koidula. As early as 1942, with Estonia still under German occupation, plans began in Moscow for transferring the nineteenth-century poet's remains from her grave on Kronstadt Island to Tallinn. On December 24, 1943, the centennial of Koidula's birth, a Soviet Estonian newspaper (printed in Moscow) featured the poet's portrait and her poems, among them, "My Fatherland Is My Beloved." And in early 1944, a new melody for that poem was composed by Gustav Ernesaks, who had retreated eastward with the Soviets in 1941. The song premiered in Leningrad on July 21, 1944, at the official celebration of Soviet Estonia's four-year anniversary. Its status as an official song of Soviet culture was thus indisputable, it seemed.[6] Soon afterward, however, the song shifted into a hazy area between official Soviet and non-Soviet culture.

On October 26, 1944, after the Soviet army reoccupied Estonia, the song premiered in Tallinn. Its popularity was instant. A performance at Koidula's reburial in August of 1946 elicited tears. That summer, it was performed many times as choirs prepared for the 1947 national song festival. Unlike several songs whose texts expressed explicit Soviet patriotism, "My Fatherland" was performed at both of the festival's concerts, with audience-requested encores. A newspaper carried on the interpretation of this song as an official expression of Soviet loyalty, asserting that "this song has become the first great victory song of Soviet rule."[7] But, as Soviet repression intensified, the song was removed from the official repertoire, together with many other non-Soviet songs that were not allowed at the 1950 festival. It reappeared in print only after Stalin's death in a collection of classic choral music.[8] It was sung again in Tartu at the first Gaudeamus song festival of 1956, but it was not included in the official program of the 1960 national song festival. Paul Rummo recalled the song's rehabilitation by popular demand at that festival's closing, after all of the songs in the officially approved program had been sung:

> And now the calls became demands: "My Fatherland Is My Beloved!"
> "My Fatherland Is My Beloved!" The voices became ever more insis-
> tent. . . . There was nobody on the conductor's stand to set a start-
> ing note or lift the baton. But from somewhere on the stage there
> suddenly rose the longed-for song's wistfully solemn melody. The
> members of the song festival organizing committee had to bring the
> melody's author to the conductor's stand almost by force. Through-
> out the song's first half one could hear, no, one felt with one's entire
> being, that a conductor was not necessary here: Even without a leader,
> the song's sound was so pure, so nuanced, so powerful that they knew
> that it was impossible to sing it any better. The song reverberated in a
> tremendous tide coming from thirty thousand mouths. But when the
> composer, moved to tears, moved his hand to open the third stanza,
> one felt yet again that there are no bounds to a human's capabilities.[9]

Official Soviet interpretations of the song were reiterated immediately
afterward. When Paul Rummo, quoted above, described the 1960 performance, he placed around it a frame of Soviet loyalty, comparing it
to the spontaneous singing of "The Internationale" at the declaration
of Soviet power in Estonia, and to Shostakovich's Seventh Symphony
at the siege of Leningrad. His essay probably presented the main arguments according to which "My Fatherland" would be allowed back
into the 1965 song festival's official program. In the centennial song
festival of 1969, it was placed next-to-last in the closing concert. The
choir, however, wanted to sing it once more after the concert ended, and
began chanting its title. As recounted by Priit Vesilind,

> The directors ordered the orchestra to strike up and drown out the
> chant, but no one left the stage, and few left the audience, even though
> the rain was falling once again. And then, through some mysterious
> synergy, the entire stadium began to sing in one voice, with no direc-
> tor. . . . Then they sang it again, and again. The Soviet authorities,
> to save face, eventually asked composer Gustav Ernesaks to take the
> stage and conduct.[10]

This, writes Vesilind, was the moment when, "with the sheer power of
massed voices," Estonians "defied their masters, those with the power
to dictate their lives." Singing this song openly expressed Estonian
defiance. It was non-Soviet, because the Soviets attempted to control
its performance and failed.

The interpretation of "My Fatherland" and other Estonian songs
of the Soviet period differs from that of instrumental works such as
the abovementioned Shostakovich, whose symphony could not be
proved to express blatant loyalty or its manifest content to be only "a
protective screen camouflaging a hidden truth" of dissidence.[11] The

meaning of this Estonian song's text, in contrast, was manifest. Official arguments that the "fatherland" was Soviet, together with any other attempts to attach "hidden," loyal meanings to the song were unmasked, and the song was clearly identified as non-Soviet when the Soviet government excluded it from the national song festivals of 1950, 1955, and 1960. It returned to the national stage by popular demand, against the resistance of government officials. It was this particular song, and not the Soviet Estonian anthem, that the choirs and audiences demanded as an encore, whether it was in the official program or not. "My Fatherland" had something that Soviet songs lacked, and it lacked critical elements of the Soviet Socialist Realism displayed by loyal songs. It contained truth, and omitted lies.

The song's text was non-Soviet in several ways. The first stanza's first two words, "my fatherland," sung together with the phrase "happiness and joy" in the fourth line, carry intertextual references to the banned national anthem of independent Estonia. The word "fatherland" stands alone here, while Soviet songs would typically add the modifier "Soviet" or other text to clarify that the referent was the entire USSR. The word "holy" evokes religious images and emotions, and was used in Soviet culture only in combination with explicit references to government ideology. Grammatically, the text's singer is one person, "my," "me," or "I," never "we," evoking individual, not collective, identification. The singer declares identity when the fatherland lives in the singer's heart and the fatherland's pain boils there, and this particular line's sadness is intensified by the only minor note in the melody. In the second stanza, the words "slander," "foreign," and "envy" are also sung on that minor note, connecting these causes of pain to the pain in the singer's heart. Envy, which causes harm to others with no benefit for oneself, is foreign; it is foreign to slander—in other words, it is foreign, not part of an Estonian's identity, to lie and live within a lie.

The song's meaning expanded and intensified also in the context of the centennial celebration, which solidified historical memory of pre-Soviet song festivals. Festival regalia had usually marked only the passing of five-year anniversaries since the 1940 arrival of Soviet power. But the festival's non-Soviet origins were explicitly documented on that year's program covers and in the title of Rudolf Põldmäe's history, *Estonia's First Universal Song Festival, 1869*.[12] In 1969, Estonia's unofficial national anthem, "My Fatherland Is My Beloved," precipitated an open confrontation between Soviet power

(the government administrators who did not allow it to be the concert's last song) and the Estonian public, the audience and choir who
nevertheless sang it last. Its status as a non-Soviet song was reconfirmed whenever the program overseers placed it next-to-last, not last
in the official festival program. In 1975 they placed it before "Dawn."
In 1980 it came last. In 1985, as in 1969, it was again second-to-last
in the official program.

Some of the song's meaning was carried within the person who
created and conducted it, Gustav Ernesaks. His fame as an Estonian
composer began in the pre-Soviet years of Estonia's independence,
when his humorous men's song about walking home, smoking a pipe
("Let's Go Home, Men!") became popular in the national choral repertoire. During the German occupation of Estonia in World War II,
as mentioned above, Ernesaks was in the Soviet Union, working as a
choir conductor. After the war, he returned to Estonia, and in 1947 he
debuted as a national song festival conductor, leading the men's choir
section. Besides the new version of "My Fatherland," four other compositions by Ernesaks were included in the festival program, among
them the Stalinist national anthem of Soviet Estonia.

Three of the 1947 festival's four conductors were arrested and
deported in 1949; Ernesaks was the sole survivor, and he was
appointed head conductor of the 1950 song festival. Ernesaks, composer of several Soviet anthems, and head conductor at the most
Stalinist of all song festivals, might easily be categorized as a "col-
laborator" with the occupying regime. Some of his songs explicitly
declared loyalty to Stalin. And yet, from his Soviet debut in 1947,
Ernesaks's song festival work existed on two levels, both of them in
public view. In James and Maureen Tusty's recent documentary film,
Singing Revolution, Lennart Meri commented on the complicated
maneuvers that were necessary under Soviet rule: "I asked him what
will be the future of the song festivals with people singing about
Lenin and Stalin and Karl Marx and Friedrich Engels and so on . . .
and Ernesaks said, 'Don't be afraid. The main thing is to preserve the
tradition. To preserve the tradition which every five years is uniting
the nation.' And I am so grateful for Gustav Ernesaks' words because
he was, of course, right."[13]

As head conductor among the 1950 song festival organizers, Ernesaks was the only person who could take the initiative
to include a couple of songs by non-Soviet composers in the program: Friedrich Saebelmann's "Most Beautiful Songs" and Miina

Härma's "I Dedicate It All to My Beloved." Several other pre-Soviet composers continued to live in Estonia during the Soviet period, and, since they had not been arrested, they could now be construed as "Soviet" composers and their earlier songs sung. For example, Aleksander Läte's 1890 "Song to Joy" was retained in 1950 as it had been retained in 1947; perhaps this song preserved memories of its popularity as an opening song of Independence-era festivals. And in 1950, perhaps, it also carried an echo of its 1947 performance, when it was conducted by Tuudur Vettik, who was now a political prisoner. This song would return again, prominently placed next-to-last in the program of the 1955 song festival. Here, too, responsibility for the song's inclusion lay on the shoulders of Gustav Ernesaks, head conductor.

Another song from the pre-Soviet period, but composed by a now-"Soviet" composer, was Mihkel Lüdig's "Lullaby." It, too, was retained in the song festivals of 1950 and 1955, as Ernesaks continued to support this composer's songs, through them also supporting the composer himself, because he would receive an honorarium for his song's performance. Lüdig's "Dawn," which had been sung at the closing of the first Independence-era festival, returned to the song festival repertoire in 1960, two years after the composer's death, conducted by Ernesaks in a cluster of four songs at the end of the last concert. Missing in 1965, "Dawn" returned to open and close the centennial celebration of 1969. As the first concert's first song, performed before the lighting of the festival flame, it was sung even before the mandatory opening song, "Lenin's Party." "Dawn" had now become the Estonian National Song Festival's anthem, always sung before the songs of Soviet loyalty; truth before lies.

These songs were not explicitly anti-Soviet. In fact, they might all be construed to fit portions of the big picture of Soviet socialist realism: Saebelmann's "Most Beautiful Songs," which clearly stated that freedom had arrived, was thus strong in its "idea-ness," and "Dawn," which included the grammatical form of the first-person- plural "we," displayed "collectiveness" on top of its great optimism. "People-ness" was covered by the songs' strong ties to earlier national traditions. Their loyalty to the current Soviet state could also be construed with arguments that the composer had been an early progressive thinker, or, better yet, that the composer had displayed his allegiance after World War II by remaining a citizen of Soviet Estonia and not emigrating to the West. But the texts themselves were all unclear in their attitude toward Soviet power. Under a strict reading of Soviet socialist realist rules, these texts would be excluded because they were vague in their "party-ness" and allowed multiple interpretations. Soviet censors attacked ambiguous textual meanings for good reason. They were the door of opportunity through which singers could walk into a space of true expression.

These texts carried the historical memory of the pre-Soviet song festivals where they had once been sung. In the 1920s and 1930s, the words "fatherland" and "our land" had referred to independent Estonia, a fact that was not lost on government administrators or the conductors and singers. Historical memory of independence was a primary meaning, with mass resonance whenever Estonians sang pre-Soviet songs. Singers were aware of the people who sang in the non-Soviet past, and if they felt themselves outside of the official, explicitly described Soviet identity, then songs such as these allowed open expression of true identity. When a younger generation began composing new choral works, they injected still more explicit, truthful texts into the national singing traditions. Most prominent among all Baltic composers who lived and created within a world of unambiguous truth is the Estonian composer Veljo Tormis.

ESTONIA: "I WANT TO SING MY OWN SONG"

Songs, Veljo Tormis recounts, acquired non-Soviet political meanings in a variety of ways. Some meanings were covert. The nineteenth-century Russian scholar Nikolai Dobroliubov identified one such means of hidden expression. If it is not possible to speak the truth, one can loudly speak the opposite of one's true thoughts. For example, Tormis's song that proclaimed, "Our happiness is secure! Life is good in our land!" effectively evoked a feeling of irony whenever sung by an unhappy singer. A second kind of hidden meaning was furthered by intermusicality, melodic quotations which called up meanings of earlier works and their texts. Tormis definitely intended to include both kinds of hidden meanings in his songs. "I confess my guilt in both of these sins!," declares Tormis, but then he adds that such secret meanings were always secondary.[14] The primary meaning of his songs was carried on the surface, in unambiguous words. Tormis recounts a long list of titles and textual excerpts that he set to music from 1964 to 1991, among them the following:

I thought a bit, I'm no longer able, I'm no longer able to stand and hesitate in silence, where the bad must be called good! ("Hamlet's Songs," 1965, words by Paul-Eerik Rummo)

This entire Russian country was skewed, the cabbage garden was upside down ("Men's Songs," 1964–65, folk poetry)

On the hill the hammers strike stones and a foreign tongue sounds, you see them over the sea and branches, beneath them names and countries disappear ("Ballad of Mary's Land," 1969, words by Jaan Kaplinski)

True equality of nations, the right of nations to self-determination ("Lenin's Words," 1972, words by Vladimir Lenin)

Then crash right by the ear, so that every one would get a fright, so that black things would fall down from black hands, and so that a clear heart can laugh inside when all the water will start pouring down from the sky all of a sudden ("Litany to Thunder," 1974, words by Ain Kaalep)[15]

Who wants to be liked, must crawl, must say "yes" while thinking "no" ("Juhan Liiv's Sarcasms," 1979, words by Juhan Liiv).

Each of these songs, and many others by Tormis, included kernels of truth. In the examples above, truthful words presented a description of "living within a lie" (1 and 6); the nature of Soviet history (examples 2 and 3); a propaganda phrase that was exclaimed with hyperbolic enthusiasm for ironic effect, because truthful theory was contradicted by Soviet practice of Russian as "first among equals" and squelched national self-determination (4); and the attempt of a person with a clear, truthful heart to destroy untruthful evil through incantations of powerful words (5). Tormis did not create words of his own but rather gave voice to truthful texts that he found in published literature and oral folklore. He did so also in his Russian-language works, for example, in his arrangement of a Russian folk song with the lyrics "Oh, you broad steppe, expansive steppe, you have reached out expansively, oh motherland" (Rhapsody of the Friendship of Nations, 1982), a text that subverted a well-known song of Soviet patriotism, "Broad Is My Country of Birth." By quoting published or archival texts, Tormis ensured that the censors and political police could not pin a political crime on him. When a text was in print, then it had already passed government censorship and was supposedly approved for use in Soviet life. "The stories are as I sang them, the words were as I set them down," he would quote another folk song, to point out that he was responsible only for the musical notes. When the head of the Communist Party's Department of Culture said that the problem with Tormis's works was his choice of texts by Estonian poet Hando Runnel, Tormis rejoined, "Why don't you speak with Runnel instead of me?"[16]

Tormis's debut on the Estonian national song festival stage took place at the opening of the 1969 centennial with the cantata "The Beginning of Song." Here, too, he quoted explicit words from a published poem by Hando Runnel to express the true meaning of the song festival and of Estonian singing traditions as a whole.[17] The song's melody began in unison, with the choir invoking the weight of centuries to pronounce a definitive history on a single, repeated note. Then the sentence expanded into polyphony, concluding in complex harmony sung by a powerful, modern Estonian choir: This song, sung at the 1969 song festival, was a song that began centuries earlier:

BEGINNING OF SONG

Listen, now!
In faraway centuries, on the shores of Estonia, there once began,
A song began.

In the language of mothers, in the spirit of fathers, it carried across to us.
In sonorous language, in the spirit of a million, it lives on.

This song began in a misty time, born in the work of the voiceless ones.
This song began in a lowly house, and it rose as an oath in the night.
A powerless clan began listening, this song was good for the soul,
For it spoke a heavenly story, that freedom must come to them.

And the powerless clan awoke, and felt the heads on their shoulders.
This song will not die, nor this story, this song for us is good.
This song for us is good.
    Leelo, leelo, leelo, leelo.

I stepped out to start my voice, ringing on the rocky hillside,
    Leelo, leelo
Lifting up the celebration, cheering up the ring of friends,
    Leelo, leelo.

I know my friends by their eyes, I know my foes by their power,
    Leelo, leelo.
I do not want enemies, wars have worn me out completely.
I want, I want to be, I want to sing my own song.
Singing in the tongue of this land, where I have my pretty home.
Here my cradle gently rocked, here my bed was softly swinging,
Over fields light children running.
    Leelo, leelo.

(repeat first stanza)

In the song's retelling of history (or description of the 1969 present), the enslaved nation heard a song that recited the story of future freedom. Here, after the third stanza, Tormis quoted Aleksander Kunileid's melody for the poem by Lydia Koidula, "You, until Death." It was sung without words—only a person who knew Koidula's original poem and its song would understand the meaning. An insider would also immediately notice that, by hook or by crook, that particular song had been inserted into the 1969 concert! "You, until Death," was non-Soviet, even if it had been published in a Soviet-era collection of choral songs.[18] It had not yet been sung at a Soviet-era song festival, and now it appeared only this once, at the 1969 centennial celebration, to be excluded again for the next two decades.

The words of Tormis's cantata were as explicitly nonviolent as they were non-Soviet. The Estonian national aspiration was . . . to sing. Here, Tormis doubled the effect of the words by quoting melodies of archaic *regilaul*, traditional songs that are unique to Estonia. The word *leelo* is a refrain word from these folk songs, used in national tradition as a shorthand reference to the heritage of folklore. At the 1969 centennial concert, Mart Saar's folk song arrangement titled "Leelo" was placed immediately after "You, until Death." Tormis borrowed folk melodies—the voice of the Estonian nation—when he playfully but explicitly rejected opposition to enemies as a component of national identity. Enemies did exist; the singer knew them by their "power," just as friends were recognized by their eyes. But the singer was tired of fighting wars, because the national mission was not battle. The quoted folk song's melody came from pre-Soviet folk tradition, and its words rejected the endless images of heroic battle that permeated everyday life in the USSR. It must be noted, however, that the song was not "anti-Soviet," or a hostile attack on enemies. It simply placed these enemies and their tactics outside of the Estonian frame of national identity.

A new wave of repression began in Estonia in 1980. Dissidents were imprisoned, one of them killed in a psychiatric hospital. A group of forty Estonian intellectuals wrote an open letter calling for public discussion of the Soviet government's ethnic policies, and the political police moved quickly to silence them.[19] Tormis, who had not signed the letter ("My work was the forty-first signature"), wrote a series of songs which were confiscated by the political police. Among these suppressed works was "Song of the Aborigine," which embodied Soviet rules of censorship. The song's only word was "taboo" repeated many times, indicating that the singers were not allowed to speak anything they wanted to truly say.[20]

Tormis was not the only non-Soviet composer in Estonia. But he, more than any other artist, aligned the Estonian national song repertoire into a non-Soviet configuration. In "The Beginning of Song," a song that defined national singing traditions in their entirety, Tormis quoted Kunileid, Koidula, Runnel, and *regilaul*, to place all of these authors and songs into an unambiguous, non-Soviet context. After Tormis, any song could serve as an expression of non-Soviet identity. Even blatant texts of submissive loyalty to Soviet power were reframed after Tormis's ironic hyperbole of "Lenin's Words" (in example 4 above). That song's subversive irony was multiplied when it earned Tormis the Lenin Prize. In Estonia, after Tormis, any composer or singer could create or recreate any song and live within the truth, if she or he wished.

LATVIA, A SINGING FORTRESS OF LIGHT

In Latvia, "One wanted to live, and singing was a means of being away, outside of Soviet time," writes Laima Muktupāvela; she asked Haralds Mednis, the leading conductor of the late Soviet period,

> "Tell me, Maestro, you became the head conductor in 1950; you climbed up on the conductor's stage in Komunāru Square. But a year before that, in 1949, there were the deportations. Maestro, you were once a conductor of the Defense League choir, a former Boy Scout; how could your hands rise up to conduct at the official festival of the Soviet regime, how could you let yourself do that?" "What else was I supposed to do?" answered Mednis. "Crouch in the forest? Wait for the English to come? Should the nation not sing, and be quiet? They'd put us all in cattle cars for resistance, and deport us. And what did we sing? The same songs: 'Fortress of Light,' 'Broken Pines.'"
>
> It's crazy, absurd, that the nation expressed inner protest with classic songs, but nobody could touch the singers because the Soviet officials sat in the first rows.
> It's good that somebody convinced them that "Broken Pines" is a song in which the choir praises the happy, victorious Soviet life, that the nation has finally received the opportunity to live in the reality envisioned by the red Latvian revolutionaries, that the song is about the fulfillment of the nation's dreams under the leadership of the great Stalin. That, you see, is what they told the officials and *nachalniki*. Everything and anything. The main thing was that there would be song. Either the officials and *nachalniki* were stupid, or they decided

to let the Latvians at least sing. A nation that sings is not dangerous. But we all knew what the nation was singing: "You can splinter us, you can break us." What else could those thousands of people do, who each had a family member, a relative deported? It can be called singing opposition, yes it can.[21]

The first two Soviet Latvian song festivals of 1948 and 1950, as mentioned in the previous chapter, were unusual in the era of Stalinist repression. Unlike the Estonian concerts of 1950, many Latvian folk songs lived on in the national song festival repertoire under Stalinism; unlike the Lithuanians in 1950, Latvians retained many songs well known from pre-Soviet nationalist tradition. Among the new texts that entered the national repertoire during the Soviet era was "This Day Is Song's Great Day." It was this first poem by a young schoolteacher, Arvīds Skalbe, that won the 1947 competition for new songs.[22] Its music was one of the last works by Pēteris Barisons, a popular independence-era composer appointed to head the Latvian conservatory's composition program in 1944.[23] The song was created, and Barisons passed away, before the Zhdanovist purges and arrests began. Although its text was open to diverging interpretations, as will be discussed below, its credentials as a song of the Soviet period were clean. Beginning with the First Song Festival of Soviet Latvia, it became the festival's opening anthem:

> This day is song's great day,
> The whole land resounds.
> Many voices, and a single thought
> Make the nation dear to me.
>
> Bright strings of the ancient kokle
> Freely sound again,
> Here by our beautiful Rīga
> Latvians find strength in song.
>
> Enemies will never rise!
> Our fields will flourish green,
> The gift earned by the nation's sweat
> Will be lifted toward a bright day.
>
> (repeat first stanza)

The song's optimism (green fields flourishing, progress toward a "bright day") and "collective-ness" ("many voices, a single thought") were explicit, and its "people-ness" was bolstered by references to the musical instrument, the kokle, and the city of Rīga. On the other hand, this lyrical text did not mention any other Soviet nations, and thus, literally, "the nation" only referred to the singing Latvians, who "find strength," while "Many voices . . . make the nation dear to me." Nor was the "gift" clearly defined; it could refer to the coming of Soviet power, or the fruits of agricultural labor, or the opportunity to sing in spite of Soviet power. The text's "single thought" could be a feeling of pride in Latvian culture, or in all-Soviet culture. Hazy references like these, and the absence of the explicit key words Stalin, Lenin, Party, or Soviet, would have signaled a deficiency in "party-ness" had the judges followed Zhdanovite rules of Soviet socialist realism. The poem nevertheless won the 1947 competition, and was subsequently performed at all Soviet Latvian song festivals, Stalinist and posttotalitarian alike. The song's meaning then emerged alongside, and in contrast with, other songs whose "party-ness" was explicit. The fact that explicit loyalty to Soviet power was absent allowed singers to define "nation" and its "single thought" as non-Soviet, if they so pleased, and to live within the truth while singing these words.

A folk song from the classic national repertoire acquired new meanings during the Soviet period. "Oh Wind," by Andrejs Jurjāns, was already recognized as a masterpiece of Latvian choral music at its debut in the national song festival of 1910. The song, wrote Andrejs Jurjāns, resembled the ebb and flow of wind, with rare pauses for the singers' breaths, the music beginning softly, each stanza gradually rising in volume to a crescendo in the sixth stanza, then receding to a calm conclusion.[24] Its haunting melody was certainly one reason why the song reentered Latvian national oral tradition, bolstered by its publication in choral scores and popular songbooks, and why it became well known in Estonian after it was translated by Mart Pukits. Its first two words acquired strong patriotic connotations when the national poet Rainis used them as the title of a play written in 1914. During the Soviet period, the song was included in the official song festival programs of 1948, 1950, 1955, and 1960, where it acquired tacit meanings that caused it to be dropped in subsequent years; it reappeared in the official concert program only once, at the centennial of 1973. But folk history recalls that, after the end of every song festival of the Soviet era, the audience stood and sang this song together with the festival choir, without a conductor. This song, like "My Fatherland Is My Beloved" in Estonia, was the unofficial Latvian national anthem.

> Oh wind, blow, wind, carry my boat,
> Carry me to Kurzeme.

There, a woman promised me
Her dear daughter as my bride.

She did promise, but she refused,
She called me a shameful drunkard.

She called me a shameful drunkard,
And a gambling horse racer.

Where's the tavern that I drank dry,
Whose good horse did I run down?

I myself pay for my own drink,
I myself ride my own horse.

Oh wind, blow, wind, carry my boat,
Carry me to Kurzeme.

In earlier folk tradition, the text would have been understood to describe a singer who could marry because he had acquired sufficient property. Kurzeme was the name of Latvia's western region, but for Rainis in 1914, the song's words expressed a longing to return to Latvia from political exile, and a wish to carry his nation "into a new horizon where it becomes free." In the Soviet period, Rainis's connotations of a forbidden country and unfree nation remained, strengthened in 1973 by a very popular film adaptation (with music by Imants Kalniņš) and a 1977 opera composed by Arvīds Žilinskis.[25] The earlier folk reference to love and wealth transformed into a national metaphor. The song's semantic weight grew as the singer was slandered, and culminated in his proud declaration of independence ("I myself . . . "). This was the singers' reply to slander. At the peak of the song's melodic crescendo in the sixth stanza, they proudly rejected lies and spoke truth.

The place name, Kurzeme, was used as a euphemism or metaphor of Latvia in other songs, too, most notably "Fortress of Light" (translated in chapter 3), which also premiered in 1910. From that song's first performance at a Soviet song festival in 1948 through the festivals of 1950 and 1955, it had non-Soviet connotations.[26] It was excluded for a decade after Nikita Khrushchev's purge of Latvian "national Communists," then reappeared in 1970 and in the centennial celebration of 1973. It was again excluded in 1977, sung in 1980, and excluded in 1985. Popular memory recalls that, whenever "Fortress" was cut, its non-Soviet meanings were the reason for doing so.

The history of "Fortress of Light" in the late Soviet period was linked tightly to the patriarch of twentieth-century Latvian choral traditions,

Figure 11. Haralds Mednis conducting an unofficial encore of "Oh Wind" at the Latvian national song festival, July 21, 1985. Mednis was excluded from the official program, but the choir called him to conduct "Fortress of Light." Photo by Valdis Lavrinovičs. Courtesy of the Literature and Music Museum, Rīga.

Haralds Mednis, who first achieved national fame in 1938 when his choir sang this song to win the national competition of rural choirs.[27] Mednis conducted at the first Song Festival of Soviet Latvia in 1948, but he would not get to conduct "Fortress" at the festival until 1980. That year, the festival was attended by the composer's wife, Annija Vītola, who, together with her husband, had fled the Soviet occupation and lived in the West since 1944. Unending audience applause called Mednis back for two encores. Soon afterward, he was again out of government favor, and neither he nor "Fortress" was included in the official program of the 1985 song festival. Nevertheless, at the end of the festival concert, the choir and audience, en masse, began chanting "Mednis! Mednis! Mednis!" and "Fortress of Light! Fortress of Light! Fortress of Light!" not stopping until he himself stepped to the stage and conducted the song. That performance was officially not planned or sanctioned. The singers, audience, and conductor all knew this. This was a memorable moment of non-Soviet truth in Latvian song.[28]

Like the Estonian centennial of 1969, the Latvian centennial of 1973 was a critical event in which pre-Soviet national heritage was

publicly revived. Official festival regalia contrived a connection to the
fifty-year anniversary of the founding of the Union of Soviet Socialist Republics (actually, it was the fifty-first, not fiftieth anniversary of
the 1922 USSR treaty). As in Estonia, after 1973, Soviet Latvian song
festival programs and souvenir pins still announced jubilees of Soviet
power, but popular memory recalled a different past. The true history
was most forcefully narrated in a song that premiered at the centennial, "To My Homeland," a poem by Jānis Peters set to music by Raimonds Pauls. The work presents a historical sequence from song to
politics, from the first song festival of 1873 to the 1905 Revolution
(referenced with the title of Rainis's 1905 book of poetry, *Sowing of
Storm*), and on to the 1915–18 military mobilization of the Latvian
Riflemen. The poem did not, however, explicitly specify *which* Latvian Riflemen. At the end of World War I, these military units split up.
Some joined the army that won Latvia's independence, while others
fought in the Bolshevik Red Army. The song's primary reference was
in its last stanza, which asserted that the symbol of national awakening, "Fortress of Light," would rejoice forever. The song by Peters and
Pauls was performed thereafter at the conclusion of every Soviet-era
song festival. Peters's prose introduction was often omitted at concerts, but it was recited in the song's first published sound recording,
once again planting the song festival's founding year deep in popular
memory:

> I see men in gray homespun suits coming toward me. It is the year
> 1873. Rīga rings, and the first Latvian Singing Festival has begun.

> Daugava River told me,
> Winding like Destiny,
> Song holds its own festival,
> Song and brother now rise upward.
> Thus sang our dear brother,
> His song challenged destiny—
> In his song, the century
> Gains the colors of a lifetime.

> 1905 shall come,
> Rain of blood shall fall,
> And the wind shall break
> The tallest pine trees.
> We'll be Riflemen,
> Song will sow a storm.
> Forever, fortress of light
> Shall sing on the hill.

Let the voices intertwined
Travel out across the land.
Song holds its own festival,
Song and brother now rise upward.
Thus sang our dear brother,
His song challenged destiny—
In his song, the century
Gains the colors of a lifetime.

Through our beating hearts
Broken pines shall grow,
New mornings call us
Onward to new paths.
Toward eternity,
Singing, we shall go.
Forever fortress of light
Shall sing on the hill.

The song's words, written in the meter of Latvian folk songs, evoke two other songs of the Latvian national movement: "Broken Pines" and, of course, "Fortress of Light." And thus, even when they were excluded from the 1977 festival, Pauls's song defiantly kept alive the memory of these two absent songs. In 1985, it was after "To My Homeland" that the audience and choir summoned Haralds Mednis to conduct the officially excluded song, "Fortress of Light."

LITHUANIA: "GOD ALONE KNOWS ITS DEEP SILENT THOUGHTS"

The history of anthems is different in Lithuania. Here, the pre-Soviet national anthem was renewed after the war as Soviet Lithuania's anthem, and sung at the song festival of 1946. After 1950, when the new anthem was decreed, it became illegal to sing "Lithuania, Our Fatherland." Lithuanian partisans and the underground resistance continued to sing it and other pre-Soviet nationalist and religious songs, but these songs were erased from public life, and were rarely taught to younger generations.

The unofficial Lithuanian national anthem, "Dear Lithuania," emerged in public differently from its Baltic counterparts. The Estonian and Latvian texts of "My Fatherland Is My Beloved," "Fortress of Light," and "Oh Wind" had been well established at pre-Soviet national song festivals, and were also included in the official Soviet song festival programs of 1947 and 1948, to be learned or relearned, with government support, by thousands of singers throughout the land. Even if from then on these songs would sometimes be officially excluded from song festivals, they were never officially banned nationwide, and unofficial meanings established in the early Soviet years could still be remembered by older singers and choirs over whom the government exerted less control. In contrast to the Estonian and Latvian unofficial anthems, "Dear Lithuania" became popular on the mass level without any initial impulse from national song festivals.

An early version of the song's text was written in 1888 by Maironis, and revised several times until the words as sung today were first published in the 1920s.[29] Its musical setting was published in 1905 in Seinai, by Maironis's longtime friend Juozas Naujalis, who during Lithuania's independence became the leading Lithuanian composer and head organizer of the first song festival of 1924.[30] Many songs by Maironis and Naujalis were sung at the three independence-era festivals, but "Dear Lithuania" was not among them. Its popularity increased in the 1930s, when it was sometimes sung, standing, as a second national anthem.[31] It was not sung at Soviet Lithuanian song festivals after World War II.[32]

"Dear Lithuania," like its author Maironis, remained on the margins of official Soviet tradition.[33] It was not included in concert programs, but it reappeared in print soon after Stalin's death.[34] The conductor Vladas Bartusevičius and the Vilnius University Song and Dance Ensemble are remembered for singing it in the mid-1960s, when others feared or were forbidden to perform it. Then, around 1966, it appeared on stage at regional events, and on July 6, 1968, it was sung at the Gaudeamus festival in Vilnius.[35]

The song stood firmly in the classic traditions of Lithuanian patriotic songs. Its symbols—heroes, history, and fatherland—appeared also in the banned national anthem, and its river landscapes resembled those of the censored song, "Where Šešupė Flows." Unlike those first-person-plural ("our fatherland") songs, "Dear Lithuania" expressed a more intimate, first-person-singular connection to "my fatherland." The second stanza embedded singers in the Lithuanian national landscape of green fields and forests, embraced by the personified Dubysa and Nevėžis Rivers. The fourth stanza asserted that the ancestors, like the current singers, also praised and defended the land.

> Dear Lithuania, land of my fathers,
> Land where the heroes rest in their graves;
>   Beautiful in the blue of your sky!

Loved, because you endured through the ages. (repeat two lines)

Beautiful valleys of swift Dubysa,
Hills, green with woods like garlands of rue;
    Over the hilltops sisters sing softly
    Bittersweet, lovely song melodies.

There, deep in thought, dark Nevėžis River
Wraps like a sash around the green meadows;
    Rippling slowly in its deep channel,
    God alone knows its deep, silent thoughts.

You, my dear fatherland, are beautiful,
Land where the heroes lie in their graves!
    Not in vain did the ancestors guard you,
    Not in vain did the bards sing your praises!

The main reason that the song's appearance on stage was impossible during the Stalinist years, and was still dangerous after Stalin's death, was the word "God" in the third stanza, in a line that assumes that God's wisdom is infinite. Some Lithuanians recall an attempt to erase religion by changing the line to "Nobody knows its [the river's] deep thoughts" (*Jo gilios minties nežino niekas*), noting that this change misplaced the grammatical accent on *mintiés* and sounded clumsy. A different option was to simply delete the offending stanza, but an effort to change the text, if it existed, was half-hearted.[36] And so, this positive reference to "God," unimaginable in any other public utterances in the Soviet Union, clearly marked the text as non-Soviet. When singing this song, Lithuanians could express not only a national identity but also true religious belief.

In 1975, the song quickly skipped past the established Soviet processes of review and entered the national song festival, after a single informal meeting between the director of the Lithuanian SSR People's Art Center, Salamonas Sverdiolas, and the minister of culture, Lionginas Šepetys. Two decades later, Sverdiolas recalled their conversation: "The Estonians have their Mu Isamaa, the Latvians have their Līgo. We also need to have fundamental patriotic songs in our repertoire, as a nucleus for our song festival. One such song is 'Dear Lithuania,' another such song is 'Where Forests Stand Green.'" Šepetys in turn wrote in his memoirs that their brief discussion quickly moved from political considerations to practical logistics: "It's not in the approved repertoire? No problem, we'll write it in ourselves; this isn't the first time we've done something like that! Not much time left? Will the choirs be able to learn it? Everybody knows it already." It was as simple as that. Once the song appeared in the official list, it came out of the closet everywhere, overnight.[37]

Lithuania's unofficial anthem had, after all, tested the censorship waters a decade earlier, at the Baltic university student song festival, Gaudeamus. In 1956 in Tartu, too, Gaudeamus thawed the silence imposed on "My Fatherland Is My Beloved." The festival (named after the nineteenth-century internationally sung academic anthem) was a place where young Balts met each other, and, particularly during after-hours parties, learned firsthand that they shared similar song festival traditions. They could easily comprehend the meanings of each other's non-Soviet unofficial anthems, even if they did not speak each other's languages. The core component of the national identity of each nation—singing—catalyzed a regional, three-nation Baltic identity.

Thus it was fitting that in 1988, Gaudeamus was the place where Estonian singers pulled their Lithuanian and Latvian peers into the non-Soviet-flag-bearing singing revolution. The blue-black-white banner had been officially legalized one week earlier in Estonia; Estonians brought it, and also Lithuanian and Latvian flags, to Vilnius, precipitating an instantaneous visual transformation that simplified later interpretations of Baltic songs. Whereas before 1988 a historian had to reconcile prominently displayed red flags and slogans of loyalty with hypothetical "non-Soviet" interpretations of "unofficial anthems," after July of 1988, these songs and singing were manifestly non-Soviet. This was the truth that prevailed in Vilnius, when Soviet power over Baltic choral culture ended.

SINGING OUTSIDE OF THE SOVIET UNION, 1987–1989

Discussions between Baltic officials and the central Soviet government in Moscow had long been a one-way street. The former Lithuanian minister of culture, Lionginas Šepetys, recalled his first meeting with Mikhail Gorbachev, who in his former capacity as all-Soviet secretary of agriculture made an official visit to Lithuania's national song festival in 1980. The central Soviet government's view of non-Russian national cultures was illuminated by Mikhail Gorbachev's patronizing lip service to the friendship of the Soviet peoples, in concert with Raisa Gorbachev's chauvinist contempt:

> Now I'm sitting next to the guest, in my role as chairman of the festival committee. I've even slighted him a bit: While giving the opening

speech, I mixed up his name and patronymic. Lithuanians don't do well with those patronymics. . . . His wife Raisa . . . saw it as negligence and was offended. We had reasons to be offended, too. During the ceremonial celebration of the Soviet republic's forty-year anniversary, our wives, who sat with Raisa in the central area, were angered by her inattentiveness to everything: Besides her own husband, she didn't listen to any of the speakers (she didn't use the translation headphones), and instead demonstratively admired her rings. . . .

When we were seeing the high guest off at the airport, the tables were loaded with everything needed for this farewell, the political battle against alcoholism notwithstanding. The all-Soviet secretary devoted extensive praise to our festival, to the procession, to the national costumes, and to the anthem of the USSR, which he heard for the first time as a mass choir performance. (Back then it didn't occur to either him or us that we were first to sing it as a mass choir [in 1946], and we would also be first to formally repudiate it. Forever.)

We felt it to be our duty, to not only nod in rhythic agreement to his litany of praise, but to also try to interrupt his monologue with a word or two. No success. We weren't able to intervene in the flow of his words even when he posed the question of how much a festival like this cost. . . . He asked, and then, without waiting for an answer, he moved elsewhere, to matters of agriculture.[38]

It was thus no great surprise that in the summer of 1985, soon after Gorbachev was appointed general secretary of the Communist Party of the Soviet Union, little changed in the three Baltic national song festivals. In fact, displays of Soviet domination intensified. In Latvia, "Fortress of Light" and its most popular conductor, Haralds Mednis, were omitted from the official program, and a Soviet military chorus and marching band were highlighted as guest performers. In Estonia, too, guest performances of Soviet army veterans and Russian children's choirs were injected into the concerts, leaving in the program only forty-eight Estonian songs out of eighty-two in all.[39] Friction was in the air in Lithuania. American folklorist Elena Bradūnas recalled signs of conflict between Lithuanian singing and dancing on the one hand, and official displays of Soviet power on the other:

At the beginning of the parade, all of the portraits of Brezhnev and the others were carried, all black and white, almost as if death masks, with the orchestra way behind. So, this entire silence, just deadly silence, following this whole parade of portraits, all of the Moscow dignitaries. Just that subtle placement of the dancers and singers in that parade made a statement to everybody.[40]

Soon afterward, Gorbachev initiated a discussion about Soviet governance. "Working people must have complete and truthful information," he wrote in 1987, and the government must engage truth. "We have come to realize the necessity of learning to overcome the inveterate discrepancy between the reality and the proclaimed policy. It is this major shift in the moral sphere that makes up the emotional content and the essence of the present socialist revolutions in our society."[41] It was as if Gorbachev had read Vaclav Havel's essay about the transformation of society, and now aimed to start "living within the truth." But whereas Havel imagined democratization as society's self-organization in multiple directions, Gorbachev asserted that it should be based on Soviet loyalty: "In my opinion, any honest, open talk, even if it arouses doubts, should be welcomed. But if you try to fit somebody else's suit on us, beware! Glasnost is aimed at strengthening our society." Persons who acted outside of the boundaries set by the Soviet government, wrote Gorbachev, would be "far removed from the people's interests."[42] A companion volume clarified the nature of Perestroika, reiterating the leading role of the Russian nation and adding that local sovereignty movements were an enemy plot:

> The natural and unavoidable process of cultural internationalization and blending of the population sometimes brings about an unhealthy response. In places where this process is proceeding with particular intensity, a few representatives of some nationalities perceive it as a threat of losing their national uniqueness, culture, language, etc. From this emerge attitudes of traditionalism, failure to correctly evaluate the significance of the Russian language as a means of international communication, and an attempt to recede into the narrow frame of their own national culture. These fears and attitudes are exploited—and for the most part unsuccessfully—by nationalistic elements and foreign secret services.[43]

The latter sentences sent an unmistakable signal regarding the Baltic, where "open talk" had begun with letter writing campaigns, petitions, and popular songs about environmental protection. That kind of activism was allowed under Glasnost a year after the Chornobyl disaster, and it was supported personally by Gorbachev.[44] But the Baltic discourse rapidly expanded deep into problems of historical and political truth, topics not foreseen under the Soviet plan.

A decade earlier, the Soviet Union had signed the 1975 Helsinki Accords, formally agreeing to allow freedom of speech within its borders. Little changed, however, in Soviet repression of dissidents. In spring of 1987, a group of Latvians calling themselves Helsinki 86 announced to the Soviet and Western mass media that they would publicly commemorate the 1941 Soviet mass deportations, testing

Gorbachev's sincerity and the Soviet Union's commitment to the 1975 treaty. The known leaders of Helsinki 86 were arrested shortly before June 14, 1987, but the demonstration nevertheless took place on the planned date. Seven group members emerged from secrecy and, wearing lapel buttons with the colors of Latvia's flag, they walked to Latvia's Freedom Monument in Rīga. There, they displayed rudimentary banners with the words "In Memory of the Victims of June 14," "For Fatherland and Freedom," and "God Bless Latvia," and gave public speeches about the date's significance. An unexpectedly large crowd of over one thousand people formed a tight circle around the demonstrators, holding police at a distance. When the group knelt before the monument for a moment of silence, the Soviet police blasted an amplified radio broadcast. But the public sang "Oh Wind," overwhelming the loudspeakers. Crowds remained near the site for about six hours, walking across the square one by one or in small groups to place flowers before the monument. Soon after midnight, police with clubs drove the remaining people away. This was the first of the "calendar demonstrations," a series of mass public meetings held on dates whose historical significance had been concealed under Soviet rule. In the course of the year that followed, Soviet police would arrest members of Helsinki 86 and deport them to the West, but new persons joined the group at its public meetings, and still others emerged from the underground network throughout 1987 and 1988. Police escalated physical force to break up Helsinki 86 demonstrations on August 23 (commemorating the 1939 Nazi-Soviet Pact) and November 18 (Latvia's 1918 declaration of independence), each of which nevertheless attracted a crowd of about ten thousand.[45]

The calendar demonstrations spread to Estonia and Lithuania, where former political prisoners successfully held mass meetings on August 23, 1987. In Tallinn's Hirve Park, they attracted about five thousand participants, who witnessed, for the first time, political speeches about historical truth. A participant displayed a large banner with the names of the three Baltic countries, each of them decorated with the colors of its banned flag. Participants sang "Be Free Estonia's Sea," "My Fatherland Is My Beloved," and "People of Kungla," but singing was not this event's strong point. This was a revolution of free speech, but not yet a mass movement or the Singing Revolution. The event's organizer, Tiit Madisson, was deported to Sweden. In Vilnius, the August 23 meeting was subdued, but nevertheless attracted a core of about five hundred participants and two thousand onlookers.[46]

In Latvia on March 25, 1988, the Helsinki 86 group held another demonstration at the Freedom Monument, commemorating the mass deportations of that date in 1949. Despite police attempts to break up their meeting by force, the participants sang, for the first time in public, Latvia's national anthem. That day, the scope of Latvian civic activism expanded dramatically. The Latvian Writers Union, a large, legal organization with the political clout to prevent police interference, organized a second demonstration in the national cemetery, attracting about twenty-five thousand participants. Four weeks later, on April 19, another symbol of independent Latvia came out into the open, when the flag was displayed at the funeral of Gunārs Astra, a political prisoner whom the Soviets liberated shortly before his sudden death. At this event, attended by about two thousand, participants again sang the national anthem, accompanied by a brass band. Two months later, on June 14, a member of Helsinki 86 carried the flag at the head of a procession organized by the Environmental Protection Club; he was arrested and deported. But a month later, the flag reappeared on the streets of Rīga on July 13, together with those of Lithuania and Estonia, in the procession of the Baltica Folklore Festival. During the festival, a mass "rehabilitation" of the flag was held on the song festival stage, and after that event, the flag's display was no longer repressed.[47]

The national colors of all three Baltic countries came out of hiding that spring and summer. In Estonia, the flag emerged on April 17 as three separate colored banners displayed together in front of the Heritage Protection Society's mass procession in Tartu. Then in May and June, a sea of blue-black-white flags sprang up at rock concerts in Tartu and Tallinn. The Soviet Estonian government moved quickly to appropriate the grassroots movement's flag, declaring it to be the Estonian national flag on June 23, 1988. From that point on, the flag was legally permitted and often displayed prominently, although the red flag and anthem retained their official status as symbols of the Soviet state until Estonia's declaration of independence in 1990. In Lithuania, the tricolor emerged in Vilnius at a commemoration of the June 14 deportations, and, as mentioned above, after July 1 it was omnipresent at mass demonstrations. It and the national anthem, "Lithuania, Our Fatherland," were formally legalized on August 17 and then adopted as official symbols of the Lithuanian SSR on November 18, 1988. In Latvia, the flag and the anthem, "God Bless Latvia," were adopted as official symbols of Soviet Latvia on February 15, 1990.[48]

Public use of non-Soviet national symbols was spurred in 1988 by three new nongovernmental national organizations: the Estonian Popular Front (Rahvarinne) began mobilizing support on April 13 and held its first congress on October 1; Latvia's Popular Front (Tautas fronte) formed on June 1 and held its congress on October 8; and the Lithuanian organization, Sąjūdis, was initiated on June 3 and held its congress on October 22. Throughout 1988 and 1989, public demonstrations held by these three organizations mobilized hundreds of thousands of supporters for their political activities. In 1990, they would transform themselves into political parties to contest, and win, the national elections.

The three national nongovernmental organizations, in turn, derived power from song traditions. Jānis Peters, chairman of Latvian Popular Front's founding congress, would later recall the critical role played by choir singers. They had an enormous repertoire of songs ready to be sung from memory. They could adapt performances at a moment's notice. The songs they sang at the mass meeting on the eve of the Popular Front's founding congress would represent the nation both to itself and to observers from abroad:

> Song was at the very foundations of the demonstration in Mežaparks
> [song festival grounds] on October 7, 1988. Singing by the entire nation.
> We invited choir singers to sing the repertoire that was needed. The
> entire golden repertoire. With the greatest and most eminent conductors.
> It was they, the conductors and choir singers, who ensured the singing
> spirit of the Popular Front's mass meetings, and the nonviolent spirit
> of the barricades. If the golden repertoire hadn't been there, ready for
> improvisation at moment's notice, within the all-encompassing People's
> Choir, and in the gestures of Mednis, Račevskis, Derkēvica, Dūmiņš,
> and the Kokars brothers, then the Popular Front would not have had
> much success in showing the world the means and the style by which the
> Latvians wish to attain what they want.[49]

In a closing speech on the congress's last day, the newly elected chairman of the Popular Front, Dainis Īvāns, explicitly linked singing to nonviolence, setting a course for the next three years of political action: "I believe we shall be unified. I believe we shall continue to grow. We shall win, if we believe, and if we grow as our belief grows—if our revolution will be, and will remain a revolution of songs, love, and spiritual activity."[50]

The revolution did remain a revolution of songs, and its songs branched out into diverse styles; at different moments, different singing styles—choral, rock, or folk—moved to the fore. During

the summer of 1988 in Estonia, rock music was king. Its technical equipment was well suited for amplified messages to reach massive audiences, bringing unity to tens or hundreds of thousands of
euphoric people. But rock music derived part of its national meaning from the places where it was performed, stages that for decades
had been the setting of choral festivals. Estonian rock musician Alo
Mattiisen wrote songs that quoted and revised earlier choral traditions; for him, the rocking, singing revolution was a direct descen-
dant of the 1869 national song festival. The public, too, felt this
connection.[51] In some ways, rock was better suited for mass demonstrations, because its poetry (to be discussed in the next chapter),
could quickly adapt to express the feelings and explicitly address
very specific issues that resonated at a particular moment. But in
other ways, rock lacked something. Audiences might sing along the
simple words of a refrain, for example, "I am Estonian!" and perhaps they even knew all of the words to some popular rock songs of
nationalism. But they also needed to sing songs of their own. The
well-known choral conductor Tõnu Kaljuste sensed this when he
was invited onto the stage during one of the Night Song Festivals of
June 1988:

> Alo Mattiisen came to me and said, "You should sing something,
> too!" He went to the conductor's stage and introduced me, that I'm a
> conductor who has also stood on this stage at song festivals, and now
> I would be leading the next song. I had to think quickly, in a panic,
> what should I do. . . . At that moment it occurred to me that we could
> sing the song with the lines "The snow has melted now, the winter
> frost is gone; the children freed from jail indoors can now play on
> the lawn." I went to the stage and sang the first line, "Now the little
> birds," and after that everybody sang along. Afterwards Alo said that
> that song had more to it than seemed at first.[52]

The children's song resonated differently from the nationalism songs
that were so popular in 1988. Its words about the "jail" which kept
children indoors during the cold winter acquired a new meaning in June
1988, when Estonians gained freedom of speech. But that summer there
were hundreds of openly patriotic songs and speeches; "singing between
the lines" was not needed. "Now the Little Birds" had another meaning,
as critical to the Singing Revolution as other songs' explicitly nationalist texts. This was a song that everyone could sing, because every Estonian child had learned it in school. It had truthful political meaning,
but it was at the same time also a bit silly, and fun, to boisterously sing
the informal, childish text together with everybody on the song festival

grounds. The act of group singing created unity. Perhaps that is the reason why this particular song was memorable.[53]

Choral music remained at the foundation of Baltic singing traditions, even when rock bands took center stage. Through the summer of 1988, all false songs (and false interpretations of songs) fell away. The "unofficial" anthems now became true anthems, proving that their meanings persisted when the independence they symbolized could be discussed openly. A new wave of composers emerged to create music unhindered by government administrators and censors.

Among the most significant events in choral music was the premiere of "Time of Awakening," by René Eespere. The song's melody was simple; the words, too, were simple, like a parent's conversation with a child. They told a concise, intensely personal story of a better life that was broken by war and Soviet terror. It concluded, in the tradition of Estonian national song poetry, in an individual, first-person-singular pledge of loyalty, but the country that was addressed in the second-person singular was different. "Fatherland" became more intimate, true in a more personal sense because it was extracted from the realm of theoretical ideologies and placed into a very tangible context of one's family. "Mom and dad's land," the land of one's parents, was loved in the childish way that a father and mother are loved:[54]

The sea here
Stood still,
Halted by someone;
Shoreline pushed
Water back,
There began the land:

Level,
Golden,
Rocky,
Earthy,
Cloudy,
Windy,
Full of hope.

Next, the first mom and dad
Came together here,
Working hard, they built a home,
And brought children home.
There was mirth, there was joy,
There were laughs, there were tears,
There was work, there was pain,

In this land.

> (refrain:)
> Estonia, Estonia,
> You are my homeland,
> You are close to my soul.
> Estonia, Estonia,
> You are my homeland,
> You are deep in my heart.

With sword, with fire
Came a foreign man,
Bringing pain, wickedness,
Eating people's bread.
Dad was killed, mommy too,
Brother too, still a child,
The whole land flooded, soaked in tears.

> (refrain)

Father's soul, mother's tongue
I'll hold in this land,
Daddy's land, mommy's land,
From the very start:
Level, golden, rocky, earthy,
Cloudy, windy, full of hope.

> (refrain)

"Time of Awakening" was a key song at the culminating mass meeting of 1988 in Estonia, the day-long Song of Estonia celebration of singing and political speeches on September 11. Many of the choral songs that were introduced in chapter 3 were sung here, as were country music hits and folk songs from oral tradition. The concert's dramatic tone was set by rock music and the euphoria of hope. Some historians of the independence movement mark this as the Singing Revolution's "grand finale," after which the movement supposedly transformed into a rational process driven by parliamentary procedure and international negotiations.[55] While euphoria and rock music ruled the day, however, the event's closing was as sober as it was moving: "My Fatherland Is My Beloved," sung by choir and public, conducted by Gustav Ernesaks. Two summers later, with independence still a tantalizing glimmer over the mountaintops, the rock songs would recede into memory, but this true and explicit choral anthem would still hold its power.

In Latvia, the summer of 1989 saw the premiere of the song "Saule, Pērkons, Daugava" at the School Children's Song Festival. Composer

Mārtiņš Brauns set to music a text written by Rainis in 1919, during Latvia's war for independence.[56] Like "Time of Awakening" in Estonia, the song recalled history, but while the Estonian song moved from a mythical past into present-day family, this Latvian history positioned the present in mythical time, affirming an eternal, sacred bond between Latvians and their country. Rainis had once revived in poetry what he believed to be surviving fragments of ancient Latvian mythology: a folktale about animals digging the Daugava, and legends about God's battles against the devil. The poem's landscape was Latvia, a gateway to the Baltic Sea (the word "Baltic" in Latvian resembles the word for "white"), whose ports have for centuries been an object of foreign military conquest. A higher power intervened to drive out the foreigners and established a home for the Latvian nation. The song affirmed a Latvian mission of persistence and survival as decreed by the great powers of nature: the Sun (Saule), Thunder (Pērkons), Dieviņš (God), and the River Daugava.[57] Its effect was heightened in performance by dramatic melodic shifts. The creation story was told in muted unison, in varied combinations of only five notes; Thunder's battles against demons expanded into a forceful polyphony. The last stanza expressed the national identity first in the hushed unison of the creation, then finally as a divine mission in the harmonies of a celestial battle:

Saule seated Latvia
At the place where ends meet:
White sea, green land,
Latvia holds the key to the gate.

Latvia holds the key to the gate,
Daugaviņa, standing guard.
Foreign people broke the gate,
And the key fell into the sea.

Pērkons cast blue flames of lightning,
Took the key back from the demons,
    Latvia bridged death and life:
    White sea and green land. (repeat two lines)

Saule seated Latvia
At the edge of the white sea,
Winds carried the drifting sand,
Latvian children were thirsty.

Saule ordered Dieviņš
To dig the Daugaviņa.

Animals dug, Dieviņš poured
Life's water from a cloud.

Water of life, water of death
Flowed into the Daugava.
I touched the water's surface,
I feel both in my soul:
Water of death, water of life:
We feel both in our soul.

Saule is our mother,
Daugaviņa soothes the pain,
Pērkons, slayer of the devil—
He is our father.
(repeat concluding stanza)

Mythological anthems such as "Saule, Pērkons, Daugava" or "Time of Awakening" anchored the nations, solidifying people's resolve to continue the independence movement. But the primary songs that expressed the objective and mission of the movement were the national anthems of Estonia, Latvia, and Lithuania. These three songs reentered the national singing repertoire in 1988. Latvia's national anthem was easiest to learn and was well established in popular memory by early summer in 1988— it is, after all, only two short stanzas with a total of twenty-eight words, with each stanza repeated twice. The three long stanzas of the Estonian anthem took a while to sink in. A video recording taken at the Song of Estonia concert on September 11 documented that some choir singers were reading their parts while they sang.[58] Lithuania's national anthem, four stanzas with no repetitions, was learned over the course of the summer. When Lithuanians played a recording of the national anthem at a mass meeting on June 24, 1988, Vytautas Landsbergis recalls, the words were not yet well known:

> The mood was marvelous, and even when the rain began falling quite
> heavily, we simply did not feel it. It seemed as if all the clouds had dis-
> persed, and the sun was shining everywhere in Lithuania again! I had
> brought an American record of the Lithuanian national anthem with
> me, and we caught this wonderful mood by playing it over the loud-
> speakers. It turned out to be a contribution that completed our elation.
> This was the first time that it had been heard openly at any public
> meeting for more than forty years, and because of this the younger
> people had some difficulty in finding the right words. Older people
> simply could not restrain their tears.[59]

At a mass meeting on July 7, 1988, Sąjūdis distributed thirty thousand copies of the anthem to help people sing along. In August, as recalled by a participant, the choir on stage at a mass meeting at Vingis Park sang the whole anthem, but many in the audience knew only the first stanza.[60] By December, all three national anthems had set deep roots. The non-Soviet identity of Estonia, Latvia, and Lithuania's national choral repertoire was manifest, framed by the revived national anthems and marked visually by the ever-present national flags.

In October that year, the Soviet official Aleksandr Yakovlev reiterated that Soviet political reform should be left to the USSR's political leaders, and not the public. Proposals coming from "performers and musicians and people of this sort"—probably a reference to the Balts—were out of touch with reality, unrealistic and not worth discussing.[61] The idea of peacefully persuading Gorbachev to enter true dialogue did not hold promise. Long after his first meeting with Gorbachev at the 1980 Lithuanian song festival, Lionginas Šepetys would still remember that the Soviet leader's mind was closed to other people's ideas:

> Mikhail Gorbachev accomplished much in democratization, openness, and the resuscitation of life. But a decade after our [1980] conversations, at the decisive moment, he was as deaf as ever to our nation's voice—supposedly he hadn't seen nor heard anything about January 13 [1991]. He continued to hear himself, while painting his own image; true, now he painted with more modest strokes and with less self assurance.[62]

Violence loomed on the horizon, and the prospects of avoiding it were not good. Gorbachev's troops reasserted the violent foundations of Soviet power at a mass demonstration in Tblisi, Georgia, on April 9, 1989, where soldiers killed twenty people and injured hundreds more. In Lithuania, when young men refused to obey conscription orders from the Soviet Army, they were arrested by force. In early 1990, bombs exploded by monuments and military bases as the Soviets attempted to construct an image of chaos that would justify a military crackdown in the Baltic.

1990: SINGING INDEPENDENCE, FORMAL AND INFORMAL

The Baltic mass rallies continued into early 1990, when the three national nongovernmental organizations transformed into political parties to compete against the Communist Party in the Soviet Union's first-ever open elections. Voters made their choice based on a single issue: independence from the Soviet Union versus remaining within the Soviet Union. The former platform won, and the three newly elected parliaments declared independence, reclaiming power over the republics whose sovereignty was suspended after the Soviet occupation and annexation in 1940. Attention shifted from mass mobilization to parliamentary procedure, a process based on the rule of law, both domestic and international. "We couldn't sing a constitution," remarks the historian Egidijus Aleksandravičius.[63]

In 1990, the political future of the three Baltic countries was unpredictable. In April, a few months before the Estonian national song festival, prime minister Indrek Toome wrote,

> I am writing these lines in early spring, when no one of us knows
> exactly what Estonia's status will be in summer when we meet at the
> Song Festival Amphitheatre. Maybe the fete will become the First
> National Song Festival of the restored Republic of Estonia. Maybe it
> will be the last in the Estonian SSR. There is one thing, however, that
> we can be sure of: the song festivals have been with us through dif-
> ferent times for 121 years already, always demonstrating our unity
> and continuity, and that is the way it will be now and in the future.
> The violently separated voices of Estonians here and in the rest of the
> world will now be united. This time we will sing the praises of nei-
> ther the foreign rule nor the compulsory friendship. This time we will
> not connect our festival with dates that do not remind us of joy but
> rather of shame and sorrow. I believe that this time we will really see
> the dawn glimmering at the mountain tops, as it says in the anthem of
> song festivals, "Dawn."[64]

The three countries were balanced between the shadow of past repression and the dawn of liberty. Although their political independence was not yet certain, Balts were free to speak and sing what they pleased. They were no longer speaking and singing on the two levels of lies and truth. The anthems sung here were the true anthems that the people wanted to sing, and encores came only at the audience's unfettered request.

This is the context in which the Estonian, Latvian, and Lithuanian national song festivals took place in the summer of 1990. It was a moment when the cultural process of nation building, as regards the national repertoire of songs, was complete. All of the important choral songs of the independence movement were placed on stage. New, nationally resonating choral songs would not emerge between then and August of 1991, when the movement for political independence would conclude, leaving Soviet history behind.

Figure 12. Estonian national song festival opening concert, June 30, 1990, Tallinn. A conductor dressed in white stands on a small stage in front. Photo by Guntis Šmidchens.

At the Estonian song festival's closing concert on July 1, the next-to-last song in the printed program was "Time of Awakening," by René Eespere. Two years after its premiere, it retained its power. The public demanded an encore that had not been planned by the organizers. The program announcer started to introduce the finale ("Estonia's Flag"), but he was drowned out by loud, incessant applause. "The Time of Awakening" was repeated a second time, with the audience singing along.

Then the printed program concluded with "Estonia's Flag," but songs continued. The first encore was "God Protect Estonia," whose composer, Juhan Aavik, passed away in exile in Sweden. His song now returned home to the land where it had only recently been banned. Long applause signaled that the audience was nowhere near feeling that the concert was over. All of the conductors were crowned with wreaths of oak leaves. Indrek Toome's words of closing, compared to his words of welcome printed in the program, took one step forward, expressing optimism in more specific terms: "Today we are allowed to sing freely, but we are not yet free. I am certain that the entire Estonian nation believes that the next song festival will be the festival of a truly free people." The audience and choir replied with long applause, affirming that Toome had correctly expressed their belief. Finally, he announced,

"The Song Festival has ended! Long live Estonia's Song Festival!"

But the festival did not end. The orchestra struck up a marching tune that transitioned into an accompaniment for "Homeland" and the public on the song festival grounds sang along. Another moment of deep silence descended as the festival fire was extinguished in the tower. On stage, the white-bearded Mikk Mikiver and a teenaged girl, Leiki, stepped to the microphone. Mikiver lived in Estonia, and the girl had come to the song festival from the city of her birth, Toronto. His answers to her questions (in Estonian) served as the festival's closing speech:

Leiki: What will happen when it goes out?

Mikiver: The flame may go out,

but it will not disappear.
It will divide up into each of our hearts.
Its power and warmth will go into the people,

into the trees,
into the land.
This flame will burn the soles of all
who in the future will walk on this land
and not know its story.

Leiki: But what will become of us?

Mikiver: If you mean
you and me—
then I will remain here,

to do work,
to love,
to have doubts,
to fight for freedom.

[applause]

We
will remain here.

You

will go back to Toronto.

And I hope
    that the time will come
    when you will be able to choose freely,
    just as every person in this world should be able to
    choose freely
    where he goes,
    where he belongs.
Nobody will be able to force you
    to continue living in Toronto,
    if you want to live in Estonia.
You must know
    that here there is a land,
    a people,
    a language.
Following the blood of your ancestors,
    you belong here.

Leiki: Is freedom coming?

Mikiver: No,
    freedom is not coming.
    We

        are going

        toward freedom.
    And one day we will get there.

[extended applause]

Leiki: Why are you certain of this?

Mikiver: Leiki,
    it is because
    we

    have decided so.
    This is a sufficient argument.

[applause].

    And over these two days
        I,
        and you too,

have seen,
or better, felt
all of Estonia,
its sons
and daughters.
I believe that you agree with me,
they are very beautiful,
and they are made beautiful by
their love for this land
about which they sing.
Leiki, we love this land,
we are finally moving to change it,
and if all goes well
some of us may become its song.
Perhaps a song like the song that is now coming.

Take this song with you, Leiki.
This is the song of our heart.
It has helped us
endure
very dark times.
Today we still sing this song on the borders between
shadow and light,
but the light is growing.

The applause was long, indicating that Mikiver's sentences in the first-person plural, "we," included tens, perhaps hundreds of thousands of Estonians in the choir and audience. A moment of silence, and they rose. The gray haired Gustav Ernesaks moved his raised hand nearly imperceptibly, and the song began on a soft, low note, in unison, "My fatherland is my beloved," then rose and expanded into a harmony of many voices, soprano, alto, tenor, and bass, and the audience was singing, too, "To whom I gave my heart."

Three minutes of applause were followed by still more songs with orchestra accompaniment as the singers (on and off stage) gradually shifted from sacred national identity to an everyday, lighthearted attachment to the land. The orchestra accompanied "Be Free, Estonia's Sea!" to its end, but the singers kept singing, repeating the refrain three more times without accompaniment. The orchestra struck up another song about the seasons and returning home to one's sweetheart, a song that had become popular during World War II:

> I wish to be at home when the apple trees are in bloom,
>   And then their rosy-pink blossoms will decorate my hair (repeat line)
>
> I wish to be at home when the grain fields turn to green,
>   And golden brown grain in the grain fields whispers in the wind.
>
> I wish to be at home when the birch groves' leaves turn gold,
>   And swans soar high in the blue sky, flying south to home.
>
> I wish to be at home when snowflakes carpet the land,
>   And frost-covered branches of spruce trees glimmer in moonlight at
>   night.
>
> I wish to be at home when my sweetheart is with me,
>   And she and I together could spend our time happily.

As the applause quieted down, a men's choir on stage called out an additional stanza from Soviet-era folklore, formerly subversive because it mentioned the unmentionable names of pre-Soviet statesmen and national currency: "I wish to be at home when Päts is President, / and Laidoner leads the army, / and the money's the Estonian cent!" A wave of laughter tickled the festival grounds. The orchestra struck up an introduction to another informal unified song, "My Dear Fatherland," followed by "The Tender Nightingale," and a song of farewell, "So the Wheel of Time Has Turned Around."

Finally, all sang the national anthem.

But then, the singing continued without orchestra accompaniment: "People of Kungla," and, for a second time, "Be Free, Estonia's Sea!" And, finally, last in this sequence of unofficial songs was a ditty of rhymed couplets about love for a woman, though its refrain also proclaimed love for Saaremaa Island, a place in Estonia.[65] It is a fun song, a long song, one that can be sung when a person simply wants to keep singing and not stop:

> I watch through a telescope from afar,
> How distant my boat is from Saaremaa. (repeat stanza)
>
> (refrain, sung twice:)
> There is no place better anywhere
> Than Saaremaa in summertime.
>
> As white as a dove is my bride;
> I saw her again in summertime.

    (refrain)

Her neck so white, her hair so black,
And a satin kerchief around her neck.

    (refrain)

I'll sip salty water from the sea
And to my dear one the truth I'll speak:

    (refrain)

If being my wife is what you want,
You must row out to Saaremaa.

    (refrain)

During the Estonian song festival procession in Tallinn on June 30, a
tiny fragment of a Lithuanian song rose up through the roaring cheers
of the Estonian public, "Water the horses, water the horses. . . ." Popular in oral tradition for most of the twentieth century, this song was
hardly ever performed on stage.[66] Its cheerful, bright melody would
energize mass meetings and processions. The opening stanza of riding Lithuanians gave the song a proud, military feeling, but the text
turned to love:

    On the hill, walls of stone—
    Lithuanians ride.
    Riding, riding, Lithuanians,
    Carrying, carrying to the young girl
    A wreath made of rue,
    A wreath made of rue.

    Now they ride up to
    Father-in-law's courtyard.
    Wake up, wake up, sister-in-law,
    Go wake up your little sister,
    Water the horses,
    Water the horses.

    I won't wake up,
    It's not day yet!
    My dear mother told me
    Not to talk to soldiers.
    I obey dear mother,
    I obey my heart.

Lithuanians have not been able to explain to me why this particular song was sung so frequently at public gatherings. Intellectuals

inevitably comment that this is not an "authentic" folk song. The words about boy-girl relations don't seem suitable for nationalism research, either. This was the same tradition, perhaps, that was first observed by the Lithuanian folklorist Stanevičius in the early nineteenth century: a song that appears at first glance to have military meaning is actually about love. In 1990, in the procession whose explicit purpose was nationalism, these particular Lithuanians were singing a love song, and not one about marching toward liberty, or conquest, or heroism in battle. In light of Herder's idea that warlike nations sing feats while gentle nations sing love, and with the benefit of today's hindsight, the song foreshadowed a nonviolent Lithuanian response to Soviet military power six months after the song festival. But we didn't know that then.

In 1990, Moscow's blockade of Lithuania encumbered the national song festival. The *Encyclopedia of Lithuanian Music* pithily summarizes the July 6–8 events, in which, despite a gasoline shortage caused by the Soviet energy embargo, a total of 31,328 performers congregated in Vilnius, among them 18,679 singers from 579 choirs:

> The Thirteenth Song Festival of Lithuania, now named National,
> took place in 1990 during the USSR's economic and visa block-
> ade. Although the majority of Lithuanian song-and-dance ensembles
> abroad were not allowed to come to Lithuania, and although the festi-
> val's traditional competitions could not take place, this song festival's
> program was one of the largest ever.[67]

The festival's program was printed before the blockade, and its words of welcome to Lithuanians from abroad, unfortunately, did not reach people to whom the Soviet government denied entry visas. But the bridge built back to Lithuania's pre-Soviet independence and first song festival was successful. Conductor Kostas Gurevičius concluded his printed greeting with words from the national anthem:

> Dear singers! With all of my heart I rejoice at the rebirth of
> our Fatherland, Lithuania, and the song which again resounds
> freely. . . . This festival reminds me of the First Song Festival of Lithu-
> ania in 1924, where I, too, had the opportunity to conduct. Back then,
> having walked for barely six years on the road of independence, Lithu-
> ania, still nursing many wounds of war and fragmentation, proved to
> all that it was alive, and determined to create and maintain its spiritual
> values.
>   I am happy to be able to greet the singers, dancers, and musi-
> cians of all Lithuania at this significant festival, and I eagerly await its
> opening. Let the echoes of the song festival resound throughout dear

Lithuania, strengthening the hope: "In the name of Lithuania, let unity blossom." [68]

The program declared that in Lithuania, the festival choir would sing the true national repertoire that had been forbidden since the beginning of the Soviet occupation fifty years earlier: "Today we meet at the Thirteenth Lithuanian National Song Festival, the First Song Festival of Resurrected Lithuania. Here we will sing, dance, and play what we like, what is dear to us."[69] Very wet weather did not lessen participants' enthusiasm, which is audible in the published live recording. As the rain poured down, they sang the canonical national repertoire, beginning with the national anthem and "Where Forests Stand Green." This classic underground song was forbidden in the early Soviet years because its image of a young man singing in the woods evoked partisans fighting Soviet forces in the deep forests of Lithuania; it was back in print in 1970, and "rehabilitated" on stage in 1975:[70]

My home is where forests stand densely green,
Where Nemunas borders Fatherland's shores.
There lies my bright country, my dear Fatherland,
Some do not see why it is so beautiful.
The forest's greenness gives senses delight,
The twittering birdsong, charming to the heart.
There by the Nemunas, shorelines green as rue,
The songs of a young man brightly ring out!

The song speaks the words of Fatherland's fate,
Its bittersweet melody saddens the heart.
Reawakening feelings for Fatherland,
Eternally holding its strong memory.
I devote all my songs to Fatherland.
To Fatherland I wish happier days.
May you live and prosper, oh our Fatherland,
As one we shall all live in unity!

"Dear Lithuania" came at the concert's conclusion, followed by "We Were Born Lithuanians," the early twentieth-century song that was banned under Stalinism, to be revived in 1988 when Sąjūdis adopted it as the independence movement's anthem. Soon, with independence restored, the Lithuanian national radio would play it at the end of each broadcast day, as had been the tradition before the coming of the Soviets in 1940. It expressed a grand feeling of inherited pride, and the singers' determination to persevere:

We were born Lithuanians,

We want to be Lithuanians!
At birth, we received that honor,
And we must not let it die!

Strong as the oak by the Nemunas,
The Lithuanian shall not bend nor bow!
Green as the spruce tree by the Šešupė,
Flourishing green in cold and storm.

(repeat first stanza, last line repeated twice)

Each of the three Baltic national song festivals of 1990 had its own unique spirit. In Vilnius, pouring rain did not extinguish enthusiasm, but it certainly diluted feelings of a sacred national ritual that might have otherwise prevailed. In Tallinn, the relaxed Estonian public moved around freely during the two four-hour concerts, sometimes sitting on the benches in front or relaxing in the sun on the grassy hillside, then retreating to a picnic among the trees and food stands during one of five informal intermissions while the combined choir left the stage and the boys' and men's choirs stepped up, to be replaced in turn by the women's choirs and the children's choir.

In Latvia, concerts began at seven o'clock in the evening and lasted late, with no intermissions. The festival grounds at nighttime became an enormous concert hall whose ceiling reached into the sky, its sunset colors gradually fading into darkness, blending into the softly swaying dark pine forests around the edges. The audience sat in numbered seats, dressed in their Sunday best, not walking about or moving from their seats until the concert's end. The movement of singers on stage, when necessary, was planned so that the music would not pause. Over four days, the singers performed three full concerts with different programs, two of them repeated twice; there were a total of eighty-six songs in the festival repertoire: eight sung by all choirs together, forty-five by the mixed adult choirs (thirteen of them with orchestra accompaniment), fourteen by women's choirs, sixteen by men's choirs, and three by combined men's and women's choirs. This was a deeply nuanced, multifaceted cultural performance, carefully choreographed to the smallest artistic detail. Each of the three concerts was a work of art based on a theme: "Song of Fate," "Folk Song," and "Song of Life." The program notes explained, for example, the opening concert's theme:

> Song has expressed the joy and the pain of its nation and its era. It
> has pulsed alongside the fate of Latvia, hiding a deeply hidden, true
> premonition of the nation's consciousness. It has been our conscience,

spurring our steps at decisive moments, mourning our losses. Song
spoke as a conscience, it breathed the nation's longings when it was
fated or ordered to be silent. And when our eyes opened two years ago
for the Third Awakening, then the words that were needed to express
it had to be found anew, but the song came of its own into our streets,
homes, and squares. It came immediately, pure, with no need to
change. Because it had never closed its eyes. And the Third Awakening
is also called the Singing Revolution.[71]

This concert, continued the artistic director Pēteris Pētersons, would
present familiar songs. It would not narrate a story or compile a history of singing but rather its songs would be a means of gently touch-
ing heroes and wounds of the past. The concert's seven thematic chapters would rise and fall in waves of elation and despair; "This wavelike
motion of rising and falling could also be called the creation of Latvia":

    I.   Rise! The tricolored sun will rejoice (two songs beginning with
          "Blue Forever," conducted by Haralds Mednis)
   II.   Dreams fade. A harsh sword glitters in the hand (four songs
          recalling World War I and the 1918–20 War for Independence)
  III.   The land is ours, the cities are ours (four songs of national
          independence between 1918 and 1940)
  IV.   Back into the waters of nonexistence (five songs of World War II)
   V.   To survive—with song, with silence (three songs of the Soviet
          period)
  VI.   Awakening in Singing—a time of hope (four songs)
 VII.   Finale—May You Live Forever, Latvia! (four songs)

In waves of ovations between songs, the audience called conductors and composers for a second bow, requesting—and receiving—
encores of particularly beloved songs. The choir, too, would break
into applause, at times addressing the conductor with the spontaneous refrain in four-part harmony, "Long may he live, long may he
live, may he live long!" while he or she walked from the stage, arms
weighed down by the flowers presented, with a kiss, by a long line of
singers and audience members who gathered by the stage after each
song.

The seventh chapter began with "Our Land" ("Daugava's Two
Shorelines"), sung together by the audience and choir. Next, "Saule,
Pērkons, Daugava," was followed by three minutes of ovations from
the choir and audience, summoning the composer, Mārtiņš Brauns,
to stage before an encore. After the third song, "To My Homeland,"
its composer Raimonds Pauls, too, was called to the stage by lengthy
applause. Then came the grand crescendo of "May You Live Forever,

Latvia!" a song not performed in Rīga since its premiere at the national song festival of 1938. It was conducted by the oldest song festival conductor, Leonīds Vīgners (son of Ernests Vīgners, song festival conductor in 1888 and 1895).

Applause after the concert, interspersed with the refrain "Long May He Live," gradually faded, transitioning into the soft notes of "Oh Wind" sung by the choir and the standing audience. Scattered applause flickered after the last, hummed stanza, but then silence descended as the choir and audience softly dispersed.

The mass concerts continued for four days. On July 8, toward the finale of the closing concert, the choir sang the Lord's Prayer, set to music by Lūcija Garūta, followed not by applause but by nearly a minute of intense silence, as would be the custom at the conclusion of church services. The last song in the program was the national anthem, also a song of prayer, and it, too, was followed by a minute of silence, softly broken by the announcement: "Our nation's Twentieth Song Festival has ended. Until we meet again at the next one!"

The singing continued, however. The audience and choir joined in unison in "Daugava's Two Shorelines," followed by "I'll Sing of You, Oh Land of My Fathers." A conductor stepped to the stage to lead the song that resonated most deeply this year, "Saule, Pērkons, Daugava," accompanied by the orchestra. Here, the choir applauded loudest, calling the composer up to the stage one more time. The audience's applause faded, but the choir continued, louder than before, chanting the name of Ivars Bērziņš, its favorite conductor. Bērziņš had not been selected to conduct this song during the regular concerts, but now, summoned by the singers, he led the choir without orchestral accompaniment.

As in Estonia, songs transitioned from a sacred atmosphere to everyday cheer. "Oh Wind," sung in four part harmony by choir and audience, was first. As the choir slowly filed off of the stage, they sang "Time to Go Home," followed by the most popular informal song during the song festival procession a few days earlier, "This Is Latvia." This song listed, to a light waltz tune, a series of popular national symbols: oak trees, the Gauja River, agrarian life, Midsummer Night—and beer:

> Here, where great oak trees raise their branches green,
> Here, where stand the men who do not fear death:
>
> (refrain, repeat twice:)
> This is Latvia, Gauja's shores are here,
> Homeland where our fathers once were born.

On the grassy hill, a cowherd whistling,
Farmer plows his field, digging furrows deep.

   (refrain)

Then at Midsummer, we come together,
And we drink some beer, and we sing some songs.

   (refrain)

But when destiny takes us forever apart,
Our last mug of beer we'll drink to Latvia.

   (refrain)

The singing gradually broke up into smaller, singing rivulets in a river
of people walking from the song festival stage through the park to
the trams that took the singing crowds back into town. My cassette
recordings contain fragments of many songs, nearly all of them songs
of love: "I'll take the most beautiful girl, and we'll live happily," "We
fit together like the sea and the wind," "I cut two fields of clover," "I
put on white stockings and went into the garden," and "I didn't come
here to sleep! . . . "

THE TRUTH OF SINGING

The three national song festivals of 1990 were a culmination of
the Baltic Singing Revolution. Nonviolent revolutions rest on the
shoulders of disciplined, unified masses of people. They depend
upon each individual's active participation, and on an awareness
of the importance of one's own voice among many others. The
two central rituals of the national song festival—the procession
and the mass concert—balanced between individual participation
and disciplined mass action. What better metaphor for active, participatory, nonviolent democracy than the image of thousands of
spectators lining a street along which walk thousands of performers, mingling, gifting flowers to each other, seeking out and finding
many familiar, individual faces among the masses of the nation?
Or the image of thirty thousand singers on stage and another hundred thousand people in the audience, each participating according
to his or her own wishes, singing from the heart, with or without a
conductor, in harmony?

One truth that is immanent at the song festival, in the formal songs
led by a conductor as well as in the informal public songs with no

individual leader, is the fact that each Balt sings, first of all, for the pleasure of artistic self-expression. Much of this pleasure comes from hearing voices in harmony or in unison with one's own. National singing traditions offer every Estonian, Latvian, and Lithuanian a unique instrument to express emotional attachment to other humans, sung together with other humans in a shared language. Feelings of national unity, and of ties that bind people to one another and to their native land, derive from the pleasure of singing. These emotions were a reason why song festivals were created and maintained over the past century and a half. These feelings are expressed in the words and melodies of songs, and in the act of singing together.

Estonian, Latvian, and Lithuanian singers sing differently, and each song festival has its own distinctive spirit expressed in three very different languages. And yet the people can easily understand each other. The Estonian composer Veljo Tormis came to the 1990 Latvian song festival to hear the premiere of his song, and added to the song's meaning in a concise, bilingual speech:

> Three stars,
> Three sisters,
> Three song festivals;
>
> One suffering,
> One hope,
> One liberty.
>
> Let our voices sound as one,
> Let our hearts be born as one,
> Let the song resound as one.[72]

The song's words by Latvian poet Māra Zālīte refer to three stars delicately held in the hands of the statue at the spire of Latvia's Freedom Monument. On the nearby square is a clock tower, a popular landmark for rendezvous. If one hasn't met the person before, one might agree to hold flowers or a book, "So that you'll know me!" The poem proposes such a meeting, not between two humans but between liberty and an individual who may choose to meet her or not. The Estonian composer Tormis's song, sung by the Latvian women's chorus, asserts that the core values of work, will, song, honor, and language are shared by the Baltic national independence movements:

> I will wait for you.
> But not by the clock tower.

By Time.
Up in the sky I will stand,
And in my slender hand
Will be three stars,
So that you would know me,
So that you would know me.

I shall wait for you.
By Work I shall wait, and by Will.
By Song, Honor, Language, I shall wait,
By our love.

(repeat first stanza)

"Yes," Veljo Tormis would later write, "This song's general context at that time of change (1989) was definitely a respect for freedom and universal human values. But for me, personally, nevertheless, 'Three Stars' was a song of love."[73] And so, for the song's creator, and perhaps also for its singers, the emotions of national revival are akin to the visceral feelings of deep, romantic love.

CHAPTER SEVEN

Living within the Truth in Rock Songs

The Singing Revolution began in Estonia on May 14, 1988, at the Tartu Music Days, an annual venue for cutting-edge rock music on the westernmost margins of permitted Soviet culture. That day, the nonconformist sprit of rock converged with explicit nationalism and civic disobedience when audience members unfurled two illegal Estonian flags. On the next day, a sea of blue, black, and white fluttered above the crowd. The flags were edited out of television broadcasts, but news of the revolutionary demonstration spread instantaneously. Three weeks later, in Tallinn, at the Old Town Days from June 4 to June 11, police at first removed sporadic flags, but soon so many thousands of people were wearing blue, black, and white clothes, carrying ribbons and banners and raising the colors on flagpoles, walls, and towers, that the Soviets gave up trying to stop them.[1]

A year earlier, the Old Town Days participants had begun a late-night tradition of walking to the national song festival stage on Tallinn's outskirts, where they sang and played music until dawn. In 1988, these informal Night Song Festivals convened again, with the number of participants growing from several thousand participants on June 4 to sixty or seventy thousand on Saturday evening, June 11, an event documented in Jim and Maureen Tusty's film *The Singing Revolution*.[2] Participants sang many songs in varied music styles. Among the many performers who stepped to the microphone was the rock musician Alo Mattiisen. It was his "Five Fatherland Songs" sung by Ivo Linna that became the voice of popular sentiment after their premiere at the flag-bedecked Tartu Music Days; a decade later, at the

Figure 13. Estonian flags appear at the Tartu Music Days, May 14, 1988. On stage is Alo Mattiisen and his band, performing the premiere of "Five Fatherland Songs." Photo by Toomas Volmer.

Smithsonian Folklife Festival, the Estonians would play two of Mattiisen's songs in their portion of the Singing Revolution celebration.

Back in spring of 1988 on the song festival stage, Estonia's 120-year-old choral traditions converged with rock music. But while choral music under Soviet government had often balanced between official and unofficial cultural traditions, rock did not carry such ideological baggage. Rock songs broke out from Soviet norms from the very beginning.

"SUNG POETRY" VERSUS SOVIET CENSORSHIP

The history of rock music in the Soviet Union grew out of the history of jazz. A Lithuanian KGB report about the repression of rock fans in 1962 called the music "ultra-modern jazz," and indeed, post-totalitarian Soviet attacks on rock music resembled earlier Stalinist attacks on jazz.[3] The mechanisms by which the music was considered to have an evil effect on the brain and on human behavior were straightforward. It stimulated the "basest instincts and sexual urges," thus corrupting the rational, nonerotic character of the new Soviet human. Loud rock music "possessed" dancers, breaking down self-control, leading to destructive violence.[4] In Latvia in 1963, dancing a few rock steps was reason enough for three young people to be arrested, and the brief career of the rock group Katedrāle ended after the sudden deaths of its two leaders.[5] Mass media hardly ever mentioned rock, and then only to attack it as a product of the rotting West. But just as elements of jazz were absorbed into government cultural programs of the late 1950s, so also a decade later Soviet policy toward rock music changed.

Around 1966, the director of Vilnius High School number 23 purchased drums and electric guitars for an amateur student ensemble, and he most certainly was not alone among school administrators.[6] At age fifteen, one of the school's students, Vytautas Kernagis, was one of many Lithuanian youths to establish an amateur rock group, but his band Aisčiai, became a star on the Vilnius youth scene. "That was the life at our school. From one dance to another. From one fantastic New Year's carnival to another. We played at these events, lying on the floor, or holding the guitars above our heads," like the Beatles whose songs they played. Kernagis also learned songs by the Rolling Stones, the Animals, and many others from LP records sent to him by an American uncle. The band would transcribe the English-language words as best they could, with form being more important than content. Refrains were relatively precise, a band member recalls, but "everything else that was murmured and hummed into the microphone wasn't that important. What was important was that they could play the melody."[7] The group's one song in Lithuanian was Maironis's classic poem about the ruins of the medieval capital city of Lithuania, "Trakai Castle," to the melody of the 1964 Animals hit "House of the Rising Sun":

> With mould and lichen overgrown,
> Behold, revered Trakai!
> Its great lords lie in graves unknown,
> The castle though stands high . . . [8]

Students remember this as the band's standard opening song, and some assert that it was their school's unofficial anthem. It's unclear if the idea of combining the 1892 poem with the 1964 rock melody came from anonymous children's folklore or was invented by Kernagis, but band members recall that it was he who suggested omitting Maironis's sad last stanza.[9] The song's romantic lament over the lost grandeur of Lithuania's golden age was less important than the youthful bravura with which sacred national verse was modernized alongside Western hits. "Our playing in Aisčiai can't be characterized as [political] resistance," remembered Kernagis, "but neither

was it just fooling around. Maybe there was also a hidden, unac-
knowledged tendency toward national identity inside us, but for us,
the music was first of all a form of self expression, an opportunity to
stand out, to rise in the eyes of the girls."[10] And playing rock music
seems to have compensated for possessing what was at that time
seen as a physical defect: thick-rimmed eyeglasses. A band member
recalled, "The girls were stuck on us. On everybody who played,
Kernagis, too. Nobody cared about eyeglasses. Just look at the Rolling Stones—they're horrifying, but they're gods. That's what it was
like for us. You stand on stage with a guitar, you sing, Jesus Maria,
they were fainting for us."[11]

Kernagis rejected outright the idea that he and his friends could
be called political "dissidents."[12] For them, the meaning of rock was
above all in its form: loud, cocky, unruly, and different from the main-
stream estrada. Most of the English song texts that they sang were
not comprehensible to the band, much less their audiences, and even
in English they weren't explicitly political. The Soviet police thought
otherwise, however, and recruited spies among Kernagis's classmates
to compile a file of his transgressions. Among the denunciations was a
secret report alleging that at summer camp he once sang a parody of
"The "Internationale":

> The red, the green, and the yellow
> Are colors of our liberty;
> Smetona will return from exile,
> Lithuania will again be free.
> This is the final battle,
> The decisive campaign;
> We'll drive out the Maskoliai and
> Lithuania will be free.[13]

This text from oral tradition was subversive in the sense that children's
folklore is usually subversive: it spoke words forbidden by school
authorities.[14] The song did, however, also carry images of national
mobilization. Its references to the colors of independent Lithuania's
flag, to the country's former president, and to "Maskoliai" (a nineteenth-century code word for "Russians") presented a counterworld
to official symbols of Soviet power. Its political meaning, and the
meaning of Kernagis's songs, intensified after the Soviets officially pronounced the singer to be deviant. A provocateur convinced Kernagis
to sign the founding statement of a fictional organization called Free
Lithuania, after which the KGB manipulated Kernagis's schoolmates

into a vote to expell him from the Komsomol. The final police report stated, "The students themselves correctly understood the conversations organized by the KGB, admitted their mistakes, and promised to not allow similar behavior in the future."[15] Expulsion meant that Kernagis would not be admitted into an institution of higher education, but he was injured more deeply by his classmates' betrayal. He left the school to instead enroll in an evening program.

Kernagis found new, truer friends in the "big beat" band Rupūs Miltai. Because they were not sponsored by any cultural institution, the group played only at dances and never at official competitions or festivals. When they played, it was not unusual for dancers to stop, stand, and listen. Among the band's last performances was a 1970 *popseišinas* (from English "pop session") attended by several hundred hippies and musicians from Lithuania, Latvia, and Estonia. Around that time, Kęstutis Antanėlis transcribed from Kernagis's LP the parts to Andrew Lloyd Webber's 1970 rock opera *Jesus Christ Superstar* and assembled about twenty performers to rehearse in secret (Kernagis's voice was too low for the part of Jesus and too high for Caiaphas, so he sang in the chorus). The rock opera's premiere on December 25, 1971, was flooded by a crowd so large that the KGB agents could not squeeze through to get inside; after the one-hour concert, the performers escaped through a secret exit. Two years later, they performed the opera again in Lithuanian translation.[16]

Kernagis often played his guitar and sang while hanging out with teenaged friends on "Brodas" (the slang name for Vilnius's main street, an abbreviation of "Broadway"). Their "anthem," writes Rūta Oginskaitė, was "Song of the Road," Kernagis's "scream" to awaken people from complacency.[17] Where the poem's author Strielkūnas had written, "If we have voices, we sing a song," Kernagis challenged his audience, "If we have hearing, we hear a song."[18] The road to the unknown future is difficult, possibly dangerous, but there is also a glimmer of hope:

> You didn't weep, and you didn't quarrel.
> We won't come back, and we won't return.
> We move ahead if we have a road,
> If we have hearing, we hear a song.
>
> All of us sang, best as we could.
> All of us silent, each one as needed.
> The road runs on, dusty and clouded.
> Will we be lucky, or meet a bullet?

Wind blows against us. The road is long.
We travel on, loving the land.
Don't you start crying, don't you be sad –
There's room enough to lay your head down.

(repeat first stanza)

The song and its singer rose to national fame in the 1971 movie *A Small Confession*, in which Kernagis was assigned the eerily auto-biographical supporting role of Ben, a student expelled from school for "silly reasons," who played guitar and sang songs to express others' feelings. "Everybody understood," an acquaintance recalled, that "something illegal had made it to the movie screen. . . . We didn't think much about the film as a whole. But everybody went to see Kernagis sing."[19] A line spoken in the film, "Ben, let's go to Nida!" became a proverb in youth slang.

Kernagis was only one of many young musicians on the 1960s Baltic rock scene. In Latvia in 1967, Raimonds Pauls began composing for another high school band, Eolika.[20] More than fifty "guitarist ensembles" emerged in Estonia, where future stars such as Ivo Linna and Tõnis Mägi played covers of hits by the Beatles, the Rolling Stones, James Brown, and later, Deep Purple, Black Sabbath, and, of course, Led Zeppelin. Finnish television broadcasts carried a constant stream of information about Western life into northern Estonia.[21]

Soviet censorship of public concerts intensified after the 1968 revolution in Czechoslovakia. But electric guitars and drums were still allowed, even if the words "rock and roll" were usually replaced by the euphemisms "big beat," "vocal-instrumental ensembles," "contemporary youth music," "electric guitar songs," or "popular dance music."[22] A harbinger of the new policy was the 1967 film *Prisoner of Kavkaz*, in which not only was music played on electric guitars and drums but popular actors danced a variant of the Twist. Soviet rock journalist Artemy Troitsky characterized the new official attitude as, "Of course it's all nonsense, and the music is for idiots, but let them fool around, it's nothing terrible."[23]

What was unacceptable, however, was rock's tendency to move ahead without official sanction, bypassing the "leading role" of the Communist Party and Soviet cultural institutions. Another 1967 rock-music film produced in Latvia presented a different motive for the new Soviet policy. In *Four White Shirts*, a Communist Party leader pointed out, "The experiments characteristic of youth should not, I think, be stifled, but they should be guided into the correct direction, comrades.

Is that not so?"[24] Talented musicians could be lured out of the underground and into institutionally supported performances that guaran-
teed a stable source of income in return for submission to the government's official processes of repertoire control.[25] They would thus make
concessions to "party-ness," and work with the leadership (and censorship) from above. Vytautas Kernagis did not.

Like the "bard" Marek Grechuta, whose records he acquired
from Poland, Kernagis pioneered "sung poetry," which placed more
emphasis on words than on innovative melodies. Like the Russian
bards Alexander Galich, Bulat Okudzhava, and Vladimir Vysotsky,
Kernagis was often shunned by the Soviet cultural administration.[26]
The ambiguous Soviet policy toward this genre and its performers
remains a riddle. Kernagis's first LP record was published not as
music but rather as a declamation of written literature.[27] Kernagis
was allowed to produce records, but his songs were not permitted
on radio or television broadcasts. The Soviet censors' reasons have
not been documented. The fact that Kernagis was not a member of
the Composers Union probably played a role.[28] It is likely, however,
that his charisma as a free, non-Soviet thinker was most to blame.
Giedrius Kuprevičius explains the ban by describing the genre's
nature: "Isn't it clear that sung poetry, and not pop music, was what
stimulated our thought?"[29]

Kernagis wrote around two hundred songs, many of them humorous.[30] He mastered in particular the art of hyperbolic irony. Among
his most popular works was the 1983 song based on a poem by Juozas
Erlickas, "Colorado Beetles." The beetle (Leptinotarsa decemlineata)
is a potato pest that spread to Europe in the second half of the twentieth century; in the Soviet Union, the pestilence was rumored to have
been caused by an American plot, and the propaganda battle against
it was both agricultural and political. Kernagis's song exaggerated the
eradication campaign into an absurd parody. Stock heroes of everyday Soviet culture—the brigadier of a farming crew, a milkmaid, and
the accordionist—became caricatures of themselves when they were
inserted into a text that spouted Soviet administrative clichés. In the
song's overenthusiastically optimistic chorus, the eradication plan is
fulfilled beyond the wildest of expectations, when the beetles are not
merely eradicated but smashed to pieces. A grammatical form turns the
government goal of "advancing agriculture" into a silly, past-perfect-
tense boast about a completed task, and the enthusiastic promise to
"sing from the heart" mocks the singer's sincerity. The song concludes

with a hysterically animated image of technology personified, perhaps deified to a superlative degree: a singing tractor in heaven.

> Up on the blue and lofty river shore
> It's nice to dream a bit and drink;
> The kolkhoz workers will arrive and sing
> And tell about the annual harvest,
> And the report on task completion methods
> Will be presented by brigadier Rapolas;
> He'll tell about the new potato species
> That doesn't fear the Colorado Beetle.
> The willow trees on both riverbanks
> Will hear and sigh about their happiness.
> The head accordionist will play and
> Accompany a song that he created.
>
> > We'll smash into pieces
> > Those Colorado beetles,
> > And the potatoes will bloom again.
> > And having advanced agriculture
> > In our dear kolkhoz, we
> > Shall sing from the heart.
>
> A wandering star above a twittering nightingale,
> The moon shall reflect in the bottle,
> And on the old and lengthy railroad tracks
> With little sparks a train shall glimmer.
> And going out into the kolkhoz fields
> I'll take a horse, a milkmaid, and a lyre.
> Now she is singing, and with her sing I,
> And a tractor is singing in the sky.
>
> > We'll smash . . . (refrain)

It is a strange twist of irony that what resonated with the public was this song's enthusiastic optimism, and not the ironic parody of Soviet life. The song lived on into the Singing Revolution and beyond, when the Soviet propaganda that it mocked became a thing of the distant past. In a similar vein, another song that ironically professed Soviet complacency with the refrain "Our days are like a festival!"[31] was embraced by audiences who latched onto it as an anthem of joy.

> Here I was born and I felt the meaningful, racing years,
> Here I sang with everyone about how happy and beautiful I am.
> The forests resound, oh they resound with our laughter and love,
> If someone is very sad, you absolutely must come here . . .

Kernagis had the gift of writing songs that expressed happiness—
it would be much easier, he later said, to write dissatisfied songs,
because one is usually alone and ready to compose when one is brood-
ing or angry. Happiness, in contrast, usually strikes at moments when
a person is with others and has no time to write. Kernagis's happiness
was not the explicit, ideologically based optimism that was officially
propagated in Soviet society. Hyperbole and irony recontextualized
empty official clichés, exposing the incongruity, indeed the absurdity,
of the Soviet order. Kernagis's humor united Lithuanians on a sincere,
human level.[32]

"I rescue people," Kernagis's character Ben once remarked in the
1971 film, in a line that would come to characterize Kernagis's life as
a whole. Rolandas Rastauskas wrote, "Even when he turned into a
comic he remained himself—a reactionary romantic calling upon the
mole to lift its head and think standing up, with back straightened
out," And Rūta Oginskaitė concludes, "He rescued people—from
hopelessness, from routine, and simply from a bad mood. He changed
people's attitude about things in life that were not going to change
soon, but it was possible to laugh a bit, because 'we'll smash it into
pieces'! He rescued you, simply because with him, you felt the power
of togetherness."[33]

"My politics," recalled Kernagis, "were always based on the idea
that, in a critical situation, a human with a good soul will choose the
correct path. What sung poetry accomplished was a movement of the
soul, and this was very big politics, particularly in the so-called frozen
period." Kernagis was not a person who could write explicit political
slogans in songs or articles; he preferred instead the politics of Jaroslav
Hašek's *Good Soldier Schweik*, who made comments as if in passing.[34]
After 1986, it was other singers who sang the explicitly political songs
needed by the massive movement for political independence. But Kernagis's songs retained their power, too. On January 11–13, 1991, Soviet
troops attacked and occupied mass media institutions in Vilnius, and
Lithuanians prepared to defend their national parliament, constructing
barricades and arming a small contingent of guards inside the building for a symbolic last stand. Vytautas Kernagis was invited to perform
an informal concert in the lobby. He discovered, not much to his surprise, that "Colorado Beetles" was still among the audience's favorite
requested songs. Even at this time of national crisis and the threat of an
overwhelming Soviet military attack, the laughter and human togetherness that Kernagis had always nurtured were needed.[35]

The two late-sixties films mentioned above—*Prisoner of Kavkaz* and *Four White Shirts*—exemplify two paths taken by rock music in the Soviet Union of the late 1960s. *Prisoner* was a blockbuster hit; it told a story of wacky humor and clean-cut youths in happy-go-lucky love, dancing to the tune of Twist melodies. *Four White Shirts*, in contrast, was not permitted to be shown on public screens for two decades; it told the story of a songwriter squelched by government censors. The reasons for censorship were never stated, and it is unknown whether the decision to stop the film was made in Latvia or in Moscow. It is likely that a key offense was a lack of "party-ness" in the scene mentioned above, because a Communist Party committee meeting was portrayed negatively. Colleagues urged the film's director to cut this episode, but he refused.[36] Another reason for censoring the film might have been a clash with Soviet moral norms. The lead character wrote a song about premarital sex; he danced the "Shake" (a non-Soviet dance) with his girlfriend, and their love ended a few weeks after they met. These elements were softened in a 1968 version of the story published by the screenplay's author, Gunārs Priede.[37]

The film's songs, however, lived on in semilegal concerts organized by the composer Imants Kalniņš. Beginning in 1968, Kalniņš would assemble a group, and, when that group was banned from stages, regroup with a new set of performers. The banned film's songs were their stable repertoire, and some but not all of them were finally published a decade later on an LP record.[38] The words by Māris Čaklais often combined the themes of love and politics. For example, one song spoke on one level of memories that remained after love was gone, but on another level served as the songwriter's defiant response to the repression of his creative independence by the Communist Party committee:

> Thoughts as clean as the falling snow
> And among them, some are unclean, too.
> Naked openness
> Facing wickedness.

The film's title song, "Four White Shirts," metaphorically exposed people who betrayed the songwriter and disfigured his art. Dirty shirts could be washed, but their stained conscience could not be cleansed,

> And will there be any point
> To remind him then
> What the song is about:
> Not shirts, but consciences.

Rock music provided refuge from Soviet life. While the Party committee eviscerated his work, the songwriter Kalniņš escaped into a daydream accompanied by another song, "Cuckoo Bird's Voice." The song's landscape was unmistakably Rīga. The film's director, too, moved the camera out of the meeting room to show hazy landscapes of his beloved city, an alternate world of beauty that consoled a defeated artist.[39] The cuckoo's voice is a sign that spring is coming; a true hope persisted, muffled by the clatter of technology, frozen by cold, seemingly exotic and naïve, an irrational phenomenon that many did not comprehend.

> In the tangle of girls, cars, and engines
> On street corners, freezing in cold
> Among sirens and whistles and roars,
> A greeting or nightmare?
> Cuckoo bird's voice.
>
> What a funny one, wandering the city,
> Why do you walk barefoot in snow?
> No, your naïve "ku-ku" is old-fashioned,
> So we threw it out long ago!
>
> We dug it deep down in the heart,
> But when frost gave way to the thaw
> Like a naïve narcissus it peeked out,
> Cuckoo bird's voice.
>
> Then we gave it to a girl,
> She pressed it in a book to dry;
> So, if it's not frozen in snow,
> It's dried between the pages,
> Cuckoo bird's voice.
>
> Go, fanatic,
> And therefore, a free man,
> Past the signs announcing "market" and "circus."
> Do not buy the "Shake" or "Hully Gully,"
> Buy just one voice of the cuckoo!
>
> But if the girl shrugs her shoulders
> Don't you stay there anymore;
> You can't ask that they all understand
> What the naïve "ku-ku" means to you!

Rock music, like the "cuckoo bird's voice," carried the songwriter out of the Soviet world, allowing him to live within the truth. The voice proclaimed a simple truth: that the spring thaw would come. The word "naïve," which would to a Marxist-Leninist ideologue

mean "childish" or "uninformed," was here turned upside down.
This voice was unsullied by political demands, stood outside the
realm of money and entertainment ("market" and "circus"), and
was desired by the free man. Nor was it of foreign origin, like the
popular dances mentioned in the fifth stanza.[40] It persisted where one
would not expect survival, even in extreme frost, or pressed and dried
like a flower between the pages of a book, or perhaps between the
poem's lines. And the "girl" who preserved these memories gained
concrete form in the film by Rolands Kalniņš. The song played in
the soundtrack while the camera panned across the Rīga skyline as
seen from the Academy of Sciences Building, halting at the words,
"We gave it to a girl," when the distant, hazy shadow of the pre-
Soviet Freedom Monument arrived at center screen. The figure of the
woman who stands at the top of this monument was not in focus,
but Latvians would know that she was there, nevertheless, a symbol
of independence from wicked censorship, sullied consciences, and
the Soviet Union.

ROCK SONGS REJECT THE LEADING ROLE
OF THE COMMUNIST PARTY

Two massive celebrations in the summer of 1980 gave no sign that
ethnic issues were coming to a head in Estonia. The national song
festival was held earlier than usual, on July 5–6, to accommodate the
Summer Olympics, whose sailing events were hosted in Tallinn from
July 22 through August 1. Major renovations added to the excitement. In addition to the construction of hotels and sailing facilities,
the entire city was painted, its façades and streets renovated and
repaired. But tensions were building below the surface. The year 1978
saw a shift regarding Soviet policy toward non-Russian nationalities.
The Central Committee of the Communist Party decreed that Russian-
language instruction and use should be intensified at all levels of education, from kindergarten to university. The head of the local Estonian Communist Party was removed, to be replaced by Karl Vaino, an
ethnic Estonian born in Russia who did not speak Estonian. Policies
of economic development produced a steady stream of Russian-speak-
ing immigrants, attracted by apartments and jobs that were denied to
Estonians.[41]

The seeming calm dissipated on September 22, when mass protests
broke out after a cancelled rock concert. It began calmly enough, with

an exhibition soccer game between the employees of Estonian Radio and Estonian Television in Tallinn's Kadriorg Stadium. To increase attendance, the organizers invited the popular band Propeller to perform during intermissions. Instead of the usual small group of friends and relatives, about seven thousand people arrived at the stadium, not to watch the game but for the concert. Propeller's lead singer, Peeter Volkonski, recalled,

> Some people came onto the grass, waving hands to the music. This scared them. The supposed reason was that they'd tear up the grass. Lord God! There weren't thousands of people out there on the grass. Some ran on the grass, but I said that "the game is beginning, we'll play again afterwards. Please return to your seats." Everybody went back to their seats very calmly. There was no problem. But somebody got nervous. I don't know who gave the orders, but we were sent notice that we weren't allowed to play after the match. I said that "we have to obey orders, but you'll see for yourself what happens afterwards." We packed up our equipment.
>
> And then the match ended, I don't even remember if the radio or television team won. The prizes were vegetables. Carrots, cabbages, turnips and so on. And then the winning team made a joke, and just like primadonnas and great actors who toss their flowers into the crowd, they tossed those carrots, cabbages and turnips to the public. It was very funny. But the public began to chant, "Propa! Propa!" Because that was the promise. And I had told them, too, that we'd be playing. And suddenly they started throwing those carrots, cabbages and turnips. A policeman got hit in the head with a cabbage or turnip.[42]

About thirty people were on the field when ten police cars surrounded and arrested them. Events snowballed into a larger protest against Soviet power through October, when two hundred factory workers went on a sympathy strike supporting Solidarity in Poland. Several thousand secondary school students took to the streets, shouting slogans that called for Estonia's freedom from Russian rule.[43] Popular memory records that during these two weeks of disorder, two trams were overturned, red flags were torn down, and a crowd shouted "Free Estonia!" "Russian language out of schools!" "Down with Gretškina (Minister of Education)!" and "Brezhnev, Retire!" [44] Many more arrests followed. The soccer game's organizers, Estonian Radio manager Tiit Karuks and announcer Mart Ummelas, lost their jobs because of "lax political vigilance" and failure to prevent the disorders. Propeller was banned, again, and its music forbidden in broadcasts (a joke maintained that all airplane propellers were confiscated at the airport, too).[45] Police used physical force to stop the demonstrations, and participants were all branded violent "hooligans," despite the fact that very few had in fact taken part in vandalism. An open letter signed by forty Estonian cultural and scholarly leaders declared that the problem was related to the recent changes in Soviet nationalities policy, and called for public discussion of ethnic issues in Estonia. Their letter was followed by two others in 1982. These Estonian calls for openness were not answered; instead, the forty signers were punished by police and employers. Another Communist Party resolution in 1983 decreed measures to expand Russian-language teaching. Government repression of political dissidents intensified. Mart Niklus and Jüri Kukk, supporters of the call for a North European nuclear free zone, were arrested, and Kukk died in prison shortly afterward.[46]

Rock music in Estonia existed somewhere between official and unofficial cultures. Estonian bands played at the cutting edge of 1970s Soviet rock music, and many of them were integrated into the professional music circuit: among others, Tõnis Mägi, Ivo Linna, Jaak Joala, Anne Veski, and the bands Fix, Apelsin, and Kuldne Trio traveled on concert tours to Russia and other Soviet republics, and their performances were broadcast on television. At a time when rock was rarely published officially, the Estonian branch of Melodiya produced many cassette recordings. Illegal nighttime access to a professional studio yielded high-quality underground recordings that even slipped into radio broadcasts. In 1979, rock gained an institutional foothold at Tartu University, where Rein Lang, Erki Berends, and Riho Illak started an annual overview concert of Estonian bands and occasional guests from outside the country. Attendance was by invitation only and restricted to four hundred persons. Tartu Music Days performers received only lodging and food, and yet they competed intensely for an invitation to this "laboratory" of innovative music where nighttime jam sessions were even more exciting than the scheduled daytime concerts. Estonian administrators were scolded in Moscow for allowing such an event to take place at all, but they replied that the music could better be controlled if it was in full view on stage and not in secret, informal concerts.[47] Estonian rock's influence reached beyond the country's borders. Among many others, the Latvian rocker Pīts Andersons, and Lithuanians such as Vytautas Kernagis recalled that they would hitchhike to Tallinn to watch Finnish TV and to see Estonians performing their own rock. But for Estonians themselves, the musical form's effect was multiplied by the words.[48]

Rein Rannap, leader the Estonian band Ruja (established 1971), recalls, "Everything we did was, of course, self-expression, but on the other hand we tried to wake and disturb people, to disturb them in the sense that they would not be at peace, to make them think."[49] In a 1981 song, Ruja's lead singer Urmas Alender spat out words with no melody, accompanied by harsh punk guitar, making images of prosperity sound ugly:

> Yesterday I saw Estonia!
> Finnish saunas, summer cottages,
> I saw bars, I saw beaches,
> I saw fancy garages!
> Yesterday I saw Estonia!
>
> Yesterday I saw Estonia!
> Broad, smooth asphalt,
> Tight breasts and butts
> in nylon and texa-pants!
> Yesterday I saw Estonia!
>
> Yesterday I saw Estonia!
> Cresting waves of oil slicks,
> Flocks of numbered cattle.
> No shadows, time enchanting!
> Yesterday I saw Estonia!

At first glance, the song corresponds nicely to Soviet government campaigns against evil Western culture: grating music denigrated American-sounding "texa-pants" and "Finnish" saunas. Anticapitalism and anticonsumerism were officially allowed. In line with government ideas, the song seemed to attack the widespread subservience to Western fashions such as jeans and nylons. But the line about "smooth asphalt roads" was incongruous, because the Soviet streets and roads were notoriously full of potholes. Perhaps the song conjured up the city of Tallinn spruced up for the 1980 Olympics, with an artificial mask of painted facades and one well-renovated road from the city center to the regatta harbor. Perhaps the song presented Estonia in the enticing images seen on Finnish television that were, in reality, beyond the reach of Estonians. Oil slicks spilled on the sea exposed careless environmental damage that one could see in any Soviet harbor, and the disconcerting image of cattle with numbers stamped on their backs was associated with a slaughterhouse. The song's text was not explicit. It carried multiple meanings, but all of them were as disturbing as the music, spoiling the complacency of everyday life in the Soviet Union. It rejected Soviet socialist realist "idea-ness" and "optimism."

The song also had another meaning that didn't, and still doesn't, translate easily into other languages. It referred back to an early twentieth-century poem by Juhan Liiv, who wrote in the tradition of incisive, sarcastic self-criticism that is deeply rooted in Estonian culture. Liiv's poem once described an Estonian intellectual wasteland, "Place of snoozing and deformity, spiritual world so dim and silent."[50] In this intertextual context, Ruja's attack on images of extravagant, materialistic leisure targeted neither the Soviet Union nor the West but rather engaged a long-standing self-reflexive discourse within the traditions of Estonian nation building, a world apart from Soviet or Western culture. Just as Liiv had subverted romantic nationalist images of an idyllic country life, so Ruja unveiled the ugliness of an Estonia that might be based on the consumption of material things, Soviet or not. Ruja sang many equally unsettling texts, published and unpublished. The music erased the ambiguity from the poems' printed versions, transforming ideas once hidden between the lines into clear expressions of truth. Rannap would later recall, "Our basic weapon was irony, anger, and scorn; we sang about all kinds of government officials and about the system. We also turned attention to fatherland themes and spiritual issues; we sang about UFOs, god, and everything that was forbidden."[51]

Other Estonian rock groups, too, openly broke Soviet social norms and moral rules. Band names such as Coma (*Kooma*) and Drug Addict (*Narkomaan*) were common until government agencies simply began assigning benign names. On stage, only scripted and approved words were allowed, but the rule was not observed. In between songs, for example, a singer in the band Apelsin would call out the name of the city where they performed, and the audience would respond enthusiastically; the singer was told to stop, but he continued until the band's performance permit was revoked. In the mid-1970s, Joel Steinfeldt broke a microphone stand on stage; at another concert, he sang, "I brush my teeth with blood!" and spat red liquid. Others told political jokes between songs, or sang a Soviet schoolchildren's song, "Lenin Is With Us," accompanied by obscene gestures. Peeter Volkonski of Propeller read official Soviet poetry aloud, exposing its vacuous content.[52] Police stopped performances for seemingly trivial reasons. Around 1979 in Tallinn, police shut off electricity to silence an audience's enthusiastic calls for encores. After another concert, a bottle of water on stage—supposedly alcohol—and bottle corks found on the hall floor were the official reason for cancelling Ruja's rehearsal and performance permits. In Estonia, it was considered a mark of honor for a group to have been banned at least once, and most singers and groups were punished repeatedly. Performance or broadcast bans varied from several months to several years, but rock musicians usually regained legal status because their concert proceeds gave the philharmonic a critical source of income.[53]

The Soviets attacked other aspects of rock culture with mixed results. Regarding the traditional energy sources of rock music worldwide –sex, drugs, and alcohol—little could be done other than policing behavior at concerts. Hippie fashions such as bell-bottom jeans were too widespread to stop, but the policy toward real hippies was mixed: they were often arrested, beaten, and forced to get haircuts; some were committed to insane asylums and subjected to painful medication. People wearing punk chains or spiked hair were treated as "asocial elements" and held under legal provisions that were tenuous even by Soviet law. One Estonian punk rocker, for example, recalled that in 1985 he was arrested and, based on a fabricated dermatological diagnosis, locked up at a clinic for communicable sexual and skin diseases. Such arrests continued into the early months of 1987.[54] The words of rock songs were subject to the traditional Soviet rules. There could be no compromise regarding Western rock poetry's ideological core, which rejected an older generation's conservative political and moral values. Such content challenged the Communist Party's leading role, and was censored.

But young audiences could see and hear the difference between the purportedly free, exuberant performances of officially approved Soviet bands and the true rock songs that surged through cracks in the system. Singers and audiences were unambiguously told by Soviet officials when their music did not conform to Soviet norms. And so, if one wished to disengage from Soviet power, all one needed to do was break the rules: play "overly loud," "unmelodic" music; listen to songs sung in an unschooled voice or in English; wear a mohawk or uncombed, shoulder-length hair. In the West, rock's nonconformist essence could be absorbed by the ideology of liberal democracy, but in the Soviet world, a single person's refusal to participate in the official structures was a threat to "collective-ness," and, along with that, a threat to the entire ideological system. Rock music offered more than simply a youthful rebellion against the older generation. Ryback convincingly argues that it was one of the only available outlets for open expression. For the two decades from the mid-sixties to the mid-eighties in the Soviet Union, rock music was a refuge, a place where a person could live within the truth and find others who did the same. William Husband adds that rock thus also gave people rudimentary experience in group mobilization and group protest.[55]

Change was brewing in the Communist Party and the Soviet government. In 1982, Leonid Brezhnev passed away, to be replaced by Yurii Andropov, a leader whose public image maintained that he enjoyed "jazz" music but who oversaw a wave of repression against political dissidents and rock musicians alike. After Andropov's sudden death fifteen months later, power passed to the aging conservative Konstantin Chernenko, who himself passed away in March of 1985. Then, Mikhail Gorbachev stepped to power and announced a new program of economic restructuring ("perestroika") to be supported by open public discussion of policy ("glasnost"), and, "in a moment of gentle candor," he revealed that he was an admirer of John Lennon. Glasnost relaxed the censorship of art and lifted restrictions on rock music's access to public stages and the mass media.[56]

Estonian punk rocker Villu Tamme was quick to respond with the song "Hello, Perestroika." The song's first stanza proclaimed hyperbolically enthusiastic support for the new government campaign. But then, as if in passing, the song spoke the truth about the Soviet system: It was a dictatorship, not democracy. The red flag was a symbol of grisly violence. Newspapers lied. Films and music were banned. Punks were persecuted.[57]

> The sky is cloudless now, the sea is bright and blue,
> Every human breathes now with a full chest too.
> The hammer and the sickle don't hit us anymore,
> Nowadays they signify only joyful work.
>
> > Hello, perestroika and democracy.
> > A land slips from the sharp claws of dictatorship,
> > Hello, perestroika, hello, peak of joy,
> > The red flag just doesn't feel grisly anymore.
>
> The tractor plows the field, and the tree bears fruit;
> *People's Voice* does not lie, its mouth does not breathe smoke.
> Forbidden films are running in every theater.
> Forbidden bands' music is also everywhere.
>
> > Hello, perestroika and democracy,
> > It's nice to slip from the sharp claws of dictatorship.

> Hello, perestroika, hello, liberty,
> Everyone now sings the songs of Pioneers.
> Auuu auuu
>
> The policeman's uniform no longer makes you retch;
> Nowadays it glimmers like a silver brooch.
> Look, now the policeman and the punk are friends,
> Happily they're shaking one another's hand.
>
> > Hello, perestroika, tralla trallallee,
> > The land now belongs to only you and me.
> > Every year a jubilee—the Great Month of Booze,
> > The people all jubilate, yippee auuu
> > Auuu auuu.
>
> The wells in Virumaa will never go dry,
> By the Mausoleum an airship now can fly.
> Well what do you say now, democracy's so big,
> You are so amazed now, your mouth it hangs agape.
>
> > Hello, perestroika, joyful homeland true,
> > I will say hello to you, as long as I get you.
> > Hello, perestroika, and democracy,
> > Hello perestroika, come give your paw to me.

If Soviet repression was truly coming to an end, then drunken jubilation was due. But Tamme expressed some doubt: "I'll say hello to you, as long as I get you," he commented, hinting that perestroika was a sham. In conversational Estonian, the expression "Give me your paw" was an informal, friendly invitation to shake hands, but the song's ironic tone redefined that phrase, instead reminding the public that it faced a dangerous partnership, possibly shaking hands with a wolf in sheep's clothing.

In 1987, a glasnost-era documentary film by Latvian director Juris Podnieks, *Is It Easy to Be Young?* broke the public silence on issues formerly banned from the mass media. Rock music gives the film its artistic frame. It opens at a rock concert, with a surging audience barely held back by security guards, and stone-faced elderly people looking on. Afterward, masses of youths crowd into a commuter train, and then the rhythmic rumble of metal wheels on steel tracks accompanies desolate shots of a train's vandalized interior.[58] Podnieks tracked down and interviewed persons he filmed at the concert, weaving them into an impressionistic collage that confirmed Soviet beliefs in rock's detrimental effect on human behavior:

"That music got everybody there started—it's natural."

"What do you now think about that concert?" "If it were a song festival, it wouldn't be anything special, just a song festival. Everything
according to the norm. But now, after that concert, young people go
crazy like that, they do terrible things."

"You were in such ecstasy there, I think I've filmed you more than
anybody else!" "I was just very excited about Pērkons. This was an
isolated incident, I believe."

"At this moment I feel like a beast. In all of my behavior, in my
attitude, I still feel like a beast. I haven't yet grown up to where I
should."[59]

The apparently aggressive behavior of Pērkons fans introduces Podnieks's documentary about young people in the Soviet Union. Students,
artists, punks, drug addicts, a morgue employee, disabled veterans of
the war in Afghanistan, Hare Krishna, and an attempted suicide all
speak candidly in front of the camera, capturing the spirit of the times.
The young people feel alienated, but anomie gives way to optimistic
energy. A teenaged girl has a baby, and feels responsibility. Youths vol-
unteer to clean up the Old Town. An amateur filmmaker documents
his generation's fears and hopes, and clips of his film are inserted in
Podnieks's documentary. Boys become firemen after military service.
And the violence with which the film began is punished: seven young
men are tried for vandalism in a show trial where six are released on
probation, and one sentenced to three years in a labor camp.

Is It Easy To Be Young? was a key text in the history of perestroika,
produced while the reforms were underway, intended for immediate
consumption both within and outside of the USSR.[60] It announced
that public discussion was now permitted regarding formerly taboo
topics—suicide, drugs, punks, death, teen pregnancy, and the war in
Afghanistan. The film also carried a message that youths were optimistic, and that their idealism could be harnessed to rejuvenate Soviet
society.[61] To Soviet audiences, the film presented people who spoke
their minds freely, giving a sense of what real democracy could be.[62]

Regarding the film's portrayal of rock, however, the music historian Māris Ruks writes, "There are good episodes, a good sequence
of images, but the true essence somehow slipped away. The director is
like a programmed guide, who, while showing the Egyptian pyramids
or Roman amphitheaters or the London Metro, continues telling a dil-
igent narrative about the Kremlin of Kazan."[63] The film included rock
music but did not unlock the riddle of its meaning in the Baltic, or, for
that matter, in the Soviet Union. Did rockers instigate vandalism, as

the film insinuated? And, by extension, would rock music's popularity in the Baltic foment nationalist aggression in the massive independence movements that soon emerged? Its form—loud, uncontrolled, and offensive to the ears—seemed to forebode violence in the Baltic Singing Revolution.

Soviet censors followed a belief that Western rock music not only led to sexual depravity but also caused violence, and that it should not be allowed. This official view remained in place from the late 1960s to the late 1980s.[64] Antirock policies seemed to be justified in the mid-1980s by Soviet rumors about fascist Baltic punks beating and killing ethnic Russians; Timothy Ryback, historian of Soviet rock, quotes the unsubstantiated rumors as if they were a shocking fact.[65]

The Latvian band Pērkons, whose concert was documented in Podnieks's film, did not cause violence, even if Soviet officials said so when they banned Pērkons from the stage for four years. The group started in 1980, when three musicians from Imants Kalniņš's group, Menuets, established their own band. Juris Kulakovs, Juris Sējāns, and Raimonds Bartaševics were joined by the singer Ieva Akurātere, who proposed the group's name, Pērkons ("Thunder").[66] Pērkons's musical credo was a poem by that title, written a century earlier by the classic poet Rūdolfs Blaumanis: "It fills my heart with passion, walking through the halls of nature, ever pleasant and uplifting, beauty unified with power." Most of the group's first song texts were poems published in 1978 by their friend Māris Melgalvs, who nurtured warm humanity in an ugly environment of piglike beasts:

No matter if it's friends or beasts
Who stand ahead of you,
The main thing is a budding branch
That blossoms inside you.

Another song that would later be misconstrued by the Soviet police as a violent attack on ("red") Communism was in fact about squelched pangs of conscience. "Ballad about a Swan" revived an image from the banned 1967 film *Four White Shirts* in which hunters senselessly kill a swan in a metaphor of the Soviet destruction of artistic freedom.[67] Heavy metal guitar blasted the accompaniment for Ieva Akurātere when she screamed the final, ironic words of the swan killer who continues his senseless violence:

Bony crow
On a wet tombstone,

It rattles its own truth at me.
Did it really not understand that all of this is just for fun?
　　How very dumb
　　To kill a swan
　　And dumber yet if there's regret,
Then it gets stupider than hell—a red swan glows in each sunset
　　So stupidly it glows that
　　You must hit again.

The group performed at small venues, its concerts advertised only by word of mouth. On January 31, 1983, police heavily patrolled the first of six planned concerts in Rīga, and on the next day, an official order was given to cancel the concerts. Kulakovs was summoned to the Ministry of Culture. He later recalled that Vladimirs Kaupužs, the minister himself, screamed at him, "I'll stick you into prison! I'll stick you into prison for traumatizing the hearing of Soviet citizens!" Kaupužs issued a report and a decree:

> During the concert on January 31, 1983, at 20:00 o'clock, the behavior of a portion of the concert audience surpassed generally accepted norms (noise, whistling and shouting in the hall, as well as other hooligan transgressions). It must be emphasized that the manner of performance, with overly loud, stupefying sound, and the behavior of the ensemble members on stage, as well as their appearance (hair, stage apparel), encouraged and attracted a certain category of audience. This created unbearable conditions in the hall. . . .
>   The concerts planned for February 2, 1983, were cancelled, to prevent the repetition of similar incidents. It is characteristic that the author of a majority of the works performed was the group's leader, J. Kulakovs. It is his compositions in particular that evoked the unhealthy reaction of a certain portion of the audience. . . .
>   1. Taking into account the low ideological and artistic level of the concert program, revoke the right of the . . . ensemble to perform concerts until a new program is prepared and approved according to the required process.[68]

Immediately after the banned concert, the group converted Ieva Akurātere's apartment into a recording studio and produced a cassette that diffused with lightning speed throughout the Latvian underground market. One of the cassette's twenty songs, titled "Song to Protest Environmental Pollution," was an unpublished 1978 poem by Māris Melgalvs that was unambiguous in its scorn for the Soviet authorities, with the last line screamed three times, "And there's really nothing fatter than the pigs that we honor!"[69] The song countered the Soviet government's censorship policy ("Shut your mouth!") with a liberating folk incantation, "Bonds upon bonds hold you, I untie them all," and taunted adversaries with a parody of a children's game song, turning free speech into a fart that stank up Soviet space.

> Whoever must, whoever must, whoever must fall in the pit,
> Nobody anywhere can ever kill them easily. (repeat stanza)
>
> And if by some chance it does happen to somebody,
>
> Shut your mouth shut your mouth, shut your mouth up in your pocket. (repeat line three times)
>
> Maybe some day some good use may turn up somewhere for your mouth,
> Maybe patching up an old coat, propping up a falling house. (repeat stanza)
>
> Bonds upon bonds hold you, I untie them all.
>
> Me and my little game stunk up the entire room. (repeat line three times)
>
> On the table, sweet sweet milk,
> Honey too, thick but transparent.
> If you don't get lost in porridge,
> You can grab the honey then.
> (repeat stanza)
>
> And there's really nothing nicer
> Than the big big honey pot,
>   And there's really nothing fatter than the pigs that we honor! (repeat line three times)

That year, Kulakovs was not allowed to take the final exams at the conservatory. He did not heed this official hint that he should withdraw from his studies, and returned the following year to pass his exams. In 1985, two years after the first ban, Pērkons found a new sponsor at a collective farm that, ironically, carried the name "Soviet Latvia." In principle, the band's legal status was now renewed, but in practice their "Category 3" classification limited their performances to the sponsor's community hall. In other words, Pērkons was still not allowed to perform anywhere in Latvia, although some concert organizers ignored this rule. On July 6, 1985, after the concert filmed by Juris Podnieks, the band's confrontation with Soviet power came to a head.

The content of Pērkons's songs, whether sung, crooned, screamed, or growled, was hardly violent. In *Is It Easy to Be Young?* the crowd surged toward the stage during "Noise," a song about a desperate search for peace and quiet.[70] The film's concluding song, "By a Blank Page," longed for "one tender caress" and words that would help people meet each other.[71] The Latvian audience's unacceptable behavior—rushing up and dancing by the stage—was one pretext for Soviet cultural administrators to ban the group's public performances. But the film shows only several hundred teenagers standing by the stage, smiling, dancing, and clapping or clasping hands in the air. Several thousand more remained seated. The musicians remember that the audience at this concert, like many others before it, was calm, sincere, and friendly; there was no vandalism on the concert grounds, and this was the only Pērkons concert ever followed by any vandalism at all. The disorder on the train after the concert might have been the work of government provocateurs.[72]

The official version remained, however, that Pērkons and rock music had instigated violence in Latvia. The second secretary of the Communist Party Central Committee, Valentin Dmitriev, ordered the minister of culture to halt the group's performances, and reprimanded the minister of the interior for the policemen's failure to maintain order. The Central Committee summoned Kulakovs to a meeting, where the head of the propaganda bureau told him that his song about the swan, quoted above, was actually a song about "hitting" the "red," in other words, it encouraged anti-Soviet violence. He was told to emigrate to the West, where rock stars like he would be worshipped. He was later again not allowed to take exams at the conservatory, and all cultural agencies in Latvia were forbidden to give him a job. Kulakovs did not obey the order to leave Latvia, however, and survived on his working wife's income. The group's musicians were banned from Latvia's stages, reemerging in public only two years later, at the February 1987 funeral of the murdered Latvian poet Klāvs Elsbergs.[73]

Meanwhile, heavy metal music was breaking out onto public stages, and a song by the band Līvi, "Native Language," grew to massive popularity. Official critics were irritated by the rough, cutting voice of Jānis Grodums. "A voice like that," recalls rock historian Uldis Rudaks, "comes from smoking a lot and drinking lots of strong drink."[74] In earlier years, Soviet government agencies could manipulate the results of annual "popularity polls," and the practice was still present in 1986. Rock music was still officially expected to be "beautiful" in form. Radio Latvia's musical editor warned the band that they needed to replace their lead singer, or their song would be pushed out of first place. But Imants Kalniņš, composer of the second-most-popular song, threatened to withdraw from the competition—and third in line would be another song by Līvi. The competition organizers conceded defeat, and "Native Language" was awarded first prize.[75]

Behind the scenes, it was probably not only the singer's voice but also the song's text that raised red flags among judges. The Soviet Union advertised itself as the home of flourishing national cultures, but "Native Language" called that image into question. Its understood reference was to Latvia's population crisis, which, as in Estonia, stemmed from the mass killings, deportations and emigration of the Stalinist era, exacerbated in the 1970s by Soviet Russian language policy and the continued mass immigration of persons who did not speak Latvian; Latvians were fast being turned into a minority in all urban centers.[76] The song presented a national identity of Latvians as an endangered nation. Images of death and silence warned that the language could die, and, along with it, the nation:

All the people weep
In a shared language
In a shared language—
They laugh, too.
Pain is only stilled
In the native language,
To the world it gives
Happiness in songs.

    (refrain:)
    In your native tongue
    Mother is mother
    In your native tongue
    Wine tastes sweeter.
    In your native tongue
    Laugh quietly to yourself.

And when you cannot
Laugh nor weep,
When you cannot do
Anything no more,
You'll be silent, silent
Like the sky and earth,
It will be in the
Language of your birth.

    (refrain)

The song drew on a core principle of nationalism, that language was fundamental to every person's identity and existence. The first word that humans learn is "mother," and it does not feel the same in languages other than one's own. Language-based national identity was not uniquely Latvian; the song's words in fact were adapted from a poem by Moldovan poet Grigore Vieru, as translated by Imants Ziedonis.[77] It was an anguished lament, "Softly weeping, then taking flight, pulling along everything on earth into the sky; Grodums sounded like an organ, like an orchestra of organs, expanded by the others' voices in the refrain."[78] The song gave voice to pain, and identified a threat of the Latvian nation's destruction under Soviet rule.

In 1986, while Podnieks was completing *Is It Easy to Be Young?* in Rīga, Lithuanian director Artūras Pozdniakovas created another Glasnost-era rock film, *Something Just Happened.* Here, a series of eleven songs fell into three chapters: "Retro," "Festival," and "Dreams." Relegated to the humorous "Retro" chapter were two older songs by "the founder of sung poetry," Vytautas Kernagis, filmed in the jerky style and quirky costumes of early twentieth century cinema. Kernagis himself regretted that these songs did not reflect his current repertoire, but in the film, they were a foil, museum antiquities that contrasted with the music that followed.[79] In the "festival" chapter, two contemporary rock bands, Foje and Antis, played outdoors at Kalnų Park in Vilnius. Their standing, cheering audience was held back by a line of policemen, but the film did not linger on the audience. Its focus was the songs, and particularly the songs sung by Antis's leader, Algirdas Kaušpėdas, whom the emcee on stage hyped as "photogenic and scenographic, a person who is able to speak and, it seems, has something to say." His first song told the personal moral conflict of living within a lie:

> Classmates are trying to convince me—be an actor
> The teacher is trying to convince me—be an actor
>   Why?
>   Don't you know why?
> I will need to talk according to the script every day
> I will have to cry sadly every night . . . [80]

Antis's second song, "Something Just Happened," gave the film its title. On one level, this was a song about love, addressing Martynas, a loser whose hopes of winning the girl of his dreams will be mercilessly dashed to pieces. A line from the triumphantly scornful refrain "Not for you, Martynas, the blue sky above," soon passed into conversational folklore as a proverbial expression commenting on silly, unrealistic hopes.

> Something just happened—a girl was angered,
> In the middle of a movie, she skipped out on a boy.
> The boy Martynas, in the middle of the movie,
> Tried to catch the girl and stop her by the door.
> > Ho-ho, ho-ho, ho-ho-ho
> > Ho-ho, ho-ho, ho-ho-ho
>
> Something just happened—the boy was shaken,
> He cannot forget her, that lovely lady.
> He struggled to please her, bought some wine for her,
> Again he made an error—and the girl was angered.
>
> > (refrain:)
> > Not for you, Martynas, the blue sky above,
> > Not for you, my friend, the rose-petal pathway,
> > You'll have to go back home now by yourself,
> > Martynas, go look for a simpler lady.
>
> Something then happened, the boy just withered,
> Conversations go wrong, everywhere he screws up.
> The damned little lady—how to find the right key,
> How can he get back now his one and only hope?
>
> > (refrain, repeated twice)

On another level, the song's words rejected the notion that youths could be co-opted to support the older generation's political power. Something really did happen in 1986. For the first time in Soviet history, the government allowed free speech to a younger generation, probably hoping to engage, and then bribe, woo, or seduce their music into service to the state. Things were going well in Moscow. Artemy Troitsky recalled that a benefit rock concert supporting the victims of Chornobyl "established rock as a positive social force and proved that rockers are not just a doubtful bunch of hooligans but real patriots." He enthusiastically quoted the words of Antis's leader: "We are called a 'Gorbachev' band in Lietuvania [sic!]"[81] But the name "Antis" is the Lithuanian word for "duck," a word used in slang to mean "false story released by the government." It could also mean "anti-S" ("against-Soviet"), and on stage and on screen, Kaušpėdas's smirking, stone-cold face threw icy water on Gorbachev's intents, rejecting prospects for a happy marriage of generations. The political effects of free speech in rock music multiplied with each new concert. Antis's Lithuanian audiences would come to associate Martynas with the Soviet government in Moscow, a crude boy whose clueless attempt to win the sympathies of Lithuania was doomed to failure. Others would sing the refrain ironically, associating it with Moscow's coarse rebuttal of Lithuania's (Martynas's) desire for freedom.[82] In either case, the song's words could not be loyal to Soviet power in Lithuania.

In the film, the audience's warm reception and cheering fade away, yielding to a rapid series of gripping visual and verbal images in the third chapter, "Dreams," more aptly described as five song-nightmares. "Zombies" accompanies images of a vampire-like creature before whom, motionless, a beautiful woman gazes at the film's audience. He sharpens a razor. In the flash of the song's shocking last seconds, he cuts out the woman's eyes; she is awake, but does not resist.

The melody was an adaptation of the 1980s hit by Men at Work, "Land Down Under," speeded up with a horn section playing the original's flute part in a surreal, cheerfully ominous harmony.[83] Kaušpėdas's death-mask visage disinterestedly reports that zombies are all around, transforming humans into mindless creatures like themselves. The only means of protecting oneself is to "live cleanly."

> Danger came with no warning,
> Rumors fly: Zombies are coming.
> The nerves don't let me sleep at night,
> Zombies prepare to give a painful bite.
>
>> Live as cleanly as you can,
>> The evil ones wake in the tundra.
>> Listen now, listen now can you hear—
>> Zombies are rolling in, thundering.

The nightmarish words intensify through three more Antis songs and documentary clips of war: soldiers attacking with bayonets, faces contorted in rage; fighter planes flying and bombs exploding, leaving burned-out ruins, corpses, and listlessly crawling, emaciated children. The film ends suddenly, leaving its audience in shock.

Something Just Happened did not give an explicit political message other than a general vision of destructive, ugly war, and the idea that war became possible when a society was blinded and turned into "zombies." Audiences might have understood the film to reject militarized society, and, possibly, the Soviet invasion of Afghanistan, but such connotations are difficult to document. The film's political statement was disquieting, even if specific referents were ambiguous. But its stance on rock music was clear. Rock did not cause violence, as implied by the introductory clips of Podnieks's *Is It Easy To Be Young?* Rock music was the genre chosen by a singer "who has something to say," because it offered a means of exposing harsh truths. Antis connected powerfully with audiences in this way. Kaušpėdas recalled, "I like to see people smile during the concert, as if they've just heard some good news which they've wanted to hear for a long time. This was particularly apparent in the time of the Soviet Union."[84]

NATIONAL AWAKENINGS

The purpose of Gorbachev's glasnost was to restructure and strengthen the Soviet economy; open public discussion of environmental policy was allowed within this frame. In the Baltic, however, environmental issues were tied to questions of sovereignty over the country's natural resources, and public discussion inevitably shifted to national sovereignty. Gorbachev hinted that glasnost could now extend into previously censored "blank spots" of Soviet history; in the Baltic, this led to public rejection of the Soviet government's historical legitimacy. It is not surprising that rock songs quickly filled every crack that opened in Soviet censorship during the early Gorbachev era; rock musicians could compose, perform, record, and broadcast new songs more quickly (and loudly) than choral composers and choirs.

On February 25, 1987, an Estonian television broadcast broke news of a massive plan to expand the strip mines in the Virumaa District of northeastern Estonia, for the purpose of extracting phosphorites to be used in agricultural fertilizer. The project would poison an enormous region's groundwater and rivers, destroy large areas of the landscape, and bring in thirty to forty thousand immigrants. Estonian public reaction compounded quickly, creating an unprecedented unity among local environmental clubs, scientists, and progressive members of the Estonian Communist Party.[85]

Rock musician Alo Mattiisen's song "Not a Single Land Is Alone" carried the movement's message. It was aired on the radio only once, against the broadcast manager's orders, several weeks before its live premiere at the Tartu Music Days. This one broadcast sufficed to bring the song national fame. Then, although banned from Soviet airwaves, the song was picked up by Finnish radio stations and broadcast south back across the border.[86]

A lineup of popular musicians recorded this series of stanzas about each of Estonia's districts ("lands"), concluding with Virumaa (Viruland). Through a play of words, the song's political meaning extended beyond the immediate objective of halting the destruction of nature, and revived the idea of Estonian sovereignty over the territory of Estonia. In the last stanza, the meaning of "land" switched from a place-name suffix to "land" as a synonym for "country." If the strip mining plan were to be stopped and Viru-*land*'s groundwater were to remain unpolluted, "Only then I'll be able to say that I live in my own *land*." Not only were all local districts of Estonia called to unite to defend one of their own, but all of the singers in Estonia were considered a single political unit:

> If all the wells of Viru-land
> Can keep their water clean and clear,
> Then I'll be able to say
> That I live in my own land,
> I live in my own land.
>
> > Nature knows, fatherland knows:
> > We must all help each other now.
> > Not a single land is alone,
> > I don't want, can't abandon you, Viru-land!
> > Not a single land is alone.

In the Soviet Union before 1987, policy related to natural resources was directed by the central government in Moscow, not by the national republics. And so, as the "phosphorite war" gained force, it became clear that Estonians were claiming the right not only to stop this particular project but to reclaim sovereignty over their national territory. Just as the song's last stanzas switched from one meaning of "land" to another, so also the environmental movement's meaning expanded from defending one district's local environment to staking a claim on the entire "land" of Estonia.[87]

Meanwhile, rock music was surfacing on public stages, attracting ever larger audiences to concerts organized by leaders who stood outside of official Soviet institutions. In the summer of 1987, a group of nongovernment individuals organized an international "heavy rock" festival, with twenty-six bands and an audience of fifteen thousand. Rock music was liberated, but political expression was restricted to the Soviet frame. Somebody briefly displayed the banned Estonian flag, foreshadowing the national demonstrations that would begin in the following year, but glasnost in 1987 did not include free speech on national issues, and the flag disappeared.[88] The rock musician best known for "fatherland" themes, Ruja's leader Rein Rannap, came under political pressure and emigrated to the USA; he would return to Estonia only after independence was restored.

And in May of 1988, Alo Mattiisen's "Five Fatherland Songs" premiered at the flag-bedecked Tartu Music Days, performed by the singer Ivo Linna, the rock group In Spe, and a vocal sextet, Kiigelaulukuuik. Mattiisen's five songs declared Estonian identity and ideology, and rose together with the blue-black-white flags to fly as a banner of the Estonian Singing Revolution. Linna sang those songs again in June at the Old Town Days and Night Song Festivals in Tallinn, and then toured the country, performing to audiences of unprecedented size. Seven thousand came to the concert in Räpina, for example, exceeding that town's total population by two thousand. This was a new kind of rock music. It broke the age barrier, attracting entire families, from toddlers to elderly grandparents. Alcohol was conspicuous by its absence. The audiences' exuberant energy was also unprecedented, with the cheering and applause often drowning out the music, like the western "Beatlemania" of decades past.[89]

In the memory of many, one phrase from the fifth song's refrain, "I Am Estonian!" encapsulated the meaning of Mattiisen's five songs as a whole; it declared the awakened national identity of each Estonian in the audience. But the texts deserve a closer look, because they expressed, in a concentrated form, ideas basic to Estonian nationalism in 1988. They defined both Estonian identity and the identity of the "other," and proposed action.

The songs built a musical bridge between the heritage of the nineteenth-century national awakening and contemporary politics. An unaccompanied choir or solo singer quoted nineteenth-century songs (marked below by italics), adding a self-aware echo of the national movement's history. Rock was the medium that brought this past into the present.[90]

The first song quoted a poem set to music a century earlier by Friedrich Saebelmann. To the classic nationalist's declaration that he was singing the most beautiful songs, contemporary poet Jüri Leesment added an editorial comment that national culture was never complete, because "the most beautiful songs remained unsung." Modern time melted into mythic time. The image of torches burning at both ends came from the Estonian national epic's prophetic conclusion, where such torches signaled the return of the national hero, Kalevipoeg, to lead the Estonian people to happiness.[91] The recipe for action was clear: Help would not come from above. Those who did not fear threats and who sought freedom would be the ones who moved the nation ahead on its never-ending path.

I give to you the most beautiful songs,
Loved by my ancestors, dear homeland!
My heart beats strongly in my chest
When I sing to you, fatherland!

The most beautiful songs remained unsung,
Lost in endless slogans and pledges and flags.
The most beautiful wishes were not fulfilled,
Lost in harmful senselessness and rubles and sloth.

The longed-for dream, held for eternity,
Torn by winds from all sides,
Something suddenly moved in the bosom—
Did this force come from inside?

The most beautiful songs are still unsung,
And alienation is still undefeated.
The torches that have never yet burned
Now all must ignite at both ends.

I give to you the most beautiful songs,
The most beautiful songs.

The most beautiful speeches remained unheard,
Lost in stupid explanations, accusations, and obfuscations.
The most beautiful melodies remained unplayed,
Lost in low scoldings, sorrows, and senselessness.

Whoever begged for freedom from above,
Feeble and pathetic is he.
Whoever quenched thirst, unmindful of danger,
Clears stones from the road!

(repeat fourth stanza)

Mattiisen's second song, "Go High Up atop the Hills," inverted a nineteenth-century poem by Mihkel Veske. Whereas the older song's refrain exclaimed, "You are beautiful, oh homeland!" the new song's text saw an "ulcer" on the natural landscape: the ugly, mass-produced apartment highrises in Tallinn's suburbs.[92] These city districts, named after "hills," as indicated by the suffix -*mäe* (Lasnamäe, Õismäe, and Mustamäe, meaning Lasna Hill, Õis Hill, and Musta Hill), gave the song a new referent. Immigrants, not Estonians, had preferred access to apartments in these new buildings, and thus the districts around them turned into islands of Soviet culture. The song's declaration that

"Lasna Hill must stop now!" called for a stop to the Soviet government's plans to increase immigration.

As an expression of Estonian ideology in 1988, the song is useful
in its description of the "other," the person whose actions were seen
as contrary to the national mission. The "migrant" was a person who
felt no attachment to the local land, "does not feel or know or see,"
a symptom of the disease inflicted on Estonia by the foreign Soviet
power. For Estonians, the first step was to stop further immigration,
as they had done in 1987 when plans to expand phosphorite mining
were halted (as above, lines quoted from the earlier, quoted song are
marked by italics):

> *Go high up atop the hills,*
> Musta, Õis, or Lasna Hill,
> Gaze down on the people's spirit
> Through the mute and foreign power.
> See there how the heart is aching,
> Wickedness has seized the hand!
>
> > *Shout it loudly to the valley*
> > With all your strength.
> > *Shout it loudly to the valley*:
> > Lasna Hill must stop now!
> > *Shout it loudly to the valley*:
> > Stop it now!
>
> Look, the people's wounded spirit
> Does not heal, there is no cure.
> Any medicine that comes now
> Will arrive much too late.
> Cliff-top city, like an ulcer,
> Endless, far as eyes can see.
> Let's all shout down to the valley
> With all our strength.
>
> > Let's all shout down to the valley:
> > Lasna Hill must stop now!
> > Let's all shout down to the valley:
> > Lasna Hill must stop now!
>
> *Go high up atop the hills,*
> *To the wafting breath of wind.*
> *Gaze below into the valley*
> *Past the splendor of the flowers.*
>
> Look, it's all completely foreign—
> Is this really home to you?

Through the dim and drafty streets
the migrant wanders aimlessly.
Look into his empty eyes,
He doesn't feel or know or see.
Let's all shout down to the valley
With all our strength:

> Let's all shout down to the valley:
> Lasna Hill must stop now!
> Let's all shout down to the valley:
> Stop it now!
> Stop it now!
> Lasna Hill.

Mattiisen's third song reached back through time to the nineteenth-century awakening, while at the same time expressing doubts whether that historical epoch could, in fact, be useful to present actions. It quoted stanzas from Lydia Koidula's poem "You, until Death," whose choral arrangement by Aleksander Kunileid premiered at the first national song festival of 1869, but, as noted in the previous chapter, was sung only once at a Soviet-era festival. It was not a choir who sang the old song, however, but rather a modern singer's solo vulnerable voice testified his identity. The melody shifted. A pensive rock tune accompanied a modern voice questioning the nineteenth-century poem's relevance. But, just as clover and aspen in the landscape were the same then as now, so people still needed to communicate on a personal level of truth and trust, as Koidula had once done in her poem: "What comes from a soul, reaches the soul." The song found a unity among Estonians of the present and poets and singers of Estonia's past. One of the singers, Riina Roose, remembers that, for her, this was the most beautiful song of the five:[93]

Until my death I shall hold you
As my beloved one,
My blossoming Estonian path,
My fragrant fatherland!

Oh land, how tenderly you carry
Your children on your arms,
You give them bread and shelter,
And a final resting place!

> Can these same words, and their tune
> Hold us all together?
> Nowadays, just like back then,

Clover blooms and aspens quake.

But yet, in your eyes
I often find your tears?
To hope, oh My Estonia,
That times are changing now!

Just the same words, and their tune,
These persistent signs,
Just as simply as back then,
Clover blooms and aspens quake.

So pious are your sons,
How brave and strong they are!
Your daughters are like flowers,
So beautiful, they bloom!

Can the same words and their tune
Hold us all together?
Nowadays, just like back then,
What comes from the soul, reaches a soul.[94]

The fourth song, "Guarding the Fatherland's Beauty" (translated in chapter 1), quoted lines from the national epic by Friedrich Kreutzwald, as set to music by K. A. Hermann (translated in chapter 4). It presented the national movement's ideology: that every Estonian should assume individual responsibility and morality, and continue the mission inherited from the nineteenth century. The performance was a ritual in folk song style, where line by line was chanted by the lead singer, then repeated by thousands in the audience. The fifth "Fatherland Song" concluded the series with an optimistic pledge of allegiance to the nation, "I Am Estonian" (also translated in chapter 1), a line borrowed from another nineteenth-century song.

In June of 1988, the potential for real change was tangible, first of all, in the simple fact that there was true freedom of speech and assembly. Radically new perspectives opened up a few months earlier on February 24, when, for the first time under Soviet occupation, a public commemoration of Estonia's Independence Day was not stopped by the Soviet police. On April 1–2, the Estonian creative unions adopted a formal statement criticizing the Communist leaders of Estonia, and a speaker publicly proposed that Estonia could again exist outside the USSR. The movement to establish a national nongovernmental organization, the Estonian Popular Front (Rahvarinne) was initiated on April 13. On April 14–17 in Tartu, the Estonian Heritage Society displayed the illegal blue, black, and white colors as three separate banners, and a young actor, Jaak Johansen, revived the words to the song "Estonia's Flag."[95] Within a few more weeks, flags at the Tartu Music Days and at the Night Song Festivals in Tallinn confirmed the exhilarating awareness that true independence really was possible.

But 1988 also saw the activization of organizations aiming to preserve Soviet power in Estonia, and an intensified surge of anti-Estonian and anti-Baltic propaganda. In the Russian-language mass media as well as internationally, Soviet officials energetically disseminated an image of Estonians, Latvians, and Lithuanians and their nonformal organizations as "fascists" intent on sowing national hatred and ethnic violence.[96] They prepared the ground for violent repression, if the Soviet government were to use violence in the future.

The best defense against Soviet defamation, and, indeed, the only possible defense, was an intensification of nonviolent politics. The first public statement to explicitly define the Baltic nations' massive political awakening as a nonviolent singing movement was an editorial by the Estonian artist Heinz Valk. On the morning of June 12, after the Night Song Festival, he drank his morning coffee and penned the historic essay that was published on June 17, giving it a title that gave the movement its name:

Singing Revolution

The current revolutionary process in Estonia has a powerfully intellectual character. The likely reason for this is a small nation's instinctive shrewd choice, recognizing its deficit of power, to make a revolution with the help of powerful pressure from large masses of people. It is impossible to even imagine in Estonia's city streets the riots, barricades, burning automobiles, and similar features of mass revolt by large nations. This is not our way! Our only weapon is the mind, and up to now we have used it admirably. . . .

For a long time, song was the only available and legal means for Estonians to openly express their thoughts and protests. For several decades one such expression has been "My Fatherland Is My Beloved." The song festivals' goal and purpose came to be the experiencing of unity among thousands of people in this song's solemn, intoxicating performance. This is, perhaps, a unique event in world history: to prepare extensively for five years, to come together from all over the country, to swallow the whims and impediments of the weather and the powers that be, and to endure all of this enormous work and worries, just to have the opportunity to sing this song, to hear it, and to carry it on in the heart! This is our nation's most glorious form of self expression, a cultural phenomenon worthy of presentation to all peoples! . . .

And now the most recent event, the Estonian people's Night Song Festival on the Song Festival Stage on June 10 and 11, 1988! I will say from the outset that participation in this festival compensated for decades of humiliation and self-denial. This was a most magnificent demonstration, the likes of which has never been seen in film or on television, in dreams or awake. A singing, rhythmically moving, happy mass of people, tens upon tens of fluttering national flags, smiles on their faces, unity, no malice, no hostility, only one word in the heart: Estonia! I said it was a happy mass of people. No! This word is too weak to express what truly happened there. This was happiness multiplied a million times; it was something even larger and even more essential. A film of the event should be broadcast throughout the Soviet Union. Then it wouldn't be possible to follow the provocateurs and stupid agitators and call us nationalists, enemies of socialism, fascists, and devil knows what else.

A nation who makes its revolution by singing and smiling should be a sublime example to all. A people like this should not be scorned, mocked, or—worst of all, pressed anew into the slavery of dictatorship! A people like this should never again be beaten down with its face in the mud! With their actions, they have earned the irrefutable right to exist under their blue sky on their hereditary fatherland. I am proud to be a member of such a people![97]

Emotions ran deep at the mass events of 1988. Tears flowed freely. "It was emotionally such an important moment, you truly don't need to explain to yourself why, what you are fighting for, why the tear comes to the eye, but that's how it was. For many this was somehow a very pure and clear, sublime moment," recalled Immo Mihkelson.[98] A leader of the movement, Marju Lauristin, saw danger: "I was sitting there and looking at the people and it was like an ocean. With every speech that ocean began to wave more and more because the emotions were coming higher and higher. It was a moment of great risk. If someone had lit a match, it could have easily caused a fire that no one could have safely extinguished."[99] Any act of violence, large or small, could provoke a Soviet decree to establish martial law. Rock musicians recognized that threat, too, and spoke explicitly to their audiences:

Emotions are the blood that pulses in the veins of these events, but we do not want to see actual blood. . . . It is not difficult to imagine what a large, skillfully provoked brawl might bring with it. It would be immediately exploited in the political battle, and definitely not in the interests of democratization or of the Estonian people. . . . Let's keep our hearts burning, but let's keep our heads cool."[100]

Soviet Estonia's government legalized the blue-black-white in response to a display of flags that it could not stop. In July, the flag revolution spread by chain reaction to Estonia's Baltic neighbors, when Estonians carried not only their own flags but also the still-banned Lithuanian and Latvian flags, to the Gaudeamus choral festival in Vilnius and the Baltica Folklore Festival in Rīga. That summer, rock musicians became national standardbearers there, too. In Lithuania, Antis spearheaded the emerging mass movement. The group awakened civic activism in the "Rock March" of 1987, a national tour of rock bands that raised money for the Lithuanian Cultural Foundation. In 1988, Antis displayed the yellow-green-red flag of independent Lithuania to declare non-Soviet identity; that year's Rock March mobilized political support for Sąjūdis and Lithuanian independence.

The Latvian singing revolution found its center on August 23, 1988, at the premiere of the rock opera *Bearslayer*. Staged on the national epic's centennial, the libretto by Māra Zālīte revived and retold the 1888 national hero's life story to match current political challenges. Whereas the original Bearslayer had been a warrior who defeated enemies in battle, in 1988 he rejected violence and no longer killed his rivals. His nemesis, the Black Knight, attacked with a fog of blindness, deafness, and muteness—alienation and a loss of communication with other humans, akin to Antis's "zombies" in Lithuania, and Mattiisen's "migrant" in Estonia. Bearslayer's countertactics, as expressed in the aria sung by Igo Fomins, awakened human consciousness on an individual level, calling for the revolution's guiding emotion to be love:

> Frozen wishes, wake up!
> Hope, get up and sleep no more!
> Ashes of submission, scatter!
> Memory, come back, return!
>
> Frozen, exiled people, rise up!
> Become warm and living flesh!
> Whoever broke away, return!
>
> (repeat first stanza)
>
> Consciousness, snap the leash!
> May your thoughts be clean and pure!
> Love, open up your eyes!
> Frozen, exiled people, rise up!
> Return! Return!

Bearslayer's fiancée, Laimdota, was the nation personified. Her aria, sung by Maija Lūsēna, was a prayer for the emotions that would help Latvians regain their humanity: faith, hope, and love. These words in the song's fourth stanza resembled a passage of the New Testament, but this was not intentional: Māra Zālīte explains, "It emerged out of a consciousness of the situation. There was a lack of faith that something could be changed, and hopes were too weak. Love for Latvia was the strongest component. But it was passive! It seemed necessary to activate it with faith and hope, and also with love's opposite."[101]

> Don't leave me, oh rising sun,
> Don't leave me in the shade.
> Give strength to my loved ones,
> Take their weakness away.
>
> Give my loved ones loving eyes,
> Give them souls that are pure.
> In the women, put your sunlight,
> Put your fire in the men.
>
> Give pride to my loved ones.
> Give them a brave smile.
> Give them hatred, too, oh sun,
> Give them hatred, too.
>
> Don't leave me, oh rising sun,
> Do not leave us all.
> Give us faith, give us hope,
> We ourselves have love.
>
> Don't leave me, oh rising sun,
> Do not leave us all.
> Don't leave me, oh rising sun,
> Do not leave us all.

Love's opposite—hatred—recalls Zālīte, was necessary. Hatred was aimed not at individual people but at the Soviet regime's policies:

> Let's not forget that at that time, a part of society was deeply enmeshed in collaboration with the system; it had just begun to love Latvia, but was still afraid of hating the regime. Or at least to openly admit it. Without this "hatred" Laimdota's Song would be too sweet and harmonious, it would not express the necessary hatred for everything that the Soviet regime had done to us. That was the thought. I admit that "hatred" and "sun" are not words that fit well together, but their dissonance is exactly what helps one even notice this.[102]

Hatred did not translate into revenge against individual collaborators but rather provided a mechanism by which collaborators could step out of the Soviet system. The national traitor Kangars was not punished by others; after betraying the national hero, he suffered only the pain of his own conscience.[103]

The rock opera *Bearslayer* premiered on August 23, 1988, and ran for forty-three sold-out performances attended by a total of 180,000 people. It is remembered as a central event, perhaps the central event of the Latvian Singing Revolution.[104] At this critical high point, the rock opera offered a vision of a national hero who was not armed, and who fought to awaken humanity without using violence against his enemies. It is not important to decide which came first, the new, nonviolent national hero or public consensus regarding nonviolent ideology. The rock opera either shaped the public's values or resonated deeply with values that were already present, but subsequent political developments derived from this nonviolent ideology of 1988.[105]

Earlier that year, Ieva Akurātere temporarily left Pērkons to emerge as a solo "bard," singing poetry that she accompanied on acoustic guitar. She found the movement's voice during a live broadcast in the spring of 1988, when, instead of an expected and approved song, she sang a song of prayer, "For My Nation," that was forbidden on Soviet stages both for its religious content and because its authors were Latvian American.[106] The audience called Akurātere back for two encores. On October 7, Akurātere sang the song again at the mass concert celebrating the founding of Latvia's Popular Front:[107]

> My thoughts fly around at night in all directions,
> Forward and backward, often in circles;
> I feel that my roots are not growing as they should;
> Even in rich earth they wither and bend.
>
> My nation is withering, scattered worldwide,
> Without its land, it struggles and splinters.
> My nation is withering, scattered worldwide,
> Even in its own land it cannot grow.
>
> (refrain:)
> Come, God, come help, come, God, come help
> All the Latvian people,
> Bring them back home to the shores of the Daugava,
> Bring them back home.
> Come, God, come help, come, God, come help
> Our Latvian people
> Grow roots in the land of a free Latvia.
>
> Every day dawns with pain for the Latvian people,
> Scattered apart, the song resounds sadly,

Every day dawns with pain for the Latvian people,
Scattered apart, our flame slowly fades.

(refrain)

The congress's opening speaker, Ēvalds Valters, added new words and meaning to the refrain's prayer: "Come, God, come help, come, God, come help. Come, God, come help lead our nation to liberty. To the country's independence. And into the bright daylight."[108] Nationalism and religion were both freed from censorship in the summer of 1988, and they merged in a public prayer for independence. National and religious meanings likewise converged in the name of the Popular Front's newspaper, *Atmoda* ("Awakening"). The second issue, published December 16, 1988, carried on its first page the poem "Prayer," written by Leonīds Breikšs before he was deported and killed by the Soviets. His words, set to music by Imants Kalniņš, were first sung by Ieva Akurātere in February of 1989, during her concert tour in North America.[109] This was the song that the Latvians recalled a decade later at the Smithsonian festival of 1998 (translated in chapter 1).[110]

Rock singers also stretched Estonian, Latvian, and Lithuanian national identity to include a shared Baltic unity. To be sure, unified political action depended on the coordinated work of the three national nongovernmental organizations, the Estonian Popular Front, the Latvian Popular Front, and the Lithuanian Sąjūdis, which came together to organize the Singing Revolution's largest mass demonstration: the "Baltic Way" of August 23, 1989, in which a million Balts formed a six-hundred-kilometer human chain connecting Tallinn, Rīga, and Vilnus, declaring unity while remembering the Soviet-Nazi treaty that had ceded their countries to Stalin on that date fifty years earlier. The three national organizations coordinated logistics, but ultimately the success of the event depended on massive voluntary public participation, which in turn would only happen if one million individuals felt a shared Baltic identity.

A memorable mover of this expanded identity was the trilingual rock song "Baltic Awakening," sung by Latvian, Lithuanian, and Estonian musicians. Stanzas in each of the three languages presented pan-Baltic symbols. Here, a literal translation of the first, Latvian-language stanza shows the shared content:

Three sisters standing by the sea,
Overcome by powerlessness and exhaustion;
The land and souls are trampled there,

The three nations' honor and mind.
But bells of fate toll in the towers,
And the sea begins to swell;
Three sisters have woken from their sleep,
And come to defend the land.
    Baltija is awakening, Baltija is awakening:
    Lithuania, Latvia, Estonia!

The three stanzas, each in its own language, proposed that the Baltic nations were like sisters by the sea; a bell rang, the sea moved, and they woke to defend themselves. These images resonate with classic, transnational components of national identity and nationalism: kinship, geography, a heritage of sad history now arriving at a transformative historical moment (marked by a bell). The dramatic situation (agitated sea) called for a shared political awakening and grassroots activism (the Estonian refrain was an imperative call, "Awaken, Baltic lands!"). Language, a core symbol in Baltic nationalism, was foregrounded in performance: each nation sang in its own language, thereby expressing unity with the two other nations singing in their own languages, sharing a belief that all Balts sang the same song. The song, like the "Baltic Way" human chain, linked national cultures together in a transnational Baltic identity. The singers urged Balts to awaken and defend their nations' honor. Other songs fueled a particular mechanism of national defense: nonviolent political action.

SINGING FOUNDATIONS OF THE NONVIOLENT, NON-SOVIET BALTIC INDEPENDENCE MOVEMENT

There is a consensus that Mattiisen's five songs were the core of the Estonian Singing Revolution, but the mechanism by which the songs affected people has not been described. It is clear that the songs of the Baltic Singing Revolution had two political functions. First, they expressed national identity, and second, they proposed action derived from that identity. Rock musicians were a critical conduit. Sabrina Ramet writes,

> Rock musicians figured—in the Soviet and East European context of the 1980s—a bit like prophets. That is to say, they did not invent or create the ideas of revolution or the feelings of discontent and disaffection. But they were sensitive to the appearance and growth of these ideas and feelings and gave them articulation, and in this way they helped to reinforce the revolutionary tide.[111]

The content of Singing Revolution songs was different from that of the songs described by Ramet. Contrary to what might be expected, revolution, discontent, and disaffection were not common themes in the Baltic after 1988.[112] The nuanced irony of Kernagis's "We'll smash into pieces those Colorado Beetles," the angry scream of Pērkons's "There's really nothing fatter than the pigs that we honor!" and the aggressive hyperbole of Tamme's "Hello, Perestroika" were things of the past. These had indeed once been attacks on the Soviet system, and their poets had articulated discontent and disaffection. But when censorship dissolved, the anger, irony, and cynicism in rock songs did not linger.

Pērkons returned to national prominence in 1989, continuing traditions that had once made the band non-Soviet in the eyes of government officials and audiences alike. "We didn't sing *against*, because that would be destructive action. We sang and were *for*. For love, *for* social issues, *for* good rock music. Latvia's independence was one item in the mission, but not the only one."[113] The band was in tune with the Latvian public; in 1989, it was their song that won first place in the annual "Mikrofons" song poll, and not, as might be expected, "Baltic Awakening" or other forceful calls for liberty, political independence, or Baltic unity.[114] The Pērkons song "We Live Because of Each Other " stepped outside of the perestroika politics that aimed to fill the empty Soviet food stores through massive economic restructuring. The song walked instead into the light that grew when two people communicated on a sincere, human level:

> We live because of each other,
> And not because of food products,
> And the light that comes from your eyes
> Is brighter than light from candles.

Pērkons's songs were still as subversive as before, but, as before, their mechanism was not aggressive violence, as Soviet authorities had alleged; the fact that they placed individual, personal relations above collective experience in issues of love, trust, and responsibility made them non-Soviet at their very foundations.

Instead of expressing feelings of discontent, Baltic rock turned to the construction and consolidation of national identity and ideology rather than the destruction of its opponents. The components of national identity followed a well-known transnational checklist of nationalism. Their songs asserted that these nations had a rich heritage of language, culture, and history, and that they were tied to an ancestral homeland. Songs engaged the nation's tragic history, and projected a belief that the nation was further endangered by Soviet rule. Song texts also constructed a democratic, nonviolent path to a political revolution.

Songs did not exist apart from political tactics. Concurrently with the mass meetings that stirred emotions, Balts were planning political action of the concrete, rational kind. On June 17, 1988, when Heinz Valk's editorial "Singing Revolution" defined the nonviolent principles of Estonian political action, a second editorial by Heino Kiik appeared on the same page of the newspaper, identifying a concrete and urgent goal: "In a democratic state, the people have only one path to taking power in their own hands: the election of their own parliament. The longer the process is dragged on, the more political energy is wasted, and faith and inspiration are weakened."[115] It was the "hot summer of 1988," writes Toivo Raun, and the heat was tangible in both climate and politics. As Valk and Kiik were submitting their editorials for publication, the local Soviet government that they challenged was on its way out. On June 16, Gorbachev removed the unpopular head of the Estonian Communist Party, and, for the first time since 1950, a native Estonian, Vaino Väljas, was appointed to the position. Old-guard leaders were replaced by new, smiling Communists in Latvia and Lithuania as well. The three new local Soviet leaders responded to popular opinion, quickly adopting some of the movement's demands, among them "rehabilitating" the three national flags, confirming the historical memory of the Nazi-Soviet Pact of 1939, and establishing the national languages as the official languages of the three Soviet republics. These dramatic developments were celebrated on September 11 at the Song of Estonia, a day-long festival of songs and political speeches that Rein Taagepera calls the summer's grand finale.[116]

But in September of 1988, the Soviet political system remained intact, with local governments appointed by Moscow, not elected by the people. The three nonformal national organizations that emerged through democratic processes had not yet gained any real political power. Heinz Valk concluded his speech at the Song of Estonia event with a soon-to-be-famous saying that expressed both short-term disappointment and long-term optimism: "Nevertheless, one day we will win!"[117] That one day was long in coming. Soviet power would remain in place for three more years.

On this long path of political developments, it is difficult to tell if the songs gave voice to popular feeling or shaped that feeling. The role of individual artists and creativity in the songs' success is also unclear. Mattiisen selected a charismatic singer, Ivo Linna, to perform the solo part of his "Five Fatherland Songs," but Estonians agree that it could just as well have been somebody else. The rock journalist Immo Mihkelson finds parallels with American music of an earlier era, where Bob Dylan sang in the spirit of the times while rejecting the idea that he himself was somehow special: "He simply did what felt best at that time. The man had the good luck to say everything most precisely, in the sense that people understood it and perceived it to be a summary. To them it seemed that Dylan knew something that nobody else knew, that he was like a Messiah."[118] Sabrina Ramet's interpretation of rockers as prophets rings true. Estonian singer Tõnis Mägi recalls that his role was very much akin to that of a prophet in the religious sense, a person through whom passed words generated by a higher power. He categorically denies that individual will or creativity played any role at all. "Some kind of powers were present there," he comments,

> I say this because I experienced it myself. I sang "Creator, Protect Maarjamaa"—"Prayer'" is the song's name. When I sang it, my hands were raised, and this energy—it was as if I held two hedgehogs in my hands. My palms turned a fiery red. . . . It was some sort of power in song, it was a spiritual matter. This has nothing to do with everyday reality; at times it felt like a dream, unreal. There were some kind of powers present there. The more time passes, the more I feel this to be true.[119]

Mägi recalls that his song was a prayer in the spirit of anthems such as "God Save the King."[120] It was a heartfelt prayer that belonged to Mägi's individual experience as a born-again religious believer in the group called Word of Life. His prayer was ecumenical, addressing the higher power of several different religious as well as secular historical traditions. In the text, the name that was once ascribed to the Baltic territory by Roman Catholic crusaders, Maarjamaa (Mary's Land), was synonymous with the country's present name, Estonia, the wished-for "home" of "homeless" Estonians. Their Creator protected not only the land, but also the sacred groves of pre-Christian pagan rituals. An intertextual reference to the New Testament, "Blessed are those who have not seen and yet have believed," merged religious belief with a secular movement that had few rational reasons to hope for success.[121] The final stanza of Mägi's song assumed first-person-singular responsibility for creating and defending the land.[122] Thus individual religious identity, national identity, and secular social consciousness merged in the text, all subsumed to a higher power:

PRAYER (CREATOR, PROTECT MAARJAMAA)

Creator, protect Maarjamaa
And forgive us our mistakes.
Creator, defend Estonia;
I clasp my hands in prayer.

Creator, guard the sacred groves,
Their crowns leaning low to the ground;
Creator, defend those without a home;
One day they will return again.

In the Great Book of Time it is written that
Blessed are they who don't see,
If, believing that nothing is possible,
Somebody walks.

I create, I protect Maarjamaa,
I create and I hope, for I know
Why those tree crowns are arched
Like my hands clasped in prayer—

That the Creator would protect Maarjamaa.

In the Baltic, rock songs articulated the public's ideas and feelings, but songs also created ideas and feelings, generated political action, and shaped ideology. While writing the "Five Fatherland Songs," Alo Mattiisen realized that, if he were to join one of the competing political factions, these songs could shape the political movement's course.[123] The Latvian rock opera *Bearslayer* disarmed that nation's national warrior hero, adding a powerful, explicitly nonviolent symbol to the nationalist discourse. Songs defined goals and tactics, and reformulated nationalism when they placed emphasis on individual conscience and responsibility, or excluded anonymous mass action and submission to an authoritarian leader.

In Lithuania, Antis was not a passive transmitter of public sentiment. The band shaped the political movement when they placed core images of Lithuanian nationalism within a nonviolent frame. "Shoreline," for example, took well-known images of the landscape as a carrier of cultural wealth and ancient heritage, juxtaposing them with the painful history ("tears") as motivation for political action to achieve justice. The singer, however, did not call for revenge, because the medicine for historical pain was love. Grand Duke Vytautas, the medieval military conqueror of vast territories, was remembered for his calm serenity, not the defeat of his enemies. In 1988, the objective was a political awakening ("move frozen blood in the veins") to ensure "Fatherland's continuity." The song's basic, unquestioned assumption was that the Lithuanian movement would be nonviolent, and therefore an absolute opposite to the outdated Soviet concept of military force and violent revolution as prime movers of historical change: "How strange our army: No weapons, young people only." The song took nonviolent tactics for granted, stressing a determined fight for justice despite what appeared to be an insurmountable imbalance in power: "How many left . . . don't ask, we'll forget the purpose."

> Shoreline where my hopes are placed
> Will be the judge and arbitrate;
> A fantastic linden-tree street landscape,
> Pronouncer of justice oh so painful,
> My shoreline.
>
> Vytautas's serenity,
> In the forests the farmer's integrity,
> Faces and rivers, our own eternity,
> Water and tears, the Fatherland's continuity,
> My shoreline.
>
> (refrain:)
> We march, one-two-three, one-two-three,
> On the water's smooth surface;
> How many left, one-two-three, one-two-three,
> Don't ask, we'll forget the purpose.
> How strange our army:
> No weapons, young people only.
> We'll move frozen blood in the veins
> Toward a great goal again.
>
> Shoreline in silence immersed,
> Along the seacoast a white stork soars,
> The grass of hillforts turned into forests,
> Forgotten celebrations, ancient stories,
> My shoreline.
>
> Broad distances, abandoned,
> Roots wounded, await longing,
> Searching for the ship approaching,
> It's the only medicine, love medicine,
> My shoreline.
> We march, one-two-three, one-two-three . . . (refrain)

Kaušpėdas "pushed his vocal cords to their very limits," expressing the desperate wish for independence that Lithuanians kept alive for the next three years.[124] In songs, Antis forcefully defined a Lithuanian national culture that excluded revenge and violence, and in this way they helped establish nonviolent ideological foundations for political action. In 1989, the band projected a vision of political independence onto the public when they challenged audiences to repeat the magic words of a new song's title: "The Country, Lithuania. / Try pronouncing it. / The Country, Lithuania." Sąjūdis went on to win the national elections on a platform of independence. Then, on March 11, 1990, the new parliament declared that Lithuania had renewed its independence, and the government placed its national security policy on foundations of civilian-based defense, not violent resistance.[125] Ten months later, in January of 1991, when Soviet military forces began attacks on mass media offices in Vilnius, Antis sang to the public assembling on barricades, unarmed by choice, to defend their national parliament.

The test of Latvian nonviolent ideology also came in January of 1991. Soviet military forces had killed Lithuanian civilians in Vilnius and moved to take over mass communication hubs and the Latvian Ministry of the Interior in Rīga. The people of Latvia built barricades around the national parliament, and thousands of unarmed individuals gathered around bonfires to serve as a human shield, should the Soviets attack. Pērkons was there, too, performing daily.[126] Their "Green Song," with words by Māris Melgalvs, resonated with the public. Every person, like a tiny ray of sunshine, was necessary for the warm power of life to prevail:

> Touch the land, the land is white.
> The land is white, not long ago it was green.
> Give it your warmth, again it'll be green.
> Remember, remember, remember—your part is green.
> Remember, remember—it's all in your power.
>
>   (refrain, repeat twice:)
>   Hail is still hail, frost is still frost,
>   Fog is still fog over everything still.
>
> On which hill will we light a fire,
> Where will we winter this summer?
>
> What do you think, what big role,
> What big role can one bonfire play?
> Icicle, what will you do, icicle, when

When you are pierced by a tiny needle of sun?
When you are pierced by a tiny needle of sun?

   (refrain)

As many fires as there are on each hill,
That is how long we shall live here. (repeat stanza four times)

   (refrain, repeated three times)

While rock songs shaped the intellectual content of Baltic nationalism, they also shaped the emotions of participants in the Singing Revolution. Memoirs and contemporary descriptions agree that songs and singing were what broke the repressive fear that had prevailed under Soviet rule, opening the floodgates of free expression.[127] Songs both induced and strengthened a feeling of euphoria at mass meetings. These events were akin to religious revivals, when strong feelings of national identity emerged through ecstatic experiences. But by year's end those emotions were subsiding. Freedom of speech and freedom of assembly came to be taken for granted. The political process dragged on. Kiik had warned in June of 1988 that, without new infusions of energy, faith in the movement's success could falter. New songs might revive the movement's emotional foundations, but they were slow in coming. A composer can't simply sit down and write a song that will resonate with the masses, unifying and energizing them.[128] This was the context in which Tõnis Mägi had another flash of inspiration. He suddenly knew an entire song, then forgot it, then found it again. The song, he believes, was an expression of mass feeling, not individual creativity:

> I wrote as quickly as possible, because it was coming from somewhere. When I later looked at the text, it felt damn funny, as if it were a very old thing, as if it hadn't been created now. . . . The song went to the people very instantaneously. Wherever we sang it, the people already knew the words by heart. I don't know how that's possible. It hadn't been published on a record. Was the text published in a newspaper somewhere? I don't know. It happened as if by itself. It simply went, and that's how it started spinning.
>   They sang it, they stood up when they sang, and people were saying that this was a new anthem or something like that. They began to call it the hymn of the new era of freedom; many people said this.[129]

"Dawn" began with the words "It's time again," in a sober realization that the work of nation building was not complete. The idea would now be repeated every time the song was sung. The road to liberty still lay ahead, long, seemingly endless, but dawn glimmering on the mountaintops beckoned and energized the traveler to take one more step, and another one, toward the distant goal.

It's time again
To straighten the back
And cast off the robes of a slave,
So that everything
Can be born once again.

It's dawn,
Majestic blaze,
Victory of light
Awakens the land.
Free
Is the sky's bright edge,
The very first ray
Falling on our land.

The call—
We all call out,
To breathe again
As free people.
Look,
The ice has cracked;
Let's hold out our hands,
And join forces.

With mind,
Unified mind,
Unified power
We can do all.
Ahead,
The only road,
The road of liberty;
There's no other road.

Power,
The power of light,
Freedom's clan,
Let us go together,
A cry
Of joy on our lips,
Look,
The great giant
Has freed his hand from stone.

Faith
Leads us ahead,

The heavenly ray
Directs us on.
And so,
To victory,
Only one step more,
One short step, step.

Land,
Land of our fathers,
This land is holy,
And becoming free.
Song,
Our victory song,
It shall ring on,
You'll see a free Estonia!

Step by step, Estonians were moving toward liberty; their measure of time was on a mythical, not an earthly scale. As they walked along, they could imagine that alongside them walked the "the giant"—Estonia's national hero Kalevipoeg, his hand freed from the stone where it was fastened at the end of the 1857 national epic.

Rock songs had always offered refuge to people seeking a life other than that of official Soviet culture. But the rock songs of the Singing Revolution were a new kind of non-Soviet song. Explicit images of national unity, liberty, and a common path toward national independence were not a means of escaping reality into a world of imagination; rather, they formulated and maintained a vision of true distancing from Soviet power. Songs energized people, "awakening" political activism, mobilizing long-term commitment in the large numbers of individuals who were necessary for the success of the nonviolent, parliamentary path to Baltic freedom.

Among all singers, rockers could most easily and quickly adapt to changing political contexts. Tõnis Mägi's "Dawn" exemplifies the fact that a song could be written, rehearsed and performed, recorded, and reach a mass radio audience within a matter of days, something that was impossible in national choral traditions and song festivals. Thus Mägi's song captured public sentiment at one critical historical moment in 1989. In a broader context, the song documented the tactics of Baltic nationalism over the three years from 1988 to 1991. It expressed a determination to move as a nation, step by step, patiently, toward the goal of political liberty. Doubt gave way to a conviction that "there's no other road," and to faith in the movement's success. Months of patient organizing work passed from the beginnings of the Singing Revolution to the truly democratic elections of March 1990, after which the three elected governments passed declarations of renewed independence: Lithuania on March 11, Estonia on March 30, and Latvia on May 4, 1990.

CHAPTER EIGHT

Living within the Truth in Folk Songs

In the Baltic, summer nights are short and days are long. It was still broad daylight in Rīga at 8:00 pm on July 13, 1988, when the opening concert of the Baltica Folklore Festival ended and the festival participants walked in a procession from the Riga Sports Castle to Dom Square. It was a public display like none before it: they carried the flags of Estonia, Latvia and Lithuania that they had smuggled into the opening concert and unfurled, together, on stage, under the noses of the highest Soviet officials. Whereas in Tallinn, the blue-black-white flag had already been given legal sanction three weeks earlier, and in Vilnius, too, the yellow-green-red banner was released in the streets on July 1, the red-white-red flag was still illegal in Rīga. The person who carried it down this very same street on June 14 was ejected from the Soviet Union only three days before the 1988 Baltica festival began. Soviet police stood by, reluctant to repress people before the eyes and cameras of the festival participants from the West.[1]

Red banners, without a doubt, still walked first in line, together with the guest flags from abroad. But right behind them the group carrying Latvia's flag paused without warning, leaving a gap between themselves and the Soviet symbols. The red flags stopped to allow them to catch up, but the Latvian flagbearer, Dainis Stalts, also stopped and waited. When it became clear that the gap would not close, the two processions continued on, with the space between them gradually expanding. Spectators first saw a small island of red Soviet flags, and then a mass of thousands led by non-Soviet colors.

Figure 14. Baltica Folklore Festival procession near the crossing of Dzir-
navu and Ļeņina Streets, Rīga, Latvia, July 13, 1988. In the center is Dainis Stalts, a leader of the Skandinieki folkore ensemble. Photo by Gunārs
Janaitis.

The procession walked three kilometers up Lenin Street to the
Lenin Monument, as did most Soviet parades in Rīga. But then,
instead of taking a right turn according to Soviet custom, it walked
straight ahead for another block down the boulevard, to non-Soviet
Latvia's Freedom Monument (built in 1935), and participants began,
informally, to place flowers at the base of this true national shrine.
Here, only a half year earlier, police had dispersed demonstrators with
clubs. Under the glasnost rules of mid-1988, the new procession route
had official permission. But the singers carried illegal flags, publicly
declaring that this, the first parade in Rīga to leave the customary
Soviet path, was stepping further, outside of Soviet structures. They,
like the students at the choral song festival in Vilnius and like the rock
music audience in Tartu, were not loyal Soviet citizens following Gorbachev's plan to restructure the USSR.

The folklore ensembles sang as they walked. Their audience cheered
and smothered them with armloads of flowers, and the Latvian public
realized that there was a tangible possibility of political change from
the grassroots upward, not directed by the Soviets. This is what made
the opening procession, more than any concert, the culminating event
in the memories of many. A Lithuanian participant recalled that music
louder than singing was needed for them to be able to hear themselves
through the public applause:

> I won't forget that moment at the Baltica festival, when we stepped
> out of the sports hall, and all the streets were full of people, they were
> in balconies, too, with flowers; they wept, they cheered. And we're
> going by the fatherland monument, and we had two sets of shepherd's
> horns. I said, "Men! We're not singing. Let's play!" And man, the
> chills are going up the spine, and we stopped by that monument with
> the horns, and we played. This was something.[2]

Folklore ensembles derived their power from sources different from
choral or rock music. They were a singing subculture within the Singing Revolution. The Baltica festival's outward appearance may have
been that of a mass event, but in its essence, it was a gathering of many
individuals in many small, face-to-face communities. Folklore performances developed in constant tension with and, indeed, in opposition
to officially sanctioned Soviet mass culture. The subversive nature of
folk songs lay in the simple fact that anybody, regardless of professional training, could sing them, and amplification, stage, or conductor were not necessary. In folklore, everybody is a participant, and
nobody is a passive onlooker. This was the spirit of the folklore movement that began several decades before the famous Baltica festival of
1988.

DISCOVERING A SINCERE VOICE IN LITHUANIA

In the late fifties and early sixties, most of the Lithuanian students
attending Vilnius University had strong family ties to the folk speech,
narratives, and songs of rural villages. Many had themselves been
born in the countryside, only a generation or two removed from
vibrant oral traditions.[3] Between lectures, they would gather outdoors to sing, and they would spend evenings in the dormitories,
singing. Students studying language, literature, or history were
required to go on fieldwork expeditions, documenting the folklore
of preindustrial village life. The young students were enthusiastic
fieldworkers. Professor Donatas Sauka would later recall that, beginning with the thaw of 1957, Vilnius University "boiled and bubbled"
with newly established groups of amateur ethnographers and folklorists. "In the summers there were mass folklore expeditions, and
during the academic year, there were cheerful, friendly, meaningful
evenings of singing and dancing, and performances by folk singers.
Beautiful years! Their sincerity and energy brought the students' cultural tastes to maturity."[4]

Fieldwork expanded into a new phase in 1963, when ten students led by Norbertas Vėlius organized the first "complex expedition," combining students' individual specialization in linguistics, folklore, or ethnography to produce an interdisciplinary description of Zervynos, a rural community in southeastern Lithuania. Using personal money, they published a book about the village. The Local Heritage Study Society (Kraštotyros draugija) that they had founded in 1961 grew rapidly, coordinating annual summer expeditions that each produced a new published book. Other student organizations of the time—the Hikers (Žygeiviai) and tourist clubs—also traveled in the Lithuanian countryside, learning local history and reviving the memories of monuments that survived from pre-Soviet times.[5]

History and Lithuanian culture came to life in informal lectures that transpired while walking or by the light of campfires. Veronika Povilionienė vividly recalled, for example, the rainy-day hike when she first heard the song "Oh Don't Weep, Dear Mother" sung by the linguist Kazimieras Eigminas.[6] During ethnographic interviews, students met eyewitnesses of Stalinist terror and the partisan war; sometimes they would gain the trust of these country people and hear about events that were concealed or misrepresented in the official lessons at school.[7] Folklore archives reveal that many of the songs that emerged at the mass meetings of the Singing Revolution were also collected during the expeditions of the late 1950s and the 1960s.

The students experimented with new research methods. Instead of simply writing down songs and filing them in urban archives, they stayed in the field for long periods, spending time with the people they studied in order to learn their customs and folklore. Vilnius University's ethnographic expeditions culminated in 1970 and 1971, when about 150 young scholars of history, ethnography, psychology, sociology, art, and folklore traveled together to study rural Lithuanian communities.[8] Their groups now also included students from Vilnius Conservatory and other institutions of higher education. The encounter with folklore was a life-changing experience. Among the students, for example, was a future movement leader, Zita Kelmickaitė:

> And the very first expedition, when I had just finished my first year at the Conservatory, was fateful. Because I went to Dzūkija. We went on an expedition to Kriokšlio Village, Varėna District. . . . I encountered such musical women in that village, who, for example, could sing seventy songs in one day, easily, sitting down. And I was stunned by that. Because for them, the songs came one after the other. But not just the

knowledge and skill at singing, but the desire. Desire, and pride. They
understood that they had something of value. And one after the other,
they remembered them and sang.[9]

Expeditions documented and archived memories of folk traditions,
but they were also a path to rediscovery and revival. Jonas Trinkūnas
would later write, "Neither the collection of materials in expeditions, nor the evening performances could satisfy the thirsty soul. We
sensed that there were deep, neveraging ideas hidden in the traditions.
We understood that the folk song is not merely a musical art, but an
expression of a better culture and way of thought."[10] Trinkūnas first
gained permission to establish the Friends of India Society on February
18, 1967, with the official purpose of furthering Soviet-Indian diplo-
macy and friendship based on shared Indo-European cultural roots.
The true goal, however, was to have a legal organization for the study
and revival of ancient Lithuanian culture. In June, the society organized a summer solstice (Rasos) celebration. About twenty or thirty
people traveled forty kilometers northwest of Vilnius to the cluster of
medieval fortress hills at Kernavė, a small town on the shores of the
Neris River. This celebration and the ones that followed were simple:
participants spoke little, sang many songs, particularly songs about
the sun, and recited poetry; they made a fire, and spoke wishes when
they placed flowers into the fire. Women wove flower wreaths that
they would set in the river later that night. They stayed awake until
dawn. There was a feeling of silent conspiracy; people recall that the
group seemed to materialize out of nowhere and then melt away afterward.[11] Others remember vivid moments of drama related to nationalism. Emilija Stanikaitė, for example, recalled that she once stood by
the fire, her face covered by a sack to hide her identity, and recited a
poem about the ancient Lithuanian bard, the *vaidila*, "On this night
appeared a vision of the ancient Rambynas. . . . " A friend later told
her that it was a beautiful poem, but instead of being pleased, she
was mortified to know that somebody had recognized her. At another
celebration, probably in 1970, somebody shot three flares into the
dark sky: yellow, green, and red—the colors of the forbidden Lithuanian flag. The KGB agents who surrounded the event that year ran
toward the flares, but the person who lit them swam across the river
to safety.[12]

Around this time back in Vilnius, Veronika Povilionienė began
meeting informally with two other women interested in learning
and performing folk songs. They were particularly drawn to the

Figure 15. Bonfires among medieval fortress hills at the Lithuanian mid-summer (Rasos) celebration in Kernavė, June 1968. Photo by Vilius Naujikas.

polyphonic, syncopated sounds of *sutartinės*, a genre that had nearly gone extinct in oral tradition. Veronika would later recall that the prominent ethnomusicologist Jadvyga Čiurlionytė came to their informal concert in March of 1968, and that afterward she kissed them and exclaimed, "Girls, just keep singing! Don't give up, and keep singing those sutartinės!"[13] She and her friends also moved the university choir's assistant director, Aldona Ragevičienė, who often recalled a train trip where she first heard Veronika singing the wedding song "Nine Years Passed":

> Nine years passed by, not only one day,
> Nine years passed by, not only one day, since I was in the garden.
>   (repeat line)

My green rue grew up, grew up so tall, (repeat as above)
With five and six branches.

On every rue branch, a little cuckoo
Cuckooed in early morning.

Cuckooed and cuckooed until her father,
Father dear gave a dowry.

They take the daughter, the earth is rumbling
Mother is weeping bitterly.

Ragevičienė later told an interviewer, "It was so unexpected and very good to hear them sing an authentic folk song. And when the girls fell silent, I began to think, why are we ashamed of our true, old folk songs, why do we sing them so rarely and shyly?" In autumn that year, Ragevičienė requested and received permission to establish the Vilnius University Student Ethnographic Ensemble.[14] A laconic newspaper report about their December premiere recorded an extraordinary atmosphere of sincerity and openness, without the cold formality of high art, or the impersonal feel of mass concerts:

> In the candlelight on a low stage, the games, songs, and legends of the winter festival, forgotten by most, came back to life. The concert resembled a folk gathering of old, when the young village men and women gathered and told stories of demons and witches, sang songs, and cast lots to discover when they would marry. . . . The young performers interacted with the audience, shunning theatrical elements, sincerely and simply, letting the program sound in a note of authenticity. An atmosphere of directness prevailed in both concerts, which received warm applause from the audience.[15]

They sang the old songs on stage and off, passing on the experience to an ever-larger circle of young Lithuanians. One student remembered for the rest of her life a moment of awakening in September of 1971, when she first heard oral performance of folk songs:

> My image of folk songs was always, well, operatic singers singing with a contrived voice. And I disliked it very much; it was not pretty at all. And when my older friends who graduated before me came to Vilnius, and they were singing with Veronika in the folklore movement, and they wrote letters that "there is a group here called Ramuva, and we sing folk songs," I thought, phoo! How can they sing like that? And when I enrolled at the university, in 1971, right away, an acquaintance of mine said on September 1, "We're going to celebrate the beginning of the academic year." . . .

And they were taking us to the place where people were meeting; it was a small group of students, some younger, some older. And we walked across the fields, and Veronika started to sing. Outdoors. With her voice. I— So, for me, it was the first time I had ever heard an authentic folk song like that, and what's more, it was sung by *Veronika*. I had no understanding—I knew only operatic singing of folk songs. I remember it shook me tremendously. What a feeling. For the rest of my life I won't forget Veronika's singing. Of course, others were also singing, but it was Veronika. That was such a powerful emotional impression, and it stayed with me for my whole life. And of course, then I got interested in folklore, and I learned songs, and I even met my husband through singing.[16]

The Soviet secret police monitored the student fieldwork expeditions, the intimately youthful, "sincere" concerts, and other extracurricular activities. As early as 1962, the KGB had four agents and three "dependable informers" among the Vilnius University language and literature students; a police report that year recommended expanding secret information-gathering.[17] The 1970 Rasos celebration at Kernavė was under open surveillance. Agents circulated in the crowd, taking photographs, and participants were later interrogated by the KGB. A Communist Youth League leader attacked unsanctioned student activities:

> Sometimes the students sing songs of doubtful content on their hikes; often our tourism groups are joined by nonmembers. This is the result of poor organization. The hike routes should be kept under more strict control, and precise lists of club members should be maintained. . . . Other rude violations also occur. In the spring, there appear "cultural" evenings organized by amateurs, dances on the territory of the dormitories. We have severely punished these noisemakers, seekers of depraved romance, and we will continue to punish them.[18]

The Lithuanian Communist Party Central Committee Bureau pointed out ideological flaws in the Local Heritage Study Society's publications, noting that the group paid too much attention to history and too little attention to current Soviet life. The 1970 expedition's book manuscript was confiscated and destroyed; a secret copy would be published only two decades later.[19] Norbertas Vėlius was forbidden to lead student expeditions. In 1971, Jonas Trinkūnas was dismissed from the Vilnius University faculty. The Heritage Society was annexed by Soviet functionaries, its membership restricted, its expeditions no longer open to nonmembers, and its activities directed toward the collection of politically correct Soviet folklore. Although members certainly continued to gather useful ethnographic materials and maintained the memory of historical sites, their activities no longer had the broad public effect they had before.[20] Then, at midsummer in 1972, Soviet police closed down the area around the Kernavė fortress hills, ostensibly to protect the historical monument.

Rasos celebrations continued, nevertheless. In the years when Lithuanians were not allowed to have celebrations in Kernavė, they would gather somewhere nearby. "The organizers tried very hard to do everything subtly," recalled Jonas Vitkūnas. "They didn't do any politics or mass demonstrations. The behavior, the spiritual atmosphere that prevailed there, said everything. This was sufficient for the people who gathered. . . . For a person who didn't understand the celebration's meaning, it would only be people singing some boring folk songs." But insiders knew the gathering's non-Soviet meaning. In 1971, they began a tradition of singing "Dear Lithuania" at Rasos. And in 1987, the celebration at Kernavė would be the first public occasion where Lithuania's national anthem was sung.[21]

The folklore ensembles founded from 1968 to 1971 survived, winning their first victory simply by not being closed down. These groups, however, were administratively integrated in a framework of officially organized "amateur art activities," and were thus subject to repertoire control by the government agencies that permitted their performances and paid their leaders. Specialists evaluated the quality and suitability of ensembles at annual review concerts that were usually organized as "competitions."

SINGING AUTHENTICALLY ON STAGE AND BEYOND

In 1974, Lithuanian traditional culture gained an institutional foothold in the newly opened outdoor ethnographic museum at Rumšiškės. Estonia's Open Air Museum's folklore ensemble, Leigarid, had shown how exhibits of log houses and farmsteads could be enhanced, and tourists entertained, with folklore contemporary to those buildings. The Lithuanian museum also needed folk culture, and thus the Vilnius Youth Theater's musical ensemble led by Povilas Mataitis was converted into the Baltic's first full-time professional folklore ensemble.[22] The group's formal recognition set a precedent, overturning arguments that urban folklore ensembles were artistically "regressive." The Rumšiškės Museum became a second home for all folklore ensembles, not only as a venue for their concerts but also as a refuge where they could bring traditions to life, deepening their ethnographic knowledge and experience of material culture and traditional calendar customs.

Professional ethnomusicologists joined the movement, too. When Laima Burkšaitienė took over leadership of the Vilnius University Ethnographic Ensemble, she taught diverse melodic traditions of Lithuania's ethnographic regions, and shifted the source of the group's repertoire from published books to archival recordings.[23] A reviewer in 1975 marvelled that the ensemble reproduced complex regional styles with scholarly precision while singing "in the folk style, with rich, unstaged voices," "with youthful enthusiasm."[24] It was at this time that the students revived a hay-cutting song, "Oh, the Hay Field," transforming agricultural tradition to a battle-ready weapon for cultural mobilization. In the field recording made by two students, the song was performed by a small group of elderly women. But the text ("we . . . boys") implied that its earlier singers were not women; powerfully performed by the ensemble's men, the song spread nationwide. The group performed it in typical Lithuanian oral style: a lead singer called the stanza's first line, and the group joined in to repeat the line and add another line, also repeated twice. The leader's voice stood a third interval above the other singers, always audible, even if the singing expanded, as it often did, to a roomful of people. Anybody could sing along and feel, firsthand, the harmony resonating within the chest and head:

> Oh, the hayfield, hayfield (repeat each line)
>   Oh, the hayfield, the green meadow.
>
> Oh, we shall go cut the hay,
>   Boys, we'll go cut hay, we'll cut the hay.
>
> Oh, we'll ride to Rīga,
>   Boys, we shall ride out to Rīga.
>
> A great city, Rīga,
>   Boys, but Warsaw city is greater still.
>
> Enemies stand like brick walls,
>   Boys, the enemies stand like brick walls.
>
> Bullets buzz around like bees,
>   Boys, the bullets buzz around like bees.
>
> Enemies fall like brick walls,
>   Boys, the enemies fall like brick walls.
>
> Blood, it flows like waterfalls.

Boys, the blood, it flows like waterfalls.

Dogs, they lap it up like lions,
  Boys, the dogs, they lap it up like lions.

The song's ties to national history and nationalism were clear. Although the first stanza spoke of hay cutting, it was a war song, not a hay-cutting song. Its text explicitly bragged about a military victory where the enemy's blood "flows like waterfalls," and dogs "lap it up like lions." This was not a Soviet battle, however, because wars against Rīga and Warsaw belonged to the much earlier historical epoch of an independent state, the Grand Duchy of Lithuania.

When ethnomusicologist Zita Kelmickaitė took over the ensemble's lead in 1976, she revived the ethnographic expeditions in which students encountered oral traditions firsthand. Her own sonorous voice offered a visceral understanding of how folk songs work: when a student found her or his own voice, along with it came the exhilarating, liberating, and empowering feeling of oral poetry performance.[25] Before the students' eyes and ears, Kelmickaitė transformed expedition materials into successful stage performances. Her agenda, she later remarked, was also political. "I think that every job well done is the best politics of all."[26] If every student learned to sing, the mission was accomplished. Regarding repertoire, their sole objective was to study and perform folklore from archaic oral tradition, and they did this extraordinarily well. The movement's core repertoire, however, remained apart from Soviet socialist realism traditions, without the explicitly loyal songs required of other amateur singers. Traditional wedding and courtship songs, for example, lacked explicit "partyness" and "idea-ness," and were wholly non-Soviet in content. These were the songs that attracted ever-larger audiences.

The university ensemble was one of the engines that spread the folklore movement nationwide: students learned the traditions of ethnographic research and singing, graduated and dispersed throughout Lithuania, and established new groups. Over two decades, but particularly over the decade from the late seventies to the late eighties, the Lithuanian folklore movement expanded to 1,220 ensembles.[27] The mechanism by which the movement spread was face-to-face performance, with little if any stimulus from the Soviet government. Performers invited the audience to sing and dance along, and the barriers between stage and audience crumbled. Musicians had an endless repertoire of dances whose steps were easy to learn, even for novices, and there was no limit to the number of times a dance could be repeated. When energy was high, they continued late into the night. Nonformally trained dancers and singers, physically tired but inspired, would then join the ensemble or start their own groups.[28]

In the early eighties, another campaign against folklore ensembles was announced in Lithuania, but with little real effect.[29] Lithuanians would later recall that Leonid Brezhnev supposedly declared, "Enough of this ethnographism!" but no such phrase appears in his speeches; it seems more likely that the antifolklore campaign coincided with the repression of dissidents under Soviet leader Yurii Andropov. Andropov was quoted by the head of the Lithuanian Communist Party in his attack on folklore ensembles in January 1983, writing in the vague, but clearly aggressive style typical of such Soviet ostracism:

> In the general context of our culture, as new spiritual values are created, there is also a return to historical-ethnographic elements and phenomena. We see this in art, architecture, film. This is a natural attempt to strengthen the cultural memory. But sometimes this attempt turns into fashion and stylization, when, with no respect for the needs of the present, for socialist content, with no attempt at selection, efforts are made to revive and reestablish everything that has ever existed. This has occurred in various projects of the Restoration Board, and in the uncontrollable onslaught of ethnographic ensembles.
> . . .
> Dear comrades! Soviet Lithuanian culture, socialist in content and national in form, marches on a path of bountiful ideological principles and artistry. The future of its prosperity is affirmed by the political and moral conscience of our cultural workers and creative intelligentsia, by the sincere and devoted work of the entire nation, by the just and consistent politics of the Communist Party.[30]

But a party secretary no longer could boast of having the "leading role" stipulated by Soviet law. Singers and administrators ignored the Communist Party leader's orders, and did nothing to end the "uncontrollable onslaught" of folklore ensembles. Zita Kelmickaitė later recalled that she asked the minister of culture, Dainius Trinkūnas, what to do; he replied that folklore ensembles should continue singing as before, but that they should avoid coverage in the mass media. Thus, in the 1980s Lithuania—where official decrees were followed by benevolent inactivity—differed dramatically from Latvia, to be discussed below.

On stage, folklore ensembles coexisted with "song-and-dance ensembles" whose highly choreographed dances and songs exemplified Soviet "folk creativity." Friction between the two performance

styles and the issue of authenticity sparked public debates that continued into the 1980s. Sometimes the new folklore ensembles gained the
upper hand. In 1976, the city of Vilnius's Skamba, Skamba Kankliai
festival followed the Soviet model of mass spectacles. A handful of
smaller folklore groups were dwarfed on the enormous song festival
stage by flashy Soviet song-and-dance ensembles. But after the formal
concert, the evening dissolved into an "unofficial festival" of informal, off-stage dancing and singing until midnight. A new kind of festival was born.[31] Three years later, the whole festival revolved around
smaller, more intimate folklore ensemble performances scattered
throughout the labyrinth of picturesque Old Town Vilnius courtyards.
The two folklore performance styles would clash again in 1987, with
a similar outcome, at the first Baltica Folklore Festival.

Baltica's foundations were laid in Tallinn in July of 1985, at a conference of the UNESCO affiliate, the International Council of Folklore
Festival Organizations (CIOFF). Its basis in Soviet culture was stated
in the government decree:

> With the purposes of propagating the Leninist national and cultural
> policies of the Soviet government, the maintenance and development
> of folk art traditions, the broadening of cultural collaboration with
> foreign countries in the area of folklore, in order to strengthen friend-
> ship and mutual understanding among nations: The festival, "Baltica,"
> is to be founded in the republics of the Soviet Baltic, with the partici-
> pation of collectives and performers from abroad.[32]

The three Baltic people's art centers planned to hold a conventional
festival of Soviet song-and-dance ensembles. The five-day event on
July 14–19, 1987, brought to Lithuania 300 performers from the
USA, France, Sweden, Poland, the German Democratic Republic, and
Hungary; 400 more from the Russian Federation, Belarus, Latvia, and
Estonia; and an additional 2,500 persons from Lithuania, of which
one fifth were in folklore ensembles. As a festival of both stylized and
unstylized folklore, Baltica 1987 replicated the experiences of the Vilnius Skamba Kankliai festival ten years earlier. Four massive concerts
on July 18 and 19 (at 12:00 noon and 9:30 pm both days) left many
participants with exhausting memories of endless rehearsals, long
waits in line to get onto stage, and brief, tenminute performances that
interspersed a spectacular array of stylized, balletlike dances and contemporary song arrangements. A Lithuanian reviewer pointed out that
this massive stage unavoidably led to a cultural confrontation. Song-
and-dance ensembles did not belong at a folklore festival, because

their performances made folk singers look "pale and inorganic." This, the reviewer thought, was in fact what organizers had intended when they put the two styles of singing alongside each other on the massive stage.[33]

Smaller-scale concerts in Vilnius's Old Town and at the Rumšiškės Museum came closer to folklore's spirit, but the Singing Revolution had not begun yet in the summer of 1987. A videotape preserved by the Lithuanian Folk Art Center documents a concert in the Vilnius University courtyard, with five twenty-minute performances by three leading Baltic groups and two guest ensembles from France.[34] The stage, albeit smaller than an amphitheater, towered two meters above the ground; singers sometimes descended to invite others to dance, but most of the audience sat silently and passively in their seats. In smaller groups off-camera and offstage, as was the tradition in Vilnius, singing and dancing continued late into the night, and still another "Baltica" emerged in the performers' dormitories, where small groups of individuals continued informal music making until morning. It was also very much an informal festival among Baltic folklore performers, for Baltic folklore performers.[35] Guest performers from abroad often went to sleep early; they were interesting, but not essential. One foreign group's political demonstration, however, foreshadowed dramatic events to come. All Baltic participants later remembered that, even if the official Soviet announcers consistently introduced Ronsed Mor as a representative of France,[36] that group's members would adamantly point out that they were not French but Breton. And in processions and concerts, they carried their own non-French flag, resembling the Balts who would carry non-Soviet flags at the Baltica festival in 1988.

INCANTATIONS FOR LATVIA'S INDEPENDENCE

In 1987, Vizma Belševica, a Latvian poet persecuted by the Soviets for saying and writing what others didn't dare think,[37] published a poetic summary of Latvian history: it was a series of "thou shalt" and "thou shalt not" imposed by foreign conquerors, concluding at the Midsummer Night's celebrations, where people were drowning in bitter fear and alcohol. She continued, however:

> But in the darkened fields, Skandinieki walk,
> But in the midnight meadows, in the starry, golden dew,
> The pure breaths sing—Look, they sing without liquor,

Without beer they sing. . . .

The land rises in waves, like Skandinieki singing,
And in the starry dew remains the trail of song.
Across the dark black fields—a tiny path.[38]

Belševica, a poet who gave others courage to think and speak the truth, herself drew strength from the folklore ensemble Skandinieki and their songs. In late 1986, when her poem was going to press, nobody foresaw that Latvians would soon seize liberty, or that the Soviet Union would crumble. The 1986 battle against the Daugavpils hydroelectric station, for example, was still taking place in newspapers and at closed meetings, but not yet at mass public meetings.[39] Public celebrations of Midsummer (Jāṇi) were still forbidden.[40] In February of 1987, the KGB gave a public warning to Latvian free thinkers when Belševica's son, Klāvs Elsbergs, editor of a new youth literary magazine, was killed and investigations of his death were suppressed by Soviet courts.[41] A thin strand of hope and a breath of freedom were openly carried by the folklore ensemble Skandinieki, who proudly celebrated Jāṇi and sang folk songs with no deference to Soviet power or Soviet culture. In 1988, it would be Skandinieki who would unfurl the forbidden flag of independent Latvia at the opening of the Baltica festival in Rīga. Alongside them stood Estonian and Lithuanian folklore ensembles. In their wake, the Singing Revolution began in Latvia.

The birth of Skandinieki as fearless speakers of truth was catalyzed by a crisis of the Livonian nation. In the late 1970s, the Liv population of Latvia had dwindled to a fraction of its pre-Soviet number; many Livs had been killed and scattered in World War II, after which return to their ancestral villages was forbidden by the Soviet government.[42] Whereas in earlier years Livs could register their nationality on their passports, a 1977 change in Soviet ethnic policy removed them from the list of Soviet nations. The Livs were officially extinct, and each Liv would have to choose a new identity. Two members of the Liv choir Līvlist led an effort to renew their nation's official status.[43] Dainis and Helmī Stalte circulated a petition and presented it to the Soviet government. Political repression followed, but they also achieved a small, political, victory: Livs were eventually allowed to write "Livonian" in their passports.[44]

Inspired by Hellero, a Finno-Ugric folklore ensemble whom they had met in Estonia, and dissatisfied with Līvlist's conservative and submissive leaders, Dainis and Helmī Stalts established Skandinieki,

Latvia's first urban folklore ensemble, on November 11 (the banned Latvian military heroes holiday), 1976. Three years later, they established a partner organization, the Friends of Folklore Club, which aimed to revive folklore traditions as a "way of life." The Club met on the twenty-first of each month, so that their meetings, which were open to the public, would coincide with the solstices and equinoxes around which calendar customs revolve. Like Imants Ziedonis's published descriptions of folk singers, or the 1978 concert of ethnographic ensembles that was organized by Academy of Sciences folklorists, Skandinieki was embraced by Latvian literary and artistic circles.[45]

The group's name carried powerful meaning. The Stalts family learned this word from a 1787 book, whose author, Gotthard F. Stender, coined *skandinieki* to designate "vowels." Stender's linguistic terminology became obsolete in the twentieth century; today's word for "vowels" is *patskaņi*, literally, "those which/who resound independently." This was the meaning that the leaders associated with the group from its inception.[46] In situations in which Soviet conformism would have been expected and obligatory, Skandinieki chose open confrontation. In 1979, for example, during a live performance on Latvian Television, the group dropped the censor-approved program and sang instead a folk song of war that began with the lines, "I laid my head down on the ground, defending my fatherland." At a concert of the Finland-USSR friendship society, Dainis Stalts read out loud a letter written by Maksim Gorkii to the Finnish artist Akseli Gallen-Kallela, warning him about the dangers of collaborating with Russia's government.[47] At public concerts in the early 1980s, Skandinieki quoted folk beliefs about insects to call for an end to the Soviet ("red") occupation: "To get rid of cockroaches, one must say the words, / 'Little red masters, move on, there's no room for you here!'"[48] And when the cultural administrators tried to steer the Latvian folklore movement onto a path of stylized, "beautiful" official Soviet folklorism, Skandinieki redoubled their efforts to popularize the loud, unrefined style of ethnographic singing.[49]

The group first performed outside of Rīga in the late seventies, touring in the countryside with concerts of Latvian folk songs sung to the accompaniment of *kokles* and guitar, often singing songs about war, among them "Our Troops Are Not So Great in Number" (translated in chapter 1). It was not a song from archaic rural traditions, but this was not an issue for Skandinieki; for them, the struggle for authentic folklore was part of a larger political battle for Latvia's independence from Soviet control.

In 1981, the director of the Ethnographic Open-Air Museum on the outskirts of Rīga offered affiliation, and Skandinieki began to sing to growing numbers of tourists from Latvia and abroad. In the museum setting, Skandinieki revived calendar customs such as the midsummer traditions that were forbidden elsewhere.[50] Like Rumšiškės in Lithuania, the Ethnographic Museum became a refuge for folklore ensembles who performed (and celebrated) folk customs in the log farmsteads.

The museum also gave Dainis and Helmī Stalte jobs as ethnographic researchers, offering them their first stable employment since the official reprisals that began during the Liv petition campaign. They began intensive fieldwork in the Latvian countryside, recording an archive full of songs and melodies. According to Soviet ideology, folk medicine, supernatural beliefs, magic rituals and mythology should have died out, giving way to science, but they persisted, nevertheless.[51] For Dainis Stalts, encounters with such traditions were sometimes a mystical experience:

> But once, well, this might be interesting for you to hear. I had been walking tremendous distances, and my back really hurt. And now I start to talk to her, she's telling me about the thrice-nine knots, and she's showing me how to take away that *dzērkste*, or *džērkste*, if you have pain in a joint. She's demonstrating all of that, and then we discussed some song, and my back was hurting so badly. And a little bit of time passed, and she only raised her head and asked, "Well, how is it, did it go away?" I hadn't said a single word about my pain. Believe it or not, there is such a thing.[52]

Skandinieki sang and danced in an intense aura of magical ritual. Lithuanians would recall the deep impression that Skandinieki left with its first Vilnius performance at the Skamba Kankliai festival of 1981. Unlike groups that revived only a few external characteristics of oral tradition, Skandinieki demonstrated that folklore was, for them, solidly grounded in supernatural beliefs, a true "way of life." In Latvia, too, the group shocked some onlookers in Rīga when they carried a real baby on stage and performed songs and rituals of *krustabas*. At real funerals, they revived funeral songs from oral tradition and found, again, that the songs resonated deeply with people's true feelings.

Supernatural experiences and beliefs gave them spiritual foundations. But their primary battle was for national survival. Wherever Skandinieki performed, they urged the public to create new groups to maintain local heritage and folklore. Their favorite strategy for convincing others—both group members and audiences at concerts—was to uncover each person's tie to folk traditions and singing, and awaken a personal interest in one's individual, local heritage:

Dainis Stalts: When we went to Talsi, we began by sincerely thanking the people of Talsi for the wealth that they've given their nation. — "How so?" — "You see, these songs and legends, they're all from the Talsi district. And we thank you from the bottom of our heart."

Helmī Stalte: These people felt a bit uncomfortable. Here we are, thanking them for something about which they know nothing. And they simply awoke there. In every place, a small group awoke. And that was our most important task.

Skandinieki's goal was to nurture self-esteem, both individual and national. A recurrent motif in the group's history is a member who could not sing when he or she joined, then opened up: "People came to us who hadn't ever even sung in choirs," remarked Helmī Stalte, "and they could barely squeak. And after three or four months he was such a lead singer." Dainis added, "People have come to us who couldn't even hold a key. Well, and now several of them lead their own groups."[53]

At Skandinieki concerts, performers and audiences merged when, like their Lithuanian peers, they walked off stage and chose partners, breaking down barriers between active stage and passive seats, creating bonds among audience members. "The Stalts family does not merely lead a folklore group but rather they incessantly break down, destroy, and fragment the mistrust that exists among people," a journalist would write while the Singing Revolution was breaking out in Latvia.[54]

The attraction to authentic songs was contagious. The Latvian folklore movement expanded in the years 1980 and 1981; some new groups, like the Skandinieki of Madona, were direct offshoots of the Rīga ensemble, while others, such as the University of Latvia's folk dance group Dandari, appeared independently. Members of Skandinieki established parallel ensembles such as Iļģi, founded by Ilga Reizniece in 1981. They sang in the loud, hearty voice typical of ethnographic style, which, as in Lithuania, they called "authentic," in contrast to "stylized" singing of choirs and opera. This voice became the major point of public contention. A scholar at the Latvian Academy of Sciences attacked the singing vociferously, asserting that such "screaming at the top of one's lungs" had never existed in the Latvian countryside.[55] There were no Latvian ethnomusicologists to whom they could turn for professional advice; the leading scholars had been repressed under Stalin, and by 1977 ethnomusicological scholarship in Latvia had come to a standstill.[56]

As in Lithuania and Estonia, a more sinister battle for power underlay the debates about authenticity, folk songs, and the performance of folklore. Professional scholars at the Latvian Academy of Sciences Folklore Archive knew that unsanctioned attempts to revive folklore traditions would be severely punished. In 1972, two young folklorists organized summer and winter solstice celebrations, and, what is more, travelled to Vilnius and informally met Lithuanian folklorists and Local Heritage Study Society activists. A secret KGB report to the head of the Communist Party listed their crimes:

> The group's organizers decided to gather each month to systematically, as they said, raise the national self-esteem of participants. Believing that there is a policy of Russification and extermination of their culture in the Soviet Baltic republics, the group's active participants set as their objective a struggle to preserve the Latvian nation's cultural heritage and unique characteristics. Thus, in essence, from the legal standpoint they covertly acted against Soviet power in Latvia.

The report went on to describe the group's celebrations and meetings, summarizing the content of lectures and discussions held in private apartments. These folklorists, asserted the KGB official, were probably hostile enemy agents:

> Some members of the group utilized the Academy of Sciences building to learn old dances as well as songs and customs of nationalist content that they performed at meetings. . . . The members of the abovementioned group did not have direct contact with foreigners, however their activities follow in form as well as content the directives of the leaders of Latvian émigré organizations abroad.[57]

The director of the Folklore Archives, Elza Kokare, received an official reprimand. One of the two young folklorists was reassigned to a different job, in effect halting her dissertation research. In subsequent years, although Latvian folklorists most definitely encouraged performances by rural ethnographic ensembles, the new urban folklore revival could not find refuge under the wing of academics as it did in Lithuania and Estonia.

In January of 1983, the Communist Party's daily newspaper, *Cīņa*, published a declaration of war against the "sentimental romantics" who revived Latvian folklore. It opened with an unmistakable threat:

> I was born authentically,
> And I died authentically,
> I was buried authentically
> In a real, authentic grave.
>
> . . . Voices are heard calling for consistent "authenticity" in the work of the folklore ensembles, that is, the need to preserve folklore heritage in its "pure" (authentic) form. The consequential result of such a concept is the archaization of folklore, the mechanical repetition of ancient social traditions. We see this in the praxis of several ensembles.
> . . .
>
> [W]e cannot evaluate folklore heritage from abstractly aesthetic, ethnographic positions; it must be evaluated from the consequential positions of the Party doctrine.[58]

The author, believed to be the minister of culture Vladimirs Kaupužs writing under a pseudonym, attempted to assert the leading role of the Communist Party and its ideology. He recounted Marx's and Lenin's writings on the reactionary romanticization of feudal society, and concluded that the "petty bourgeois," "naive and reactionary" folklore revivalists lacked Marxist methodology and needed to study the classics of scientific Communism and recent Marxist-Leninist theory. The ideological attack was followed by concrete action. Among others, Valdis Muktupāvels's ensemble, Savieši, was disbanded. The first and highly successful republic-wide folklore festival took place in 1982, but plans for another festival were halted for the next three years.[59] The director of the Ethnographic Museum, Aivars Ronis, was ordered several times to fire Dainis and Helmī Stalte, but he refused. The Stalti home was searched and their library of old books confiscated, never to be returned; Dainis and Helmī were interrogated at KGB headquarters, and their home was placed under open surveillance. Anonymous telephone threats and harassment by the municipal government continued into the second half of the 1980s.

A decade of torment sharpened powerful feelings that sustained Dainis and Helmī: an unshakable trust in each other, in their own clan, and in Skandinieki—all of which the KGB attempted to infiltrate and break apart—and an unbending scorn and mistrust of all persons who bowed to the pressure of Soviet agencies in situations in which the Stalti refused to collaborate. Among Dainis and Helmī's favorite songs was a magical incantation that protected a singer from the *skauģis* (in folk belief, the "envious one," a person with the evil eye) and turned evil energy back upon itself. Each line was repeated twice, making the song easy for large groups to sing along:

> Skauģis has his aspen trees, and I have my own black-bay horses;
> Every evening skauģis came and tried to count up my good horses;
> Go and count your own trees, skauģi, leave alone my black-bay horses!

> When I'm riding down the road, the devil hides among the bushes;
> But what can the devil do now to my horses or to me?
> Serpent wove my horse's bridle, grass snake wove my riding whip,
> I was born on the fifth morning, and my horse on the fifth evening.

> Skauģis's children all are crouching at the entrance of my road,
> Move away, you skauģis children, or my horse will trample you!
> Skauģis digs a hole for me now, at the edges of my road—
> Dig it good and deep now, skauģi, you'll fall in and break your own
>   neck!

Folklore ensembles began to return to public life in 1985, at celebrations marking the 150-year anniversary of Latvian folklorist Krišjānis Barons. Throughout Latvia that year, the folk song compiler was honored at events that usually included songs, dances, and games led by folklore ensembles. At the Latvian national song festival that summer, it dawned on the poet Jānis Peters that the folklore movement had remained independent and was closer to the essence of Latvian culture than even the song festival's choral concerts: "It seems that the folklore ensembles' morning performance at the Open-Air Museum was closest to unique creativity and improvisation. The organizing committee deserves thanks for this, because this event was by its nature the warmest of all commemorations of Krišjānis Barons in his anniversary year."[60]

Latvian folk music specialists emerged to defend the folklore ensembles. Andrejs Krūmiņš, for example, asserted that these new groups were performing in the true style of rural singers, a style that was well known not only in Latvia, but throughout Eastern Europe:

> The traditional singing style is real. It was inherited along with all folklore. I know that not everyone likes it. I wish to emphasize that the unique beauty of the ethnographic singing style may be heard only by persons who do not evaluate it from the point of view of the academic singing style. In general, there is presently a lack of thorough research about ethnographic singing. In the absence of such scholarly studies, it is difficult to defend performers of folklore from the unfounded accusations of "screaming at the top of one's lungs."[61]

Folklore ensembles were gaining allies among Latvian artists, authors, and scholars. But the battle continued in vicious attacks from high Soviet officials. An article signed by the head of the language and literature section of the Latvian Academy of Sciences attacked the "ancestorishness" (*senciskums*) and "falsely contrived attempts at authenticity" practiced by Skandinieki. Matters such as these, he wrote, should be left to the professional folklorists. The folklore movement was a mere fad that would soon pass, but, he said, "We, the scholars, will continue the systematic collection and classification, the publication and study, and analysis of the contributions to which Krišjānis Barons devoted his life."[62]

Cultural administrators would continue to attack folklore ensembles for two and a half more years. 1985 nevertheless saw a turning point. Folklore ensembles were still not given much official support, but they were no longer harassed by the political police. For Skandinieki in early 1988, war songs continued to set the tone in the struggle for authentic folklore and national survival. On January 20 of that year, for example, the group performed three songs that they would remember a decade later at the Smithsonian festival.[63] Soon, a battle broke out at the very heart of Soviet life, in the People's Art Center at the Ministry of Culture. Thanks to the free speech that was emerging in the mass media, the government organizers of the Baltica Folklore Festival could no longer isolate themselves from public opinion. The organizing committee split into two factions, with conservative administrators favoring stylized Soviet folk culture, and newcomers supporting the folklore movement.[64]

The conservatives stood firmly behind the argument that, from the scholarly point of view, the activities of the folklore ensembles could not be called "authentic folklore," and therefore they were simply art of poor quality, undeserving of support or display at an international festival. But musicologist Arnolds Klotiņš broke from the ranks of the Academy of Sciences and spoke out in defense of the folklore ensembles, basing his arguments on Russian folklorism scholarship.[65] The task of moderating fell to the chair of the committee, Anatolijs Gorbunovs, who at that time was the ideology secretary of the Latvian Communist Party.[66] His Party now stepped in to take a leading role in the movement it had recently opposed. No minutes were recorded at the organizational meetings, but a participant recalled that, whenever a conflict arose, they would meet with Gorbunovs. He would listen to both sides of the argument, and consistently decide in favor of the committee's newcomers. And so, it was officially decided that the festival would highlight Latvian folklore ensembles and ethnographic ensembles. Song-and-dance groups would not be automatically disqualified, and were encouraged to prepare programs of unstylized folklore. Thus, the committee now explained, they would follow guidelines set by the International Council of Folklore Festival Organizations (CIOFF), which strictly distinguished between performances of stylized folklore and those that were close to oral tradition.[67] The 1988 Baltica festival was still to be a very large event of international scope, but there would no longer be a mass "ethnoshow" like the one that had overshadowed Baltica in Vilnius. Instead, from July 13 to 17 the festival would take place among ten cities in Latvia, with only one large opening concert in the Rīga Sports Stadium featuring the international ensembles and a few Latvian groups. But even this concert, it was hoped, would be more intimate than typical Soviet festivals, because there would be no flashy song-and-dance ensembles on stage.

Igor Tõnurist, leader of the Estonian folklore ensemble Leegajus, was at an organizational meeting in Rīga on April 19, 1988. His notes document plans for the opening concert as presented by its artistic director, Māra Zālīte. The concert would be a celebration of the sun; the meaning of all songs should be "Sun, come!" The stage would be placed in the hall's center, with the audience surrounding it on all four sides. Norwegian, Finnish, Swedish, émigré Latvian, Estonian, and Lithuanian folklore ensembles would dance onto the stage in a long line, forming a circle. There would be three Baltic texts performed at this moment, among them the Latvian incantation, "Go away, rain, rumbling and howling, across the Daugava, tearing up earth. Come, dear sun, glimmering!" Such was the original plan for the July 13 concert, in which Skandinieki chanted a variant of the incantation, "Shine, sun, shimmering!" that they sang again in 1998 at the Smithsonian festival. At the organizational meeting in April 1988, however, the national flags of Estonia, Latvia, and Lithuania were never mentioned. The decision to bring them on stage was made by members of three Baltic folklore ensembles on July 13, moments before the concert's beginning, without approval from the festival's organizers; in fact, they were warned minutes before the concert not to do anything political. The flags were smuggled in under women's scarves and unfurled when they stepped on stage. At this moment, several high Soviet Latvian officials in the audience stood up and left the hall.[68] It was now, officially, a non-Soviet event.

When the concert ended, the participants, still holding flags high, lined up as planned and walked out into the streets of Rīga. Dainis and Helmī Stalti later vividly remembered the incantation that Skandinieki sang when they walked past the KGB headquarters at the corner of Lenin and Engels Streets (today Brīvības and Stabu Streets).[69] Folk song accomplished the impossible, and folk song defended its singers (each pair of lines is repeated twice):

> Other people may have words,
> I myself have mighty words:
>
> I stopped the Daugava River,
> Pushed a stake into the center,
>
> I was stabbed and I was beaten,
> Like a wooden block of oak;
>
> Stabs and beating did not wound me,
> Like a tempered block of steel.
>
> All the pathways burn in fire,
> All the roads are locked in irons;
>
> With dear Dieviņš helping me,
> I want to pass through it all.

That day, Soviet censorship still prevailed in Latvia's newspapers. The flags were illegal, and therefore they did not appear in published photographs. The newspaper *Padomju Jaunatne* reported, for example, that the opening concert was attended by Communist leaders Boris Pugo, Jānis Vagris, V. Sobolev, and Leonards Bartkēvičs, but didn't note that they left their seats a few minutes after the concert began. It quoted the Communist Party ideology secretary Anatolijs Gorbunovs's speech about international friendship but did not describe what happened onstage. A photograph showed Dainis Stalts carrying a flagpole, but Latvia's flag could be recognized only if a reader knew what it was. By the next day, however, unambiguous photographs and news hit print, and the last shards of Soviet political censorship crumbled to dust.[70]

On July 16, an unofficial mass ceremony on the song festival stage "rehabilitated" Latvia's national flag. The event had not been planned in the officially approved Baltica program. Speakers from home and abroad confirmed in words what the festival procession had stated in action: this was now the flag of Latvia, and it was not Soviet. The festival continued through the week, flags and all, in ten cities, with informal dancing and singing in the streets from dawn to dawn. And so it happened that in Latvia two national symbols—unstylized folk songs and the national flag—emerged from the shadows into sunlight together, each providing a non-Soviet context for the other.

Not all singers and dancers at Baltica carried flags. People's Art Center administrators threatened leaders of song-and-dance ensembles that if they carried flags they would lose their jobs, and they in turn told their members that any persons who dared to break the law would be expelled. After the festival, high government officials and scholars convened to pronounce damning curses upon Skandinieki and its leaders. The folklore movement, sputtered one speaker, was a "rotting fish," and the "fish's head, where the rot begins," was the Stalts couple. "Hooligans of the stage" who improvised unplanned performances at public events must be stopped, shouted another. Two years later, Helmī would remember that meeting and smile, "For us, that was a compliment."[71]

On July 11, 1991, beneath the ancient oaks and the linden tree at the Baltica festival's opening, Dainis Stalts invoked the spirit of Johann Gottfried Herder, discoverer of folk songs. Helmī's voice chanted a fire-lighting song. Skandinieki repeated each line, with men's voices droning accompaniment on a single note, like a bagpipe:

> I began a little fire,
>
> Burning nine kindling twigs,
>   (I began a little fire, burning nine kindling twigs, burning nine
>   kindling twigs, burning nine kindling twigs).
>
> Dievs and Laima warm themselves,
> Laima, maker of my fate,
>   (repeat as above)
> [. . .]
> Thrice times nine burning sparks,
> Rising up toward the sky,
>
> Let misfortune all burn up,
> Like the little spark of fire.
> [. . .]

Skandinieki had also sung this song a few weeks earlier at their midsummer celebration in western Latvia. I later watched a video recording of that event with them.[72] At Helmī's words "Thrice times nine burning sparks rising up toward the sky" a burning wreath rose up from the flames, dancing in the heat, with sparks flying twenty or thirty feet above the ground, remaining aloft for the song's duration. "Do you remember that?" they remarked. It was, somebody said, a *Skandinieku brīnums*, "Skandinieki miracle."

POLITICS OF EXPERIMENTAL SINGING IN ESTONIA

Veljo Tormis's revival of Estonian folk songs in choral music is well known. He found his unique composing style in a cycle of traditional calendar songs that he created in 1966, and his numerous arrangements of Estonian folk songs (*regilaul*) entered the popular choral canon, injecting oral style and harmonies into modern high culture.[73] But while choral music flourished and grew, archaic *regilaul* singing faded from memory. The poet Jaan Kaplinski wrote in 1969, "It is, in a way, surprising how thoroughly the Estonians have been able to forget their own folk songs. . . . Ignoring and forgetting [these songs] testifies not to the high level of our musical taste but to our carelessness and snobbism."[74]

Kaplinski's published essay is remembered as a turning point, but it was only the crest of a wave rising all around. A milestone in *regilaul* research was reached in 1965, when Herbert Tampere published the last of five volumes in his definitive collection of oral folk song melodies.[75] In Tallinn, Tampere organized concerts by Estonian folk musicians from various parts of Estonia, attracting a regular audience for weekend events at the Museum of Theater and Music.[76] Beginning in 1971, a weekly radio program featured field recordings of *regilaul* with commentary by Tormis, Ottilie Kõiva, Ingrid Rüütel, and the young ethnographer Igor Tõnurist. "These were times," Tõnurist would later remember, "when we were told that . . . we shall have one unified Soviet nation and Soviet culture which is primarily based on the Russian language community cultural traditions." In this context, any divergent public statements encouraged cultural activists like himself to persist in their work.[77]

"I believe that the old folk song is a living art," Tormis declared in 1971. "It is hidden inside us, it is in our blood, we need to only begin singing, and we will once again recognize it." For Tormis, singing wasn't to be limited to staged performances by choirs. "From personal experience," he wrote in 1972, "I know that singing together . . . provides excitement and pleasure, inner happiness, and a thirst for this activity. . . . Perhaps more of us should actually try out these communal song traditions which are, in fact, ours; they are majestic, and attainable by all." Tormis enjoyed breaking the stiff posturing of composers' and musicologists' meetings by standing up to lead *regilaul*. He came to be seen as a "contemporary shaman," a modernday equivalent of the FinnoUgric medicine men of the past, who healed the public by means of music and archaic songs.[78] Tormis sought to convince all Estonians, not only musical virtuosos, that they could sing, and that their singing could come as easily as it once had flowed in oral folk tradition. In 1975, Tormis co-edited a pocket-sized *regilaul* collection for everyday use:

> Lately there has been a growth of public interest toward folklore as a genuine, independent cultural phenomenon, toward folk song as a single, complete form of art. . . . They are met with interest and approval. This is what has inspired us to compile this selection intended for peo-ple interested in singing regilaul. The "Regi-songbook" is not a read-ing book or a poetry compilation (those, too, can be compiled out of folk song texts, there have been and will be more of them), but rather, this is a *songbook*.[79]

In Estonia as in Lithuania, there appeared folklore ensembles that aimed to reconstruct and revive traditional singing. They were, as in Lithuania, tightly bound to academic research. Unlike in Lithuania, however, only a handful of Estonian ensembles found refuge under the sponsorship (and with the active participation) of professional folklorists and ethnomusicologists. Outside of scholarly circles, Soviet Estonian cultural institutions did not support such amateur folklore ensembles, and archaic singing did not grow into a mass movement of ensembles, as it did in Lithuania. Nevertheless, its effect on national culture was profound.

Two folklore ensembles, Leigarid and Leegajus, were born as academic research projects.[80] In 1969, the director of Tallinn's Open-Air Ethnographic Museum decided to sponsor a new ensemble to entertain the steadily increasing number of Western tourists, and invited Kristjan Torop, a graduate of Tartu University and a specialist in stylized folk dance, to create and lead the group. Torop accepted the position, and then delved into all of the ethnographic materials that he could find.[81] He decided that the ensemble that he named Leigarid ("Minstrels") would remain as close as possible to village folk dance traditions of the preindustrial past. They would sing *regilaul*, too.

Torop's intents clashed with those of Soviet government cultural agencies, which expected him to follow the repertoire guidelines of the established folk song-and-dance ensembles. All of the performances were to include, for example, explicit "friendship of nations" (preferably expressed in Russian songs) and praise for the Soviet state (in songs created by Soviet poets and composers). Unwillingness or refusal to perform such materials was interpreted as dissent. The demonstrative reprimand came in August of 1974, when Leigarid participated in an all-Soviet competition of amateur art ensembles in Moscow. After the performance, the ensemble's leaders were invited to a "discussion" performed by an administrator at the Soviet Ministry of Culture, who, among other things, told them that Torop should be removed. The lecture, like so many acts of Soviet censorship, was delivered only orally.[82] But three members of the group—Torop, Tõnu Ruus, and Paavo Saar— reconstructed its content immediately after they left Moscow, typed it, and filed it in the ensemble's archives. It documents Soviet socialist realist principles as applied to folklore performance in 1974: "party-ness" and "idea-ness" stood above all, and the conversation's intentionally humiliating conclusion asserted the Soviet government's power to dictate even the smallest details of individual human interaction. The Soviet official's lecture presented a list of eight transgressions:

1. At the beginning of your program, you didn't greet the people of Moscow;

2. You had a decoration on stage. I have been to Saaremaa Island, and I know that it was a fence. But not everybody knows this, and you should have explained what it is and why it is there;

3. The title of your program was "Whoever doesn't remember the past lives without a future." Lenin said something similar. You should have written it as Lenin said it, and written underneath that Lenin said it;

4. (Regarding the poem read at the beginning of the performance): The silence before the festival! You have silence! What silence are you talking about? Devil take it! When all around, everything is rumbling and reverberating etc.;

5. You did not have Lenin in the program; the Party was not mentioned. Presently it is a time when this is necessary, because anti-Soviet elements still exist;

6. You display only the old, but you should also show contemporary folk creativity. (In response to Torop's remark that we differentiate between modern individual creativity and true folk creativity): Is this not folk creativity, the works

written today by authors! This goes right back to the folk. In the olden days, it was also an individual who wrote (or created) a story. I don't understand what these scholars are thinking when they differentiate like that and don't recognize today's (individual) creativity as folk creativity. Modern creativity employs the very same steps; a person has only two legs and can't invent anything truly new. If it is presented in such beautiful traditional clothes as you have, isn't it folk creativity all the same;

7. I know that your ensemble is talented. I saw how you carried along the audience on Saaremaa Island, and enlivened them. I believe and hope that you are able to learn something modern. The ensemble is only as good as the leader in front of it, comrades scholars;

8. (We gave Comrade Danilova a guest book, in which all of the ensemble members in Moscow had signed their names. Underneath, I wrote the date and "Leigarid" Tallinn): But it isn't written here that the book was given to me. Nobody will believe that this was given to me as a gift. You must write: To L. A. Danilova, for the conversation.

After news of the Moscow "conversation" arrived back in Estonia, Leigarid's performances outside of the museum were heavily restricted. A planned tour to Sweden was cancelled minutes before departure.[83] Torop was officially told to resign his position, but he refused and continued teaching as before, ignoring the Soviet principles of "folk creativity" and progress in folklore performances. Administrators openly looked for a new leader, but everybody refused the invitations, knowing that Torop would be fired if they accepted. The official disapproval of Leigarid's activities was public knowledge in Estonia, resulting in even more popularity for the group and its leader. But few ventured to create new folklore ensembles, and existing song-and-dance ensembles stuck to Soviet folklore performance traditions, fearing repercussions from above if their repertoire might include too much old folklore.

While Leigarid focused on folk dance, a second group, Leegajus, was founded in 1970 to explore *regilaul* singing. Its statutes stipulated that the group's singing would be based solely on ethnographic and ethnomusicological principles. But they also subsisted on a viscerally felt singing experience. Tõnurist himself awakened to folk song performance in the late 1960s as a student at the Institute of Ethnography in

Moscow, where he heard Lithuanian women singing at student gatherings. It was here that the idea first occurred to him, "Why couldn't we start doing the same thing?"[84]

The new group found a compromise between official Soviet rules and authentic folklore. Tõnurist recalled that he was summoned to the Ministry of Culture and told that his work was "nationalist," not conforming to Soviet culture. The official lecture about acceptable forms of Soviet art included veiled threats and demands that he change the repertoire. He and Leegajus responded on several levels; they included authentic Russian, Latvian, Lithuanian, Georgian, and other folk songs, experimenting with a variety of oral styles while fulfilling the official requirement for "friendship of the Soviet nations." Leegajus rejected demands that the ensemble sing newer arrangements of archaic traditions in the spirit of Soviet "folk creativity." Tõnurist argued that the group's sole purpose was a scholarly experiment, and he was supported by the ethnomusicologist Vaike Sarv (the sister-in-law of Leegajus founder Ain Sarv), who explained that the ensemble's singing was not for the artistic entertainment of audiences but rather was an experimental means of experiencing dying song traditions from the "insider's perspective":

> Folklorists have found a new form of working with folk music. This is the method of experimentation in which the conditions and results are not controlled unilaterally by the material to be studied. The role of intuition becomes greater, with the scholar sometimes taking on the role of artist. We could call Leegajus an extraordinary research group that has come into existence as a result of an extreme shortage of authentic folk singers and folk song tradition.[85]

The group's LP record brought to life one such song from Kuusalu District. A careful listener will hear that the singers revived more than words and melodies; they followed an old custom of singing with their arms and shoulders locked in a circle, stepping slowly to turn the wheel, as described in archival sources. A lead singer called each eight-syllable line, and the group (their voices marked below by parentheses) joined her on the last two syllables, then repeated the whole line. This two-syllable overlap of voices, called a *leegajus*, produced a three-minute song unbroken by pauses for breaths. Archaic *regilaul*'s poetic form appears simple at first glance—there are eight trochaic syllables per line. But each line has two or three words that alliterate. The folk poet's mastery appeared when a line was paraphrased in the line that followed it, in eight syllables of new, alliterated words. Sometimes the oral poet squeezed a syncopated ninth syllable into the line, and sometimes she stretched a one-syllable word to cover the space of two, but she never missed a beat in the long, long song (the English translation below sometimes cuts the eighth syllable, a metric modification that would not be allowed in *regilaul*). Leegajus revived and enacted the singer's boast about her prowess as a poet. The final four lines, for example, repeat the same idea, "Now I sing as skillfully as a bird," in four variations:

> When I start to sing (a song, when I start to sing a song),
> Sing a song, pronounce a (poem, sing a song, pronounce a poem),
> Village people come to (listen...), (repeat each line as above)
> City people come to see,
> Where did this child learn to sing,
> Put the words to melodies?
> She went to hear these songs in Harju,
> Visited Viru to learn the words.
> I thought quickly, and I answered:
> I didn't hear these songs in Harju,
> Nor visit Viru to learn words.
> May the mother thrive in good health,
> Who took me to witness weddings,
> Made me come to marriages,
> Brought me with her on her bosom,
> Lifted me up on her lap,
> Steered me to the room of singers,
> To the meeting of musicians.
> I sipped from the glass of singers,
> From the mug of the musicians,
> So I added to my singing,
> Made the words for melodies.
> Now I sing in songbird language,
> I quack quickly in duck language,
> I speak softly in hen language,
> My voice goes into grouse language!

Leegajus concerts had multiple, coexisting meanings. They were academic experiments at reconstructing oral performances, and here they found a small niche that was officially tolerated. But they also accumulated non-Soviet meanings, particularly on November 16, 1977, ostensibly a celebration of the Bolshevik Revolution's sixty-year anniversary. A brief newspaper report commented that "the multiplicity of relations that exist between master and serf" was a theme that "can be interpreted in many ways":

In a dark room overflowing with people, there resounds the old voice
of singer Liisu Orik, recorded in Tõstamaa in 1964:

> Oh, we are sad slaves at nighttime,
> Slaves at nighttime, serfs in daytime,
> Servants trapped in shiny shackles,
> Laborers locked up in fetters . . .

. . . In the light of a lantern (from Raikküla) a man reads fragments
about the life of Estonian peasants as recorded by others. One of them
is from J. Chr. Petri's work *Ehstland und die Ehsten*, which discusses
the rural people's life in 1802:

> "The miserable house in which he lives is not his own. The field
> that he cultivates by the sweat of his brow, and the fruit, do not
> belong to him. All that he has—his flock, servant, even his wife and
> children—are the property of his master."[86]

It was not, however, solely a lamentation or protest over hard times,
but also included satire and simple humor: "Love of life, resistance
under the most difficult conditions, these appeared in every song," the
reviewer wrote. Over the next decade, Leegajus would repeat the program several times, and again during the Singing Revolution. Later,
Igor Tõnurist and Ain Sarv confirmed that this performance was not
only about serfdom but also about the Soviet "masters" and a critique of Soviet society, in which each person knew that "the miserable
house he lives in is not his own."

Whenever Leegajus came under the scrutiny of cultural administrators and security agents, it was Tõnurist's responsibility to speak for
the group; Ain Sarv called him the "diplomat" who ensured that the
group would not be banned while at the same time not making compromises regarding repertoire and singing style.[87] Tõnurist's defense of
Leegajus was bolstered by his degree from Moscow State University,
and also by his membership in the Communist Party; he had both academic credentials and the official status needed to defend his ensemble
when it was criticized for "nationalistic activity."[88] It is important to
note that the group's activities did resemble cultural "nationalism"
movements as studied by Western scholars, but in Soviet-era discourse
the term "nationalist" meant "fascist" or "chauvinist," and Leegajus
was most certainly not "nationalist" in that sense:

> I have never been a nationalist, and I could never be one, either, sim-
> ply because of my own situation. An Estonian ethnographer who has
> gone all his life to Russian-language schools, and speaks Russian at
> home, simply cannot be a nationalist. But still, as much as I have been

> able to, I have always fought for the preservation of my culture and its
> uniqueness, and for its continuation.[89]

Over its first decade, Leegajus acquired a tremendous repertoire of
songs from which the group could, with little preparation, call up
songs appropriate to any context. In 1981, in their printed ten-year
anniversary concert program, the group took stock: 1,000 rehearsals
and 300 performances; 600 songs, 130 of them recorded at the Estonian Radio Archive; 30 television broadcasts, 3 published records,
and performances in Moscow, Leningrad, Dubna, Kirish, Voronezh,
Barnaul, Minsk, Karelia, Lithuania, Latvia, Georgia, Azerbaidzhan,
the German Democratic Republic, Sweden, and Hungary. Over the
next decade, Leegajus's song repertoire would more than double in
size.[90]

The Estonian public's interest in *regilaul* grew steadily, but there
was no massive surge of new ensembles comparable to those in Lithuania or Latvia. Estonians offer a variety of explanations for this, stat-
ing, for example, that the characteristic Estonian reservedness made
them shy away from singing in the loud style of oral *regilaul*; others
pointed out that the texts were often in nonstandard dialects and, perhaps, difficult for the average Estonian to understand. But audiences
did, in fact, find deep connections to Leegajus's songs. The emotional
effect of their singing remains today only in memory. "I'm sad that we
didn't record more—it was difficult to record," recalls Igor Tõnurist,
"Complete programs that we did were never recorded. Long projects—that's what they were called, projects.... Back then we would be
doing a concert, and people would start to wipe tears from their eyes.
Starting with children's songs. Lullabies, game-songs. And people
would start to cry. We asked them later, why?—Grandmother came
to mind."[91] It is more likely that more Estonian folklore ensembles did
not appear because the Soviet Estonian Ministry of Culture and its
affiliate, the People's Art Center, did not support or even discouraged
such groups from coming into being. Policy changed and new ensembles emerged only after the 1985 CIOFF conference at which plans
began for the Baltica Folklore Festival.

Archaic *regilaul* remained Leegajus's focus for two decades, with
few changes even during the Singing Revolution. In Estonia in June
of 1988, Leegajus performed a folklorized game-dance variant of the
nineteenth-century nationalism song "My Dear Fatherland," and
revived the 1977 "slave program" discussed above. But on public
stages that summer, the explicit songs of nationalism performed by

choirs and rock groups ruled the day. Leegajus's repertoire was less amenable to euphoric mass meetings.

Later that year came Leegajus's most dramatic moment of political expression before their largest-ever live audience, at the Song of Estonia concert on September 11. Here, Tõnurist recombined *regilaul* texts to address the Soviet Estonian government, using archaic song as a means of calling for democracy:

> Oh you, our illustrious lords,
> Oh you, our marvelous masters,
> Stand up, get up from your seats,
> Go and gaze out at the people,
> Come to watch over your country,
> See how the districts despair,
> See how the regions unravel,
> Small ones suffer, the weak are weary.
>
> Oh, you illustrious lords of Tallinn,
> Courageous kings of the capital city,
> Seek out new slaves for yourself,
> Search and find some other servants,
> Hire new working hands to help you.
> Summon new people to serve!
> My years now come to an end,
> Days of work are done for me,
> Weeks of work are now wrapped up.
> Pay me now, give me my wages
> My slave's salary, pauper's pain!
>
> If you don't pay now and here
> Don't settle your servant's accounts,
> I don't want my pay in heaven,
> I don't want Mary to pay me.
>
> I'll look for a better master,
> I will find a better boss,
> Better place to earn my bread,
> I'll go work for someone else,
> Every day I'll have a new shirt,
> Every week I will wear new pants.
>
> Oh you, our marvelous masters,
> Queenly ladies with gold crowns,
> I'll repeat, I'll say again,
> One more time, repeatedly:
>
> If you don't pay now and here,
> Don't settle your servant's accounts,

> I don't want my pay in heaven,
> I don't want Mary to pay me.
> Seek out new slaves for yourself,
> Search and find some other servants,
> Who will work for you for no food,
> Do your work with no good clothes,
> I cannot live without eating,
> Or do your work without clothes!

The song's creative adaptation of folk song texts notwithstanding, Leegajus's unaccompanied, monophonic song was barely noticed in the day-long concert of dramatic, explicitly patriotic texts performed by choirs and rock bands.[92] Tõnurist later remembered, "It was getting dark, not possible to film, no lights, and people were getting tired. For me the content was important, but how much got to the audience, I can't say now."[93] The experiment was successful: centuries-old oral poetry lived on as political rhetoric in the new era of democratization. During the Singing Revolution, Leegajus continued to break new ground in folk song performance but caused hardly a ripple in the ocean of contemporary political activism. In 1989, the group was the first to revive Christian folk hymns from both Protestant and Orthodox oral traditions, breaking Soviet-era censorship of this genre, but, perhaps needless to say, they again did not attract much public attention. Leegajus's main activities in 1990 and 1991 were located not on stage before mass audiences but rather in small community halls and schools. There, they continued to popularize unamplified *regilaul* as a tradition of enjoyable, personal, face-to-face oral poetry that invited active audience participation.

Two decades before the Singing Revolution, Leegajus, Leigarid, and, of course, Veljo Tormis pioneered the revival of *regilaul*, attuning the Estonian public to the traditional eight-syllable, alliterated meter and call-response style. By 1988, this oral poetry was well known and easily recognized as a uniquely Estonian and core form of poetic expression that spoke for the nation, to the nation. When rock musician Alo Mattiisen adapted *regilaul* in the fourth of his "Five Fatherland Songs," the archaic form was part of what electrified the Estonian public.

The year 1989 saw the collapse of the centralized Soviet administration, and the freedoms of public assembly and association were appropriated by hundreds of thousands of people. Among the many new Baltic organizations were national folklore societies in each of the three countries hosting the Baltica festival. On April 15, 1989, the three national folklore societies established the Baltica Association and applied for membership in the International Council of Folklore Festival Organizations (CIOFF). The application was seconded by Nordic delegates; although admission up to that point had been open only to United Nations member states, CIOFF's executive board and legal commission gave its support, and, overriding the Soviet delegation's protests, the CIOFF general assembly voted to grant membership in September of 1990. Thus the Baltica Association was the first Baltic organization to independently join an international organization where the the USSR was also a member-state.[94]

CIOFF and UNESCO declarations on endangered cultures offered a theme for the July 1989 Baltica festival in Tallinn. The Estonian organizers highlighted Finno-Ugric peoples who were fewer in numbers than their own nation. The Mari, Mordvin, and Udmurt performers from the Russian Federation faced heavy pressure to assimilate into Russian culture, and the festival was their advocate, helping audiences study and learn about endangered languages and worldviews. Ingrid Rüütel pointed out,

> We will not organize grand spectacles and pompous shows, as this is not relevant to folklore, at least [not] in our region. We do not aim at commercial profit, nor do we want to stage a demonstration of Soviet international friendship. Baltica '89 attempts to be a folklore festival in the real sense of the word—orientated to man, to the inner values of folklore, to preservation of cultural traditions rather than the exterior and spectacular.[95]

Foregrounded in the Baltica '89 festival program was the motto song "Sing as Long as You Live." This particular variant was a recording of ninety-three-year-old Liisu Orik in 1965, but it echoed a much longer history in Estonia's national culture. A choral arrangement premiered at the national song festival of 1896, and it was usually listed among the first songs in 1920s and 1930s school textbooks.[96] In the 1989 Baltica festival program, Ingrid Rüütel pointed out that this song encapsulated the folklore festival's essential idea: it was both "man-centered" and "nation-centered." A singing person or a singing people is alive. And if a person or a people is alive, then singing gives meaning to their life:

> Sing now, sing now, my little mouth,
> Twitter now, my little bird's tongue,
> Mull it over, my little mind,
> And be happy, my little heart!
>
> Soon enough you shall be silent

> When you slip beneath the black sod,
> Placed inside a pretty coffin,
> In between the long white boards.

In 1990, Lithuania's Baltica was cancelled during the economic crisis caused by the Soviet blockade. But one year later, in July of 1991, Baltica returned to Latvia. The enthusiastic, euphoric mass meetings of the early Singing Revolution had faded into the past. Six months earlier, in January, Soviet soldiers had killed civilians in Vilnius and Rīga, and they continued to regularly attack Latvian and Lithuanian border-control posts, beating customs officials and burning down their offices. The Baltic response was nonviolent. Ingrid Rüütel, the president of the Baltica Association, declared,

> We, the small nations of the Baltic countries, cannot rely on physical force. For us of greatest importance is our intellectual composure and inward superiority even in the most difficult situations. The Baltic nations confront military force and the arms with persistence, strength of soul, and feeling of solidarity, which are invigorated and deepened with the help of our songs and dances.[97]

SONGS MEET VIOLENCE

In a diary entry for New Years Eve, December 31, 1988, an American exchange student described Lithuanians singing a war song beneath the branches of a towering oak tree in Rumšiškės Museum:

> "This is the place where all celebrations at Rumšiškės start," Virginia whispered to me. "It is our holy place—like a church. We come here to pray, to look for strength, to seek guidance." Vytautas leaned his back against the oak and took his kanklės onto his lap. Everyone gathered around him in a circle. He began to sing.

The diarist, Laima Vince, noted, "People believe these lyrics. They believe that the independence movement will ripple outward to the world outside the city of Vilnius. It is the de facto anthem of the singing revolution."[98] The song was even more popular in 1990, when it was printed in two festival songbooks:

> Oh, on the hill, on the high hill stands a royal white banner,[99]
>   Oi oi oi, stands a royal white banner.

> By that royal white banner stands a pale gray stone; (repeat as above)
> On that pale grey stone sit a father and a mother.

> They sit, they weep, dressing their son for war:

Oh our dear son, oh proud rider, Oh where will you lie down,
Oh where will you lie down, Oh where will you find a blanket?

I will lie down on the cold dew, and the fog will be my blanket.

Oh dear son, oh proud rider, go and ride to Vilnius city,
Go and ride to Vilnius city, buy yourself three trumpets,
When you sound the first horn, your father and mother shall weep.
When you sound the second horn, Vilnius city shall wake up.
When you sound the third horn, you shall move the entire world.

Two decades later, in 2008, Zita Kelmickaitė and Dalia Kutavičienė produced *Power of Song*, a documentary film about Lithuania's Singing Revolution from 1988 to 1991. The narrative starts at an enormous mass demonstration in Lithuania in August of 1988. Gold-green-red flags flutter in the wind, and thousands call in unison, "Lithuania! Be Free! Lithuania! Be free!" The rhythmic chant gives way to a song urging the nation to prepare for war. There is a reason to fight. Even if a soldier might die, the song declares, Lithuania will live on:

Oh brothers, saddle your steeds,
    Oh brothers, saddle your steeds,
    Oh brothers, saddle your steeds,
    You must ride to war.
        Oh brothers, saddle your steeds,
        You must ride to war.

Oh sister, give me my sword, (repeat as above)
    I must strike the foe.

If I shall not return,
    My horse will bring me home.

And on my sandy grave
    A birch tree will grow.

And in the birch's branches
    A cuckoo will sing.

And in that little cuckoo
    A small heart will beat.

And in that little heart
    A song will resound.

And in that song will echo
    All Lithuania.

In 1988, it was not a foregone conclusion that nonviolence would prevail in the struggle for national liberation. What was certain was that singing expressed unity under the independent flag of Lithuania. Singing also allowed every individual person to experience the exhilaration of free speech. Only a few people dared to step to the microphone and speak words that recently would have been suppressed by the political police, for example, criticizing the Soviet government's plan to expand the nuclear reactor at Ignalina, or rejecting Bolshevik ideology, or calling for Lithuania's independence. But such political rhetoric was available to singers in a song that had been well known in oral tradition for many decades, "Sister, Sow the Rue So Green." Its simple, repetitive poetic structure ensured that even people who had never heard it before could instantly join in. The rhyme scheme allowed the infinite adaptation and improvisation of new, witty stanzas that transformed any current political issue into a song. Folklorists have documented variants sung from 1989 to 1991, some with as many as seventeen stanzas. But in Kelmickaitė's documentary, the singers gave a concise performance of three memorable verses:

> Sister, sow the rue so green,
>> Sister, sow the rue so green,
>>> Sister, sow the rue so green,
>>> So Lithuania will be free!
>>>> Sister, sow the rue so green,
>>>> So Lithuania will be free!
>
> Sister, sow carnations thick, (repeat as above)
>> To get rid of Bolsheviks!
>
> Sister, sow the flax so blue,
>> So Ingnalina won't go boom!

In 1988, mass demonstrations, flags, speeches, and songs notwithstanding, Lithuania was not free. But at public assemblies over the next years, speech by speech, song by song, Lithuanians drew strength, bringing suppressed images from the past into the open present. The experience of mass deportations under Stalin came to life in songs once sung by the victims. Among them, "In Springtime the Birds Fly" found a firm place in national tradition when one of its more than fifty oral variants was printed in the songbook of the 1990 song festival. A decade later, at the Smithsonian festival, Veronika Povilionienė and the singers from Marcinkonys Village recalled that this was a key text. It reconstructed historical memory while at the same time describing the present: Soviet life was meaningless. But singers could imagine a time in the future, when Lithuania would be "a slave no more," and life would again have purpose (each pair of lines is repeated):

> In springtime the birds fly back to the homeland,
> But will we ever return?

> Our days and our precious youth will run past,
> Only pain in the heart will remain.

> Our life crawls along behind bars of steel,
> But life is no longer the same.

> Now all Lithuania is in Siberia,
> And who will bring freedom again?

> In sunshine of freedom, a future of peace,
> When she'll be a slave no more.

> Who will reach a hand out to help her in bondage,
> To rescue from a terrible foe?

> Oh dear God above, is it truly forbidden
> To love the fatherland?

> Will we really never again get to see
> Our dear Lithuania free?

> In springtime the birds fly back to the homeland,
> But will we ever return?

> What use are our days, and our precious youth,
> If our fatherland is not free?

In the Singing Revolution from 1988 to 1991, Lithuanians identified the meaning of their struggle for liberty, and they prepared for battle. Songs, and war songs in particular, fueled courage to again struggle and die for the country's political independence. Lithuanians remembered the suffering of the deportees, the bravery of the partisans, and the sense of mission created by past nation builders.

And then, shortly before noon on January 11, 1991, Lithuanian cameramen filmed Soviet troops, clubs and rifles at the ready, lined up in front of the Vilnius newspaper printing plant. Facing them on the building steps was a wall of Lithuanian women and men, elbows locked, singing with bravura the song about a father who wanted his sons to be plowsmen:

> Don't you worry, oh dear father,
>   Don't you worry, oh dear father,

Figure 16. Singing Lithuanian civilian defenders flash victory signs at Soviet soldiers preparing to occupy the Vilnius Press Center, shortly before noon, January 11, 1991. Photo by Paulius Lileikis. Courtesy of the Central State Archives of Lithuania, LCVA 0-108094.

Don't you worry, oh dear father,
Your son will soon grow up bigger,
Your son will soon grow up bigger.

Your son will soon grow up bigger,
Your son will soon grow up bigger,
Your son will soon grow up bigger,
He'll be Lithuania's soldier,
He'll be Lithuania's soldier.[100]

Lithuania's soldiers were not holding guns. The outcome of the military offensive was never in doubt. Minutes later, the soldiers would beat and shoot a passage through the crowd to occupy the building and shut down its printing presses. The country's mass media, however, was not yet silenced. A clip of a Soviet officer strafing the building with bullets, and images of the brave, smiling, unarmed, singing Lithuanian soldiers were broadcast nationwide. Thousands of volunteers flooded into Vilnius to join their ranks.

A day later, shortly past midnight on January 12–13, Juris Podnieks and his crew filmed another Lithuanian singing event.[101] At that

moment of crisis, too, folk songs were the weapon of choice: there was
no equipment to amplify rock music, and people pressed together too
densely in the dark for a choral performance. In freezing weather, an
elderly woman poured a hot drink from a thermos bottle, and a mass
of voices sang, their faces invisible in the shadows:

> Dear son, the Fatherland calls you,
> Dear son, the Fatherland calls you,
> Lithuania will be free again.
> Lithuania will be free again.
>
> But if some day I must depart
> From this dear country that I love,
> Girl, don't you mourn for me, because
> I will return to you again.

The pavement shuddered under a roar of engines and tank treads.
Gunshots and screams filled the dark. The song morphed into a rhythmic chant, "Lie-tu-va! Lie-tu-va! Lie-tu-va!" Lithuanian TV went off
air. Podnieks carried his film through a five-hour drive over icy roads,
his car's windows all broken, to Rīga, where it was broadcast on Latvian TV, picked up by Western news stations, and rebroadcast around
the world. On television in Bloomington, Indiana, we saw Soviet soldiers advancing, pointing automatic rifles, bullet tracer lights flashing
behind them. A bearded young man implored, "Do you really have no
shame? Come to your senses!" A soldier held his gun by the barrel and
clubbed the bearded man over the head. There were more screams,
and rifle shots, and then bodies lying on the ground, lifeless eyes star-
ing up into the sky.[102] That night in Vilnius, fourteen civilians were
killed and hundreds more wounded.

Hours later, thousands of Lithuanian civilian defenders gathered in
the square around the national parliament building. Several hundred
meters beyond them, another hostile crowd of Soviet soldiers in civilian
clothes was gathering. The speech by Vytautas Landsbergis in parliament
was amplified throughout the square over loudspeakers, reiterating the
national tactics of nonviolent struggle:

> And in case they begin to attack you, if they throw something or hit some-
> body, our biggest weapon would be if you did not answer with the same.
> You are our shield, not our sword. We have always won because we held
> back. Let us hold back. . . .
>   Many of you probably feel humiliation and hatred in your hearts,
> directed at the scoundrels who are doing this to Lithuania. But

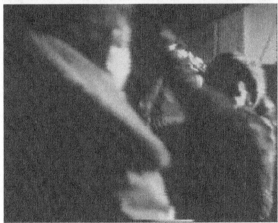

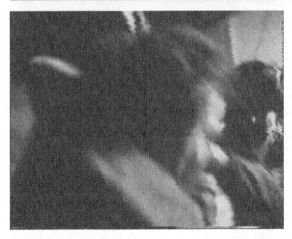

Figure 17. Three stills from Juris Podnieks documentary film *Postscriptum,* 1991. A civilian defender at Vilnius Radio and Television Studios entrance implores, "Do you really have no shame? Come to your senses!" and is clubbed by a Soviet soldier, January 13, 1991. Filmed by Aleksandrs Demčenko. Images by Juris Podnieks Studio, Rīga, Latvia.

nevertheless, suppress that anger, turn your backs to them, look at each other, but not at the enemy. Look into the eyes of the person who is close to you, your comrade, and sing. Song helped us; it helped for many centuries. And now, too, let's sing something, let's sing sacred hymns, only let's not bicker or swear or allow ourselves to be pulled into a brawl. Let there be more calm in our hearts, more light and faith. But let us leave the evil feelings and crimes to them. Let's be what we must be, and our Lithuania will be bright and happy! Let's not pay attention to that shooting, let's sing![103]

In Latvia's capital city Rīga, hundreds of thousands came to the public meeting by the Daugava River on January 13. "We have come together," summarized Romualds Ražuks, "to say the words that must be said to ourselves, must be said to the world, must be said to our government. Now I ask you one more time. Will we defend our supreme council and government?" The people roared, "Yes!" "Will we defend the radio and television of our Latvia?" "Yes!" The meeting closed with the song "Daugava's Two Shorelines," and Lutheran pastor Juris Rubenis prayed for warmth and compassion to enter icy hearts.[104]

People flowed from the banks of the Daugava into the streets of the Old Town. Throughout the day, heavy cargo trucks arrived in Rīga to park in a wall around the buildings that housed Latvia's government and parliament. Welders and construction crews built concrete barricades and steel grids to slow attacking soldiers and tanks. People settled in around bonfires, waiting, if needed, to become human shields. Day after day they waited, passing the time listening to news and speeches on portable radios. On impromptu stages, singers performed songs of all styles. Juris Kulakovs recalls that Pērkons performed often:

> I don't exactly remember how it all took place—there were little stages—I don't know who coordinated it—there were telephone calls, at such and such time be at such and such place—actually, every night we were either in one place or the other (often in both places, one after the other)—we weren't at Zaķusala TV tower, though—the concerts varied—I think the stage by the Council of Ministers had drums—but in Dom Square, sound recordings (as far as I remember) with microphones, singing along.
>
> The feelings at that time were very unique—every time, while driving there, we understood that they might shoot at us (some were killed—among them my friend Andris Slapiņš, cameraman).[105]

Choirs provided organizational infrastructure. On January 13, Haralds Mednis's choir issued a call for all singers to come to the barricades. In their rehearsal hall, they set up a central office to coordinate round-the-clock patrols in Rīga and to staff first aid stations (six of the choir's singers were medical doctors). Needless to say, they, too, sang on the barricades to bolster morale, and Haralds Mednis, aged eighty-five, came to conduct in the freezing weather.[106] Juris Podnieks filmed a choir in Old Town Rīga singing a popular folk song whose arrangement premiered at the 1990 song festival, cheerfully boasting the identity of a Latvian singer and the singing generations who gave her the songs:

> Mother dear, this is your doing
> That I grew to be a singer,
>   Ai-rai-ridi-rā, rai-ridi-rā, ral-lal-la!
>   That I grew to be a singer:
>
> Mother dear, you perched my cradle
> Near a singing nightingale,
>   Ai-rai-ridi-rā, rai-ridi-rā, ral-lal-la!
>   Near a singing nightingale!

Baritone Raimonds Baltakmens would later write, "Songs defeated war in the 'Bard of Beverīna.' The same was true in Old Town Rīga, where the tanks might have been able to break down the barricades but not the song."[107]

January of 1991 saw Baltic nonviolent principles tested by fire. Murder, interpreted as innocent martyrdom, easily inflames violent, vengeful emotions. But three days after the events in Vilnius, Lithuanian poet Justinas Marcinkevičius spoke at the funeral,

> Our hearts do not call for revenge. They call for justice, if it still exists in this world. For humanness, if it is not yet trampled into the dirt. Let the enemies of independence know that we have become even more firm in our belief and in our struggle, because our dead never abandon us, they remain with us, they support not only us but also liberty, justice, democracy, and the universal principles of truth and humanity. How powerful we are when my hand is in your hand, and your hand is in his hand. In this chain of hands embracing all of Lithuania, we will forever also feel the hands of those who perished; they will stand with us as they did on that night of January 13, against tanks and automatic rifles, against darkness and violence, against shameless lies and libel.[108]

This was the culmination of the Singing Revolution, the critical moment that tested whether the movement grounded in national identity and culture, conceived as a civilian-based struggle, and dedicated to nonviolent principles, could endure. Revenge and violent retaliation were explicitly rejected.[109] Had vengeful emotions taken hold, the Singing Revolution would have ended, and war begun.

Public singing in Lithuania shifted to religious hymns. A frequently sung song was Maironis's prayer for the Virgin Mary to rescue Lithuanians from a terrifying foe.

Soviet soldiers continued to kill people. On January 20 in Rīga, five civilians, among them two of Podnieks's cameramen, were shot and killed. Periodic attacks on customs offices at Lithuania's borders culminated on July 31, when a Soviet special forces unit captured seven customs officials and policemen at Medininkai. The Lithuanians followed their government's orders not to use their guns, and surrendered without resisting. The Soviet soldiers made them lie down on the ground and shot a bullet into the back of each man's head.[110]

On August 19, television broadcasts from Moscow displayed a committee sitting on stage at a long table, announcing that it had assumed control. In the center sat the group's chairman, coffee cup trembling in his hands. To his far right was minister of the Interior (and head of the KGB) Boris Pugo, unmoving, hair disheveled, eyes fixed on the camera lens and the millions of people behind it. In Old Town Rīga, armored vehicles and young soldiers with automatic rifles surrounded the Latvian national parliament. The national radio studios and telephone central were occupied and communication disconnected. Radio Latvia, however, somehow continued to broadcast throughout the night from mobile transmitters, interspersing news with song recordings, among them Skandinieki singing the war song that they would sing in 1998 at the Smithsonian festival, "Brother Dear, Oh Brother Dear."[111]

Then, on August 20, Russia's president Boris Yeltsin took command of the former Soviet military, ordering the violence in the Baltic to stop. On August 21, one last truckful of Soviet soldiers raced around the Lithuanian parliament, wounding two guards and killing a third, Artūras Sakalauskas. This last murder, committed after the collapse of Soviet power, was an act of spiteful revenge. But the killings from January to August were failed attempts to provoke a violent response from Lithuanians, Latvians, and Estonians. Baltic restraint and commitment to nonviolent principles ensured that the end of Soviet power would not turn into a mass bloodbath.

On August 21, 1991, the rain that had been drizzling the previous few days cleared up and the sun came out. The Soviet military melted back into its barracks, firing a few scattered shots here and there, leaving deep tank treads in the fields around the Vilnius TV tower, and broken windows and bullet holes in building façades.

CHAPTER NINE

Nonviolent National Singing Traditions

James and Maureen Tusty's film *Singing Revolution* documents a critical moment on May 15, 1990, when several hundred Interfront demonstrators broke down the gates of the Estonian parliament and streamed inside, tearing down the blue-black-white flags of independence. Edgar Savisaar, speaker of the parliament, appealed to the public in a radio broadcast, "Toompea is under attack!" and thousands of Estonians gathered within minutes, chanting "Freedom! Freedom! Freedom!" There were many more Estonians surrounding the building than Interfront activists inside. The threat of a violent clash was palpable. Nevertheless, the massive Estonian crowd soon parted to open a narrow path for the Interfront group's sheepish retreat, unscathed, out and away from the building. Afterward, Estonian leader Marju Lauristin spoke to the people in the square, reaffirming the significance of their nonviolent response to violence: "A big, big thank you to you! We knew that we could depend on you. That if you came to help us, you'd do so exactly as you did. With your intelligence, with your song, with your heart. And this is exactly what makes us strongest of all. Thank you, thank you, thank you!"[1] The Estonian leaders knew their public. If an adversary tried to provoke violence, Estonians would not respond in kind. They would instead follow well-established traditions of nonviolent national identity. The people in the square sang an answer to Lauristin's speech, and their song was not new. It was Martin Körber's nineteenth-century pledge to honor his fatherland in song, a text whose ideological roots reached back into the late eighteenth century.

NONVIOLENT NATIONAL SONG TRADITIONS,
FROM HERDER TO THE SMITHSONIAN FOLKLIFE FESTIVAL

National identity and the national culture that surrounds and shapes it are not primordial, ageless phenomena. They are constructed in a tradition of nation building. The historical roots of the Baltic Singing Revolution reach back more than two centuries, to Johann Gottfried Herder's discovery of folk songs. Nineteenth-century European nationalists were inspired by Herderian ideas of folk songs as a valuable heritage, as an expression of a nation's spirit, and as a means of giving voice to a national struggle for liberation from foreign tyrants. These ideas, and more, were cornerstones of the Singing Revolution.

Intertextual connections between Johann Gottfried Herder's *Volkslieder* and the commemorative concert at the 1998 Smithsonian Folklife Festival are easy to point out. Herder and the Balts presented some remarkably similar songs. At the Smithsonian festival, for example, the Latvians began their performance with "Shine, Sun, Shimmering," an incantation for the sun to defeat darkness. Herder, too, had once selected and translated the Latvian folk song, "Will You Shine Still, Dearest Sun?" presenting a nation that was, in its poetry, close to nature and the sun's mythological power. The Lithuanians opened their segment with "On the Hill, a Maple," a song mirroring Herder's series of three Lithuanian songs telling the tragic story of a bridegroom killed in war. And the Estonian performance of Mattiisen's "Guarding the Beautiful Fatherland" drew power from folk poetry to reject selfish greed and subservience to "landlords." Herder, too, had once harnessed folk poetry's empathetic power when he published "Lament about the Tyrants of the Serfs," giving voice to singers locked in chains at their greedy landlord's whipping post. Herder's song shook the inhumane institution of serfdom. Mattiisen's song shook the foundations of collectivist, materialist Soviet power, in a call-and-response pledge of allegiance to individual responsibility, trust, and truth.

Nonviolent identity, like national identity, is constructed by culture builders. Individual activists shape the image of a peaceful society, and sustain nonviolent mechanisms for handling conflict.[2] In the Baltic, the mechanism was based on an idea that songs and singing are the nation's preferred "weapons." When Herder discovered and celebrated the local folk poetry, he also planted hardy seeds of nonviolence in the field of Baltic nation building. The Lithuanian songs that he published offered evidence of a peaceful nation singing about love, not war, and this compelling argument soon entered the Lithuanian national discourse. An Estonian "Song about War" in Herder's *Volkslieder* publicized an individual soldier's trauma; that same song later found new life in Kreutzwald's national epic. Herder's friend and pupil Garlieb Merkel continued the folk song project, publishing Latvian songs and studying the history of singing in the Baltic region. Merkel highlighted a medieval account of a singer who stopped a war, and this key motif inspired Auseklis's poetic line "The nation was saved by the power of song," which was set to music by Jāzeps Vītols, held from public performance by the Soviets, and finally revived at the Latvian song festival of 1990.[3] Herder's notion that poetry should be "heard, not seen" first blossomed in mass choral traditions. Choirs revived traditional folk songs in urban contexts, and the Baltic folklore movement continued this Herderian tradition in a new, effective oral style. Choral traditions of "sung poetry" expanded powerfully in twentieth-century rock and roll. All of these currents of song flowed into the Singing Revolution.

Why was it called a "singing" revolution? What songs did Balts sing? And how, exactly, did songs and singing move historical events? The 1998 Smithsonian Folklife Festival's Singing Revolution concert engaged these questions. This book therefore now returns to where it began, to the sixteen songs that 150 representatives of Estonia, Latvia, and Lithuania performed at the commemorative concert in Washington, DC, on July 4, 1998.[4] Using as a starting point the interpretive frame outlined by folklorist Alan Dundes, the meanings and functions of the sixteen songs will be derived from performance contexts, from song texts, and, finally, from the texture of singing.[5] "Context" is defined as the specific setting in which songs were performed. It includes what Dundes termed "oral literary criticism," native interpretations regarding what songs meant and did; when such commentary was spoken from 1988 to 1991, it was rhetoric that shaped the movement's nonviolent course. Song "texts" are here defined as that portion of songs which are easily translatable into English because words in both languages denote the same thing. English translations may reproduce, for example, explicit or metaphorical expressions of national unity and national objectives, definitions of outsiders and adversaries, and rhetoric that is explicitly violent or nonviolent.[6] Song "texture," the sound of the text when it is performed (including melodic tone and register of a singing voice, as well as rhythm, rhyme, and other

phonetic features of language), was also laden with meaning and rhetorical function.

SIXTEEN BALTIC SONGS, REMEMBERED IN THE CONTEXT OF NONVIOLENT NATIONALIST ACTION

In 1998, Smithsonian festival organizers and Baltic performers agreed
that the primary context of the "Singing Revolution" concert was historical memory. Events that had taken place a decade earlier had an
important message for the present and the future: the Balts would
create an inspiring example of a successful nonviolent political struggle that intersected with the highest American ideals. In the festival's
printed program, the secretary of the Smithsonian Institution noted,
"The Baltic countries each demonstrate the richness of their cultural
life, and its importance in sustaining the struggle to regain their freedom and independence only a decade ago." On stage before the July
4 concert, festival coordinator Kerry Stromberg emphasized a connection to the United States: "They want to share their story with you,
and I think it's a perfect opportunity to be telling it on the National
Mall, in Washington, DC, on Independence Day." Latvian participant
Dainis Stalts, speaking for all three Baltic delegations, remarked that
this was a once-in-a-hundred-years opportunity for Estonians, Latvians, and Lithuanians to share their message with Americans.[7]

"The victorious, bloodless singing revolution of a small nation
is unique in the history of the world," Ingrid Rüütel began. It was
a singing revolution, because "song was a weapon," asserted Zita
Kelmickaitė, and Dainis Stalts concurred. "We had weapons: the wisdom, the conscience, and the song of the nation." Songs were defen-
sive, not offensive, weapons. When Lithuanians gathered to protect
their bases of free speech and democracy, Kelmickaitė concluded,
"Their only shield was the song." Her words, along with introductions by Rüütel and Stalts, echoed words spoken and sung by Balts
during the Singing Revolution a decade earlier, as quoted in previous
chapters of this book.[8]

The Singing Revolution's weapon and shield was singing, and its
objective was political independence, signified by the flags that gave
context to songs from 1988 to 1991. The last song that Estonians sang
at the concert on July 4, 1998, was a song about their flag, a physical witness to history. Baltic performances at the Smithsonian festival
reproduced the context of flags, sometimes even against the wishes of

their American hosts.[9] Flags declared, visually, that the people gathering, speaking, and singing around them were acting outside of the Soviet system. The Soviet police who arrested flagbearers in May and June of 1988, and the editors who initially censored the flags from officially published newspapers and broadcasts confirmed that these were, indeed, non-Soviet symbols.[10] Soviet policies would later try to annex the flags. In June of 1988, the Soviet Estonian government decreed that the blue-black-white flag was an officially approved symbol (but did not remove the red flag); in August of 1988 and February of 1990, respectively, the Soviet Lithuanian and Soviet Latvian governments even decreed that the national flags replaced official Soviet heraldry. But such attempts to disarm flags as symbols of non-Soviet independence did not succeed. From the spring of 1988 on, the presence of national flags, and the absence of explicitly loyal red Soviet flags, left a permanent visual gap to subvert any official Soviet images of a unified state.[11]

Baltic flags also signified nonviolence. In May of 1990 the anti-independence demonstrators used a Soviet flagpole as a battering ram to break through the Estonian national parliament's gates, but the flags of Estonia, Latvia, and Lithuania were not used this way. They gave the Singing Revolution the visual symbol of self-recognition that is critical to nonviolent mass movements. The political action that surrounded the flags from 1988 to 1991 was nonviolent: singing, walking in processions, speaking the truth at peaceful public assemblies, self-organization and elections, parliamentary procedure, and negotiations with the adversary in Moscow. The context of singing and flags was consistently, explicitly nonviolent political action. [12]

EXPLICIT RHETORIC IN SONG TEXTS: NATIONALISM, VIOLENCE AND NONVIOLENCE

A direct relation between people's ideology and the words that they sing is usually taken for granted. Herder believed that folk song texts were a key to knowing a people's national spirit. Current scholarship usually follows this Herderian tradition of interpretation: whenever historians quote a song, it is to show that a mass of people shared a political idea. For related reasons, political leaders often institutionalized singing to disseminate official ideology and silence dissent, and convened singing events where the public would ritually display submission to power. The orchestrated songs of Soviet Stalinism are not evidence of their singers' true feelings. But in the Baltic, after Balts seized the freedoms of speech and assembly in 1987, it is safe to assume that publicly performed songs expressed the singers' ideologies.

Most of the Singing Revolution songs that the Balts commemorated in 1998 expressed nationalism. The texts defined national identity by kinship, territory, and language, and presented the nation's historical mission as a struggle for liberty. Songs embraced national geography in phrases such as "Estonia's sea," "Estonia's shore," "the birch grove of your birthplace," "Dear Lithuania, land of my fathers," and "Daugava's two shorelines, joined as one forever." Songs identified the singers' ethnic identity and language: "I am and I'll stay Estonian"; "the language that is ours." Poetry joined native people and landscapes with liberty, presenting a national ideal of freedom from foreign rule: "Free like our forefathers," "Sacred soil, free sea, native farmsteads," "Be free, Estonia's sea, be free, Estonia's shore!" A struggle for freedom contained the moral principles of "truthful teachings, objective justice," and their metaphors, light and sunlight: "Shine, sun!" "The sun will glimmer brightly!" "Sunlight shimmers on each face," "Your sun should always shine," "See the sun gleam in my sword." Images of national landscapes, kinship, and history had roots in the poetry and songs of nineteenth- and early twentieth-century nation builders.[13] Liberty, often associated with truth and light, was also a common ideal in the century-old national song repertoire.[14]

A nonviolent political movement, it seems, should be fueled by songs containing nonviolent rhetoric. While relying on a sense of mutual responsibility, evincing stubborn noncooperation with unjust systems, and displaying the ethos of being an underdog, nonviolent rhetoric should, it seems, also empathize with opponents, and it should avoid violent metaphors. Songs should center on themes of perseverance and unity; singing should help prepare psychologically for action, and that action should be, for example, marching, voting, or sitting in prison, but not killing.[15] "Lithuanians are a very peaceful nation," Zita Kelmickaitė asserted at the Smithsonian festival concert. The texts that they and the other Balts sang, however, gave mixed signals. Military confrontation was a dominant metaphor for the struggle against Soviet power. Song texts were explicit: "Guarding the beautiful fatherland, fighting against the enemy," "Take the sword in your hand, and defend your fatherland," "So that I may honorably defeat the enemy." The struggle had two possible conclusions: either defeat of enemies, or death in battle. These images were inherited from earlier nationalist songs.[16]

Songs identified adversaries: historical "crusaders" who invaded from abroad to end liberty, "foreign shackles come and bind our hands." Enemies had long been commonplace in Baltic nationalist songs.[17] In the past, however, they were often identified ethnically as Poles, Russians, Germans, Prussians, Belarusians, or even Estonians. In this historical context, it is notable that the Singing Revolution's songs did not continue earlier traditions of identifying specific ethnic groups as enemies.[18] Now, adversaries were defined by actions, most notably invasion and subjugation, but also "slick stories," "mad howling," "cursing," "snitching," "greed," "scolding," and "false stories." "Groveling," and "bowing" to money (rubles) would exclude a person from the national community. Insiders could also become "others" if they chose to be passive bystanders and didn't join the struggle: "Life is good at home, they know," but "to renounce your own nation is like selling yourself into slavery."

The singers identified themselves as underdogs: "A thousand times one thousand people" (only one million people), "the smallest of people," "Our Troops Are Not So Great in Number," "We do not have many soldiers." Their weakness would be overcome by superhuman forces: "The scales of fate are tipping." Higher powers had decreed the situation: "I was created Estonian," and those higher powers were summoned to help in the struggle: "If you are in pain, in danger, lift your eyes up to the sky"; "So we pray to you, oh Lord"; "Lead me, God, on my pathway, and protect my body"; "Laima, grant your favor"; "Shine, sun, shimmering . . . / drive darkness to the sea, let the daughters of the sea strike it with their oaken clubs"; "Maria, . . . rescue from the terrible foe"; "angels of heaven lift each fallen man." Enemies "will go to Hell."

Nevertheless, success depended on mortal humans: "If you lose your land, / Even prayer won't give you another." Death was a real danger: "Laid his head down for his fatherland"; "Dear son, dear soldier, why did you turn into an oak?"; "killed in war"; "Many sons fell there." Fear of death was a real emotion, symbolically expressed in tears: "Why do you weep, my dear sister?" "Don't weep, dear mother." But fighters chose to join the struggle of their own free will: "Should they ride, or should they wait, / should they turn and stay at home?"; "Better I be killed in war, than I die beside the road"; "Promised that their wedding soon would be, / But he rode to war." They were motivated by conviction that their struggle was meaningful: "Not in vain did the ancestors guard you"; "the words they've spoken / By the nation's heart and blood." They needed, and found, courage: "Courage will be powerful"; "like those courageous men"; "Fear not snow nor storm"; "Let Estonian households echo / with brave minds"; "Father, give us strength, and bravery, and unity, we pray." Praise of courage and courageous death in battle, as well as prayer for divine assistance, were common images in the national song repertoire of past eras, too.[19]

Bravery in the national struggle coexisted with violence directed at enemies. As song texts prepared the nation for war and possible death, they also urged soldiers to defeat enemies. One of the songs remembered at the Smithsonian festival, "Oh, Don't Weep, Dear Mother," proposed violent retaliation when it declared that "many sons fell there" but that the "enemy blood that flowed there" would fill a river. Veronika Povilionienė later confirmed that the threat was a real one: "I think Maironis used this to say that we shall resist. Don't come, because you'll get bashed over the head."[20] Although not common, violent retaliation existed also in other Baltic songs of the Singing Revolution.[21]

From 1990 to 1991, a potential for violent resistance loomed large. Had Soviet soldiers broken through the mass of civilians that surrounded Lithuania's national parliament on January 13, 1991, inside the building they would have met defenders armed with hunting rifles and Molotov cocktails.[22] In January of that year, Soviet military forces began regular attacks on Lithuanian and Latvian border posts. Baltic guards were tempted to answer in kind. So, for example, on May 18, 1991, after a civilian-clothed Soviet policeman shot his pistol at the Šalčininkai border control post, a Lithuanian guard returned fire, shooting the policeman dead. The violence escalated on the next day in a rapid wave of Soviet attacks on Lithuanian border posts, during which a Lithuanian guard, Gintaras Žagunis, was killed.

Even if Heinz Valk asserted that violence is "not our way," in 1988 one could not have predicted with certainty that the Baltic independence movements would remain nonviolent. Massive violence could have broken out even if the Balts or their elected leaders remained nonviolent. Such was the case, for example, on May 15, 1990, in Rīga (a few hours before the Tallinn events described at the beginning of this chapter). That morning at about 10:00 o'clock, Latvia's parliament was stormed by a large number of Soviet military cadets wearing (identical) civilian clothes, carrying posters written in identical handwriting on identical sheets of cardboard, chanting "Sovetskii Soiuz!" ("Soviet Union!" in Russian).[23] Dainis Īvans, leader of the Latvian Popular Front, would later write that he did not call masses of Latvians to defend the parliament, because it seemed at the time that even if the crowd broke through the parliament doors, the worst they could do was beat up the people inside. Soviet police officers stood by while the cadets surged toward the national parliament's front door, pushing aside the civilians who tried to block their way. (The film *Baltic Requiem* by Juris Podnieks documents the cadets singing a stanza of "The Internationale," and a uniformed Soviet military officer covering the lens of a camera recording his presence.) A line of unarmed Latvian security guards, elbows interlocked, blocked their path, and by the building's entry stood the Latvian Women's League choir, singing. Then, a group of "black berets" (Soviet special forces soldiers) started to beat both the unarmed Latvian guards and the Soviet military cadets. Īvans noted that loyal Soviet newspapers subsequently praised the Soviet Ministry of Interior for establishing order between feuding camps.[24] One of the Latvian guards commented to a newspaper reporter that the clash of black berets and military cadets seemed to be "a theater performance planned in advance."[25] Later, in January of 1991, Latvian military veterans planned a civilian-based defense of the national parliament: if Soviet troops were to attack, their task was to disarm attacking soldiers as they passed through the narrow passageways of the barricades. The Latvian guards turned away amateur defenders who occasionally appeared on the barricades with improvised firebombs and hand weapons, and they were trained to stop the violent provocateurs who might appear among them.[26]

Violent resistance is sometimes welcomed or staged by authoritarian regimes, because it legitimizes violent repression. Soviet news wires regularly reported explosions supposedly caused by "nationalist fighters." Soviet soldiers in the Rīga special forces unit (Otriad Mobil'nyi Osobogo Naznacheniia, or OMON) base were told that Latvians had abducted and raped the wife of one of their officers.[27] If the Soviet military investigated these news stories, then the records are not available. But a potential for true violent resistance might have influenced the Soviet leaders' decision to hold back on the use of force.[28]

Whatever the factors were that cooled the heads of Soviet military commanders, the Baltic Singing Revolution did come to a peaceful conclusion. The simple fact borne out by history is that nonviolence prevailed. Baltic participants remember, however, that war songs played a critical role. The song texts sometimes depicted the violent defeat of enemies in battle. Like the movements themselves, the songs seemed to hold the potential for both nonviolent and violent resistance.[29] From 1988 through 1991, war songs mobilized the public, but no public violence appeared. As events unfolded, it became clear that the singing Balts were mustering martial bravery for nonviolent struggle, and not for violent, vengeful war. Somehow, war songs strengthened the public's resolve to continue on a nonviolent course. Singing must have had meaning beyond these surface texts.

TEXTS BEYOND THE NATIONAL STRUGGLE: LOVE, HOPE, AND FAITH, BASIC (AND SUBVERSIVE AND NONVIOLENT) HUMAN EMOTIONS

The singing repertoire of the Singing Revolution included much more than songs of nationalism and liberation. Between these texts there were many others.[30] Love songs, for example, were not highlighted at the 1998 Smithsonian concert; an Old Prussian courtship song was introduced as a lament for an extinct nation. But courtship and wedding songs were, in fact, performed many times over the two-week folklife festival. They, too, were part of the singing repertoire that undermined Soviet power in the Baltic. Love songs formed a powerful undercurrent in Baltic choral, rock, and folk music singing traditions. Love was what singers wanted to sing about, and love songs were what audiences wanted to hear. Soviet power typically censored romance from official festival programs, but love songs continued in unofficial family or community singing traditions, and in informal public singing events such as the song festival processions and post-concert songs described in chapter 3. Among the reasons why rock music became so popular was the fact that it gave voice to young people's romantic love, offering a counterworld to the official Soviet songs of collective identity and socialist production that youths were required to learn and perform at school. When the Latvian song "We Live Because of Each Other" placed first, ahead of powerful political texts, in the national popularity polls of 1989, it was the tip of the iceberg; when Soviet censorship collapsed, the love songs that were released catalyzed yet another singing revolution when they abandoned asexual socialist realist prescriptions for poetry and music. And a love song, "Nine Years Passed," stood at the cradle of the Baltic folklore movement in 1968 when it inspired the Vilnius University

Ethnographic Ensemble's founder. Folk songs of courtship and marriage would always comprise a large part of every folklore ensemble's
repertoire.

When Lithuanian, Latvian, and Estonian singers sang love songs,
were they expressing non-Soviet identity, or national identity, or were
they individuals who sang about romantic love for another individual?
Or were they portraying love stories in a detached, proverbial world
of songs? Or maybe the song's content was unimportant, and the festival context defined the songs' meaning as simply "feeling happy and
singing together with other singers"? The answer is, probably, all of
the above.[31] But these songs' textual content, nevertheless, was love,
and not, for example, war heroism—in Herder's scheme of humankind, they sang an identity of "gentle" nations. And when Baltic singers rehabilitated love as a basic human value, they wielded the power
of the powerless, as envisioned by Vaclav Havel, subverting the Soviet
system of collective identity by stepping into a non-Soviet counterworld of individual relationships. Love alone, however, would not be
enough to guide the independence movement to a successful conclusion. In the Latvian rock opera of 1988, the nation's embodiment,
Laimdota, sang "We ourselves have love," but she prayed for faith
and hope.

Religion, too, was an emotional force that fueled the mass movement,
particularly at some of its most critical moments. Zita Kelmickaitė concluded her 1998 narrative about the Singing Revolution with one song
that repelled despair: "When it was very, very difficult for Lithuanians,
they would always turn to Maria." Religion merged with Estonian and
Latvian nationalism in songs such as "Creator, Protect Maarja's Land"
and "Lord, You Hear Each Tiny Blade of Grass." It is difficult, if not
impossible, to distinguish when and where individuals might have felt
nationalist or religious emotions. Both were repressed by the Soviets,
and both were released at the same moment, in the euphoric summer of 1988. National and religious symbolism shared the image of
being born again: Lithuanian Sąjūdis named its newspaper "Rebirth"
(Atgimimas), the Latvian Popular Front named its newspaper "Awakening" (Atmoda), and Estonians sang the massively popular choral
song "Time of Awakening." Regardless of whether the "awakening"
was religious or national or both, it gave the movement faith and hope,
two emotions that must be sustained for a nonviolent movement to
succeed. These emotions were, in turn, strengthened whenever Balts
joined in songs of national prayer.

In the summer of 1988, at rock concerts, choral concerts, and folk-lore concerts, Balts sang and danced throughout the days and nights. They delivered and listened to long speeches, and they prayed and wept publicly. They discarded forever the official symbols of Soviet power and replaced them with symbols of national independence, in a revolution of non-Soviet public solidarity. Spine-tingling feelings may have come not so much from the content of words spoken and sung by participants as from the fact that people could gather and speak without fear of government reprisal.[32] But the euphoria soon calmed, and singing would also disappear from Baltic historiography. Some authors report that the Singing Revolution ended with the Song of Estonia concert in September of 1988; others argue that it ended in October of that year, at the founding of the Popular Front of Lat-via and Sąjūdis in Lithuania, moments in which historians agree that "cooler heads" prevailed, and Baltic politics shifted from singing to "parliamentary" tactics.[33]

Such misconceptions about the Singing Revolution's end date come from a misunderstanding of how nonviolent political movements work. Nonviolence takes time. Mass euphoria played a role. Intense feelings of transcendence, religious or otherwise, continue to affect people's actions long after the feelings fade.[34] To succeed, nonviolent movements had to transition from dizzy happiness to the more mea-sured emotions related to patience and persistence. For parliamen-tary tactics to succeed in the Baltic, leaders needed to know and to show that hundreds of thousands of people stood behind them, ratio-nally prepared and emotionally ready, if needed, to die at the hands of Soviet power. Here, songs and poetry continued, as before, to rein-force the deep ideological foundations of the independence move-ments, cementing a national, nonviolent identity that Ingrid Rüütel described in 1998 as "stubborn and obstinate, but at the same time levelheaded and determined."

In the Baltic, the Singing Revolution continued for three years. The Estonian declaration of economic sovereignty in November of 1988 encountered fierce resistance from Moscow. Lithuania's decla-ration of renewed independence in March 1990 brought an energy embargo, forcing the government to declare a "moratorium" in June. And, finally, after the military crackdown in January 1991 came a long, tense spring and summer of regular military attacks on customs posts set up by the independent Baltic governments. Negotiations with Moscow dragged on with little result.[35] Through the years and months until August of 1991, Mikhail Gorbachev and the central Soviet government gave no reason to think that the Baltic independence movements would succeed in the forseeable future. But Balts hoped, nevertheless. Even if intense, euphoric feelings waned after people became accustomed to free speech and free assembly, songs did not fade from public life after the autumn of 1988. The three national song festivals of 1990 were powerful, calm, cheerful, and hopeful displays of national unity.

At the 1998 Smithsonian festival, Balts remembered singing songs of prayer to the Sun, to God, to the Lord, to Laima-Goddess of Fate, and to the Virgin Mary. These songs and many others like them sustained feelings of hope from 1988 through 1991.[36] Faith in the movement's success came from imagining that the Singing Revolution was part of a larger, cosmic plan. Songs anchored Balts alongside the national heroes Kalevipoeg, Bearslayer, and the serene Grand Duke Vytautas, together with the nurturing, shimmering Sun and the demon-killer Thunder, and in the realm of the Creator, of Our Father in Heaven, and Maria, most beautiful lily. In the context of mythical time, it didn't matter if freedom would come one, two, or many years later. Patience and persistence, a fundamental requirement for a nonviolent mass movement to succeed, emerged from hope and faith. Hope and faith, in turn, emerged in singing.

MEANINGS BEYOND TEXTS AND CONTEXTS

The Singing Revolution's song repertoire included both violent and nonviolent texts, and both were meaningful to the singers whose ideology proved to be nonviolent. Perhaps the songs fed nationalism, and the emotional bonds created by nationalism were a resource for peaceful mass politics: "nonviolence and passionate ethnic identity need not be incompatible," argues Mark Beissinger.[37] There remains a possibility that singing and nationalism could have gone either way, supporting either nonviolent or violent action. But if *all* of the songs that Balts sang from 1988 to 1991 are considered, then the ideological interpretations of the songs' words fall apart. Many songs of the Singing Revolution did not have political texts. When people sang informally during the 1990 song festival, they sang myriad folk songs about love, courtship, and marriage, and even children's songs!

While singers walking in song festival processions sang, they shared meanings among themselves and with the audiences who lined the streets, singing along. For all of these song performers, meanings extended beyond texts, including an unspoken comment, as explicated by Richard Bauman, "Interpret what I say in some special sense; do not take it to mean what the words alone, taken literally, would say." A song's meaning included the fact that many people could sing along, and each singer recalled memories of previous performances and traditions of singing, which all provided context for any particular song.[38] Singing held memories of songs as symbols of national identity, and as nonviolent weapons in the struggle for national culture.

A song's text did not need to contain explicit ideology. Under Soviet rule, unofficial national anthems emerged, partly because of what they said, but also because of what they did not say. They omitted explicit declarations of Soviet loyalty that were required in official songs. Singing offered a mechanism for stepping away from the officially imposed Soviet identity. But there was more to the political meaning of songs than national separatism.

The musical act of singing must also be interpreted apart from its words. Several texts performed at the 1998 Smithsonian festival referred to singing, presenting it as a basic form of being Estonian, Latvian, and Lithuanian: Latvians ask God, "Do you hear us singing sweetly?" Estonians celebrate with "ringing songs of joy," and Lithuanian "sisters sing." Singing has long been an explicit image in the three national song repertoires, associated with the idea that these are "nations of singers."[39] The style of singing—choral, rock, or folk—is not critical. Ingrid Rüütel pointed out that singing was a self reflexive national pastime in a variety of styles. Her words are echoed by many Balts who confirm that style was not a consideration during the Singing Revolution—they went to folklore performances, choral song festivals, and rock concerts with equal enthusiasm. The Baltic songs at the Smithsonian concert offered a representative sample: choral ("Daugava's Two Shorelines," "Dear Lithuania," "Stay Free, Estonia's Sea," "Estonia's Flag"); rock/pop ("I Am Estonian," "Lord, You Hear Each Tiny Blade of Grass"); and folk ("High Up in the Air, Two Doves," "On the Hill a Maple," "Oh, Dear Son, Dear Soldier"). Sometimes choral, rock, and folk styles merged in a single song, such as "Guarding the Beautiful Fatherland."

Song meanings are related to emotions. But singers themselves often find it difficult to describe the emotional effect of their own singing. The erudite statesman and scholar Rein Taagepera, for example, remembers the powerful song he sang on September 8, 1991, "Be Free

Estonia'a Sea," with the text recently adapted to fit a new context. The words "be free again" were changed to "stay free" after Estonia won its independence in August that year. Taagepera disappoints a historian who would try to pin down his emotions. The song's performance definitely included them, and those emotions were clearly part of the meaning that affected his political actions. But, Taagepera writes, "That feeling I cannot convey."[40] He is not alone in his inability to incorporate songs into a rational history of the Singing Revolution.

Songs and singing have multiple meanings, some rationally explicit and others emotionally felt, and it is difficult to prove which meanings were foremost in any given singer's mind from 1988 to 1991. It is useful, however, to explore how singing functioned, and what it did for Balts and their Singing Revolution, because what the singing Balts did, Gene Sharp reminds us, "stands as a major milestone in the history of the modern world."[41]

WHAT DOES SINGING DO? HOW DID SONGS AFFECT INDIVIDUALS? WAS SINGING NECESSARY IN THE BALTIC SINGING REVOLUTION?

Scholars of many disciplines agree that music can both express and induce emotional states of happiness, sadness, fear, anger, and love.[42] There is less consensus beyond this preliminary observation. Some are wary of singing. Mark Beissinger, for example, writes that Estonian concerts during the summer of 1988 were an "orgy" of nationalism.[43] The word "orgy" suggests that singing is a regression from enlightened thought to irrational animal behavior. Anthropologists, too, look for the evolutionary origins of human singing in animal calls. Some have noted singing's similarities to the chirping of birds, which is an instrument of claiming territory and attracting mates. Others point to the "singing" of mated gibbons, which claims territory and displays the monogamous pair's bond, or to the calls of gorillas and chimpanzees, which function to maintain dominance in group relationships and regulate physical distance between individuals.[44] An imagined causal relation between such animal calls and group cohesion is sometimes transferred to human music.

Studies of music in political movements often stress its role in group behavioral control. Steven Brown points out, for example, that music homogenizes social behavior; it reinforces group ideologies by persuasion and manipulation; it defines and reinforces social identity; and it creates group-level cooperation.[45] Whether these responses to music are involuntary or voluntary is unclear, but research weighs toward the latter. In the Baltic, singing did not always produce the effects listed by Brown. Stalinist ideologues of Soviet socialist realist rituals did intend to modify the behavior of Balts, to manipulate them into a Soviet identity, and to create group-level cooperation that would homogenize them into the culture and society of the Soviet Human, but the Soviet experiment in behavioral control failed.[46] Even if the Singing Revolution did see national ideological cooperation based on shared identity, singing in and of itself did not cause such things to happen.

Some scholars turn attention away from collective behavior, focusing instead on the experience of individual persons, speculating as to what happens in each singer's mind. Benedict Anderson imagines an individual's selfless transcendence into an imagined existence among the nation's millions, "no matter how banal the words and mediocre the tunes": "How selfless this unisonance feels! If we are aware that others are singing these songs precisely when and as we are, we have no idea who they may be, or even where, out of earshot, they are singing. Nothing connects us all but imagined sound."[47] Other observers sense that mass singing may have evil consequences: if these singers with no sense of self were to be manipulated by evil conductors, they could turn into fascists and Nazis. The journalist Anatol Lieven, for example, hints that the Latvian national song festival of 1990 might have been a racist ritual where "General Will" overpowered individual, cosmopolitan liberty.[48]

Ethnomusicological and psychological research also describes how music bonds people, but the picture is different from Anderson's or Lieven's. Monique Ingalls argues that, when many people sing together, Anderson's imagined community becomes "temporarily emplaced, embodied by actions and expressions" of the participants.[49] Music creates feelings of "boundary loss" and trust among people, and the experience is based in each individual's emotions, grounded in that person's personal choices.[50] Even at the massive rock concerts of 1988, audience members felt themselves to be individual participants, and not a mass of passive followers.[51] The idea that singing is selfless is roundly rejected by performers. Conductor Elaine Brown, for example, knows that a choir consists only of individuals:

> Too often . . . we view choirs as masses or *walls of people that we "conduct."* We tend to conduct anonymously. Imagine, if you will,

that there is a piece of string or tether connecting from your center to each person in the choir. In other words, a one-to-one connection with each singer. They are lines of communication from your center to each person in the choir. And it is a two-way street: you communicate to them and they communicate to you on a one-to-one basis. I and Thou, you and me. Honest and direct. There is no other way.[52]

Latvian conductor Māris Sirmais elaborates, "A conductor must work with each person individually, teaching that person not only how to sing correctly but how to emotionally project yourself so intensely that what you do as a unit, as a personality, speaks to listeners. So that each person standing in this energy circuit would feel these energetic charges all around, next to themselves on the right and on the left."[53] Singing does not erase individual identity. To the contrary, it erases anonymity and connects the individual singer very directly and personally to other individuals.[54]

Singing enhances individual health and emotional well-being. Music's effect on human health has been documented, although the mechanisms are not well understood. It relaxes patients, allowing anaesthetic doses to be reduced. It may reduce stress and lower the likelihood of repeated heart attacks. Its therapeutic effects in treating mental disorders are well established. Singing enhances the body's immune functions.[55] The field of music therapy originally aimed to reduce symptoms in an individual but now has expanded to explore health benefits for individuals in singing communities, involving emotions related to "participation and performance; responsiveness and responsibility; relationship and belonging; enablement and empowerment."[56] The Baltic Singing Revolution may also be analyzed in light of these findings of Community Music Therapy. Singing affected and changed singers' emotions, healing trauma and fortifying self-assurance for actions that shaped historical events.

Everyday stress and emotional problems can lead to anxiety that lowers the quality of performance.[57] Singing performance, on the other hand, can counteract a person's emotional problems. Psychologists agree that the act of singing enhances human self-esteem, which in turn helps heal depression and related social ills. Music therapy and group singing have improved the lives of homeless people, crime-prone street youths, adults with severe physical disabilities, and individuals suffering from grief or depression.[58] In the Baltic, singing could melt the heritage of Soviet domination. It could counter traumatic memories of the cruel mass violence inflicted by Joseph Stalin, and calm a mind-numbing everyday clash between official Soviet propaganda and lived experience.

Singing's effect on self-esteem also played a role. Nonviolence tactician Robert L. Helvey identifies the "absence of self-confidence" as a key reason why oppressive rulers can convince populations to obey them, and adds that that low self-confidence is lowered even further by fear of punishment. The Soviet Union was no different. Schools attempted to implant in every child a collective Soviet identity that would supersede individual, family, or ethnic identity. Submission to the collective was the rule. A common motif I have heard in Baltic life stories is of the Soviet-era teacher who ordered a child to lip-synch while the class sang, to keep their voice from sticking out from the choir. But singing from the heart, if it occurred and was not squelched by a conformist teacher, would give a person feelings of individual empowerment, which would in turn lead to the courage that an individual needed to publicly step out of the submissive crowd.

The mechanism of how, physiologically, this takes place, hasn't been documented, but song performers have delved deeply into what happens when a person sings. James Jordan writes, "Music making is constructed of correct notes, correct rhythms, dynamics and articulation. But the mortar of music is human trust (of self and others), belief in self and others, and love of self." If a performer fails to find the right state of mind, then "human nature will thrust his spirit to a place of anger, mistrust of the ensemble, mistrust of self, inhumaneness, varying degrees of violence in both gesture and words (especially gesture), and a general state of frustration," and all of the above will be audible in a choir's singing. This is why professional singers train themselves to go to "that place" of vulnerability, openness, and self-acceptance: "In order to make music, one must be able to meet others on the equal ground of trusting and loving. In order to accomplish that goal, one must be able to look inward and realize the trust and love that already exists in oneself."[59] During the Singing Revolution, millions of Baltic singers found "that place," together.

Singing gives courage. Robert Helvey describes one mechanism by which singing overcomes fear at nonviolent public demonstrations: songs and chants provide "a constant reminder that no one is alone."[60] But the Baltic experience showed that there's more to it than that. Songs do more than merely signal one's presence to others in the group; in the Baltic, singing created courage within each individual. Songs began to affect people's behavior long before the Singing

Revolution began. In 1990, leading singer Ilga Reizniece explained that folklore revival had been bolstering Latvian courage for a decade or more:

> Our people have been frightened into submission, terribly frightened, to the extent that they are afraid even to talk to other people. . . . I'm talking to you, I don't have any complexes, I can talk to you, right? Skandinieki are all like that. . . . But the average Latvian cannot do that. . . . This probably comes from the Stalinist period, when people couldn't talk to others because there could be terrible consequences. . . . Folklore took all of that away. And this is why folklore is needed at the political events, because it creates a feeling of liberation.[61]

It is difficult to sing in a hunched, submissive position. One must straighten out the back to get the songs out. The effect of standing up straight, physically and emotionally, was described by Vaclav Havel in his essay about the power of the powerless: you must simply "straighten your backbone and live in greater dignity as an individual."[62]

In 1991, individual courage, multiplied by the thousands, motivated thousands of people standing on the barricades in Lithuania, Latvia, and Estonia, unarmed, each of them preparing to receive their Soviet adversary's violence, and hoping to awaken their attackers' conscience. The leaders of the independence movements depended on this show of strength, the "people power" that stood around them, one by one. Without these thousands of brave individuals blocking the path of Soviet tanks and guns (under the watchful gaze of journalists from around the world), military action could have been swift and efficient. A mere several hundred parliamentary leaders could have been easily removed or coopted, and Soviet order reinstated.

EXPERIENCING THE SINGING REVOLUTION

What does singing feel like, and how does it affect a singer? The singers with whom I have discussed this question, like Rein Taagepera quoted above, cannot say. When asked, instead of answering the question, they typically invite you to sing with them. "If you were there with us," argues Bella in Gunārs Priede's 1968 play about censored songs, "you would have been singing along with us and feeling the same as we felt. . . . In things like this, you have to be inside, and not observe from outside. . . . You were listening, not loving anybody and participating only with your intellect, cool and distant, and you thought you were objective . . . while the living people all around you were laughing and crying."[63] A reader who doubts that singing produces feelings of love, well-being, self-esteem, and courage, is hereby instructed to follow the methods of Estonian experimental folkloristics, as described in chapter 8, "Sing!" For a beginner, any song will do. Producing correct notes and rhythm is less important than finding "that place" which all singers do find, a place of openness, vulnerability, and belief in self . . . and creative joy. And this is a starting point for nonviolent political action.

In chapter 1, native participants and leading singers offered sixteen songs as a window into their experiences during the Singing Revolution. The English translations, perhaps, echo the voices of the singers who sang them. If you read them aloud or sing them to, or with, other people, perhaps you'll find that the fears that inhibit such actions will fall away, as predicted in Alo Mattiisen's song, and "courage will be powerful." If you summon Maria, Most Beautiful Lily, you may feel how she helped rescue Lithuanians from a terrifying foe. And if, in a moment of deep depression, you chant the incantation "Shine, Sun, Shimmering" thrice nine times, you may encounter light. Look and listen for other singers around you, and a movement begins. Since the nineteenth century, Balts have nurtured such singing traditions in their national identity. Under Soviet government, singing offered a meeting place for free people. When the opportunity arose, Balts drew on their national singing traditions and stepped forward, individual singer by individual singer, by the thousands or hundreds of thousands, to declare their independence nonviolently, disarming Soviet power in a singing revolution.

CONCLUSION

The Baltic Singing Revolution recedes into history.[64] It is only one chapter in a much longer narrative of nonviolent political action worldwide. Every case is uniquely shaped and adapted to a local context and culture, and yet all share common roots. All societies have the potential for nonviolent action. Dainis Īvāns writes that in this particular "war" for independence, people successfully applied, sometimes consciously, sometimes unconsciously, the methods of nonviolent, spiritual resistance that had once been planted by Henry David Thoreau and advanced, in turn, by Leo Tolstoy, Mahatma Gandhi, and Martin Luther King. And they discovered "peace, and the power that lies within it. It is the last and most powerful weapon that a nation has, a gift that God gives at a moment when silent prayer no longer helps, nor enduring hope, nor diplomatic negotiations, nor weapons."[65]

As Īvāns gazes at a photograph taken during a pivotal mass demonstration, he notices that individual faces at the procession's front (his own among them) melt into a massive river of human generations, past and present. In the Baltic Singing Revolution, individual leaders were less important than the national singing traditions that brought together and energized many thousands of individuals.[66] National traditions allowed each singer to discover the value of her or his own voice, and to hear music that was most beautiful when many different voices converged in harmony. As these national traditions developed from the nineteenth century through the end of the millennium, they established in Estonia, Latvia, and Lithuania powerful identities and traditions of political and cultural activism that were nonviolent at their very foundations.

The map was created using ArcGIS® software by Esri. Data sources include HELCOM—The Helsinki Commission; OpenStreetMap; and Microsoft Bing Maps. Facsimiles of the planning maps for the August 23, 1989, Baltic Way demonstration were published by Lembit Koik in *Balti kett* (Tallinn: Eesti Entsüklopeedia Kirjastus, 2004), 78–79.

APPENDIX I: INDEX AND MAP OF PLACE NAMES

Asterisks (*) mark pages where place names are mentioned in songs.

13,000 years ago	Glaciers recede; first human settlement
6,000 years ago	Possible arrival of the Finno-Ugric ancestors of Estonians and Livs; Estonian *regilaul* singing may have emerged about 2,000 years ago
5,000 years ago	Possible arrival of the Indo-European ancestors of Old Prussians, Lithuanians, and Latvians; they honored the god Percon/Perkūnas/Pērkons and may have droned in harmony when they chanted oral poetry
1198–1290	Baltic crusaders conquer Livonia (present-day Estonia and Latvia), establishing a German-speaking nobility
	Battle halted by a singer in Beverīna fortress (1208); Letgallians (inhabitants of Northeast Latvia) carry a red-white-red flag to battle (1279)
1200s–1400s	Lithuanian tribes unite to repel crusader attacks and expand the borders of the Grand Duchy of Lithuania; Grand Duke Jogaila (Jagiełło) crowned king of Poland (1386)
	Lithuanian Grand Duke Vytautas defeats the crusaders at the Battle of Žalgiris (1410)
1500s–1600s	Reformation and Counter-Reformation
	Universities established in Königsberg (1544), Vilnius (1579), and Tartu (1630); first printed Lutheran hymnals in Lithuanian (1547), Latvian (1587), and Estonian (1637)
1709–11	Plague and famine decimate East Prussia's population; Lithuanians become a minority in the region that comes to be called "Lithuania Minor"
1700s	Russian Empire expands, conquering Estland and Lifland from Sweden (1710), and annexing Vitebsk (1772); Kovno, Kurland, and Vilna (1795); and Suvalki (1815) Provinces. Herder lives in Rīga (1764–69), encounters oral folk song

traditions, and publishes Baltic songs in *Volkslieder* (1778–79); Merkel portrays the ancestors of Estonians and Latvians as peaceful, singing nations in *Die Vorzeit Lieflands* (1798)

1800–60s   Emergence of singing Balts

First Estonian book of war songs printed for the Napoleonic war (1807); Rėza begins teaching at Königsberg University (1807); emancipation of Estonian and Latvian serfs (1816–19); Seinai seminary (1826) and Cimze seminar (1839) established, and future cultural leaders study at University of Tartu;

Valančius's poem "Biruta" enters Lithuanian oral tradition (1820s); Polish and Lithuanian revolutions (1831 and 1863); emancipation of Lithuanian and eastern Latvian (Latgallian) serfs (1861); Russian imperial ban on Lithuanian-language books and secular associations, including choirs (1864–1904)

1860s–1900   Nation building

First Estonian Song Festival and national anthem premiere (1869); First Latvian Singing Festival and national anthem premiere (1873); "People of Kungla" and "Bard of Beveriņa" emerge to build identity of singing nations

Vītols begins teaching composition at Saint Petersburg Music Academy (1886), educates many Baltic composers

Birutė Society established in Lithuania Minor (1885); book smuggling across border to Lithuanian areas of Russian Empire; Kudirka publishes Lithuanian national anthem (1898)

1890s–1920   Revolutions and war

"Internationale" translated into Estonian, Latvian, and Lithuanian (1904–05); during the 1905 Revolution, congress delegates sing the future Estonian, Latvian, and Lithuanian national anthems; in 1910, Estonian and Latvian national song festivals, and Lithuanian regional song festival in Kaunas feature many native poets and composers

During World War I (1914–18), Daugava River is the front line between the Russian Empire and Germany (1915–17); Latvian riflemen units established

1918   Declarations of independence by Lithuania (February 16), Estonia (February 24), and Latvia (November 18)

Public education established, including national singing curriculum; national conservatories established to yield a generation of teachers, performers, and composers

1923–24   First independence-era national song festivals in all three countries; 1938 sees the last independent national song festivals in

Tallinn (17,000 singers and musicians) and Rīga (16,000 singers); a regional Lithuanian song festival in Klaipėda gathers 2,000 singers

1939–45   World War II

August 1939–

June 1941   Nazi-Soviet treaties confirm Soviet interests in Latvia, Estonia, and Finland (August 23), and in Lithuania (September 25); Soviet Union invades Poland and Finland (September-November 1939), and annexes Estonia, Latvia, and Lithuania (1940); Balts conscripted into Soviet army; first mass deportations to Siberia (June 14, 1941)

1941–45   Nazi-Soviet war; Germany occupies the Baltic (1941); the Holocaust; Balts conscripted into labor and military service; Soviets reoccupy the Baltic (1944–45); Soviet Ministry of Interior troops fight Baltic partisans until 1953

1944–55   Stalinist government

First Soviet-era national song festivals (1946–48); unofficial national anthems emerge in Estonia ("My Fatherland Is My Beloved") and Latvia ("Oh Wind," and "Fortress of Light")

Second wave of mass deportations (1948–49); Zhdanovite purge of culture; Stalinist repertoire enforced at national song festivals (1950)

1955–85   Post-totalitarian government

Selected choral classics republished (1955–59) but not performed at song festivals for another decade; Soviet ban on jazz music softens (1956–57); informal student ethnographic expeditions in Lithuania (1958–71)

Estonian song festival choir calls Gustav Ernesaks to informally conduct "My Fatherland Is My Beloved" (1960); Soviet ban on rock music softens (1966); first midsummer (Rasos) revival in Kernavė, Lithuania (1967); folklore ensembles established in Lithuania (1968) and Estonia (1969–70); Estonian song festival centennial, premiere of Tormis's "Beginning of Song" (1969)

Four White Shirts, Latvian film about rock music censorship, produced but banned from public screening (1968); "Dear Lithuania" sung at Lithuanian Rasos celebration; police tighten surveillance and punish participants (1971)

Informally organized performance of the rock opera *Jesus Christ Superstar* in Vilnius (1971)

Latvian song festival centennial, premiere of "To My Homeland" (1973); Lithuanian unofficial anthems "Dear Lithuania" and "Where Forests Stand Green" are added to the
national song festival program (1975)

Latvian folklore ensemble Skandinieki established (1976);
Vilnius folklore festival moves to smaller stages and informal music making in Old Town

Tartu Music Days rock festival established (1979); interrupted rock concert in Tallinn leads to riots (1980)

Latvian song festival choir calls Haralds Mednis to informally conduct "Fortress of Light" (1985)

Latvian rock group Pērkons concert in Ogre (1985) filmed by
Juris Podnieks, featured in his film *Is It Easy to Be Young?*
(1987); Pērkons banned from stage (1985–87)

1985–88   "Perestroika"

                    First nonformal public political demonstrations; organizers
                    deported to the West (1986–87); censorship ends (1987–
                    88), opening the way for public performances of uncensored
                    music; arrests of punk rockers and hippies end

1988–89   Singing Revolution begins

May 14, 1988   Blue, black, and white flags displayed during Mattiisen's
                    "Five Fatherland Songs" at the Tartu Music Days

June 4–11,
1988   Tallinn Old Town Days, Night Song Festivals; Heinz Valk
                    publishes the editorial "Singing Revolution" (June 17)

July 1–3, 1988   Estonian, Lithuanian, and Latvian flags unfurled during
                    Gaudeamus Baltic students' choral festival, Vilnius

July 13, 1988   Flags unfurled during Baltica Folklore Festival procession in
                    Rīga

June–August
1988   National anthems revived; Mattiisen's "Five Fatherland
                    Songs" tour Estonia; Antis leads "Rock Marches" in Lithu-
                    ania; premiere of Latvian rock opera *Bearslayer* (August 23)

September–
October 1988   Song of Estonia concert, Tallinn (September 11); mass choral
                    concerts at the founding congresses of the Popular Fronts of
                    Estonia and Latvia, and Sąjūdis of Lithuania

Summer 1989   Premiere of the trilingual rock song "Baltic Awakening";
                    "Baltic Way" hands-across-the Baltic demonstration (August
                    23)

1990	Elected governments declare renewed independence of Lithuania (March 11), Estonia (March 30), and Latvia (May 4)
June–July 1990	First uncensored national song festivals
1991	Soviet military repression
January 2	Military takeover of printing plant in Rīga, Latvia
January 11–13	Military takeover of press center and television broadcast facilities in Vilnius, Lithuania, with fourteen civilian defenders killed; Baltic governments organize civilian barricades around national parliaments.
January 13	President Boris Yeltsin establishes bilateral relations between the Russian Federation and Estonia, Latvia, and Lithuania
January 20	Soviet special forces units attack the Latvian Ministry of Interior in Rīga; five killed, among them two cameramen in Juris Podnieks's crew
Spring–summer	Soviet military attacks on Baltic customs posts
July 29	Lithuania and the Russian Federation sign treaty recognizing each other's independence (ratified by Lithuania on August 19, 1991, and by the Russian Federation on January 17, 1992)
July 31	Soviet special forces unit executes seven customs and border patrol officers at Medininkai, Lithuania
August 19	Coup by Soviet hardliners in Moscow
August 21	Soviet coup attempt fails; Soviet troops withdrawn to bases; international recognition of Baltic independence
1991–92	Constitutional assemblies, elections
1993–94	Russian Federation troops withdrawn from the Baltic

APPENDIX III: SONG ANNOTATIONS AND INDEX

Format of entries (songs with an asterisk are translated in this book):

English title: Original title (original language: Est. = Estonian, Ger. = German, Lat. = Latvian, Lit. = Lithuanian, Rus. = Russian; author of words/composer, musical group), source used in this book. Published variants. Pages in this book (asterisk indicates pages containing the full text).

Bubelis and Tarmo Pihlap), *Mikrofons 89* (Melodiya C60 29483004,
1989), track 1. *249–50, 251, 403n6

*Bard of Beveriņa: Beveriņas Dziedonis, *also* Beverīnas Dziedonis (Lat.
Auseklis 1873 / Vītols 1891), J. Lapiņš, ed., *Ausekļa kopoti raksti*
(Riga: A. Gulbis, 1923), 254. Maija Rožlapa, ed., *Mana tauta dziedāja,
tāpēc nenosala: XX Vispārējie dziesmu svētki, Koru koncertu dziesmu
teksti* (Rīga: E. Melngaiļa Tautas mākslas centrs, Zinātne, 1990), 100–
101. 57, 59, *100, 101, 305

Bearslayer (rock opera). *See* Return! *and* Laimdota's Song

Be Free Estonia's Sea. *See* Stay Free, Estonia's Sea!

*Beginning of Song: Laulu Algus (Est. Runnel/Tormis 1968), cassette
recording, Tallinn song festival stage, June 30, 1990. *171, 172–73

Beveriņas Dziedonis. *See* Bard of Beveriņa

*Biruta: Biruta (Lit. Valiūnas 1823 / Kaszewski 1816, Beresnevičius approx.
1860), Valiūnas, *Ant mariu krašto*, 31–33. *66–67, 95–96

*Black Poplar Standing by the Roadside: Šalyj Kelio Jovaras Stovėjo (Lit. folk
song recorded in 1935), Abaris, *Užaugau Lietuvoj*, 3. R. Ambrazevičius,
ed., *Skamba, skamba kankliai* (Vilnius: Littera, 1990), 1. *107

Bloom, Rye Blossom: Ziedi, Ziedi Rudzu Vārpa (Lat. folk song). 52

*Blue Forever: Mūžam Zili (Lat. Skalbe/Dārziņš 1909), Maija Rožlapa,
*Mana tauta dziedāja, tāpēc nenosala: XX Vispārējie dziesmu svētki,
Koru koncertu dziesmu teksti* (Rīga: E. Melngaiļa Tautas mākslas
centrs, Zinātne, 1990), 9. 118, *119, 204

Boże, Cóś Polskę. *See* God Who Holds Poland

Bozhe, Tsaria Khrani. *See* national anthem: Russian Empire

Bridesong: Brautlied (Ger. translation of Lit. folksong, *Volkslieder*, vol. 2,
book 2, no. 4). English translation in Algirdas Landsbergis, ed., *The
Green Linden* (New York: Voyages Press, 1964), 83. 40

Broad Is My Country of Birth: Shiroka Strana Moia Rodnaia (Rus.). 170

*Broken Pines: Lauztās Priedes (Lat. Rainis 1901/ Dārziņš), V. Greble et al.,
eds., *Cīņas dziesmas* (Rīga: Latvijas PSR Zinātņu Akadēmijas Izdevniecība,
1957), 135; Rožlapa, *Mana tauta dziedāja*, 12. *117, 142, 156, 173, 179

*Brother Dear: Ai Bāliņi (Lat. folk song, sung by Skandinieki),
Manischewitz, *Singing Revolution Special Program*, B-5. *13–14, 122,
306, 312–13, 399n63

Brother's War Tale. *See* Song about the War

Bunda Jau Baltija. *See* Baltic Awakening

*But for the Golden Summer Days: Kad Ne Auksinēs Vasaros (Lit. folk
song). Abaris, *Užaugau Lietuvoj*, 11. Songs 73–76 in *Lietuvių liaudies
dainynas* 19:160–64. *129–30

By a Blank Page: Pie Baltas Lapas (Lat. Melgalvs/Kulakovs, Pērkons). 232

Cantata to the Decade of Soviet Lithuania: Kantata Tarybų Lietuvos
Dešimtmečiui (Lit. J. Švedas). 148

Castle of Light. *See* Fortress of Light

Ciemā teku. . . . *See* Where Are You Running?

Classmates Are Trying to Convince Me: Klasėj Mane Kalbina (Lit. Kaušpėdas/Antis, 1986). 234

*Colorado Beetles: Kolorado Vabalai (Lit. Erlickas/Kernagis 1983). 215, *216, 217, 251

The Country, Lithuania: Lietuvos Valstybė (Lit. Kaušpėdas/Antis 1989), Antis et al., *Roko maršas per Lietuvą '89* (Melodiya C60–30637–8, 1989). 256

Creator, Protect Maarjamaa. *See* Prayer (Creator, Protect Maarjamaa)

*Cuckoo Bird's Voice: Dzeguzes Balss (Lat. Čaklais/Kalniņš), Rolands Kalniņš, "Elpojiet dziļi." *119

Dainų Šventei, also Dainų Dainelės. *See* To the Song Festival

*Daugava's Two Shorelines, also Our Land: Daugav' Abas Malas, *also* Mūsu Zeme (Lat. Rainis 1916 /Norvilis 1935), Manischewitz, *Singing Revolution Special Program*, track B:24. Rainis, *Kopoti raksti* 12:477; Rožlapa, *Mana tauta dziedāja*, 38. *21, 124, 204–5, 304, 312–13, 320

*Dawn: Koit (Est. Kuhlbars/Lüdig 1923), Vahter and Variste, eds., *Eesti koorilooming*, 2:23. *102, 168, 194

*Dawn: Koit (Est. Mägi, 1988), *Meie Repertuaar*, no. 7 (July 1989): 3–4. Rinne, *Laulev revolutsioon*, 326. 257, *258–59

*Dear Lithuania: Lietuva Brangi (Lit. Maironis/Naujalis), Manischewitz, *Singing Revolution Special Program*, track B:21. Maironis, *Pavasario balsai*, 166–67, 295–97; A. Gimžauskas, ed., *Kur lygūs laukai: Dainos chorams* (Vilnius: Valstybinė Grožinės Literatūros Leidykla, 1959), 6. *19–20, 179, *180–81, 182, 202, 269, 312, 314, 320

Dear son, the Fatherland calls you. *See* Linden Trees Bowed Low

Decorate Estonian Homesteads: see Estonia's Flag

Devyni Metai. *See* Nine Years Passed

Dievs, Svētī Latviju. *See* national anthem: Latvia

Div' Dūjiņas. *See* High Up in the Air, Two Doves

Div' Pļaviņas. *See* I Cut Two Fields of Clover

Don't Leave Me, Oh Rising Sun. *See* Laimdota's Song

Dzeguzes Balss. *See* Cuckoo Bird's Voice

Dziesmai Šodien Liela Diena. *See* This Day Is Song's Great Day

Dziesma par Četriem Baltiem Krekliem. *See* Four White Shirts

Dziesma par Sapumpurotu Zaru. *See* No matter if it's friends or beasts

Dzimtā Valoda. *See* Native Language

Eesti Lipp. *See* Estonia's Flag

Eestlane Olen. *See* Five Fatherland Songs: (5) I Am Estonian

Eile Nägin Ma Eestimaad. *See* Yesterday I Saw Estonia!

Einige Hochzeitslieder. *See* A Few Wedding Songs

Ei Ole Üksi Ükski Maa. *See* Not a Single Land Is Alone

Černiauskas, *Europos tautų nacionaliniai himnai*, 113. *98, 99, 141,
143, 147, 163, 179–80, 186, 192–93, 202, 269, 374n28, 385n48
*Lithuanian SSR: Anthem of the Lithuanian SSR: Lietuvos TSR Himnas
(Lit. Venclova/Dvarionas and Švedas 1950), Antanas Venclova,
Raštai, vol. 1 (Vilnius: Valstybinės Grožinės Literatūros Leidykla,
1955), 17–18. 141, *143, 145, 156, 179
*Russian Empire: God Protect the Tsar: Bozhe, Tsaria Khrani (Rus.
Zhukovskii/L'vov 1833), Semenov, *Rodnye zvuki*, 1–2. 63, *64, 83,
87, 90, 101, 123
*Soviet Union: state anthem of the USSR: Gosudarstvennyi Gimn SSSR
(Rus. Mikhalkov/Aleksandrov 1944). *139, 140–42, 145, 147, 149,
152, 156, 183
Sweden: Du Gamla, Du Fria (Dybeck, 1844). 77
*Native Language: Dzimtā Valoda (Lat. adaptation of Vieru, translated by
Ziedonis/Virga, Līvi 1986), *Mikrofons 86* (Melodiya C60 29483 004, 1986),
track 1. Klass Vāvere, *Līvi* (Riga: Tandems, 1997), 66. 232, *233, 234
Nav Skaitā Lieli Mūsu Pulki. *See* Our Troops Are Not So Great in Number
Nedod Dievs, Vītolam. *See* I'll Take the Most Beautiful Girl
Nightingale Wove a Crown: Lakstīgala Kroni Pina (Lat. folk song),
Rožlapa, *Mana tauta dziedāja*, 76. Song 408 in Barons, *Latvju dainas*.
305
*Nine Years Passed: Devyni Metai (Lit. folk song), Veronika Povilionienė,
video-recorded interview, April 8, 2010. Povilionienė knows a variant
sung to a different melody, and wasn't sure which one she sang in 1968,
but Meilutė Ramonienė confirmed that the variant quoted here was the
one she learned at Vilnius University in 1971. *266–67, 316
Noise: Troksnis (Lat. Bērziņš 1972/ Kulakovs, Pērkons 1981). 231
No matter if it's friends or beasts: *Line from* Dziesma par Sapumpurotu
Zaru (Lat. Melgalvs 1978/ Kulakovs, Pērkons 1981), Pērkons, *Dziesmu
izlase*, track 1. Melgalvs, *Meldijās iešana*, 54. 229
Not a Single Land Is Alone: Ei Ole Üksi Ükski Maa (Est. Leesment/
Mattiisen 1987), Rinne, *Laulev revolutsioon* 315–16. 237–38
Now, Men, Let Us Be Strong (Est. Winkler 1807). 111–12
Now the Little Birds: Juba Linnukesed (Est.). 188–89
Nu Ardievu, Vidzemīte. *See* Farewell Now, Dear Vidzemīte
O Alte Burschenherrlichkeit (Ger. Höfling 1825). 369n69
O Bursi Hiilgus Endine. *See* O Alte Burschenherrlichkeit
*Oh Brothers, Saddle Your Steeds: Balnokit Broliai Žirgus (Lit. folk song),
Kelmickaitė and Kutavičienė, *Dainos galia*. Song 14 in *Lietuvių liaudies
dainynas* 18:63–64. In April of 1991, Julija Gelažis documented
that Lithuanians in Lithuania would add a final stanza, "And in that
Lithuania, Lithuanians shall sing," in Julija Gelazis, "Vakarone: A

*Prayer (Creator, Protect Maarjamaa): Palve (Looja, Hoia Maarjamaa)
(Est. Kangur/Mägi 1987), *Meie Repertuaar*, no. 7 (July 1989): 5–7.
Rinne, *Laulev revolutsioon* 325. 253, *254, 317, 319, 395n122

*Prayer (Lord, You Hear Each Tiny Blade of Grass: Lūgšana (Kungs,
Kas Zāles Čukstus Dzirdi) (Breikšs/Kalniņš, Akurātere 1989),
Manischewitz, *Singing Revolution Special Program*, track B:8.
Atmoda, December 16, 1988, 1. *14–15, 249, 312–4, 317, 319–20,
*393n110

Prayer of the Russians. *See* national anthem: Russian Empire

Preobrazhenskii Regiment anthem. 98

Pretskauģu Dziesma. *See* Anti-Skauģis Song

Projām Jāiet. *See* Time to Go Home

Protesta Dziesma. *See* Song to Protest Environmental Pollution

Pulcējaties, Latvju Dēli. *See* Strömt herbei, ihr Völkerscharen

Pūt, Vējiņi. *See* Oh Wind, Blow, Wind

Rahvahulgad, Tulge Kokku. *See* Strömt herbei, ihr Völkerscharen

Requiem (Mozart). 70

Restlessness. *See* Blue Forever

*Return! *also* Bearslayer's Aria: Atgriešanās (Lat. Zālīte/Liepiņš 1988),
Liepiņš and Zālīte, *Rokopera Lāčplēsis*, 25. *246

Rhapsody of the Friendship of Nations (Rus. and other folk songs / Tormis,
1982). 170

Rifleman's Song: Strēlnieka Dziesma (Lat. Rokpelnis/Ozoliņš 1941), Fricis
Rokpelnis, *Vējš cērtas vaigā: Izlase* (Riga: Liesma, 1969), 117. 127,
404n21

Rīga Dimd. *See* Rīga Rings

Rīga girls now have sorrowful faces. *See* Oh, Farewell, My Little Friend

*Rīga Rings: Rīga Dimd! (Lat. folk song / Cimze 1872), *Pirmee
wispahrigee*, 55–56. Rožlapa, *Mana tauta dziedāja*, 66; Song 7892–2
in Barons, *Latwju dainas*. *88, 90, 142

*Ruin in the Garden: Iškada Daržely (Lit. folk song, adapted by Rhesa
1825), Rėza, *Lietuvių liaudies dainos*, 94–97. *See also* Song of the
Maiden *and* Lament of the Maiden. 61

*Saaremaa Island: Saaremaa (Est. folk song). Cassette recording, July 1,
1990, Tallinn song festival stage. Kuresoo, *Kostke, laulud*, 46. *199–
200, 385n65

Saa Vabaks. *See* Stay Free, Estonia's Sea!

Šalyj Kelio Jovaras. *See* Black Poplar Standing by the Roadside

*Saule, Pērkons, Daugava (Lat. Rainis 1919 / Brauns 1989), Rožlapa, *Mana
tauta dziedāja*, 39–40. Brauns omitted the stanza about Dieviņš and
animals digging the Daugava in a version that he wrote for the choir,
Sindī Putnu Dārzs; Mārtiņš Brauns, e-mail to author, April 27, 2013.
190, *191–92, 204–5, 385n57

Še, Kur Līgo. *See* Here, Where Pine Forests Grow

Šeit Ir Latvija. *See* This is Latvia

Sēk, Sesute. *See* Sister, Sow the Rue So Green

*Shine, Sun, Shimmering!: Spīguļo, Saulīt! (Lat. folk song sung by L.
  Bērziņa 1978, recorded by D. Stalts), Manischewitz, *Singing Revolution
  Special Program*, track B:3. Helmī Stalte, ed., *Līgo: Gadskārtu ieražas*
  (Rīga: E. Melngaiļa Tautas mākslas centrs, 1989), 36; Song 34028 in
  Barons, *Latwju dainas*. *11–12, 55, 283, 308, 312–13, 326, 399n51

Shiroka Strana Moia Rodnaia. *See* Broad Is My Country of Birth

*Shoreline: Krantas (Lit. Antis 1988), Antis, *Geriausios dainos* (Zona
  Records ZNCD 075, 2006), track 13. 254, *255, 256

Sind Surmani. *See* Five Fatherland Songs: (3) You, until Death

*Sing as Long as You Live: Laula, kuni Elad (Est. folk song sung by Liisu
  Orik), *Baltica '89*, 3. *296–97

Singer of Beverīna. *See* Bard of Beverīna

*Singer's Childhood: Lauliku lapsepōli (Est. folk song / Härma). *104

*Sister, Sow the Rue So Green: Sēk, Sesute, Žalią Rūtą (Lit. folk song),
  Kelmickaitė and Kutavičienė, *Dainos galia*. Songs 197, 198, and 199 in
  Lietuvių liaudies dainynas 19:309–13. 128, *299

Slavs'ia, Slavs'ia. *See* Glory, Glory to Our Russian Tsar!

Soldiers Are Uneasy: Karavīri Bēdājas (Lat. folk song). 116

So the Wheel of Time Has Turned Around: Nii Ajaratas Ringi Käind (Est.
  Saarik/Türnpu). 199

*Something Just Happened: Kažkas Atsitiko (Lit. Kaušpėdas/Antis 1986),
  A. Pozdniakovas, *Kažkas atsitiko* (Lietuvos Kinostudija 1986, Bomba
  Video BBV 015, 1996). Antis, *Geriausios dainos*, track 3. 234, *235

*Song about the War: Lied vom Kriege; (Ger. transl. of Est. folk song,
  Volkslieder, vol. 2, book 3, no. 10), Herder, *Werke in zehn Bänden*,
  3:384–86. *33–35, 108–9, 112–13, 309

Song for Stalin: Laul Stalinile (Est. Ernesaks). 150

Song of Solomon (Biblical text). 28–30, 42

*Song of the Aborigine: Pärismaalase Lauluke (Est. Tormis 1981). *172–73

*Song of the Maiden about Her Garden: Lied des Mädchens um ihren
  Garten (Ger. transl. of Lit. folk song, *Volkslieder*, vol. 1, book 2, no.
  2), Herder, *Werke in zehn Bänden*, 3:121. *See also* Lament of a Maiden
  and Ruin in the Garden. *31, 59, 61, 308

*Song of the Road: Kelio Daina (Lit. Strielkūnas/Kernagis), Kernagis,
  Akustinis (VK CD 001), track 20. Jonas Strielkūnas, *Vėjas rugiuos*
  (Vilnius: Vaga, 1971), 27. *213–14

*Song of the Young Warrior: Lied des Jungen Reuters (Ger. transl. of Lit.
  folk song, *Volkslieder*, vol. 1, book 2, no. 3), Herder, *Werke in zehn
  Bänden*, 3:122–23. Reuter may also be translated as "cavalryman."
  *31–32, 308

NOTES

INTRODUCTION

1. Heinz Valk, "Laulev revolutsioon," *Sirp ja Vasar*, June 17, 1988, reprinted in Mart Laar, Urmas Ott, and Sirje Endre, eds. *Teine Eesti: Eeslava. Eesti iseseisvuse taassünd 1986–1991. Dokumendid, kõned, artiklid.* Documents, Speeches, Articles (Tallinn: SE&JS, 1996), 425–26; excerpts quoted in Harri Rinne, *Laulev revolutsioon: Eesti rokipõlvkonna ime*, trans. Sander Liivak (Tallinn: Varrak, 2008), 262–63.

2. Gene Sharp, "The New Challenge," in *The Baltic Way to Freedom: Non-Violent Struggle of the Baltic States in a Global Context*, ed. Jānis Škapars (Riga: Zelta Grauds, 2005), 424.

3. Andrejs Plakans, *A Concise History of the Baltic States* (Cambridge: Cambridge University Press, 2011), 386–401; Andres Kasekamp, *A History of the Baltic States* (Palgrave Macmillan, 2010), 160–71.

4. Olgerts Eglitis, *Nonviolent Action in the Liberation of Latvia* (Cambridge, MA: The Albert Einstein Institution, 1993); G. Miniotaite, *Nonviolent Resistance in Lithuania: A Story of Peaceful Liberation* (Boston, MA: The Albert Einstein Institution, 2002); Mark Beissinger, "The Intersection of Ethnic Nationalism and People Power Tactics in the Baltic States, 1987–91," in *Civil Resistance and Power Politics: The Experience of Non-Violent Action from Gandhi to the Present*, ed. Adam Roberts and Timothy Garton Ash (Oxford University Press, 2009).

5. Priit Vesilind, *The Singing Revolution* (Tallinn: Varrak, 2009); Vance Wolverton, "Breaking the Silence: Choral Music of the Baltic Republics. Part One: Estonia," *Choral Journal* 38, no. 7 (1998): 21–28; Vance Wolverton, "Breaking the Silence: Choral Music of the Baltic Republics. Part Two: Latvia," *Choral Journal* 38, no. 9 (1998): 37–44; Vance Wolverton, "Breaking the Silence: Choral Music of the Baltic Republics. Part Three: Lithuania," *Choral Journal* 38, no. 10 (1998): 23–29; David Puderbaugh, "How Choral Music Saved a Nation," *Choral Journal* 49, 4 (2008): 28–43.

6. James Peacock, "Geertz's Concept of Culture in Historical Context: How He Saved the Day and Maybe the Century," in *Clifford Geertz by His Colleagues*, ed. Richard Shweder and Byron Good (Chicago: University of Chicago Press, 2005), 54.

7. Anthony D. Smith, *Ethno-Symbolism and Nationalism: A Cultural Approach* (Florence, KY: Routledge, 2009), 16.

8. J. Manischewitz, ed. *Singing Revolution Special Program,* unpublished sound recordings FP-1998–CT-0284A and FP-1998–CT-0284B (Washington, DC: Ralph Rinzler Folklife Archives and Collections, 2009).

9. John Miles Foley, *How to Read an Oral Poem* (Urbana: University of Illinois Press, 2002), 45.

10. Peter Ackerman and Jack DuVall, *A Force More Powerful: A Century of Nonviolent Conflict* (New York: St. Martin's Press, 2000); Gene Sharp, *There Are Realistic Alternatives* (Boston, MA: Albert Einstein Institution, 2003).

11. Graham Kemp and Douglas P. Fry, eds., *Keeping the Peace: Conflict Resolution and Peaceful Societies around the World* (New York: Routledge, 2004); Elsie Boulding, *Cultures of Peace: The Hidden Side of History* (Syracuse, NY: Syracuse University Press, 2000); Leslie E. Sponsel and Thomas Gregor, eds., *The Anthropology of Peace and Nonviolence* (Boulder, CO: Lynne Rienner, 1994).

12. Ellen W. Gorsevski, *Peaceful Persuasion: The Geopolitics of Nonviolent Rhetoric* (Albany: State University of New York Press, 2004); Kerran L. Sanger, *"When the Spirit Says Sing!" The Role of Freedom Songs in the Civil Rights Movement* (New York: Garland, 1995); Joe Street, *The Culture War in the Civil Rights Movement* (Gainesville: University Press of Florida, 2007). Many books chronicle song authors' names and dates when selected songs were produced and performed, but do not analyze the poetics or content of a movement's song repertoire.

13. Manfred Steger, *Gandhi's Dilemma: Nonviolent Principles and Nationalist Power* (New York: St. Martin's Press, 2000).

14. Beissinger, "Intersection of Ethnic Nationalism and People Power," 232.

CHAPTER 1

1. Author's field notes, July 4, 1998; Manischewitz, *Singing Revolution Special Program.* Words spoken and sung by performers were transcribed and translated by the author. Descriptions of performance context are given in square brackets.

2. "Oh, it floated, floated, And floated across, From the town of Gillija, A yellow little boat. Oh, little brother, little brother, My little brother, Where will we turn our boat, Where will we sail? To the sea, Or to the lagoon, Or to the village Where my maiden lives? Not to the sea, Not to the lagoon, Only to the village Where my maiden lives." The old Prussian song was published, accompanied by a Latvian translation that was used for this translation to English, in Valdis Muktupāvels, *Rasa: Prūšos manas kājas autas* (Rīga: Latvijas Kultūras Fonds, 1989), 15. The published variant has two additional stanzas.

3. Little information was published about the 150 Balts at the Smithsonian Folklife Festival. The Festival's Program lists names of group members and themes of performances. Reports in English-language publications are

sparse; to my knowledge, only one scholarly description appears in a brief published review, James I. Deutsch, "Smithsonian Folklife Festival on the National Mall," *Journal of American Folklore* 113, no. 447 (2000): 99–100. The Baltic mass media produced several general accounts; the Smithsonian Institution's Ralph Rinzler Folklife Archives contain many hours of video and sound recordings from the Festival.

4. Tape-recorded interview, Tallinn, June 20, 2000.

CHAPTER 2

1. This and other passages written in the present tense are based on my notes taken during fieldwork in 1990–91. Uģis Niedre of the Latvian Open-Air Museum estimates that the oaks described here are about 200 years old, and the linden is about 120 years old; the linden's circumference is 360 centimeters, and the oaks measure 350 centimeters and 275 centimeters around; email to author, March 4, 2009.

2. For brevity, only Herder's titles are given here, although some titles include several songs; numerals refer to the volume, the book, and the number of the particular song. Page numbers in parentheses refer to Johann Gottfried Herder, *Sämtliche Werke*, ed. Bernhard Suphan, 33 vols. (Hildesheim, Germany: Georg Olms, 1967–68), 25. Estonian songs: 2.2.1 "Einige Hochzeitlieder" (399–401); 2.2.2 "Klage über die Tyrannen der Leibeignen" (401–3); and 2.3.10 "Lied vom Kriege" (496–98). Latvian songs: 2.2.7 "Fragmente lettischer Lieder" (409–11); and 2.2.8 "Frühlingslied" (411–12). Lithuanian songs: 1.1.3 "Die kranke Braut" (143–44); 1.1.4 "Abschiedslied eines Mädchens" (144–45); 1.1.5 "Der versunkene Brautring" (145–46); 1.2.2 "Lied des Mädchens um ihren Garten" (186); 1.2.3 "Lied des jungen Reiters" (187–88); 1.2.4 "Der unglückliche Weidenbaum" (188–89); 1.2.23 "Die erste Bekanntschaft" (242); and 2.2.4 "Brautlied" (404–5). An Estonian song, "Jörru, Jörru" and a Latvian song, "Es pa zellu raudadams," are quoted within prose descriptions of song traditions in the introduction to volume 2, book 2 (391, 394). See also "Lettisches Singe," in Herder's first, unpublished folk song collection of 1774 (ibid., 25:91), and Herder's manuscripts of two songs published in the posthumous *Stimmen der Völker in Liedern*: "Der Hagestolze" (589–90) and "Schmeichellied auf die Herrschaft" (ibid., 25:579–80).

3. Kurt Stavenhagen, "Herder in Riga," in *Abhandlungen des Herder-Instituts zu Riga* (Riga: G. Löffler, 1925) 1:1–22; Leonid Arbusow, "Herder und die Begründung der Volksliedforschung im deutschbaltischen Osten," in *Im Geiste Herders: Gesammelte Aufsätze zum 150. Todestage J. G. Herders*, ed. Erich Keyser (Kitzingen am Main: Holzner Verlag, 1953), 129–256; Hermann Strobach, "Herders Volksliedbegriff: Geschichte und Gegenwärtige Bedeutung," *Jahrbuch für Volkskunde und Kulturgeschichte* 21 (1978): 9–55.

4. Johann Gottfried Herder, *Werke in zehn Bänden*, ed. Martin Bollacher et al., 10 vols. (Frankfurt am Main: Deutscher Klassiker Verlag, 1985–2000) 1:98, lines 6–7, quoted by Ulrich Gaier, ibid., 3:892–93.

5. Ibid., 3:73, lines 24–33.

6. Ibid., 2:457, lines 36–37; 2:458, lines 1–2.

7. Before Herder, Hamann wrote that hearing the "monotonous" rhythms of Latvian work songs helped one understand the meters of ancient Greek poetry, and that "poetry is the mother tongue of the human race." Hamann inspired Herder's unpublished essay, in which textual borrowing is evident, for example, in a reference to the "monotonous" rhythm of folk songs, and in a declaration that "the mother tongue of the poet is the song"; also from Hamann are ideas about the ancient interdependence of song, music and dance; Arbusow, "Herder," 134–35.

8. Neither Herder nor Hmann knew Latvian, and at this time they did not know the content of Latvian folk poetry; Stavenhagen, "Herder in Riga," 15n18.

9. Arbusow, "Herder," 140. Herder's text is quoted by Ludis Bērziņš, *Greznas dziesmas* Folkloristikas Biblioteka (Riga: Zinātne, 2007), 81.

10. Ulrich Gaier, in Herder, *Werke in zehn Bänden*, 3:895.

11. Letter 88, August 31, 1770, Johann Gottfried Herder, *Briefe: Gesamtausgabe, 1763–1803*, ed. Wilhelm Dobbek and Günter Arnold, 9 vols. (Weimar: Böhlau, 1977–88), 1:200, lines 134–39, 147–50. The letter is also quoted by Caroline von Herder in her *Erinnerungen aus dem Leben Joh. Gottfrieds von Herder*, ed. Johann Georg Müller, vol. 1 (Tübingen: Cotta, 1820), 158. Digital facsimile published by books.google.com (accessed July 25, 2008).

12. Forty-six of these songs would later make up one fourth of Herder's two volumes of *Volkslieder*. The table of contents of the Silver Book, with notes on songs published in *Volkslieder*, appears in Herder, *Sämtliche Werke*, 29:vii–ix.

13. Herder, *Erinnerungen*, 236, 246, 257.

14. Herder, *Briefe*, 3:157. See also Herder, *Werke in zehn Bänden*, 3:895–97.

15. Herder referred to Lessing explicitly, for example, when he noted "how much sensitive language rhythm" is contained in Lithuanian songs; he had not changed this view in 1773 when he asserted, "The Lithuanian maiden who parts with all of her house, and portrays from her eye and heart the entire world of a bride, is a greater poetess than the most comical fabricator of a farewell speech." Herder, *Werke in zehn Bänden*, 2:458, 12–15; 3:67, 29–32.

16. Kreutzfeld first provided four German translations in a printer's proof that, it turned out, was never published, and when Herder asked for more, he sent three songs in a manuscript. Hans V. Müller, "Die 'Preußische Blumenlese' von 1775, eine Quelle von Herders 'Volksliedern,'" *Zentralblatt für Bibliothekswesen* 34, no. 5/7 (1917): 186–87; Herder to Hamann, August 25, 1775, Letter 181, Herder, *Briefe*, 3:205, lines 135–37.

17. "Von Ähnlichkeit der mittlern englischen und deutschen Dichtkunst nebst verschiedenem das daraus folget," Herder, *Werke in zehn Bänden*, 2:562, lines 9–24. I have translated the songs and discussed intertextual connections to Herder's love letters and the Song of Solomon in Guntis Šmidchens, "Herder and Lithuanian Folk songs," *Lituanus* 56, no. 1 (2010): 51–67.

18. Robert Thomas Clark, *Herder: His Life and Thought* (Berkeley: University of California, 1955), 252–57.

19. "Über die Wirkung der Dichtkunst auf die Sitten der Völker in alten und neuen Zeiten," in Herder, *Werke in zehn Bänden*, 4:200, lines 8–13 (emphasis in original).

20. This idea first appeared in the unpublished *Alte Volkslieder* (1774), ibid., 3:60, lines 8–12. Here, *unpolicierte* is translated as "unregimented"; Stefan Grief translates the word as "not bound by rigid bureaucracy" and illuminates Herder's critique of Enlightenment poetics, which is embedded in this phrase, in Hans Adler and Wulf Koepke, eds., *A Companion to the Works of Johann Gottfried Herder* (Rochester: Camden House, 2011), 158.

21. Herder, *Werke in zehn Bänden*, 2:560–61, lines 8–25, 35–37, 1, 6–7, 17–23. "Theogony" studies the origins of the gods, and "cosmogony" studies origins of the earth.

22. Richard Kurin, *Reflections of a Culture Broker: A View from the Smithsonian* (Washington, DC: Smithsonian Institution Press, 1997), 18.

23. "Fragment Über Die Ode" in Herder, *Werke in zehn Bänden*, 1:98, lines 25–28, quoted by Ulrich Gaier in ibid., 3:842–43.

24. Herder, *Werke in zehn Bänden*, 4:167, lines 4–7.

25. Songs of four nations predominate, comprising 66 percent of the entire collection: German (37 songs), English (35 songs), Spanish (18 songs), and Scottish (17 songs). The remaining fourteen nations are represented by a few songs each: Norse/Scaldic (10 songs); Lithuanian (8 songs); Greek (6 songs); French (5 songs); Danish, Morlackian (Croatian), and Latin (4 songs each); Estonian and Italian (3 songs each); Latvian and Lapp (Sámi) (2 songs each); Greenlandic (Inuit), Peruvian (Inca), and Wendish (1 song each).

26. Herder, *Werke in zehn Bänden*, 3:427, lines 9–10, 920; Suphan, "Herders Volkslieder," quoted by Gaier in ibid., 3:920. Arbusow regrets that Herder abandoned ethnographic grouping when he revised *Alte Volkslieder* to create *Volkslieder*; Arbusow, "Herder," 174.

27. Herder, *Werke in zehn Bänden*, 3:922–24. The themes of the first volume's books 2 and 3 were, according to Gaier, "passivity and activity in natural and supernatural relations" and "liberation in love, battle and art."

28. Šmidchens, "Herder and Lithuanian Folk songs," 63–64.

29. The first and second song were sent to Herder in the sequence that he repeated in *Volkslieder*, but he revised Kreutzfeld's punctuation for the second song, adding three lines to indicate that he thought it was incomplete. He then set the remaining two songs aside for a later section, and took the song about a rider's death from Kreutzfeld's second packet. Müller, "Die 'Preußische Blumenlese' von 1775."

30. Caroline later recalled that some called him a coward, in *Erinnerungen*, 23–24, 33, 69. Digital facsimile downloaded from books.google.com on August 19, 2008.

31. Herder, *Werke in zehn Bänden*, 3:1150.

32. Ibid., 3:60, lines 27–30. Emphasis in original.

33. Ibid., 2:560, lines 29–30.

34. Ibid., 3:1001.

35. Ibid., 3:230, lines 11–13; and 3:244, lines 19–20.

36. Ibid., 3:293, lines 10–12; and 3:295, lines 23–25.

37. Ibid., 3:420, lines 9–15.

38. Although Herder credited Hupel for the Latvian songs, it was actually Gustav Bergmann and Heinrich Baumann who provided most of those texts. Bērziņš, *Greznas dziesmas*, 130; Andrejs Johansons, *Latvijas kultūras vēsture, 1710–1800* (Stockholm: Daugava, 1975), 419–27; and Herder, *Werke in zehn Bänden*, 3:979–80, 1118–22.

39. "Journal Meiner Reise im Jahr 1789," in Herder, *Sämtliche Werke*, 4:362. See also Herder's quote from a 1778 novel by T. G. von Hippel in the second volume of *Volkslieder*: "Kurland is home to both slavery and freedom," Herder, *Werke in zehn Bänden*, 3:297, lines 9–10.

40. If Herder had given each Estonian song a separate number, the "book's" total number of songs would have risen to thirty-three, disrupting the structure of thirty songs per book in volume 2.

41. Herder, *Werke in zehn Bänden*, 3:301–3, 402, lines 16–20. Herder omitted line 15 from the text sent to him, "Der Ferkel grunzt in der Schürze" (The piglet grunts in her apron), perhaps for aesthetic reasons (cf. note from Herder's manuscripts, *Sämtliche Werke*, 25:402.).

42. "Acht alte estnische Volkslieder (aus Herders Nachlass)," *Verhandlungen der gelehrten Estnischen Gesellschaft zu Dorpat* 16, no. 2 (1896): 256.

43. Juhan Kahk, "Peasant Movements and National Movements in the History of Europe," *Acta Universitatis Stockholmensis: Studia Baltica Stockholmensia* 2 (1985): 15–23.

44. Helen Liebel-Weckowicz, "Nations and Peoples: Baltic-Russian History and the Development of Herder's Theory of Culture," *Canadian Journal of History* 21, no. 1 (1986): 22; Ingeborg Solbrig quotes the "Lament about the Tyrants of the Serfs" in a discussion of Herder's disappointment at the American Revolution's failure to emancipate the slaves, in "Herder and the 'Harlem Renaissance' of Black Culture in America: The Case of the 'Neger-Idyllen.'" in Ingeborg Solbrig, *Herder Today: Contributions from the International Herder Conference, Nov. 5–8, 1987, Stanford, California*, ed. Kurt Mueller-Vollmer (Berlin: Walter de Gruyter, 1990), 408. Gaier points out that this song had a political, not aesthetic, function, in Herder, *Werke in zehn Bänden*, 3:859. And Mechthild Keller observes that Herder's comments were directed at Baltic Germans, expressing shock at their cruelty as oppressors, in "'Politische Seeträume': Herder und Russland," in *Russen und Rußland aus deutscher Sicht, 18. Jahrhundert: Aufklärung*, ed. Mechthild Keller (Munich: Wilhelm Fink Verlag, 1987), 381. Roger Bartlett reconfirms that the Baltic problem of serfdom was first formulated in terms of nationality by Herder's acquaintance Garlieb Merkel, "Russische und baltische Publizistik gegen die Leibeigenschaft: Aleksandr Radiščev, 'Reise Von St. Petersburg Nach Moskau,' und Garlieb Merkel, 'Die Letten', und 'Rückkehr Ins Vaterland', in Jörg Drews, ed., *"Ich werde gewiss grosse Energie zeigen": Garlieb Merkel (1769–1850) als Kämpfer, Kritiker, und Projektemacher in Berlin und Riga* (Bielefeld, Germany: Aisthesis, 2000), 35.

45. Herder, *Werke in zehn Bänden*, 3:420.

46. Herder, *Sämtliche Werke*, 9:534. See also his introduction to *Alte Volkslieder*, in Herder, *Werke in zehn Bänden*, 3:67, lines 29–33.

47. Herder, *Werke in zehn Bänden*, 3:306, lines 35–39.

48. In his translation, Herder also edited the content of the oral song in which the singer rode to "Prussia," not to "foreign lands"; Bērziņš, *Greznas dziesmas*, 108.

49. Herder, *Werke in zehn Bänden*, 3:445–46, lines 26–27, 6–7, 15–17.

50. Ibid., 3:307, lines 23–26.

51. Ibid., 3:297, lines 23–25.

52. Bērziņš, *Greznas dziesmas*, 124–25.

53. In 1791, Herder attacked the Baltic "yoke of servitude" explicitly: "Perhaps centuries will pass before it is removed from them, and as compensation for the abominations through which these peaceful nations were robbed of their land and their freedom, they will, out of humanity, once again be given freedom for their enjoyment and productive use"; Herder, *Werke in zehn Bänden*, 6:689, lines 18–23.

54. Ibid., 3:427, lines 16–22.

55. Ibid., 3:248, lines 4–6.

56. August Wilhelm Schlegel an Herder, May 22, 1797, as quoted by Ulrich Gaier in Herder, *Werke in zehn Bänden*, 3:842.

57. As discussed by Steven D. Martinson in Koepke, *Companion*, 24.

58. Herder, *Werke in zehn Bänden*, 4:194–96; 214, lines 19–20; ibid., 3:426, lines 35–36.

59. Heinz Röllecke, "Über Volks- und geistliche Lieder bei Herder," in *Johann Gottfried Herder: Aspekte seines Lebenswerkes*, ed. Martin Kessler and Volker Leppin (Berlin: De Gruyter, 2005), 115–28.

60. Caroline to Johann Friedrich Hartknoch, November 14, 1799, Letter 31 in Herder, *Briefe*, 8:419, lines 25–26. Also quoted in Wilhelm Dobbek, *Karoline Herder: Ein Frauenleben in klassischer Zeit* (Weimar: Böhlau, 1967), 73.

61. Herder, *Werke in zehn Bänden*, 10:804, lines 1–8, emphasis in original. Also quoted in Gerhard Sauder's essay about Herder's views on poetry, in Koepke, *Companion*, 324.

62. Herder, *Werke in zehn Bänden*, 3:429, line 9.

63. Ibid., 10:831–32, lines 33–34, lines 1–3.

64. "Hoffnungen eines Sehers vor dreitausend Jahren," ibid., 10:107, lines 20–21.

65. Damon Linker, "The Reluctant Pluralism of J. G. Herder," *Review of Politics* 62, no. 2 (2000): 283–85. Retrieved from JSTOR.

66. Herder, *Werke in zehn Bänden*, 3:906.

67. Ibid., 10, 1386.

68. Stavenhagen, "Herder in Riga," 13–15. Bērziņš, *Greznas dziesmas*, 93.

69. Johann Gottfried von Herder, *Stimmen der Völker in Liedern*, ed. Johann von Müller (Tübingen: Cotta, 1807), vi.

70. As pointed out in 1885 by Carl Redlich in "Einleitung," in Herder, *Sämtliche Werke*, 25:xvii–xviii.

71. As pointed out by Ulrich Gaier in Herder, *Werke in zehn Bänden*, 3:904–5.

72. From a variant stanza recorded in 1924: "Bridges built by fathers' fathers / We the children cross the bridges; / Children when you cross the

bridges, / Keep enough to last a lifetime"; Jēkabs Vītoliņš, *Bērnu dziesmu cikls: Bēru dziesmas* (Riga: Zinātne, 1971), 187.

73. "Family Rituals and Celebrations in Latvian Folklore," in *Baltica '91. Starptautiskais folkloras festivāls / International Folklore Festival 9.–14. VII. 1991* (Riga: E. Melngaiļa Tautas Mākslas Centrs, 1991), 17.

74. "Association 'Baltica'—independent member of CIOFF," in *Baltica '91. Starptautiskais folkloras festivāls / International Folklore Festival 9.–14. VII.1991* (Riga: E. Melngaiļa Tautas Mākslas Centrs, 1991), 5.

75. Herder, *Werke in zehn Bänden*, 3:247, line 14, emphasis in original.

CHAPTER 3

1. Cassette tape recording, Tallinn, June 30, 1990. The three fragments presented here are from the most frequently sung songs. Four of the groups passing by sang "People of Kungla," four others sang "Be Free Estonia's Sea," and two others sang "My Dear Fatherland."

2. Cassette tape recording, Rīga, July 7, 1990. The three fragments presented here are from the most frequently sung songs. Fifteen of the groups passing by sang "This Is Latvia," and twelve sang "Here, Where Pine Forests Grow," which concludes with the vow, "I Am a Latvian." The refrain "Long May He Live" was repeated too many times and by too many groups to be counted. The four folk song fragments are from the songs "Where Are You Running?" (sung by five passing choirs), "I Cut Two Fields of Clover" (five choirs), "Bloom, Rye Blossom" (four choirs), and "A Swift River Flowed" (sung by four other choirs). Songs sung by other groups included "Āvu, Āvu," "Bēdu Manu," and "Līgo" (each three times); "Jūriņ Prasa," "Līgo Laiva," "Mirdzot Šķēpiem," "Sijā Auzas," and "Tautiet's Mani Pavadīja" (each twice); and "Aiz Ezera Balti Bērzi," "Div' Dūjiņas," "Dziedot Dzimu," "Es Dziedāšu par Tevi, Tēvu Zeme," "Lai Slava Tam," "Kumeliņi, Kumeliņi," "Ķemermiestiņā," "Ozolīti Zemzarīti," "Projām Jāiet," "Seši Mazi Bundzenieki," "Skaista Ir Jaunība," "Tōli Dzeivoj," and "Tautiešami Apsolīju" (each once).

3. Benedict Anderson, *Imagined Communities: Reflections on the Origin and Spread of Nationalism*, rev. ed. (London: Verso, 2006), 37–46.

4. Anthony D. Smith, *The Cultural Foundations of Nations: Hierarchy, Covenant, and Republic* (Malden, MA: Blackwell Publishing, 2008), 30–31.

5. Albertas Juška, "Lietuvininkų kalba: Lietuvškai kalbančių žmonių skaičius," in *Mažosios Lietuvos enciklopedija*, ed. Zigmas Zinkevičius et al. (Vilnius: Mažosios Lietuvos Fondas, 2003), 594–95.

6. The first history of Lithuanian-language hymnals was written by Ostermeyer in 1793. The *kantička* hymnals, and melodic variation, are described in Algirdas Ambrazas, ed., *Lietuvos muzikos istorija, I knyga: Tautinio atgimimo metai, 1883–1918* (Vilnius: Lietuvos Muzikos Akademija, 2002), 60–65.

7. Gottfried Herder (1706–1763) and Anna Pelz (1717–1772).

8. Daiva Kšanienė, *Muzika Mažojoje Lietuvoje: Lietuvių ir vokiečių kultūrų sąveika (XVI a.–XX a. 4 dešimtmetis)* (Klaipėda, Lithuania: Mažosios Lietuvos Fondas, Klaipėdos Universiteto Leidykla, 2003), 146–50.

9. Regimantas Gudelis, *Chorinis menas visuomenės kultūroje: Europos chorinė tradicija ir jos įsitvirtinimas Lietuvoje* (Klaipėda: Klaipėdos Universiteto Leidykla, 2001), 172–79.

10. Heidi Heinmaa, *Protestantlik kantoriinstitutsioon Tallinnas 16.–17. sajandil,* Eesti Muusikaloo Toimetised 4 (Tallinn: 1999), 34–59.

11. Siret Rutiku, "Über die Rolle des deutschen Kirchenliedes in der estnischen Kulturgeschichte," in *Kulturgeschichte der baltischen Länder in der Frühen Neuzeit, Mit einem Ausblick in die Moderne,* ed. Klaus Garber and Klöker (Tübingen: Max Niemeyer Verlag, 2003), 249–55; "Dziesmu grāmata," in *Latvju enciklopēdija,* vol. 1, ed. Arveds Švābe (Stockholm: Apgāds Trīs Zvaigznes, 1950–51), 564.

12. Luther and Zinzendorf quoted by Friedriech Blume, *Protestant Church Music: A History* (New York: Norton & Company, 1974), 13–14, 600.

13. Stenders published secular songbooks in 1774, 1783, and 1789; Gotthard Friedrich (Vecais Stenders) Stender, *Ziņģes* (Riga: Zinātne, 1990); Bērziņš, *Greznas dziesmas,* 61–65, 71.

14. Karl Leichter, "Muusikakultuur Eestis XVIII sajandil," in *Eesti Muusika I,* ed. Artur Vahter (Tallinn: Eesti Raamat, 1968), 18; Jānis Bērziņš, *Dziesmotais novads: Ieskats Madonas novada kordziedāšanas vēsturē* (n.p., 2003), 8–9; J. Vītoliņš and L. Krasinska, *Latviešu mūzikas vēsture* (Rīga: Liesma, 1972), 116–17; Leichter, "Eesti koorilaulu tekkimine," 26–30; Valentīns Bērzkalns, *Latviešu Dziesmu svētku vēsture, 1864–1940* (New York: Grāmatu Draugs, 1965), 15–16.

15. Bērziņš, *Dziesmotais novads,* 10–17.

16. Smith, *Cultural Foundations,* 34–35.

17. Paulius V. Subačius, "Inscribing Orality: The First Folklore Editions in the Baltic States," *European Studies* 26 (2008): 81; Dace Bula, *Dziedātājtauta: Folklora un nacionālā ideoloģija* (Riga: Zinātne, 2000), 48–49; Dace Bula, "Johans Gotfrīds Herders un tautas dzejas interpretācijas Latvijā," in *Herders Rīgā,* ed. Māra Siliņa (Riga: Rīgas Doma Evaņģēliski Luteriskā Draudze, 2005), 13.

18. Albinas Jovaišas, *Liudvikas Rėza* (Vilnius: Vaga, 1969), 230–31; Alfonsas Šešplaukis, *J. G. Herderis ir baltų tautos: Mokslinė studija* (Vilnius: Mokslo ir Enciklopedijų Leidykla, 1995), 53–54.

19. Haralds Biezais, ed. *Die erste Sammlung der lettischen Volkslieder von Gustav Bergmann. Mit einer historischen Einleitung über die Ausgaben der lettischen Volkslieder* (Uppsala: Senatne, 1961), 99.

20. In 1787, Schlegel published thirteen Estonian songs in *Der Teutsche Merkur,* adding rhetorical arguments for emancipation; A. Vinkel, ed., *Eesti kirjanduse ajalugu,* vol. 1 (Tallinn: Eesti Raamat, 1965), 250–51. Merkel's "Über Dichtunggeist und Dichtung unter den Letten," in *Der Teutsche Merkur,* 1797, Latvian translation in Garlībs Merķelis, "Par latviešu dzejas garu un dzeju," *Kultūrvēsturiski raksti* (Riga: Zvaigzne, 1992), 199.

21. Endre Bojtár, *Foreword to the Past: A Cultural History of the Baltic People* (Budapest: Central European University Press, 1999), 312–17; Johansons, *Latvijas kultūras vēsture,* 319–28.

22. Garlieb Merkel, *Die Vorzeit Lieflands: Ein Denkmal des Pfaffen- und Rittergeistes,* 2 vols. (Berlin: Vossische Buchhandlung, 1798–1999), 1:49, 162, 226. Retrieved from EEVA Tekstid, http://www.utlib.ee/ekollekt/eeva/ (accessed February 12, 2013).

23. Herder, *Sämtliche Werke,* 20:288. In one of his last essays about the history of humankind, Herder also quoted from Merkel's *Vorzeit Lieflands;* Herder, *Werke in zehn Bänden,* 10:436–39.

24. Ludwig Jedemin Rhesa, *Prutena, oder preussische Volkslieder und andere vaterländische Dichtungen* (Königsberg: Heinrich Degen, 1809; reprint copy downloaded from books.google.com), 45–48; see also Jovaišas, *Liudvikas Rėza,* 21, 205–16.

25. Ludvikas Rėza, *Lietuvių liaudies dainos I* (Vilnius: Valstybinė Grožinės Literatūros Leidykla, 1958), 358–59.

26. Rhesa, *Prutena,* 173. Rėza was a leader in his local chapter of the Freemasons, and his writings on Lithuanian mythology and folk poetry often included the Masonic key words "naturalness," "sincerity," "beauty," and the numbers 1, 2 and 3; Laima Kiauleikytė, "Freimaurerlied atgarsiai L. G. Rėzos (1776–1840) kūryboje," *Kultūrologija* 10 (2003): 136–37.

27. Rėza mentioned Lessing and Herder in his letter asking Goethe to help get the book published; Jovaišas, *Liudvikas Rėza,* 42.

28. Rėza, *Lietuvių liaudies dainos,* 358–59; Jovaišas, *Liudvikas Rėza,* 303.

29. Subačius, "Inscribing Orality," 83; Bojtár, *Foreword to the Past,* 238.

30. Jovaišas, *Liudvikas Rėza,* 312–16. Goethe's review appears in *Sämtliche Werke: Briefe, Tagebücher und Gespräche,* ed. Dieter Borchmeyer (Frankfurt am Main: Deutscher Klassiker Verlag, 1985), 38:153–54.

31. Jaan Undusk, "Hamanni ja Herderi vaim eesti kirjanduse edendajana: Sünedohhi printsiip," *Keel ja Kirjandus* no. 9 (1995): 584.

32. Indrek Jürjo, *Liivimaa valgustaja August Wilhelm Hupel, 1737–1819* (Tallinn: Riigiarhiiv, 2004), 400–3.

33. Johann Heinrich Rosenplänter, ed., *Beiträge zur genauern Kenntniß der ehstnischen Sprache,* vol. 2 (1813), 73–74. Retrieved from EEVA tekstid (July 26, 2009).

34. Ibid., vol. 6 (1816), 17; Undusk, "Hamanni ja Herderi vaim," 585.

35. Ibid., 584–87.

36. A. K., "Dritter Brief," in Rosenplänter, *Beiträge,* vol. 9 (1817), 14; Vinkel, *Eesti kirjanduse ajalugu,* 1:336.

37. Risto Järv, "Kristfrid Gananderi 'Mythologia Fennica' saksakeelsest tõlkest" *Keel ja Kirjandus* 44, no. 3 (2001): 177.

38. Christian Jaak Peterson, "Christfrid Ganander Thomassons Finnische Mythologie, aus dem Schwedischen übersetzt, völlig umgearbeitet und mit Anmerkungen," in Rosenplänter, *Beiträge,* vol. 14 (1822), 26. Retrieved from EEVA tekstid (December 29, 2011).

39. Bula, *Dziedātājtauta,* 64–65.

40. Subačius, "Inscribing Orality."

41. Simonas Stanevičius, *Dainos žemaičių* (Vilnius: Lietuvių Literatūros ir Tautosakos Institutas, 1999), 17; Jakob Hurt, ed. *Setukeste laulud,* Monumenta Estoniae Antiquae (Helsinki: Suomalaisen Kirjallisuuden Seura, 1904),

1:3–10; Krišjānis Barons began his monumental collection of Latvian songs with the thematic grouping, "[Songs] about Songs and Singing: Songs and singing are the shared by the whole nation, and accompany a person's life"; Krišjānis Barons, ed., *Latwju dainas* (Riga: Liesma, 1985), 1:1–34.

42. F. Gunther Eyck, *The Voice of Nations: European National Anthems and Their Authors* (Westport, CT: Greenwood Press, 1995), 13.

43. Richard S. Wortman, *Scenarios of Power* (Princeton: Princeton University Press, 1995), 1:388–90; N. A. Soboleva, "The Composition of State Anthems of the Russian Empire and the Soviet Union," *Russian Social Science Review* 50, no. 2 (2009): 74.

44. Wortman, *Scenarios*, 2:46, 221, 226, 476.

45. Eyck, *Voice of Nations*, 41–42.

46. Best known is Germany's "Watch on the Rhine."

47. Jovaišas, *Liudvikas Rėza*, 30, 329.

48. Laura Mason, *Singing the French Revolution: Popular Culture and Politics, 1787–1799* (Ithaca, NY: Cornell University Press, 1996), 94–101.

49. East Latvia (Latgale) was part of Vitebsk Province, annexed by the Russian Empire in 1772; Kurland, Vilna and Kovno Provinces were annexed in 1795. Suvalki Province was first annexed by Prussia in 1793, then by the Russian Empire in 1815.

50. Slawomir Żurawski, ed., *Literatura polska, encyclopedia PWN: Epoki literackie, prądy i kierunki, dzieła i twórcy* (Warsaw: Wydawnyctwo Naukowe Pwn, 2007), 192; Bogdan Zakrzewski, *Boże, Coś Polskę Alojzego Felińskiego* (Wrocław: Zakład Narodowy Imienia Ossolińskich, 1983), 15–16; Norman Davies, *God's Playground: A History of Poland*, 2 vols. (Oxford: Clarendon Press, 1981), 2:19.

51. Silvestras Valiūnas, *Ant marių krašto* (Vilnius: Vaga, 1976), 31–33, 217–18; Regina Mikšytė, *Silvestras Valiūnas* (Vilnius: Vaga, 1978), 186–93; Kšanienė, *Muzika Mažojoje Lietuvoje*, 222–24.

52. Giedrius Viliūnas, "Vytauto Didžiojo kultas tarpukario Lietuvoje," *Lietuviu Atgimimo istorijos studijos* 17: Nacionalizmas ir emocijos (2001): 79, 93.

53. Jūratė Petrikaitė, "Silvestro Valiūno 'Birutės' folkloriniai variantai," *Tautosakos Darbai* 25 (2008): 179.

54. Ruth-Ester Hillila and Barbara Blanchard-Hong, *Historical Dictionary of the Music and Musicians of Finland* (Westport, CT: Greenwood Press, 1997), 239, 292–93, 340–41.

55. Dieter Düding, "The Nineteenth-Century German Nationalist Movement as a Movement of Societies," in *Nation Building in Central Europe*, ed. Hagen Schulze (Leaminton Spa, England: Berg, 1987); Dieter Düding, Peter Friedmann, and Paul Münch, eds., *Öffentliche Festkultur: Politische Feste im Deutschland von der Aufklarung bis zum ersten Weltkrieg*, Rowohlts Enzyklopädie: Kulturen und Ideen (Hamburg: GmbH, 1988), 67–88, 166–90.

56. Kšanienė, *Muzika Mažojoje Lietuvoje*, 52–58; Baiba Jaunslaviete, "Ieskats vācbaltiešu dziesmu svētku vēsturē," *Mūzikas Akadēmijas Raksti* 3 (2007): 32–52. Jörg Hackmann, "Voluntary Associations and Region Building: A Post-National Perspective on Baltic History," Center for European

Studies Working Paper Series 105 (2002), http://aei.pitt.edu/9047/1/Hack-mann.pdf (accessed February 19, 2011).

57. Jannsen translated F. W. Krummacher's *Zionsharfe*, published with the title *Sioni-Laulo-Kannel* vols. 1–3, 1845–60; Madli Puhvel, *Symbol of Dawn: The Life and Times of the Nineteenth-Century Estonian Poet Lydia Koidula* (Tartu, Estonia: Tartu University Press, 1995), 23–24, 41.

58. Quoted by Leichter, "Eesti koorilaulu tekkimine," 31.

59. Cimze's teachers were C. W. Harnisch (a student of J. H. Pestalozzi), and professor F. A. W. Diesterweg.

60. Raimonds Baltakmens, "Vīru koru korifejs Mednis un 'Dziedonis,'" in *Gaismas pils augšāmcēlējs Haralds Mednis*, ed. Raimonds Baltakmens and Dzintars Gilba (Riga: Valters un Rapa, 2006), 125–26.

61. Among them were such Estonians as C. R. Jakobson (graduated 1869), author of a popular Estonian reading textbook and some song festival song-books; Aleksander Saebelmann Kunileid (1868), composer of popular song melodies and head conductor of the first Estonian national song festival; Aleksander Läte (1879), head conductor of the Fourth National Song Festival; composers Friedrich August Saebelmann (1871) and Aleksander Eduard Thomson (1865), and teachers Andreas Erlemann (1856) and Joosep Kapp (1853). Among the Latvian students were the future national poet Auseklis (1871) and national anthem author Kārlis Baumanis (1856); Juris Neikens (1846), organizer of the first regional Latvian song festival in Dikļi; Indriķis Zīle (1867), head conductor at the first three Latvian national song festivals; and conductors Atis Kauliņš and Jānis Sērmūkslis (1874).

62. Arveds Švābe, *Latvijas vēsture, 1800–1914* (Stockholm: Daugava, 1958), 171–73, 404. Beginning in 1857, Latvian songbooks of translated German popular songs were published by Kārlis Vērichs (*Dziesmu vaiņaks*, reprinted four times) and J. Kaktiņš, as summarized in Bērzkalns, *Latviešu Dziesmu svētku vēsture*, 17–18.

63. Rudolf Põldmäe, *Esimene Eesti üldlaulupidu 1869* (Tallinn: Eesti Raa-mat, 1969), 23.

64. Johann Voldemar Jannsen, *125 uut laulo neile, kes hea melega laul-wad ehk laulo kuulwad* (Tartu Estonia: H. Laakmann, 1860). Retrieved from http://books.google.com (accessed August 21, 2009).

65. M. Kalda writes that Jannsen based his Estonian song on a German adaptation by G. Schultz-Bertram, "Was Ist des Ehsten Vaterland?" in Endel Nirk, ed., *Eesti kirjanduse ajalugu: XIX sajandi teine pool* (Tallinn: Eesti Raa-mat, 1966), 2:154. I do not have the text of that song. The source of Jannsen's images is less important here than the differences between the songs as they were sung in Estonian or German.

66. Jannsen commented that the word denoted not only Estland Province, today's northern Estonia: "This word, 'Eestima,' wherever it appears in songs here, does not refer only to Tallinn Province, but rather, to all of the Estonian fatherland, where Estonians live and eat their daily bread while listening to the word." Jannsen, *125 uut laulo*, 9.

67. Indrek Elling, "Eesti Üliõpilaste Seltsi tekkimise tagamad. Saksa ja baltisaksa eeskujud," in *Tartu, baltisakslased ja Saksamaa*, ed. Helmut

Piirimäe and Claus Sommerhage (Tartu, Estonia: Tartu Ülikooli Kirjastus, 1998), 196–204.

68. Ibid., 194–96; Švābe, *Latvijas vēsture*, 375; Hackmann, "Voluntary Associations and Region Building." Curonia appeared earlier at the University of Jena. In Saint Petersburg, Fraternitas Nevania was established in 1847. At the University of Tartu, students from the Grand Duchy of Finland organized Finnonia in 1810. For simplicity, the word "fraternity" is here used as a loose translation for the various terms referring to student organizations (Landsmannschaft, Corporation, Fraternitas, Corps, corporation, *korporatsioon*, *korporācija*).

69. The translation of two German songs into Latvian and Estonian, "Strömt herbei, ihr Völkerscharen" ("Pulcējaties, latvju dēli"/"Rahvahulgad, tulge kokku") and "O, alte Burschenherrlichkeit" ("Ak, vecā buršu greznība"/"O bursi hiilgus endine"), is documented by Tiina Metso, "German Influence on Estonian and Baltic German Corps Traditions in Tartu," *Acta Historica Tallinnensia* 8 (2004): 32–35.

70. J. Lapiņš, ed., *Ausekļa kopoti raksti* (Riga: A Gulbja Apgādībā), 104–6.

71. "Wir hatten gebauet ein stattliches Haus," text 1231, and "Ich hab mich ergeben mit Hertz und mit Hand," text 1230, in "Volksliederarchiv," Müller-Lüdenscheidt-Verlag, http://www.volksliederarchiv.de/ (accessed September 13, 2011).

72. Aarne Vinkel, *Martin Körber: Elutee ja töö* (Tallinn: Eesti Teaduste Akadeemia Underi ja Tuglase Kirjanduskeskus, 1994), 36, 72.

73. A new stanza appeared in 1886, inserted before Körber's last stanza: "Oh, land of my fathers, May you flourish long! Oh, land with ample courage, and spiritual wealth!"; ibid., 77. Ingrid Rüütel, ed. *Eesti uuemad laulumängud*, 2 vols. (Tallinn: Eesti Raamat, 1980–83), 405–13.

74. Toivo U. Raun, "Nineteenth- and Early Twentieth-Century Estonian Nationalism Revisited," *Nations and Nationalism* 9, no. 1 (2003): 134–35, 140. Translated German songs were praised in Jannsen's day, but they were later scorned as foreign borrowings. Miina Härma's new melody for Körber's words was propagated by schoolbooks and song festivals, but it did not displace the original German tune in popular tradition; Vinkel, *Martin Körber*, 77, 80–81.

75. *Eestirahwa 50-aastase Jubelipiddo-Laulud* (Tartu, Estonia: Wannemuine-selts, 1869), 21.

76. Eyck, *Voice of Nations*, 200.

77. Johann Voldemar Jannsen, "Veel natukke Tallinna laulo piddust," in *Eesti rahvaluuleteaduse ajalugu: Välitud tekste ja pilte*, ed. Eduard Laugaste (Tallinn: Eesti Riiklik Kirjastus, 1963), 178.

78. Smith, *Cultural Foundations*, 36–38; Anderson, *Imagined Communities*, 145; Miroslav Hroch, *Social Preconditions of National Revival in Europe* (Cambridge: Cambridge University Press, 1985); Toivo U. Raun and Andrejs Plakans, "The Estonian and Latvian National Movements: An Assessment of Miroslav Hroch's Model," *Journal of Baltic Studies* 21, no. 2 (1990): 131–44; Mart Laar, *Äratajad: Rahvuslik ärkamisaeg Eestis 19. sajandil ja selle kandjad* (Tallinn: Grenader, 2006), 383–91, 397–98.

79. Toivo U. Raun, *Estonia and the Estonians* (Stanford: Hoover Institution Press, 2001), 57–59; Andrew Plakans, *The Latvians: A Short History* (Stanford: Hoover Institution Press, 1995), 89–90.

80. Debates over Germanization are mentioned by Švābe, *Latvijas vēsture*, 173–74; Andrejs Plakans, "Peasants, Intellectuals, and Nationalism in the Russian Baltic Provinces, 1820–90," *Journal of Modern History* 46 (1974): 458; and Raun and Plakans, "Estonian and Latvian National Movements," 134. The imperial context for native-language newspapers is discussed in Wortman, *Scenarios*, 2:24.

81. Peterson's petition called on the Russian government to control land rental and sale agreements; to eliminate Baltic German control of the courts and allow the use of Estonian language during trials; to remove Estonian education from the control of the Baltic German clergy; and to abolish corporal punishment; Puhvel, *Symbol of Dawn*, 51–52 and 262n1.

82. Ibid., 58.

83. Koidula's poem may have been inspired by the German poet August Heinrich Hoffmann von Vallersleben's poem "My Fatherland Is My Bride," but the two texts have few similarities other than their titles; Paul Rummo, "Ühe laulu lugu," *Looming* 1 (1961): 118–19.

84. Also quoted by Puhvel, *Symbol of Dawn*, 57.

85. Kristin Kuutma, "Laulupeod rahvusliku identiteedi kandjana," *Maetagused* 1 (1996), http://folklore.ee/tagused/nr1/internet.htm (accessed July 11, 2009).

86. Põldmäe, *Esimene Eesti üldlaulupidu 1869*, 23–38.

87. Quoted in ibid., 106.

88. *Eesti Postimees* 28, July 18, 1869, quoted in ibid., 121.

89. Ibid., 123–25.

90. Ibid., 157–58.

91. Carl Robert Jakobson, *Wanemuine kandle healed. Neljahealega meeste koorid. Eesti laulupühaks 1869* (1869).

92. Foley, *How to Read an Oral Poem*, 50–52.

93. Ants Viires, "Pseudomythology in Estonian Publicity in the Nineteenth and Twentieth Century," *Ethnologia Europaea* 21, no. 2 (1991): 140.

94. *Pirmee Latweeschu dzeedaschanas swehtki Rihgâ no 26ta lihdz 29 juhnijam 1873* (Riga: K. un M. Busch Brahļu Apgahdeenâ), 2; Juris Neikens recalled in his memoir that 120 men and 120 children sang at the event, as quoted in K. Dzirkalis, ed. *Pirmo Latviešu Dziesmu svētku 75 gadu atceres svinības Dikļos* (Riga: Pagalms, 1939), 7. Both books downloaded from dziesmusvetki.lndb.lv (accessed September 18, 2011).

95. Bīlenšteins is named as the organizer of the 1870 Dobele festival in *VI. Latvju vispārējie dziesmu un muzikas svētki* (Riga: Latvju Dziesmu un Muzikas Svētku Preses un Propagandas Sekcijas Izd, 1926), 6. Downloaded from dziesmusvetki.lndb.lv (accessed September 18, 2011).

96. Matīss Kaudzīte, *Atmiņas no tautiskā laikmeta* (Riga: Zvaigzne ABC, 1994), 112, 84; *Pirmee Latweeschu dzeedaschanas swehtki*, 9, 27.

97. *Pirmee Latweeschu dzeedaschanas swehtki*, 12. Revised version in *Latviešu kordziesmas antoloģija*, 12 vols. (Riga: SIA SOL, 1997), 1:25–26.

The Latvian word *diet* is translated as "rejoice" as it was used by Latvian poets in the late nineteenth century; in folklore and in later usage, the word meant "dance"; Konstantīns Karulis, *Latviešu etimoloģijas vārdnīca* (Riga: Avots, 1992), 1:215.

98. Some contemporaries criticized the melody as a weak mixture of the Russian anthem, the English anthem, and a German folk song, Vizbulīte Bērziņa, *Tautas muzikālā atmoda latviešu publicistu skatījumā* (Riga: Zinātne, 1983), 83. Whatever the melodic connotations might have been, in 1874 the anthem was banned from public performance until the early twentieth century. Valda Kvaskova, "Latvijas Valsts vēstures arhīva dokumenti—Dziesmu svētku tradīcijas glabātāji," *Latvijas Arhīvi* 2 (2008): 84.

99. *Pirmee Latweeschu dzeedaschanas swehtki*, 12.

100. Ibid., 14. The event is also remembered by Kaudzīte; Kaudzīte, *Atmiņas*, 187.

101. F. Abt's song "Es lebe hoch" is discussed in the introduction to Cimze, *Dziesmu rota, izlase* (Riga: Liesma, 1973), 8; Kevin C. Karnes, "A Garland of Songs for a Nation of Singers: An Episode in the History of Russia, the Herderian Tradition, and the Rise of Baltic Nationalism," *Journal of the Royal Musical Association* 130, no. 2 (2005): 197 (accessed August 18, 2007, from Research Library database, document ID: 955884811).

102. Kaudzīte, *Atmiņas*, 189–90, 193, 211.

103. Ibid., 192–93.

104. Lapiņš, *Ausekļa kopoti raksti*, 75. Kaudzīte mentions Vēbers as a great public speaker, but does not mention this particular speech; Kaudzīte, *Atmiņas*, 316–36.

105. Auseklis sang first bass in the men's choir of Lielvārde; *Pirmee Latweeschu dzeedaschanas swehtki*, 35.

106. Lapiņš, *Ausekļa kopoti raksti*, 434.

107. *Latviešu kordziesmas antoloģija*, 1:29.

108. Vītols omitted Auseklis's third and eighth stanzas; ibid., 1:51.

109. Juhans Āviks, «Atmiņas par profesoru Vītolu,» and Vlads Jakubēns, "Profesors Jāzeps Vītols un lietuvju mūziķi," both in *Jāzeps Vītols tuvinieku, audzēkņu un laikabiedru atmiņās* ed. Oļģerts Grāvītis (Riga: Zinātne, 1999), 116, 132.

110. Estonia: 1869, 1879, 1880, 1891, 1894, 1896; Latvia 1873, 1880, 1888, 1895.

111. Leszek Belzyt, *Sprachliche Minderheiten im preußischen Staat, 1815–1914: Die preußische Sprachenstatistik in Bearbeitung und Kommentar* (Marburg: Herder-Institut, 1998), 24–26, 73, 78, 80.

112. Irena Tumavičiūtė, "Jurgis Zauerveinas—skelbęs santaiką visam pasauliui," in *Nuo Mažvydo iki Vydūno: Karaliaučiaus krašto šviesuoliai*, ed. Vytautas Šilas (Vilnius: Mintis, 1998).

113. Ambrazas, *Lietuvos muzikos istorija*, 1:110; Vilius Kalvaitis, ed., *Prūsijos Lietuvių dainos* (Lietuvių Literatūros ir Tautosakos Institutas, 1998), 361.

114. Tumavičiūtė, "Jurgis Zauerveinas," 110, 116–17.

115. Sauerwein's translation into Sorbian was set to music by Korla Awgust Kocor; Oskar Vistdal, *Georg Sauerwein: Europear og døl: Ein dokumentasjon*

(Bergen: Norsk Bokreidingslag, 2000), 199–201. Thanks to Heather Short for help with the translation from Norwegian.

116. Tomas Balkelis, *The Making of Modern Lithuania* (London: Routledge, 2009), 41–42.

117. Vytautas Landsbergis, "Maironis dainius. Kalba konferencijoje Maironio lietuvių literatūros muziejuje, Kaunas 2002–11–14," Lietuvos Respublikos Seimas, http://www3.lrs.lt/pls/inter/w5_show?p_r=914&p_d=21836&p_k=1 (accessed September 16, 2012).

118. Vytautas Landsbergis, "Maironis ir muzika," in *Maironis*, ed. Jonas Lankutis (Vilnius: Vaga, 1990), 181–82.

119. Maironis was the first to identify the Lithuanian Grand Duke Jogaila as a national traitor who had taken the Polish crown and established the union between Poland and Lithuania; Alvydas Niženkaitis, "Jogailos įvaizdis lietuvių visuomenėje," *Lietuvių Atgimimo istorijos studijos* 17 (2001): 62.

120. Balkelis, *Making of Modern Lithuania*, 27.

121. Aleksandras Merkelis, *Didysis varpininkas Vincas Kudirka* (Chicago: Vydūno Jaunimo Fondas, 1989), 307.

122. Ambrazas, *Lietuvos muzikos istorija*, 1:245–47.

123. Maironis, *Raštai*, 3:520.

124. Ambrazas, *Lietuvos muzikos istorija*, 1:348.

125. Vytautas Landsbergis, as quoted in ibid., 249.

126. Quoted by Gudelis, *Chorinio meno*, 283.

127. Vytautas Jakelaitis, *Lietuvos dainų šventės* (Vilnius: Vaga, 1970), 22–32.

128. Lapiņš, *Ausekļa kopoti raksti*, 390; emphasis in original.

129. Bērzkalns, *Latviešu Dziesmu svētku vēsture*, 169–70. This episode is also recounted in a fictional novel by Ernests Aistars, *Savā zemē* (New York: Grāmatu Draugs, 1975), 241–42.

130. Konstantin Päts, "Aulikud piduosalised!" *Päevaleht*, June 29, 1990, 1.

131. Algirdas Ambrazas, *Lietuvos muzikos istorija*, 2:198–200; Jakelaitis, *Lietuvos dainų šventės*, 68.

132. Quoted by Gudelis, *Chorinis menas*, 243–45.

133. Ambrazas, *Lietuvos muzikos istorija*, 2:189–201; Jakelaitis, *Lietuvos dainų šventės*, 42–48, 52–68.

134. W. Tamman, ed., *Kooli laulmiseraamat. Metoodiliselt korraldatud ja piltidega kaunistatud kooli laulmise materjaal* (Tartu, Estonia: Postimees, 1920), 174–75. See also Artur Vahter and Jüri Variste, eds., *Eesti koorilooming*, vol. 2 (Tallinn: Eesti Riiklik Kirjastus, 1955), 9–11.

135. Vita Zalče, "IX Latviešu dziesmu svētki—Kārļa Ulmaņa Latvijas mūžibas zvērests," *Latvijas Arhīvi* 2 (2008): 112, 121–24; Silvija Radzobe, "Song of Renewal—and the Tradition of Political Mystery," in *Latvia and Latvians: A People and a State in Ideas, Images, and Symbols*, ed. Ausma Cimdiņa and Deniss Hanovs (Riga: Zinātne, 2010); Vladas Sirutavičius, "Šventės nacionalizavimas: 'Tautos šventės' atsiradimas Lietuvos respublikoje XX amžiaus 4-ajame dešimtmetyje," *Lietuvių atgimimo istorijos studijos* 17 (2001): 133–45.

CHAPTER 4

1. Pranė Dundulienė, *Lietuvių liaudies kosmologija* (Vilnius: Mokslas, 1988), 11–12. Norbertas Vėlius, *The World Outlook of the Ancient Balts*, trans. Dalija Tekorienė (Vilnius: Mintis, 1989), 194–201, 13–18.

2. Anthony David Smith, "War and Ethnicity: The Role of Warfare in the Formation, Self-Images, and Cohesion of Ethnic Communities," *Ethnic and Racial Studies* 4, no. 4 (1981); Smith, *Cultural Foundations*, 45–46.

3. Epp Annus, *Eesti kirjanduslugu* (Tallinn: Koolibri, 2001), 56.

4. The mobilization campaign failed because local nobles did not pay for the troops' provisions or clothes; Rein Helme, *1812. Aasta Eestis ja Lätis* (Tallinn: Olion, 1990), 133.

5. Reinhold Johann Winkler, *Eesti-ma Ma-wäe söa-laulud* (Tallinn: Gressel, 1807), 7, digital scan retrieved from EEVA tekstid, August 16, 2010; Vinkel, *Eesti kirjanduse ajalugu*, 298.

6. Peterson, " Christfrid Ganander Thomassons Finnische Mythologie," 64–65; on Peterson's influences from Herder, see Vinkel, *Eesti kirjanduse ajalugu*, 395–96.

7. Peterson's source was Rosenplänter, *Beitrage* 4 (1815), 136; see also Rosenplänter, *Beitrage* 7 (1817), 47–50.

8. Ninth Tale, lines 329–37; Twentieth Tale, lines 198–201; Felix J. Oinas, *Surematu Kalevipoeg*, ed. Jaan Undusk (Tallinn: K/K, 1994), 90–105.

9. Song 9 in Friedrich Reinhold Kreutzwald, *Kalevipoeg: An Ancient Estonian Tale*, trans. George Kurman (Moorestown, NJ: Symposia Press, 1982), 118.

10. Guntis Šmidchens, "National Heroic Narratives in the Baltics as a Source for Nonviolent Political Action," *Slavic Review* 66, no. 3 (2007): 491.

11. Voldemar Tammann and Juhan Aavik, *Kooli-koor. I jagu* (Tartu, Estonia: V. Tamman, 1928), 71. "Fatherland Commemoration" is the first song in a sixth-grade textbook compiled by Tamman and Aavik, *Kooli leelo VI* (Tartu, Estonia: Loodus, 1936), 3, and the second song in an eighth-grade textbook by Riho Päts, *Lemmiklaulik 8* (Tallinn: Kooli-kooperatiiv, 1939), 7.

12. Bula, *Dziedātājtauta*, 73. Brīvzemnieks attacked a passage in *Volkslieder*, mistakenly ascribing to Herder himself words that the philosopher quoted from others; Fricis Brīvzemnieks, "O narodnoi poezii latyshei," in *Sbornik antropologicheskikh i etnograficheskikh statei*, ed. V. A. Dashkov (Moscow: 1873), 13–15.

13. On June 27 and August 31, 1991, I recorded Skandinieki singing the song with different words in the last stanza: "Singing songs and playing music, / they'll defeat the enemy; / singing songs and playing music, / they'll return home from the war."

14. Cimze, *Dziesmu rota, izlase*, 52.

15. Tālis Pumpuriņš, *Sarkanbaltsarkanās—Latvijas karoga krāsas: Pētījumi, atmiņas un dokumenti par Latvijas valsts karoga tapšanas vēsturi* (Cēsu Vēstures un Mākslas Muzejs, 2000), 34–54.

16. *Latvijas Padomju Enciklopēdija* (Riga: Galvenā Enciklopēdiju Redakcija, 1981), 4:303. At least five Latvian translations circulated in the early

twentieth century. An Estonian translation by V. Grünstamm was published in 1905, and a second translation by H. Pöögelmann appeared in 1906; the song was translated into Lithuanian by Juozas Baltrušaitis-Mėmelė in 1905 and first published in the United States.

17. V. Greble, E. Kokare, and Jēkabs Vītoliņš, eds., *Cīņas dziesmas* (Riga: Latvijas PSR Zinātņu Akadēmijas Izdevniecība, 1957), 135, 290.

18. Rainis, "Vienīgā zvaigzne," first published in 1902; Jānis Rainis, *Kopoti raksti* (Riga: Zinātne, 1980), 1:127, 483; quoted by Jānis Krēsliņš, Sr., "Vēlreiz par augstākām idejām," *Diena*, February 3, 2005, 16.

19. Greble, Kokare, and Vītoliņš, *Cīņas dziesmas*, 96, 277.

20. Ackerman and DuVall, *Force More Powerful*, 13–39.

21. Šmidchens, «National Heroic Narratives,» 498.

22. Zane Gailīte, ed., *Mēness meti, saules stīga. Emīls Dārziņš* (Riga: Pils, 2006), 78–79.

23. Rhesa, *Prutena*, 163. M. Biržiška, ed., *Liudo Rėzos Dainos. Pirmo lietuviško dainyno III leidimas, I dalis* (Kaunas: Vytauto Didžiojo Universiteto Humanitarinių Mokslų Fakulteto Leidinys, 1935), 157.

24. Simonas Stanevičius, *Raštai* (Vilnius: Vaga, 1967), 72; Stanevičius, *Dainos žemaičių*, 15–16.

25. Kalvaitis, *Prūsijos Lietuvių dainos*, 379.

26. Tumavičiūtė, "Jurgis Zauerveinas," 118.

27. Maironis, *Pavasario balsai*, 69–70, 236–37; Abaris, *Užaugau Lietuvoj*, 18–19.

28. D. Andriulis et al., eds., *Dainuojam: Dainų rinkinys kariams, šauliams, moksleiviams ir jaunimui* (Kaunas: Kariuomenės Štabo Spaudos ir Švietimo Skyriaus Leidinys, 1935), 30–31; "Where the Plains Are Level" was third in this military songbook, after the national anthem and "We Were Born Lithuanians."

29. Tallat-Kelpša omitted Maironis's last stanza in the song: "It is horrific there still, and frightening by night! Even grown men try to avoid it: people say there are graves of ancient giants, whose ghosts sometimes walk about."

30. A. Hinnoms, "Ar latviešu strēlniekiem pasaules karā," *Latviešu Strēlnieki* 31 (1940): 3145. Latvian Riflemen would later recall yet another morale-building song, "Viens saucējs sauc pie Daugavas," from the war's early years. Voldemārs Krauklis, "Kara laika atmiņas," *Latviešu Strēlnieki* 29 (1939): 2919; Jānis Gulbis, "Kā es atceros latviešu strēlnieku laimetu," *Latviešu Strēlnieki* 29 (1939): 2958. Several of the Latvian Riflemen's regimental flags quoted songs, among them "God Bless Latvia" and "On the Ground by the Field I Laid My Head"; Igors Vārpa, *Latviešu karavīrs zem Krievijas impērijas, Padomju Krievijas un PSRS karogiem* (Riga: Nordik, 2006), 35–36.

31. Jaan Wahi, ed. *Uued Sõjalaulud* (Tartu, Estonia: K. Jaik, 1914), 7–9, 12, 13.

32. Vita Ivanauskaitė, "Tarpukario Lietuvos dainos: Kolektyvinės ir individualiosios kūrybos sintezė," in *Lietuvių liaudies dainynas* (Vilnius: Lietuvių Literatūros ir Tautosakos Institutas, 2004), 18:15–16.

33. "Kaitseväelased mälestavad tuntud marsilaulu autorit," Kaitsevägi— Uudised, September 30, 2004, http://www.mil.ee/et/arhiiv/4886 (accessed August 19, 2013).

34. Rainis, Kopoti raksti, 12:222, 477, 484.

35. Darius Staliūnas, "Žuvusių karių kultas tarpukario Lietuvoje," Lietuviu Atgimimo istorijos studijos 17.

36. Ivanauskaitė, "Tarpukario Lietuvos dainos," 28–31, 47.

37. Ibid., 31–43.

38. Viliūnas, "Vytauto Didžiojo kultas," 89–90.

39. Ibid., 96.

40. "Kulkosvaidis" and "Kulkosvaidininkas," in Andriulis, Dainuojam, 82–83.

41. Živilė Ramoškaitė, «Antrojo Pasaulinio karo ir pokario dainos,» Lietuvių Liaudies Dainynas 19:30–31.

42. Ibid.

43. Ibid., 34–35.

44. Romuald J. Misiunas and Rein Taagepera, The Baltic States: Years of Dependence 1940–1990, rev., expanded ed. (Berkeley: University of California Press, 1993), 83–94.

45. Ramoškaitė, "Antrojo Pasaulinio karo ir pokario dainos," 47.

46. Lionginas Baliukevičius, "August 1948," in The Diary of a Partisan: A Year in the Life of the Postwar Lithuanian Resistance Fighter Dzūkas (Vilnius: Genocide and Resistance Research Centre of Lithuania, 2008), 46.

47. Ramoškaitė, "Antrojo Pasaulinio karo ir pokario dainos," 25.

CHAPTER 5

1. Kasekamp, History of the Baltic States, 124–31; Aldis Purs, "Soviet in Form, Local in Content: Elite Repression and Mass Terror in the Baltic States, 1940–1953," in Stalinist Terror in Eastern Europe, ed. Kevin McDermott and Matthew Stibbe (Manchester: Manchester University Press, 2010), 22–29; Aleksandras Shtromas, "The Baltic States as Soviet Republics: Tensions and Contradictions," in The National Self-Determination of Estonia, Latvia, and Lithuania, ed. Graham Smith (London: Macmillan, 1994). Finland rejected the Soviet ultimatum, and was invaded by the Red Army in the Winter War; Soviet military bases were established there in the early months of 1940; Jason Edward Lavery, The History of Finland (Westport, CT: Greenwood Press, 2006), 114–17.

2. Primary sources on the Holocaust and Nazi occupation are compiled by Andrew Ezergailis, The Holocaust in Latvia, 1941–1944: The Missing Center (Riga: Historical Institute of Latvia and Washington, DC: United States Holocaust Memorial Museum, 1996); and Alfonsas Eidintas, Jews, Lithuanians, and the Holocaust (Vilnius: Versus Aureus, 2003). The mass murder of Jews was organized and carried out by the security police (Sicherheitsdienst, SD), under orders from the Nazi government in Berlin. Local ethnic collaborators joined auxilliary SD killing units, motivated by personal gain (stealing the property of those they killed, earning money for killing, or evading

punishment for Soviet collaboration) rather than by national, religious, or racial ideology; Eidintas, *Jews, Lithuanians, and the Holocaust*, 253–73; Ezergailis, *Holocaust in Latvia*, 79–115. Documents related to the military conscription of Estonians and Latvians into the Estonian and Latvian legions are compiled by Andrew Ezergailis, ed. *The Latvian Legion: Heroes, Nazis, or Victims?: A Collection of Documents from OSS War-Crimes Investigation Files, 1945–1950* (Riga: Historical Institute of Latvia, 1997); and Andrew Ezergailis, ed., *Stockholm Documents: The German Occupation of Latvia, 1941–1945: What Did America Know?* (Riga: Historical Institute of Latvia, 2002), 350–53. The failed military mobilization in Lithuania is described by Saulius Sužiedėlis, "The Military Mobilization Campaigns of 1943 and 1944 in German-Occupied Lithuania: Contrasts in Resistance and Collaboration," *Journal of Baltic Studies* 21, no. 1 (1990): 33–52.

3. Arvydas Anušauskas, ed., *The Anti-Soviet Resistance in the Baltic States* (Vilnius: Du Ka, 1999); David J. Smith, *Estonia: Independence and European Integration* (New York: Routledge, 2001), 37; Artis Pabriks and Aldis Purs, *Latvia: The Challenges of Change* (New York: Routledge, 2001), 30–31; Thomas Lane, *Lithuania: Stepping Westward* (New York: Routledge, 2001), 64–67.

4. Robert Conquest, *Stalin: Breaker of Nations* (New York: Penguin, 1991), 299.

5. Kasekamp, *History of the Baltic States*, 141–46.

6. Composers unions were established as a Soviet institution in 1932; their use as instruments of Stalinist terror was first demonstrated in 1936, in the public persecution of Dmitry Shostakovich; Richard Taruskin, *Defining Russia Musically: Historical and Hermeneutical Essays* (Princeton: Princeton University Press, 1997), 513–16.

7. Order 158 of the Board of Artistic Affairs, in Andrejs Plakans, ed. *Experiencing Totalitarianism: The Invasion and Occupation of Latvia by the USSR and Nazi Germany, 1939–1991: A Documentary History* (Bloomington, IN: Authorhouse, 2007), 67.

8. Heinrihs Strods, *Politiskā cenzūra Latvijā, 1940–1990*, 2 vols. (Riga: Jumava, 2010), 1:13, 153. A secret order to purge Lithuania's libraries was given in December of 1949; Romualdas Bagušauskas and Arūnas Streikus, eds., *Lietuvos kultūra sovietinės ideologijos nelaisvėje, 1940–1990: Dokumentų rinkinys* (Vilnius: Lietuvos Gyventojų Genocido ir Rezistencijos Tyrimo Centras, 2005), 131–34.

9. S. Frederick Starr, *Red and Hot: The Fate of Jazz in the Soviet Union, 1917–1991* (New York: Limelight Editions, 1994), 194–202, 14; "Lietuvos TSR Valstybinės filharmonijos direktoriaus P. Sagaičio pranešimas partinės organizacijos atvirame susirinkime, svarščiusiame VKP(b) CK nutarimą dėl dramos teatrų repertuaro ir priemonių jam pagerinti," and Z. Kumpienė, "Kalba Lietuvos TSR Tarybinių kompozitorių Sąjungos susirinkime, skirtame 1948 m. vasario 10 d. VKP(b) CK nutarimo dėl V. Muradelio operos 'Didžioji draugystė' aptarimui, 1948 m. kovo 1 d.," in Laima Kiauleikytė and Violeta Tumasonienė, eds., *Muzika 1940–1960, Dokumentų rinkinys* (Vilnius: Lietuvos Archyvų Generalinė Direkcija, 1992), 98, 250, 311n17; and Timothy W.

Ryback, *Rock around the Bloc: A History of Rock Music in Eastern Europe and the Soviet Union* (New York: Oxford University Press, 1990), 10–14, 30, 52–53, 103–4, 214.

10. Rinne, *Laulev revolutsioon,* 30. The folk memory may stem from Valgre's 1949 revision of his "Saaremaa Waltz," as discussed by Valter Ojakäär, *Vaibunud viiside kaja: Eesti levimuusika ajaloost* (Tallinn: Eesti Entsüklopeediakirjastus, 2000), 396.

11. Robert C. Tucker, *The Soviet Political Mind: Stalinism and Post-Stalin Change* (New York: W. W. Norton, 1971), 143–66. Stalin's support for Lysenko's and Pavlov's ideas, and his assertion that language is a means of enacting politics, are documented by Ethan Pollock, *Stalin and the Soviet Science Wars* (Princeton: Princeton University Press, 2006), 41–71, 104–67. See also Ryback, *Rock around the Bloc,* 8. Pavlov himself rejected Stalin's use of violence to consolidate Soviet power: "Have you given enough thought to the possibility that many years of terror and unrestrained, arbitrary power will transform our character—which is already quite Asiatic—making it shameful and slavelike? Can much good be accomplished by slaves? Pyramids can be built, yes. But not true, shared, human happiness"; D. K. Burlaka et al., eds., *I. P. Pavlov: Pro et contra* (Saint Petersburg: Izdatel'stvo Russkogo Khristianskogo Gumanitarnogo Instituta, 1999), 720.

12. Caryl Emerson, *The Cambridge Introduction to Russian Literature* (New York: Cambridge University Press, 2008), 200–201.

13. Felix Oinas, *Essays on Russian Folklore and Mythology* (Columbus, OH: Slavica Publishers, 1984), 131–79; Dana Prescott Howell, *The Development of Soviet Folkloristics* (New York: Garland, 1992), 341–42; Guntis Šmidchens, "Folklorism Revisited," *Journal of Folklore Research* 36, no. 1 (1999): 51–70.

14. R. Pelše et al., eds., *Latviešu padomju folklora* (Riga: Latvijas PSR Zinātņu Akadēmijas Izdevniecība, 1953), 3; A. Medne-Romane, "Darba tautas cīņa ar apspiedēju latviešu vēstītājā folklorā," in *Folkloras Institūta Raksti* (Riga: Latvijas PSR Zinātņu Akadēmija, 1950), 92; Rolfs Ekmanis, *Latvian Literature under the Soviets, 1940–1975* (Belmont, MA: Nordland Publishing Company, 1978), 177–80; Laura Olson, *Performing Russia: Folk Revival and Russian Identity* (London: Routledge Curzon, 2004), 40–41.

15. Quoted by Ieva Kalniņa, "Latviešu padomju folkloras konstrukcija," in *Kultūra un vara: Raksti par valodu, literatūru, tradicionālo kultūru,* edited by Janīna Kursīte et al. (Riga: LU Akadēmiskais Apgāds, 2007), 39.

16. Emerson, *Cambridge Introduction to Russian Literature,* 202.

17. Ekmanis, *Latvian Literature under the Soviets,* 51–52, 106–7, 117–18, 236–38. Terry Martin traces the origins of Soviet images of Russians as "first among equals" in the USSR and "the most talented nation in the world" to an unpublished 1933 speech by Stalin and an announcement published in 1936, in Terry Martin, *The Affirmative Action Empire: Nations and Nationalism in the Soviet Union, 1923–1939* (Ithaca, NY: Cornell University Press, 2001), 452–53.

18. Jiří Fukač, "Socialist Realism in Music: An Artificial System of Ideological and Aesthetic Norms," in *Socialist Realism and Music,* ed. Geoffrey Chew and Petr Macek (Prague: KLP, 2004), 19–20.

19. G. G. Soboleva, as quoted by Olson, *Performing Russia*, 54–55.

20. The Latvian Soviet Socialist Republic's anthem was approved by decree on July 19, 1945, and the Estonian SSR anthem was approved on the following day, July 20, 1945.

21. "Himnas," *Mažioji Lietuviškoji Tarybinė Enciklopedija* (Vilnius: Mintis, 1966), 1:629; "Valstybės himnas," *Tarybų Lietuvos Enciklopedija* (Vilnius: Vyriausioji Enciklopedijų Redakcija, 1988), 4:440.

22. "From the Minutes of the Bureau of the Central Committee of the Latvian Communist Party Concerning the Contents of the Antherm of the Latvian SSR," in Plakans, *Experiencing Totalitarianism*, 150.

23. Email to author, March 8, 2010.

24. The Latvian translator of the all-Soviet anthem did capture Stalinist biological principles: "Mūs audzēja Staļins" means "Stalin cultivated us" in the agricultural sense.

25. Alexei Yurchak, *Everything Was Forever until It Was No More: The Last Soviet Generation* (Princeton: Princeton University Press, 2006), 24–26.

26. Geoffrey Chew and Petr Macek, eds., *Socialist Realism and Music* (Prague: KLP, 2004), 15. Yurchak confirms that nonparticipation in official loyalty rituals would bring about serious repercussions; Yurchak, *Everything Was Forever*, 27.

27. Fukač, "Socialist Realism in Music," 19.

28. Decisions and actions often attributed to Andrei Zhdanov were dictated by Stalin, who continued the Soviet cultural policies of the 1930s. The only new aspect of "Zhdanovism" was that the censorship mechanism was made public; "Resolution of the TsK VKP(b) Orgburo 'On the journals Star and Leningrad,'" August 14, 1946 (published in *Pravda* August 21, 1946), in Katerina Clark et al., eds., *Soviet Culture and Power: A History in Documents, 1917–1953* (New Haven, CT: Yale University Press, 2007), 349–51, 423; "Lietuvos TSR tarybinių kompozitorių sąjungos narių susirinkimo, skirto 1946 m. rugpiūčio 24 d. VKP(b) CK nutarimo dėl žurnalų 'Zvezda' ir 'Leningrad' aptarimui, protokolas. 1946 m. rugsėjo 15 d.," in Kiauleikytė and Tumasonienė, *Muzika 1940–1960*, 80–82.

29. Māris Rauda, "'Stalin, we are following you . . . ': The Poet Jānis Sudrabkalns," *Occupied Latvia Today* (1986): 46–53, 103; Vita Gruodytė, "Lithuanian Musicology in Historical Context: 1945 to the Present," *Journal of Baltic Studies* 39, 3 (2008): 267.

30. The Lithuanian line about Stalin was changed by Vacys Reimeris to "The Party leads us to happiness and power." The Latvian line was changed to "We will go forever with the flag of October." In Estonian, the "Stalinist path" was replaced by the "path of communism." The USSR anthem was revised more extensively: The refrain was now uniform, its second line repeating "Friendship of nations" instead of "Happiness" or "Glory," and its third and fourth lines changed to "Lenin's Party, the people's power, leads us to the triumph of communism." In the song's second stanza, the last two lines now omitted Stalin and continued Lenin's contributions: "He lifted nations to the just cause, / Inspired us to work and heroic deeds!" The third stanza was revised in its entirety: "In the victory of communism's immortal ideas, / We see

the future of our country, / And to the red banner of our glorious Fatherland, / We will always be selflessly true!"

31. Entries on Moiseev and the ensemble in B. A. Vvedenskii, ed., *Bol'shaia sovetskaia entsiklopediia*, vol. 12 (1952), 310–12, and vol. 28 (1954), 74. The leader of the Lithuanian national dance ensemble (later named Lietuva) travelled to Moscow in 1941 to consult with the Moiseev ensemble; Kazys Poškaitis, *Lietuvių šokio kelias į sceną* (Vilnius: Vaga, 1985), 59–60. Soviet Latvia's professional dance ensemble was Daile, established in 1968; Soviet Estonia did not have a professional song-and-dance ensemble, but Moiseev was also the model for amateurs; Sille Kapper, "Pärimus ja jäliendus: Postkolonialistlik katse mõista rahvatantsu olukorda Eesti NSV-s ja pärast seda," *Methis* 7 (2011): 125.

32. Jakelaitis, *Lietuvos dainų šventės*, 97.

33. Ibid., 100; Mindaugas Černiauskas, *Europos tautų nacionaliniai himnai* (n.p.: Versus Aureus, 2006), 118; "Himnas," in *Mažioji Lietuviškoji Tarybinė Enciklopedija* (Vilnius: Mintis, 1966), 1:629. Lionginas Šepetys states that the 1946 Lithuanian song festival saw the new Soviet anthem's first-ever performance by a mass choir; *Neprarastoji karta: Siluetai ir spalvos* (Vilnius: Lietuvos Rašytojų Sąjungos Leidykla, 2005), 153. At that event, it was probably sung in Lithuanian translation; *Tarybų Sąjungos himnas* (Moscow: LTSR Valstybinė Leidykla, 1944).

34. Karen Petrone, *Life Has Become More Joyous, Comrades: Celebrations in the Time of Stalin* (Bloomington: Indiana University Press, 2000), 16–18.

35. Quoted in Jakelaitis, *Lietuvos dainų šventės*, 98.

36. *Mažioji Lietuviškoji Tarybinė Enciklopedija*, 2:418 and 1:352–53. The independence-era heritage was reclaimed in 1970, when Vytautas Jakelaitis published the first book-length study of Lithuanian song festival history, in which the Soviet festival of 1946 is described under the title "Fourth Song Festival 1946—The First in the Soviet years"; Jakelaitis, *Lietuvos dainų šventės*, 94.

37. Teodoras Brazys, Mikas Petrauskas, Česlovas Sasnauskas, Kazimieras Banaitis, Julius Štarka, Antanas Vanagaitis, Juozas Žilevičius, and Aleksandras Kačanauskas.

38. "Lietuvos TSR tarybinių kompozitorių sąjungos . . . ," in Kiauleikytė and Tumasonienė, *Muzika 1940–1960*, 80–82.

39. "A. Klenicko pranešimas Lietuvos TSR tarybinių kompozitorių Sąjungos susirinkime, skirtame 1948 m. vasario 10 d. VKP(b) CK nutarimo dėl V. Muradelio operos 'Didžioji draugystė' aptarimui" (March 1, 1948), "Muzikologės Z. Kumpienės kalba . . . ," "J. Tallat-Kelpšos pranešimas . . . ," in Kiauleikytė and Tumasonienė, *Muzika 1940–1960*, 95–96, 99, 105–6.

40. Gruodytė, "Lithuanian Musicology in Historical Context," 266; her source is Kiauleikytė and Tumasonienė, *Muzika 1940–1960*, 92–109.

41. Toivo Ojaveski, Mart Puust, and A. Põldmäe, eds., *130 aastat eesti laulupidusid* (Tallinn: Talmar & Põhi, 2002), 116–17.

42. Raun, *Estonia and the Estonians*, 171.

43. Quoted by Mare Põldmäe, "Kaks laulupidu, 1947 ja 1950," *Teater. Muusika. Kino* 3 (1990): 33.

44. Ojaveski et al., *130 aastat*, 251.

45. *Eesti muusika biograafiline leksikon* (Tallinn: Valgus, 1990), 79, 193, 287.

46. Ojaveski et al., *130 aastat*, 250–51.

47. Ibid., 129.

48. Põldmäe, "Kaks laulupidu, 1947 ja 1950," 32–35.

49. Petrone, *Life Has Become More Joyous*, 23–24, 35–39.

50. Ekmanis, *Latvian Literature under the Soviets*, 120–26.

51. *Latvijas PSR Mazā Enciklopēdija* (Riga: Zinātne, 1957), 1:597, 2:367.

52. Segejs Kruks, *Par mūziku skaistu un melodisku! Padomju kultūras politika, 1932–1964* (Riga: Neptuns, 2008), 22–24, 127–28.

53. Martin Boiko, "Muzikoloģija/Mūzikas Zinātne: A Critical History of Latvian Musicology," *Journal of Baltic Studies* 39, no. 3 (2008): 330; Vizbulīte Bērziņa, *Daudz baltu dieniņu . . . : Jēkaba Graubiņa dzīvesstāsts* (Riga: Atēna, 2006), 211–28.

54. Smith, *Estonia*, 37; Pabriks and Purs, *Latvia*, 32; Lane, *Lithuania*, 61–63.

55. I. Plotke et al., eds. *Padomju Latvijas 15 gadi* (Riga: Latvijas Valsts Izdevniecība, 1955), 38–39.

56. Yurchak, *Everything Was Forever*, 126–28, 290.

57. Petrone, *Life Has Become More Joyous*, 4.

58. Laura Olson also argues that state-sponsored folk culture should not be studied solely in the context of Stalinist fakelore; Olson, *Performing Russia*, 13.

59. Czeslaw Milosz, *The Captive Mind*, trans. Jane Zielonko (New York: Vintage Books, 1990), 64–69.

60. Aili Aarelaid-Tart, *Cultural Trauma and Life Stories* (Helsinki: Aleksanteri Institute, 2006), 212.

61. Vaclav Havel et. al., *Power of the Powerless: Citizens against the State in Central-Eastern Europe* (Armonk, NY: M. E. Sharpe, 1985), 31.

62. Ibid., 72.

63. Ryback, *Rock around the Bloc*, 17–18; "Iš Lietuvos TSR Kultūros Ministro įsakymo gerinti estradinės muzikos padėtį respublikoje," and "Iš Lietuvos TSR Kultūros Ministro įsakymo įsteigti Lietuvos TSR Valstybinės Fillharmonijos estradinį orkestrą," in Kiauleikytė and Tumasonienė, *Muzika 1940–1960*, 69–71, 265, and 317n40; Starr, *Red and Hot*, 245–56. The Rīga Estrada Orchestra was established in 1957; Daiga Mazvērsīte, *Pieskāriens: Raimonds Pauls un latviešu mūzikas kultūra* (Riga: Madris, 2006), 12–14.

64. Recordings of two banned Pauls concerts were smuggled to the West and published; Raimonds Pauls, *Edgars Liepiņš: Rīga toreiz—Rīga šodien*, 2 LP record set (Hamburg: Kultūras Glābšanas Biedrība, 1981); and Raimonds Pauls, *Mūžīgais unisons*, LP record (Hamburg: Kultūras Glābšanas Biedrība, 1983). In 1988, Pauls rehabilitated the songs of a banned pop singer, Eduards Rozenštrauhs (1918–1992); Andžils Remess and Jānis Peters, *Maestro: Raimonds Pauls* (Riga: Jumava, 2010), 55–57, 88–91.

65. Havel, *Power of the Powerless*, 28.

66. "Lietuvos TSR Varlstybinės filharmonijos direktoriaus P. Sagaičio pranešimas partinės organizacijos atvirame susirinkime, svarsčiusiame VKP(b) CK nutarimą dėl dramos teatrų repertuaro ir priemonių jam pagerinti" (September 28, 1946), in Kiauleikytė and Tumasonienė, *Muzika 1940–1960*, 252.

67. *Dziesmu svētku mazā enciklopēdija* (Riga: Musica Baltica, 2004), 45–47.

68. Joachim Braun, "Reconsidering Musicology in the Baltic States of Lithuania, Latvia, and Estonia: 1990–2007," *Journal of Baltic Studies* 39, no. 3 (2008): 235. The 1949 instrumental work "Variations on a Theme by Jāzeps Vītols" was based on a popular church chorale by the composer who had fled to the West to escape the Soviet occupation. The quotation of religious music, and in particular the piece's culmination in a funeral march, most explicitly did not display the optimistic spirit of socialist realism.

69. Havel, *Power of the Powerless*, 58. A fellow prisoner recalled that the Latvian composer discussed above, Jēkabs Graubiņš, said, "If the conscience is clean, there is no need to fear anything"; Bērziņa, *Daudz baltu dieniņu*, 221, 24–25.

70. Bagušauskas and Streikus, *Lietuvos kultūra*, 430–32.

71. In the 1950s, Soviet scholars began to falsify Vītols's biography, writing that the aging, allegedly senile composer was fooled into emigrating; Kevin C. Karnes, "Soviet Musicology and the 'Nationalities Question': The Case of Latvia," *Journal of Baltic Studies* 39, no. 3 (2008): 297–98.

72. Heinrihs Strods, "Non-Violent Resistance in Latvia (1945–1985)," in *Regaining Independence: Non-Violent Resistance in Latvia, 1945–1991*, ed. Valdis Blūzma, et al. (Riga: Latvian Academy of Sciences, 2009), 91.

73. Havel, *Power of the Powerless*, 39, 64–65. Emphasis in original.

74. Ibid., 27–43, 78–81.

75. Ibid., 47, 82.

76. Ibid., 92–93.

77. The Soviets arrested, among many others, Bruno Javoišs, a twenty-two-year old who raised a Latvian flag on the Rīga radio tower on December 5, 1963. He was sentenced to seven years in a labor camp for "anti-Soviet agitation"; Ieva Nikoleta Dāboliņa, "Dzīvie pieminekļi. Atceroties Gunāru Astru," *Ir*, October 21, 2011, www.ir.lv (accessed October 21, 2011).

CHAPTER 6

1. A. Shakhov, "Vse flagi v gosti k nam," *Sovetskaia Litva*, July 2, 1988, p. 3. A picture of three participants holding flags was published on page 1 of the Estonian newspaper *Sirp ja Vasar*, July 8, 1988. The Latvian participant Valdis Holms notes that the Lithuanian flag at the opening concert was in the form of three long ribbons unfurled by the singers at the front of the choir; he also describes the performance of Latvia's national anthem, with orchestra accompaniment, at the festival concert; "Nākotnē ejamais ceļš: Baltijas studentu dziesmu svētki *Gaudeamus*," *Latvija Šodien* 1988, 69–70. The confrontations between the singers and the police, who refrained from violent force, were recalled by a Latvian participant, Dita Kanapinska, in a

conversation with author, autumn 2009, and by a Lithuanian eyewitness, Silvestras Gaižiūnas, email to author, May 19, 2010.

2. Tape-recorded conversation with Leidi Veskis, Astrid Vartina, and Juta Ruud, during the concert on June 30, 1990.

3. Imants Ziedonis, *Raksti* (Riga: Nordik, 1996), 3:102.

4. Similarities between (unofficial) national and loyal Soviet songs are pointed out by Kanni Labi, "Isamaalaulud ja okupatsioonirežiim—nostalgia, utoopia ja reaalsus," *Methis* 7 (Spring 2011): 115.

5. Martin, *Affirmative Action Empire*, 444.

6. Rummo, "Ühe laulu lugu," 120–21.

7. *XII Üldlaulupeo Teataja* 9, 1947, as quoted in ibid., 126.

8. The collection was edited by the conductors Artur Vahter and Jüri Variste; Vahter and Variste, *Eesti koorilooming*, 2:63.

9. Rummo, "Ühe laulu lugu," 111; Ojaveski et al., *130 aastat*, 253; Vesilind, *Singing Revolution*, 99.

10. Vesilind, *Singing Revolution*, 104.

11. Taruskin, *Defining Russia Musically*, 487.

12. Põldmäe, *Esimene Eesti üldlaulupidu 1869*. Note the capitalized word *Eesti*, which means "Estonia" and not "Estonian."

13. Quoted in Vesilind, *Singing Revolution*, 97.

14. Veljo Tormis, *Lauldud sõna* (Tartu, Estonia: Ülikooli Kirjastus, 2000), 118–19; Tormis quotes analyses of his works published by the musicologists Mark Rais and Toomas Siitan.

15. Excerpt from "Litany to Thunder" translated into English by Kristin Kuutma, in liner notes to the CD by Veljo Tormis, *Litany to Thunder*, Estonian Philharmonic Chamber Choir, Tõnu Kaljuste (ECM New Series 1687, 1999).

16. Tormis, *Lauldud sõna*, 119; Mimi S. Daitz, *Ancient Song Recovered: The Life and Music of Veljo Tormis* (Hillsdale, NY: Pendragon Press, 2004), 220.

17. Daitz, *Ancient Song Recovered*, 85.

18. Vahter and Variste, *Eesti koorilooming*, 2:130–32.

19. Raun, *Estonia and the Estonians*, 196; Sirje Kiin, Rein Ruutsoo, and Andres Tarand, eds., *40 kirja lugu* (Tallinn: Olion, 1990).

20. Tormis, *Lauldud sõna*, 123–24; Daitz and Tormis, *Ancient Song Recovered*, 201.

21. Laima Muktupāvela, *Brāli brāli: Balsu burvji brāļi Kokari* (Riga: Dienas Grāmata, 2008), 93–94.

22. Viktors Hausmanis, ed., *Latviešu rakstniecība biogrāfijās* (Riga: LZA Literatūras, Folkloras un Mākslas Institūts, Latvijas Enciklopēdija, 1992), 295.

23. Bērzkalns, *Latviešu Dziesmu svētku vēsture*, 447–48. *Latvijas PSR Mazā Enciklopēdija*, vol. 1 (Riga: Zinātne, 1967), 187.

24. J. Wihtols, ed., *Pamahziba kà V. Latweeschu Wispahrigo dseesmu swehtku dseesmas jamahza* (Jelgawa: G. Landsbergs, 1904), 13–14.

25. J. Rainis, *Raksti* (Västerås, Sweden: Ziemeļblāzma, 1952), 1:8; Rainis, *Kopoti raksti*, 10:310, line 62, 507–12. The play saw hundreds of

performances in the Soviet period, with new versions staged in Latvia in 1944, 1945, 1947, 1948, 1953, 1955, 1957, and 1968; a musical performance in 1960; and an opera by A. Žilinskis in 1977. G. Piesis directed the 1973 film with a screenplay by Imants Ziedonis and music by Imants Kalniņš.

26. Raimonds Baltakmens asserts that "Fortress of Light" was "forgotten" and not sung in 1950; Baltakmens, "Vīru koru korifejs Mednis," 179.

27. Ibid., 79.

28. Ibid., 181–82. The episode is not mentioned by Ilma Grauzdiņa and Arnis Poruks, *Dziesmu svētku gara gaita* (Riga: E. Melngaiļa Tautas Mākslas Centrs, 1990), 71.

29. Maironis, *Pavasario balsai*, 166–67, 295–97.

30. Onė Narbutienė, *Juozas Naujalis: Straipsniai. Laiškai. Dokumentai. Amžininkų atsiminimai. Straipsniai apie kūrybą* (Vilnius: Vaga, 1968), 242, 318.

31. Remembered by Victor Lapatinskas in a conversation in spring 2010.

32. See 1924–65 song festival programs in Jakelaitis, *Lietuvos dainų šventės*.

33. The official Soviet view was documented in a 1962 decree by the Lithuanian Communist Party Central Committee, on the occasion Marionis's centennial:

> "Maironis belonged to the bourgeois clerical class and held high positions in the religious hierarchy. In several works he expressed a negative view of the class struggle, propagated for the unity of the nation, and opposed the socialist movement. On the other hand, in Marionis's best poetic works there is reflected the people's hatred for tsarism. The poet's lines about battles against the crusaders are very popular. They played an important role in the Lithuanian people's struggle against the Kaiser's occupiers and the hitlerite invaders. Maironis's best poems became songs. They sing about love for the homeland and its nature. In some of his satires written during the years of bourgeois rule, the poet unmasked bourgeois politikers, condemned careerism and avarice, and the political and moral degeneration of the rulers." Bagušauskas and Streikus, *Lietuvos kultūra*, 308–9

34. A. Gimžauskas, *Kur lygūs laukai: Dainos chorams* (Vilnius: Valstybinė Grožinės Literatūros Leidykla, 1959), 6.

35. Jakelaitis, *Lietuvos dainų šventės*, 195.

36. I have not found published documentation of the changed text; Giedrius Subačius recalled that in the 1970s his schoolchildren's choir sang the song without this stanza (conversation, spring 2011). A 1968 songbook cut the last three stanzas of "Where Šešupė Flows" but kept "Dear Lithuania" in its entirety; A. Zakaras, ed. *Kur giria žaliuoja* (Vilnius: Vaga, 1968–70), 1:6, 67–68.

37. "'Ir laivas plaukia . . . per laikus': Ilgametį Centro direktorių Salomoną Sverdiolą kalbina Juozas Mikutavičius," in *Liaudies kultūra: Lietuvos liaudies kultūros centrui—60* (Vilnius: Lietuvos Liaudies Kultūros Centras, 2001), 39; Šepetys, *Neprarastoji karta*, 150; Egidija Ramanauskaitė, "Lithuanian Youth Culture versus Soviet Culture," in *The Baltic Countries under Occupation: Soviet and Nazi Rule, 1939–1991*, ed. Anu Mai Kõll (Acta Universitatis

Stockholmiensis, 2003), 327; Jakelaitis, *Lietuvos dainų šventės*, 195; Vaidotas Karlonas, ed., *Dainų šventė* (Vilnius: Vaga, 1980), 196, 198.

38. Šepetys, *Neprarastoji karta*, 152–53.

39. Ojaveski et al., *130 aastat*, 206–7, 56.

40. Unpublished 1998 documentary film, Smithsonian Folklife Festival.

41. Mikhail Gorbachev, *Perestroika: New Thinking for Our Country and the World* (New York: Harper & Row, 1987), 75–76.

42. Ibid., 79.

43. *Sovetskoe obshchestvo segodnia: Voporsosy i otvety* (Moscow: Izdatelstvo Politicheskoi Literatury, 1987), 129. The book's last page reports that it was submitted to the censors on June 15, 1987, approved for print on September 14, 1987, and printed in 200,000 copies.

44. Juris Dreifelds, "Two Latvian Dams, Two Confrontations," *Baltic Forum* 6, no. 1 (1989): 11–24; Robert Smurr, *Perceptions of Nature, Expressions of Nation: An Environmental History of Estonia* (Saarbrücken, Germany: Lambert Academic Publishing, 2009), 281–345; Katrina Schwartz, *Nature and National Identity after Communism: Globalizing the Ethnoscape* (Pittsburgh: University of Pittsburgh Press, 2006), 69–71.

45. Misiunas and Taagepera, *Baltic States*, 307–11; Juris Dreifelds, *Latvia in Transition* (Cambridge: Cambridge University Press, 1996), 55–60; Valdis Blūzma, "The Period of Awakening and Non-Violent Resistance (1986–4 May 1990)," in *Regaining Independence: Non-Violent Resistance in Latvia, 1945–1991*, ed. Valdis Blūzma et al. (Riga: Latvian Academy of Sciences, 2009), 299–300; Pāvils Brūvers, "1987. gada 14. jūnijs Rīgā," and documents 1, 2, and 11, *Latvija Šodien* (1987): 1–9, 130, 133.

46. Punk rocker Merle Jääger recalls that tears came to her eyes when she heard elderly women singing patriotic songs in Hirve Park. Lagle Parek comments, "There was an attempt to sing. No big deal that it didn't turn out very well." Eve Pärnaste remembers that singers didn't know all of the words to "Be Free Estonia's Sea," but that it went well nevertheless. That song was interrupted by an impromptu speaker from the crowd; another speaker defended the Communist Party and attacked this song as a "fascist" song, but others pointed out that he was attacking a different song, not "Be Free." See *Hirvepark 1987: 20 aastat kodanikualgatusest, mis muutis Eesti lähiajalugu.* (Tallinn: MTÜ Kultuuriselts Hirvepark, 2007), 126, 40, 58, 66, 95, 219, 22–23. Descriptions of the demonstrations in Tallinn and Lithuania also appear in Michael Tarm and Mari-Ann Rikken, eds., *Documents from Estonia: Articles, Speeches, Resolutions, Letters, Editorials, Interviews Concerning Recent Developments from April 1986 to March 1989* (New York: Estonian American National Council, 1989), 14–15; Misiunas and Taagepera, *Baltic States*, 308–9; and Alfred Erich Senn, *Lithuania Awakening* (Berkeley: University of California Press, 1990), 19–22.

47. Dreifelds, *Latvia in Transition*, 57–58. Eyewitness accounts of demonstrations in Rīga from March to June 1988 appear in *Latvija Šodien* 1988, 23–24, 30–31; 47–53.

48. "Obsuzhdeny voprosy natsional'noi simvoliki," *Sovetskaia Litva*, August 18, 1988, p. 1; "V tsentral'nom Komitete Kommunisticheskoi partii

Litvy i Sovete Ministrov Litovskoi SSR," *Sovetskaia Litva*, August 20, 1988, pp. 1, 3; "Zakon Litovskoi Sovetskoi Sotsialisticheskoi Respubliki Ob izmenenii statei 168 i 169 Konstitutsii Litovskoi SSR," *Sovetskaia Litva*, November 19, 1988, p. 1 (the anthem's ninth line was changed to "Let the sun in Lithuania overcome the darkness"); "Zakon Latviiskoi Sovetskoi Sotsialisticheskoi Respubliki O vnesenii izmenenii v Konstitutsiiu (Osnovnoi Zakon) Latviiskoi Sovetskoi Sotsialisticheskoi Respubliki," *Sovetskaia Latviia*, February 20, 1990, 2. The official Russian-language translation differs slightly from the Latvian original: "God, bless our fatherland, eternal Latvia, Let your daughters bloom, let your sons sing and the people live in happiness in Latvia."

49. Astra Mille, *Te un citadelē: Jānis Peters. Tumšsarkanā* (Riga: Atēna, 2006), 52–53.

50. *Latvijas Tautas fronte: Gads pirmais* (Riga: Latvijas Tautas Fronte, 1989), 199; Dainis Īvāns, *Gadījuma karakalps* (Riga: Vieda, 1995), 179.

51. Rinne, *Laulev revolutsioon*, 246.

52. Kajar Kase, "Mälestused öölaulupeost: Tõnu Kaljuste," *Postimees*, August 15, 2008, http://oolaulupidu.postimees.ee/?id=27055 (accessed July 9, 2010).

53. Remembered, for example, by Riina Roose, in Rinne, *Laulev revolutsioon*, 254.

54. Here the lines of the song are broken up in the first stanza, to show the pauses in the melody as performed by the choir.

55. Rein Taagepera, *Estonia: Return to Independence* (Boulder, CO: Westview Press, 1993), 142.

56. Daugava, in Rainis, *Kopoti raksti*, 12:188, lines 256–83.

57. Rainis wrote in 1915, "The gods are alive, because they are phenomena of nature, not personas." "The Latvian faith cannot die, because we cannot forget that the sun is the sun, not a persona, thunder is thunder, not a persona"; Rainis, *Kopoti raksti*, 24, 668–69.

58. *Uus Ärkamisaeg Eestimaal*, edited by Ain Haas and Ed Haas (n.p.: 1989?), a set of two VHS videotapes in the personal archive of Ain Haas; see also *Eestimaa laul*, DVD video recording (Tallinn: LunaVista Productions, 2008).

59. Vytautas Landsbergis, *Lithuania Independent Again*, trans. Anthony Packer and Eimutis Šova (Seattle: University of Washington Press, 2000), 113.

60. Senn, *Lithuania Awakening*, 89; Seattle resident Irena Blekys recalled the August event during a conversation in spring of 2010.

61. Yakovlev quoted in ibid., 238.

62. Šepetys, *Neprarastoji karta*, 153.

63. Santara šviesa seminar, September 6, 2008, Lemont, Illinois.

64. *The Twenty-first Estonian Song and the Fourteenth Folk Dance Festival: A Reference Book*, trans. Ülle Leis (Tallinn: Eesti Raamat, 1990), 3.

65. In 2009, a ninety-year-old Estonian woman in Seattle recalled that in the 1920s and 1930s this song was not sung in polite company, because of its suggestive stanzas about a woman's neck and hair.

66. *Lietuvių liaudies dainynas*, 18:371–72; Ivanauskaitė, "Tarpukario Lietuvos dainos," 48–49. Friends of Vytautas Kernagis remembered a class

skit that parodied this song; in Rūta Oginskaitė, *Nes nežinojau, kad tu nežinai: Knyga apie Vytautą Kernagį* (Vilnius: Tyto Alba, 2009), 67.

67. Vytautas Jakelaitis, "Dainų šventės," in *Muzikos enciklopedija A–H*, ed. Juozas Antanavičius (Vilnius: Lietuvos Muzikos Akademija, 2000), 298–301.

68. *Dainų šventė: XIII Lietuvos tautinė dainų šventė* (Vilnius: Mintis, 1990), 6.

69. Ibid., 13.

70. D. Linčiuvienė, ed., *Kur giria žaliuoja*, 2:3.

71. *XX Vispārējie latviešu dziesmu svētki: Koncertu programma* (Riga: E. Melngaiļa Tautas Mākslas Centrs, 1990), 4.

72. Cassette recording, Latvian song festival concert, Rīga, July 6, 1990.

73. Email to author, May 5, 2011.

CHAPTER 7

1. Endel Pillau, ed. *Eestimaa kuum suvi 1988: Ajakirjanduskroonika* (Tallinn: Olion, 1989), 76–77; Ivo Linna, Riho Illak, and Riina Roose, quoted in Rinne, *Laulev revolutsioon*, 125, 236–38, 241. Estonia's flag revival, including earlier displays and government censorship, is documented in detail by Laar, Ott, and Endre, *Teine Eesti*, 299–310.

2. Vesilind, *Singing Revolution*, 124; Rinne, *Laulev revolutsioon*, 242, 341–44; Laar, Ott, and Endre, *Teine Eesti*, 353–56; Jüri Leesment, "Mälestused öölaulupeost," *Postimees*, July 30, 2008, http://oolaulupidu.postimees.ee/?id=23390 (accessed July 6, 2010).

3. "LSSR KGB pažyma apie šiuolaikinės vakarų muzikos mėgėjų grupės atskleidimą ir poveikio priemonės prieš jos narius, Vilnius, 1962 m. lapkričio 14 d.," in Bagušauskas and Streikus, *Lietuvos kultūra*, 314, 15, 16.

4. Starr, *Red and Hot*, 194–202, 14; Z. Kumpienė, "Kalba," in Kiauleikytė and Tumasonienė, *Muzika 1940–1960*, 98, 311n17; and Ryback, *Rock around the Bloc*, 10–14, 30, 52–53, 103–4, 214.

5. Māris Ruks, *No zemes un debesīm: Pērkons* (Riga: Antava, 2006), 37–38. Artemy Troitsky reports that the first rock group in the Soviet Union was a Latvian high school band, Revengers, established 1961, soon followed by the Estonian band Junior, established 1963, and mentions that a 1965 concert by a Latvian band, Melody Makers, was cancelled a few hours before it was to begin; Troitsky, *Back in the USSR: The True Story of Rock in Russia* (Boston: Faber and Faber, 1987), 21–22, 26.

6. The school director, Juozas Petkevičius, is remembered by Vytautas Kernagis; in Oginskaitė, *Nes nežinojau*, 96–97. Lithuanian "middle school," which included grades nine through twelve, is here translated as the American equivalent, "high school." Ryback summarizes the 1966 changes in all-Soviet policy regarding Komsomol dance clubs in Ryback, *Rock around the Bloc*, 107.

7. Oginskaitė, *Nes nežinojau*, 74, 99–100, 105.

8. Translated by Peter Tempest, in Vytautas Kubilius, ed. *The Amber Lyre: Eighteenth–Twentieth-Century Lithuanian Poetry* (Moscow: Raduga Publishers, 1983), 32–33. Vello Salumets notes that the Animals melody also became

popular in Estonia, where singers sang Koidula's poem "Meil aiaäärne tän-avas"; Salumets, *Rock-rapsoodia* (Tallinn: Eesti Entsüklopeedia Kirjastus, 1998), 129.

9. Oginskaitė, *Nes nežinojau*, 70–71.

10. Kernagis quoted in ibid., 100. Ryback agrees that rock was a "visceral, rather than political experience"; Ryback, *Rock around the Bloc*, 34.

11. Rytis Gustaitis, quoted in Oginskaitė, *Nes nežinojau*, 107.

12. Kernagis, quoted in ibid., 119.

13. Ibid., 127.

14. Simon Bronner, *American Children's Folklore* (Little Rock, AR: August House, 1988), 95–97.

15. Oginskaitė, *Nes nežinojau*, 135.

16. Ibid., 185–88; Ryback, *Rock around the Bloc*, 149.

17. Ibid., 155.

18. Jonas Strielkūnas, *Vėjas rugiuos* (Vilnius: Vaga, 1971), 27. The song's third stanza was omitted in the film *A Small Confession*, as discussed later in the book.

19. Oginskaitė, *Nes nežinojau*, 192.

20. Mazvērsīte, *Pieskāriens*, 18.

21. Salumets, *Rock-rapsoodia*, 28, 286–87, 412–13; see also Jaak Kilmi's 2009 documentary film *Disco and Atomic War*.

22. Ryback, *Rock around the Bloc*, 51, 103–4; Troitsky, *Back in the USSR*, 25, 28, 97.

23. The film directed by Leonid Gaidai (1923–1993), *Kavkazskaia Plen-nitsa* (released in English as *Kidnapping, Caucasian Style*), is mentioned in Troitsky, *Back in the USSR*, 26–27.

24. Rolands Kalniņš, "Elpojiet dziļi," *Rolanda Kalniņa aizliegtās filmas*, DVD (Jura Podnieka Studija, 2009).

25. As described by Ryback, *Rock around the Bloc*, 150–52.

26. Ibid., 43–49; Troitsky, *Back in the USSR*, 63; Rinne, *Laulev revo-lutsioon*, 123–24.

27. Zina Nutautaitė, quoted in Oginskaitė, *Nes nežinojau*, 270.

28. Troitsky describes an intensified professionalization campaign in 1983 that in fact aimed to exclude rock songwriters from official music production; Troitsky, *Back in the USSR*, 95–96.

29. Quoted in Oginskaitė, *Nes nežinojau*, 313.

30. Among his favorite poets were Juozas Erlickas, Marcelijus Martinaitis, Sigitas Geda, and Dalia Saukaitytė.

31. The refrain quotes a 1929 poem by Salomėja Nėris, who would later become a Stalinist troubadour; "Mūsų dienos kaip šventė," in Salomėja Nėris, *Raštai* (Vilnius: Valstybinė Grožinės Literatūros Leidykla, 1957), 1:75; Oginskaitė, *Nes nežinojau*, 427–29.

32. Yurchak argues that late-Soviet Russian humor based on overidenti-fication "cannot be understood simply as a form of resistance to authorita-tive symbols because it also involves a feeling of affinity and warmth toward them." Such humor, argues Yurchak, did not explicitly challenge Soviet power, and in fact it made the Soviet system seem "all the more immutable

and predictable," even if it placed the performer and audience in an ambiguous place "inside/outside" (*vnye*) the Soviet discursive parameters; Yurchak, *Everything Was Forever*, 131–33, 250–51, 95. In Lithuania, however, ambiguous "inside/outside" humor did challenge and reject Soviet identity, because the parallel discourse of independence from the Soviet Union shifted its weight to "outside."

33. Oginskaitė, *Nes nežinojau*, 203.

34. Quoted in ibid., 431–32.

35. Quoted in ibid., 441.

36. Rolands Kalniņš, 1995 interview, *Rolanda Kalniņa aizliegtās filmas*. Inga Pērkone quotes Kalniņš's diary to document his apprehension upon finishing the screenplay in 1966. She argues that the film was shelved either because Kalniņš refused to cut offensive scenes, or because he disliked the film director's artistic interpretation and did not give permission to distribute it. Regardless, the order to pull it from distribution and to destroy all copies was given on December 19, 1969. Inga Pērkone et al., *Inscenējumu realitāte: Latvijas aktierkino vēsture* (Riga: Mansards, 2011), 102, 104–5, 181.

37. In the published version, the Communist Party meeting took place off stage, and the songwriter declared his love for his girlfriend in the final scene. The play was first staged in 1966, but the script for that show has not been published.

38. Ruks, *No zemes un debesīm*, 35–39; Māris Čaklais, *Im Ka: Imants Kalniņš laikā un telpā* (Riga: Jumava, 1998), 109–18. A 1970 document ordering local officials to terminate Kalniņš's "illegally organized and ideologically ill-prepared" band is published in Plakans, *Experiencing Totalitarianism*, 332. Imants Kalniņš, *Dzeguzes Balss: Dziesmas ar M. Čaklā vārdiem* LP record (Melodiya, 1979).

39. Rolands Kalniņš, 1995 interview, *Rolanda Kalniņa aizliegtās filmas*.

40. Ieva Lešinska-Geibere recalled that these dances were popular in Latvia in the 1960s and 1970s; email to author, June 13, 2010.

41. Estonian CP documents related to the 1978 policy are quoted in Kiin, Ruutsoo, and Tarand, *40 kirja lugu*, 171–78; Smith, *Estonia*, 41–42.

42. Quoted in Rinne, *Laulev revolutsioon*, 68–69.

43. Misiunas and Taagepera, *Baltic States*, 242; Raun, *Estonia and the Estonians*, 196; Kiin, Ruutsoo, and Tarand, *40 kirja lugu*, 18–26. Troitsky writes only that "young concert-goers kicked up a ruckus"; Troitsky, *Back in the USSR*, 84.

44. El'sa Robertovna Gretshkina (born 1932), Estonian SSR minister of education from 1980 to 1988, was seen as the main administrator of Russification policies in Estonia; Toivo Miljan, *Historical Dictionary of Estonia* (Lanham, MD: Scarecrow Press, 2004), 171–72.

45. Rinne, *Laulev revolutsioon*, 70–73.

46. Kiin, Ruutsoo, and Tarand, *40 kirja lugu*, 3–7, 84–120; Smith, *Estonia*, 42; Raun, *Estonia and the Estonians*, 196; Rein Taagepera, *The Death of Jüri Kukk: A Case Study in Erratic Repression* (Irvine: University of California, 1981); Rein Taagepera, *Softening without Liberalization in the Soviet Union: The Case of Jüri Kukk* (Lanham, MD: University Press of America,

1984). The secret CPSU resolution of May 26, 1983, is quoted in Strods, "Non-Violent Resistance," 89.

47. Rinne, *Laulev revolutsioon*, 147–80, 198–202; Troitsky, *Back in the USSR*, 62, 82, 91; Aleksandr Kushnir, *100 magnitoal'bomov sovetskogo roka, 1977–1991: 15 let podpol'noi zvukozapisi* (Moscow: Lean, Agraf, Kraft, 1999), 82–83.

48. Andersons quoted in Troitsky, *Back in the USSR*, 26; Troitsky notes that important meanings of Estonian songs were not accessible to him because he did not speak the language; *Back in the USSR*, 84. Kernagis quoted in Oginskaitė, *Nes nežinojau*, 148–49. Latvian veteran punk rocker Dambis (Raimonds Lagimovs) asserts that, for him, the message always took precedence over musical form; in Uldis Rudaks, *Rokupācija: Latviešu rokmūzikas vēsture* (Riga: Dienas Grāmata, 2008), 415.

49. Quoted in Rinne, *Laulev revolutsioon*, 40.

50. Yesterday I Saw Estonia!

I saw saunas and shacks,
I saw baggage and sacks,
Fieldstones piled in stacks—
Yesterday I saw Estonia!

Yesterday I saw Estonia!
Decayed farmsteads!
Faint plowed furrows!
Scrubby alder and juniper!
Yesterday I saw Estonia!

Yesterday I saw Estonia!
Overgrown bushes and scrub,
Place of snoozing and deformity,
Spiritual world so dim and silent –
Yesterday I saw Estonia!

Juhan Liiv, "Eile nägin ma Eestimaad!" *Teosed: Proosa, Luule* (Tallinn:
    Eesti Riiklik Kirjastus, 1956), 332.

51. Quoted by Rinne, *Laulev revolutsioon*, 40–42.

52. He described one such performance in 1980, at the event that sparked riots in Tallinn: "It was 'March of the Soviet Soccer Players' or 'Soccer Players' Song' or something like that. It was a completely unbelievable song that I found in a Pioneers songbook. A thick book, very funny. I read other texts from it at other Propeller concerts, too. Infinitely idiotic. And if they confronted me on why I'm reading them—'Can't I read Soviet poetry, composed under Soviet rule??' The words were something like, 'Into the English and Scotsmen's goal, from Moscow flies the victorious ball'"; ibid., 68.

53. Ibid., 22–23, 31–32, 38–40, 42–43, 52, 116.

54. Villu Tamme, quoted in ibid., 75–78; Strods, "Non-Violent Resistance," 111–12; Amanda Jeanne Swain, "A Death Transformed: The Political and Social Consequences of Romas Kalanta's Self Immolation, Soviet Lithuania, 1972" (PhD diss., University of Washington, 2013), 46, 174.

55. William B. Husband, "Review of Timothy Ryback's *Rock around the Bloc*," *Russian Review* 49, no. 4 (1990): 522.

56. Troitsky, *Back in the USSR*, 95–99, 116, 123–25, 137; Yurchak adds that Andropov's speechwriters listened to Vysotsky; Yurchak, *Everything Was Forever*, 124; Ryback, *Rock around the Bloc*, 3.

57. Rinne, *Laulev revolutsioon*, 47, 96.

58. Cameraman Aleksandrs Demčenko reports that the train in the film was not the one vandalized at Ogre; in Tatjana Fasta, *Juris Podnieks: Vai viegli būt elkam?* (Riga: Kontinents, 2010), 122.

59. Juris Podnieks, *Vai viegli būt jaunam? Is It Easy to Be Young?* DVD (Riga: Jura Podnieka Studija, 2007), chapter 1. The English subtitles and Russian dubbing omit the band's name, Pērkons, which is spoken in Latvian.

60. Andrew Horton, *The Zero Hour: Glasnost and Soviet Cinema in Transition* (Princeton: Princeton University Press, 1992), 72–76, 155–56. The film was informally screened in Latvia in 1986, but officially premiered the following year in Moscow. It was shown throughout the Soviet Union, and a dubbed English-language edition was produced for distribution in the West by IFEX Films (New York), in the Soviet Cinema Today series.

61. Gorbachev also wrote, "There is every ground to believe that our young people wholeheartedly welcome the revolutionary changes, which have been started in the country, and that they are ready to promote them with their youthful energy and passionate dedication"; Gorbachev, *Perestroika*, 116.

62. Abrams Kļeckins interview, Podnieks, *Is It Easy to Be Young?*

63. Ruks, *No zemes un debesīm*, 111.

64. A 1980 KGB report to the Latvian Communist Party stressed rock music's "negative psychic effect on youth"; in Plakans, *Experiencing Totalitarianism*, 337. Yurchak reproduces an official list of ideologically harmful Western bands that was circulated in 1985 by the All-Soviet Komsomol organization; Yurchak, *Everything Was Forever*, 214–15.

65. Ryback, *Rock around the Bloc*, 112, 64–66; Ryback writes, "During the early 1980s, Baltic punks took to the streets, offending, assaulting, and on occasion, killing Russian residents and tourists." "During the spring of 1985, three massive anti-Russian protests broke out in the Latvian capital; on May 9, May 15, and again on July 15, up to five hundred young Latvians clashed with local militia in pitched street battles throughout Riga. Rumors circulated that during the confrontations several Russian nationals who challenged the Latvian youths were beaten to death"; ibid., 215, 218. Māris Ruks writes that Latvian punks intended to offend onlookers with their ugly appearance and loud language, but not with physical violence; Ruks, *No zemes un debesīm*, 100–104. Ruks later adds, "Documentation of Ryback's report would require research in the militia and court archives. I've also heard about these things, but, based on my research, and also as an eyewitness of that time period, I do not know of any evidence for Ryback's assertion that Russians were killed. There would have then been loud court trials in Latvia. There were none. There were some fights and clashes, but not massive numbers of people. I think that the KGB intentionally flooded the Western countries with information about murders of Russians, because the Western countries were accused of creating and activating

the anti-Soviet punk movement"; email to author, September 26, 2011. In Pod-nieks's *Is it Easy to Be Young?* filmed in 1985, a Latvian punk grimly stares at the camera, but then the flicker of a friendly smile crosses his face.

66. The group is not discussed by Troitsky, who makes only a brief ref-erence to the film *Is it Easy to Be Young?* in his overview of Latvian rock; Troitsky, *Back in the USSR*, 86–87, 160.

67. Māris Čaklais's 1963 poem about a swan, "Wings," was published in Gunārs Priede, "Trīspadsmitā," in *Septiņas lugas* (Riga: Liesma, 1968), 360–62.

68. Ruks, *No zemes un debesīm*, 7–13. The document's first page is repro-duced among the illustrations between pages 56 and 57. Pērkons was attacked at a time when Soviet cultural institutions intensified efforts to control and repress rock bands throughout the USSR, as described in Troitsky, *Back in the USSR*, 95–99.

69. The "pigs" stanza was censored in Melgalvs's book *Meldijās iešana: Dzejoļi, 1975–1980* (Riga: Liesma, 1980), 27, but Kulakovs learned the uncensored song words from typewritten manuscripts given to him by both Melgalvs and Klāvs Elsbergs; email to author, October 12, 2011.

70. The soundtrack is not synchronized with the visual images; partici-pants remember that the actual song which brought the crowd to their feet was "Rush Hour," a song about finding peace in a noisy, crowded city; its refrain called for individual human responsibility. Ruks, *No zemes un debesīm*, 107–8.

71. Melgalvs, *Meldijās iešana*, 42.

72. Juris Kulakovs, email to author, April 4, 2011.

73. Ruks, *No zemes un debesīm*, 105–21, 35–37.

74. Quoted Anda Burve-Rozīte, "Elita gribēja vest mājās," *Ir*, June 16, 2010, http://ir.lv/2010/6/16/elita-gribeja-vest-majas (accessed June 26, 2010).

75. Klass Vāvere and Signe Neimane, *Līvi* (Tandems, 1997), 45–47; Rudaks, *Rokupācija*, 56.

76. Strods, "Non-Violent Resistance," 78; Blūzma, "Period of Awaken-ing," 241–45.

77. Grigore Vieru, *Piektdienas zvaigzne: Dzejoļi* (Riga: Liesma, 1988), 110.

78. Vāvere and Neimane, *Līvi*, 46.

79. Kernagis also had high respect for Antis, "whose songs and music made the audience think, not dance," as quoted in Oginskaitė, *Nes nežinojau*, 429.

80. Translated by Rimas Žilinskas, "The Rockin' Revolution: The Role of Rock Music in Mobilizing Soviet Lithuania's National Awakening," unpub-lished paper presented at the 2006 Conference on Baltic Studies, Georgetown University.

81. Troitsky, *Back in the USSR*, 125, 35.

82. Algirdas Kaušpėdas, interviewed by Toma Pagojutė, "A. Kaušpėdas: išbandymas šlove ir kulkomis," *Lietuvos Rytas*, March 11, 2012, retrieved from www.lrytas.lt (accessed March 18, 2012).

83. "The Land Down Under" also contains the word "zombie," denoting marijuana, not the living dead. The image of thunder is the only image shared in the words of the two songs.

84. Marius Listopadskis, "Atrieda atidunda," *Ore*, December 1, 2003, http://www.ore.lt/article.php?action=get&id=200534 (accessed June 26, 2010).

85. Smurr, *Perceptions of Nature*, 281–99; Misiunas and Taagepera, *Baltic States*, 303–4.

86. Rinne, *Laulev revolutsioon*, 215–22; Smurr, *Perceptions of Nature*, 303–8.

87. Smurr, *Perceptions of Nature*, 309–16.

88. Rinne, *Laulev revolutsioon*, 223–32, 274.

89. Ivo Linna, quoted in ibid., 268–70; Laar, Ott, and Endre, *Teine Eesti*, 400.

90. The Singing Revolution's revival of nineteenth-century choral songs was discussed in chapter 6; some of these classic texts were also revived in new rock arrangements, for example, the Kuldne Trio performed a popular version of Körber's "My Dear Fatherland," as recalled by Ivo Linna in Rinne, *Laulev revolutsioon*, 124.

91. Kreutzwald, *Kalevipoeg*, 266.

92. Ivo Linna, quoted in Rinne, *Laulev revolutsioon*, 255.

93. Ibid., 255, 271; Jüri Leesment recalled that Alo Mattiisen chose Ivo Linna to sing the five fatherland songs because he was truly "Estonian-minded."

94. Mattiisen changed the order of Koidula's stanzas 3 and 4, and omitted four of her original stanzas as follows:

> Until my death . . . (as above)
> My Estonian meadows and rivers,
> And my mother tongue:
> I want to praise you highly
> Even at my hour of death!
>
> Oh land, how tenderly . . . (as above)
> Truly I would rather live and breathe here,
> On your bosom, Maarjamaa,
> Than live my life on foreign soil
> In honor and in joy!
>
> So pious are your sons . . . (stanza four above),
> And your wind and your sun
> Sustain your blossoming
> The wings of a high-flying hawk
> Shield you so tenderly!
>
> But yet, in your eyes . . . (stanza three above)
> The hours of the future
> Will bring us affirmation!
> Go firmly! Head up high!
> Time will give advice!
> Lydia Koidula, *Luuletused* (Tallinn: Eesti Raamat, 1969), 86–87.

95. Laar, Ott, and Endre, *Teine Eesti*, 305.

96. Misiunas and Taagepera, *Baltic States*, 309–10; Blūzma, "Period of Awakening," 275–76, 79–81.

97. *Sirp ja Vasar*, June 17, 1988; reprinted in Laar et al., eds. *Teine Eesti: Eeslava*, 425–26; excerpts of the editorial are quoted in Rinne, *Laulev revolutsioon*, 262–63.

98. Tears and emotions are also described by Ivo Linna and others, Rinne, 241, 50–52, 74, 80.

99. Quoted in Vesilind, *Singing Revolution*, 134.

100. Pillau, *Eestimaa kuum suvi 1988*, 104. The declaration by nine leading singers, among them Mägi, Mattiisen, and Linna, is also quoted in Rinne, *Laulev revolutsioon*, 275.

101. 1 Corinthians 13:3; Zālīte, email to author, October 23, 2006.

102. Ibid.

103. Guntis Šmidchens, "Notes on the Latvian National Hero, Lāčplēsis," *Journal of Folklore Research* 43, no. 3 (2006): 276.

104. Klass Vāvere, "Latviešu roks 13, 'Lāčplēsis,'" Liesma (1990): 18.

105. Zālīte writes, "Does writing emerge from life, or does life emerge from writing? I don't know. I only write"; inscription in my copy of Zālīte's book, *Divas dramatiskas poēmas* (Riga: Liesma, 1987), quoted from a 1985 play in that book, p. 52.

106. In an interview recorded by Indra Ekmanis, Akurātere reports that she first heard the song recorded by the Latvian American group Dzintars on an LP record given to her around 1986 by Alfreds Stinkurs; Indra Ekmanis, *The Sound of Protest*, DVD (bachelor's thesis, Arizona State University, 2011).

107. Ieva Akurātere, *Manai tautai* (Riga: Pētergailis, 2007), 89–90.

108. *Latvijas Tautas fronte: Gads pirmais*, 5.

109. Ieva Akurātere, email to author, October 19, 2011.

110. Ieva Akurātere, *Ieva Akurātere* (Riga: Melodiya (C6028197009), 1989). "Prayer," as composed by Imants Kalniņš and sung by Akurātere, was five stanzas longer than Julgī Stalte's version at the Smithsonian festival. The words were published on page one of the Latvian Popular Front's newspaper, *Atmoda*, December 16, 1988 (first stanza as Stalte sang it at the 1998 Smithsonian festival; only stanzas omitted in chapter 1 are translated here):

> Lord, you hear each tiny blade of grass. . . (chapter 1, stanza 1)
> Lord, we believe that you desire, and it is your sacred wish
> That this nation should continue here, and take harvest from this land
> That the Latvian tongue should always sound out on these hills and
>   vales,
> The land whispers, each stone speaks this to me,
> Each stone speaks this to me.

> It can't be your wish . . . (chapter 1, stanzas 2 and 3)
> Therefore come defend us when the guard in the tower sounds alarm,
> When a friend dies, taken by death's scythe, in the arms of a friend,

394 Notes to Pages 250–52

When the swarms of leaden bullets fly to tear and sting Latvians,
When unseen hands will raise white groves of crosses on the tombs.

[The song by Kalniņš and Akurātere omitted one of Breikšs's
    stanzas published in 1988: "Too late then to unite us, if today
    we're torn by hate, / Through the land the Latvian nation's
    anguished lament will sound, / Must a brother know his brother
    only when they are in chains, / And is it our only destiny, to walk
    the path of slaves?"]

Is this freedom only one faint dream upon our nation' path,
And in years to come, will foreign masters make us into slaves again?
One cannot believe this, no, this thought gives pain to the heart
So we pray to you on this day, come down from your throne, oh Lord!

Come and walk across this land, while it still can feel the sun,
Come and forge us into cliffs, so noone can shatter us,
Come and bless us, and unite us, and give us strength to work,
So that in the fateful hour, dreadful punishment won't come,
dreadful punishment won't come.

So we pray to you. . . . (chapter 1, stanzas 4 and 5)

See also commentary about this poem's 1933 version published 1935,
in Leonīds Breikšs, *Dzīve un darbi* (Riga: Enigma, 1998–), 1:375–76;
2:411–12.
    111. Sabrina Petra Ramet, "Rock: The Music of Revolution (and Politi-
cal Conformity)," in Sabrina Ramet, ed. *Rocking the State: Rock Music
and Politics in Eastern Europe and Russia* (Boulder, CO: Westview Press,
1994), 2.
    112. Steven J. Pierson also argues that Estonian song festival traditions
were "prophetic"; "We Sang Ourselves Free: Musical Experience and Development among Christian Estonians from Repression to Independence," *Acta
Universitatis Stockholmiensis, Studia Baltica Stockholmiensia* 23 (2003):
380–82.
    113. Juris Kulakovs, "Pērkons: Grupas īsa vēsture," Latvian Television,
n.d., posted by vm8383 on YouTube, November 30, 2008, http://www.you-
tube.com/watch?v=dmjER-9oxrw (accessed July 9, 2010).
    114. *Mikrofons '89*, LP record C60 29483004 (Riga: Melodiya, 1989).
Latvian nonformal organizations also paid little attention to economic issues,
as discussed in Blūzma, "Period of Awakening," 289n140.
    115. Heino Kiik, "Õitsiöö mõtteid," *Sirp ja Vasar*, June 17, 1988, 3.
    116. Raun, *Estonia and the Estonians*, 224. The WeatherOnline historical
archive reports that temperature highs in Tallinn from mid-June to mid-July
surpassed eighty degrees Fahrenheit, ten degrees above the average for that
time of year; www.weatheronline.co.uk (accessed July 7, 2010). Taagepera,
Estonia: Return to Independence, 127–44; Smith, *Estonia*, 45–46; Rinne,
Laulev revolutsioon, 16, 280.

117. Vesilind, *Singing Revolution*, 134.

118. Quoted in Rinne, *Laulev revolutsioon*, 256.

119. Quoted in ibid., 277.

120. Villu Tamme recalls that this was Mägi's intent; quoted in ibid., 120.

121. John 20:29, 1; Peter 1:8.

122. The Estonian language shifts responsibility from creator to self with untranslatable ease, by merely inserting the letter *n*: *Looja, hoia* means "Creator, protect," and *loon ja hoian* means "I create, I protect."

123. Quoted in Rinne, *Laulev revolutsioon*, 308.

124. Austė Nakienė, "'Lietuva, tu mums šventa!' Antitarybinis rokas ir patriotinis hiphopas," *Tautosakos Darbai* 32 (2006): 184.

125. Miniotaite, *Nonviolent Resistance in Lithuania*, 73–76.

126. Ruks, *No zemes un debesīm*, 166–68.

127. Valk, "Laulev revolutsioon"; Heinz Valk, "Mäletused öölaulupeost," *Postimees* (2008), http://oolaulupidu.postimees.ee/24243/maletused-oolaulupeost-heinz-valk/ (accessed October 12, 2012).

128. Rinne, *Laulev revolutsioon*, 268–69, 293, 297.

129. Quoted in ibid., 273–74.

CHAPTER 8

1. Helmī and Dainis Stalts, tape-recorded interview, July 15, 1997. Photographs of Konstantīns Purpurs carrying the flag on June 14 were published together with his account of the event in "Taisni uz priekšu pa brīvības ielu 14.6.1988," *Latvija Šodien* (1988): 47–53.

2. Stanislovas Kavaliauskas, in Zita Kelmickaitė and Dalia Kutavičienė, *Dainos galia* (Lietuvos TV, 2008).

3. Up to 1970, more than half of the Lithuanian population still lived in the countryside; urbanization of the Latvian and Estonian population took place at least two decades earlier; Misiunas and Taagepera, *Baltic States*, 364–65.

4. Donatas Sauka, *Lietuvių tautosaka* (Vilnius: Mokslas, 1982), 254.

5. Vacys Milius, "Bendražygis"; Irena Seliukaitė, "Kraštotyros baruose"; and Dalia and Laima Šilainytė, "Bendravimo su žmonėmis mokykla"; in Perla Vitkuvienė, ed., *Norbertas Vėlius* (Vilnius: Mintis, 1999), 121–30, 133–47; Tadas Šidiškis, «Keturiasdešimt metų su žygeiviais,» *Liaudies kultūra*, no. 3 (2008): 56–63.

6. Video-recorded interview, Vilnius, April 8, 2010.

7. See, for example, a song about the mass deportations recorded by Norbertas Vėlius in 1959, song 159 in *Lietuvių liaudies dainynas*, 19:266.

8. Milius, "Bendražygis," in Vitkuvienė, *Norbertas Vėlius*, 124. Some expeditions were described by Norbertas Vėlius, "Ekspedicija Kernavėje," *Literatūra ir Menas*, August 23, 1969; A. Pociulpaitė, "Kraštotyrininkų dešimtoji," *Literatūra ir Menas*, August 14, 1971; Zita Kelmickaitė, "Ir tapom kraštotytininkais," *Literatūra ir Menas*, September 4, 1976. The folklore ensembles that emerged soon afterward consulted Kraštotyra Society books, as well as the five-volume scholarly publication of folklore texts; K.

Korsakas, ed. *Lietuvių tautosaka* (Vilnius: Valstybinė Politinės ir Mokslinės Literatūros Leidykla, 1962–68).

9. Cassette-recorded interview, Vilnius, October 10, 1991. Kelmickaitė told the same story to a journalist seven years earlier; Povilas Krikščiūnas, "Dar neišdainuotos visos dainos," *Kultūros barai* 235, no. 7 (1984): 41–42.

10. Jonas Trinkūnas, "Ramuvai—20 metų," *Ramuva* (1989): 5.

11. Saulė Matulevičienė, "Iš Rasos šventės istorijos," in *Liaudies kultūra*, no. 3 (2007): 68.

12. Emilija Stanikaitė, tape-recorded interview, Kernavė, Lithuania, June 21, 1997. Stanikaitė recited the line "Šią naktį regėjosi senovės Rambynas."

13. "Veronika," *Liaudies kultūra*, no. 1 (2007): 55–56.

14. Linas Medelis, "8 metai—ne viena diena," *Jaunimo Gretos* 8, no. 381 (1976). Around this time, new folklore ensembles also appeared in Moscow, among them the Shchurov Trio (founded 1962; produced a record in 1968) and the Pokrovskii Ensemble (1973); Olson, *Performing Russia*, 80–83.

15. Jacinevičius, L., [untitled], *Literatūra ir Menas*, December 28, 1968, 11.

16. Meilutė Ramonienė, video-recorded interview, Vilnius, April 8, 2010.

17. Bagušauskas and Streikus, *Lietuvos kultūra*, 283.

18. V. Žeimantas, "Šeimininkavimo mokykla: Universiteto studentų profsąjungos komiteto pirmininko V. Žeimanto atskaitinis pranešimas," *Tarybinis studentas*, October 29, 1971.

19. Norbertas Vėlius et al., eds., *Gervėčiai: Monografija* (Vilnius: Mintis, 1989).

20. Irena Seliukaitė, "Kraštotyros baruose," in Vitkuvienė, *Norbertas Vėlius*, 134–45.

21. Jonas Vitkūnas and Rimantas Matulis, quoted in Matulevičienė, "Iš Rasos šventės istorijos," 69.

22. Austė Nakienė, "Lietuvių folkloro teatras: Autentiškas dainavimas, metaforinė išraiška ir įspūdingas scenovaizdis," *Tautosakos Darbai* 22 (2005): 166–79. The Communist leader of Soviet Lithuania, Antanas Sniečkus, is sometimes credited with projects that strengthened Lithuanian national identity; Misiunas and Taagepera, *Baltic States*, 206. Sniečkus's personal support for this professional folklore ensemble was reported to me by Povilas Mataitis, tape-recorded interview, December 6, 1991.

23. Leaders of many folklore ensembles often did research at the Academy of Science folklore archives in Vilnius.

24. Arvydas Karaška, "Lietuva: Dainų kraštas," *Kultūros barai* 11 (1975): 74.

25. Olson documents a similar experience in Russia, where "shy, polite" urban youths "found their voices" in folklore ensembles; Olson, *Performing Russia*, 85, 97–100.

26. Tape-recorded interview, November 24, 1991.

27. Guntis Šmidchens, "A Baltic Music: The Folklore Movement in Lithuania, Latvia, and Estonia, 1968–1991" (PhD diss., Indiana University, 1996), 275–84.

28. Olson describes similar, informal diffusion of traditions at the Pokrovskii Ensemble's "studio" in Moscow; Olson, *Performing Russia*, 97.

29. Bagušauskas and Streikus, *Lietuvos kultūra*, 417, 25, 26.

30. Lionginas Šepetys, "Tarybinė Kultūra—Kultūra liaudžiai, liaudies kultūra," *Tiesa*, January 28, 1983.

31. Albertas Girnius, "Skambink, sese, dar linksmiau," *Literatūra ir Menas*, June 5, 1976, 6.

32. Ministerstvo kul'tury SSSR. Prikaz No 241, 05.06.86, Moskva. Ob uchrezhdenii festivalia folklora "Baltika" v respublikakh Sovetskoi Pribaltiki. Mimeographed, five-page document in the files of the Estonian People's Art Center. Živilė Ramoškaitė-Sverdiolienė recalled that the name Baltica might have been suggested by Salomonas Sverdiolas, email to author, January 14, 2012.

33. Ž. Ramoškaitė, "Pirmasis tarptautinis," *Pergalė* 10 (1987): 181; Živilė Ramoškaitė, email to author, February 29, 2012.

34. The Vilnius Civil Engineering Institute group led by Evaldas Vyčinas, Skandinieki from Latvia, Ronsed Mor from Bretagne, and Lo Gerbo Baudo from Confolens. The Lithuanian host, Ratilio, performed last.

35. The Estonian folklore ensembles, Leigarid and Leegajus (to be discussed below) also performed at the Baltica '87 festival.

36. The two groups from France are described in the festival's printed program, *Baltica '87: International Folklore Festival of the Baltic Republics* (Vilnius: Mintis, 1987), 36.

37. Rolfs Ekmanis, "Some Notes on Vizma Belševica," *World Literature Today* (1998); Astrida Stahnke, "A Note about Vizma Belševica, a Latvian Poetess," *Lituanus* 47, no. 3 (2001).

38. Vizma Belševica, *Dzeltu laiks. Dzeja* (Riga: Liesma, 1987), 30.

39. Nīls R. Muižnieks, "The Daugavpils Hydro Station and 'Glasnost' in Latvia," *Journal of Baltic Studies* 18, no. 1 (1987): 63–70.

40. Midsummer celebrations were banned after the Communist purge of the Latvian government in 1960. The Soviets also attempted to censor passages that mentioned Jāņi from classic works of Latvian literature; Strods, *Politiskā cenzūra Latvijā*, 1:219. In 1964, Latvian poet Ojārs Vācietis led a petition campaign that attempted to legalize the midsummer celebrations, and was supported by Andrei Sakharov and other Russian intellectuals, among them Lev Kopelev, "Ligo- znachit radost,'" *Druzhba Narodov* 7 (1966): 251–53. In the seventies, public celebrations were not explicitly forbidden, but they were censored from the mass media and intentionally disrupted, for example, by school and university administrators who scheduled final exams on June 24. What traditions remained were often blurred by alcohol. In the early 1980s, Skandinieki revived the celebration, ostensibly as a performance for tourists, in the Latvian Folklife Museum, but for the general public, the official ban continued until spring of 1988. Māris Čaklais, "Oficiāli Līgo svēki- tas ir normāli," *Literatūra un Māksla*, April 22, 1988, 5; Jānis Stradiņš, "Par Jāņu svinēšanu un Jāņu apkarošanu: Raksts laikrakstā 'Lauku Avīze' 1988. gada 18. jūnijā," in *Trešā atmoda: Raksti un runas 1988.–1990. gadā Latvijā un par Latviju* (Riga: Zinātne, 1992) 302–6; Janīna Kursīte, "Atslēgas

vārds—Jāņi: Folklorā, dzīvē, fotogrāfijās " in *Jāņu fotoalbums*, ed. Pēteris and Ligita Leja Korsaks (Riga: Norden, 2007), 161–62.

41. Ieva Lešinska, "Atrast pareizo balsi," *Latvija Šodien* (1987): 44–49; Māris Rauda, "In Memoriam: Klāvs Elsbergs, 1958.3.I–1987.5.II," *Latvija Šodien* (1987): 49–50; Vizma Belševica, *Bille* (Ithaca, NY: Mežābele, 1992), 230–35.

42. Censuses of the Liv population on the northwest coast of Latvia document their decreasing numbers: 2,324 in 1852; 962 in 1930; and 800 in 1948. In 1959, there were 185 Livonians on the coast, of whom 87 knew the Livonian languge, but in 1989 the language was spoken by only a handful of 135 persons who identified themselves as Livs; Valda Marija Šuvcāne, *Lībiešu folklora* (Riga: Jumava, 2003), 9.

43. The attempt to regain official recognition of Livonians as an ethnic group is mentioned by Valda Marija Šuvcāne, *Lībiešu ciems, kura vairs nav* (Riga: Jumava, 2002), 185, 419–20.

44. Dainis and Helmī Stalte, tape-recorded interview, July 25, 1990.

45. Imants Ziedonis, "Kurzemīte, Otrā grāmata," in *Raksti*, 2:281–84.

46. Dainis and Helmī Stalts, interview, July 25, 1990; Gotthard Friedrich (Vecais Stenders) Stender, *Bildu àbice* (Riga: Liesma, 1977), 26–27. Stender's contrastive term for consonants, *neskaņi* nowadays implies "the ones who sound badly." The word *skandinieki* has undocumented connotations of "minstrels" and "travelling singers." Karulis, *Latviešu etimoloģijas vārdnīca*, 2:26.

47. "The fact is, that if you live next to a greedy person, immoral and profane, you must know that that person is always your enemy and—no matter how softly he may speak, no matter what he may promise—he is lying, he will betray you, the scoundrel that he is! . . . The government of Finland has forgotten with whom it is dealing—this is a mistake, I think. The government of Finland must always think about the needs of its people, it should worry itself with organizing defense in case of a possible attack from the side of the Russian government, and not play games, flirt with this government, as the Finnish Senate has done more than once"; Maksim Gorkii, *Sobranie sochinenii* (Moscow: Gosudarstvennoe Izdatel'stvo Khudozhestvennoi Literatury, 1953), 24:20–23.

48. Valdis Muktupāvels, "Varas un pretestības valoda, zīmes un simboli 20.gs. 80. gadu folklorisma mūzikā un muzicēšanā," in *Kultūra un vara*, ed. Janīna Kursīte et. al (Riga: LU Akadēmiskais apgāds, 2007), 100.

49. Dainis took inspiration from an earlier, failed Latvian national renaissance by two Rīga ensembles in 1957, Saulgrieži and Sakta, who performed stylized folklore, but added subtle underground meanings that their audiences understood. It was also general knowledge that the leader of Saulgrieži, Jēkabs Graubiņš, had recently returned from five years of exile in Siberia. The audience laughed to express support for significant phrases on stage, for example, when, during a supposed performance of wedding customs, a guest on stage called out, "There's no meat! We want meat!" speaking out loud the truth about food shortages in everyday Soviet life.

50. Tape-recorded interview, August 14, 1991.

51. The official interpretation of folk beliefs and magic incantations, for example, was that "the human living at a lower stage of economic evolution correctly sensed that it is possible to affect and change the weather, but he had approached this problem with incorrect methods and incorrect technology, because he lacked knowledge"; H. Vaita, "Latviešu tautas meteoroloģija," *Folkloras Instrūta Raksti* I (1950): 268–69. That article also quoted a variant of the incantation "Shine, Sun, Shimmering," which Skandinieki performed at the 1988 Baltica Folklore Festival and at the 1998 Smithsonian Folklife Festival.

52. Dainis Stalts, tape-recorded interview, July 27, 1990.

53. Tape-recorded interview, July 27, 1990.

54. Andris Bergmanis, "Tautasdziesmā viss ir pateikts," *Skola un ģimene* 7, no. 295 (1988): 1–3.

55. Vilis Bendorfs, "Folkloras noliktava?," *Padomju Jaunatne* (1986): 4.

56. Martin Boiko, "Latvian Ethnomusicology, Past and Present," *Yearbook for Traditional Music* 26 (1994): 53. Repression of ethnomusicologists was highest in the late 1950s, when Nikita Khrushchev ordered the purge of the the Latvian Communist Party's disobedient leadership. The Communist "purge" spread to all sectors of Latvian political and cultural life; Misiunas and Taagepera, *Baltic States*, 140–46, 172–76.

57. Beatrise Reidzāne, "Zinātniece laikmeta ainā (personīgas pieredzes stāsts): Elzai Kokarei—90," *Letonica* 21 (2011): 134–35.

58. G. Atvars, "Kā atrast 'sinkrēto vērtību veselumu': Polēmiskas piezīmes par ētiskā ideāla meklējumu kritikā un publicistikā," *Cīņa* 27 (January 1983): 2. Muktupāvels documents a similar article published in 1984, in Muktupāvels, "Varas un pretestības valoda," 96.

59. Māra Vilceniece, "Folkloras dzīve Latvijā," in *Latvija Šodien 1984* (Rockville, MD: World Federation of Free Latvians, 1984); see also Misiunas and Taagepera, *Baltic States*, 300–301.

60. Jānis Peters, "Dvēseles acugaisma," in *Paliekamdziesma: Krišjānim Baronam 150*, ed. Ligita Bībere and Māra Misiņa (Riga: Liesma, 1987), 222.

61. Andrejs Krūmiņš, "Savstarpēji saprasties!," *Padomju Jaunatne*, December 30, 1986.

62. Viktors Hausmanis, "Svētki beigušies, darbs turpinās," *Cīņa*, December 24, 1985, 3.

63. "Brother Dear," "High Up in the Air, Two Doves," and "Our Troops Are Not So Great in Number" are listed in the concert program approved by the government censor, a document in my personal archive.

64. Māra Zālīte, "Pirms festivāla," *Literatūra un Māksla*, July 22, 1988, 3.

65. Arnolds Klotiņš, "Folklora un dejas," *Literatūra un Māksla*, April 22, 1988.

66. Two years later, Gorbunovs was elected chairman of the Latvian Supreme Council, and in 1993 he became the chairman of the Saeima (Parliament of Latvia).

67. Liāna Ose quoted in Gita Lancere, "Kādi mēs to sagaidīsim?" *Cīņa*, July 6, 1988.

68. As recalled by Māra Zālīte in a conversation in Seattle on May 18, 2011.

69. Dainis and Helmī Stalte, tape-recorded interview, July 15, 1997.

70. "Ar saules motīvu," *Padomju Jaunatne*, July 14, 1988. Lithuanian reports of the festival included photographs that clearly documented the three flags, for example, Jonas Albertavičius, "Austros medžio pavėnėje," in *Kalba Vilnius*, no. 33 (1988): 4–5. Soon afterward, Latvian newspapers published flag photographs; *Pionieris*, July 15, 1988, 8; and *Padomju Jaunatne*, July 16, 1988, 1. Copies of the articles downloaded from http://baltica.llkc.lt/index.php?220283062 (accessed July 17, 2010).

71. Helmī Stalte, tape-recorded interview, July 27, 1990.

72. That particular videotape, filmed by Valdis Kupris, no longer exists, because it was stolen from the Stalts home along with their entire collection of ethnographic field recordings. It is likely that another copy exists, but I have not been able to find out what happened to Valdis Kupris's film archive after his death.

73. Urve Lippus, quoted in Daitz, *Ancient Song Recovered*, 135; Marja Liidja, "Juttu Veljo Tormisega," *Õhtuleht*, November 3, 1974.

74. Jaan Kaplinski, "Pärandus ja pärijad," *Sirp ja Vasar*, February 28, 1969. The lines quoted here were underlined in a clipping of the article that Igor Tõnurist, to be discussed later in the book, saved in his personal archive. Kaplinski's essay is translated in full in Daitz, *Ancient Song Recovered*, 60–62.

75. Herbert Tampere, ed. *Eesti rahvalaule viisidega* (Tallinn: Valgus, 1956–65).

76. Pille Kippar, "Osalemisrõõmust," *Sirp ja Vasar*, September 28, 1979, 7.

77. Igor Tõnurist, "'Ma laulan mere murusta!': Ingrid Rüütel and Estonian Folklore Movement," in *Individual and Collective in Traditional Culture*, ed. Triinu Ojamaa, Andreas Kalkun, and Ingrid Rüütel (Tartu, Estonia: Eesti Kirjandusmuuseumi Etnomusikloloogia Osakond, 2006), 220–21.

78. Igor Tõnurist, "Laaliku minu isädä. . . . ," *Sirp ja Vasar*, August 13, 1971; Daitz, *Ancient Song Recovered*, 71–72; Uno Uiga, "Veljo Tormis ja rahvalaul," *Sirp ja Vasar*, May 18, 1973; Vaike Sarv, "Artist in the Role of Contemporary Shaman," in *Traditional Belief Today: Conference Dedicated to the Ninetieth Anniversary of Oskar Loorits* (Tartu: Estonian Academy of Sciences, 1990).

79. Ülo Tedre and Veljo Tormis, *Regilaulik* (Tallinn: Eesti Raamat, 1975), 6, emphasis in original.

80. The "excellent contribution toward introducing folk song" by these two folklore ensembles was mentioned by Tormis in 1972, translated in Daitz, *Ancient Song Recovered*, 72–73.

81. Kristjan Torop, tape-recorded interviews, Tallinn, January 20 and February 11, 1992.

82. Strods, *Politiskā cenzūra Latvijā*, 1:26.

83. Kalev Järvela, "Kristjan Torop ja 'Leigarid,'" in *Kristjan Toropit meenutades*, edited by Heino Aassalu (Tallinn: n.p., 1998), 45.

84. Cassette-recorded interview, February 27, 1992. "Haridus- ja Teadusala Töötajate Maja rahvamuusikaansambli 'Leegajus' põhikiri," typed document in Igor Tõnurist's personal archive.

85. Vaike Sarv, "Leegajus," *Sirp ja Vasar*, October 20, 1978. In Moscow, Dmitrii Pokrovskii also described his ensemble as an "experiment"; Olson, *Performing Russia*, 84.

86. Vaike Sarv, "Leegajus." The passage from Petri's book was quoted from Eduard Laugaste, *Saaksin ma saksa sundijaks* (Tallinn: Eesti Raamat, 1976), 33.

87. Ain Sarv, tape-recorded interview, Tallinn, March 30, 1992.

88. Tõnurist joined the Communist Party in 1973, for idealistic reasons: "For many years, there was no possibility for the intelligentsia, and the Academy scholars in particular, to join the Party. And there was a general trend at this time, that, like in Lithuania earlier, 'Let's join the Party and take more power into our own hands,'" tape-recorded interview, March 25, 1992.

89. Tape-recorded interview, February 27, 1992.

90. When I interviewed Ain Sarv on March 30, 1992, he estimated that the ensemble's repertoire had grown from 600 pieces in 1981 to about 1,500 in 1992, a figure that seems accurate. The repertoire has been well documented throughout the past two decades, thanks to the thoroughness with which Igor Tõnurist kept records of the group's activities. The standard "diaries" required of amateur ensembles by the Soviet cultural bureaucracy include every rehearsal and performance from 1972 to 1991, with frequent notes about the songs rehearsed or performed. Before concerts, Igor would often type up a small slip of paper with the songs to be performed, and afterward, he would usually write the date on the wrinkled program list and place it in a folder. In 1992, the file contained 104 lists with a total of at least 750 items (500 songs, 50 game songs, 180 dances and instrumental pieces, and 17 foreign songs). Offstage, Leegajus's informal repertoire was much larger. Šmidchens, *Baltic Music*, 332–35.

91. Video-recorded interview, Tallinn, March 26, 2010.

92. Leegajus members appeared near the stage for a few seconds in a videotape that documented the event, but their song was not included in that recording; a recent book includes photographs of Leegajus, and notes that they sang three songs. Two folk songs (but not the song quoted here) are included in the book's companion CD; Elme Väljaste and Enno Selirand, eds., *Eestimaa laul 88: Kõned, fotod, meenutused*, CD (Tallinn: MTÜ Eestimaa Laul, 2011), 24–25, 36–37, 61; *Eestimaa laul*, DVD.

93. Videotaped interview, March 26, 2010.

94. "Eesti Folkloori Seltsi Põhikiri," *Meie Repertuaar*, no. 4 (April 1989): 7–8; Ingrid Rüütel, "Association "Baltica"—Independent Member of CIOFF," in *Baltica'91. Latvija* (Riga: E. Melngaiļa Tautas Mākslas Centrs, 1991).

95. Ingrid Rüütel, "The Main Principles of 'Baltica '89,'" in *Baltica'89*, ed. K. Kuutma (Tallinn: Eesti Kultuurikomitee, 1989), 4. Rüütel later argued that the festival should grapple with the problem of "national and cultural pluralism as the main basis of the richness and multiplicity of the world culture as a whole," in "About Finno Ugric Folk Music Activities in Estonia," *Proceedings of the Estonian Academy of Sciences; Social Sciences* 39, no. 1 (1990): 18–25.

96. Among other textbooks, see Miina Hermann, *Laulmise õpetus koolidele I* (Tartu, Estonia: n.p., 1923), 11; Miina Hermann, *Laulmisõpetus koolidele I*

(Tartu, Estonia: Loodus, 1931), 12; J. Aavik and V. Tamman, *Leelo VI: Alg-kooli VI klassi lauluvara* (Tartu, Estonia: V. Tamman, 1932), 17; J. Aavik and V. Tamman, *Kooli Leelo VI* (Tartu, Estonia: Loodus, 1936), 21; Päts, *Lemmiklaulik 6* (Tallinn: Kooli-kooperatiiv, 1937), 5.

97. Rüütel, "Association 'Baltica,'" 4–5.

98. Laima Vince, *Lenin's Head on a Platter: An American Student's Diary from the Final Years of the Soviet Union, September 1988–August 1989* (Vilnius: Lithuanian Writers' Union Publishers, 2008), 101.

99. The word *karūna* means "crown" in everyday language, but in folk songs it may also mean "banner"; *Lietuvių liaudies dainynas*, 9:611. An alternative translation for this line would be "stands a white crown."

100. The event is documented in Kelmickaitė and Kutavičienė, "Dainos galia."

101. "Postscriptum," in *Homeland*, DVD (Riga: Juris Podnieks Studio, 2005). Hedrick Smith introduced and commented the first American broadcast of Podnieks's film, titled *Baltic Requiem*, on June 24, 1991; Walter Goodman, "On the Baltics and the Persian Gulf," *New York Times*, June 24, 1991 (late edition, East Coast), C14.

102. Cameraman Aleksandrs Demčenko's account is recorded in Fasta, *Juris Podnieks*, 225–27.

103. Excerpt from the minutes of the twenty-second meeting of the Lithuanian Supreme Council, January 13, 1991; in Vytautas Landsbergis, ed. *Nauji dokumentai apie Sausio 13-ąją* (Vilnius: Baltijos Kopija, 2003), 106–7.

104. Radio Latvia, January 13, 1991. Recording rebroadcast by *Ir*, http://www.ir.lv/barikades/?date=0&audio=0 (accessed January 15, 2011).

105. Juris Kulakovs, email to author, September 27, 2010.

106. Raimonds Baltakmens, "Dziesmu vairogs atsita bultas," in *Barikādes: Latvijas mīlestības grāmata*, ed. Viktors Daugmalis (Riga: BAF, 2001), 309.

107. Ibid.

108. K. Saja et al., eds., *Lietuva 1991.01.1: Dokumentai, liudijimai, atgarsiai* (Vilnius: Valstybinis Leidybos Centras, 1991), 69.

109. Vytautas Landsbergis, "1991 m. sausio 16 d. Kalba Aukščiausios Tarybos posėdije," in *Laisvės byla 1990–1991: Kalbos, pranešimai, užrašai, laiškai, pokalbiai, interviu, įvairūs dokumentai* (Vilnius: Lietuvos Aidas, 1992), 206–7. The "Appeal to the People of Lithuania" published by the Government of the Republic of Lithuania on February 2, 1991, was one of many national policy documents that rejected revenge as a motivation for violence: The foreign aggression against the Lithuanian state and the Lithuanian nation continues. The behavior of Soviet troops may become more brazen, cruel and provocative. We are convinced that in this decisive period of trial Lithuania has only one effective and undefeatable weapon, expressive of our Baltic and Christian culture—that of nonviolent protest, of people's self-control and calm endurance. We appeal to all the people of the country, the youth in particular, who are most conscious of injustice, and we urge all to resist provocations of the foreign troops, to refrain from any acts of physical resistance so desired by the enemy. We shall win by maintaining the honor of the Lithuanian state in the face of the world community of nations." (*Lietuvos*

Aidas, February 2, 1991, as translated in Miniotaite, *Nonviolent Resistance in Lithuania*, 77)

110. Landsbergis, *Lithuania Independent Again*, 281; "Six Found Dead at Lithuanian Customs Post, OMON Denial," BBC Summary of World Broadcasts, August 1, 1991; "Lithuania: Mikhailov, Another Two Former Riga OMON Officers Killed Medininkai Guards—Prosecutor," Baltic News Service, March 30, 2011 (retrieved from LexisNexis Academic on April 8, 2011); "Medininkai Suspects Charged with War Crimes," Baltic News Service, July 27, 2011 (retrieved from LexisNexis Academic on September 22, 2011).

111. Author's diary, Rīga, August 19–21, 1991. Another song broadcast several times that night was "Klusa, klusa latvju sēta": "Latvia, Latvia, victory comes glimmering; after the very last shot has rung out, Latvia shall be free!"

CHAPTER 9

1. James Tusty and Maureen Tusty, *The Singing Revolution* (Docurama Films, 2007), 1:11:30; Vesilind, *Singing Revolution*, 145–47.

2. Kristin Dobinson, "A Model of Peacefulness: Rethinking Peace and Conflict in Norway," in Kemp and Fry, *Keeping the Peace*, 165.

3. The "Bard of Beverīna" (originally spelled Beveriņa) was sung at pre-Soviet national song festivals in 1895, 1910, 1926, 1933, and 1938, but only once during the Soviet era, in 1960.

4. The discussion refers to the texts of songs as Balts sang them in 1988–91, and not the abbreviated or revised texts remembered and performed in 1998. Lithuanians in Lithuania, for example, never abbreviated songs as they did on stage in 1998; chapters 3 and 4 fill in the missing stanzas that were actually sung. Before September 1991, the Estonian song "Stay Free, Estonia's Sea!" began with a different word, "be free" (i.e., "become free"), not "stay free," because the country was not free yet.

5. Alan Dundes, "Texture, Text, and Context," *Southern Folklore Quarterly* 28, no. 4 (1964): 251–65.

6. The trilingual 1989 song "Baltic Awakening" (discussed in chapter 7) shows that Balts also believed that a text could be translated and keep its meaning.

7. I. Michael Heyman, "The Festival: On the Mall and Back Home," in *1998 Smithsonian Folklife Festival on the National Mall, Washington, D.C., June 24–28 & July 1–5* (Washington, DC: Smithsonian Institution, 1998), 2. Here and below, quotations from the July 4, 1998, concert are transcribed and translated from the archived recording edited by J. Maniszewitz, *Singing Revolution Special Program.*

8. Among others, see Heinz Valk: "Our only weapon is the mind," in his June 1988 editorial, "Laulev revolutsioon"; Vytautas Landsbergis, who in January 1991 spoke to the unarmed defenders of the national parliament, "our shield, not our sword," in Landsbergis, *Nauji dokumentai*, 106–7; and Dainis Īvāns, who in October 1988 predicted victory "if our revolution . . . will remain a revolution of songs, love and spiritual activity," *Latvijas Tautas fronte: Gads pirmais*, 199.

9. In 1998, Baltic flags also expressed nonviolent resistance to the organizers of the Smithsonian festival. The Balts brought flags with them to Washington, DC, and requested that festival staff help provide flagpoles; the Smithsonian staff, however, was intent on keeping national politics separate from folklore, did not provide flagpoles, and tried to dissuade Balts from carrying flags at the opening ceremony. "But we are representing a country!," exclaimed Helmī in an interview I recorded on June 24, 1998. "And it was the Americans, the organizers of this festival, when they met with us in Rīga, who stressed the path of singing opposition as a phenomenon in world culture. Not with explosives and terrorism, but with a song. But together with this song we also had our national flags. For us it was, it is, a unified whole!" The Balts sidestepped Smithsonian officials and asked Baltic American acquaintances to help get flagpoles. And they came to the opening concert, flags fluttering in the wind.

10. Laar, Ott, and Endre, *Teine Eesti*, 304–9.

11. Lithuanians recalled that after their government made the yellow-green-red flag official in 1988, organizers of official functions in Moscow would place it upside down so that the red side would blend in with the other Soviet flags.

12. Speeches, display of flags, and singing are numbers 1, 18, and 37 on the well-known list by Gene Sharp, "198 Methods of Nonviolent Action," Albert Einstein Institution, http://www.aeinstein.org/organizations103a.html (accessed February 9, 2013).

13. See "song contents and contexts" in the index for references to national territory, regions, rivers, flora, and kinship.

14. See "song contents and contexts" in the index for references to liberty, truth, and light. The ubiquitous mention of liberty in Soviet loyalty songs was parodied in the punk song "Hello, Perestroika."

15. Gorsevski, *Peaceful Persuasion*, 75; Kenneth E. Boulding, "Nonviolence and Power in the Twentieth Century," in Stephen Zunes, Lester R. Kurtz, and Sarah Beth Asher, eds., *Nonviolent Social Movements: A Geographical Perspective* (Malden, MA: Blackwell, 1999), 15; Sanger, *"When the Spirit Says Sing!"* 134–49.

16. See "song contents and contexts" in the index for references to battle.

17. See "song contents and contexts" in the index for references to enemies. Crusaders were established as villains by eighteenth- and nineteenth-century German abolitionists such as Garlieb Merkel.

18. Benedict Anderson points out that nationalist songs rarely, if ever, express fear and loathing of a specific enemy; Anderson, *Imagined Communities*, 142.

19. See "song contents and contexts" in the index for references to God and the heavens, courage, and tears.

20. Video-recorded interview, April 8, 2010.

21. See "song contents and contexts" in the index for references to killing enemies. In Latvia, at the October 9, 1988 mass demonstration organized by the Popular Front, a songsheet printed in 100,000 copies contained texts that threatened, "For you, oh tyrant on the throne, our sword was sharpened long

ago," and "Whoever hopes to capture us gets a bullet in the forehead." Latvijas Tautas Fronte, *Tautas manifestācija "Par tiesisku valsti Latvijā" Piektdien, 1988. gada 7. oktobrī 15:00: Dziesmu teksti līdzdziedāšanai*, facsimile published in *Latvija Šodien* 1988, 85–87.

22. Landsbergis, *Lithuania Independent Again*, 246–47.

23. N. Kabanovs, "Demonstranti civiltērpos," *Atmoda* May 22, 1990, 3.

24. Īvāns, *Gadījuma karakalps*, 281–83. KGB General Johansons writes in his memoir that, in 1991, it was unclear who was giving orders to OMON; Edmunds Johansons, *Čekas Ģenerāļa piezīmes. Atmoda un VDK* (Riga: 1991. Gada Barikāžu Dalībnieku Biedrība, 2006), 113, 18, 20–25.

25. "Liecina Gatis Jurkāns, LNNK kārtības sargs," *Atmoda* May 22, 1990, 3.

26. Documents confirming the Latvian government's policy of civilian-based defense are published in Eglitis, *Nonviolent Action in the Liberation of Latvia*, 45–68. Tactical planning is described, for example, by colonel Vilnis Zvaigzne, in Modris Ziemiņš, ed. *Rīgā deg ugunskuri, Maskavā brūk padomju impērija* (Riga: Modris Ziemiņš, 2001), 204–14.

27. Steven Zunes and Lester R. Kurtz, "Conclusion," in Zunes, *Nonviolent Social Movements* 311; Īvāns, *Gadījuma karakalps*, 332–44.

28. It was rumored that Soviet troops attacked only one Estonian border post because they believed that Estonians would fight back. A tactical commander in Old Town Rīga, Auseklis Pļaviņš, recalls that he intentionally lied to a Soviet military informer that Latvians were well armed with grenades, and that snipers with armor-piercing weapons stood on guard, prepared to shoot down Soviet helicopters; in Ziemiņš, *Rīgā deg ugunskuri*, 293. Latvian customs officer Aivars Gulbis recalled that after OMON brutally beat up a customs official on July 28, 1991, he summoned OMON commander Cheslav Mlinnik to his office and hinted that, if OMON were to again harm people, he could not guarantee the safety of Mlinnik's parents; Aigars Urtāns, "Gads, kad dega robeža," *Diena*, May 20, 2006, 24.

29. Dace Bula argues that there is nothing inherently nonviolent in the act of singing, which can be a means of attaining national unity for peaceful as well as violent purposes. She compiles a list of national characteristics that appeared in a lengthy 1993–94 discussion of Latvian folk songs and notes that the list did not include nonviolent characteristics such as "forgiving" or "slow to anger"; in Bula, *Dziedātājtauta*, 24, 76–77.

30. Linda Dégh, following the methods of her teacher Gyla Ortutay, stressed the importance of studying a community's entire repertoire, in Linda Dégh, *Narratives in Society: A Performer-Centered Study of Narration* (Helsinki: Suomalainen Tiedeakatemia, 1995), 10–11; John Miles Foley reminds us to "read both behind and between the signs" in John Miles Foley, *How to Read an Oral Poem*, 139–41; Henry Glassie has long pursued ethnography as "an integrated treatment of the whole repertory of a community," in Henry Glassie, *The Stars of Ballymenone* (Bloomington: Indiana University Press, 2006), 423; Barre Toelken, too, argues that any tradition of a "whole group of people" is best understood as part of the total repertoire of folklore, in Barre Toelken, *The Dynamics of Folklore* (Boston: Houghton Mifflin, 1979), 183–84.

31. Thomas DuBois demonstrates that rigorous interpretation of what a song means to a singer must travel along three axes: associative (singers associate a song with their personal or other people's experience), situational (the song may narrate a known historical event or describe a proverbial or typical situation), and generic (categories of songs may be identified by content or by context); Thomas DuBois, *Lyric, Meaning, and Audience in the Oral Tradition of Northern Europe* (South Bend, IN: University of Notre Dame Press, 2006), 2–5.

32. Anatol Lieven indicates that free speech was what moved emotions at demonstrations—"the songs, the tears, the sense of relief as people were able to say in public things which for fifty years they had been scared even to whisper in private." Anatol Lieven, *The Baltic Revolution: Estonia, Latvia, Lithuania, and the Path to Independence*, 2nd ed. (New Haven, CT: Yale University Press, 1994), 219.

33. Plakans, *Concise History of the Baltic States*, 392. Taagepera writes that on September 11, 1988, the Singing Revolution "reached its grand finale"; Taagepera, *Estonia: Return to Independence*, 142; Kasekamp, *History of the Baltic States*, 160–71.

34. Alf Gabrielsson's survey of 953 people found that intense music experience is associated with both physical reactions (tears, shivers, goosebumps) and transcendental experiences; 15 percent recalled nonreligious transcendental experiences, and 11 percent recalled religious feelings. Many commented that music gave them new insights and feelings of confirmation; music's ability to generate a feeling of community was mentioned by 18 percent of the respondents; Alf Gabrielsson, "Strong Experiences with Music," in *Handbook of Music and Emotion: Theory, Research, Applications*, ed. Patrick N. Juslin and John A. Sloboda (Oxford: Oxford University Press, 2010), 554–65.

35. Alfred Erich Senn, *Gorbachev's Failure in Lithuania* (New York: St. Martin's Press, 1995), 115–57.

36. See "song contents and contexts" in the index for references to hope and prayer.

37. Beissinger, "Intersection of Ethnic Nationalism and People Power," 232.

38. Richard Bauman, *Verbal Art as Performance*, with supplementary essays by Barbara A. Babcock et al. (Prospect Heights, IL: Waveland Press, 1984, ©1977), 9.

39. Dace Bula documents the notion, taken for granted from the nineteenth century to the present day, that Latvia is a "nation of singers"; Bula, *Dziedātājtauta*, 60, 68. See "song contents and contexts" in the index for references to singing, metaphors of the cuckoo and the nightingale, and musical instruments.

40. Taagepera, *Estonia: Return to Independence*, 208.

41. Sharp, "New Challenge," 424.

42. The mechanisms of "distraction" and "perceived control" do not adequately explain music's effect, which is mediated by music's effect on the emotions; Patrick N. Juslin and John A. Sloboda, "The Past, Present, and Future of Music and Emotion Research," in *Handbook of Music and Emotion: Theory,*

Research, Applications, ed. Patrick N. Juslin and John A. Sloboda (Oxford: Oxford University Press, 2010), 940.

43. Beissinger, "Intersection of Ethnic Nationalism and People Power," 234.

44. Steven Mithen, *The Singing Neanderthals: The Origins of Music, Language, Mind, and Body* (Cambridge, MA: Harvard University Press, 2006), 112–15.

45. Steven Brown and Ulrik Volksten, eds., *Music and Manipulation: On the Social Uses and Social Control of Music* (New York: Berghahn Books, 2006), 4–5.

46. Music psychologists agree that Pavlovian behaviorism does not explain how music changes behavior; Shannon de l'Etoile, "Processes of Music Therapy: Clinical and Scientific Rationales and Models," in *The Oxford Handbook of Musical Psychology*, ed. Susan Hallam, Ian Cross, and Michael Thaut (Oxford: Oxford University Press, 2009), 494–95.

47. Anderson, *Imagined Communities*, 145.

48. Lieven, *Baltic Revolution*, 113, 394n6.

49. Monique Ingalls, "Singing Heaven Down to Earth: Spiritual Journeys, Eschatological Sounds, and Community Formation in Evangelical Conference Worship," *Ethnomusicology* 55, no. 2 (2011): 263.

50. Mithen, *Singing Neanderthals*, 208–11.

51. Rinne, *Laulev revolutsioon*, 126, 223, 48; Ramanauskaitė, "Lithuanian Youth Culture," 332.

52. Elaine Brown, quoted in James Jordan, *The Musician's Soul: A Journey Examining Spirituality for Performers, Teachers, Composers, Conductors, and Music Educators* (Chicago: GIA Publications, 1999), 91.

53. Interviewed by Anita Mellupe; Anita Mellupe, *Kamēr . . . Māris Sirmais un Latvija dzied!* (Riga: Likteņstāsti, 2008), 121.

54. A Russian singer told fieldworker Laura Olson, "One does not feel the group as a hindrance to one's freedom; rather, one feels that one's relation to the collective provides the safety that allows the expression of individuality"; Olson, *Performing Russia*, 103.

55. Suzanne B. Hanser, "Music, Health, and Well-Being," in *Handbook of Music and Emotion: Theory, Research, Applications*, ed. Patrick N. Juslin and John A. Sloboda (Oxford: Oxford University Press, 2010); G. Kreutz et al., "Effects of Choir Singing or Listening on Secretory Immunoglobulin A, Cortisol, and Emotional State," *Journal of Behavioral Medicine* 27 (2004): 623–35.

56. Brynjulf Stige et al., "When Things Take Shape in Relation to Music: Towards an Ecological Perspective on Music's Help," in *Where Music Helps: Community Music Therapy in Action and Reflection*, ed. Brynjulf Stige, Gary Ansdell, Cochavit Elefant, and Mercédès Pavlicevic (Burlington, VT: Ashgate, 2010), 302.

57. Dianna T. Kenny, and Bronwen Ackermann, "Optimizing Physical and Psychological Health in Performing Musicians," in *The Oxford Handbook of Music Psychology*, ed. Susan Hallam, Ian Cross, and Michael Thaut (Oxford University Press, 2009), 393–96.

58. Betty Bailey and Jane Davidson, "Amateur Group Singing as a Therapeutic Instrument," *Nordic Journal of Music Therapy* 12, no. 1 (2003): 18–32; Hanser, "Music, Health, and Well-Being," 865–68. See chapters by Mercédès Pavlicevic, "Crime, Community, and Everyday Practice: Music Therapy as Social Activism"; and Cochavit Elefant, "Giving Voice: Participatory Action Research with a Marginalized Group"; in Stige and van den Hurk, *Where Music Helps*; and José van den Hurk, "Music Therapy Helping to Work through Grief and Finding a Personal Identity," *Journal of Music Therapy* 36, no. 3 (1999): 222–52.

59. Jordan, *Musician's Soul*, 7, 32, 111–12.

60. Robert L. Helvey, *On Strategic Nonviolent Conflict: Thinking about the Fundamentals* (Washington, DC: The Albert Einstein Institute, 2004), 23, 104.

61. Tape-recorded interview, July 6, 1990.

62. Havel, *Power of the Powerless*, 65.

63. Priede, "Trīspadsmitā," 367–68.

64. Aili Aarelaid-Tart, "The End of Singing Nationalism as Cultural Trauma," *Acta Historica Tallinnensia* 8 (2004): 77–98.

65. Īvāns, *Gadījuma karakalps*, 9.

66. Histories of Estonia, Latvia, and Lithuania rarely, if ever, mention the individuals whose songs are highlighted in this book, for example, Ieva Akurātere, Urmas Alender, Ott Arder, Mārtiņš Brauns, Māris Čaklais, Rene Eespere, Juozas Erlickas, Jānis Grodums, Imants Kalniņš, Algirdas Kaušpėdas, Zita Kelmickaitė, Vytautas Kernagis, Juris Kulakovs, Jüri Leesment, Zigmārs Liepiņš, Ivo Linna, Tõnis Mägi, Justinas Marcinkevičius, Alo Mattiisen, Haralds Mednis, Māris Melgalvs, Raimonds Pauls, Jānis Peters, Veronika Povilionienė, Rein Rannap, Brigita Ritmane, Andris Ritmanis, Hando Runnel, Ingrid Rüütel, Julgī Stalte, Helmī Stalte, Dainis Stalts, Villu Tamme, Igor Tõnurist, Veljo Tormis, Kristjan Torop, Norbertas Vėlius, and Māra Zālīte. Histories of the 1988–91 Baltic independence movements rarely, if ever, mention earlier poets and composers whose songs were popular during the movements, among them Auseklis, Kārlis Baumanis, Leonīds Breikšs, Jānis Cimze, Emīls Dārziņš, Juozas Gudavičius, Carl Hermann, Johann Voldemar Jannsen, Andrejs Jurjāns, Lydia Koidula, Martin Körber, Friedrich Kreutzwald, Mihkel Lüdig, Vincas Kudirka, Friedrich Kuhlbars, Aleksander Kunileid, Maironis, Emilis Melngailis, Juozas Naujalis, Viktor Oxford, Rainis, Ksaveras Sakalauskas-Vanagėlis, Česlovas Sasnauskas, Georg Sauerwein, Kārlis Skalbe, Juozas Tallat-Kelpša, and Jāzeps Vītols.

BIBLIOGRAPHY, DISCOGRAPHY,
AND FILMOGRAPHY

Aarelaid-Tart, Aili. *Cultural Trauma and Life Stories.* Helsinki: Aleksanteri Institute, 2006.

———. "The End of Singing Nationalism as Cultural Trauma." *Acta Historica Tallinnensia* 8 (2004): 77–98.

Aassalu, Heino, ed. *Kristjan Toropit meenutades.* Tallinn: n.p., 1998.

Abaris, Leonidas, ed. *Užaugau Lietuvoj: Lietuvių liaudies dainos.* Vilnius: Lietuvos Liaudies Kultūros Centras, 1990.

"Acht alte estnische Volkslieder (aus Herders Nachlass)." *Verhandlungen der gelehrten Estnischen Gesellschaft zu Dorpat* 16, no. 2 (1896): 243–67.

Ackerman, Peter, and Jack DuVall. *A Force More Powerful: A Century of Nonviolent Conflict.* New York: St. Martin's Press, 2000.

Adler, Hans, and Wulf Koepke, eds. *A Companion to the Works of Johann Gottfried Herder.* Rochester, NY: Camden House, 2011.

Aistis, Jonas, ed. *Laisvės kovų dainos.* New York: Lietuvos Nepriklausomybės Fondas, 1962.

Akurātere, Ieva. *Ieva Akurātere.* LP record, C6028197009. Riga: Melodiya, 1989.

———. *Manai tautai.* Riga: Pētergailis, 2007.

Albertavičius, Jonas. "Austros medžio pavėnėje." In *Kalba Vilnius,* no. 33 (1988), 4–5. Digital copy posted by Lithuanian Folk Culture Centre, "Baltica 1988, Atgarsiai spaudoje," http://www.baltica.llkc.lt/index. php?2655362138. Accessed February 9, 2013.

Ambrazas, Algirdas, ed. *Lietuvos muzikos istorija, I knyga: Tautinio atgimimo metai, 1883–1918.* Vilnius: Lietuvos Muzikos Akademija, 2002.

———. *Lietuvos muzikos istorija, II knyga: Nepriklausomybės metai, 1918–1940.* Vilnius: Lietuvos Muzikos ir Teatro Akademija, 2009.

Ambrazevičius, R., ed. *Skamba, skamba kankliai.* Vilnius: Littera, 1990.

Anderson, Benedict. *Imagined Communities: Reflections on the Origin and Spread of Nationalism.* Rev. ed. London: Verso, 2006.

Andriulis, D., et al., eds. *Dainuojam: Dainų rinkinys kariams, šauliams, moksleiviams ir jaunimui.* Kaunas: Kariuomenės Štabo Spaudos ir Švietimo Skyriaus Leidinys, 1935.

Annus, Epp. *Eesti kirjanduslugu.* Tallinn: Koolibri, 2001.

Antis. *Dovanėlė.* LP record, C60–29335–6. N.p.: Melodiya, 1989.

———. *Geriausios dainos.* CD ZNCD 075. Vilnius: Zona Records, 2006.

Antis et al. *Roko maršas per Lietuvą '89.* LP record C60–30637–8. N.p.: Melodiya, 1990.

Anušauskas, Arvydas, ed. *The Anti-Soviet Resistance in the Baltic States.* Vilnius: Du Ka, 1999.

"Ar saules motīvu." *Padomju Jaunatne,* July 14, 1988.

Arbusow, Leonid. "Herder und die Begründung der Volksliedforschung im deutschbaltischen Osten." In *Im Geiste Herders: Gesammelte Aufsätze zum 150. Todestage J. G. Herders,* edited by Erich Keyser, 129–256. Kitzingen am Main: Holzner Verlag, 1953.

Atvars, G. "Kā atrast 'sinkrēto vērtību veselumu': Polēmiskas piezīmes par ētiskā ideāla meklējumu kritikā un publicistikā." *Cīņa,* January 27, 1983, 2–3.

Āviks, Juhans. "Atmiņas par profesoru Vītolu." In *Jāzeps Vītols tuvinieku, audzēkņu un laikabiedru atmiņās,* edited by Oļģerts Grāvītis, 111–17. Riga: Zinātne, 1999.

Bagušauskas, Romualdas, and Arūnas Streikus, eds. *Lietuvos kultūra sovietinės ideologijos nelaisvėje, 1940–1990: Dokumentų rinkinys.* Vilnius: Lietuvos Gyventojų Genocido ir Rezistencijos Tyrimo Centras, 2005.

Bailey, Betty, and Jane Davidson. "Amateur Group Singing as a Therapeutic Instrument." *Nordic Journal of Music Therapy* 12, no. 1 (2003): 18–32.

Baliukevičius, Lionginas. *The Diary of a Partisan: A Year in the Life of the Postwar Lithuanian Resistance Fighter Dzūkas.* Translated by Irena Blekys and Lijana Holmes.Vilnius: Genocide and Resistance Research Centre of Lithuania, 2008.

Balkelis, Tomas. *The Making of Modern Lithuania.* London: Routledge, 2009.

Baltakmens, Raimonds. "Dziesmu vairogs atsita bultas." In *Barikādes: Latvijas mīlestības grāmata,* edited by Viktors Daugmalis, 304–9. Riga: BAF, 2001.

Baltakmens, Raimonds, and Dzintars Gilba, eds. *Gaismas pils augšāmcēlējs Haralds Mednis.* Riga: Valters un Rapa, 2006.

Baltica '87: International Folklore Festival of the Baltic Republics. Vilnius: Mintis, 1987.

Barons, Krišjānis, ed. *Latwju dainas.* 6 vols. Riga: Liesma, 1985.

Bauman, Richard. *Verbal Art as Performance,* with supplementary essays by Barbara A. Babcock et al. Prospect Heights, IL: Waveland Press, 1984, ©1977.

Beissinger, Mark. "The Intersection of Ethnic Nationalism and People Power Tactics in the Baltic States, 1987–91." In *Civil Resistance and Power Politics: The Experience of Non-Violent Action from Gandhi to the Present,* edited by Adam Roberts and Timothy Garton Ash, 231–46. New York: Oxford University Press, 2009.

Belševica, Vizma. *Bille.* Ithaca, NY: Mežābele, 1992.

———. *Dzeltu laiks. Dzeja.* Riga: Liesma, 1987.

Belzyt, Leszek. *Sprachliche Minderheiten im preußischen Staat, 1815–1914: Die preußische Sprachenstatistik in Bearbeitung und Kommentar.* Marburg: Herder-Institut, 1998.

Bendorfs, Vilis. "Folkloras noliktava?" *Padomju Jaunatne,* November 12, 1986, 4.

Bergmanis, Andris. "Tautasdziesmā viss ir pateikts." *Skola un ģimene* 7, no. 295 (1988): 1–3.

Bērziņa, Vizbulīte. *Daudz baltu dieniņu . . . : Jēkaba Graubiņa dzīvesstāsts.* Riga: Atēna, 2006.

———. *Tautas muzikālā atmoda latviešu publicistu skatījumā.* Riga: Zinātne, 1983.

Bērziņš, Jānis. *Dziesmotais novads: Ieskats Madonas novada kordziedāšanas vēsturē.* N.p.: Mantojums, 2003.

Bērziņš, Ludis. *Greznas dziesmas.* Riga: Zinātne, 2007.

Bērzkalns, Valentīns. *Latviešu Dziesmu svētku vēsture, 1864–1940.* New York: Grāmatu Draugs, 1965.

Biezais, Haralds, ed. *Die erste Sammlung der lettischen Volkslieder von Gustav Bergmann. Mit einer historischen Einleitung über die Ausgaben der lettischen Volkslieder.* Uppsala: Senatne, 1961.

Biržiška, M., ed. *Liudo Rėzos Dainos. Pirmo lietuviško dainyno III leidimas, I dalis.* Kaunas: Vytauto Didžiojo Universiteto Humanitarinių Mokslų Fakulteto Leidinys, 1935.

Blume, Friedriech. *Protestant Church Music: A History.* New York: Norton & Company, 1974.

Blūzma, Valdis. "The Period of Awakening and Non-Violent Resistance (1986–4 May 1990)." In *Regaining Independence: Non-Violent Resistance in Latvia, 1945–1991,* edited by Valdis Blūzma et al., 229–69. Riga: Latvian Academy of Sciences, 2009.

Boiko, Martin. "Latvian Ethnomusicology, Past and Present." *Yearbook for Traditional Music* 26 (1994): 47–65.

———. "Muzikoloģija/Mūzikas Zinātne: A Critical History of Latvian Musicology." *Journal of Baltic Studies* 39, no. 3 (2008): 325–40.

Bojtár, Endre. *Foreword to the Past: A Cultural History of the Baltic People.* Budapest: Central European University Press, 1999.

Boulding, Elsie. *Cultures of Peace: The Hidden Side of History.* Syracuse, NY: Syracuse University Press, 2000.

Boulding, Kenneth E. "Nonviolence and Power in the Twentieth Century." In *Nonviolent Social Movements: A Geographical Perspective,* edited by Stephen Zunes, Lester R. Kurtz, and Sarah Beth Asher, 9–17. Malden, MA: Blackwell, 1999.

Braun, Joachim. "Reconsidering Musicology in the Baltic States of Lithuania, Latvia, and Estonia: 1990–2007." *Journal of Baltic Studies* 39, no. 3 (2008): 231–38.

Breikšs, Leonīds. *Dzīve un darbi.* 4 vols. Riga: Enigma, 1998.

Brīvzemnieks, Fricis. "O narodnoi poezii latishei." In *Sbornik antropologicheskikh i etnograficheskikh statei,* edited by V. A. Dashkov, vol. 2, 7–15. Moscow: Obshchestvo Liubitelei Estestvoznaniia, Antropologii i Etnografii, 1873.

Bronner, Simon. *American Children's Folklore.* Little Rock, AR: August House, 1988.

Brown, Steven, and Ulrik Volksten, eds. *Music and Manipulation: On the Social Uses and Social Control of Music.* New York: Berghahn Books, 2006.

Brūvers, Pāvils. "1987. gada 14. jūnijs Rīgā." *Latvija Šodien* (1987): 1–9.

Bula, Dace. *Dziedātājtauta: Folklora un nacionālā ideoloģija.* Riga: Zinātne, 2000.

———. "Johans Gotfrīds Herders un tautas dzejas interpretācijas Latvijā." In *Herders Rīgā,* edited by Māra Siliņa, 12–19. Riga: Rīgas Doma Evaņģēliski Luteriskā Draudze, 2005.

Burkšaitienė, Laima, and Danutė Krištopaitė, eds. *Aukštaičiu melodijos.* Vilnius: Vaga, 1990.

Čaklais, Māris. *Im Ka: Imants Kalniņš laikā un telpā.* Riga: Jumava 1998.

———. "Oficiāli Līgo svēki- tas ir normāli." *Literatūra un Māksla,* April 22, 1988, 5.

Černiauskas, Mindaugas. *Europos tautų nacionaliniai himnai.* N.p.: Versus Aureus, 2006.

Chew, Geoffrey, and Petr Macek, eds. *Socialist Realism and Music.* Prague: KLP, 2004.

Cimze. *Dziesmu rota, izlase.* Riga: Liesma, 1973.

Clark, Katerina, Evgeny Dobrenko, Andrei Artizov, and Oleg Naumov, eds.

Soviet Culture and Power: A History in Documents, 1917–1953. New Haven, CT: Yale University Press, 2007.

Clark, Robert Thomas. *Herder: His Life and Thought*. Berkeley: University of California, 1955.

Conquest, Robert. *Stalin: Breaker of Nations*. New York: Penguin, 1991.

Dāboliņa, Ieva Nikoleta. "Dzīvie pieminekļi. Atceroties Gunāru Astru." *Ir*, October 21, 2011, www.ir.lv. Accessed October 21, 2011.

Dabrila, K. J. *Vai lėkite dainos*. Facsimile printing of songbook published in Marijampolė, 1940. Edited by V. Pakarskas. Vilnius: Eksperimentinė Technikos Paminklų Restauravimo Įmonė, 1990.

Dainų šventė: XIII Lietuvos tautinė dainų šventė. Vilnius: Mintis, 1990.

Daitz, Mimi S. *Ancient Song Recovered: The Life and Music of Veljo Tormis*. Hillsdale, NY: Pendragon Press, 2004.

Davies, Norman. *God's Playground: A History of Poland*. 2 vols. Oxford: Clarendon Press, 1981.

Dégh, Linda. *Narratives in Society: A Performer-Centered Study of Narration*. Helsinki: Suomalainen Tiedeakatemia, 1995.

de l'Etoile, Shannon. "Processes of Music Therapy: Clinical and Scientific Rationales and Models." In *The Oxford Handbook of Musical Psychology*, edited by Susan Hallam, Ian Cross, and Michael Thaut, 493–502. Oxford: Oxford University Press, 2009.

Deutsch, James I. "Smithsonian Folklife Festival on the National Mall." *Journal of American Folklore* 113, no. 447 (2000): 99–100.

[Divdesmitie] XX Vispārējie latviešu dziesmu svētki: Koncertu programma. Riga: E. Melngaiļa Tautas Mākslas Centrs, 1990.

Dobbek, Wilhelm. *Karoline Herder: Ein Frauenleben in klassischer Zeit*. Weimar: Böhlau, 1967.

Dobinson, Kristin. "A Model of Peacefulness: Rethinking Peace and Conflict in Norway." In *Keeping the Peace: Conflict Resolution and Peaceful Societies around the World*, edited by Graham Kemp and Douglas P. Fry, 149–66. New York: Routledge, 2004.

Dreifelds, Juris. *Latvia in Transition*. Cambridge: Cambridge University Press, 1996.

———. "Two Latvian Dams, Two Confrontations." *Baltic Forum* 6, no. 1 (1989): 11–24.

Drews, Jörg, ed. *"Ich werde gewiss grosse Energie zeigen": Garlieb Merkel (1769–1850) als Kämpfer, Kritiker, und Projektemacher in Berlin und Riga*. Bielefeld, Germany: Aisthesis, 2000.

DuBois, Thomas. *Lyric, Meaning, and Audience in the Oral Tradition of Northern Europe*. South Bend, IN: University of Notre Dame Press, 2006.

Düding, Dieter. "The Nineteenth-Century German Nationalist Movement as a Movement of Societies." In *Nation Building in Central Europe*, 19–49. Edited by Hagen Schulze. Leaminton Spa, England: Berg, 1987.

Düding, Dieter, Peter Friedmann, and Paul Münch, eds. *Öffentliche Festkultur: Politische Feste im Deutschland von der Aufklarung bis zum ersten Weltkrieg*. Hamburg: GmbH, 1988.

Dundes, Alan. "Texture, Text, and Context." *Southern Folklore Quarterly* 28, no. 4 (1964): 251–65.

Dundulienė, Pranė. *Lietuvių liaudies kosmologija*. Vilnius: Mokslas, 1988.

Dziesmu svētku mazā enciklopēdija. Riga: Musica Baltica, 2004.

Dzintars. *A Faraway Song*. LP record. Portland, OR: N.p., 1978.

Dzirkalis, K., ed. *Pirmo Latviešu Dziesmu svētku 75 gadu atceres svinības Diklos*. Riga: Pagalms, 1939. Retrieved from http://dziesmusvetki.lndb.lv/, February 9, 2013.

Eestimaa laul. DVD video recording. Tallinn: LunaVista Productions, 2008.

Eesti muusika biograafiline leksikon. Tallinn: Valgus, 1990.

Eestirahwa 50–aastase Jubelipiddo-Laulud. Tartu, Estonia: Wannemuineselts, 1869.

Eglitis, Olgerts. *Nonviolent Action in the Liberation of Latvia*. Cambridge, MA: The Albert Einstein Institution, 1993.

Eidintas, Alfonsas. *Jews, Lithuunians, and the Holocaust*. Vilnius: Versus Aureus, 2003.

Ekmanis, Indra. *The Sound of Protest*. DVD. Bachelor's thesis, Arizona State University, 2011.

Ekmanis, Rolfs. *Latvian Literature under the Soviets, 1940–1975*. Belmont, MA: Nordland Publishing Company, 1978.

———. "Some Notes on Vizma Belševica." *World Literature Today* (Spring 1998): 287–96.

Elling, Indrek. "Eesti Üliõpilaste Seltsi tekkimise tagamad. Saksa ja baltisaksa eeskujud." In *Tartu, baltisakslased ja Saksamaa*, edited by Helmut Piirimäe and Claus Sommerhage, 190–206. Tartu, Estonia: Tartu Ülikooli Kirjastus, 1998.

Emerson, Caryl. *The Cambridge Introduction to Russian Literature*. New York: Cambridge University Press, 2008.

Eyck, F. Gunther. *The Voice of Nations: European National Anthems and Their Authors*. Westport, CT: Greenwood Press, 1995.

Ezergailis, Andrew. *The Holocaust in Latvia, 1941–1944: The Missing Center*. Riga: Historical Institute of Latvia / Washington, DC: United States Holocaust Memorial Museum, 1996.

———, ed. *The Latvian Legion: Heroes, Nazis, or Victims?: A Collection of*

Documents from OSS War-Crimes Investigation Files, 1945–1950. Riga: Historical Institute of Latvia, 1997.

————, ed. *Stockholm Documents: The German Occupation of Latvia, 1941–1945: What Did America Know?* Riga: Historical Institute of Latvia, 2002.

Fasta, Tatjana. *Juris Podnieks: Vai viegli būt elkam?* Riga: Kontinents, 2010.

Foley, John Miles. *How to Read an Oral Poem.* Urbana: University of Illinois Press, 2002.

Fukač, Jiří. "Socialist Realism in Music: An Artificial System of Ideological and Aesthetic Norms." In *Socialist Realism and Music,* edited by Geoffrey Chew and Petr Macek, 16–21. Prague: KLP, 2004.

Gabrielsson, Alf. "Strong Experiences with Music." In *Handbook of Music and Emotion: Theory, Research, Applications,* edited by Patrick N. Juslin and John A. Sloboda, 547–74. Oxford: Oxford University Press, 2010.

Gailīte, Zane, ed. *Mēness meti, saules stīga. Emīls Dārziņš.* Riga: Pils, 2006.

Gelazis, Julija. "Vakarone: A Lithuanian-American Musical Experience." Master's thesis, Wesleyan University, 1991.

Gimžauskas, A. *Kur lygūs laukai: Dainos chorams.* Vilnius: Valstybinė Grožinės Literatūros Leidykla, 1959.

Girnius, Albertas. "Skambink, sese, dar linksmiau." *Literatūra ir Menas,* June 5, 1976, 6.

Glassie, Henry. *The Stars of Ballymenone.* Bloomington: Indiana University Press, 2006.

Goodman, Walter. "On the Baltics and the Persian Gulf." *New York Times,* June 24, 1991 (late edition, East Coast), C14.

Gorbachev, Mikhail. *Perestroika: New Thinking for Our Country and the World.* New York: Harper & Row, 1987.

Gorkii, Maksim. *Sobranie sochinenii.* Vol. 24. Moscow: Gosudarstvennoe Izdatel'stvo Khudozhestvennoi Literatury, 1953.

Gorsevski, Ellen W. *Peaceful Persuasion: The Geopolitics of Nonviolent Rhetoric.* SUNY Series in Communication Studies. Albany: State University of New York Press, 2004.

Grauzdiņa, Ilma, and Arnis Poruks. *Dziesmu svētku gara gaita.* Riga: E. Melngaiļa Tautas Mākslas Centrs, 1990.

Greble, V., E. Kokare, and Jēkabs Vītoliņš, eds. *Cīņas dziesmas.* Riga: Latvijas PSR Zinātņu Akadēmijas Izdevniecība, 1957.

Gruodytė, Vita. "Lithuanian Musicology in Historical Context: 1945 to the Present." *Journal of Baltic Studies* 39, no. 3 (2008): 263–82.

Gudelis, Regimantas. *Chorinis menas visuomenės kultūroje* (2001) and *Chorinio meno atspinžiai XIX a. pabaigos–XX a. pirmosios pusės publicistikoje* (2003). Klaipėda, Lithuania: Klaipėdos Universiteto Leidykla, 2001.

Gulbis, Jānis. "Kā es atceros latviešu strēlnieku laimetu." *Latviešu Strēlnieki* 29 (1939): 2958.

Haas, Ain, and Ed Haas, eds. *Uus Ärkamisaeg Eestimaal.* Unpublished VHS videotape, 1989.

Hackmann, Jörg. "Voluntary Associations and Region Building: A Post-National Perspective on Baltic History." Center for European Studies Working Paper Series 105 (2002), http://aei.pitt.edu/9047/1/Hackmann. pdf. Accessed February 19, 2011.

Hanser, Suzanne B. "Music, Health, and Well-Being." In *Handbook of Music and Emotion: Theory, Research, Applications,* edited by Patrick N. Juslin and John A. Sloboda, 849–77. Oxford: Oxford University Press, 2010.

Hausmanis, Viktors. *Latviešu rakstniecība biogrāfijās.* Riga: LZA Literatūras, Folkloras un Mākslas Institūts, Latvijas Enciklopēdija, 1992.

——. "Svētki beigušies, darbs turpinās." *Cīņa,* December 24, 1985, 3.

Havel, Vaclav, et. al. *Power of the Powerless: Citizens against the State in Central-Eastern Europe.* Armonk, NY: M. E. Sharpe, 1985.

Heinmaa, Heidi. *Protestantlik kantoriinstitutsioon Tallinnas 16.–17. sajandil.* Tallinn: Eesti Keele Instituut, 1999.

Helme, Rein. *1812. Aasta Eestis ja Lätis.* Tallinn: Olion, 1990.

Helvey, Robert L. *On Strategic Nonviolent Conflict: Thinking about the Fundamentals.* Washington, DC: The Albert Einstein Institute, 2004.

Herder, Caroline von. *Erinnerungen aus dem Leben Joh. Gottfrieds von Herder.* Edited by Johann Georg Müller. Vol. 1. Tübingen: Cotta, 1820. Digital facsimile by books.google.com. Accessed July 25, 2008.

Herder, Johann Gottfried. *Briefe: Gesamtausgabe, 1763–1803.* Edited by Wilhelm Dobbek and Günter Arnold. 9 vols. Weimar: Böhlau, 1977–88.

——. *Sämtliche Werke.* Edited by Bernhard Suphan. 33 vols. Hildesheim, Germany: Georg Olms, 1967–68.

——. *Stimmen der Völker in Liedern.* Edited by Johann von Müller. Tübingen: Cotta, 1807.

——. *Werke in zehn Bänden.* Edited by Martin Bollacher et al. 10 vols. Bibliothek deutscher Klassiker. Frankfurt am Main: Deutscher Klassiker Verlag, 1985–2000.

Heyman, I. Michael. "The Festival: On the Mall and Back Home." *1998 Smithsonian Folklife Festival on the National Mall, Washington, D.C., June 24–28 & July 1–5,* 2. Washington, DC: Smithsonian Institution, 1998.

Hillila, Ruth-Ester, and Barbara Blanchard-Hong. *Historical Dictionary of the Music and Musicians of Finland.* Westport, CT: Greenwood Press, 1997.

Hinnoms, A. "Ar latviešu strēlniekiem pasaules karā." *Latviešu Strēlnieki* 31 (1940): 3145.

Hirvepark 1987: 20 aastat kodanikualgatusest, mis muutis Eesti lähiajalugu. Tallinn: MTÜ Kultuuriselts Hirvepark, 2007.

Horton, Andrew. *The Zero Hour: Glasnost and Soviet Cinema in Transition.* Princeton: Princeton University Press, 1992.

Howell, Dana Prescott. *The Development of Soviet Folkloristics.* New York: Garland, 1992.

Hroch, Miroslav. *Social Preconditions of National Revival in Europe.* Cambridge: Cambridge University Press, 1985.

Hupel, August. *Topographische Nachrichten.* 3 vols. Riga: Johann Friedrich Hartknoch, 1774–82.

Hurt, Jakob, ed. *Setukeste laulud.* Monumenta Estoniae Antiquae, vol. 1, no. 1. Helsinki: Suomalaisen Kirjallisuuden Seura, 1904.

Husband, William B. "Review of Timothy Ryback's Rock around the Bloc." *Russian Review* 49, no. 4 (1990): 522.

Ingalls, Monique. "Singing Heaven Down to Earth: Spiritual Journeys, Eschatological Sounds, and Community Formation in Evangelical Conference Worship." *Ethnomusicology* 55, no. 2 (2011): 255–79.

"'Ir laivas plaukia . . . per laikus,' Ilgametį Centro direktorių Salomoną Sverdiolą kalbina Juozas Mikutavičius." In *Liaudies kultūra: Lietuvos liaudies kultūros centrui—60,* 30–45. Vilnius: Lietuvos Liaudies Kultūros Centras, 2001.

Ivanauskaitė, Vita. "Tarpukario Lietuvos dainos: Kolektyvinės ir individualiosios kūrybos sintezė." In *Lietuvių liaudies dainynas,* vol. 18, 7–50. Vilnius: Lietuvių Literatūros ir Tautosakos Institutas, 2004.

Īvāns, Dainis. *Gadījuma karakalps.* Riga: Vieda, 1995.

Jakelaitis, Vytautas. "Dainų šventės." In *Muzikos enciklopedija A-H,* edited by Juozas Antanavičius, 298–301. Vilnius: Lietuvos Muzikos Akademija, 2000.

———. *Lietuvos dainų šventės.* Vilnius: Vaga, 1970.

Jakobson, Carl Robert. *Wanemuine kandle healed. Neljahealega meeste koorid. Eesti laulupühaks 1869.* Saint Petersburg: C.R. Jakobson, 1869.

Jakubēns, Vlads. "Profesors Jāzeps Vītols un lietuvju mūziķi." In *Jāzeps Vītols tuvinieku, audzēkņu un laikabiedru atmiņās,* edited by Oļģerts Grāvītis, 132–34. Riga: Zinātne, 1999.

Jannsen, Johann Voldemar. *125 uut laulo neile, kes hea melega laulwad ehk laulo kuulwad.* Tartu, Estonia: H. Laakmann, 1860.

———. "Veel natukke Tallinna laulo piddust." In *Eesti rahvaluuleteaduse ajalugu: Välitud tekste ja pilte*, edited by Eduard Laugaste, 178. Tallinn: Eesti Riiklik Kirjastus, 1963.

Järv, Risto. "Kristfrid Gananderi 'Mythologia Fennica' saksakeelsest tõlkest." *Keel ja Kirjandus* 44, no. 3 (2001): 173–80.

Jaunslaviete, Baiba. "Ieskats vācbaltiešu dziesmu svētku vēsturē." *Mūzikas Akadēmijas Raksti* 3 (2007): 32–52.

Johansons, Andrejs. *Latvijas kultūras vēsture, 1710–1800.* Stockholm: Daugava, 1975.

Johansons, Edmunds. *Čekas Ģenerāļa piezīmes. Atmoda un VDK.* Riga: 1991 Gada Barikāžu Dalībnieku Biedrība, 2006.

Jordan, James. *The Musician's Soul: A Journey Examining Spirituality for Performers, Teachers, Composers, Conductors, and Music Educators.* Chicago: GIA Publications, 1999.

Jovaišas, Albinas. *Liudvikas Rėza.* Vilnius: Vaga, 1969.

Jürjo, Indrek. *Liivimaa valgustaja August Wilhelm Hupel, 1737–1819.* Tallinn: Riigiarhiiv, 2004.

Juška, Albertas. "Lietuvininkų kalba: Lietuvškai kalbančių žmonių skaičius." In *Mažosios Lietuvos enciklopedija*, edited by Zigmas Zinkevičius et al., 594–96. Vilnius: Mažosios Lietuvos Fondas, 2003.

Juslin, Patrick N., and John A. Sloboda. "The Past, Present, and Future of Music and Emotion Research." In *Handbook of Music and Emotion: Theory, Research, Applications*, edited by Patrick N. Juslin and John A. Sloboda, 933–55. Oxford: Oxford University Press, 2010.

Kahk, Juhan. "Peasant Movements and National Movements in the History of Europe." *Acta Universitatis Stockholmensis: Studia Baltica Stockholmensia* 2 (1985): 15–23.

Kalniņa, Ieva. "Latviešu padomju folkloras konstrukcija." In *Kultūra un vara: Raksti par valodu, literatūru, tradicionālo kultūru*, edited by Janīna Kursīte et al., 30–40. Riga: LU Akadēmiskais Apgāds, 2007.

Kalniņš, Imants. *Dzeguzes balss: Dziesmas ar M. Čaklā vārdiem.* LP record C60-11303-4. N.p.: Melodiya, 1979.

Kalniņš, Rolands. *Rolanda Kalniņa aizliegtās filmas.* DVD. Riga: Jura Podnieka Studija, 2009.

Kalvaitis, Vilius, ed. *Prūsijos Lietuvių dainos.* Vilnius: Lietuvių Literatūros ir Tautosakos Institutas, 1998.

Kaplinski, Jaan. "Pärandus ja pärijad." *Sirp ja Vasar*, February 28, 1969, 9.

Kapper, Sille. "Pärimus ja jäljendus: Postkolonialistlik katse mõista rahvatantsu olukorda Eesti NSV-s ja pärast seda." *Methis* 7 (2011): 122–36.

Karaška, Arvydas. "Lietuva: Dainų kraštas." *Kultūros barai* 11 (1975): 74–75.

Karlonas, Vaidotas, ed. *Dainų šventė.* Vilnius: Vaga, 1980.

Karnes, Kevin C. "A Garland of Songs for a Nation of Singers: An Episode in the History of Russia, the Herderian Tradition, and the Rise of Baltic Nationalism." *Journal of the Royal Musical Association* 130, no. 2 (2005): 197–235.

———. "Soviet Musicology and the 'Nationalities Question': The Case of Latvia." *Journal of Baltic Studies* 39, no. 3 (2008): 283–306.

Karulis, Konstantīns. *Latviešu etimoloģijas vārdnīca.* 2 vols. Riga: Avots, 1992.

Kase, Kajar "Mälestused öölaulupeost: Tõnu Kaljuste." *Postimees*, August 15, 2008, http://oolaulupidu.postimees.ee/?id=27055. Accessed July 9, 2010.

Kasekamp, Andres. *A History of the Baltic States.* New York: Palgrave Macmillan, 2010.

Kaudzīte, Matīss. *Atmiņas no tautiskā laikmeta.* Riga: Zvaigzne ABC, 1994.

Kaušpėdas, Algirdas. "A. Kaušpėdas: išbandymas šlove ir kulkomis." Interviewed by Toma Pagojutė. *Lietuvos Rytas*, March 11, 2012. Retrieved from www.lrytas.lt. Accessed March 18, 2012.

Keller, Mechthild. "'Politische Seeträume': Herder und Russland." In *Russen und Rußland aus deutscher Sicht, 18. Jahrhundert: Aufklärung*, edited by Mechthild Keller, 357–95. Munich: Wilhelm Fink Verlag, 1987.

Kelmickaitė, Zita. "Ir tapom kraštotyrininkais." *Literatūra ir Menas*, September 4, 1976, 6.

Kelmickaitė, Zita, and Dalia Kutavičienė. *Dainos galia.* [Vilnius]: Lietuvos TV, 2008.

Kemp, Graham, and Douglas P. Fry, eds. *Keeping the Peace: Conflict Resolution and Peaceful Societies around the World.* New York: Routledge, 2004.

Kenny, Dianna T., and Bronwen Ackermann. "Optimizing Physical and Psychological Health in Performing Musicians." In *The Oxford Handbook of Music Psychology*, edited by Susan Hallam, Ian Cross, and Michael Thaut, 390–400. Oxford: Oxford University Press, 2009.

Kiauleikytė, Laima. "Freimaurerlied atgarsiai L. G. Rėzos (1776–1840) kūryboje." *Kultūrologija* 10 (2003): 126–43.

Kiauleikytė, Laima, and Violeta Tumasonienė, eds. *Muzika 1940–1960, Dokumentų rinkinys.* Vilnius: Lietuvos Archyvų Generalinė Direkcija, 1992.

Kiik, Heino. "Õitsiöö mõtteid." *Sirp ja Vasar*, June 17, 1988, 3.

Kiin, Sirje, Rein Ruutsoo, and Andres Tarand, eds. *40 kirja lugu.* Tallinn: Olion, 1990.

Kippar, Pille. "Osalemisrõõmust." *Sirp ja Vasar*, September 28, 1979, 7.

Klotiņš, Arnolds. "Folklora un dejas." *Literatūra un Māksla*, April 22, 1988, 4–6.

Koidula, Lydia. *Luuletused*. Tallinn: Eesti Raamat, 1969.

Koik, Lembit. *Balti kett*. Tallinn: Eesti Entsüklopeedia Kirjastus, 2004.

Kopelev, Lev. "Ligo- znachit radost.'" *Druzhba Narodov* 7 (1966): 251–53.

Korsakas, K., ed. *Lietuvių tautosaka*. 5 vols. Vilnius: Valstybinė Politinės ir Mokslinės Literatūros Leidykla, 1962–68.

Krauklis, Voldemārs. "Kara laika atmiņas." *Latviešu Strēlnieki* 29 (1939): 2919.

Kreutz, G., S. Bongard, S. Rohrmann, V. Hodapp, and D. Grebe. "Effects of Choir Singing or Listening on Secretory Immunoglobulin A, Cortisol, and Emotional State." *Journal of Behavioral Medicine* 27 (2004): 623–35.

Kreutzwald, Friedrich Reinhold. *Kalevipoeg: An Ancient Estonian Tale*. Translated by George Kurman. Moorestown, NJ: Symposia Press, 1982.

Krikščiūnas, Povilas. "Dar neišdainuotos visos dainos." *Kultūros Barai* 235, no. 7 (1984): 39–42.

Kruks, Segejs. *Par mūziku skaistu un melodisku! Padomju kultūras politika, 1932–1964*. Riga: Neptuns, 2008.

Krūmiņš, Andrejs. "Savstarpēji saprasties!" *Padomju Jaunatne*, December 30, 1986, 3.

Kšanienė, Daiva. *Muzika Mažojoje Lietuvoje: Lietuvių ir vokiečių kultūrų sąveika (XVI a.–XX a. 4 dešimtmetis)*. Klaipėda, Lithuania: Mažosios Lietuvos Fondas, Klaipėdos Universiteto Leidykla, 2003.

Kubilius, Vytautas, ed. *The Amber Lyre: Eighteenth–Twentieth-Century Lithuanian Poetry*. Moscow: Raduga Publishers, 1983.

Kuresoo, Ly, ed. *Kostke, laulud, eesti keeles*. Tallinn: Eesti Muusikaühing, 1990.

Kurin, Richard. *Reflections of a Culture Broker: A View from the Smithsonian*. Washington, DC: Smithsonian Institution Press, 1997.

Kursīte, Janīna. "Atslēgas vārds—Jāņi: Folklorā, dzīvē, fotogrāfijās." In *Jāņu fotoalbums*, edited by Pēteris and Ligita Leja Korsaks, 159–64. Riga: Norden, 2007.

Kushnir, Aleksandr. *100 magnitoal'bomov sovetskogo roka, 1977–1991: 15 let podpol'noi zvukozapisi*. Moscow: Lean, Agraf, Kraft, 1999.

Kuutma, Kristin, ed. *Eesti laulud, mängud, pillilood ja tantsud*. Tallinn: Eesti Rahvakultuuri Keskus, 1992.

———. "Laulupeod rahvusliku identiteedi kandjana." *Maetagused* 1 (1996), http://folklore.ee/tagused/nr1/internet.htm. Accessed July 11, 2009.

Kvaskova, Valda. "Latvijas Valsts vēstures arhīva dokumenti—Dziesmu svētku tradīcijas glabātāji." *Latvijas Arhīvi* 2 (2008): 69–105.

Laar, Mart. *Äratajad: Rahvuslik ärkamisaeg Eestis 19. sajandil ja selle kandjad.* Tallinn: Grenader, 2006.

Laar, Mart, Urmas Ott, and Sirje Endre, eds. *Teine Eesti: Eeslava. Eesti iseseisvuse taassünd 1986–1991. Dokumendid, kõned, artiklid.* Tallinn: SE&JS, 1996.

———. *Teine Eesti: Eesti iseseisvuse taassünd, 1986–1991.* Tallinn: SE&JS, 1996.

Labi, Kanni. "Isamaalaulud ja okupatsioonirežiim—nostalgia, utoopia ja reaalsus." *Methis* 7 (2011): 109–21.

Lancere, Gita. "Kādi mēs to sagaidīsim?" *Cīņa,* July 6, 1988, 3.

Landsbergis, Vytautas. *Laisvės byla 1990–1991: Kalbos, pranešimai, užrašai, laiškai, pokalbiai, interviu, įvairūs dokumentai.* Vilnius: Lietuvos Aidas, 1992.

———. *Lithuania Independent Again.* Translated by Anthony Packer and Eimutis Šova. Seattle: University of Washington Press, 2000.

———. "Maironis dainius. Kalba konferencijoje Maironio lietuvių literatūros muziejuje, Kaunas 2002-11-14." Lietuvos Respublikos Seimas, http://www3.lrs.lt/pls/inter/w5_show?p_r=914&p_d=21836&p_k=1. Accessed September 16, 2012.

———. "Maironis ir muzika." In *Maironis,* edited by Jonas Lankutis, 179–84. Vilnius: Vaga, 1990.

———, ed. *Nauji dokumentai apie Sausio 13-ąją.* Vilnius: Baltijos Kopija, 2003.

Lane, Thomas. *Lithuania: Stepping Westward.* New York: Routledge, 2001.

Lapiņš, J., ed. *Ausekļa kopoti raksti.* Riga: A Gulbja Apgādībā, 1923.

Latviešu kordziesmas antoloģija. 12 vols. Riga: SIA SOL, 1997.

Latvija Šodien. 20 vols. Washington, DC: World Federation of Free Latvians, 1972–91.

Latvijas Padomju Enciklopēdija. 10 vols. Riga: Galvenā Enciklopēdiju Redakcija, 1981–1988.

Latvijas PSR Mazā Enciklopēdija. 3 vols. Riga: Zinātne, 1967.

Latvijas Tautas fronte: Gads pirmais. Riga: Latvijas Tautas Fronte, 1989.

Latvijas Tautas Fronte. *Tautas manifestācija "Par tiesisku valsti Latvijā" Piektdien, 1988. gada 7. oktobrī 15:00: Dziesmu teksti līdzdziedāšanai.* Songbook facsimile published in *Latvija Šodien* 1988, 85–87.

Latvju dziesmas tēvijai. N.p.: Latvijas Mūzikas Biedrība, 1990.

Laugaste, Eduard, ed. *Kui ma pääsen mõisast.* Tallinn: Eesti Raamat, 1983.

———. *Saaksin ma saksa sundijaks.* Tallinn: Eesti Raamat, 1976.

Lavery, Jason Edward. *The History of Finland*. Westport, CT: Greenwood Press, 2006.

Leegajus. *Leegajus*. LP record C30 05807–8 Stereo. N.p.: Melodiya, 1979.

Leesment, Jüri. "Mälestused öölaulupeost." *Postimees*, July 30, 2008, http://oolaulupidu.postimees.ee/?id=23390. Accessed July 6, 2010.

Leichter, Karl. "Eesti koorilaulu tekkimine, levik ja areng XIX sajandi esimesel poolel." In *Eesti Muusika*, edited by Artur Vahter, vol. 1, 26–35. Tallinn: Eesti Raamat, 1968.

——. "Muusikakultuur Eestis XVIII sajandil." In *Eesti Muusika*, edited by Artur Vahter, vol. 1, 17–25. Tallinn: Eesti Raamat, 1968,

Lešinska, Ieva. "Atrast pareizo balsi." *Latvija Šodien* (1987): 44–49.

Liebel-Weckowicz, Helen. "Nations and Peoples: Baltic-Russian History and the Development of Herder's Theory of Culture." *Canadian Journal of History* 21, no. 1 (1986): 1–23.

Liepiņš, Zigmārs, and Māra Zālīte. *Rokopera Lāčplēsis: Programma. Pirmizrāde 1988. g. 23. augustā Rīgā*. Riga: LPSR Valsts Filharmonija, 1988.

Lietuvių liaudies dainynas. Vilnius: Lietuvių Literatūros ir Tautosakos Institutas, 1980–.

Lieven, Anatol. *The Baltic Revolution: Estonia, Latvia, Lithuania, and the Path to Independence*. 2nd ed. New Haven, CT: Yale University Press, 1994.

Liidja, Marja. "Juttu Veljo Tormisega." *Õhtuleht*, November 23, 1974.

Liiv, Juhan. *Teosed: Proosa, Luule*. Tallinn: Eesti Riiklik Kirjastus, 1956.

Linčiuvienė, D., ed. *Kur giria žaliuoja II*. Vilnius: Vaga, 1970.

Linker, Damon. "The Reluctant Pluralism of J. G. Herder." *Review of Politics* 62, no. 2 (2000): 267–93.

Listopadskis, Marius. "Atrieda atidunda," *Ore*, December 1, 2003, http://www.ore.lt/article.php?action=get&id=200534. Accessed June 26, 2010.

Maironis. *Pavasario balsai*. Vilnius: Vaga, 1982.

——. *Raštai*. 3 vols. Vilnius: Vaga, 1987–88.

——. *Rinktiniai raštai*. 2 vols. Vilnius: Valstybinė Grožinės Literatūros Leidykla, 1956.

Manischewitz, J., ed. *Singing Revolution Special Program*. Unpublished sound recordings FP-1998–CT-0284 A and FP-1998–CT-0284 B. Washington, DC: Ralph Rinzler Folklife Archives and Collections, 2009.

Martin, Terry. *The Affirmative Action Empire: Nations and Nationalism in the Soviet Union, 1923–1939*. Ithaca, NY: Cornell University Press, 2001.

Mason, Laura. *Singing the French Revolution: Popular Culture and Politics, 1787–1799*. Ithaca, NY: Cornell University Press, 1996.

Matulevičienė, Saulė. "Iš Rasos šventės istorijos." *Liaudies kultūra*, no. 3 (2007): 64–69.

Mažioji Lietuviškoji Tarybinė Enciklopedija. 3 vols. Vilnius: Mintis, 1966–71.

Mazvērsīte, Daiga. *Pieskāriens: Raimonds Pauls un latviešu mūzikas kultūra*. Riga: Madris, 2006.

Medelis, Linas. "8 metai—ne viena diena." *Jaunimo Gretos* 8, no. 381 (1976): 13–19.

Medne-Romane, A. "Darba tautas cīņa ar apspiedēju latviešu vēstītājā folklorā." In *Folkloras Institūta Raksti* 1 (1950): 47–93.

Meie Repertuaar. Tallinn: ENSV Rahvaloomingu ja Kultuuritöö Teaduslik Metoodikakeskus, 1951–91.

Melgalvs, Māris. *Meldijās iešana: Dzejoļi, 1975–1980*. Riga: Liesma, 1980.

Mellupe, Anita. *Kamēr . . . Māris Sirmais un Latvija dzied!* Riga: Likteņstāsti, 2008.

Merkel, Garlieb. *Die Vorzeit Lieflands: Ein Denkmal des Pfaffen- und Rittergeistes*. 2 vols. Berlin: Vossische Buchhandlung, 1798–99. Retrieved from EEVA Tekstid, http://www.utlib.ee/ekollekt/eeva/. February 16, 2013.

———. [Merķelis, Garlībs]. "Par latviešu dzejas garu un dzeju." *Kultūrvēsturiski raksti*. Riga: Zvaigzne, 1992.

Merkelis, Aleksandras. *Didysis Varpininkas Vincas Kudirka*. Chicago: Vydūno Jaunimo Fondas, 1989.

Metso, Tiina. "German Influence on Estonian and Baltic German Corps Traditions in Tartu." *Acta Historica Tallinnensia* 8 (2004): 20–36.

Mikrofons 86. LP record C60 25223 007. Riga: Melodiya, 1986.

Mikrofons 89. LP record C60 29483 004. Riga: Melodiya, 1989.

Mikšytė, Regina. *Silvestras Valiūnas*. Vilnius: Vaga, 1978.

Miljan, Toivo. *Historical Dictionary of Estonia*. Lanham, MD: Scarecrow Press, 2004.

Mille, Astra. *Te un citadelē: Jānis Peters. Tumšsarkanā*. Riga: Atēna, 2006.

Milosz, Czeslaw. *The Captive Mind*. Translated by Jane Zielonko. New York: Vintage Books, 1990.

Miniotaite, G. *Nonviolent Resistance in Lithuania: A Story of Peaceful Liberation*. Boston, MA: Albert Einstein Institution, 2002.

Misiunas, Romuald J., and Rein Taagepera. *The Baltic States: Years of Dependence, 1940–1990*. Revised, expanded edition. Berkeley: University of California Press, 1993.

Mithen, Steven. *The Singing Neanderthals: The Origins of Music, Language, Mind, and Body*. Cambridge, MA: Harvard University Press, 2006.

Muižnieks, Nīls R. "The Daugavpils Hydro Station and 'Glasnost' in Latvia." *Journal of Baltic Studies* 18, no. 1 (1987): 63–70.

Muktupāvela, Laima. *Brāli brāli: Balsu burvji brāļi Kokari.* Riga: Dienas Grāmata, 2008.

Muktupāvels, Valdis, ed. *Rasa: Prūšos manas kājas autas.* Riga: Latvijas Kultūras Fonds, 1989.

———. "Varas un pretestības valoda, zīmes un simboli 20. gs. 80. gadu folklorisma mūzikā un muzicēšanā." In *Kultūra un vara,* edited by Janīna Kursīte et al., 92–102. Riga: LU Akadēmiskais Apgāds, 2007.

Müller, Hans V. "Die 'Preußische Blumenlese' von 1775, eine Quelle von Herders 'Volksliedern.'" *Zentralblatt für Bibliothekswesen* 34, no. 5/7 (1917): 182–88.

Nakienė, Austė. "Lietuvių folkloro teatras: Autentiškas dainavimas, metaforinė išraiška ir įspūdingas scenovaizdis." *Tautosakos Darbai* 22 (2005): 166–79.

———. "'Lietuva, tu mums šventa!' Antitarybinis rokas ir patriotinis hiphopas." *Tautosakos Darbai* 32 (2006): 180–88.

"Nākotnē ejamais ceļš: Baltijas studentu dziesmu svētki Gaudeamus." *Latvija Šodien* (1988): 69–70.

Narbutienė, Onė. *Juozas Naujalis: Straipsniai. Laiškai. Dokumentai. Amžininkų atsiminimai. Straipsniai apie kūrybą.* Vilnius: Vaga, 1968.

Nirk, Endel, ed. *Eesti kirjanduse ajalugu: XIX sajandi teine pool.* 5 vols. Eesti Kirjanduse Ajalugu. Tallinn: Eesti Raamat, 1966.

Niženkaitis, Alvydas. "Jogailos įvaizdis lietuvių visuomenėje." *Lietuvių Atgimimo istorijos studijos* 17 (2001): 68–102.

Oginskaitė, Rūta. *Nes nežinojau, kad tu nežinai: Knyga apie Vytautą Kernagį.* Vilnius: Tyto Alba, 2009.

Oinas, Felix. *Essays on Russian Folklore and Mythology.* Columbus, OH: Slavica Publishers, 1984.

Oinas, Felix J. *Surematu Kalevipoeg.* Edited by Jaan Undusk. Tallinn: K/K, 1994.

Ojakäär, Valter. *Vaibunud viiside kaja: Eesti levimuusika ajaloost.* Tallinn: Eesti Entsüklopeediakirjastus, 2000.

Ojaveski, Toivo, Mart Puust, and A. Põldmäe, eds. *130 aastat eesti laulupidusid.* Tallinn: Talmar & Põhi, 2002.

Olson, Laura. *Performing Russia: Folk Revival and Russian Identity.* London: Routledge Curzon, 2004.

Pabriks, Artis, and Aldis Purs. *Latvia: The Challenges of Change.* New York: Routledge, 2001.

Päts, Konstantin. "Aulikud piduosalised!" *Päevaleht* (June 29, 1990): 1.

Pauls, Raimonds. *Edgars Liepiņš: Rīga toreiz—Rīga šodien.* 2 LP record set. Hamburg: Kultūras Glābšanas Biedrība, 1981.

———. *Mūžīgais unisons.* LP record. Hamburg: Kultūras Glābšanas Biedrība, 1983.

Peacock, James. "Geertz's Concept of Culture in Historical Context: How He Saved the Day and Maybe the Century." In *Clifford Geertz by His Colleagues,* edited by Richard Shweder and Byron Good, 52–62. Chicago: University of Chicago Press, 2005.

Pelše, R., et al., eds. *Latviešu padomju folklora.* Riga: Latvijas PSR Zinātņu Akadēmijas Izdevniecība, 1953.

Pērkone, Inga, Zane Balčus, Agnese Surkova, and Beāte Vītola. *Inscenējumu realitāte: Latvijas aktierkino vēsture.* Riga: Mansards, 2011.

Pērkons. *Dziesmu izlase, 1981–1982.* MRCD 006. N.p.: Microphone Records, 1994.

Peters, Jānis. "Dvēseles acugaisma." In *Paliekamdziesma: Krišjānim Baronam 150,* edited by Ligita Bībere and Māra Misiņa, 221–23. Riga: Liesma, 1987.

Peterson, Christian Jaak. "Christfrid Ganander Thomassons Finnische Mythologie, aus dem Schwedischen übersetzt, völlig umgearbeitet und mit Anmerkungen," *Beiträge zur genaurem Kenntniß der ehstnischen Sprache* 14 (1821).

Petrikaitė, Jūratė. "Silvestro Valiūno 'Birutės' folkloriniai variantai." *Tautosakos Darbai* 25 (2008): 175–83.

Petrone, Karen. *Life Has Become More Joyous, Comrades: Celebrations in the Time of Stalin.* Bloomington: Indiana University Press, 2000.

Pierson, Steven J. "We Sang Ourselves Free: Musical Experience and Development among Christian Estonians from Repression to Independence." In *The Baltic Countries under Occupation: Soviet and Nazi Rule, 1939–1991,* edited by Anu Mai Kõll, 385–418. Stockholm: Acta Universitatis Stockholmiensis, 2003

Pillau, Endel, ed. *Eestimaa kuum suvi 1988: Ajakirjanduskroonika.* Tallinn: Olion, 1989.

Pirmee wispahrigee Latweeschu dzeedaschanas swehtki Rihgâ no 26ta lihdz 29 juhnijam 1873. Facsimile printing, n.d. Latvju Mūsika, 1973.

Plakans, Andrejs. *A Concise History of the Baltic States.* Cambridge: Cambridge University Press, 2011.

———, ed. *Experiencing Totalitarianism: The Invasion and Occupation of Latvia by the USSR and Nazi Germany, 1939–1991: A Documentary History.* Bloomington, IN: Authorhouse, 2007.

———. "Peasants, Intellectuals, and Nationalism in the Russian Baltic Provinces, 1820–90." *Journal of Modern History* 46 (1974): 445–75.

[Plakans, Andrew]. *The Latvians: A Short History.* Stanford: Hoover Institution Press, 1995.

Plotke, I., et al., eds. *Padomju Latvijas 15 gadi*. Riga: Latvijas Valsts Izdevniecība, 1955.

Pociulpaitė, A. "Kraštotyrininkų dešimtoji." *Literatūra ir Menas*, August 14, 1971, 13.

Podnieks, Juris. *Homeland*. DVD. Riga: Juris Podnieks Studio, 2005.

———. *Vai viegli būt jaunam? Is It Easy to Be Young?* DVD. Riga: Jura Podnieka Studija, 2007.

Põldmäe, Mare. "Kaks laulupidu, 1947 ja 1950." *Teater. Muusika. Kino* 3 (1990): 32–35.

Põldmäe, Rudolf. *Esimene Eesti üldlaulupidu 1869*. Tallinn: Eesti Raamat, 1969.

Pollock, Ethan. *Stalin and the Soviet Science Wars*. Princeton: Princeton University Press, 2006.

Poškaitis, Kazys. *Lietuvių šokio kelias į sceną*. Vilnius: Vaga, 1985.

Pozdniakovas, A. "Kažkas atsitiko." VHS videocassette BBV 015. [Vilnius]: Bomba Video, 1996.

Priede, Gunārs. "Trīspadsmitā." In *Septiņas lugas*, 333–77. Riga: Liesma, 1968.

Puderbaugh, David. "How Choral Music Saved a Nation." *Choral Journal* 49, no. 4 (2008): 28–43.

Puhvel, Madli. *Symbol of Dawn: The Life and Times of the Nineteenth-Century Estonian Poet Lydia Koidula*. Tartu, Estonia: Tartu University Press, 1995.

Pumpuriņš, Tālis. *Sarkanbaltsarkanās—Latvijas karoga krāsas: Pētījumi, atmiņas un dokumenti par Latvijas valsts karoga tapšanas vēsturi*. Cesis, Latvia: Cēsu Vēstures un Mākslas Muzejs, 2000.

Purpurs, Konstantīns. "Taisni uz priekšu pa brīvības ielu 14.6.1988." *Latvija Šodien* (1988): 47–53.

Purs, Aldis. "Soviet in Form, Local in Content: Elite Repression and Mass Terror in the Baltic States, 1940–1953." In *Stalinist Tterror in Eastern Europe*, edited by Kevin McDermott and Matthew Stibbe, 19–38. Manchester: Manchester University Press, 2010.

Radzobe, Silvija. "Song of Renewal—and the Tradition of Political Mystery." In *Latvia and Latvians: A People and a State in Ideas, Images, and Symbols*, edited by Ausma Cimdiņa and Deniss Hanovs, 89–106. Riga: Zinātne, 2010.

Rainis, J. *Raksti*. 17 vols. Västerås, Sweden: Ziemeļblāzma, 1952.

Rainis, Jānis. *Kopoti raksti*. 30 vols. Riga: Zinātne, 1980.

Ramanauskaitė, Egidija. "Lithuanian Youth Culture versus Soviet Culture." In *The Baltic Countries under Occupation: Soviet and Nazi Rule, 1939–1991*, edited by Anu Mai Kõll, 341–46. Stockholm: Acta Universitatis Stockholmiensis, 2003.

Ramet, Sabrina, ed. *Rocking the State: Rock Music and Politics in Eastern Europe and Russia.* Boulder, CO: Westview Press, 1994.

Ramoškaitė, Živilė. "Antrojo Pasaulinio karo ir pokario dainos." In *Lietuvių liaudies dainynas* 19:7–63. Vilnius: Lietuvių Literatūros ir Tautosakos Institutas, 2005.

———. "Pirmasis tarptautinis." *Pergalė,* no. 10 (1987): 181.

Rauda, Māris. "In Memoriam: Klāvs Elsbergs, 1958.3.I–1987.5.II." *Latvija Šodien* (1987): 49–50.

———. "'Stalin, we are following you . . . ': The Poet Jānis Sudrabkalns." *Occupied Latvia Today* (1986): 46–53, 103.

Raun, Toivo U. *Estonia and the Estonians.* Stanford: Hoover Institution Press, 2001.

———. "Nineteenth- and Early Twentieth-Century Estonian Nationalism Revisited." *Nations and Nationalism* 9, no. 1 (2003): 129–47.

Raun, Toivo U., and Andrejs Plakans. "The Estonian and Latvian National Movements: An Assessment of Miroslav Hroch's Model." *Journal of Baltic Studies* 21, no. 2 (1990): 131–44.

Reidzāne, Beatrise. "Zinātniece laikmeta ainā (personīgas pieredzes stāsts): Elzai Kokarei—90." *Letonica* 21 (2011): 134–35.

Remess, Andžils, and Jānis Peters. *Maestro: Raimonds Pauls.* Riga: Jumava, 2010.

Rēza, Ludvikas. *Lietuvių liaudies dainos.* 2 vols. Vilnius: Valstybinė Grožinės Literatūros Leidykla, 1958–64.

[Rhesa, Ludwig Jedemin]. *Prutena, oder preussische Volkslieder und andere vaterländische Dichtungen.* Königsberg: Heinrich Degen, 1809. Reprint. Downloaded from books.google.com, July 7, 2008.

Rinne, Harri. *Laulev revolutsioon: Eesti rokipõlvkonna ime.* Translated by Sander Liivak. Tallinn: Varrak, 2008.

Rokpelnis, Fricis. *Vējš cērtas vaigā: Izlase.* Riga: Liesma, 1969.

Röllecke, Heinz. "Über Volks- und geistliche Lieder bei Herder." In *Johann Gottfried Herder: Aspekte seines Lebenswerkes,* edited by Martin Kessler and Volker Leppin, 115–28. Berlin: De Gruyter, 2005.

Rosenplänter, Johann Heinrich, ed. *Beiträge zur genauern Kenntniß der ehstnischen Sprache.* 20 vols. Pärnu, Estonia: n.p., 1813–1832. Retrieved from EEVA Tekstid, February 9, 2013.

Rožlapa, Maija, ed. *Mana tauta dziedāja, tāpēc nenosala: XX Vispārējie dziesmu svētki, Koru koncertu dziesmu teksti.* Riga: E. Melngaiļa Tautas Mākslas Centrs, Zinātne, 1990.

Rudaks, Uldis. *Rokupācija: Latviešu rokmūzikas vēsture.* Riga: Dienas Grāmata, 2008.

Ruks, Māris. *No zemes un debesīm: Pērkons.* Riga: Antava, 2006.

Rummo, Paul. "Ühe laulu lugu." *Looming* 1 (1961): 111–28

Rutiku, Siret. "Über die Rolle des deutschen Kirchenliedes in der estnischen Kulturgeschichte." In *Kulturgeschichte der baltischen Länder in der Frühen Neuzeit, Mit einem Ausblick in die Moderne,* edited by Klaus Garber and Martin Klöker, 245–62. Tübingen: Max Niemeyer Verlag, 2003.

Rüütel, Ingrid. "About Finno Ugric Folk Music Activities in Estonia." *Proceedings of the Estonian Academy of Sciences; Social Sciences* 39, no. 1 (1990): 18–25.

———. "Association 'Baltica'—Independent Member of CIOFF." In *Baltica '91: Latvija,* 3–5. Riga: E. Melngaiļa Tautas Mākslas Centrs, 1991.

———, ed. *Eesti uuemad laulumängud.* 2 vols. Tallinn: Eesti Raamat, 1980–83.

———. "The Main Principles of 'Baltica '89'" In *Baltica '89,* edited by K. Kuutma, 16–20. Tallinn: Eesti Kultuurikomitee, 1989.

Ryback, Timothy W. *Rock around the Bloc: A History of Rock Music in Eastern Europe and the Soviet Union.* New York: Oxford University Press, 1990.

Saja, Kazys, et al., eds. *Lietuva: 1991.01.13: Dokumentai, liudijimai, atgarsiai.* Vilnius: Valstybinis Leidybos Centras, 1991.

Salumets, Vello. *Rock-rapsoodia.* Tallinn: Eesti Entsüklopeedia Kirjastus, 1998.

Sanger, Kerran L. *"When the Spirit Says Sing!" The Role of Freedom Songs in the Civil Rights Movement.* New York: Garland, 1995.

Sarv, Vaike. "Artist in the Role of Contemporary Shaman." In *Traditional Belief Today: Conference Dedicated to the Ninetieth Anniversary of Oskar Loorits,* 132. Tartu: Estonian Academy of Sciences, 1990.

———. "Leegajus." *Sirp ja Vasar,* October 20, 1978, 11.

Sauka, Donatas. *Lietuvių tautosaka.* Vilnius: Mokslas, 1982.

Schwartz, Katrina. *Nature and National Identity after Communism: Globalizing the Ethnoscape.* Pittsburgh: University of Pittsburgh Press, 2006.

Seliukaitė, Irena. "Kraštotyros baruose." In *Norbertas Vėlius,* edited by Perla Vitkuvienė, 133–38. Vilnius: Mintis, 1999.

Semenov, Grigorii, ed. *Rodnye zvuki: Sbornik russkikh gimnov I narodnykh pesen dlia nachal'nykh uchilishch.* Riga: Ernst Plate, 1898.

Senn, Alfred Erich. *Gorbachev's Failure in Lithuania.* New York: St. Martin's Press, 1995.

———. *Lithuania Awakening.* Berkeley: University of California Press, 1990.

Šepetys, Lionginas. "Tarybinė Kultūra—Kultūra liaudžiai, liaudies kultūra." *Tiesa,* January 28, 1983, 2.

———. *Neprarastoji karta: Siluetai ir spalvos*. Vilnius: Lietuvos Rašytojų Sąjungos Leidykla, 2005.

Šešplaukis, Alfonsas. *J. G. Herderis ir baltų tautos: Mokslinė studija*. Vilnius: Mokslo ir Enciklopedijų Leidykla, 1995.

[Sestie] VI. Latvju vispārējie dziesmu un muzikas svētki. Riga: [Sesto] Latvju Dziesmu un Muzikas Svētku Preses un Propagandas Sekcijas Izd., 1926. Retrieved from http://dziesmusvetki.lndb.lv/, February 9, 2013.

Sharp, Gene. "The New Challenge." In *The Baltic Way to Freedom: Non-Violent Struggle of the Baltic States in Global Context*, edited by Jānis Škapars, 423–26. Riga: Zelta Grauds, 2005.

———. "198 Methods of Nonviolent Action." Albert Einstein Institution, http://www.aeinstein.org/organizations103a.html . Accessed February 9, 2013.

———. *There Are Realistic Alternatives*. Boston, MA: Albert Einstein Institution, 2003.

Shtromas, Aleksandras. "The Baltic States as Soviet Republics: Tensions and Contradictions." In *The National Self-Determination of Estonia, Latvia, and Lithuania*, edited by Graham Smith, 86–117. London: Macmillan, 1994.

Šidiškis, Tadas. "Keturiasdešimt metų su žygeiviais." *Liaudies kultūra*, no. 3 (2008): 56–63.

Sirutavičius, Vladas. "Šventės nacionalizavimas: 'Tautos šventės' atsiradimas Lietuvos respublikoje XX amžiaus 4–ajame dešimtmetyje." *Lietuvių atgimimo istorijos studijos* 17 (2001): 133–45.

Skandinieki. *Divi duči rotaļu kopā ar Skandiniekiem*. LP record C30 18795–6. Riga: Melodiya, 1982.

Smeijsters, Henk, and José van den Hurk. "Music Therapy Helping to Work through Grief and Finding a Personal Identity." *Journal of Music Therapy* 36, no. 3 (1999): 222–52.

Šmidchens, Guntis. *A Baltic Music: The Folklore Movement in Lithuania, Latvia, and Estonia, 1968–1991*. Ph.D. diss., Indiana University, 1996.

———. "Folklorism Revisited." *Journal of Folklore Research* 36, no. 1 (1999): 51–70.

———. "Herder and Lithuanian Folksongs." *Lituanus* 56, no. 1 (2010): 51–67.

———. "National Heroic Narratives in the Baltics as a Source for Nonviolent Political Action." *Slavic Review* 66, no. 3 (2007): 484–508.

———. "Notes on the Latvian National Hero, Lāčplēsis." *Journal of Folklore Research* 43, no. 3 (2006): 217–80.

Smith, Anthony David. *The Cultural Foundations of Nations: Hierarchy, Covenant, and Republic*. Malden, MA: Blackwell Publishing, 2008.

————. *Ethno-Symbolism and Nationalism: A Cultural Approach.* Florence, KY: Routledge, 2009.

————. "War and Ethnicity: The Role of Warfare in the Formation, Self-Images, and Cohesion of Ethnic Communities." *Ethnic and Racial Studies* 4, no. 4 (1981): 375–97.

Smith, David J. *Estonia: Independence and European Integration.* New York: Routledge, 2001.

Smurr, Robert. *Perceptions of Nature, Expressions of Nation: An Environmental History of Estonia.* Saarbrücken, Germany: Lambert Academic Publishing, 2009.

Soboleva, N. A. "The Composition of State Anthems of the Russian Empire and the Soviet Union." *Russian Social Science Review* 50, no. 2 (2009): 67–94.

Solbrig, Ingeborg. "Herder and the 'Harlem Renaissance' of Black Culture in America: The Case of the 'Neger-Idyllen.'" In *Herder Today: Contributions from the International Herder Conference, Nov. 5–8, 1987, Stanford, California,* edited by Kurt Mueller-Vollmer, 402–14. Berlin: Walter de Gruyter, 1990.

Sovetskoe obshchestvo segodnia: Voporsosy i otvety. Moscow: Izdatelstvo Politicheskoi Literatury, 1987.

Sponsel, Leslie E., and Thomas Gregor, eds. *The Anthropology of Peace and Nonviolence.* Boulder, CO: Lynne Rienner, 1994.

Stahnke, Astrida. "A Note about Vizma Belševica, a Latvian Poetess." *Lituanus* 47, no. 3 (2001): 5–10.

Staliūnas, Darius. "Žuvusių karių kultas tarpukario Lietuvoje." *Lietuvių Atgimimo istorijos studijos* 17 (2001): 120–32.

Stalte, Helmī, ed. *Līgo: Gadskārtu ieražas.* Riga: E. Melngaiļa Tautas Mākslas Centrs, 1989.

Stanevičius, Simonas. *Dainos žemaičių.* Vilnius: Lietuvių Literatūros ir Tautosakos Institutas, 1999.

————. *Raštai.* Vilnius: Vaga, 1967.

Starr, S. Frederick. *Red and Hot: The Fate of Jazz in the Soviet Union, 1917–1991.* New York: Limelight Editions, 1994.

Stavenhagen, Kurt. "Herder in Riga." *Abhandlungen des Herder-Instituts zu Riga.* Riga: G. Löffler, 1925.

Steger, Manfred. *Gandhi's Dilemma: Nonviolent Principles and Nationalist Power.* New York: St Martin's Press, 2000.

Stender, Gotthard Friedrich (Vecais Stenders). *Bildu ābice.* Riga: Liesma, 1977.

————. *Ziņģes.* Riga: Zinātne, 1990.

Stige, Brynjulf, Gary Ansdell, Cochavit Elefant, and Mercédès Pavlicevic, eds. *Where Music Helps: Community Music Therapy in Action and Reflection.* Burlington, VT: Ashgate, 2010.

Stradiņš, Jānis. "Par Jāņu svinēšanu un Jāņu apkarošanu: Raksts laikrakstā 'Lauku Avīze' 1988. gada 18. jūnijā." In *Trešā atmoda: Raksti un runas 1988.–1990. gadā Latvijā un par Latviju,* 302–6. Riga: Zinātne, 1992.

Street, Joe. *The Culture War in the Civil Rights Movement.* Gainesville: University Press of Florida, 2007.

Strielkūnas, Jonas. *Vėjas rugiuos.* Vilnius: Vaga, 1971.

Strobach, Hermann. "Herders Volksliedbegriff: Geschichte und Gegenwärtige Bedeutung." *Jahrbuch für Volkskunde und Kulturgeschichte* 21 (1978): 9–55.

Strods, Heinrihs. "Non-Violent Resistance in Latvia (1945–1985)." In *Regaining Independence: Non-Violent Resistance in Latvia, 1945–1991,* edited by Valdis Blūzma et al., 61–166. Riga: Latvian Academy of Sciences, 2009.

———. *Politiskā cenzūra Latvijā, 1940–1990.* 2 vols. Riga: Jumava, 2010.

Subačius, Paulius V. "Inscribing Orality: The First Folklore Editions in the Baltic States." *European Studies* 26 (2008): 79–90.

Šuvcāne, Valda Marija. *Lībiešu ciems, kura vairs nav.* Riga: Jumava, 2002.

Sužiedėlis, Saulius. "The Military Mobilization Campaigns of 1943 and 1944 in German-Occupied Lithuania: Contrasts in Resistance and Collaboration." *Journal of Baltic Studies* 21, no. 1 (1990): 33–52.

Švābe, Arveds. *Latvijas vēsture, 1800–1914.* Stockholm: Daugava, 1958.

———, ed. *Latvju enciklopēdija.* 3 vols. Stockholm: Apgāds Trīs Zvaigznes, 1950–1955.

Taagepera, Rein. *Estonia: Return to Independence.* Boulder, CO: Westview Press, 1993.

———. *The Death of Jüri Kukk: A Case Study in Erratic Repression.* Irvine: University of California, 1981.

———. *Softening without Liberalization in the Soviet Union: The Case of Jüri Kukk.* Lanham, MD: University Press of America, 1984.

Tamman, W. [Voldemar], ed. *Kooli laulmiseraamat. Metoodiliselt korraldatud ja piltidega kaunistatud kooli laulmise materjaal.* Tartu, Estonia: Postimees, 1920.

W. Tamman and Juhan Aavik. *Kooli-koor. I jagu.* Tartu, Estonia: V. Tamman, 1928.

———. *Kooli leelo VI.* Tartu, Estonia: Loodus, 1936

Tampere, Herbert, ed. *Eesti rahvalaule viisidega.* 5 vols. Tallinn: Valgus, 1956–65.

Tampere, Herbert, Erna Tampere, and Ottilie Kõiva, eds. *Anthology of*

Estonian Traditional Music: Recordings from the Estonian Folklore Archives. Five CDs, EKMCD 005. Tartu: Estonian Literary Museum, 2003.

Tarm, Michael, and Mari-Ann Rikken, eds. *Documents from Estonia: Articles, Speeches, Resolutions, Letters, Editorials, Interviews Concerning Recent Developments from April 1986 to March 1989.* New York: Estonian American National Council, 1989.

Taruskin, Richard. *Defining Russia Musically: Historical and Hermeneutical Essays.* Princeton: Princeton University Press, 1997.

Tarybų Lietuvos Enciklopedija. 4 vols. Vilnius: Vyriausioji Enciklopedijų Redakcija, 1985–88.

Tedre, Ülo, and Veljo Tormis, eds. *Regilaulik.* Tallinn: Eesti Raamat, 1975.

Toelken, Barre. *The Dynamics of Folklore.* Boston: Houghton Mifflin, 1979.

Tõnurist, Igor. "Laaliku minu isädä. . . . ." *Sirp ja Vasar,* August 13, 1971, 6.

———. "'Ma laulan mere murusta!': Ingrid Rüütel and Estonian Folklore Movement." In *Individual and Collective in Traditional Culture,* edited by Triinu Ojamaa, Andreas Kalkun, and Ingrid Rüütel, 219–36. Tartu, Estonia: Eesti Kirjandusmuuseumi Etnomusikoloogia Osakond, 2006.

Tormis, Veljo. *Lauldud sõna.* Tartu, Estonia: Ülikooli Kirjastus, 2000.

———. *Litany to Thunder.* ECM New Series 1687. Munich: ECM Records, 1999.

Trinkūnas, Jonas. "Ramuvai—20 metų." *Ramuva* (1989): 5.

Troitsky, Artemy. *Back in the USSR: The True Story of Rock in Russia.* Boston: Faber and Faber, 1987.

[Tryliktoji] XIII Lietuvos tautinė dainų šventė. LP records C1031343001 and C1031345006. N.p.: Melodiya, 1990.

Tucker, Robert C. *The Soviet Political Mind: Stalinism and Post-Stalin Change.* New York: W. W. Norton, 1971.

Tumavičiūtė, Irena. "Jurgis Zauerveinas—skelbęs santaiką visam pasauliui." In *Nuo Mažvydo iki Vydūno: Karaliaučiaus krašto šviesuoliai,* edited by Vytautas Šilas, 109–18. Vilnius: Mintis, 1998.

Tusty, James, and Maureen Tusty. DVD. *The Singing Revolution.* N.p.: Docurama Films, 2007.

The Twenty-First Estonian Song and the Fourteenth Folk Dance Festival: A Reference Book. Translated by Ülle Leis. Tallinn: Eesti Raamat, 1990.

Uiga, Uno. "Veljo Tormis ja rahvalaul." *Sirp ja Vasar,* May 18, 1973.

Undusk, Jaan. "Hamanni ja Herderi vaim eesti kirjanduse edendajana: Sünedohhi printsiip." *Keel ja Kirjandus,* no. 9 (1995): 577–87.

Vahter, Artur, and Jüri Variste, eds. *Eesti koorilooming.* 2 vols. Tallinn: Eesti Riiklik Kirjastus, 1954–55.

Vaita, H. "Latviešu tautas meteoroloģija." *Folkloras Institūta Raksti* 1 (1950): 239–78.

Valiūnas, Silvestras. *Ant marių krašto*. Vilnius: Vaga, 1976.

Väljaste, Elme, and Enno Selirand, eds. *Eestimaa laul 88: Kõned, fotod, meenutused, CD*. Tallinn: MTÜ Eestimaa Laul, 2011.

Valk, Heinz. "Laulev revolutsioon." *Sirp ja Vasar*, June 17, 1988, 3.

———. "Mäletused öölaulupeost." *Postimees*, August 2, 2008. http://oolaulupidu.postimees.ee/24243/maletused-oolaulupeost-heinz-valk/. Accessed October 12, 2012.

Vārpa, Igors. *Latviešu karavīrs zem Krievijas impērijas, Padomju Krievijas un PSRS karogiem*. Riga: Nordik, 2006.

Vāvere, Klass. "Latviešu roks 13, 'Lāčplēsis.'" *Liesma* (January 1, 1990): 18.

Vāvere, Klass, and Signe Neimane. *Līvi*. [Riga]: Tandems, 1997.

Vėlius, Norbertas. "Ekspedicija Kernavėje." *Literatūra ir Menas*, August 23, 1969, 9.

———. *The World Outlook of the Ancient Balts*. Translated by Dalija Tekorienė. Vilnius: Mintis, 1989.

Vėlius, Norbertas, et al., eds. *Gervėčiai: Monografija*. Vilnius: Mintis, 1989.

Venclova, Antanas. *Raštai*. 3 vols. Vilnius: Valstybinė Grožinės Literatūros Leidykla, 1955.

"Veronika." *Liaudies kultūra*, no. 1 (2007): 55–56.

Vesilind, Priit. *The Singing Revolution*. Tallinn: Varrak, 2009.

Vieru, Grigore. *Piektdienas zvaigzne: Dzejoļi*. Translated by Imants Ziedonis. Riga: Liesma, 1988.

Viires, Ants. "Pseudomythology in Estonian Publicity in the Nineteenth and Twentieth Century." *Ethnologia Europaea* 21, no. 2 (1991): 137–43.

Vīķe-Freiberga, Vaira. "Family Rituals and Celebrations in Latvian Folklore." In *Baltica '91. Starptautiskais folkloras festivāls / International Folklore Festival 9.–14. VII. 1991*, 14–17. Riga: E. Melngaiļa Tautas Mākslas Centrs, 1991.

Vilceniece, Māra. "Folkloras dzīve Latvijā." In *Latvija Šodien* (1984): 84–89. Rockville, MD: World Federation of Free Latvians, 1984.

Viliūnas, Giedrius. "Vytauto Didžiojo kultas tarpukario Lietuvoje." *Lietuvių Atgimimo istorijos studijos* 17 (2001): 68–102.

Vince, Laima. *Lenin's Head on a Platter: An American Student's Diary from the Final Years of the Soviet Union, September 1988–August 1989*. Vilnius: Lithuanian Writers' Union Publishers, 2008.

Vinkel, A., ed. *Eesti kirjanduse ajalugu*. Vol. 1. Tallinn: Eesti Raamat, 1965.

Vinkel, Aarne. *Martin Körber: Elutee ja töö*. Tallinn: Eesti Teaduste Akadeemia Underi ja Tuglase Kirjanduskeskus, 1994.

Vistdal, Oskar. *Georg Sauerwein: Europear og døl: Ein dokumentasjon.* Bergen: Norsk Bokreidingslag, 2000.

Vitkuvienė, Perla, ed. *Norbertas Vėlius.* Vilnius: Mintis, 1999.

Vītoliņš, Jēkabs, ed. *Bērnu dziesmu cikls. Bēru dziesmas.* Riga: Zinātne, 1971.

Vītoliņš, Jēkabs, and L. Krasinska. *Latviešu mūzikas vēsture.* Riga: Liesma, 1972.

"Volksliederarchiv." Müller-Lüdenscheidt-Verlag, http://www.volksliederarchiv.de/. Accessed September 13, 2011.

Wahi, Jaan, ed. *Uued Sõjalaulud.* Tartu, Estonia: K. Jaik, 1914.

Wihtols, J., ed. *Pamahziba kà V. Latweeschu Wispahrigo dseesmu swehtku dseesmas jamahza.* Jelgawa: G. Landsbergs, 1904. Retrieved from http://dziesmusvetki.lndb.lv/, February 9, 2013.

Winkler, Reinhold Johann. *Eesti-ma Ma-wäe söa-laulud.* Tallinn: Gressel, 1807. Retrieved from EEVA Tekstid, August 16, 2010.

Wolverton, Vance. "Breaking the Silence: Choral Music of the Baltic Republics. Part One: Estonia." *Choral Journal* 38, no. 7 (1998): 21–28.

———. "Breaking the Silence: Choral Music of the Baltic Republics. Part Two: Latvia." *Choral Journal* 38, no. 9 (1998): 37–44.

———. "Breaking the Silence: Choral Music of the Baltic Republics. Part Three: Lithuania." *Choral Journal* 38, no. 10 (1998): 23–29.

Wortman, Richard S. *Scenarios of Power.* 2 vols. Princeton: Princeton University Press, 1995.

Yurchak, Alexei. *Everything Was Forever until It Was No More: The Last Soviet Generation.* Princeton: Princeton University Press, 2006.

Zakaras, A., ed. *Kur giria žaliuoja.* Vol. 1. Vilnius: Vaga, 1968.

Zakrzewski, Bogdan. *Boże, Cóś Polskę Alojzego Felińskiego.* Wrocław: Zakład Narodowy Imienia Ossolińskich, 1983.

Zalče, Vita. "IX Latviešu dziesmu svētki—Kārļa Ulmaņa Latvijas mūžības zvērests." *Latvijas Arhīvi* 2 (2008): 106–48.

Zālīte, Māra. "Pirms festivāla." *Literatūra un Māksla,* July 22, 1988, 3.

Žeimantas, V. "Šeimininkavimo mokykla: Universiteto studentų profsąjungos komiteto pirmininko V. Žeimanto atskaitinis pranešimas." *Tarybinis studentas,* October 29, 1971, 3.

Ziedonis, Imants. *Raksti.* 12 vols. Riga: Nordik, 1996.

Ziemiņš, Modris, ed. *Rīgā deg ugunskuri, Maskavā brūk padomju impērija.* Riga: Modris Ziemiņš, 2001.

Zunes, Stephen, Lester R. Kurtz, and Sarah Beth Asher, eds. *Nonviolent Social Movements: A Geographical Perspective.* Malden, MA: Blackwell, 1999.

Żurawski, Slawomir, ed. *Literatura polska, encyclopedia PWN: Epoki literackie, prądy i kierunki, dzieła i twórcy.* Warsaw: Wydawnyctwo Naukowe Pwn, 2007.

GENERAL INDEX

Aavik, Juhan (1884–1982), 92, 195
Aarelaid-Tart, Aili (b. 1947), 153
Ackerman, Peter (b. 1946), 6
Aisčiai (Lithuanian rock band), 211–12
Akhmatova, Anna (1889–1966), 150
Akurātere, Ieva (b. 1958), 229–30, 248–49, 408n66
Akurāters, Jānis (1876–1937), 117
alcohol, 183, 225, 232, 239, 274. See also song contents: alcohol
Aleksandravičius, Egidijus (b. 1956), 194
Aleksandrov, Aleksandr (1883–1946), 140–42
Alender, Urmas (1953–1994), 223, 408n66
Alexander I, tsar (1777–1825), 101, 113
Alexander II, tsar (1818–1881), 64, 79
Alexander III, tsar (1845–1894), 64
Alunāns, Juris (1832–1864), 75, 79
Anderson, Benedict (b. 1936), 78, 322, 404n18. See also "imagined community"
Andersons, Pīts (b. 1946), 222
Andropov, Yurii (1914–February 1984), 162, 226, 272
Andrulis, Domas (1896–1973), 148
Animals (British rock band), 211
Antanėlis, Kęstutis (b. 1951), 213
Antis (Lithuanian rock band), 234–37, 246, 254–56, 336, 391n79
Apelsin (Estonian rock band), 222, 224
Arbusow, Leonid (1882–1951), 27
Arder, Ott (1950–2004), 223, 408n66
Arnim, Achim von (1781–1831), 69
Astra, Gunārs (1931–1988), 186
Auseklis (Miķelis Krogzemis; 1850–1879), 6, 75, 90–92, 99–100, 309, 371n108, 408n66

Baliukevičius, Lionginas (1925–1950), 131

Baltakmens, Raimonds (b. 1927), 305
Baltica Association 22, 295–96
Baltica Folklore Festival (see also CIOFF): 1987 in Lithuania, 273, 283; 1988 in Latvia, 11, 22, 47–49, 186, 246, 261–63, 275, 282–85; 1989 in Estonia, 296–97; 1990 in Lithuania, cancelled, 297; 1991 in Latvia, 24, 297
Baltic Way 1989 demonstration, 249–50, 258, 336
Banaitis, Juozas (1908–1967), 148
Banaitis, Kazimieras (1896–1963), 379n27
Barisons, Pēteris (1904–1947), 174
Barons, Krišjānis (1835–1923), 75, 281–82, 367n41
Bartaševics, Raimonds (b. 1953), 229
Bartkēvičs, Leonards (b. 1932), 284
Bartusevičius, Vladas (1927–1982), 180
Basanavičius, Jonas (1851–1927), 93, 97, 125
Bauman, Richard (b. 1940), 320
Baumanis, Jānis (1834–1891), 86
Baumanis, Kārlis (1835–1905), 86, 92, 408n66
Bearslayer (Latvian national epic), 246
Bearslayer (Latvian national hero), 114, 118, 319
Bearslayer (rock opera), 246–48, 254, 317
Beatles (British rock band), 211, 214, 239
Beissinger, Mark (b. 1954), 6, 319, 321
Belševica, Vizma (1931–2005), 274–75
Bendorius, Jonas (1889–1954), 148
Bérat, Frédéric (1801–1855), 344
Berends, Erki (b. 1955), 222
Beresnevičius, Antanas (1832–1904), 69
Bergmane, Irēna, 151

Hitler, Adolf (1889–1945), 135. *See also*
Molotov-Ribbentrop Pact
Holocaust, 135, 335, 375n2
Hupel, August (1737–1819), 37, 47, 57,
61
Hurt, Jakob (1839–1907), 8, 62, 75,
83, 92
Husband, William, 226
hymnals. *See* songbooks

Ilčiukas, Antanas (1902–1990), 155
Iļǵi (Latvian folklore group), 278
Illak, Riho (b. 1955), 222
"imagined community" 57, 61, 78–79,
84, 111–12, 153, 322
In Spe (Estonian rock band), 8, 239
Interfront (*Internatsional'nyi Front
Trudiashchikhsia,* "International
Workers' Front"), 8, 309
International Council of Folklore
Festival Organizations. *See* CIOFF
International Peace Society, 120
Īvāns, Dainis (b. 1955), 187, 315,
326–27

Jagiełło, King of Poland, Grand Duke of
Lithuania (1351–1434), 67–68, 333,
372n119
Jakobson, Adam (1817–1857), 70
Jakobson, Carl Robert (1841–1882),
81, 84
Jannsen, Johann Voldemar (1819–1890),
70–74, 76–83, 408n66
Jannsen, Lydia. *See* Koidula, Lydia
Järvela, Kalev (leader of Leigarid, b.
1960), 22
Javoišs, Bruno (b. 1941), 381n77
jazz, 137, 154, 210–11, 226
Jesus (4 BC–33 AD), 68, 213
Joala, Jaak (b. 1950), 222
Jogaila. *See* Jagiełło
Johanson, Jaak (b. 1959), 244
Jordan, James (b. 1953), 324
Jovaišas, Albinas (b. 1931), 59
Jurjāns, Andrejs (1856–1922), 92,
408n66

Kaalep, Ain (b. 1926), 347
Kačanauskas, Aleksandras (1882–1959),
379n37
Kaktiņš, Jānis (1827–1901), 85
Kalevipoeg (Estonian national epic), 79,
113, 143–44, 239, 242, 309
Kalevipoeg (Estonian national hero),
144, 239, 258–59, 319
Kaljuste, Tõnu (b. 1953), 188
Kalniņš, Alfreds (1879–1951), 155–56

Kalniņš, Imants (b. 1941), 176, 218–20,
229, 233, 249, 408n66
Kalniņš, Rolands (b. 1922), 220
Kangars (Latvian national villain),
248
Kant, Immanuel (1724–1804), 26
Käo, Henno (1942–2004), 343
Kaplinski, Jaan (b. 1941), 170, 286
Kapp, Artur (1878–1952), 92
Kappel, Johannes (1855–1907), 92
Karindi, Alfred (1901–1969), 150
Kārkliņš, Jēkabs (1867–1960), 151
Karosas, Juozas (1890–1981), 148
Karuks, Tiit (b. 1946), 221
Kaszewski, Jan (1783–1847), 66, 69
Katedrāle (Latvian rock band), 211
Kaudzīte, Matīss (1848–1926), 87, 88,
90
Kaupužs, Vladimirs (b. 1925), 230, 280
Kaušpėdas, Algirdas (b. 1953), 234–37,
408n66
Kelmickaitė, Zita (b. 1951), 15–19, 264,
271–72, 298, 310, 317, 408n66
Kernagis, Vytautas (1951–2008), 211–
17, 222, 234, 251, 385n66, 391n79,
408n66
Kęstutis, Grand Duke of Lithuania
(1300–1382), in song, 66–68
Khrushchev, Nikita (1894–1971), 176,
399n56
Kiigelaulukuuik (Estonian choir), 239
Kiik, Heino (1927–2013), 252, 257
King, Martin Luther (1929–1968), 326
Klenickis, Abelis (1904–1990), 147–48
Klotiņš, Arnolds (b. 1934), 282
Knüpffer, Arnold (1777–1843), 62
Koidula, Lydia (Lydia Jannsen; 1843–
1886), 80–81, 149, 164, 172–73,
242, 408n66
Kõiva, Ottilie-Olga (b. 1932), 286
Kokare, Elza (b. 1920), 279
Kokars, Gido (b. 1921), 187
Kokars, Imants (1921–2012), 187
Kooma (Estonian rock band), 224
Körber, Martin (1817–1893), 76, 81,
307, 408n66
Koreivienė, J. L. 69
Kraštotyros Draugija, *see* Local
Heritage Society
Kreutzfeld, Gottlieb (1745–1784), 28, 57
Kreutzwald, Friedrich Reinhold (1803–
1882), 75, 77–79, 113, 243, 309,
408n66
Kristsons, Zigmārs (1965–2009), 14
Krogzemis, Miķelis. *See* Auseklis
Kronvalds, Atis (1837–1875), 88, 90
Krūmiņš, Andrejs (1926–1999), 281